2022 CAMBRIDGE DEDICATED TEACHER AWARDS

Teachers play an important part in shaping futures. Our Dedicated Teacher Awards recognise the hard work that teachers put in every day.

Thank you to everyone who nominated this year; we have been inspired and moved by all of your stories. Well done to all of our nominees for your dedication to learning and for inspiring the next generation of thinkers, leaders and innovators.

Congratulations to our incredible winners!

WINNER

Regional Winner — Australia, New Zealand & South-East Asia
Mohd Al Khalifa Bin Mohd Affnan
Keningau Vocational College, Malaysia

Regional Winner — Europe
Dr. Mary Shiny Ponparambil Paul
Little Flower English School, Italy

Regional Winner — North & South America
Noemi Falcon
Zora Neale Hurston Elementary School, United States

Regional Winner — Central & Southern Africa
Temitope Adewuyi
Fountain Heights Secondary School, Nigeria

Regional Winner — Middle East & North Africa
Uroosa Imran
Beaconhouse School System KG-1 branch, Pakistan

Regional Winner — East & South Asia
Jeenath Akther
Chittagong Grammar School, Bangladesh

For more information about our dedicated teachers and their stories, go to
dedicatedteacher.cambridge.org

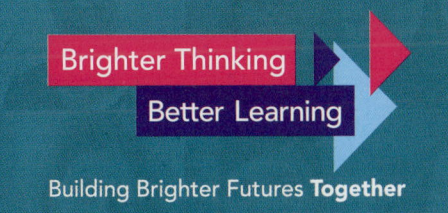

CAMBRIDGE UNIVERSITY PRESS

Brighter Thinking
Better Learning
Building Brighter Futures Together

Contents

How to use this series		vi
How to use this book		vii

Unit A Space, time and motion — 1

1 Kinematics — 2
- 1.1 Displacement, distance, speed and velocity — 3
- 1.2 Uniformly accelerated motion: the equations of kinematics — 7
- 1.3 Graphs of motion — 16
- 1.4 Projectile motion — 20

2 Forces and Newton's laws — 29
- 2.1 Forces and their direction — 30
- 2.2 Newton's laws of motion — 39
- 2.3 Circular motion — 52

3 Work, energy and power — 61
- 3.1 Work — 62
- 3.2 Conservation of energy — 70
- 3.3 Power and efficiency — 78
- 3.4 Energy transfers — 80

4 Linear momentum — 84
- 4.1 Newton's second law in terms of momentum — 85
- 4.2 Impulse and force–time graphs — 87
- 4.3 Conservation of momentum — 90
- 4.4 Kinetic energy and momentum — 93
- 4.5 Two-dimensional collisions — 97

5 Rigid body mechanics — 102
- 5.1 Kinematics of rotational motion — 103
- 5.2 Rotational equilibrium and Newton's second law — 106
- 5.3 Angular momentum — 119

6 Relativity — 125
- 6.1 Reference frames and Lorentz transformations — 126
- 6.2 Effects of relativity — 134
- 6.3 Spacetime diagrams — 143

Unit B The particulate nature of matter — 155

7 Thermal energy transfers — 156
- 7.1 Particles, temperature and energy — 157
- 7.2 Specific heat capacity and change of phase — 161
- 7.3 Thermal energy transfer — 168

8 The greenhouse effect — 177
- 8.1 Radiation from real bodies — 178
- 8.2 Energy balance of the earth — 180

9 The gas laws — 188
- 9.1 Moles, molar mass and the Avogadro constant — 189
- 9.2 Ideal gases — 191
- 9.3 The Boltzmann equation — 199

10 Thermodynamics — 205
- 10.1 Internal energy — 206
- 10.2 The first law of thermodynamics — 211
- 10.3 The second law of thermodynamics — 218
- 10.4 Heat engines — 224

11 Current and circuits — 231
- 11.1 Potential difference, current and resistance — 232
- 11.2 Voltage, power and emf — 238
- 11.3 Resistors in electrical circuits — 241
- 11.4 Terminal potential difference and the potential divider — 254

CAMBRIDGE
UNIVERSITY PRESS

Physics
for the IB Diploma

COURSEBOOK

K. A. Tsokos

CAMBRIDGE
UNIVERSITY PRESS

Shaftesbury Road, Cambridge CB2 8EA, United Kingdom

One Liberty Plaza, 20th Floor, New York, NY 10006, USA

477 Williamstown Road, Port Melbourne, VIC 3207, Australia

314–321, 3rd Floor, Plot 3, Splendor Forum, Jasola District Centre, New Delhi – 110025, India

103 Penang Road, #05–06/07, Visioncrest Commercial, Singapore 238467

Cambridge University Press is part of Cambridge University Press & Assessment, a department of the University of Cambridge.

We share the University's mission to contribute to society through the pursuit of education, learning and research at the highest international levels of excellence.

www.cambridge.org
Information on this title: www.cambridge.org/9781009071888
DOI: 10.1010/9781009071888

© Cambridge University Press & Assessment 2023

This publication is in copyright. Subject to statutory exception and to the provisions of relevant collective licensing agreements, no reproduction of any part may take place without the written permission of Cambridge University Press & Assessment.

First published 1998
Second edition 1999
Third edition 2001
Fourth edition published by Cambridge University Press 2005
Fifth edition 2008
Fifth edition (full colour version) 2010
Sixth edition 2014
Seventh edition 2023

20 19 18 17 16 15 14 13 12 11 10 9 8 7 6 5 4 3 2 1

Printed in Dubai by Oriental Press

A catalogue record for this publication is available from the British Library

ISBN 9781009071888 Coursebook with digital access
ISBN 9781009073103 Digital Coursebook
ISBN 9781009073134 Coursebook (eBook)

Additional resources for this publication at www.cambridge.org/9781009071888

Cambridge University Press & Assessment has no responsibility for the persistence or accuracy of URLs for external or third-party internet websites referred to in this publication and does not guarantee that any content on such websites is, or will remain, accurate or appropriate.

This work has been developed independently from and is not endorsed by the International Baccalaureate Organization. International Baccalaureate, Baccalauréat International, Bachillerato Internacional and IB are registered trademarks owned by the International Baccalaureate Organization.

....

NOTICE TO TEACHERS
It is illegal to reproduce any part of this work in material form (including photocopying and electronic storage) except under the following circumstances:
(i) where you are abiding by a licence granted to your school or institution by the Copyright Licensing Agency;
(ii) where no such licence exists, or where you wish to exceed the terms of a licence, and you have gained the written permission of Cambridge University Press;
(iii) where you are allowed to reproduce without permission under the provisions of Chapter 3 of the Copyright, Designs and Patents Act 1988, which covers, for example, the reproduction of short passages within certain types of educational anthology and reproduction for the purposes of setting examination questions.

Contents

Unit C Wave behaviour — 263

12 Simple harmonic motion — 264
- 12.1 Simple harmonic oscillations — 265
- 12.2 Details of simple harmonic motion — 273
- 12.3 Energy in simple harmonic motion — 279
- 12.4 More about energy in SHM — 281

13 The wave model — 286
- 13.1 Mechanical pulses and waves — 287
- 13.2 Transverse and longitudinal waves — 290
- 13.3 Electromagnetic waves — 298
- 13.4 Waves extension — 299

14 Wave phenomena — 301
- 14.1 Reflection and refraction — 302
- 14.2 The principle of superposition — 308
- 14.3 Diffraction and interference — 311
- 14.4 Single-slit diffraction — 318
- 14.5 Multiple slits — 322

15 Standing waves and resonance — 329
- 15.1 Standing waves — 330
- 15.2 Standing waves on strings — 331
- 15.3 Standing waves in pipes — 334
- 15.4 Resonance and damping — 340

16 The Doppler effect — 346
- 16.1 The Doppler effect at low speeds — 347
- 16.2 The Doppler effect for sound — 351

Unit D Fields — 357

17 Gravitation — 358
- 17.1 Newton's law of gravitation — 359
- 17.2 Gravitational potential and energy — 366
- 17.3 Motion in a gravitational field — 373

18 Electric and magnetic fields — 384
- 18.1 Electric charge, force and field — 385
- 18.2 Magnetic field and force — 395
- 18.3 Electric potential and electric potential energy — 406

19 Motion in electric and magnetic fields — 416
- 19.1 Motion in an electric field — 417
- 19.2 Motion in a magnetic field — 421

20 Electromagnetic induction — 428
- 20.1 Electromagnetic induction — 429
- 20.2 Generators and alternating current — 443

Unit E Nuclear and quantum physics — 449

21 Atomic physics — 450
- 21.1 The structure of the atom — 451
- 21.2 Quantisation of angular momentum — 457

22 Quantum physics — 462
- 22.1 Photons and the photoelectric effect — 463
- 22.2 Matter waves — 473

23 Nuclear physics — 478
- 23.1 Mass defect and binding energy — 479
- 23.2 Radioactivity — 486
- 23.3 Nuclear properties and the radioactive decay law — 494

24 Nuclear fission — 506
- 24.1 Nuclear fission — 507

25 Nuclear fusion and stars — 514
- 25.1 Nuclear fusion — 515
- 25.2 Stellar properties and the Hertzsprung–Russell diagram — 516
- 25.3 Stellar evolution extension — 523

Glossary — 529

Index — 537

Acknowledgements — 551

PHYSICS FOR THE IB DIPLOMA: COURSEBOOK

> How to use this series

This suite of resources supports students and teachers of the IB Physics Diploma course. All of the books in the series work together to help students develop the necessary knowledge and scientific skills required for this subject.

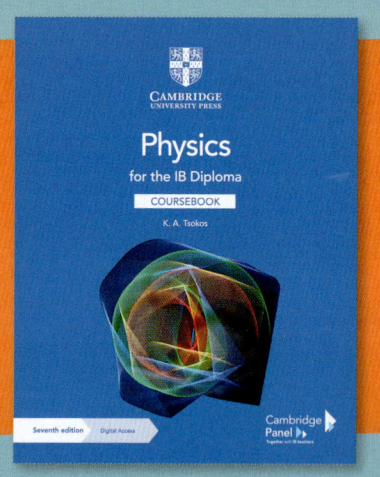

The coursebook with digital access provides full coverage of the latest IB Physics Diploma course.

It clearly explains facts, concepts and practical techniques, and uses real world examples of scientific principles. A wealth of formative questions within each chapter help students develop their understanding, and own their learning. A dedicated chapter in the digital coursebook helps teachers and students unpack the new assessment, while exam-style questions provide essential practice and self-assessment. Answers are provided on Cambridge GO, supporting self-study and home-schooling.

The workbook with digital access builds upon the coursebook with digital access with further exercises and exam-style questions, carefully constructed to help students develop the skills that they need as they progress through their IB Physics Diploma course. The exercises also help students develop understanding of the meaning of various command words used in questions, and provide practice in responding appropriately to these.

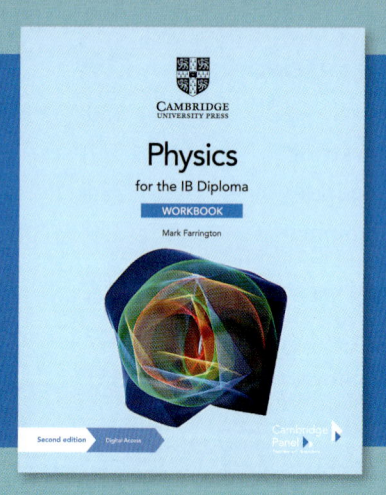

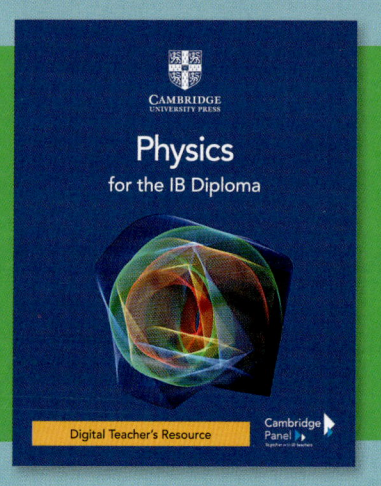

The Teacher's resource supports and enhances the coursebook with digital access and the workbook with digital access. This resource includes teaching plans, overviews of required background knowledge, learning objectives and success criteria, common misconceptions, and a wealth of ideas to support lesson planning and delivery, assessment and differentiation. It also includes editable worksheets for vocabulary support and exam practice (with answers) and exemplar PowerPoint presentations, to help plan and deliver the best teaching.

> How to use this book

Throughout this book, you will find lots of different features that will help your learning. These are explained below.

UNIT INTRODUCTION

A unit is made up of a number of chapters. The key concepts for each unit are covered throughout the chapters.

LEARNING OBJECTIVES

Each chapter in the book begins with a list of learning objectives. These set the scene for each chapter, help with navigation through the coursebook and indicate the important concepts in each topic.

- A bulleted list at the beginning of each section clearly shows the learning objectives for the section.

GUIDING QUESTIONS

This feature contains questions and activities on subject knowledge you will need before starting this chapter.

Links

These are a mix of questions and explanation that refer to other chapters or sections of the book.

The content in this book is divided into Standard and Higher Level material. A vertical line runs down the margin of all Higher Level material, allowing you to easily identify Higher Level from Standard material.

Key terms are highlighted in **orange bold** font at their first appearance in the book so you can immediately recognise them. At the end of the book, there is a glossary that defines all the key terms.

KEY POINTS

This feature contains important key learning points (facts) and/or equations to reinforce your understanding and engagement.

EXAM TIPS

These short hints contain useful information that will help you tackle the tasks in the exam.

SCIENCE IN CONTEXT

This feature presents real-world examples and applications of the content in a chapter, encouraging you to look further into topics. You will note that some of these features end with questions intended to stimulate further thinking, prompting you to consider some of the benefits and problems of these applications.

NATURE OF SCIENCE

Nature of Science is an overarching theme of the IB Physics Diploma course. The theme examines the processes and concepts that are central to scientific endeavour, and how science serves and connects with the wider community. Throughout the book, there are 'Nature of Science' features that discuss particular concepts or discoveries from the point of view of one or more aspects of Nature of Science.

PHYSICS FOR THE IB DIPLOMA: COURSEBOOK

THEORY OF KNOWLEDGE

This section stimulates thought about critical thinking and how we can say we know what we claim to know. You will note that some of these features end with questions intended to get you thinking and discussing these important Theory of Knowledge issues.

INTERNATIONAL MINDEDNESS

Throughout this Physics for the IB Diploma course, the international mindedness feature highlights international concerns. Science is a truly international endeavour, being practised across all continents, frequently in international or even global partnerships. Many problems that science aims to solve are international and will require globally implemented solutions.

CHECK YOURSELF

These appear throughout the text so you can check your progress and become familiar with the important points of a section. Answers can be found at the back of the book.

TEST YOUR UNDERSTANDING

These questions appear within each chapter and help you develop your understanding. The questions can be used as the basis for class discussions or homework assignments. If you can answer these questions, it means you have understood the important points of a section.

WORKED EXAMPLE

Many worked examples appear throughout the text to help you understand how to tackle different types of questions.

REFLECTION

These questions appear at the end of each chapter. The purpose is for you as a learner to reflect on the development of your skills proficiency and your progress against the objectives. The reflection questions are intended to encourage your critical thinking and inquiry-based learning.

EXAM-STYLE QUESTIONS

Exam-style questions at the end of each chapter provide essential practice and self-assessment. These are signposted in the print coursebook and can be found in the digital version of the coursebook.

SELF-EVALUATION CHECKLIST

These appear at the end of each chapter/section as a series of statements. You might find it helpful to rate how confident you are for each of these statements when you are revising. You should revisit any topics that you rated 'Needs more work' or 'Almost there'.

Free online material

Additional material to support the Physics for the IB Diploma course is available online.

This includes Assessment guidance—a dedicated chapter in the digital coursebook helps teachers and students unpack the new assessment and model exam specimen papers. Additionally, answers to the Exam-style question and Test your understanding are also available.

Visit Cambridge GO and register to access these resources.

Unit A
Space, time and motion

INTRODUCTION

This unit deals with Classical Mechanics. The basic concepts that we will use include position in space, displacement (change in position), mass, velocity, acceleration, force, momentum, energy and of course time. These concepts, the relations between them and the laws they give rise to are discussed in the first five chapters. This incredible structure that began with Newton's work detailed in his Principia is also called Newtonian Mechanics. The Newtonian view of the world has passed every conceivable experimental test both on a local terrestrial scale as well as on a much larger scale when it is applied to the motion of celestial bodies. It is the theory upon which much of engineering is based with daily practical applications.
Of course, no theory of Physics can be considered "correct" no matter how many experimental tests it passes. The possibility always exists that new phenomena, new observations and new experiments may lead to discrepancies with the theory. In that case it may be necessary to modify the theory or even abandon it completely in favour of a new theory that explains the old as well as the new phenomena.

This is the case, too, with Newtonian Mechanics. In chapter 6 of this unit we will see that the Newtonian concepts of space and time need to be revised in situations where the speeds involved approach the speed of light. This is not to say that Newtonian Mechanics is useless; the theory of relativity that replaces it, does becomes Newtonian Mechanics in the limit of speeds that are small compared to that of light. Laws that have been derived with Newtonian Mechanics such as the conservation of energy, the conservation of momentum and the conservation of angular momentum also hold in the theories that replace Newtonian Mechanics. There is another limit in which Newtonian Mechanics is unable to describe observed phenomena. This is the physics on a very small, atomic and nuclear scale. At these scales Newtonian Mechanics fails completely to describe the observed phenomena and needs to be replaced by a new theory, Quantum Mechanics.

Chapter 1
Kinematics

LEARNING OBJECTIVES

In this chapter you will:

- learn the difference between displacement and distance
- learn the difference between speed and velocity
- learn the concept of acceleration
- learn how to analyse graphs describing motion
- learn how to solve motion problems using the equations for constant acceleration
- learn how to describe the motion of a projectile
- gain a qualitative understanding of the effects of a fluid resistance force on motion
- gain an understanding of the concept of terminal speed.

1 Kinematics

> **GUIDING QUESTIONS**
>
> - Which equations are used to describe the motion of an object?
> - How does graphical analysis help us to describe motion?

Introduction

This chapter introduces the basic concepts used to describe motion.

First, we consider motion in a straight line with constant velocity. We then discuss motion with constant acceleration. Knowledge of uniformly accelerated motion allows us to analyse more complicated motions, such as the motion of projectiles.

We use graphical analysis when acceleration is not constant.

1.1 Displacement, distance, speed and velocity

Straight line motion in one dimension means that the particle that moves is constrained to move along a straight line. The **position** of the particle is then given by its coordinate on the straight line (Figure 1.1). Position is a vector quantity—this is important when discussing projectile motion but, while discussing motion on a straight line, we can just express position as a positive or a negative number since here the vector can only point in one direction or the opposite.

If the line is horizontal, we use the symbol x to represent the coordinate and position. If the line is vertical, we use the symbol y. In general, for an arbitrary line, we use a generic symbol, s, for position. So, in Figure 1.1, $x = 6$ m, $y = -4$ m, $s = 0$ and $y = 4$ m. It is up to us to decide which side of zero we call positive and which side of zero we call negative; the decision is arbitrary.

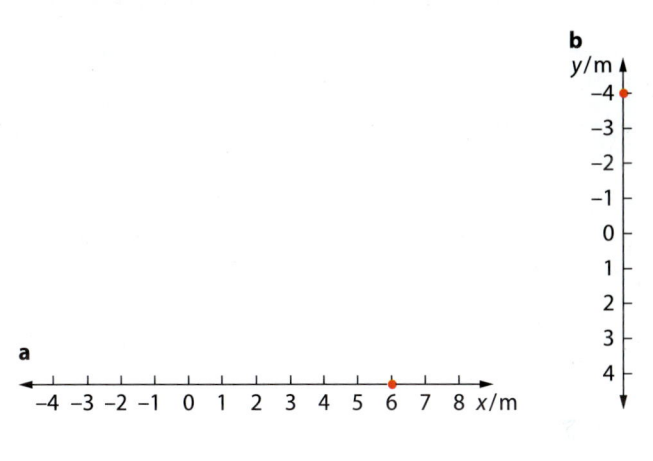

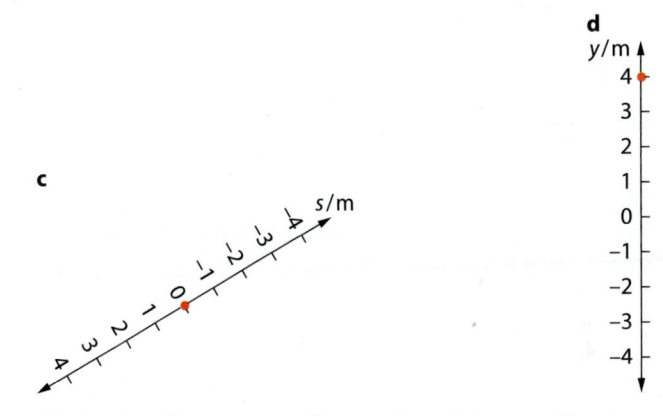

Figure 1.1: The position of a particle is determined by the coordinate on the number line.

The change in position is called **displacement**, $\Delta s = s_{\text{final}} - s_{\text{initial}}$. Displacement is a vector.

Table 1.1 shows four different motions. Make sure you understand how to calculate the displacement and that you understand the direction of motion.

Initial position	Final position	Displacement	Direction of motion
12 m	28 m	+16 m	Towards increasing s
−6 m	−14 m	−8 m	Towards decreasing s
10 m	−5 m	−15 m	Towards decreasing s
−20 m	−15	+5 m	Towards increasing s

Table 1.1: Four different motions.

Consider the two motions shown in Figure 1.2. In the first motion, the particle leaves its initial position at −4 m and continues to its final position at 16 m. The displacement is:

$\Delta s = s_{final} - s_{initial} = 16 - (-4) = 20$ m

The **distance** travelled is the actual length of the path followed (20 m).

In the second motion, the particle leaves its initial position at 12 m, arrives at position 20 m and then comes back to its final position at 4 m.

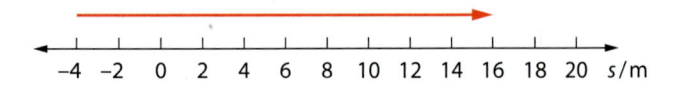

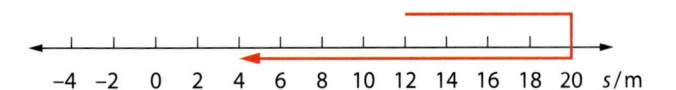

Figure 1.2

The second motion is an example of motion with changing direction. The change in the position of this particle (its displacement) is:

$\Delta s = s_{final} - s_{initial} = 4 - 12 = -8$ m

But the distance travelled by the particle (the length of the path) is 8 m in the outward trip and 16 m on the return trip, making a total **distance** of 24 m. So, we must be careful to distinguish distance from displacement:

Distance is a scalar quantity but displacement is a vector quantity.

Numerically, they are different if there is a change of direction, as in Figure 1.2.

As the particle moves on the straight line its position changes. In **uniform motion** in equal intervals of time, the position changes by the same amount.

For uniform motion the **velocity**, v, of the particle is the displacement divided by the time to achieve that displacement: $v = \frac{\Delta s}{\Delta t}$.

The **average speed** is the total distance travelled divided by the time taken.

Assume that the first motion in Figure 1.2 took 4.0 s to complete. The velocity is $\frac{20}{4.0} = 5.0$ m s^{-1}. The average speed is the same since the distance travelled is also 20 m.

Assume the second motion took 6.0 s to complete. The velocity is $\frac{-8.0}{6.0} = -1.3$ m s^{-1} and the average speed is $\frac{24}{6.0} = 4.0$ m s^{-1}. So, in uniform motion, average speed and velocity are not the same when there is change in direction.

This implies that for uniform motion:

$v = \frac{s - s_{initial}}{t - 0}$

which can be re-arranged to give:

$s = s_{initial} + vt$

(Notice how we use s for final position, rather than s_f or s_{final}, and we will write s_i for $s_{initial}$ for simplicity). So for motion with constant velocity:

$s = s_i + vt$

> **EXAM TIP**
>
> This formula can only be used when the velocity is constant.

This formula gives, in uniform motion, the position s of the moving object t seconds after time zero, given that the constant velocity is v and the initial position is s_i.

This means that a graph of *position* against *time* is a straight line and the graph of *velocity* against *time* is a horizontal straight line (Figure 1.3).

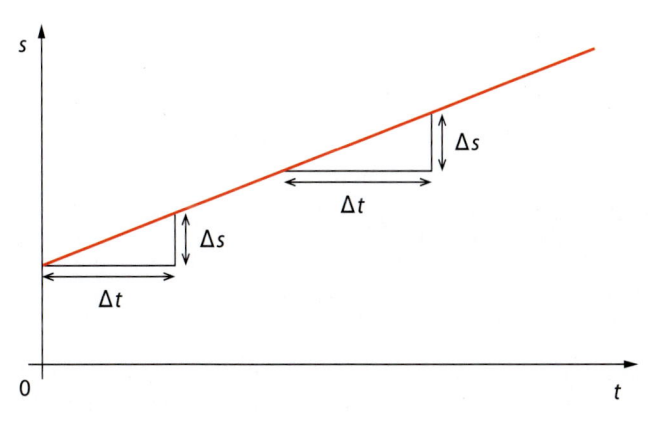

Figure 1.3: In uniform motion the graph of *position* against *time* is a straight line with non-zero gradient. The graph of *velocity* against *time* is a horizontal straight line.

Positive velocity means that the position *s* is increasing. Negative velocity means that *s* is decreasing. Observe that the area under the *v* versus *t* graph from *t* = 0 to time *t* is *vt*.

From $s = s_i + vt$ we deduce that $s - s_i = vt$ and so the area in a *velocity*-against-*time* graph is the displacement.

> **CHECK YOURSELF 1**
>
> An object moves from A to B at speed 15 m s^{-1} and returns from B to A at speed 30 m s^{-1}.
>
> What is the average speed for the round trip?

> **WORKED EXAMPLE 1.1**
>
> Two cyclists, A and B, start moving at the same time. The initial position of A is 0 km and her velocity is +20 km h^{-1}. The initial position of B is 150 km away from A and he cycles at a velocity of −30 km h^{-1}.
>
> **a** Determine the time and position at which they will meet.
>
> **b** What is the displacement of each cyclist when they meet?
>
> **c** On another occasion the same experiment is performed but this time B starts 1 h after A. When will they meet?
>
> **Answer**
>
> **a** The position of A is given by the formula $s_A = 0 + 20t$.
>
> The position of B is given by the formula $s_B = 150 - 30t$.
>
> They will meet when they are at the same position, i.e. when $s_A = s_B$. This implies:
>
> $$20t = 150 - 30t$$
> $$50t = 150$$
> $$t = 3.0 \text{ h}$$
>
> The common position is found from either $s_A = 20 \times 3.0 = 60$ km or $s_B = 150 - 30 \times 3.0 = 60$ km.
>
> **b** The displacement of A is 60 km − 0 = 60 km. That of B is 60 km − 150 km = −90 km.
>
> **c** $s_A = 0 + 20t$ as before. When *t* h go by, B will have been moving for only *t* − 1 h.
>
> Hence $s_B = 150 - 30(t - 1)$.
>
> They will meet when $s_A = s_B$:
>
> $$20t = 150 - 30(t - 1)$$
> $$50t = 180$$
> $$t = 3.6 \text{ h}$$

TEST YOUR UNDERSTANDING

1. A car must be driven a distance of 120 km in 2.5 h. During the first 1.5 h the average speed was 70 km h^{-1}. Calculate the average speed for the remainder of the journey.

2. Find the constant velocity for each motion whose position–time graphs are shown in Figure 1.4.

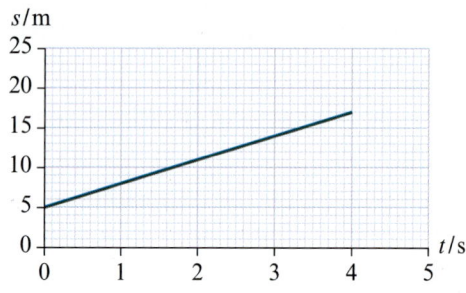

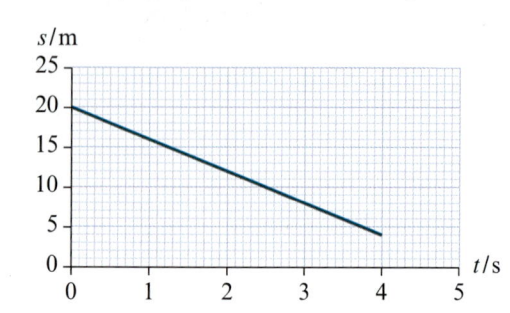

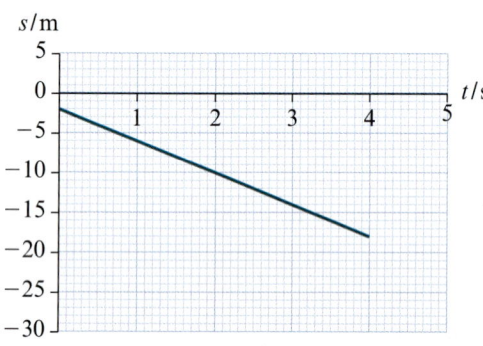

Figure 1.4

3. Draw the position–time graphs for an object moving in a straight line with velocity–time graphs as shown in Figure 1.5. The initial position is zero.

   In each case, state the displacement at 4 s.

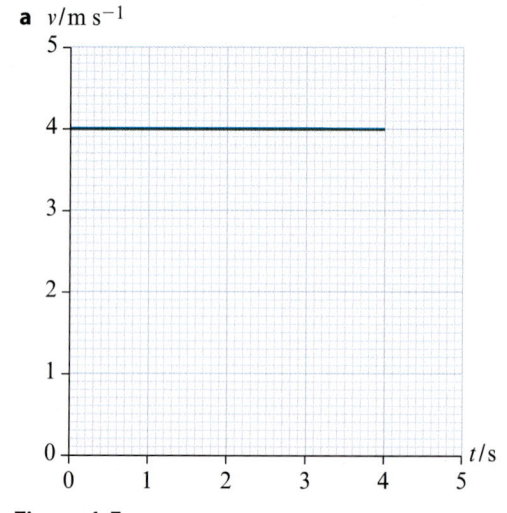

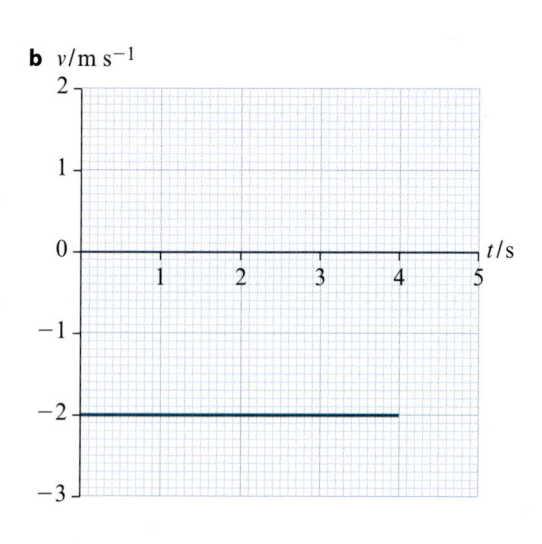

Figure 1.5

CONTINUED

4   Two cyclists, **A** and **B**, have displacements 0 km and 70 km, respectively.

   At $t = 0$ they begin to cycle towards each other with velocities 15 km h^{-1} and 20 km h^{-1}, respectively.

   At the same time, a fly that was sitting on cyclist **A** starts flying towards cyclist **B** with a velocity of 30 km h^{-1}.

   As soon as the fly reaches cyclist **B** it immediately turns around and flies towards cyclist **A**, and so on until cyclist **A** and cyclist **B** meet.

   a   Find the position of the two cyclists and the fly when all three meet.

   b   Determine the distance travelled by the fly.

1.2 Uniformly accelerated motion: the equations of kinematics

Defining velocity in non-uniform motion

How is velocity defined when it is not constant? We have to refine what we did in Section 1.1. We now define the **average velocity** as:

$$\bar{v} = \frac{\Delta s}{\Delta t}$$

where Δs is the total displacement for the motion and Δt the total time taken. We would like to have a concept of velocity at an instant of time, the **(instantaneous) velocity**. We need to make the time interval Δt very, very small. The instantaneous velocity is defined as:

$$v = \lim_{\Delta t \to 0} \frac{\Delta s}{\Delta t}$$

In other words, instantaneous velocity is the rate of change of position. This definition implies that velocity is the gradient of a *position*-against-*time* graph.

Consider Figure 1.6a. Choose a point on this curve. Draw a tangent to the curve at the point. The gradient of the tangent line is the meaning of $v = \lim_{\Delta t \to 0} \frac{\Delta s}{\Delta t}$ and, therefore, also of velocity.

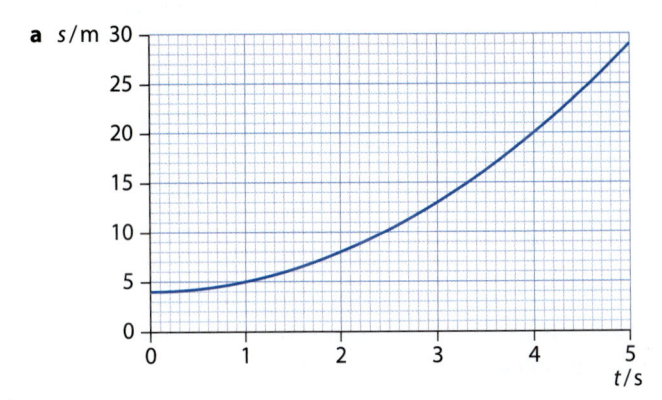

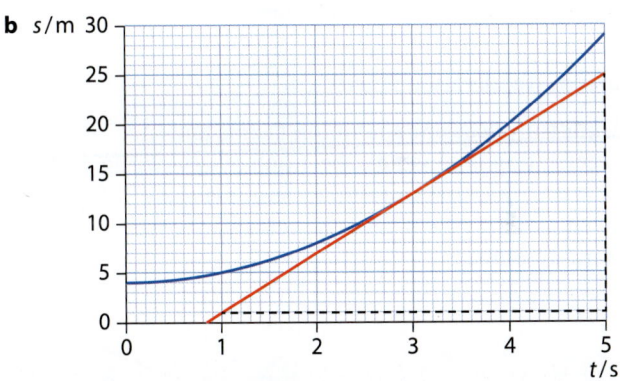

Figure 1.6: a In uniformly accelerated motion the graph of *position* against *time* is a curve. **b** The gradient (slope) of the tangent at a particular point gives the velocity at that point.

In Figure 1.6b the tangent is drawn at $t = 3.0$ s. We can use this to find the instantaneous velocity at $t = 3.0$ s.

The gradient of this tangent line is:
$$\frac{25 - 1.0}{5.0 - 1.0} = 6.0 \, \text{m s}^{-1}$$

To find the instantaneous velocity at some other instant of time we must take another tangent and we will find a different instantaneous velocity. At the point at $t = 0$ it is particularly easy to find the velocity: the tangent is horizontal and so the velocity is zero.

From now on we drop the word *instantaneous* and refer just to velocity. The magnitude of the velocity is known as the **(instantaneous) speed**.

When the velocity changes we say that we have acceleration. The average acceleration is defined as $\bar{a} = \frac{\Delta v}{\Delta t}$. So for a body that accelerates from a velocity of 2.0 m s^{-1} to a velocity of 8.0 m s^{-1} in a time of 3.0 s the average acceleration is $\bar{a} = \frac{8.0 - 2.0}{3.0} = 2.0 \, \text{m s}^{-2}$.

To define instantaneous acceleration or just simply acceleration, we use the same idea as for velocity. We let the time interval Δt get very small and define acceleration as:

Acceleration is the rate of change of velocity. $a = \lim_{\Delta t \to 0} \frac{\Delta v}{\Delta t}$. It is the gradient of a *velocity*-against-*time* graph. Acceleration is a vector.

Uniformly accelerated motion means that the acceleration is constant: the graph of *velocity* against *time* is a non-horizontal straight line (Figure 1.7). In equal intervals of time the velocity changes by the same amount.

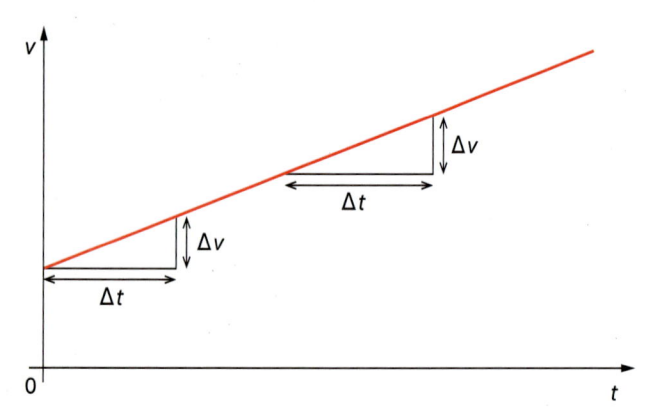

Figure 1.7: In uniformly accelerated motion the graph of *velocity* against *time* is a straight line with non-zero slope.

Figure 1.8: This fighter jet is accelerating.

When the acceleration is positive, the velocity is increasing (Figure 1.8). Negative acceleration means that v is decreasing.

For constant acceleration there is no difference between instantaneous acceleration and average acceleration.

Suppose we choose a time interval from $t = 0$ to some arbitrary time t later. Let the velocity at $t = 0$ (the initial velocity) be u and the velocity at time t be v. Then:

$$a = \frac{\Delta v}{\Delta t} = \frac{v - u}{t - 0}$$

which can be re-arranged to:

$$v = u + at$$

For uniformly accelerated motion, this formula gives the velocity v of the moving object t seconds after time zero, given that the initial velocity is u and the acceleration is a.

WORKED EXAMPLE 1.2

A particle has an initial velocity 12 m s^{-1} and moves with a constant acceleration of -3.0 m s^{-2}. Determine the time at which the particle stops instantaneously.

Answer

At some point it will stop instantaneously; that is, its velocity v will be zero.

We know that $v = u + at$.

Substituting values gives:

$0 = 12 + (-3.0) \times t$

$3.0t = 12$

Hence $t = 4.0$ s.

1 Kinematics

Consider the graph of *velocity* against *time* in Figure 1.9. Imagine approximating the straight line with a staircase. The area under the staircase is the change in position since at each step the velocity is constant. If we make the steps of the staircase smaller and smaller, the area under the line and the area under the staircase will be indistinguishable and so we have the general result that:

> **KEY POINT**
>
> The area under the curve in a *velocity* against *time* graph is the change in position; in other words, the displacement.

From Figure 1.9 this area is (the shape is a trapezoid):

$$\Delta s = \left(\frac{u+v}{2}\right)t$$

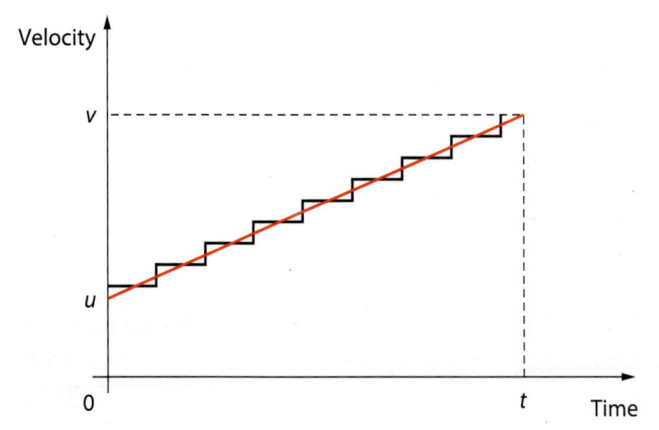

Figure 1.9: The straight-line graph may be approximated by a staircase.

But $v = u + at$, so this becomes:

$$\Delta s = \left(\frac{u+u+at}{2}\right)t = ut + \frac{1}{2}at^2$$

So we have two formulas for position in the case of uniformly accelerated motion (recall that $\Delta s = s - s_i$):

$$s = s_i + \left(\frac{u+v}{2}\right)t \text{ or } \Delta s = \left(\frac{u+v}{2}\right)t$$

$$s = s_i + ut + \frac{1}{2}at^2 \text{ or } \Delta s = ut + \frac{1}{2}at^2$$

We get a final formula if we combine $s = s_i + ut + \frac{1}{2}at^2$ with $v = u + at$.

From the second equation, we find $t = \frac{v-u}{a}$.

Substituting in the first equation we get:

$$s - s_i = u\frac{v-u}{a} + \frac{1}{2}a\left(\frac{v-u}{a}\right)^2 = \frac{uv}{a} - \frac{u^2}{a} + \frac{1}{2}\frac{v^2}{a} - \frac{uv}{a} + \frac{1}{2}\frac{u^2}{a}$$

$$= \frac{v^2 - u^2}{2a}$$

This becomes:

$$v^2 = u^2 + 2a(s - s_i) \text{ or } v^2 = u^2 + 2a\Delta s$$

Usually $s_i = 0$ so this last equation is usually written as $v^2 = u^2 + 2as$.

This formula is useful to solve problems in which no information about time is available.

In summary, for motion along a straight line with constant acceleration:

$$v = u + at$$

$$\Delta s = \left(\frac{u+v}{2}\right)t$$

$$\Delta s = ut + \frac{1}{2}at^2$$

$$v^2 = u^2 + 2a\Delta s$$

Graphs of *position* against *time* for uniformly accelerated motion are parabolas (Figure 1.10). If the parabola 'holds water' (concave up) the acceleration is positive. If its concave down, the acceleration is negative.

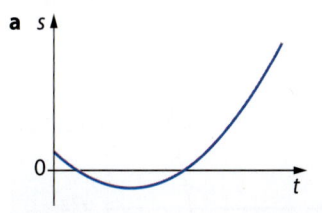

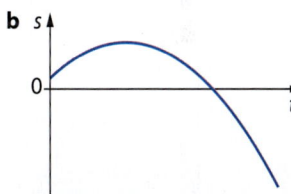

Figure 1.10: Graphs of *position* s against *time* t for uniformly accelerated motion. **a** Positive acceleration. **b** Negative acceleration.

9

PHYSICS FOR THE IB DIPLOMA: COURSEBOOK

> **EXAM TIP**
>
> Table 1.2 summarises the meaning of the gradient and area for the different motion graphs.
>
> | Graph of ... | Gradient | Area |
> |---|---|---|
> | position against *time* | velocity | |
> | velocity against *time* | acceleration | change in position, i.e. displacement |
> | acceleration against *time* | | change in velocity |
>
> **Table 1.2:** Information that can be derived from motion graphs
>
> The **equations of kinematics** can be used only for motion on a straight line with constant acceleration. (If the initial position is zero, Δs may be replaced by just s.)

> **CHECK YOURSELF 2**
>
> The graph in Figure 1.11 shows the variation of position with time.
>
> [Graph: s/m vs t/s, showing a curve that rises to ~0.75 m near t=0.5s, falls through 0 near t=1.25s, reaches minimum ~-0.75 m near t=1.75s, then rises again]
>
> **Figure 1.11**
>
> Indicate the intervals of times for which the acceleration is:
>
> **a** positive   **b** negative   **c** zero.

> **WORKED EXAMPLE 1.3**
>
> A particle has an initial velocity $2.00 \, \text{m s}^{-1}$. Its acceleration is $a = 4.00 \, \text{m s}^{-2}$. Find its displacement after 10.0 s.
>
> **Answer**
>
> Displacement is the change of position, i.e. $\Delta s = s - s_i$. We use the equation:
>
> $$\Delta s = ut + \frac{1}{2}at^2$$
> $$= 2.00 \times 10.0 + 1/2 \times 4.00 \times 10.0^2$$
> $$= 220 \, \text{m}$$

> **WORKED EXAMPLE 1.4**
>
> A car has an initial velocity of $u = 5.0 \, \text{m s}^{-1}$. After a displacement of 20 m, its velocity becomes $7.0 \, \text{m s}^{-1}$. Find the acceleration of the car.
>
> **Answer**
>
> Here, $\Delta s = s - s_i = 20$ m.
>
> So, use $v^2 = u^2 + 2a\Delta s$ to find a.
>
> $7.0^2 = 5.0^2 + 2a \times 20$
>
> $24 = 40a$
>
> Therefore, $a = 0.60 \, \text{m s}^{-2}$.

> **WORKED EXAMPLE 1.5**
>
> A body has an initial velocity of $4.0 \, \text{m s}^{-1}$. After 6.0 s the velocity is $12 \, \text{m s}^{-1}$. Determine the displacement of the body in the 6.0 s.
>
> **Answer**
>
> We know u, v and t. We can use:
>
> $$\Delta s = \left(\frac{v + u}{2}\right)t$$
>
> to get:
>
> $$\Delta s = \left(\frac{12 + 4.0}{2}\right) \times 6.0$$
>
> $$\Delta s = 48 \, \text{m}$$

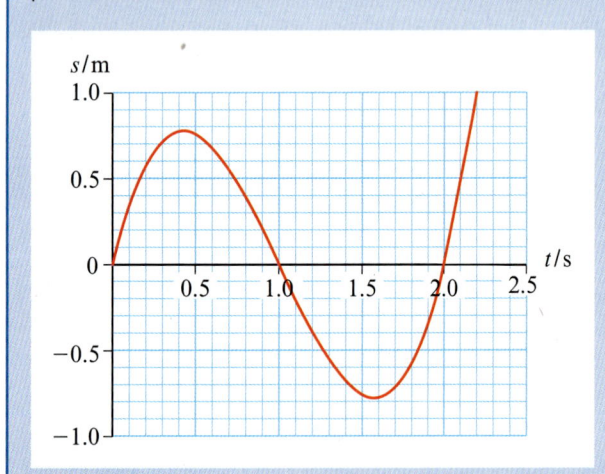

CONTINUED

A slower method would be to use $v = u + at$ to find the acceleration:

$$12 = 4.0 + 6.0a$$
$$\Rightarrow a = 1.333 \text{ m s}^{-2}$$

Then use the value of a to find Δs:

$$\Delta s = ut + \tfrac{1}{2}at^2$$
$$= 4.0 \times 6.0 + \tfrac{1}{2} \times 1.333 \times 36$$
$$= 48 \text{ m}$$

WORKED EXAMPLE 1.6

A ball, X, starts moving to the right from rest with a constant acceleration of 2.0 m s^{-2}. 2.0 s later, a second ball, Y, starts moving to the right with a constant velocity of 9.0 m s^{-1}. Both balls start from the same position.

Determine the position of the balls when they meet. Describe what is going on.

Answer

Let the two balls meet t s after X starts moving.

The position of X is:

$$s_X = \tfrac{1}{2}at^2 = \tfrac{1}{2} \times 2.0 \times t^2 = t^2$$

The position of Y is:

$$s_Y = 9(t - 2)$$

(The factor $t - 2$ must be considered because, after t s, Y has actually been moving for only $t - 2$ seconds.)

These two positions are equal when the two balls meet, and so:

$$t^2 = 9(t - 2)$$

Solving the quadratic equation we find $t = 3.0$ s and 6.0 s. At these times the positions are 9.0 m and 36 m.

At 3.0 s Y caught up with X and passed it. At 6.0 s X caught up with Y and passed it. (Making position–time graphs here is instructive.)

WORKED EXAMPLE 1.7

A particle starts out from the origin with velocity 10 m s^{-1} and continues moving at this velocity for 5 s. The velocity is then abruptly reversed to −5 m s^{-1} and the object moves at this velocity for 10 s.

For this motion find:

a the change in position, i.e. the displacement

b the total distance travelled

c the average speed

d the average velocity

Answer

The problem is best solved using the velocity–time graph, which is shown in Figure 1.12.

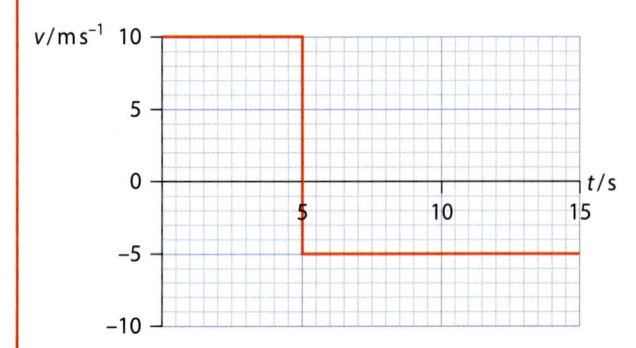

Figure 1.12

a The initial position is zero. So, after 5.0 s, the position is 10 × 5.0 m = 50 m (the area under the first part of the graph). In the next 10 s, the displacement changes by −5.0 × 10 = −50 m (the area under the second part of the graph). So the change in position (the displacement) = 50 − 50 = 0 m.

b Take the initial velocity as moving to the right. The object moved towards the right, stopped and returned to its starting position. (We know this because the displacement was 0.) The distance travelled is 50 m moving to the right and 50 m coming back, giving a total distance travelled of 100 m.

c The average speed is $\frac{100}{15}$ = 6.7 m s^{-1}.

d The average velocity is zero, since the displacement is zero.

WORKED EXAMPLE 1.8

An object with an initial velocity 20 m s^{-1} and initial position of −75 m experiences a constant acceleration of −2 m s^{-2}. Sketch the position–time graph for this motion for the first 20 s.

Answer

Use the equation $s = s_i + ut + \frac{1}{2}at^2$. Substituting the values we know, the position is given by $s = -75 + 20t - t^2$. This is the function we must graph. The result is shown in Figure 1.13.

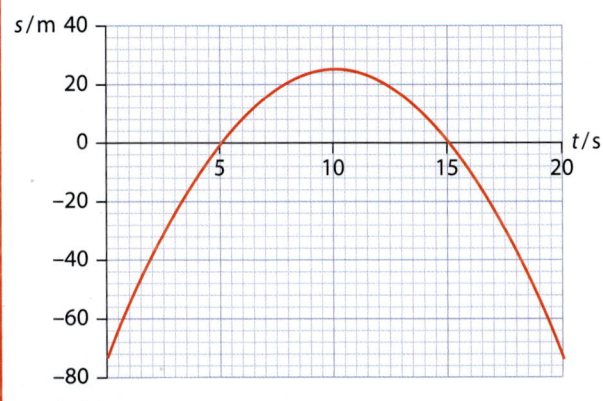

Figure 1.13

At 5 s the object reaches the origin and overshoots it. It returns to the origin 10 s later ($t = 15$ s). The furthest it gets from the origin is 25 m. The velocity at 5 s is 10 m s^{-1} and at 15 s it is −10 m s^{-1}. At 10 s the velocity is zero.

A special acceleration

Assuming that we can neglect air resistance and other frictional forces, an object thrown into the air will experience the **acceleration of free fall** while in the air. This is an acceleration caused by the attraction between the earth and the body. The magnitude of this acceleration is denoted by g. Near the surface of the earth $g = 9.8$ m s^{-2}. The direction of this acceleration is always vertically downwards. (We will sometimes approximate g to 10 m s^{-2}.)

WORKED EXAMPLE 1.9

An object is thrown vertically upwards with an initial velocity of 20 m s^{-1} from the edge of a cliff that is 25 m from the sea below, as shown in Figure 1.14.

Determine:

a the ball's maximum height

b the time taken for the ball to reach its maximum height

c the time to hit the sea

d the speed with which it hits the sea

(You may approximate g to 10 m s^{-2}.)

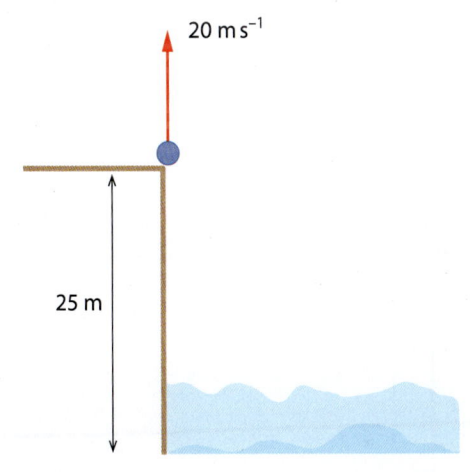

Figure 1.14: A ball is thrown upwards from the edge of a cliff.

Answer

We have motion on a vertical line so we will use the symbol y for position (Figure 1.15a). We take the direction up to be positive. The zero for position is the ball's initial position.

CONTINUED

a

b

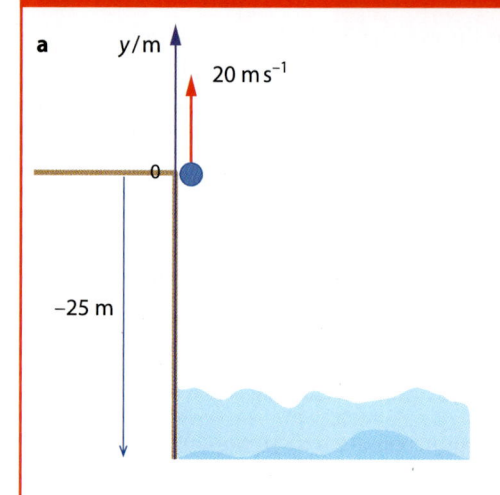

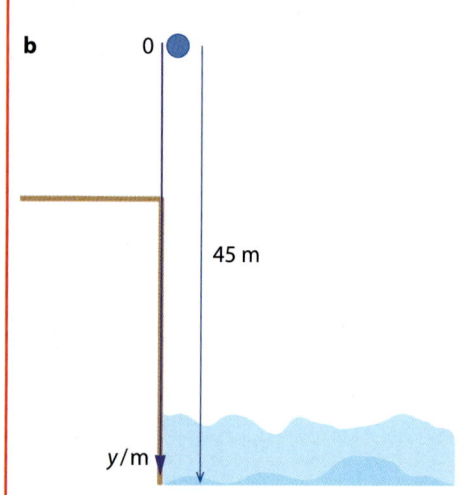

Figure 1.15: Diagrams for solving the ball's motion. **a** Displacement upwards is positive. **b** The highest point is the zero of position. Here we take displacement downwards to be positive.

---

a The quickest way to get the answer to this part is to use $v^2 = u^2 - 2gy$. (The acceleration is $a = -g$.) At the highest point $v = 0$, and so:

$0 = 20^2 - 2 \times 10y$
$\Rightarrow y = 20$ m

b At the highest point the object's velocity is zero. Using $v = 0$ in $v = u - gt$ gives:

$0 = 20 - 10 \times t$
$t = \frac{20}{10} = 2.0$ s

CONTINUED

c There are many ways to do this. One is to use the displacement arrow shown in blue in Figure 1.15a. Then, when the ball hits the sea, $y = -25$ m. Now use the formula $y = ut - \frac{1}{2}gt^2$ to find an equation that only has the variable t:

$-25 = 20 \times t - 5 \times t^2$
$t^2 - 4t - 5 = 0$

This is a quadratic equation. Using your calculator you can find the two roots as -1.0 s and 5.0 s. Choose the positive root to find the answer $t = 5.0$ s.

Another way of looking at this is shown in Figure 1.15b. Here we start at the highest point and take the direction down to be positive. Then, at the top $y = 0$, at the sea $y = +45$ m and $a = +10$ m s^{-2}. Now, the initial velocity is zero because we take our initial point to be at the top.

Using $y = ut + \frac{1}{2}gt^2$ with $u = 0$, we find:

$45 = 5t^2$
$\Rightarrow t = 3.0$ s

This is the time to fall to the sea. It took 2.0 s to reach the highest point, so the total time from launch to hitting the sea is:

$2.0 + 3.0 = 5.0$ s.

d Use $v = u - gt$ and $t = 5.0$ s to get $v = 20 - 10 \times 5.0 = -30$ m s^{-1}. The speed is then 30 m s^{-1}.

(If you prefer the diagram in Figure 1.15b for working out part **c** and you want to continue this method for part **d**, then you would write $v = u + gt$ with $t = 3.0$ s and $u = 0$ to get $v = 10 \times 3.0 = +30$ m s^{-1}.)

CHECK YOURSELF 3

A ball is thrown vertically upwards with a speed of 20 m s^{-1} and another vertically downwards with the same speed and from the same height. What interval separates the landing times of the two balls? (Take $g = 10$ m s^{-2}.)

1 Kinematics

TEST YOUR UNDERSTANDING

5 The initial velocity of a car moving on a straight road is 2.0 m s⁻¹. It becomes 8.0 m s⁻¹ after travelling for 2.0 s under constant acceleration. Find the acceleration.

6 A car accelerates from rest to 28 m s⁻¹ in 9.0 s. Find the distance it travels.

7 A particle has an initial velocity of 12 m s⁻¹ and is brought to rest over a distance of 45 m. Find the acceleration of the particle.

8 A particle at the origin has an initial velocity of −6.0 m s⁻¹ and moves with an acceleration of 2.0 m s⁻². Determine when its position will become 16 m.

9 A plane starting from rest takes 15.0 s to take off after speeding over a distance of 450 m on the runway with constant acceleration. Find the take-off velocity.

10 A particle starts from rest with constant acceleration. After travelling a distance d the speed is v. What was the speed when the particle had travelled a distance $\frac{d}{2}$?

11 A car is travelling at 40.0 m s⁻¹. The driver sees an emergency ahead and 0.50 s later slams on the brakes. The deceleration of the car is 4.0 m s⁻².

   a Find the distance travelled before the car stops.

   b Calculate the stopping distance if the driver could apply the brakes instantaneously without a reaction time.

   c Calculate the difference in your answers to **a** and **b**.

   d Assume now that the car was travelling at 30.0 m s⁻¹ instead. Without performing any calculations, state whether the answer to **c** would now be less than, equal to or larger than before. Explain your answer.

12 Two balls are dropped from rest from the same height. One of the balls is dropped 1.00 s after the other. Air resistance is ignored.

   a Find the distance that separates the two balls 2.00 s after the second ball is dropped.

   b Explain what happens to the distance separating the balls as time goes on.

13 A particle moves in a straight line with an acceleration that varies with time as shown in Figure 1.16. Initially the velocity of the object is 2.00 m s⁻¹.

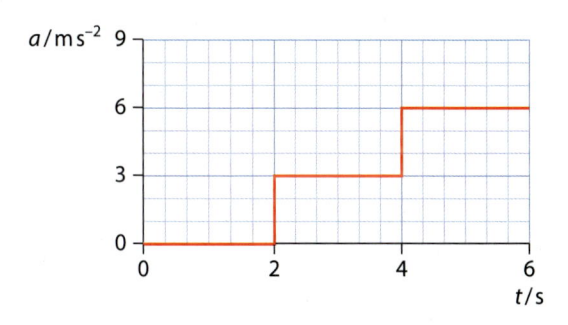

Figure 1.16

   a Find the maximum velocity reached in the first 6.00 s of this motion.

   b Draw a graph of the *velocity* against *time*.

14 The graph in Figure 1.17 shows the variation of velocity with time of an object. Find the acceleration at 2.0 s.

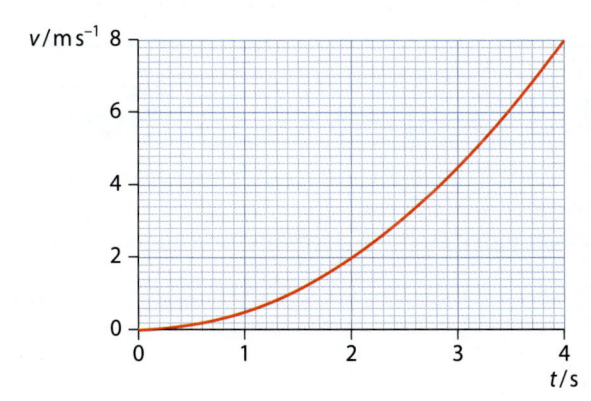

Figure 1.17

CONTINUED

15 Your brand-new convertible is parked 15 m from its garage when it begins to rain. You do not have time to get the keys, so you begin to push the car towards the garage. The maximum acceleration you can give the car is 2.0 m s^{-2} by pushing and 3.0 m s^{-2} by pulling back on the car. Find the least time it takes to put the car in the garage. (Assume that the car and the garage are point objects.)

16 A stone is thrown vertically up from the edge of a cliff 35.0 m from the sea (Figure 1.18). The initial velocity of the stone is 8.00 m s^{-1}.

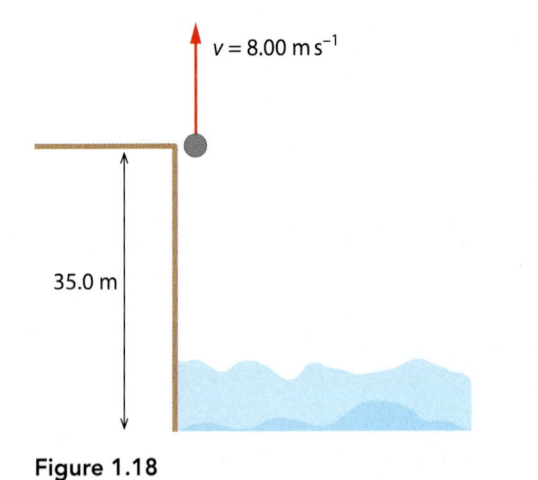

$v = 8.00$ m s^{-1}

35.0 m

Figure 1.18

Determine:

a the maximum height of the stone

b the time when it hits the sea

c the velocity just before hitting the sea

d the distance the stone covers

e the average speed and the average velocity for this motion

17 A ball is thrown upwards from the edge of a cliff with velocity 20.0 m s^{-1}. It reaches the bottom of the cliff 6.0 s later. Take $g = 10$ m s^{-2}.

a Determine the height of the cliff.

b Calculate the speed of the ball as it hits the ground.

18 A toy rocket is launched vertically upwards with acceleration 3.0 m s^{-2}. The fuel runs out when the rocket reaches a height of 85 m.

a Calculate the velocity of the rocket when the fuel runs out.

b Determine the maximum height reached by the rocket.

c Draw a graph to show the variation of

  i the velocity of the rocket

  ii the position of the rocket from launch until it reaches its maximum height

d Calculate the time the rocket takes to fall to the ground from its maximum height.

1.3 Graphs of motion

If the acceleration is constant the equations derived in Section 1.2 hold and we can use them to analyse a motion problem. But if acceleration is not constant these equations do not apply and cannot be used. But we can still analyse a motion using graphs. Our main tools will be those provided in Table 1.1.

Consider the graph of *position* against *time* shown in Figure 1.19.

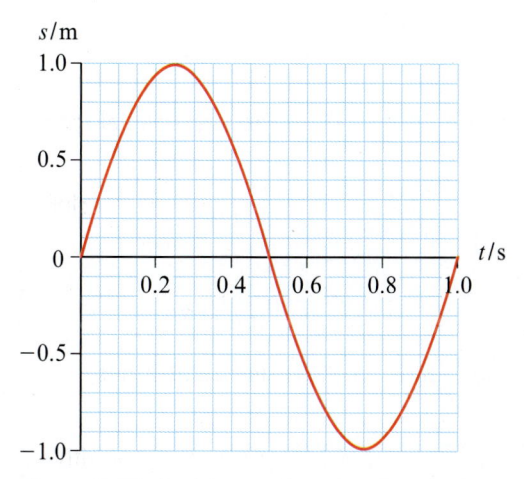

Figure 1.19: *Position* against *time* for accelerated motion.

We would like to predict the shape of the graph of *velocity* against *time*. We use the fact that velocity is the gradient of the *position*-against-*time* graph. We see that at $t = 0$ the gradient is positive. As time increases the gradient is still positive but gets smaller and smaller and at $t = 0.25$ s it becomes zero. It then becomes negative. It gets more and more negative, reaching its most negative value at $t = 0.5$ s. It remains negative past 0.5 s but the curve gets less steep and the gradient becomes zero again at 0.75 s. From then it becomes positive and increases until 1.0 s. These observations lead us to the *velocity*-against-*time* graph shown in Figure 1.20. Note that it is the shape we are after, not detailed numerical values of velocity; hence there is no need to put numbers on the vertical axis.

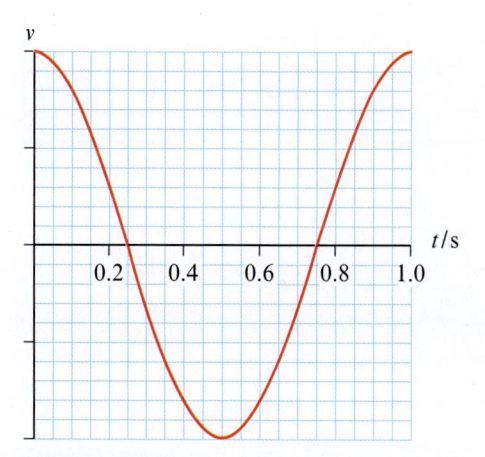

Figure 1.20: The velocity graph corresponding to the graph of Figure 1.19.

Working in exactly the same way we can find the shape of the *acceleration*-against-*time* graph by examining the gradient of the velocity graph we just obtained. The result is Figure 1.21.

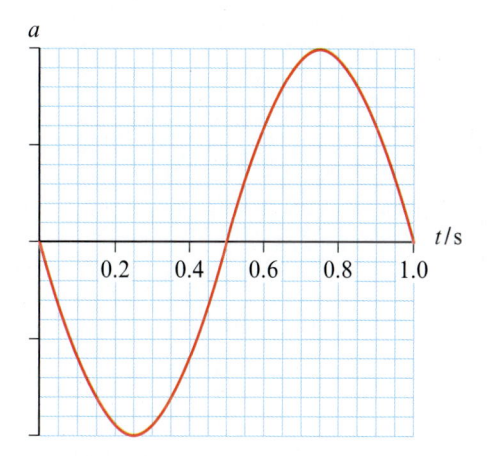

Figure 1.21: Acceleration graph corresponding to the velocity graph of Figure 1.20.

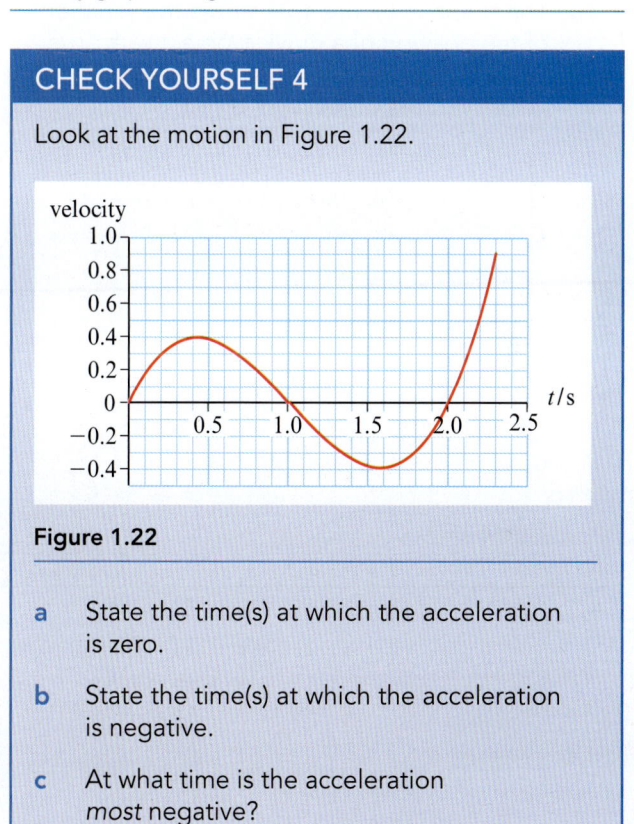

CHECK YOURSELF 4

Look at the motion in Figure 1.22.

Figure 1.22

a   State the time(s) at which the acceleration is zero.

b   State the time(s) at which the acceleration is negative.

c   At what time is the acceleration *most* negative?

d   At 2.3 s, do you expect the displacement to be positive or negative and why?

TEST YOUR UNDERSTANDING

19 The graph in Figure 1.23 shows the variation of the position of a moving object with time. Draw the graph showing the variation of the velocity of the object with time.

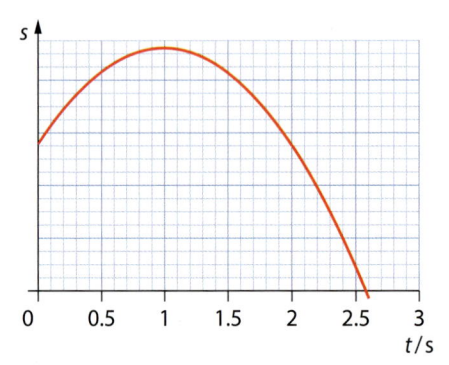

Figure 1.23

20 The graph in Figure 1.24 shows the variation of the position of a moving object with time. Draw the graph showing the variation of the velocity of the object with time.

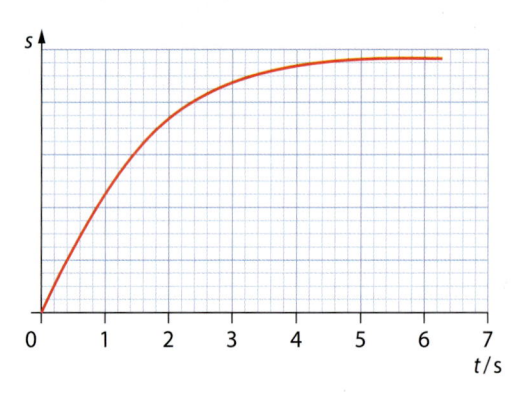

Figure 1.24

21 The graph in Figure 1.25 shows the variation of the position of a moving object with time. Draw the graph showing the variation of the velocity of the object with time.

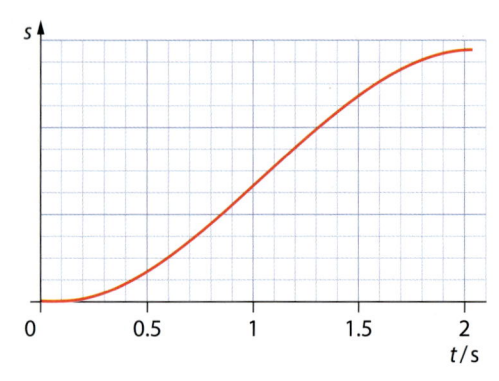

Figure 1.25

22 The graph in Figure 1.26 shows the variation of the velocity of a moving object with time. Draw the graph showing the variation of the position of the object with time. The initial position is zero.

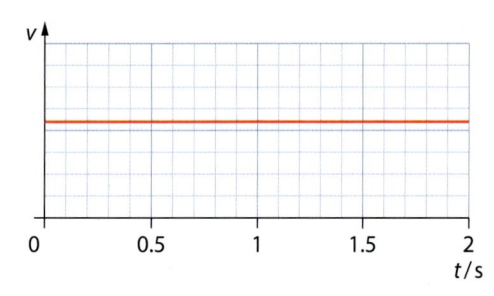

Figure 1.26

CONTINUED

23 The graph in Figure 1.27 shows the variation of the velocity of a moving object with time. Draw the graph showing the variation of the position of the object with time (assuming the initial position to be zero).

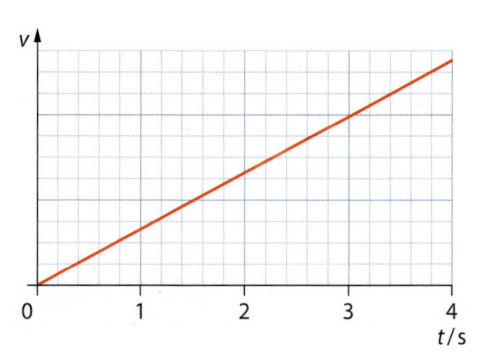

Figure 1.27

24 The graph in Figure 1.28 shows the variation of the velocity of a moving object with time. Draw the graph showing the variation of the acceleration of the object with time.

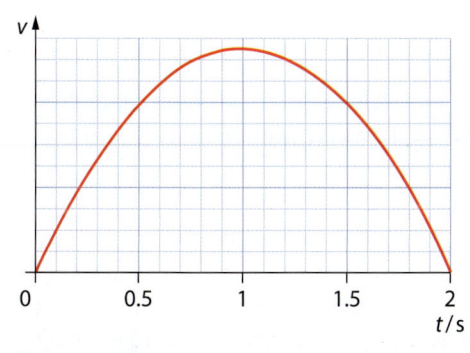

Figure 1.28

25 The graph in Figure 1.29 shows how acceleration varies with time.

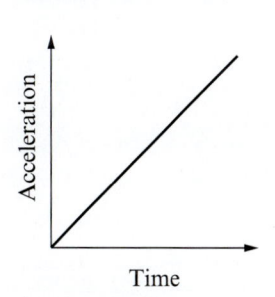

Figure 1.29

Draw a graph to show how velocity varies with time. The initial velocity is zero.

26 The graph in Figure 1.30 shows how acceleration varies with time.

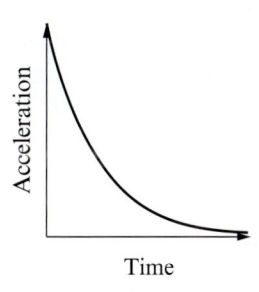

Figure 1.30

Draw a graph to show how velocity varies with time. The initial velocity is zero.

27 The graph in Figure 1.31 shows the position against *time* of an object moving in a straight line. Four points on this graph have been selected.

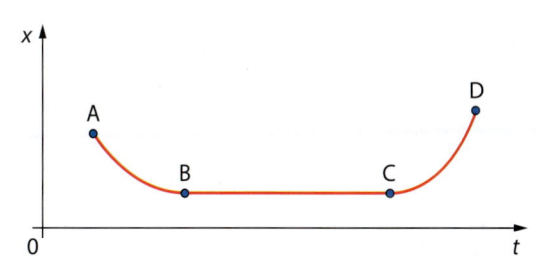

Figure 1.31

- **a** Is the velocity between **A** and **B** positive, zero or negative?
- **b** What can you say about the velocity between **B** and **C**?
- **c** Is the acceleration between **A** and **B** positive, zero or negative?
- **d** Is the acceleration between **C** and **D** positive, zero or negative?

CONTINUED

28 Sketch velocity–time plots (no numbers are necessary on the axes) for the following motions.

   a A ball is dropped from a certain height and bounces off a hard floor. The speed just before each impact with the floor is the same as the speed just after impact. Assume that the time of contact with the floor is negligibly small.

   b A cart slides with negligible friction along a horizontal air track. When the cart hits the ends of the air track it reverses direction with the same speed it had right before impact. Assume the time of contact of the cart and the ends of the air track are negligibly small.

   c A person jumps from a hovering helicopter. After a few seconds she opens a parachute. Eventually she will reach a terminal speed and will then land.

1.4 Projectile motion

Figure 1.32 shows the positions of two objects every 0.2 s: the first was simply allowed to drop vertically from rest; the other was launched horizontally with no vertical component of velocity. We see that in the vertical direction, both objects fall the **same distance** in the **same time** and so will hit the ground at the same time.

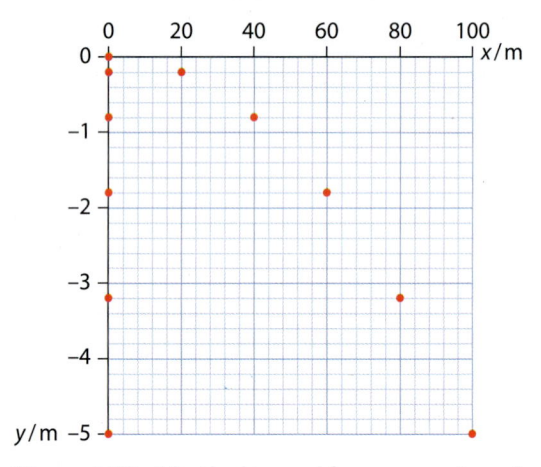

Figure 1.32: A body dropped from rest and one launched horizontally cover the same vertical distance in the same time.

THEORY OF KNOWLEDGE

How do we understand this fact? Consider Figure 1.33, in which a black ball is projected horizontally with velocity v. A blue ball is allowed to drop vertically from the same height.

Figure 1.33a shows the situation when the balls are released as seen by an observer X at rest on the ground. But suppose there is an observer Y, who moves to the right with velocity $\frac{v}{2}$ with respect to the ground. What does Y see? Observer Y sees the black ball moving to the right with velocity $\frac{v}{2}$ and the blue ball approaching with velocity $-\frac{v}{2}$ Figure 1.18b). The motions of the two balls are therefore identical (except for direction). So this observer will determine that the two bodies reach the ground at the **same time**. Since time is absolute in Newtonian physics, the two bodies must reach the ground at the same time as far as any other observer is concerned as well.

1 Kinematics

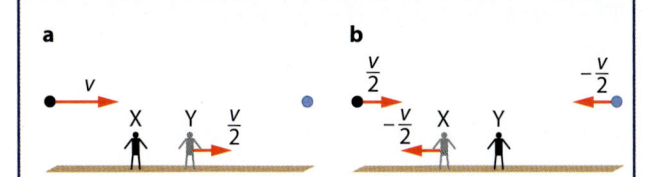

CONTINUED

Figure 1.33: a A ball projected horizontally and one simply dropped from rest from the point of view of observer X. Observer Y is moving to the right with velocity $\frac{v}{2}$ with respect to the ground. **b** From the point of view of observer Y, the black and the blue balls have identical motions.

The motion of a ball that is projected at some angle can be analysed by separately looking at the horizontal and the vertical directions. All we have to do is consider two motions, one in the horizontal direction in which there is no acceleration and another in the vertical direction in which we have an acceleration, g.

Consider Figure 1.34, where a projectile is launched at an angle θ to the horizontal with speed u.

The components of the *initial* velocity vector are $u_x = u \cos\theta$ and $u_y = u \sin\theta$.

At some later time t the components of velocity are v_x and v_y. In the x-direction there is zero acceleration and in the y-direction, the acceleration is $-g$ and so:

Horizontal direction	Vertical direction
$v_x = u \cos\theta$	$v_y = u \sin\theta - gt$

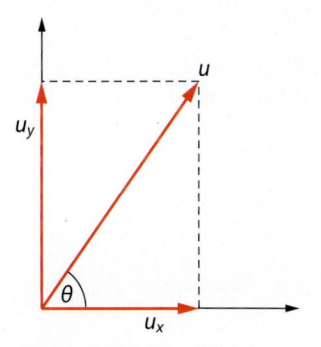

Figure 1.34: A projectile is launched at an angle θ to the horizontal with speed u.

The green vector in Figure 1.35a shows the position of the projectile t seconds after launch. The red arrows in Figure 1.35b show the velocity vectors and their components. Here the true vector nature of what we have been calling position comes into its own.

The position of the projectile is determined by the **position vector** $\vec{r}$, a vector from the origin to the position of the projectile. The components of this vector are x and y.

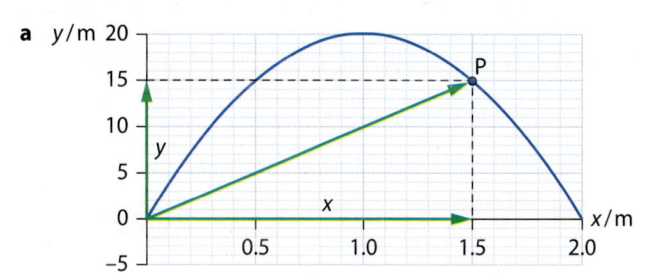

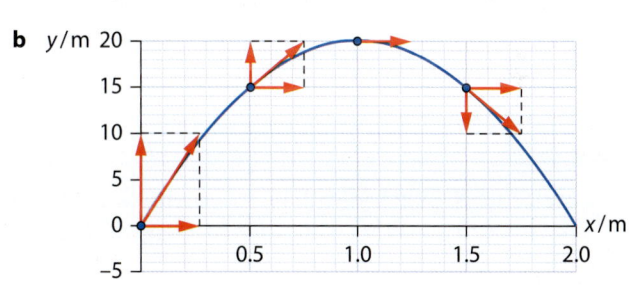

Figure 1.35: a The position of the particle is determined if we know the x- and y-components of the position vector. **b** The velocity vectors for projectile motion are tangents to the parabolic path.

EXAM TIP

All that we are doing is using the formulas from the previous section for velocity and position – $v = u + at$ and $s = ut + \frac{1}{2}at^2$ – and rewriting them **separately** for each direction x and y. In the x-direction there is zero acceleration, and in the y-direction there is an acceleration $-g$.

We would like to know the x- and y-components of the position vector. We now use the formula for position. In the x-direction:

$x = u_x t$ and so $x = ut \cos\theta$

In the y-direction: $y = u_y t - \frac{1}{2}gt^2$ and so $y = ut \sin\theta - \frac{1}{2}gt^2$.

PHYSICS FOR THE IB DIPLOMA: COURSEBOOK

In summary:

Horizontal direction	Vertical direction
$v_x = u\cos\theta$	$v_y = u\sin\theta - gt$
$x = ut\cos\theta$	$y = ut\sin\theta - \frac{1}{2}gt^2$

The equation with 'squares of speeds' is a bit trickier (carefully review the following steps). It is:

$v^2 = u^2 - 2gy$

Since $v^2 = v_x^2 + v_y^2$ and $u^2 = u_x^2 + u_y^2$, and in addition $v_x^2 = u_x^2$, this is also equivalent to:

$v_y^2 = u_y^2 - 2gy$

> **EXAM TIP**
>
> Always choose your x- and y-axes so that the origin is the point where the launch takes place.

> **CHECK YOURSELF 5**
>
> A projectile is launched with kinetic energy K at 60° to the horizontal. What is the kinetic energy of the projectile at the highest point of its path? (Kinetic energy is equal to $\frac{1}{2}mv^2$.)

> **WORKED EXAMPLE 1.10**
>
> A body is launched with a speed of 18.0 m s^{-1} at the following angles:
>
> a 30° to the horizontal
>
> b 0° to the horizontal
>
> c 90° to the horizontal
>
> Find the x- and y-components of the initial velocity in each case.
>
> **Answer**
>
> a $v_x = u\cos\theta$ $v_y = u\sin\theta$
>
> $v_x = 18.0 \times \cos 30°$ $v_y = 18.0 \times \sin 30°$
>
> $v_x = 15.6 \text{ m s}^{-1}$ $v_y = 9.00 \text{ m s}^{-1}$
>
> b $v_x = 18.0 \text{ m s}^{-1}$ $v_y = 0 \text{ m s}^{-1}$
>
> c $v_x = 0$ $v_y = 18.0 \text{ m s}^{-1}$

> **WORKED EXAMPLE 1.11**
>
> For a projectile launched at some angle above the horizontal, sketch graphs to show the variation with time of:
>
> a the horizontal component of velocity
>
> b the vertical component of velocity
>
> **Answer**
>
> The graphs are shown in Figure 1.36.

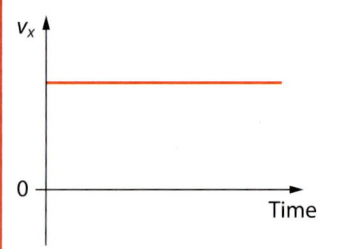

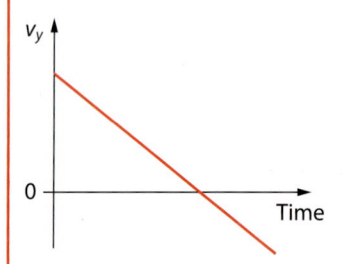

Figure 1.36: Answer to worked example 1.11

> **WORKED EXAMPLE 1.12**
>
> An object is launched horizontally from a height of 20 m above the ground with speed 15 m s^{-1}. Determine:
>
> a the time at which it will hit the ground
>
> b the horizontal distance travelled
>
> c the speed with which it hits the ground
>
> (Take $g = 10 \text{ m s}^{-2}$.)
>
> **Answer**
>
> a The launch is horizontal, i.e. $\theta = 0°$, and so the formula for vertical position is just $y = -\frac{1}{2}gt^2$. The object will hit the ground when $y = -20$ m.

CONTINUED

Substituting the values, we find:

$-20 = -5t^2$

$\Rightarrow t = 2.0\,\text{s}$

b The horizontal position is found from $x = ut$. Substituting values:

$x = 15 \times 2.0 = 30\,\text{m}$

(Remember that $\theta = 0°$.)

c Use $v^2 = u^2 - 2gy$ to get:

$v^2 = 15^2 - 2 \times 10 \times (-20)$

$v = 25\,\text{m s}^{-1}$

WORKED EXAMPLE 1.13

An object is launched horizontally with a velocity of $12\,\text{m s}^{-1}$. Determine:

a the vertical component of velocity after 4.0 s

b the x- and y-components of the position vector of the object after 4.0 s.

Answer

a The launch is again horizontal, i.e. $\theta = 0°$, so substitute this value in the formulas. The horizontal component of velocity is $12\,\text{m s}^{-1}$ at all times.

From $v_y = -gt$, the vertical component after 4.0 s is $v_y = -40\,\text{m s}^{-1}$.

b The coordinates after time t are:

$x = ut \qquad y = -\tfrac{1}{2}gt^2$

$x = 12.0 \times 4.0 \qquad y = -5 \times 16$

$x = 48\,\text{m}$ and $y = -80\,\text{m}$

EXAM TIP

Worked example 1.13 is a basic problem—you must know how to do this!

Figure 1.37 shows an object thrown at an angle of $\theta = 30°$ to the horizontal with initial speed $20\,\text{m s}^{-1}$. The position of the object is shown every 0.2 s. Note how the dots get closer together as the object rises (the speed is decreasing) and how they move apart on the way down (the speed is increasing). It reaches a maximum height of 5.1 m and travels a horizontal distance of 35 m. The photo in Figure 1.38 shows an example of projectile motion.

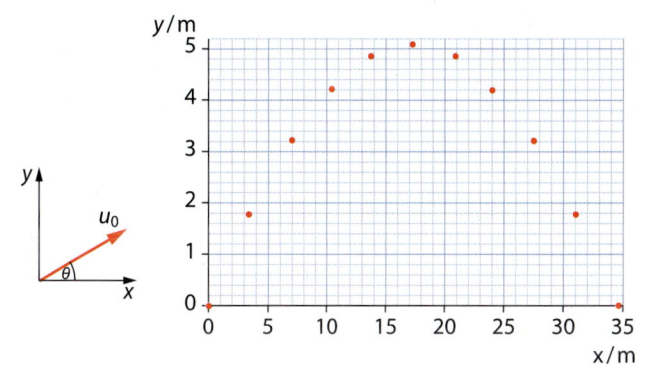

Figure 1.37: A launch at of $\theta = 30°$ to the horizontal with initial speed $20\,\text{m s}^{-1}$.

At what point in time does the vertical velocity component become zero? Setting $v_y = 0$ we find:

$0 = u\sin\theta - gt$

$\Rightarrow t = \dfrac{u\sin\theta}{g}$

Figure 1.38: A real example of projectile motion.

The time when the vertical velocity becomes zero is, of course, the time when the object attains its maximum height. What is this height? Going back to the equation for the vertical component of position, we find that when:

$t = \frac{u \sin \theta}{g}$

y is given by:

$y_{max} = u \frac{u \sin \theta}{g} \sin \theta - \frac{1}{2} g \left(\frac{u \sin \theta}{g} \right)^2$

$y_{max} = \frac{u^2 \sin^2 \theta}{2g}$

What about the maximum displacement in the horizontal direction (called the range)? At this point y is zero. We can find the time by setting $y = 0$ in the formula for y but it is easier to notice that since the path is symmetrical the time to cover the range is double the time to get to the top, so $t = \frac{2u \sin \theta}{g}$.

> **EXAM TIP**
>
> You should not remember these formulas by heart. You should be able to derive them quickly.

Therefore the range is:

$x = \frac{2u^2 \sin \theta \cos \theta}{g}$

A bit of trigonometry allows us to rewrite this as:

$x = \frac{u^2 \sin 2\theta}{g}$

One of the identities in trigonometry is $2 \sin \theta \cos \theta = \sin 2\theta$.

The maximum value of $\sin 2\theta$ is 1, and this happens when $2\theta = 90°$ ($\theta = 45°$). In other words, we obtain the maximum range with a launch angle of 45°. This equation also says that there are two different angles of launch that give the same range for the same initial speed. These two angles add up to a right angle. (Can you see why?)

> **CHECK YOURSELF 6**
>
> On earth the maximum height and range of a projectile are H and R, respectively. The projectile is launched with the same velocity on a planet where the acceleration of free fall is $2g$. What are the maximum height and range of the projectile on the planet?

> **WORKED EXAMPLE 1.14**
>
> A projectile is launched at 32.0° to the horizontal with initial speed 25.0 m s^{-1}. Determine the maximum height reached. (Take $g = 9.81$ m s^{-2}.)
>
> **Answer**
>
> The vertical velocity is given by $v_y = u \sin \theta - gt$ and becomes zero at the highest point. Thus:
>
> $t = \frac{u \sin \theta}{g}$
>
> $t = \frac{25.0 \times \sin 32.0°}{9.81}$
>
> $t = 1.35$ s
>
> Substituting in the formula for y, $y = ut \sin \theta - \frac{1}{2} gt^2$, we get:
>
> $y = 25 \times \sin 32.0° \times 1.35 - \frac{1}{2} \times 9.81 \times 1.35^2$
>
> $y = 8.95$ m
>
> Equivalently, $0 = (u \sin \theta)^2 - 2gy \Rightarrow$
>
> $y = \frac{(25.0 \times \sin 32.0°)^2}{2 \times 9.81} = 8.95$ m

> **WORKED EXAMPLE 1.15**
>
> A projectile is launched horizontally from a height of 42 m above the ground. As it hits the ground, the velocity makes an angle of 55° to the horizontal. Find the initial velocity of launch. (Take $g = 9.8$ m s^{-2}.)
>
> **Answer**
>
> The time it takes to hit the ground is found from $y = -\frac{1}{2} gt^2$. (Here $\theta = 0°$ since the launch is horizontal.)
>
> The ground is at $y = -42$ m and so:
>
> $-42 = -\frac{1}{2} \times 9.8 t^2$
>
> $\Rightarrow \quad t = 2.928$ s
>
> Using $v_y = u \sin \theta - gt$, when the projectile hits the ground:
>
> $v_y = 0 - 9.8 \times 2.928$
>
> $v_y = -28.69$ m s^{-1}

> **CONTINUED**
>
> We know the angle the final velocity makes with the ground (Figure 1.39). Hence:
>
> $\tan 55° = \left|\dfrac{v_y}{v_x}\right|$
>
> $\Rightarrow v_x = \dfrac{28.69}{\tan 55°}$
>
> $v_x = 20.09 \approx 20 \text{ m s}^{-1}$ 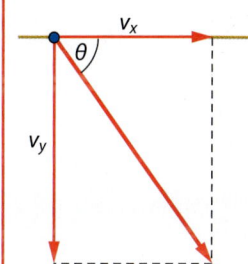
>
> $\tan \theta = \left|\dfrac{v_y}{v_x}\right|$
>
> **Figure 1.39**

Links

In projectile motion we have a single constant force whose direction is always vertical. This force is the weight of the body. When the body is projected at an angle to the vertical the result is motion along a path that is parabolic. There is one other instance where again a force that is constant in magnitude and direction acts on a body. This is the case of motion of an electric charge in a uniform electric field. So we expect that a charge projected at an angle in a region of uniform electric field will also result in motion along a parabolic path and what we have learned in this chapter will apply to that case as well. See **Chapter 19**.

Fluid resistance

The discussion of the previous sections has neglected air resistance forces. In general, whenever a body moves through a fluid (gas or liquid) it experiences a **fluid resistance force** that is directed opposite to the velocity. Typically $F = kv$ for low speeds and $F = kv^2$ for high speeds (where k is a constant). The magnitude of this force increases with increasing speed.

Imagine dropping a body of mass m from some height. Assume that the force of air resistance on this body is $F = kv$. Initially, the only force on the body is its weight, which accelerates it downwards. As the speed increases, the force of air resistance also increases. Eventually, this force will become equal to the weight and so the acceleration will become zero: the body will then move at constant speed, called **terminal speed**, v_T. This speed can be found from:

$mg = kv_T$

which leads to:

$v_T = \dfrac{mg}{k}$

Figure 1.40 shows how the speed and acceleration vary for motion with an air resistance force that is proportional to speed. The speed eventually becomes the terminal speed, and the acceleration becomes zero. The initial acceleration is g.

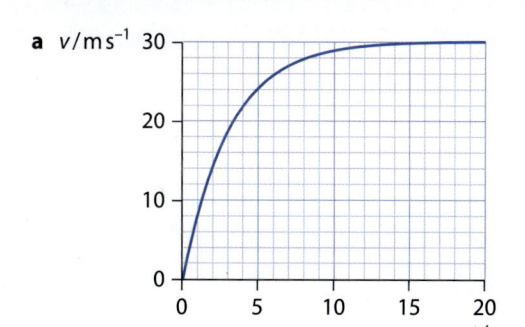

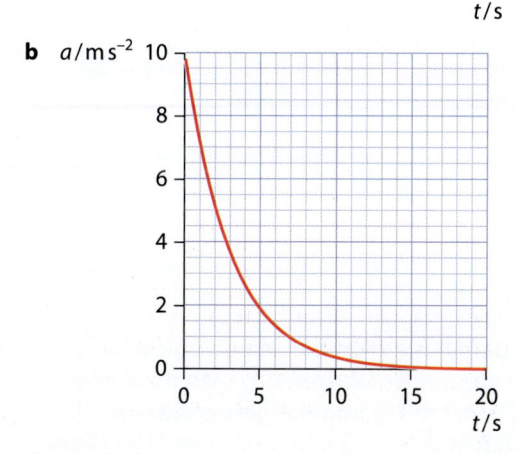

Figure 1.40: a The variation with time of a speed. **b** Acceleration in motion with an air resistance force proportional to speed.

The effect of air resistance forces on projectiles is very pronounced. Figure 1.41 shows the positions of a projectile with (red) and without (blue) air resistance forces. With air resistance forces the range and maximum height are smaller and the shape is no longer symmetrical.

The projectile hits the ground at a steeper angle.

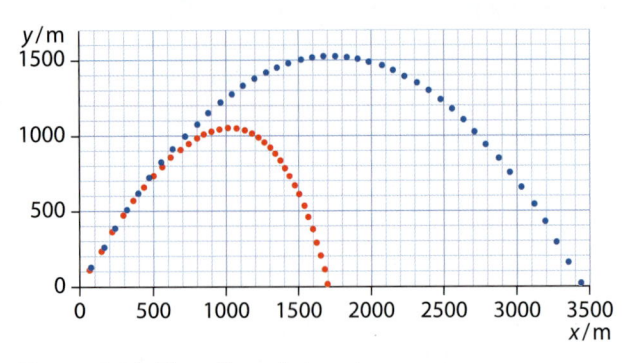

Figure 1.41: The effect of air resistance on projectile motion.

> **WORKED EXAMPLE 1.16**
>
> The force of air resistance in the motion described by Figure 1.40 is given by $F = 0.653v$.
>
> Determine the mass of the projectile.
>
> **Answer**
>
> The terminal speed is 30 m s^{-1} and is given by $v_T = \frac{mg}{k}$. Hence:
>
> $m = \frac{0.653 \times 30}{9.8}$
>
> $m \approx 2.0$ kg

NATURE OF SCIENCE

The simple and the complex

Careful observation of motion in the natural world led to the equations for motion with uniform acceleration along a straight line that we have used in this section. Thinking about what causes an object to move links to the idea of forces. However, although the material in this section is perhaps some of the 'easiest' material in your physics course, it does not enable you to understand the falling of a leaf off a tree. The falling leaf is complicated because it is acted upon by several forces: its weight, but also air resistance forces that constantly vary as the orientation and speed of the leaf change. In addition, there is wind to consider as well as the fact that turbulence in air greatly affects the motion of the leaf. So the physics of the falling leaf is far away from the physics of motion along a straight line at constant acceleration. But learning the principles of physics in a simpler context allows its application in more involved situations.

TEST YOUR UNDERSTANDING

29 A ball rolls off a table with a horizontal speed of 2.0 m s^{-1}. The table is 1.3 m high. Calculate how far from the table the ball will land.

30 Two particles are on the same vertical line. They are thrown horizontally with the same speed, 4.0 m s^{-1}, from heights of 4.0 m and 8.0 m.

   a Calculate the distance that will separate the two objects when both land on the ground.

   b The particle at the 4.0 m height is now launched with horizontal speed u such that it lands at the same place as the particle launched from 8.0 m. Calculate u.

31 For an object thrown at an angle of 40° to the horizontal at a speed of 20 m s^{-1}, draw graphs of:

   a *horizontal velocity* against *time*

   b *vertical velocity* against *time*

   c *acceleration* against *time*.

32 Determine the maximum height reached by an object thrown with speed 24 m s^{-1} at 40° to the horizontal.

33 An object is thrown with speed 20.0 m s^{-1} at an angle of 50° to the horizontal. Draw graphs to show the variation with time of:

   a the horizontal position

   b the vertical position

CONTINUED

34 A cruel man takes aim horizontally at a chimp that is hanging from the branch of a tree, as shown in Figure 1.42.

The chimp lets go of the branch as soon as the hunter pulls the trigger. Treating the chimp and the bullet as point particles, determine if the bullet will hit the chimp.

Figure 1.42

35 A ball is launched from the surface of a planet. Air resistance and other frictional forces are neglected. The graph in Figure 1.43 shows the position of the ball every 0.20 s.

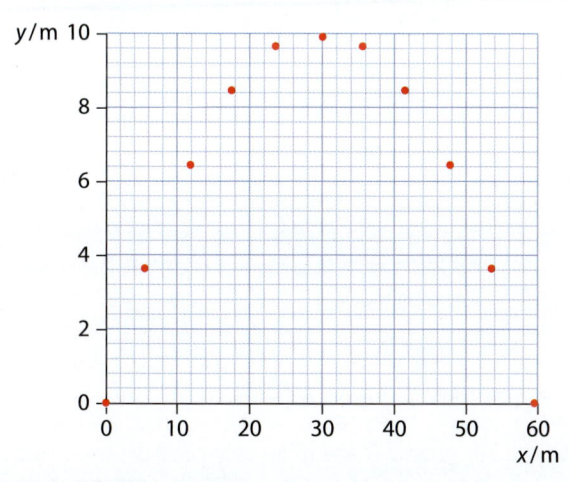

Figure 1.43

a Use this graph to determine:

  i the components of the initial velocity of the ball,

  ii the angle to the horizontal the ball was launched at,

  iii the acceleration of free fall on this planet.

b Make a copy of the graph and draw two arrows to represent the velocity and the acceleration vectors of the ball at $t = 1.0$ s.

c The ball is now launched under identical conditions from the surface of a **different** planet where the acceleration due to gravity is twice as large. Draw the path of the ball on your graph.

36 A stone is thrown with a speed of 20.0 m s^{-1} at an angle of 48° to the horizontal from the edge of a cliff 60.0 m above the surface of the sea.

a Calculate the velocity with which the stone hits the sea.

b Discuss qualitatively the effect of air resistance on your answer to **a**.

37 a State what is meant by **terminal speed**.

b A ball is dropped from rest. The force of air resistance on the ball is proportional to the ball's speed. Explain why the ball will reach terminal speed.

38 A projectile is launched with speed u at 45° to the horizontal. The projectile is at height h at two different times.

a Show that the horizontal distance separating those points is $\frac{u}{g}\sqrt{u^2 - 4gh}$.

b Deduce, using the result in part **a**, the maximum height reached by this projectile.

39 A projectile is launched with some speed at some angle to the horizontal. At 1.0 s and at 5.0 s the height of the projectile from the ground is the same. What is the maximum height reached by this projectile? (Take $g = 10$ m s^{-2}.)

SELF-ASSESSMENT CHECKLIST

I am able to …	Section	Not yet	Nearly there	Ready to move on
define and distinguish between the concepts of position, displacement, average and instantaneous velocity and average and instantaneous acceleration	1.1			
solve problems using the equations of kinematics	1.2			
analyse motion through graphs	1.3			
solve problems with projectile motion	1.4			
describe the effect of air resistance force on projectile motion	1.4			

REFLECTION

Do you understand the difference between *distance* and *displacement*? Do you understand the difference between *speed* and *velocity*? Are you confident using the *equations of kinematics*? Do you know what information a graph of position versus time gives? Do you know what information a graph of velocity versus time gives? Can you explain why a body reaches *terminal speed* if it is acted upon by a speed dependent resistance force? Do you understand how to solve problems with *projectile motion*? Can you describe the effect of *air resistance* on the path of a projectile?

EXAM-STYLE QUESTIONS

You can find questions in the style of IB exams online in the digital coursebook.

CHECK YOURSELF ANSWERS

1. Let d be the distance between A and B and t_1, t_2 the travel times back and forth. Then $d = 15 t_1 = 30 t_2$, i.e. $t_1 = 2 t_2$. The average speed is then $\bar{v} = \dfrac{2d}{t_1 + t_2} = \dfrac{2 \times 30 t_2}{3 t_2} = 20 \text{ m s}^{-1}$

2. Positive for 1.0 s on, because curve is concave up, negative for 0 s to 1.0 s and zero at 1.0 s.

3. It takes 2 s to get to the maximum height and 2 to return so the required time is 4 s.

4. a Zero at about 0.4 s and 1.6 s.
   b Negative from 0.4 s to 1.6 s.
   c Most negative at 1.0 s.
   d The displacement from 0 s to 1.0 s is about the same in magnitude as that from 1.0 s to 2.0 s so the displacement at 2.3 s will be positive.

5. $K = \frac{1}{2} m u^2$. At the highest point, KE $= \frac{1}{2} m u^2 \cos^2 60° = \frac{1}{2} m u^2 \times \frac{1}{4} = \frac{K}{4}$.

6. Both H and R are inversely proportional to the acceleration of free fall and so both are halved.

Chapter 2
Forces and Newton's laws

LEARNING OBJECTIVES

In this chapter you will learn how to:

- treat bodies as point particles
- construct and interpret free-body force diagrams
- apply the equilibrium condition, $\Sigma F = 0$
- apply Newton's three laws of motion
- solve problems involving frictional forces
- explain why we have acceleration in circular motion
- apply Newton's laws to circular motion
- identify centripetal forces.

PHYSICS FOR THE IB DIPLOMA: COURSEBOOK

> **GUIDING QUESTIONS**
>
> - What is the connection between force and motion?
> - How does knowledge of the forces on a body allow a prediction of the state of motion of a body?

Introduction

This chapter introduces Newton's laws of motion. A lot of classical physics is based on these laws. It was once thought that knowledge of the present state of a system and all forces acting on it would enable the complete prediction of the state of that system in the future. We will learn how to correctly identify the forces that act on a system, find the net force on a system, and apply Newton's laws to describe the motion that may take place.

2.1 Forces and their direction

A **force**, which we commonly associate with a pull or a push, is a vector quantity. We represent forces with arrows whose length is proportional to the magnitude of the force. It is important that we are able to correctly identify the *direction* of forces.

Forces

In this chapter we will deal with the following forces: weight, string tension, spring tension, normal contact forces, drag forces, buoyant forces (upthrust) and frictional forces.

Weight

Weight is the gravitational force between a body and the planet the body is on. The **weight** of a body is given by the formula

$W = mg$

where m is the mass of the body and g is the gravitational field strength of the planet. The unit of g is newton per kilogram, N kg^{-1}. The gravitational field strength is also known as 'the acceleration due to gravity' or the 'acceleration of free fall'. Therefore the unit of g is also m s^{-2}.

If m is in kg and g in N kg^{-1} or m s^{-2} then W is in newtons, N. On the *surface* of the earth, $g = 9.81$ N kg^{-1}—a number that we will sometime approximate by the more convenient 10 N kg^{-1}. (We almost always do this for multiple choice exam questions.) This force is always directed vertically downward, as shown in Figure 2.1.

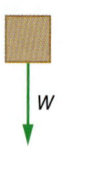

Figure 2.1: The weight of an object is always directed vertically downward.

The mass of an object is the same everywhere in the universe, but its weight depends on the *location* of the body. For example, a mass of 70 kg has a weight of 687 N on the surface of the earth ($g = 9.81$ N kg^{-1}) and a weight of 635 N at a height of 250 km from the earth's surface (where $g = 9.07$ N kg^{-1}). However, on the surface of Venus, where the gravitational field strength is only 8.9 N kg^{-1}, the weight is 623 N.

Tension

The force that arises in any body when it is stretched or compressed is called **tension**. A string that is taut is said to be under tension. This force is the result of interactions between the molecules of the material making up the string and is electrical in nature. A tension force in a string is created when two forces are applied in opposite directions at the ends of the string (see Figure 2.2).

Figure 2.2: A tension force in a string.

To say that there is tension in a string means that an arbitrary point P on the string is acted upon by two forces (the tension T) as shown in Figure 2.3. If the string hangs from a ceiling and a mass m is tied at the other end, tension develops in the string. At the point of support at the ceiling, the tension force pulls down *on the ceiling* and at the point where the mass is tied the tension acts upwards *on the mass*.

2 Forces and Newton's laws

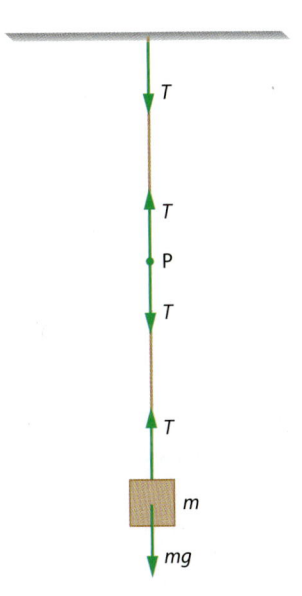

Figure 2.3: The tension is directed along the string.

In most cases we will idealize the string by assuming it is massless. This does not mean that the string *really* is massless, but rather that its mass is so small compared with any other masses in the problem that we can neglect it. In that case, the tension T is the same at all points on the string. The direction of the tension force is along the string. Further examples of tension forces in a string are given in Figure 2.4. A string or rope that is not taut has zero tension in it.

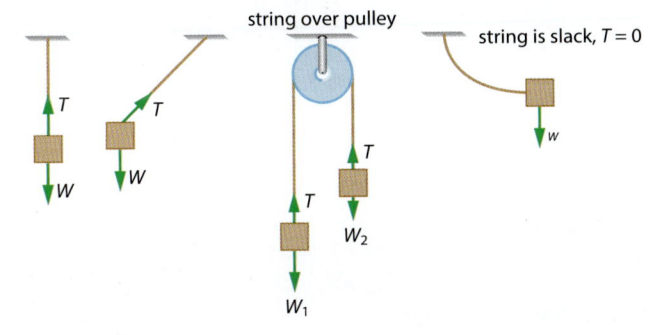

Figure 2.4: More examples of tension forces.

Springs

A spring that is pulled so that its length increases will develop a tension force inside the spring that will tend to bring the length back to its original value. Similarly, if it is compressed a tension force will again try to restore the length of the spring, Figure 2.5. Experiments show that for a range of extensions of the spring, the tension force is proportional to the extension, $T = kx$, where k is known as the spring constant. This relation between tension and extension is known as **Hooke's law**.

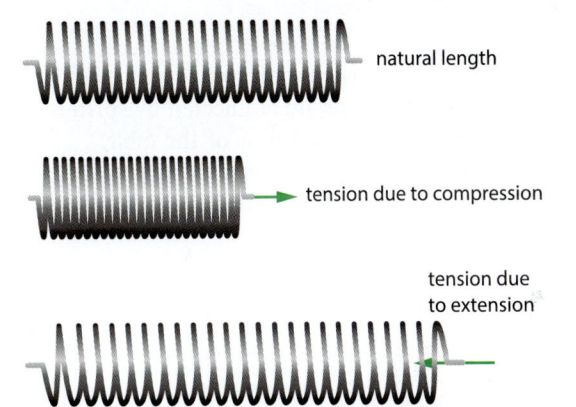

Figure 2.5: Tension is proportional and opposite to the extension or compression.

> ### CHECK YOURSELF 1
>
> A block is attached to a vertical spring. Will the extension of the spring be different on the earth and on the moon?

Normal contact forces

If a body touches another body, there is a **normal contact force** between the two bodies. This force is perpendicular to the surface of the body exerting the force, hence the name normal. Like tension, the origin of this force is also electrical. In Figure 2.6 we show the normal force R on several bodies.

31

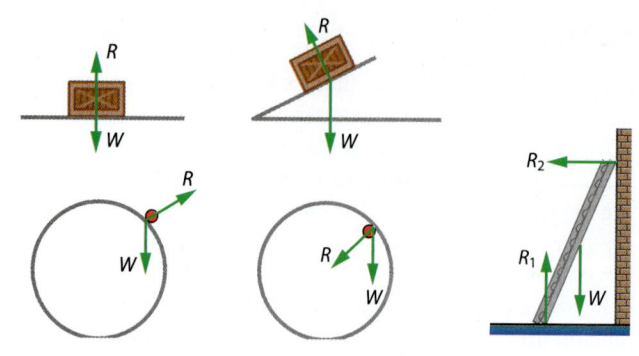

Figure 2.6: Examples of normal forces, R.

We can understand the existence of contact forces in a simple model in which atoms are connected by springs. The block pushes down on the atoms of the table, compressing the springs under the block. This creates the normal force on the block, Figure 2.7.

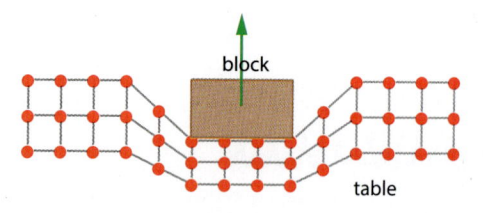

Figure 2.7: A simple model of contact forces.

Drag forces

Drag forces are forces that oppose the motion of a body through a fluid (a gas or a liquid). Typical examples are the air resistance force experienced by a car (see Figure 2.8) or plane, or the resistance force experienced by a steel marble dropped into a jar of honey. Drag forces are directed opposite to the velocity of the body and in general depend on the speed and shape of the body. The higher the speed, the higher the drag force.

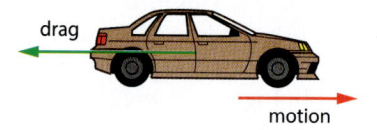

Figure 2.8: Drag forces oppose motion.

For the case of a spherical body of radius r falling through a fluid of density ρ with speed v the drag force is given by Stoke's law:

$$F_D = 6\pi\eta r v$$

where η is a quantity known as the viscosity of the fluid. (This formula applies to spherical, small objects moving through a fluid smoothly.) Viscosity is a measure of the forces between layers of the fluid that are moving relative to each other; water has a viscosity of about 10^{-3} Pa s, motor oil 0.5 Pa s and honey 1.5 Pa s. The unit is Pa s where the pascal (Pa) is the unit of pressure and equals N m^{-2}. Viscosity decreases with increasing temperature.

Buoyant forces (upthrust)

Any object placed in a fluid (liquid or gas) experiences an upward force called the **buoyant force** (see Figure 2.9). This force is given by

$$F_B = \rho g V_{imm}$$

where V_{imm} is the volume of the body that is immersed in the fluid.

If the buoyant force equals the weight of the body, the body will float in the fluid. If the buoyant force is less than the weight, the body will sink. The buoyant force is caused by the pressure that the fluid exerts on the body. The pressure is greater at the bottom compared to that at the top.

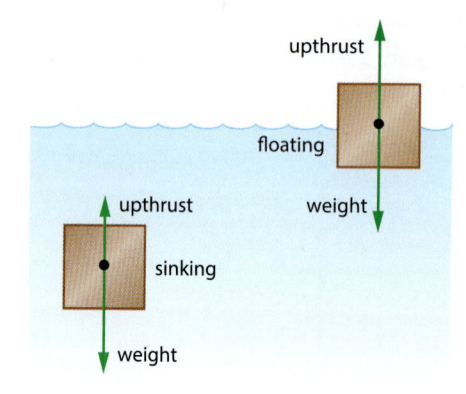

Figure 2.9: Buoyant force.

Frictional forces

Frictional forces generally oppose the motion of a body. They are also electrical in origin. (See Figure 2.10.)

2 Forces and Newton's laws

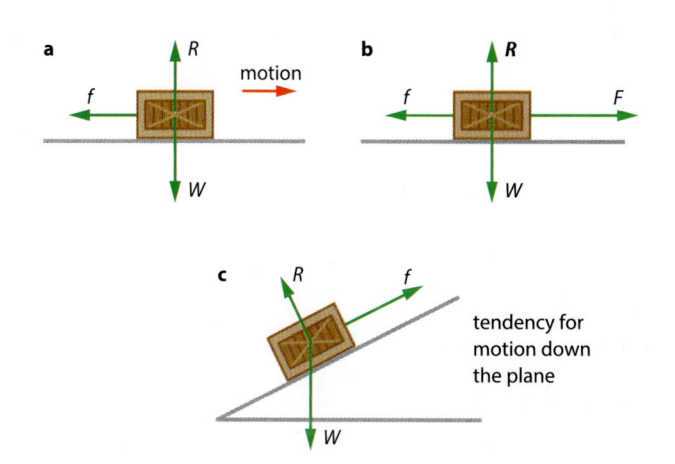

Figure 2.10: Examples of frictional forces, *f*. In **a** there is motion to the right, which is opposed by a single frictional force that will eventually stop the body. In **b** the force accelerating the body is opposed by a frictional force. In **c** the body does not move, but it does have a tendency to move down the plane, and so a frictional force directed up the plane opposes this tendency, keeping the body in equilibrium.

Friction arises whenever one body slides over another. In this case we have **dynamic friction**. Friction also arises whenever there is a tendency for motion, not necessarily motion itself. For example, a block that rests on an inclined plane has a tendency to slide down the plane, so there is a force of friction up the plane. Similarly, if you pull on a block on a level rough road with a small force the block will not move. This is because a force of friction develops that is equal and opposite to the pulling force. In this case we have **static friction**.

In the simple model of matter consisting of atoms connected by springs, pushing the block to the right results in springs stretching and compressing. The net result is a force opposing the motion, friction, Figure 2.11.

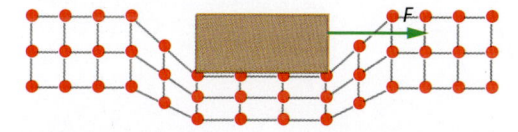

Figure 2.11: Friction in the simple atoms-and-springs model of matter.

A more realistic model involves irregularities (called *asperities*) in the surfaces which interlock, opposing sliding, Figure 2.12.

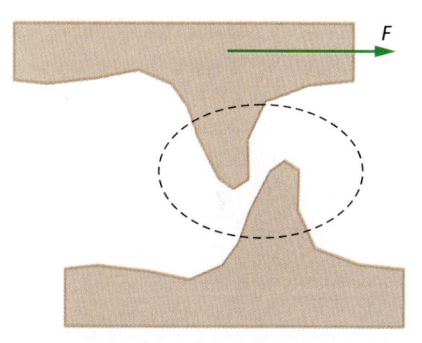

Figure 2.12: Exaggerated view of how asperities oppose the sliding of one surface over the other.

Frictional forces are still not very well understood, and there is no theory of friction that follows directly from the fundamental laws of physics. However, a number of simple, empirical 'laws' of friction have been discovered. These are not always applicable and are only approximately true, but they are useful in describing frictional forces in general terms.

The '**friction laws**' may be summarised as follows:

1. the area of contact between the two surfaces does not affect the frictional force.
2. the force of dynamic friction is equal to $f_d = \mu_d R$, where R is the normal force between the surfaces and μ_d is the **coefficient of dynamic friction**.
3. the force of dynamic friction does not depend on the speed of sliding.
4. the *maximum* force of static friction that can develop between two surfaces is given by $f_s = \mu_s R$, where R is the normal force between the surfaces and μ_s is the **coefficient of static friction** with $\mu_s > \mu_d$.

> **EXAM TIP**
>
> One of the most common mistakes is to think that $\mu_s R$ is the formula that gives the static friction force. This is not correct. This formula gives the maximum possible static friction force that can develop between two surfaces.

Figure 2.13 shows how the frictional force *f* varies with a pulling force *F*. The force *F* pulls on a body on a horizontal rough surface. Initially the static frictional force matches the pulling force and we have no motion, $f_s = F$. When the pulling force exceeds the maximum possible static friction force, $\mu_s R$, the frictional force drops abruptly to the dynamic value of $\mu_d R$ and stays

33

at that constant value as the body accelerates. This is a well-known phenomenon of everyday life: it takes a lot of force to get a heavy piece of furniture to start moving (you must exceed the maximum value of the static friction force), but once you get it moving, pushing it along becomes easier (you are now opposed by the smaller dynamic friction force).

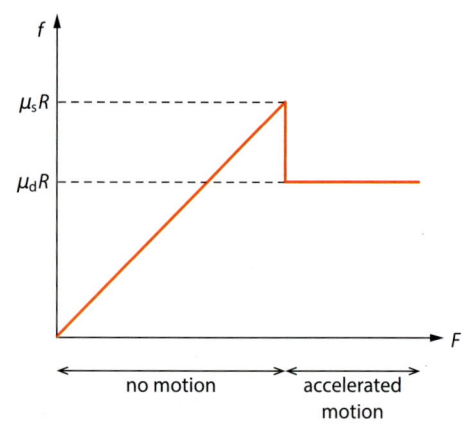

Figure 2.13: The variation of the frictional force f between surfaces with the pulling force F.

CHECK YOURSELF 2

A block of weight 5.0 N rests on a rough horizontal table. The static coefficient of friction between the block and the table is 0.60. A horizontal force of 2.2 N is applied to the block. What is the frictional force on the block?

Other forces

In later chapters we will deal with other forces, such as the electric force, the magnetic force, and the nuclear force.

Free-body force diagrams

A **free-body force diagram** is a diagram showing the magnitude and direction of all the forces acting on a chosen body. The body is shown on its own, free of its surroundings and of any other bodies it may be in contact with. In Figure 2.14 we show three situations in which forces are acting; below each is the corresponding free-body force diagram for the shaded bodies.

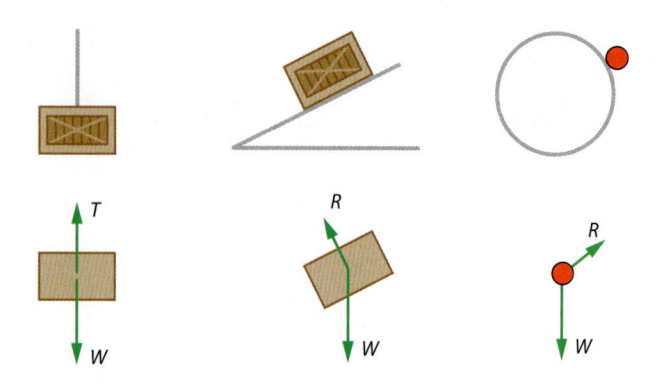

Figure 2.14: Free-body diagrams.

In any mechanics problem, it is important to be able to draw correctly the free-body force diagrams for all the bodies of interest. It is also important that the length of the arrow representing a given force is proportional to the magnitude of the force.

WORKED EXAMPLE 2.1

a Draw the free-body diagram for a pendulum when the bob is at the extreme left position.

b Draw the free-body diagram for a ball that moves on the inside surface of a vertical circle at the three positions shown in Figure 2.15.

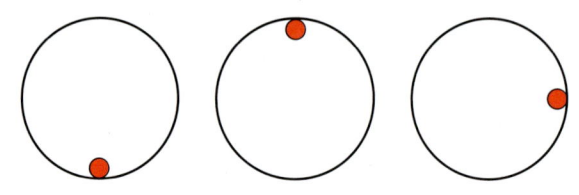

Figure 2.15: For worked example 2.1.

Answer

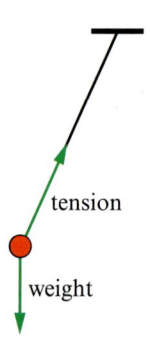

a See Figure 2.16.

Figure 2.16: The two forces on the bob.

2 Forces and Newton's laws

CONTINUED

b See Figure 2.17. The size of the normal force here will be understood when we move to Newton's second law. For now make sure you understand the direction.

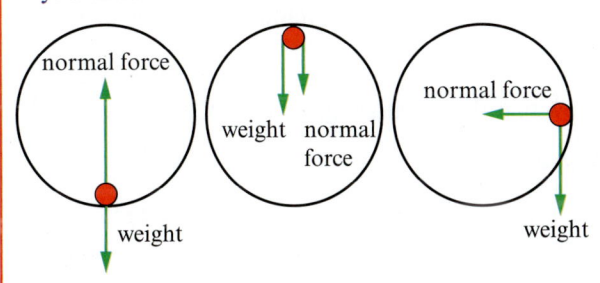

Figure 2.17: The forces on the ball.

Equilibrium

Equilibrium of a point particle means that the **resultant or net force** on the particle is zero. The net force on a particle is the one single force whose effect is the same as the combined effect of individual forces acting on the particle. We denote it by $\sum F$. Finding the net force is easy when the forces are in the same or opposite directions. In Figure 2.18a, the net force is (we take the direction to the right to be positive)

$\sum F = 12 + 6.0 - 8.0 = 10$ N.

This is positive, indicating a direction to the right. In Figure 2.18b it is (we take the direction upward to be positive)

$\sum F = 5.0 + 6.0 - 4.0 - 8.0 = -1.0$ N

The negative sign indicates a direction vertically down.

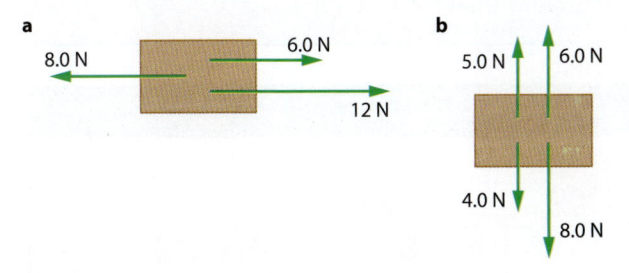

Figure 2.18: The net force is found by plain addition and/or subtraction when the forces are in the same or opposite direction.

WORKED EXAMPLE 2.2

Determine the magnitude of the force F given that the block (Figure 2.19) is in equilibrium.

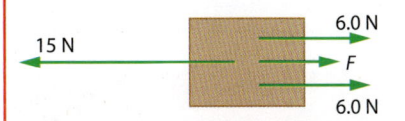

Figure 2.19: For worked example 2.2.

Answer

For equilibrium, $\sum F = 0$ and so $6.0 + F + 6.0 - 15 = 0$. This gives $F = 3.0$ N.

WORKED EXAMPLE 2.3

A brick of weight 50 N rests on a horizontal surface. The coefficient of static friction between the brick and the surface is 0.60, and the coefficient of dynamic friction is 0.20. A horizontal force F is applied to the brick, its magnitude increasing uniformly from zero. Once the brick starts moving the pulling force no longer increases. Estimate the net force on the moving brick.

Answer

The maximum frictional force that can develop between the brick and the surface is $f_s = \mu_s R$, which evaluates to $0.60 \times 50 = 30$ N. So motion takes place when the pulling force is just barely larger than 30 N. Once motion starts the frictional force will be equal to $\mu_d R$, i.e., $0.20 \times 50 = 10$ N. The net force on the brick in that case will be just larger than $30 - 10 = 20$ N.

35

PHYSICS FOR THE IB DIPLOMA: COURSEBOOK

CHECK YOURSELF 3

An ice cube floats in water in a glass. What happens to the level of the water when the ice cube melts?

WORKED EXAMPLE 2.4

An iceberg floats in seawater. The density of ice is 920 kg m^{-3} and that of seawater is 1020 kg m^{-3}. Estimate the fraction of the volume of the iceberg that is under water.

Answer

The weight of the iceberg is balanced by the buoyant force. The weight is given by

$$W = mg = \rho_{ice} gV$$

and the buoyant force is

$$F_B = \rho_{water} gV_{imm}.$$

The weight and the buoyant forces are equal and so

$$\rho_{ice} gV = \rho_{water} gV_{imm}$$
$$\frac{V_{imm}}{V} = \frac{\rho_{ice}}{\rho_{water}} = \frac{920}{1020} = 0.90$$

WORKED EXAMPLE 2.5

A small sphere of radius r and density ρ_{body} falls vertically through a viscous fluid of viscosity η and density ρ_{fluid} with constant speed v. (As we will be discussing extensively later on, motion with constant velocity is equivalent to equilibrium, and the net force is zero.)

Show that the speed v is given by $v = \frac{2}{9}\frac{(\rho_{body} - \rho_{fluid})r^2 g}{\eta}$.

Answer

The forces on the falling sphere are the weight vertically downward and the drag force and the buoyant force upward.

Hence $W = B + F_D$. Now $W = mg = \rho_{body} gV$, $B = \rho_{fluid} gV$ and $F_D = 6\pi\eta rv$ so that:

$$\rho_{body} gV = \rho_{fluid} gV + 6\pi\eta rv.$$

Now use the formula for the volume of a sphere, $V = \frac{4\pi r^3}{3}$, to get

$$\rho_{body} g \frac{4\pi r^3}{3} = \rho_{fluid} g \frac{4\pi r^3}{3} + 6\pi\eta rv$$

$$6\pi\eta rv = \frac{4\pi r^3 g}{3}(\rho_{body} - \rho_{fluid})$$

$$v = \frac{2}{9}\frac{(\rho_{body} - \rho_{fluid})r^2 g}{\eta}$$

CHECK YOURSELF 4

A car moves on a straight horizontal road with constant speed. The force due to the engine pushing the car forward is F. Is the total resistive force on the car less than F, equal to F, or greater than F?

TEST YOUR UNDERSTANDING

1. Figure 2.20 shows a block at rest on a rough table. The block is connected by a string that goes over a pulley to a second hanging block. Draw the forces on each body.

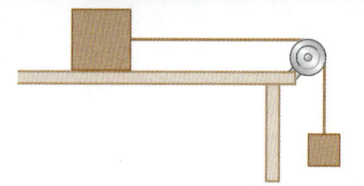

Figure 2.20: For question 1.

CONTINUED

2 a A bead is at rest at the top of a sphere, Figure 2.21. Draw the forces on the bead.

   b The bead is given a small push, and at the right-most position shown, it is just about to lose contact with the sphere. Draw the forces on the bead.

   c Draw the forces on the bead in the intermediate position.

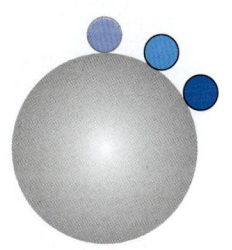

   Figure 2.21: For question 2.

3 Look at Figure 2.22. Compare the tension in the string in the two cases.

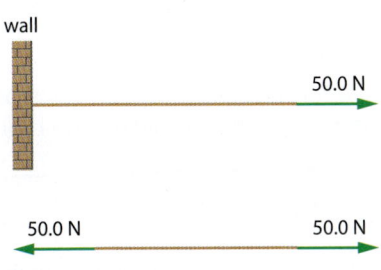

   Figure 2.22: For question 3.

4 A spring is compressed by a certain distance and a mass is attached to its right end, as shown in Figure 2.23. The mass is at rest on a rough table. On a copy of the diagram, draw the forces acting on the mass.

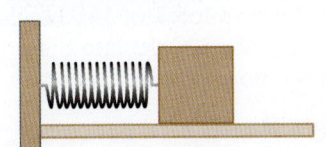

   Figure 2.23: For question 4.

5 A mass hangs attached to three strings, as shown in Figure 2.24. On a copy of the diagram, draw the forces on:

   a the hanging mass

   b the point where the strings join.

   Figure 2.24: For question 5.

6 A force of 12 N extends a spring by 3 cm. What force will extend the spring by 4 cm?

7 Two identical springs, each with a spring constant of $k = 220$ N m^{-1}, are connected to a trolley and fixed supports as shown in Figure 2.25.

   a When the trolley is in equilibrium the springs have their natural length. Calculate the net force on the trolley when it is moved 2.0 cm to the right.

   b When the trolley is in equilibrium each spring is extended by 4.0 cm. Calculate the net force on the trolley when it is moved 2.0 cm to the right.

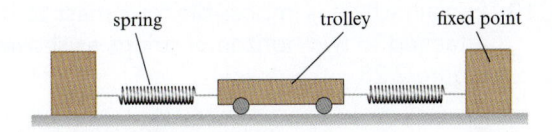

   Figure 2.25: For question 7.

8 Find the net force on each of the bodies, A–F, shown in Figure 2.26. The only forces acting are the ones shown. Indicate direction by 'right', 'left', 'up' and 'down'.

37

CONTINUED

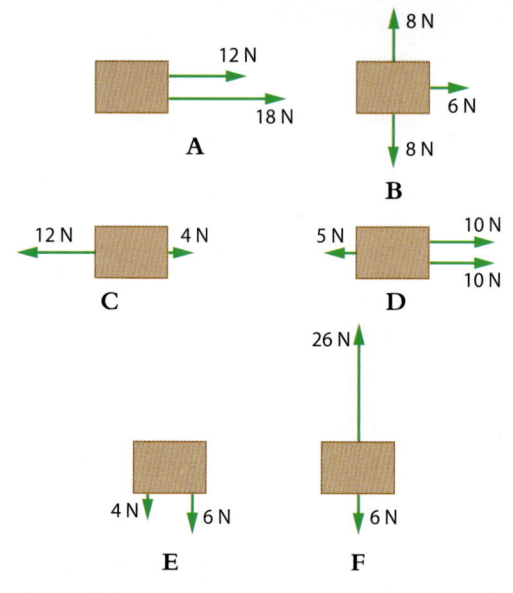

Figure 2.26: For question 8.

9 A small ball falls through a liquid at constant speed. Copy Figure 2.27, then draw and label the forces acting on the ball.

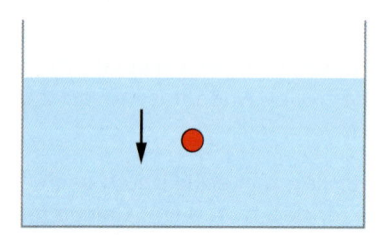

Figure 2.27: For question 9.

10 Explain why it is impossible for a mass to hang attached to two horizontal strings as shown in Figure 2.28.

Figure 2.28: For question 10.

11 A block X rests on top of another block Y (see Figure 2.29). Both blocks are on a frictionless, horizontal table. There is friction between the two blocks. In **a**, a horizontal force is applied to block Y. In **b**, the force is applied to block X. In both cases, the two blocks move together without sliding on each other.

In each case draw the *horizontal* forces acting on each block.

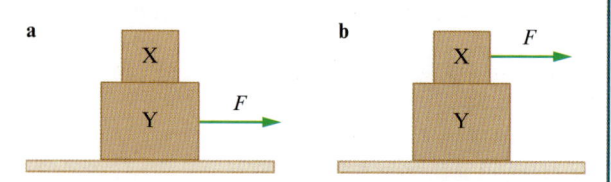

Figure 2.29: In **a** the force is applied to Y. In **b** it is applied to X. The blocks move together.

12 A mass of 2.00 kg rests on a rough horizontal table. The coefficient of static friction between the block and the table is 0.60. The block is attached to a hanging mass by a string that goes over a smooth pulley, as shown in Figure 2.30. Determine the largest mass that can hang in this way without forcing the block to slide.

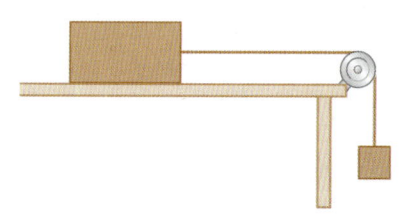

Figure 2.30: For question 12.

13 A boy tries to lift a suitcase of weight 220 N by pulling upward on it with a force of 140 N. The suitcase does not move. Calculate the normal force from the floor on the suitcase.

14 A block of weight 15 N rests on a horizontal table. A man pushes the block downward with a force of 12 N. What is the normal force of the table on the block?

2.2 Newton's laws of motion

Newton's first law of motion

Suppose you have two identical train carriages. Both are equipped with all the apparatus you need to do physics experiments. One train carriage is at rest at the train station. The other moves in a straight line with constant speed—the ride is perfectly smooth, there are no bumps, there is no noise and there are no windows to look outside. Every physics experiment conducted in the train at rest will give identical results to similar experiments made in the moving train. We have no way of determining whether a carriage is 'really at rest' or 'really moving'. We find it perfectly natural to believe, correctly, that no net force is present in the case of the carriage at rest. Therefore no net force is required in the case of the carriage moving in a straight line with constant speed.

Newton's first law of motion states that:

> **KEY POINT**
>
> When the net force on a body is zero, the body will move with constant velocity (which may be zero); in other words, it will move on a straight line with constant speed (which may be zero).

In effect, Newton's first law defines what a force is. A force is what *changes a body's velocity*. A force is *not* what is required to keep something moving as Aristotle thought.

Using the law in reverse allows us to conclude that if a body is *not* moving with constant velocity (which may mean not moving in a straight line, or not moving with constant speed or both) then a force *must be acting* on the body. So, since the earth revolves around the sun we know that a force must be acting on the earth.

Newton's first law is also called the law of **inertia**. Inertia is what keeps the body in the same state of motion when no forces act on the body. When a car accelerates forward, the passengers are thrown back into their seats because their original state of motion was motion with low speed. If a car brakes abruptly, the passengers are thrown forward, Figure 2.31. This implies that a mass tends to stay in the state of motion it was in before the force acted on it. The reaction of a body to a change in its state of motion (acceleration) is inertia.

Figure 2.31: The car was originally travelling at high speed. When it hits the wall the car stops, but the passenger wants to stay in the original high speed state of motion. This results in him hitting the steering wheel and the windshield (which is why it is a good idea to have safety belts and air bags).

Newton's third law of motion

Newton's third law of motion states that:

> **KEY POINT**
>
> If body X exerts a force on body Y, then body Y will exert an equal and opposite force on body X.

Make sure you understand that these equal and opposite forces act on *different* bodies. Thus, you cannot use this law to claim that it is impossible to ever have a net force on a body because for every force on it there is also an equal and opposite force. Here are four examples of this law:

1 You stand on roller-skates facing a wall. You push on the wall, and you move away from it. This is because you exerted a force on the wall, and in turn the wall exerted an equal and opposite force on you, making you move away (Figure 2.32).

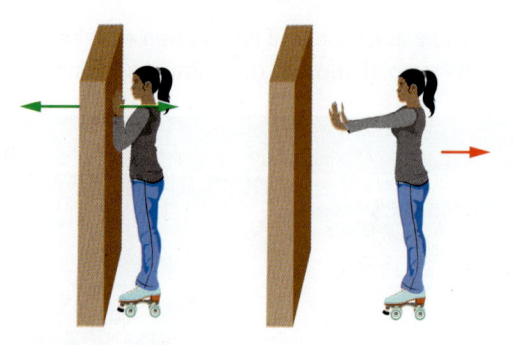

Figure 2.32: The girl pushes on the wall, so the wall pushes on her in the opposite direction.

2   You step on a scale. The scale exerts an upward force on you, and so you exert a downward force on the scale. This is the force that the scale reads (Figure 2.33).

Figure 2.33: The familiar bathroom scale does not measure mass. It measures the force that you exert on it. This force is the weight *only* when the scale is at rest.

3   A helicopter hovers in air, Figure 2.34. Its rotors exert a force downward on the air. Thus, the air exerts the upward force on the helicopter that keeps it from falling.

Figure 2.34: The upward force on the rotor is due to the force the rotor exerts on the air downward.

4   A book of mass 2 kg is allowed to fall feely. The earth exerts a force on the book, namely the weight of the book of about 20 N. Thus, the book exerts an equal and opposite force on the earth—a force upward equal to 20 N.

You must be careful with situations with two forces that are equal and opposite; they do not always have to do with the third law. For example, a block of mass 3 kg resting on a horizontal table has two forces acting on it. Its weight of about 30 N, and the normal force from the table that is also 30 N. These two forces are equal and opposite, but they are acting on the same body and so have nothing to do with Newton's third law. (The force that pairs with the weight of the block is an upward force on the earth, and the one that pairs with the normal force is a downward force on the table.)

Newton's third law also applies to cases where there is no contact between the bodies. Examples are the *electric* force between two electrically charged particles or the *gravitational* force between any two massive particles. These forces must be equal and opposite. (See Figure 2.35.)

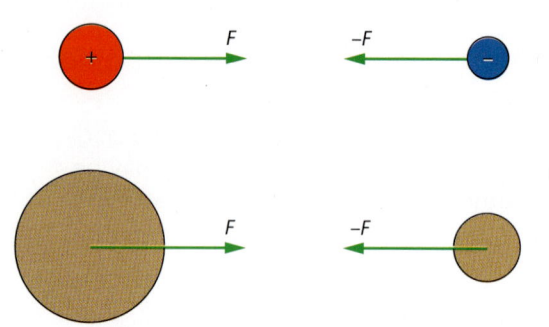

Figure 2.35: The two charges and the two masses are different, but the forces they exert on each other are equal and opposite.

SCIENCE IN CONTEXT

Helicopters, planes and rockets function because of Newton's third law.

Equilibrium

When there are angles between the various forces, solving equilibrium problems is a bit more cumbersome and will involve getting components of forces using vector methods. We choose a set of axes whose origin is the body in question and find the components of all the forces on the body. Figure 2.36 shows three forces acting at the same point. We have equilibrium, which means the net force acting at the point is zero. We need to find the unknown magnitude and direction of force F_1. This situation could represent three people pulling on three ropes that are tied at a point.

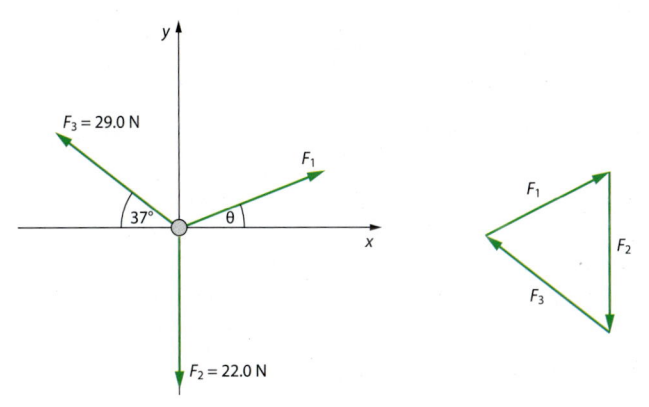

Figure 2.36: Force diagram of three forces in equilibrium pulling a common point. Notice that the three vectors representing the three forces form a triangle.

Getting components along the horizontal (x) and vertical (y) directions for the known forces, we have

$F_{2x} = 0$

$F_{2y} = -22.0$ N (put minus sign by hand)

$F_{3x} = -29.0 \cos 37° = -23.16$ N (put minus sign by hand)

$F_{3y} = 29.0 \sin 37° = 17.45$ N

Equilibrium demands that $\sum F_x = 0$ and $\sum F_y = 0$.

$\sum F_x = 0$ implies $F_{1x} + 0 - 23.16 = 0 \Rightarrow F_{1x} = 23.16$ N

$\sum F_y = 0$ implies $F_{1y} - 22 + 17.45 \Rightarrow F_{1y} = 4.55$ N

Therefore, $F_1 = \sqrt{23.16^2 + 4.55^2} = 23.6$ N. The angle is found from $\tan \theta = \dfrac{F_{1y}}{F_{1x}} \Rightarrow \theta = \tan^{-1}\left(\dfrac{4.55}{23.16}\right) = 11.1°$.

EXAM TIP

If we know the x and y components of a force, we can find the magnitude of the force from

$F = \sqrt{F_x^2 + F_y^2}$

SCIENCE IN CONTEXT

Figure 2.37: The temple of Hephaestus in Athens.

The temple of Hephaestus in Athens (see Figure 2.37) still stands after 2500 years because it was built according to the laws of equilibrium.

WORKED EXAMPLE 2.6

A body of weight 98.0 N hangs from two strings that are attached to the ceiling as shown in Figure 2.38. Determine the tension in each string.

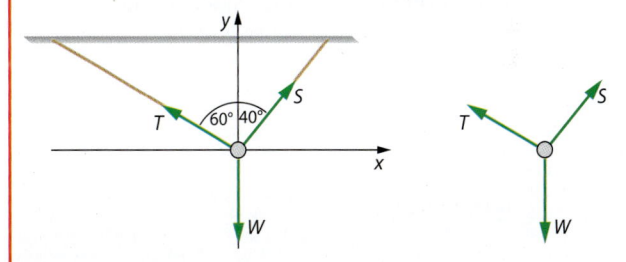

Figure 2.38: For worked example 2.6.

Answer

The three forces acting on the body are as shown, with T and S being the tensions in the two strings. Taking components about horizontal and vertical axes through the body we find:

$T_x = -T \cos 30°$	$S_x = S \cos 50°$	$W_x = 0$
$T_y = T \sin 30°$	$S_y = S \sin 50°$	$W_y = -98.0$ N

CONTINUED

Equilibrium demands $\sum F_x = 0$ and $\sum F_y = 0$:

$\sum F_x = 0$ implies $-T \cos 30° + S \cos 50° = 0$

$\sum F_y = 0$ implies $T \sin 30° + S \sin 50° - 98 = 0$

From the first equation we find that $S = T \frac{\cos 30°}{\cos 50°} = 1.3473 \times T$. Substituting this in the second equation gives

$T(\sin 30° + 1.3473 \sin 50°) = 98$

which solves to $T = 63.96 \approx 64.0$ N. Hence $S = 1.3473 \times 63.96 = 86.17 \approx 86.2$ N.

WORKED EXAMPLE 2.7

A mass of 125 g is attached to a spring of spring constant $k = 58$ N m^{-1} that is hanging vertically.

a   Find the extension of the spring.

b   If the mass and the spring are placed on the moon, will there be any change in the extension of the spring?

Answer

a   The forces on the hanging mass are its weight and the tension of the spring. Since we have equilibrium, the two forces are equal in magnitude. Therefore

$kx = mg$

$x = \frac{mg}{k}$

$= \frac{0.125 \times 9.81}{58}$

$= 0.021$ m $= 2.1$ cm

b   The extension will be less, since the acceleration of gravity is less.

Newton's second law of motion

Newton's second law of motion states that:

> **KEY POINT**
>
> The net force on a body of constant mass is proportional to that body's acceleration and is in the same direction as the acceleration.

Mathematically

$\vec{F} = m\vec{a}$

where the constant of proportionality, m, is the *mass* of the body.

Figure 2.39 shows the net force on a freely falling body, which happens to be its weight, $W = mg$. By Newton's second law, the net force equals the mass times the acceleration, and so

$mg = ma$

$a = g$

The acceleration of the freely falling body is exactly g. Experiments going back to Galileo show that indeed all bodies fall with the same acceleration in a vacuum irrespective of their density, their mass, their shape and the material from which they are made. Look for David Scott's demonstration dropping a hammer and a feather on the moon in Apollo 15's mission in 1971. You can do the same demonstration without going to the moon by placing a hammer and a feather on a book and dropping the book. If the heavy and the light object fell with different accelerations, the one with the smaller acceleration would lift off the book—but it doesn't.

Figure 2.39: A mass falling to the ground acted upon by gravity.

2 Forces and Newton's laws

The equation $F = ma$ defines the unit of force, the newton (symbol N). One newton is the force required to accelerate a mass of 1 kg by 1 m s^{-2} in the direction of the force.

It is important to realise that the force in the second law is the *net force* $\sum F$ on the body.

> **EXAM TIP**
>
> How to solve an $F = ma$ problem:
>
> **Step 1:** Make a diagram and choose the direction that you will take as positive.
>
> **Step 2:** Make a free-body diagram.
>
> **Step 3:** Find the net force by looking at the free-body diagram.
>
> **Step 4:** Set the net force equal to ma.
>
> **Step 5:** Solve for what is unknown.

Let's apply the Exam tip steps to a simple problem (Figure 2.40): a block of mass 5.0 kg is accelerated to the right on a horizontal road by a horizontal force F. The acceleration is 0.80 m s^{-2}. A frictional force of 12 N acts on the block. What is the magnitude of F?

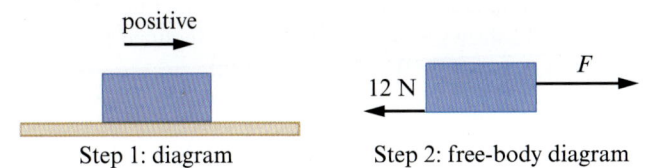

Figure 2.40: The diagram shows the horizontal forces acting on the block.

In step 3 we find the net force by looking at the free-body diagram: it is simply $F - 12$. (Because the positive direction is to the right.)

In step 4 we equate the net force to ma:
$F - 12 = 5.0 \times 0.8$.

Finally, in step 5 we solve for the only unknown quantity, F: $F - 12 = 4.0 \Rightarrow F = 16$ N.

> **CHECK YOURSELF 5**
>
> An elevator moving upwards is slowing down to a stop. Which diagram in Figure 2.41—A, B or C—shows the forces on the elevator? 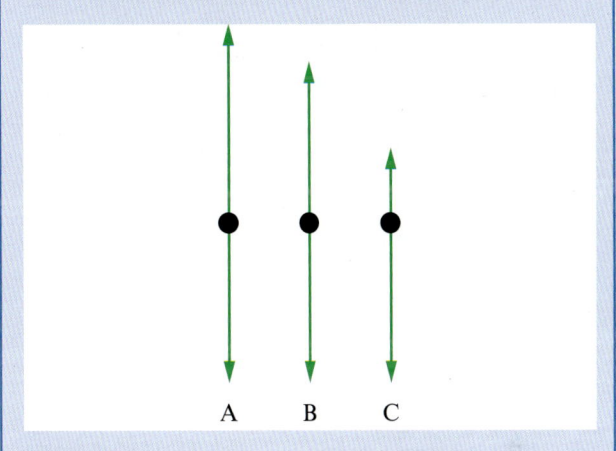
>
> **Figure 2.41:** For check yourself question 5.

> **WORKED EXAMPLE 2.8**
>
> A person of mass $m = 70$ kg stands on the floor of an elevator. Find the normal force they experience from the elevator floor when the elevator:
>
> **a** is standing still
>
> **b** moves up at constant speed 3.0 m s^{-1}
>
> **c** moves up with acceleration 4.0 m s^{-2}
>
> **d** moves down with acceleration 4.0 m s^{-2}.
>
> For simplicity, take $g = 10$ m s^{-2}.
>
> **Answer**
>
> Two forces act on the person: their weight mg vertically down and the normal force R from the floor vertically up.
>
> **a** There is no acceleration, and so by Newton's second law the net force on the person must be zero. Hence
>
> $R = mg$
>
> $\quad = 7.0 \times 10^2$ N

43

CONTINUED

b There is no acceleration and so again

$R = mg$

$= 7.0 \times 10^2$ N

c Take the up direction to be positive; then the net force is $\sum F = R_{up} - mg_{down}$.

So $R - mg = ma$ and

$R = mg + ma$

$= 700$ N $+ 280$ N

$= 9.8 \times 10^2$ N

d Take the down direction to be positive: $\sum F = mg - R$. So

$mg - R = ma$ and

$R = mg - ma$

$= 700$ N $- 280$ N

$= 4.2 \times 10^2$ N

WORKED EXAMPLE 2.9

A man of mass 70 kg is standing in an elevator. The elevator is moving *upward* at a speed of 3.0 m s⁻¹. The elevator comes to rest in a time of 2.0 s. Determine the normal force on the man from the elevator floor during the period of deceleration. Repeat for the case where the elevator goes down and then stops.

Answer

Let us take the up direction to be positive. The acceleration is

$a = \frac{v-u}{t} = \frac{0-3.0}{2.0} = -1.5$ m s⁻²

So, the net force is

$\sum F = R - mg$

Hence:

$R - mg = ma$

$R = ma + mg$

$= 70 \times (-1.5) + 70 \times 10$

CONTINUED

$= -105 + 700 = 595$ N

$\approx 6.0 \times 10^2$ N

What if, instead, the man was moving *downward* and then decelerated to rest? Take the up direction to be positive again. The net force is $\sum F = R - mg$ and

$a = \frac{v-u}{t} = \frac{0-(-3.0)}{2.0} = +1.5$ m s⁻². So,

$R - mg = ma$

$R = ma + mg$

$= 105 + 700 = 805$ N

$\approx 8.0 \times 10^2$ N

Both cases are easily experienced in daily life. When the elevator goes up and then stops we feel 'lighter' during the deceleration period. When going down and about to stop, we feel 'heavier' during the deceleration period. The feeling of 'lightness' or 'heaviness' has to do with the normal force we experience from the floor.

The inclined plane

Many problems in mechanics involve an inclined plane. Figure 2.42 shows a block at rest on an inclined plane that makes an angle θ to the horizontal.

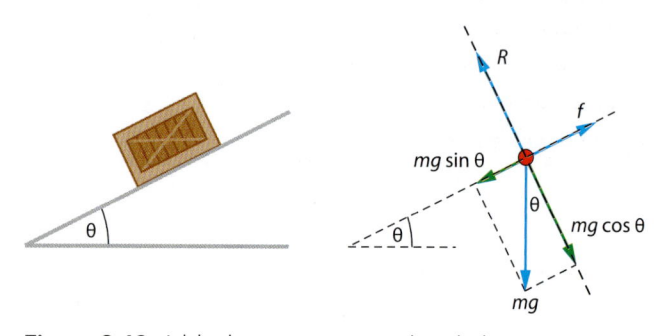

Figure 2.42: A block at rest on an inclined plane.

The free-body diagram shows the three forces acting on the block (the block is now shown as a point; it is convenient to always do that so that the forces are shown acting at the same point). The forces are the normal force R at right angles to the plane, the weight mg vertically down and a frictional force f acting up the plane. We have also drawn a set of x and y axes. The x-axis is chosen to be along the inclined plane.

This is convenient because if the block were to slide down, it would move along the x axis. In other words it is convenient to choose an axis along which motion takes or could take place.

We now need to find the components of the weight along the two axes. Along the x-axis the component is $mg \sin\theta$ and along the y-axis it is $mg \cos\theta$. Since we have equilibrium we have two equations:

$f = mg \sin\theta$ and $R = mg \cos\theta$

Now suppose that the largest angle of the inclined plane at which we can have equilibrium is θ_{max}. In other words if the angle of the inclined plane were to increase ever so slightly above θ_{max}, the block would slide down. This means that at this angle the frictional force is the largest possible and so is given by $f_{max} = \mu_s R$, i.e., $f_{max} = \mu_s mg \cos\theta_{max}$. So our first equilibrium equation becomes

$\mu_s mg \cos\theta_{max} = mg \sin\theta_{max}$

And so

$\mu_s = \tan\theta_{max}$

Consider now the case where the inclined plane is frictionless. The normal force is still $R = mg \cos\theta$, but along the x-direction we have an unbalanced force $mg \sin\theta$, and so the block will accelerate down the plane. The acceleration is found from Newton's second law:

$mg \sin\theta = ma \Rightarrow a = g \sin\theta$.

> **CHECK YOURSELF 6**
>
> A block of mass 2.0 kg slides down a frictionless inclined plane with acceleration 4.0 m s^{-2}. What is the acceleration of a 5.0 kg block sliding down the same plane?

Cases with more than one body present

We now examine cases where more than one body are present. We simply have to apply the five steps of the previous exam tip to *each* body in the problem. So consider the following situation:

Two blocks of mass 4.0 and 6.0 kg are joined by a string and rest on a frictionless horizontal table (see Figure 2.43). A force of 100 N is applied horizontally on one of the blocks. We want to find the acceleration of each block and the tension of the string joining the two blocks.

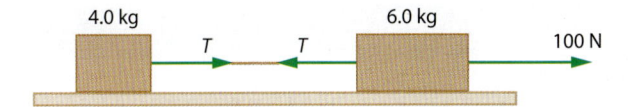

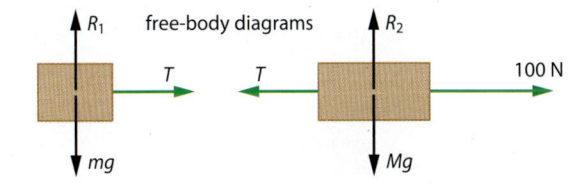

Figure 2.43: A force pulling two blocks joined by a string.

Figure A2.43 shows the forces on *each* block. The net force on the 6.0 kg block is $100 - T$ and on the 4.0 kg mass just T. Physics strings are assumed to be inextensible, which means that the two bodies move with the *same* acceleration. Thus, applying Newton's second law separately on each block,

$100 - T = 6a$

$T = 4a$

We have to unknown quantities and two equations. Solving for a (by adding the two equations side by side or using your calculator) gives $a = 10$ m s^{-2}. The tension is

$T = 4.0 \times 10 = 40$ N.

Note that the free-body force diagram makes it clear that the 100 N force acts *only* on the body to the right. It is a common mistake to say that the body to the left is also acted upon by the 100 N force.

However, in problems with more than one body it is often a simplification to treat the bodies as one. In our problem here, we may consider the two bodies as one of mass 10 kg. The net force on the body is 100 N. Note that the tensions are irrelevant now since they cancel out. (They have become *internal* forces, and these are irrelevant.) Applying Newton's second law on the single body we have $100 = 10a \Rightarrow a = 10$ m s^{-2}. But to find the tension we must break up the combined body into the original two bodies. Newton's second law on the 4.0 kg body gives $T = 4a = 40$ N.

45

CHECK YOURSELF 7

Two blocks of mass 3 kg and 5 kg are joined by a string and are allowed to fall freely, as shown in Figure 2.44.

What is the tension in the string?

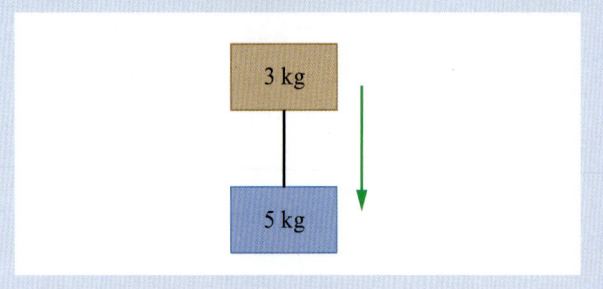

Figure 2.44: For check yourself question 7.

WORKED EXAMPLE 2.10

(Atwood's machine) Two blocks of $m = 4.0$ kg and $M = 6.0$ kg are joined together by a string that passes over a pulley. The blocks are held stationary and then released. Determine the acceleration of each block.

Answer

Intuition tells us that the larger mass will start moving downward and the small mass will go up. The acceleration of each block will be the same in magnitude since the string is assumed to be inextensible.

Method 1

Figure 2.45 shows the free-body diagrams: weight mg and tension T on m and weight Mg and tension T on M.

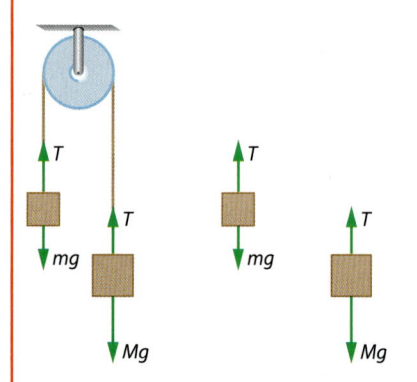

Figure 2.45: For worked example 2.10.

CONTINUED

Newton's second law applied to each mass states

$T - mg = ma$ (1)

$Mg - T = Ma$ (2)

Note these equations carefully. Each says that the net force on the mass in question is equal to that mass times that mass's acceleration. In the first equation we find the net force in the upward direction, because that is the direction of acceleration. In the second we find the net force in the downward direction, since that is the direction of acceleration in that case. We want to find the acceleration, so we simply add up these two equations side by side to find

$Mg - mg = (m + M)a$

Hence

$a = \frac{M - m}{M + m}g$

(Note that if $M \gg m$, the acceleration tends to g (because in that case we can neglect m compared to M). This shows clearly that if the two masses are equal then there is no acceleration. This is a convenient method for measuring g: Atwood's machine effectively 'slows down' g so the falling mass has a much smaller acceleration from which g can then be determined. Putting in the numbers for our example we find $a = 2.0$ m s^{-2}. Having found the acceleration we may, if we wish, also find the tension in the string, T. Putting the value for a in formula (1) we find

$T = m\frac{M - m}{M + m}g + mg$

$= \frac{2Mm}{M + m}g$

$= 48$ N

(If $M \gg m$, the tension tends to $2mg$ (we can neglect m compared to M in the denominator in which case M cancels out).

Method 2

We treat the two masses as one body and apply Newton's second law on this body (but this is trickier than in the previous example)—see Figure 2.46.

CONTINUED

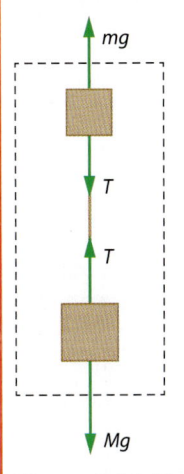

Figure 2.46: The forces on the system of the two blocks.

In this case the net force is $Mg - mg$ and, since this force acts on a body of mass $M + m$, the acceleration is found as before from $F = $ mass $\times$ acceleration. Note that the tension T does not appear in this case, being now an internal force.

WORKED EXAMPLE 2.11

In Figure 2.47, a block of mass M is connected to a smaller block of mass m through a string that goes over a pulley. Ignoring friction, find the acceleration of each block and the tension in the string.

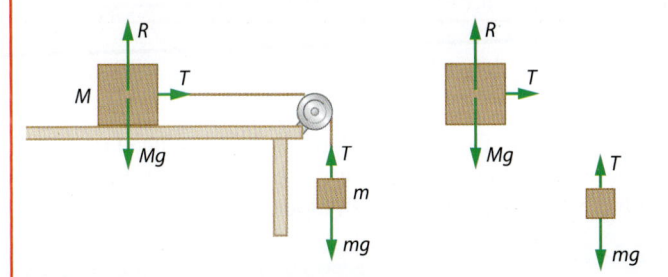

Figure 2.47: For worked example 2.11.

Answer

Method 1

The forces are shown in Figure 2.47. Convince yourself that you agree with this diagram. Thus

$mg - T = ma$

$T = Ma$

from which (adding the two equations side by side)

PHYSICS FOR THE IB DIPLOMA: COURSEBOOK

CONTINUED

$a = \dfrac{mg}{m+M}$

(If $M \gg m$ the acceleration tends to zero.) If $M = 8.0$ kg and $m = 2.0$ kg, this gives $a = 2.0$ m s^{-2}.

Hence $T = \dfrac{Mmg}{m+M}$

$= 16$ N

Method 2

Treating the two bodies as one results in the situation shown in Figure 2.48.

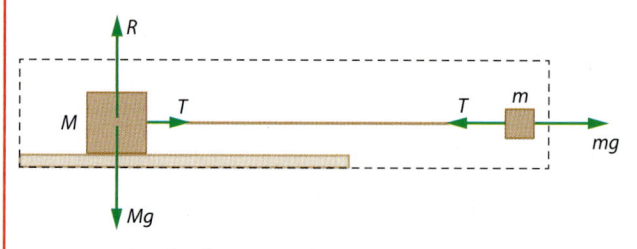

Figure 2.48: The forces on the two blocks taken as one.

The net force on the mass $M + m$ is mg. Hence $mg = (M + m)a$

$mg = (M + m)a$

$\Rightarrow a = \dfrac{mg}{m+M}$

The tension can then be found as before.

WORKED EXAMPLE 2.12

A block of 4.0 kg is placed on top of a block of mass 6.0 kg, as shown in Figure 2.49. The blocks are placed on a frictionless horizontal surface. A horizontal force of magnitude F is applied to the bottom block. The static coefficient of friction between the blocks is 0.60. What is the largest force F so that both blocks move together without sliding on each other?

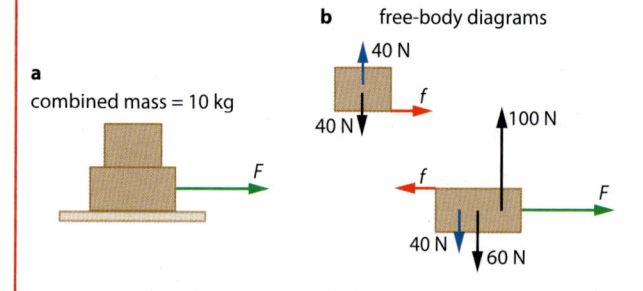

Figure 2.49: Free-body diagram for two blocks, one on top of the other and moving together.

CONTINUED

Answer

As the bottom block accelerates to the right, because of inertia, the top block wants to stay where it is, i.e., slide backwards relative to the bottom block. Thus a friction force will develop that will push the top block to the right. This gives the free-body diagrams in Figure 2.49. Forces in blue and red represent pairs according to Newton's third law.

Since we want the maximum value of F we will have to use the maximum frictional force that can develop between the two blocks, and that is $f_{max} = \mu_s N = 0.60 \times 40 = 24$ N. Applying Newton's second law to each body,

$F - 24 = 6a$

$24 = 4a$

This means that $a = 6.0$ m s^{-2} and so $F = 24 + 36 = 60$ N.

WORKED EXAMPLE 2.13

The force F in the previous example is 80 N. What is the acceleration of each block? The coefficient of dynamic friction between the blocks is 0.50.

Answer

We know that there will be sliding since the force is now larger than the maximum of 60 N found in the previous example. The force of friction will now be $f = \mu_d N = 0.50 \times 40 = 20$ N. Thus,

$80 - 20 = 6a_1 \Rightarrow a_1 = 10$ m s^{-2}

$20 = 4a_2 \Rightarrow a_2 = 5.0$ m s^{-2}

Both blocks are accelerating forward, but relative to the bottom block the top block is sliding backward.

Links

Newton's second law (for a particle of constant mass) is written as $F = ma$. In this form, this equation does not seem particularly powerful. However, if we realise that in calculus acceleration is $a = \frac{dv}{dt} = \frac{d^2x}{dt^2}$ the second law becomes $\frac{d^2x}{dt^2} - \frac{F}{m} = 0$. This is a differential equation. Given the dependence of the force on time or position, the equation can be solved to give the actual path that the particle will move on under the action of the force. For example, Newton showed that if the force depends on position as $F \sim \frac{1}{x^2}$ then the motion has to be along a conic section (ellipse, circle, and so on). Similarly, if the force depends on position as $F \sim x$ (as in a spring) then the motion will be oscillations about a fixed point. So the same equation applied to different contexts allows for the determination of the type of motion that results under the action of a force.

TEST YOUR UNDERSTANDING

15 A mass is hanging from a string that is attached to the ceiling. A second piece of string (identical to the first) hangs from the lower end of the mass (see Figure 2.50).

Figure 2.50: For question 15.

State and explain which string will break if:

a the bottom string is slowly pulled with ever increasing force

b the bottom string is very abruptly pulled down.

16 A block of mass 15.0 kg rests on a horizontal table. A force of 50.0 N is applied vertically downward on the block. Calculate the force that the block exerts on the table.

17 A block of mass M = 12 kg is connected with a string to a smaller block of mass m = 4.0 kg. The big block is resting on a smooth inclined plane as shown in Figure 2.51. Determine the angle θ of the plane so that neither mass moves.

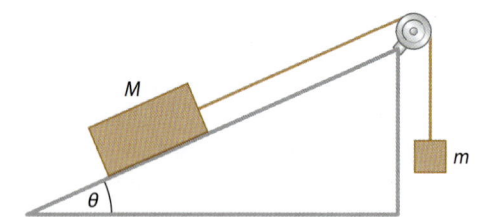

Figure 2.51: For question 17.

18 Describe under what circumstances a constant force would result in:

a an increasing acceleration on a body

b a decreasing acceleration on a body.

19 A block of mass 2.6 kg is projected with initial speed 18 m s^{-1} along a rough horizontal plane. The dynamic coefficient of friction between the block and the plane is 0.35.

a After how much time will the block stop?

b What distance will the block cover?

c Without further calculations, state how the answers to **a** and **b** would change, if at all, when the experiment is repeated with a block of double the mass.

20 A block of mass 4.2 kg is projected with speed 14 m s^{-1} up an inclined plane making an angle 28° with the horizontal. The dynamic coefficient of friction between the block and the inclined plane is 0.42, and the static coefficient is 0.55.

a After how much time will the block stop?

b What distance will the block cover?

c When the block stops, will it then slide down the plane, or will it stay at rest?

d In another experiment the same block is projected *down* the plane with the same speed as before. Will the block stop?

21 A man of mass m stands in an elevator.

a Find the normal force from the elevator floor on the man when:

  i the elevator is standing still

  ii the elevator moves up at constant speed v

  iii the elevator accelerates down with acceleration a

  iv the elevator accelerates down with acceleration a = g.

b What happens when a > g?

CONTINUED

22. Get in an elevator and stretch out your arm holding your heavy physics book. Press the button to go up. Describe and explain what is happening to your stretched arm. Repeat as the elevator comes to a stop at the top floor. What happens when you press the button to go down, and what happens when the elevator again stops? Explain your observations carefully using the second law of motion.

23. Figure 2.52 shows a person in an elevator pulling on a rope that goes over a pulley and is attached to the top of the elevator. The mass of the elevator is 30.0 kg and that of the person is 70.0 kg. ($g = 10$ m s^{-2}).

   a On a copy of the diagram, draw the forces on the person.

   b Draw the forces on the elevator.

   c The elevator accelerates upwards at 0.50 m s^{-2}. Find the normal force on the person from the elevator floor.

   d The force the person exerts on the elevator floor is 200 N. Find the acceleration of the elevator.

Figure 2.52: For question 23.

24. Two blocks X (mass 2.0 kg) and Y (mass 6.0 kg) are in contact on a frictionless horizontal table. A force of 24 N acts horizontally on block X as shown in Figure 2.53.

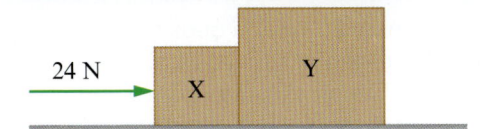

Figure 2.53: For question 24.

   a What is the acceleration of each block?

   b Determine the force X exerts on Y.

25. a Calculate the tension in the string joining the two masses in Figure 2.54.

   b If the position of the masses is interchanged, will the tension change?

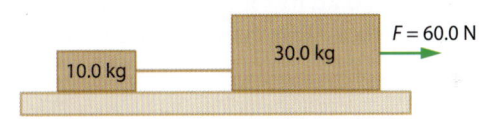

Figure 2.54: For question 25.

26. A mass of 3.0 kg is acted upon by three forces of 4.0 N, 6.0 N and 9.0 N and is in equilibrium. Convince yourself that these forces can indeed be in equilibrium. The 9.0 N force is suddenly removed. Determine the acceleration of the mass.

27. A block of mass $M = 15$ kg is connected with a string to a smaller block of mass m. The big block is on a rough inclined plane as shown in Figure 2.55. The coefficient of static friction is 0.40. The angle of the plane is $\theta = 25°$. Determine the largest and smallest mass m that can hang from the string and still have equilibrium.

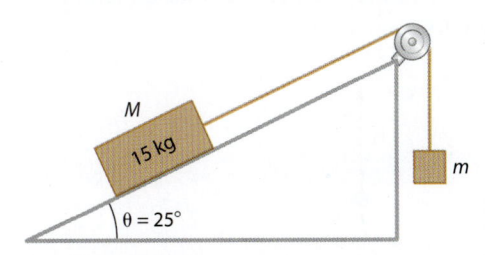

Figure 2.55: For question 27.

> **CONTINUED**
>
> 28 A block of mass 25 kg and density 2800 kg m^{-3} is fully submerged in a liquid of density 850 kg m^{-3}. The block hangs from a vertical string. What is the tension in the string?
>
> 29 A rectangular block of density 750 kg m^{-3} floats in water of density 1000 kg m^{-3}.
>
>   a What fraction of the vertical height of the block is under water?
>
>   b The block is pushed downward so it is fully submerged and is then released. What is the initial acceleration of the block?
>
> 30 A rectangular raft of mass 1200 kg and density 800 kg m^{-3} floats in water of density 1000 kg m^{-3}. How many people of average mass 50 kg can stand on the raft so that it is just about to be fully submerged?
>
> 31 A ball of density 3500 kg m^{-3} and radius 6.0 mm is released from rest in a liquid of density 920 kg m^{-3} and viscosity 0.70 Pa s.
>
>   a What is the terminal speed of the ball as it falls through the liquid? Ignore the buoyant force.
>
>   b How do you expect the answer to **a** to change if the liquid temperature is increased?
>
>   c Repeat **a** taking the buoyant force into account.

2.3 Circular motion

Circular motion is a common type of motion which includes as a very special case the motion of planets around the sun that is approximately circular. As we will see, circular motion requires the presence of a force directed towards the centre of the circle. In the case of planets going around the sun a new force had to be discovered to accommodate for this fact: the force of gravitation.

Circular motion and angular speed

Consider the object in Figure 2.56, which rotates on a circle of radius r in the counterclockwise direction with constant speed v.

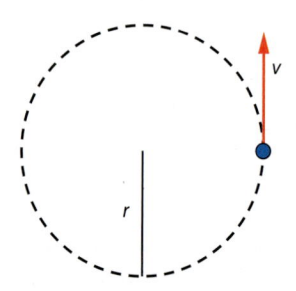

Figure 2.56: An object moving on a circle of radius r.

Let T be the time taken to complete one full revolution (or orbit). We call T the **period** of the motion. Since the speed is constant and the object covers a distance of $2\pi r$ in a time of T seconds, it follows that

$$v = \frac{2\pi r}{T}$$

We may also note that the object sweeps out an angle of 2π radians in a time equal to the period, so we define the **angular speed** of the object (denoted by ω) by (Figure 2.57)

angular speed, $\omega = \dfrac{\text{angle swept}}{\text{time taken}} = \dfrac{\Delta\theta}{\Delta t}$

For a complete revolution, $\Delta\theta = 2\pi$ and $\Delta t = T$ so that we also have

$$\omega = \frac{2\pi}{T}$$

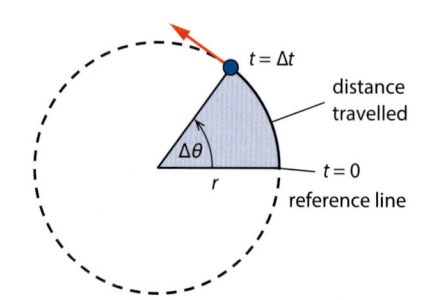

Figure 2.57: As the object rotates around the circle it sweeps out an angle measured from some arbitrary reference line.

The units of angular speed are radians per second or just s^{-1}.

We may define a quantity called the **frequency, f** of the motion. This will be useful also in the context of waves later on. Frequency is the number of full revolutions per second. Since we make one full revolution in the course of one period T, the number in one second is $f = \frac{1}{T}$.

So, in terms of frequency we also have that $\omega = 2\pi f$.

Comparing $v = \frac{2\pi r}{T}$ with $\omega = \frac{2\pi}{T}$ we see that $v = r\omega$

This is the relation between the *linear speed v* and the *angular speed ω*.

Summarising all the formulae:
$v = r\omega = \frac{2\pi r}{T} = 2\pi r f$.

Figure 2.58: As the earth rotates about its axis, stars appear to trace circles in the night sky.

THEORY OF KNOWLEDGE

The photograph in Figure 2.58 shows stars tracing arcs. Most of the ancients would explain this observation by saying that the stars rotate around the fixed earth. Today we explain this by saying that the earth rotates about its axis. Which view is correct, and how do we know? In 1851 the French physicist Leon Foucault constructed a long pendulum with a heavy bob at the end. When set into oscillation the plane of oscillation rotates slowly clockwise (in the northern hemisphere). The simple explanation for this effect is the rotation of the earth about its axis. The same reason that makes the Foucault pendulum *precess*, that is, change its plane of oscillation, is responsible for the patterns of wind and ocean currents on earth.

It is quite remarkable how *very simple* observations reveal something deep about the world around us. In the same category we have Eratosthenes' ingeniously simple method for the measurement of the radius of the earth and Olbers' observation about the darkness of the night sky leading to the abandonment of the Newtonian view of an infinite universe.

WORKED EXAMPLE 2.14

Calculate:

a the angular speed of the earth as it rotates around the sun

b the angle swept by the earth in 30 days

c the linear speed of the earth.

(The radius of the orbit is about 1.5×10^{11} m.)

Answer

a The earth completes one full revolution in approximately 365 days. We use $\omega = \frac{2\pi}{T}$ for angular speed:

$\omega = \frac{2\pi}{365 \times 24 \times 60 \times 60}$

$\omega = 1.99 \times 10^{-7} \approx 2.0 \times 10^{-7} \, s^{-1}$

b $\theta = \frac{30}{365} \times 2\pi = 0.52$ radians or approximately 30°.

c We need the relation between angular and linear speed $v = \omega r$:

$v = 1.99 \times 10^{-7} \times 1.5 \times 10^{11} = 29580 \approx 3.0 \times 10^4 \, m \, s^{-1}$

Centripetal acceleration

It is important to note right away that in circular motion even if the linear speed is constant the velocity is not: it is changing because it is changing direction. Since the velocity changes, we have acceleration. What follows is a *derivation* of the expression for acceleration in circular motion. You may want to skip the derivation and go directly to the result just before the end of this section.

Look at Figure 2.59 which shows the velocity of a particle at two points P and Q. We are making use of the fact that the velocity vector has to be tangent to the circle.

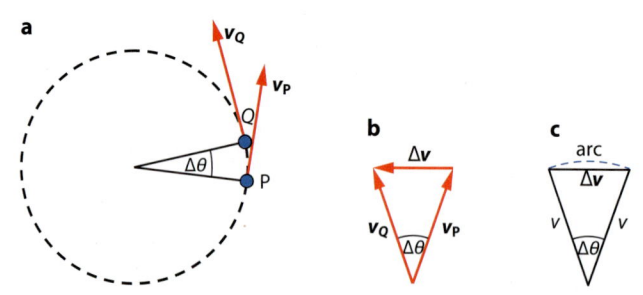

Figure 2.59: a The velocity vector changes direction as the particle moves from P to Q. **b** The change in the velocity vector from P to Q is given by the red arrow. **c** The distance travelled and the length of the arc are the same if the angle $\Delta\theta$ is very small.

The acceleration is defined as

$$\vec{a} = \frac{\Delta\vec{v}}{\Delta t}$$

where $\Delta\vec{v}$ is a vector. Thus, we have acceleration every time the velocity *vector* changes. This vector will change if:

- its magnitude changes
- or the direction changes
- or both magnitude and direction change.

For motion in a circle with constant *speed*, it is the direction of the velocity vector that changes. We must thus find the difference $\Delta\vec{v} = \vec{v}_Q - \vec{v}_P$. (Note that the magnitude of the velocity vectors at P and Q are the same—they are equal to the constant speed v of the moving particle.)

The magnitude of the vector $\Delta\vec{v}$ can be found from simple trigonometry. Look at the small triangle in Figure 2.59b. The triangle is isosceles, and two sides have length v, the speed of the particle. The third side

is $|\Delta\vec{v}|$. This is approximately an arc (Figure 2.59c) in a circle of radius v and subtending an angle $\Delta\theta$ (in radians). Hence $\Delta v = v\Delta\theta$. Therefore, using $a = \frac{\Delta v}{\Delta t}$ the acceleration has a magnitude given by

$$a = \frac{v\Delta\theta}{\Delta t}$$
$$= v\omega$$

But $\omega = \frac{v}{r}$ and so the acceleration is

$$a = v \times \frac{v}{r} = \frac{v^2}{r}$$

This gives us the magnitude of the acceleration vector for motion around a circle of radius r with constant speed v. As we see, the magnitude of the acceleration vector is constant if v is constant. But what about its direction? As Δt gets smaller and smaller, the angle $\Delta\theta$ gets smaller and smaller, which means that the vector $\Delta\vec{v}$, which is in the direction of acceleration, becomes perpendicular to $\vec{v}$. This means that the acceleration vector is normal to the circle and directed toward the centre of the circle. It is a **centripetal acceleration** (see Figure 2.60).

A body moving along a circle of radius r with speed v experiences centripetal acceleration that has magnitude $a_c = \frac{v^2}{r}$ and is directed toward the centre of the circle.

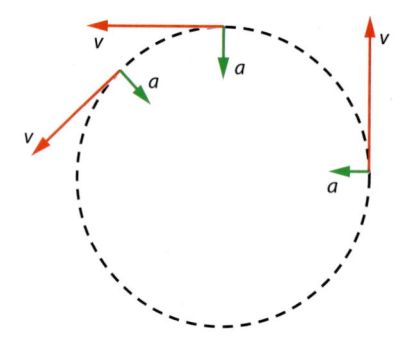

Figure 2.60: The centripetal acceleration vector is normal to the velocity vector.

We can find many equivalent expressions for the centripetal acceleration as follows. Using $v = \frac{2\pi r}{T}$ we have that

$$a_c = \frac{4\pi^2 r^2}{rT^2} = \frac{4\pi^2 r}{T^2}$$

Using $v = r\omega$, gives $a_c = \omega^2 r$.

Since $\omega = 2\pi f$ we also have $a_c = 4\pi^2 rf^2$. So we can use any one of

$$a_c = \frac{v^2}{r} \text{ or } a_c = \omega^2 r \text{ or } a_c = \frac{4\pi^2 r}{T^2} \text{ or } a_c = 4\pi^2 rf^2$$

depending on what is convenient.

2 Forces and Newton's laws

CHECK YOURSELF 8

The earth has a mass of 6×10^{24} kg and completes one revolution around the sun in a circular orbit of radius 1.5×10^{11} m. What is the gravitational force between the earth and the sun?

WORKED EXAMPLE 2.15

a A particle moves along a circle of radius 2.0 m with constant angular speed 2.1 s^{-1}. Determine the centripetal acceleration of the particle.

b The radius of the earth is $R = 6.4 \times 10^6$ m. Determine the centripetal acceleration due to the spinning earth experienced by someone on the equator.

c A mass moves in a circle with constant speed in a counterclockwise direction, as in Figure 2.61a. Determine the direction of the velocity change when the mass moves from A to B.

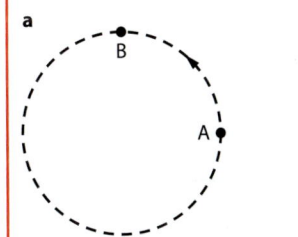

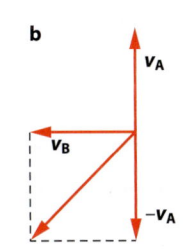

Figure 2.61: Diagram to find the change in velocity.

Answer

a We remember that $a_c = \omega^2 r$ and so $a_c = 2.1^2 \times 2.0$. Hence $a_c \approx 8.8 \text{ m s}^{-2}$.

b A mass on the equator covers a distance of $2\pi R$ in a time $T = 1$ day. Thus $v = \dfrac{2 \times \pi \times 6.4 \times 10^6}{24 \times 60 \times 60} = 4.65 \times 10^2 \text{ m s}^{-1}$ and so $a = \dfrac{(4.65 \times 10^2)^2}{6.4 \times 10^6} = 3.4 \times 10^{-2} \text{ m s}^{-2}$. This is quite small compared with the acceleration of free fall, and we are not aware of it in daily life.

c The velocity at A is vertical and at B it points to the left. The change in the velocity vector is $\vec{v}_B - \vec{v}_A$, and this difference of vectors is directed as shown in Figure 2.61b.

Centripetal forces

If we know that a body moves in a circle, then we know at once that a net force must be acting on the body, since it moves with acceleration. If the speed is constant, the direction of the acceleration is toward the centre of the circle and therefore that is also the direction of the net force. It is a **centripetal force**. Consider a car that moves on a circular level road of radius r with constant speed v. Friction between the wheels and the road provides the necessary force directed toward the centre of the circle that enables the car to take the turn. (See Figure 2.62.)

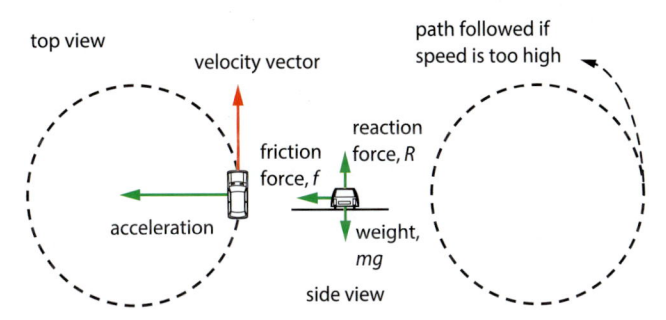

Figure 2.62: A car will skid outward (i.e., will cover a circle of larger radius) if the friction force is not large enough.

CHECK YOURSELF 9

A pendulum swings back and forth. The instant the string is vertical, is the pendulum bob in equilibrium?

WORKED EXAMPLE 2.16

a The coefficient of static friction between the tyres of a car of mass 1100 kg and dry asphalt is about 0.70. Determine the maximum speed with which a car can take a circular turn of radius 95 m.

b In wet conditions the coefficient of friction is reduced to 0.40. Predict the safe maximum speed now.

Answer

a The *maximum* frictional force is given by $f_{max} = \mu_s N$ where the normal force is N. Hence $f_{max} = 0.70 \times 1100 \times 9.81 = 7554 \approx 7.6 \times 10^3$ N. This frictional force provides the centripetal force for the car and so

55

CONTINUED

$$\frac{mv^2}{r} = f$$

$$v = \sqrt{\frac{fr}{m}}$$

$$v = \sqrt{\frac{7554 \times 95}{1100}}$$

$$v \approx 26 \text{ m s}^{-1}$$

b We may repeat part **a** or better notice that $\frac{mv^2}{r} = \mu_s mg \Rightarrow v = \sqrt{\mu_s gr}$. So the mass is not relevant, and the new speed is $v = 26 \times \sqrt{\frac{0.40}{0.70}} \approx 20 \text{ m s}^{-1}$.

EXAM TIP

It is very important that you understand worked example 2.17.

WORKED EXAMPLE 2.17

A particle is tied to a string and moves with constant speed in a horizontal circle. The string is tied to the ceiling. Draw the forces on the particle.

Answer

The common mistake here is to put a horizontal force pointing toward the centre and call it the centripetal force. When you are asked to find forces on a body, the list of forces that are available include the weight, normal forces (if the body touches another body), friction (if there is friction), tension (if there are strings or springs), resistance forces (if the body moves in air or a fluid), electric forces (if electric charges are involved), etc. Nowhere in this list is there an entry for a centripetal force.

Think of the word centripetal as simply an adjective that *describes* forces already acting on the body, *not* as a new force. In this example, the only forces on the mass are the weight and the tension. If we decompose the tension into horizontal and vertical components, we see that the weight is equal and opposite to the vertical component of the tension. This means that the only force left on the body is the horizontal component of the tension. We may now call this force

CONTINUED

the centripetal force. But this is not a new force. It is simply the component of a force that is already acting on the body. (See Figure 2.63.)

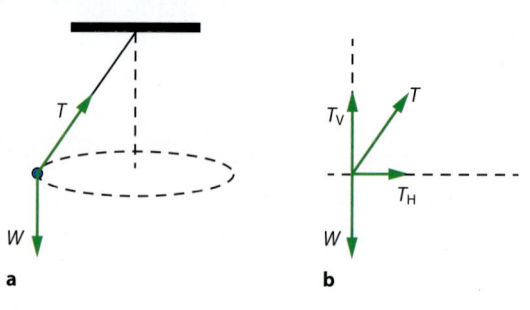

Figure 2.63: For worked example 2.17.

WORKED EXAMPLE 2.18

A mass m is tied to a string and *made* to move in a vertical circle of radius R with constant speed v (Figure 2.64).

a Determine the tension in the string at the lowest and highest points of the circle.

b Calculate the minimum speed so that the string never goes slack.

Answer

a The forces are as shown. At the lowest point, the net force is $T_1 - mg$ and so

$$T_1 - mg = m\frac{v^2}{r}$$

giving

$$T_1 = m\frac{v^2}{r} + mg$$

At the highest point, the net force is $mg + T_2$ and so

$$T_2 = m\frac{v^2}{r} - mg$$

2 Forces and Newton's laws

CONTINUED

b The string goes slack when the tension in the string becomes zero at the top. So we need $v^2 > gr$.

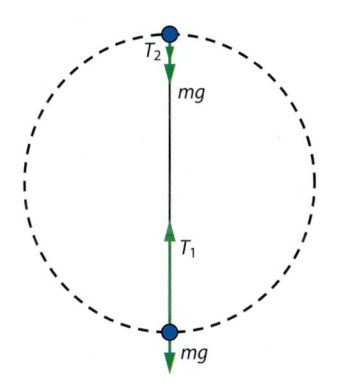

Figure 2.64: For worked example 2.18.

It is a common mistake in circular motion problems to include a force pushing the body *away* from the centre of the circle: a *centrifugal force*. It is important to stress that no such force exists. A body in circular motion cannot be in equilibrium, and so no force pushing away from the centre is required.

NATURE OF SCIENCE

Simple deductions

Newton's second law of mechanics implies that when a body moves with acceleration a net force of magnitude ma must be acting on the body and must have a direction that is the same as that of the acceleration vector. As we saw, circular motion involves an acceleration directed toward the centre of the circle. This means that the observation of the (approximate) circular motion of planets implies the existence of a force. Newton used this fact to deduce the existence of the gravitational force: the same force that is responsible for the falling of objects toward the surface of the earth is responsible for the motion of planets around the sun.

TEST YOUR UNDERSTANDING

32 **a** Calculate the angular speed and linear speed of a particle that completes a 3.50 m radius circle in 1.24 s.

   b Determine the frequency of the motion.

33 Calculate the centripetal acceleration of a body that moves in a circle of radius 2.45 m making 3.5 revolutions per second.

34 A mass moves on a circular path of radius 2.0 m at constant speed 4.0 m s^{-1} (see Figure 2.65).

   a Calculate the magnitude and direction of the *average* acceleration during a quarter of a revolution (from A to B).

   b Calculate the centripetal acceleration of the mass.

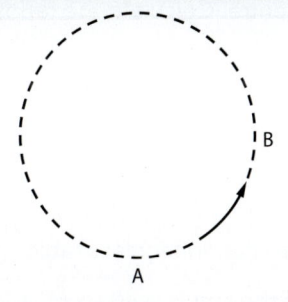

Figure 2.65: For question 34.

35 An astronaut rotates at the end of a horizontal test machine whose arm has a length of 10.0 m, as shown in Figure 2.66. The acceleration she experiences must not exceed 5g (take $g = 10$ m s^{-2}). Determine the maximum number of revolutions per minute of the arm.

CONTINUED

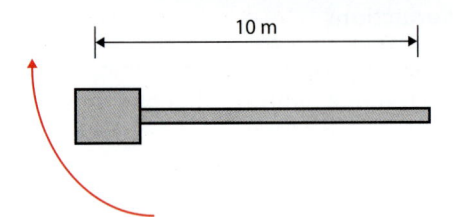

Figure 2.66: For question 35.

36 A horizontal disc of radius R rotates about a vertical axis through its centre, Figure 2.67.

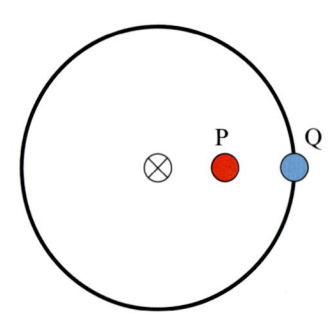

Figure 2.67: For question 36.

P and Q are two points on the disc. Q is on the circumference of the disc, and P is at a distance of $R/2$ from the centre. Calculate the ratios:

a $\dfrac{\omega_P}{\omega_Q}$

b $\dfrac{v_P}{v_Q}$

c $\dfrac{a_P}{a_Q}$

37 A body of mass 1.00 kg is tied to a string and rotates on a horizontal, frictionless table.

  a The length of the string is 40.0 cm, and the speed of revolution is 2.0 m s^{-1}. Calculate the tension in the string.

  b The string breaks when the tension exceeds 20.0 N. Determine the largest speed at which the mass can rotate.

  c The breaking tension of the string is 20.0 N, but you want the mass to rotate at 4.00 m s^{-1}. Determine the shortest length of string that can be used.

38 Estimate the length of the day if the centripetal acceleration at the equator due to the spinning earth were equal to the acceleration of free fall (g = 9.8 m s^{-2}, earth radius = 6400 km.)

39 A neutron star has a radius of 50.0 km and completes one revolution every 25 ms.

  a Calculate the centripetal acceleration experienced at the equator of the star.

  b The acceleration of free fall at the surface of the star is 8.0 × 10^{10} m s^{-2}. State and explain whether a probe that landed on the star can stay on the surface or whether it will be thrown off.

40 The earth (mass = 6.0 × 10^{24} kg) rotates around the sun in an orbit that is approximately circular, with a radius of 1.5 × 10^{11} m.

  a Estimate the orbital speed of the earth around the sun.

  b Determine the centripetal acceleration experienced by the earth.

  c Deduce the magnitude of the gravitational force exerted on the sun by the earth.

41 A plane travelling at a speed of 180 m s^{-1} along a horizontal circle makes an angle of θ = 35° to the horizontal. The lift force L is acting in the direction shown in Figure 2.68.

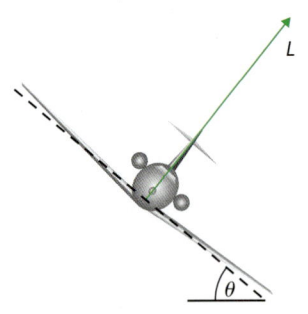

Figure 2.68: For question 41.

Calculate the radius of the circle.

42 A cylinder of radius 5.0 m rotates about its vertical axis. A girl stands inside the cylinder with her back touching the inside wall of the

58

CONTINUED

cylinder. The floor is suddenly lowered, but the girl stays 'glued' to the wall. The coefficient of friction between the girl and the wall is 0.60.

  a Draw a free-body diagram of the forces on the girl.

  b Determine the minimum number of revolutions per minute for which the girl does not slip down the wall.

43 A horizontal disc has a hole through its centre. A string passes through the hole and connects a mass m on top of the disc to a bigger mass M that hangs below the disc. The smaller mass is rotating on the disc in a circle of radius r. Determine the speed of m such that the big mass stands still. (See Figure 2.69.)

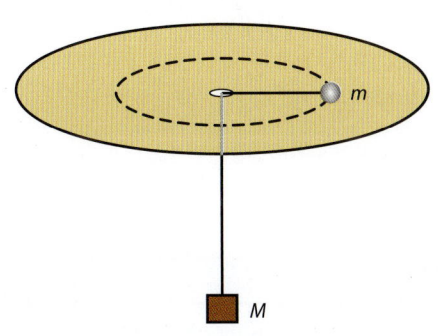

Figure 2.69: For question 43.

44 The ball in Figure 2.70 is attached to a rotating pole with two strings. The ball has a mass of 0.250 kg and rotates in a horizontal circle at a speed of 8.0 m s^{-1}. Determine the tension in each string.

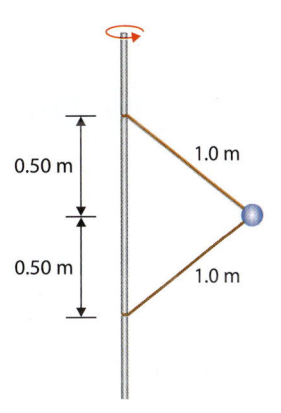

Figure 2.70: For question 44.

SELF-ASSESSMENT CHECKLIST

I am able to ...	Section	Not yet	Nearly there	Ready to move on
construct free-body diagrams showing the correct direction of forces find the net force on a body	2.1			
apply the condition for equilibrium, $\Sigma F = 0$	2.1			
understand and apply Newton's laws of motion	2.2			
solve problems when friction is present	2.2			
identify centripetal forces	2.3			
understand that a body in circular motion is not in equilibrium	2.3			
solve problems with circular motion	2.3			

PHYSICS FOR THE IB DIPLOMA: COURSEBOOK

REFLECTION

Do you know how to find the *net force* on a body? Can you draw *free-body* diagrams? Can you find the *components* of a force along given axes? Can you find the magnitude and direction of a force given its components? Can you identify forces which make a *Newton third law pair*? Can you solve problems with *Newton's second law*? Can you solve problems in which *frictional forces* are present? Can you solve problems involving forces and accelerations in a variety of situations? Do you understand why in *circular motion* a force directed towards the centre is necessary? Can you solve problems with circular motion?

EXAM-STYLE QUESTIONS

You can find questions in the style of IB exams in the digital coursebook.

CHECK YOURSELF ANSWERS

1 Yes, because the weight of the block is less on the moon.

2 The minimum force needed to move the block is 3.0 N so the block will not move. The frictional force is then 2.2 N.

3 It stays the same. The buoyant force equals the weight of the ice cube and also the weight of the displaced water. So when the ice cube melts, its volume will be that of the displaced water.

4 The net force is zero so the resistive force is equal to F.

5 C, because the net force has to be opposite to the velocity.

6 The same; the acceleration is independent of mass.

7 The acceleration of each block is g. The net force on the bottom block is $mg - T = ma$, so $T = 0$ since $a = g$.

8 The centripetal acceleration is $a_c = \frac{4\pi^2 r}{T^2} = \frac{4\pi^2 \times 1.5 \times 10^{11}}{(365 \times 24 \times 60 \times 60)^2} \approx 6 \times 10^{-3}$ m s^{-2}, and so the force is $F = Ma = 6 \times 10^{24} \times 6 \times 10^{-3} = 3.6 \times 10^{22}$ N.

9 No, the bob moves in a circular arc and so has centripetal acceleration toward the centre of the arc. Hence the tension force is greater than the weight.

Chapter 3
Work, energy and power

LEARNING OBJECTIVES

In this chapter you will learn how to:

- understand the concepts of kinetic, gravitational potential and elastic potential energy
- understand work done as energy transferred
- understand power as the rate of energy transfer
- understand and apply the principle of energy conservation
- calculate the efficiency in energy transfers.

> **PHYSICS FOR THE IB DIPLOMA: COURSEBOOK**

GUIDING QUESTION

How are we led to the law of energy conservation, and how do we use it to describe changes in systems?

KEY POINT

The work done by a force is the product of the force in the direction of the displacement times the distance travelled.

Introduction

This chapter deals with the related concepts of work, energy and power—three fundamental quantities in physics. We will find out that the work done by the net force is the change in the kinetic energy of the body. Kinetic energy is one of many forms of energy that are used to describe a mechanical system, along with gravitational and elastic potential energies. We will see how the total mechanical energy of a system (kinetic and potential) stays the same in the absence of resistive forces, leading to our first conservation law.

(Equivalently, since $s \cos\theta$ is the distance travelled in the direction of the force, work may also be defined as the product of the force times the distance travelled in the direction of the force.)

The cosine here can be positive, negative or zero; thus work can be positive, negative or zero. We will see what that means shortly.

The unit of work is the joule. One joule is the work done by a force of 1 N when it moves a body a distance of 1 m in the direction of the force. 1 J = 1 N m.

WORKED EXAMPLE 3.1

A mass is being pulled along a level road by a rope attached to it in such a way that the rope makes an angle of 34° with the horizontal. The force in the rope is 24 N. Calculate the work done by this force in moving the mass a distance of 8.0 m along the level road.

Answer

We just have to apply the formula for work done:

$W = Fs \cos\theta$

Substituting the values from the question,

$W = 24 \times 8.0 \times \cos 34°$

$W = 160$ J

3.1 Work

Work done by a force

We first consider the definition of **work done** by a constant force for motion in a straight line. By constant force we mean a force that is constant in magnitude as well as in direction. Figure 3.1 shows a block that is displaced along a straight line. The distance travelled by the body is s. The force makes an angle θ with the displacement.

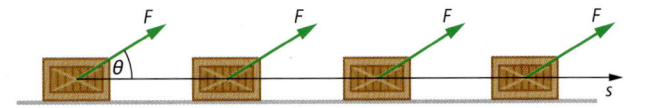

Figure 3.1: A force moving its point of application performs work.

The force acts on the body all the time as it moves. The work done by the force is defined as

$W = Fs \cos\theta$

But $F \cos\theta$ is the component of the force in the direction of the displacement and so

WORKED EXAMPLE 3.2

A car with its engine turned off moves on a horizontal level road. A constant force of 620 N opposes the motion of the car. The car comes to rest after 84 m. Calculate the work done on the car by the opposing force.

> **CONTINUED**
>
> **Answer**
>
> We again apply the formula for work done, but now we have to realise that $\theta = 180°$. So
>
> $W = 620 \times 84 \times \cos 180°$
>
> $W = -52$ kJ

> **WORKED EXAMPLE 3.3**
>
> You stand on roller skates facing a wall. You push against the wall and move away. Discuss whether the force exerted by the wall on you performed any work.
>
> **Answer**
>
> No work was done by the contact force because the point at which the force is applied has not moved. (So where did the energy you gained come from?)

Work done by a varying force

You will meet situations where the force is not constant in magnitude or direction and the path is not a straight line. Let us first discuss the case of a force varying in magnitude. Figure 3.2 shows how the magnitude of the force varies with distance travelled. Consider what happens when the force moves the body a very small distance Δs. Because Δs is so small we may assume that the force does not vary during this distance. The work done is then $F\Delta s$ and is the area of the dark brown rectangle shown. For the total work we have to add the area of the many rectangles under the curve. The sum is the area under the curve.

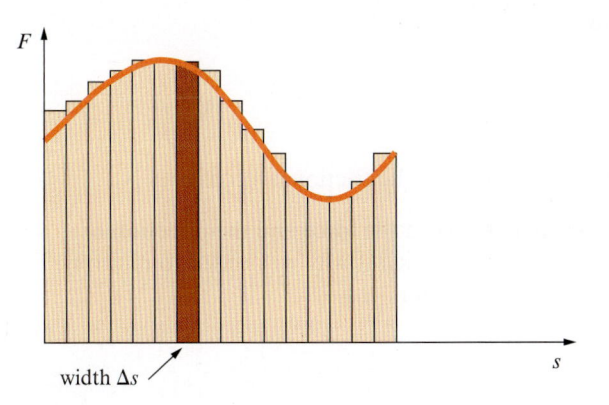

Figure 3.2: The area under the graph of force against distance is the work done.

The work done by a force is the area under the graph that shows the variation of the magnitude of the force with distance travelled.

> **WORKED EXAMPLE 3.4**
>
> A force varies with distance travelled according to the graph in Figure 3.3. What is the work done in moving a distance of 4.0 m?
>
> **Answer**
>
> The work done is the area under the graph from $d = 0$ to $d = 4$ m. This is
>
> $W = \dfrac{2.0 + 10}{2} \times 4.0 = 24$ J

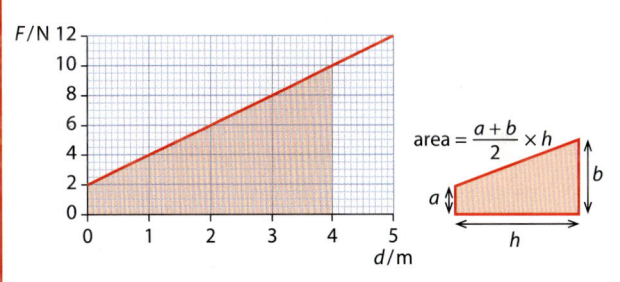

Figure 3.3: The work done is the area under the graph. The area of a trapezoid is half the sum of the parallel sides multiplied by the perpendicular distance between them.

Work done in circular motion

We know that in circular motion there must be a force directed towards the centre of the circle. This is called the centripetal force.

Figure 3.4 shows the forces pointing towards the centre of the circular path. When we break the circular path into straight segments the angle between the force and the segment is always a right angle. This means that work done along each segment is zero because $\cos 90° = 0$. So for circular motion the total work done by the centripetal force is zero.

Figure 3.4: The work done by the centripetal force is zero.

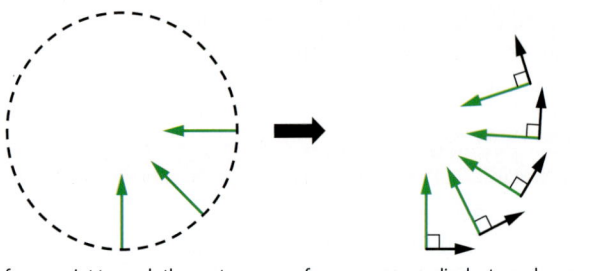

forces point towards the centre   forces are perpendicular to each segment

> **CHECK YOURSELF 1**
>
> The work done by the centripetal force in a full revolution is zero because
>
> a   the displacement is zero
>
> b   the force is at a right angle to the velocity
>
> c   the centripetal force does not move its point of application
>
> d   forces do work only when they move the body along a straight line.

The work–kinetic energy relation

Imagine a net force F that acts on a particle of mass m. The force produces an acceleration a given by

$$a = \frac{F}{m}$$

Let the initial speed of the particle be u. Because we have acceleration, the speed will change. Let the speed be v after travelling a distance s. We know from kinematics that

$$v^2 = u^2 + 2as$$

Substituting for the acceleration, this becomes

$$v^2 = u^2 + 2\frac{F}{m}s$$

We can rewrite this as

$$Fs = \tfrac{1}{2}mv^2 - \tfrac{1}{2}mu^2$$

We interpret this as follows: Fs is the work done on the particle by the net force. The quantity $\tfrac{1}{2} \times$ mass $\times$ speed^2 is the energy the particle has due to its motion, called kinetic energy. For speed v, **kinetic energy** E_K is defined as

$$E_K = \tfrac{1}{2}mv^2$$

In our example, the initial kinetic energy of the particle is $\tfrac{1}{2}mu^2$ and the kinetic energy after travelling distance s is $\tfrac{1}{2}mv^2$. The result says that the work done has resulted in a *transfer* of energy that has changed the kinetic energy of the particle.

We can write this as

$$W_{net} = \Delta E_K$$

where W_{net} is the net work done and ΔE_K is the change in kinetic energy. This is known as the **work–kinetic energy relation**.

We can think of the work done as energy transferred. In this example, the work done has transferred energy to the particle by increasing its kinetic energy.

> **WORKED EXAMPLE 3.5**
>
> A block of mass 2.5 kg slides on a rough horizontal surface. The initial speed of the block is 8.6 m s^{-1}. It is brought to rest after travelling a distance of 16 m. Determine the magnitude of the frictional force.
>
> **Answer**
>
> We will use the work–kinetic energy relation, $W_{net} = \Delta E_K$.
>
> The only force doing work is the frictional force, f, which acts in the opposite direction to the motion.
>
> $$W_{net} = f \times 16 \times (-1)$$
>
> The change in kinetic energy is
>
> $$\Delta E_K = \tfrac{1}{2}mv^2 - \tfrac{1}{2}mu^2 = -92.45 \text{ J}$$
>
> So
>
> $$-16f = -92.45$$
>
> $$f = 5.8 \text{ N}$$
>
> The magnitude of the frictional force is 5.8 N.
>
> (The angle between the force and the direction of motion is 180°, which is why we needed to multiply by cos 180°, which is –1.)

WORKED EXAMPLE 3.6

You hold a ball of mass 0.25 kg in your hand and throw it so that it leaves your hand with a speed of 12 m s^{-1}. Calculate the work done by your hand on the ball.

Answer

The question asks for work done, but here we do not know the forces that acted on the ball nor the distance by which we moved it before releasing it. But using $\Delta E_K = W_{net}$, we find

$W_{net} = \frac{1}{2}mv^2$

$W_{net} = \frac{1}{2} \times 0.25 \times 12^2 = 18$ J

WORKED EXAMPLE 3.7

Suppose that in the previous example your hand moved a distance of 0.90 m in throwing the ball. Estimate the average net force that acted on the ball.

Answer

The work done was 18 J and so $Fs = 18$ J with $s = 0.90$ m. This gives $F = 20$ N.

WORKED EXAMPLE 3.8

A mass m hangs from two strings attached to the ceiling such that they make the same angle with the vertical, as shown in Figure 3.5. The strings are shortened very slowly so that the mass is raised a distance h above its original position. Determine the work done by the tension in each string as the mass is raised.

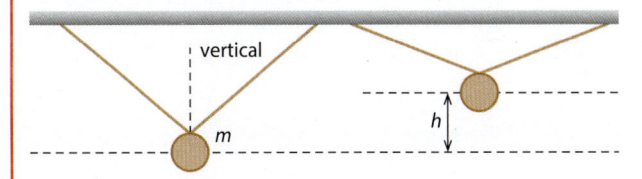

Figure 3.5: For worked example 3.8.

CONTINUED

Answer

The net work done is zero, either because the net force on the mass is zero or because the change in kinetic energy is zero. The work done by gravity is $-mgh$, and thus the work done by the two equal tension forces is $+mgh$. The work done by each is thus $\frac{mgh}{2}$.

Work done by gravity

We will now concentrate on the work done by a very special force, namely the weight of a body. Remember that weight is mass times acceleration of free fall and is directed vertically down. Thus, if a body is displaced horizontally, the work done by mg is zero. In this case the angle between the force and the direction of motion is 90° (Figure 3.6), so

$W = mgs \cos 90° = 0$

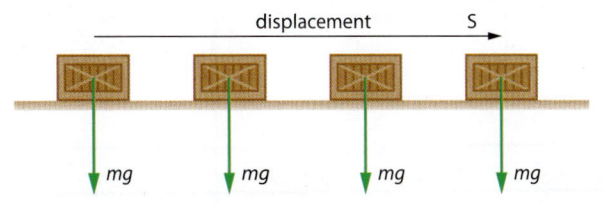

Figure 3.6: The force of gravity is normal to this horizontal displacement, so no work is being done.

> **EXAM TIP**
>
> When a body is displaced such that its final position is at the same vertical height as the original position, the work done by the weight is zero.

We are not implying that it is the weight that is forcing the body to move along the table. We are calculating the work done by a particular force (the weight) if the body (somehow) moves in a particular way.

If the body falls a vertical distance h, then the work done by the weight is $+mgh$. The force of gravity is parallel to the displacement, as in Figure 3.7a.

65

If the body moves vertically upward to a height h from the initial position, then the work done by the weight is $-mgh$ since now the angle between direction of force (vertically down) and displacement (vertically up) is 180°. The force of gravity is parallel to the displacement but opposite in direction, as in Figure 3.7b.

Suppose now that instead of just letting the body fall or throwing it upward, we use a rope to either lower it or raise it, at constant speed, by a height h (Figure 3.8). The work done by the weight is the same as before, so nothing changes. But we now ask about the work done by the force F that lowers or raises the body. Since F is equal and opposite to the weight, the work done by F is $-mgh$ as the body is lowered and $+mgh$ as it is being raised.

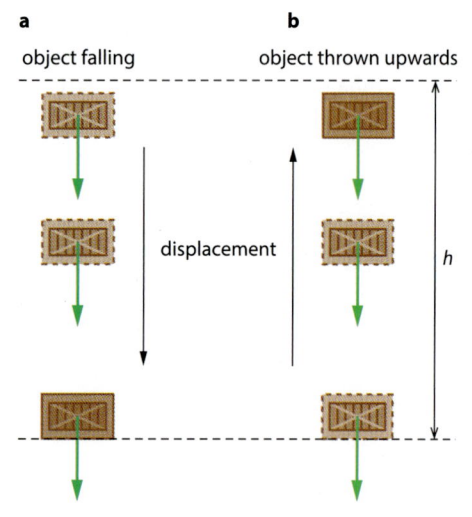

Figure 3.7: The force of gravity (green arrows) is parallel to the displacement in **a** and opposite in **b**.

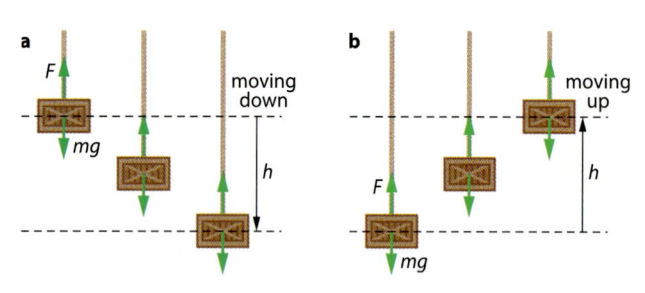

Figure 3.8: Lowering and raising an object at constant speed using a rope.

In discussing work done it is always important to keep a clear picture of the force whose work we are calculating.

Gravitational potential energy

We just saw that when a force raises a body of mass m by a vertical distance h (at constant speed) the work done by that force is mgh.

For the earth–mass system we define the **gravitational potential energy, E_P**, to be the work done by the moving force in placing a body a height h above the surface of the earth: $E_P = mgh$.

This implies that a body on the surface has zero potential energy. But as we will see (for example worked example 3.11 of the next section), we may call any horizontal surface to be the zero of potential energy and measure heights from that surface. This formula is approximate anyway and may only be used if the height h is very small compared to the radius of the earth.

> **EXAM TIP**
>
> Gravitational potential energy is the energy of a system due to its position and represents the work done by an external agent in bringing the system to that position.

Tension in a spring

Here we will meet another force to which we can associate a potential energy. It is the tension in a spring.

Consider a horizontal spring whose left end is attached to a vertical wall. If we apply a force F to the other end we will stretch the spring by some amount, x. We know from Chapter 2 that the force F and the extension x are directly proportional to each other, i.e., $F = kx$, a result known as Hooke's law, Figure 3.9.

Since the force F and the extension x are directly proportional, the graph of force versus extension is a straight line through the origin and work done is the area under the curve (Figure 3.10).

3 Work, energy and power

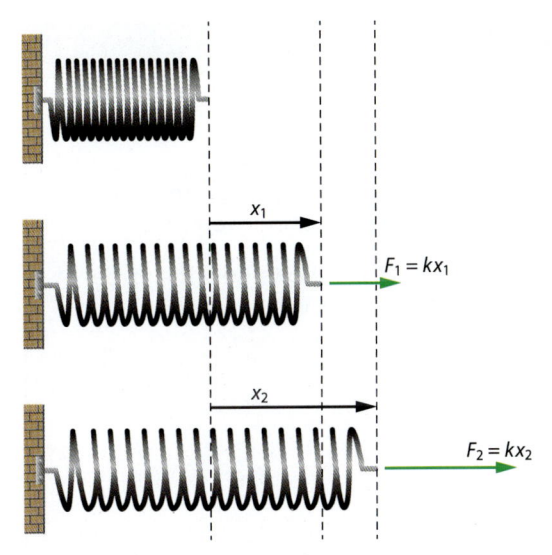

Figure 3.9: Stretching a spring requires work to be done.

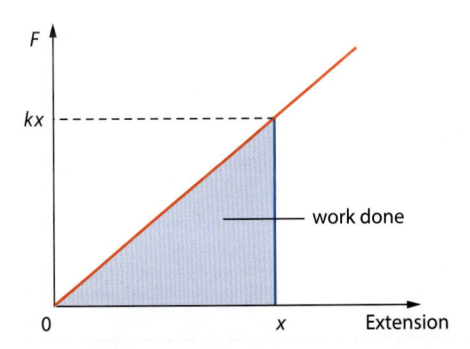

Figure 3.10: The force F stretches the spring. The force is proportional to extension according to Hooke's law.

To find the work done in extending the spring from its natural length ($x = 0$) to extension x, we need to calculate the area of the triangle of base x and height kx. Thus

area $= \frac{1}{2}kx \times x$

area $= \frac{1}{2}kx^2$

The work to extend a spring from its natural length by an amount x is thus

$W = \frac{1}{2}kx^2$

The work done in extending the spring goes into **elastic potential energy**, E_H stored in the spring. The elastic potential energy of a spring whose extension (or compression) is x is $E_H = \frac{1}{2}kx^2$. (The subscript H refers to Hooke).

> **EXAM TIP**
>
> Notice that in the data booklet the formula uses Δx in place of our x. Notice also that the work done when extending a spring from an extension x_1 to an extension x_2 (so $x_2 > x_1$) is
>
> $W = \frac{1}{2}k(x_2^2 - x_1^2)$

> **CHECK YOURSELF 2**
>
> A toy gun has a spring that is compressed by an amount e. The gun shoots a ball with speed v. What speed would the same ball have if the spring were compressed by an amount $2e$?

> **WORKED EXAMPLE 3.9**
>
> A mass of 8.4 kg rests on top of a vertical spring whose base is attached to the floor. The spring compresses by 5.2 cm.
>
> **a** Calculate the spring constant of the spring.
>
> **b** Determine the energy stored in the spring.
>
> **Answer**
>
> **a** The mass is in equilibrium so $mg = kx$. So
>
> $k = \frac{mg}{x}$
>
> $k = \frac{8.4 \times 9.8}{5.2 \times 10^{-2}}$
>
> $k = 1583 \approx 1600 \text{ N m}^{-1}$
>
> **b** The stored energy E_H is
>
> $E_H = \frac{1}{2}kx^2$
>
> $E_H = \frac{1}{2} \times 1583 \times (5.2 \times 10^{-2})^2$
>
> $E_H = 2.1 \text{ J}$

TEST YOUR UNDERSTANDING

1. A horizontal force of 24 N pulls a body a distance of 5.0 m along its direction. Calculate the work done by the force.

2. A block slides along a rough table and is brought to rest after travelling a distance of 2.4 m. A force of 3.2 N opposes the motion. Calculate the work done by the opposing force.

3. A block is pulled by a force making an angle of 20° to the horizontal, as shown in Figure 3.11. Find the work done by the pulling force when its point of application has moved 15 m.

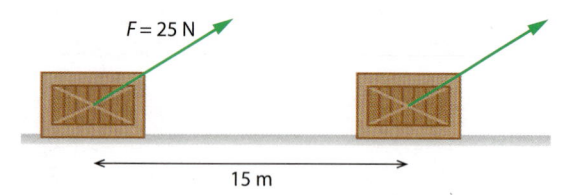

   Figure 3.11: For question 3.

4. A block of mass m slides down an inclined plane a distance d, as shown in Figure 3.12. The incline makes an angle θ to the horizontal.

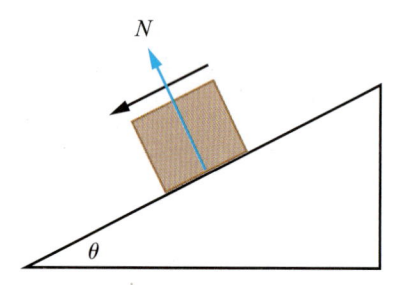

   Figure 3.12: For question 4.

   Determine the work done by the normal force N on the block.

5. A ball of mass m is tied to a string and moves on a horizontal circle of radius R with constant speed v on a horizontal table.

   a Explain carefully why the tension force does zero work during a full revolution.

   b How much work does it do in half a revolution?

6. You are holding a weight in your palm. Discuss whether you are doing work.

7. The graph (Figure 3.13) shows how the force F acting on a body varies with distance travelled x.

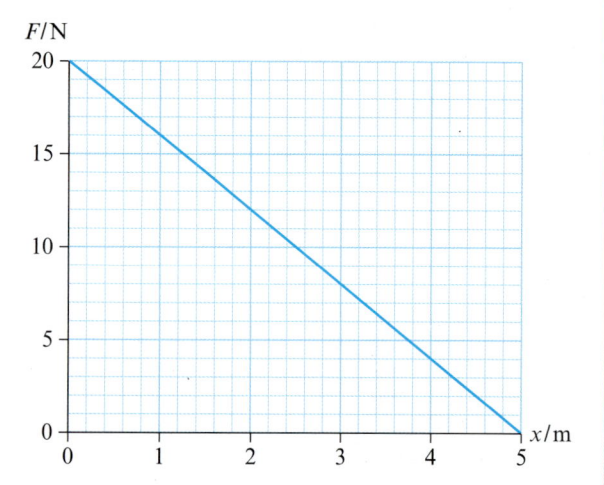

   Figure 3.13: For question 7.

   a Calculate the work done by the force after the body has been moved a distance of 5.0 m.

   b Is the speed of the body increasing or decreasing?

8. The velocity of an object moving along a straight line changes from 5.0 m s^{-1} to −5.0 m s^{-1} as the result of a force acting on the object. What is the work done by the force?

9. A block of mass 2.0 kg and an initial speed of 5.4 m s^{-1} slides on a rough horizontal surface and is eventually brought to rest after travelling a distance of 4.0 m. Calculate the frictional force between the block and the surface.

10. The graph (Figure 3.14) shows how the force F acting on a body varies with distance x travelled.

CONTINUED

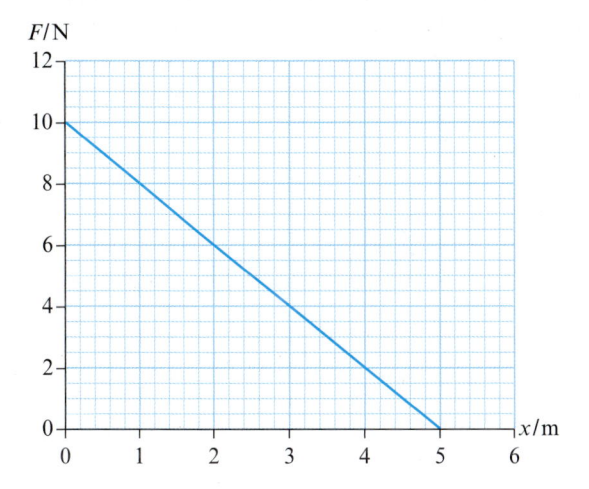

Figure 3.14: For question 10.

When the body was at $x = 0$ its kinetic energy was 5.0 J. What is the kinetic energy at $x = 5.0$ m?

11 A force F acts on a body of mass $m = 2.0$ kg initially at rest. The graph (Figure 3.15) shows how the force varies with distance travelled (along a straight line).

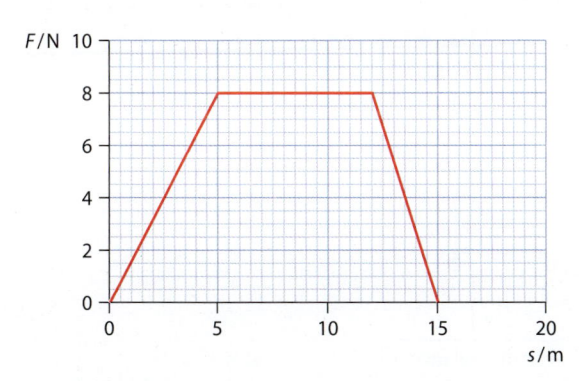

Figure 3.15: For question 11.

a Find the work done by this force.

b Calculate the final speed of the body.

12 A body of mass 3.0 kg has kinetic energy 36 J. It is brought to rest after travelling a horizontal distance of 4.0 m. A frictional force acts in a direction opposite to the velocity. Determine the magnitude of the frictional force.

13 Equal forces are applied to a 1 kg block and a 10 kg block, both of which are initially at rest. After moving a distance of 1 m, which body has the greatest kinetic energy, or is the energy the same for both?

14 A body falls freely under the action of gravity. After falling 1 m the kinetic energy increases by 1 J. What will be the change in kinetic energy after falling another 1 m?

15 A block of weight 150 N is tied to a rope. The block is lowered vertically by a distance of 12 m at constant speed. What is the work done by:

a the weight of the block

b the tension in the rope.

16 Figure 3.16 shows a block that is lowered by a vertical distance h along the curved red path.

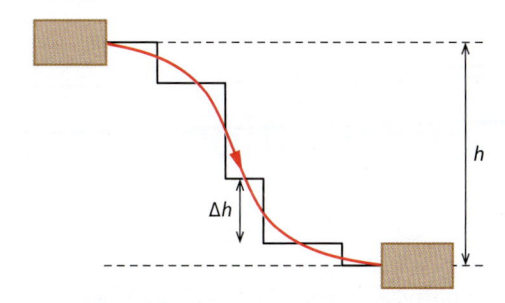

Figure 3.16: For question 16.

By approximating the red path with the 'staircase' path, argue that the work done by the weight is still mgh and so show that the work done by the weight is independent of the path followed.

17 You want to move a block to the top of an incline—from position A to position B. You can either pull it up the plane (Figure 3.17a) or raise it vertically (Figure 3.17b). In both cases, you use the same constant speed.

PHYSICS FOR THE IB DIPLOMA: COURSEBOOK

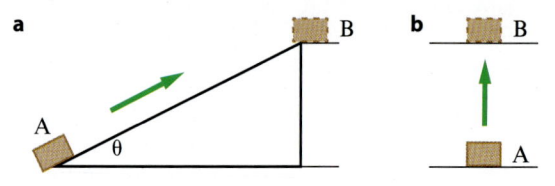

CONTINUED

Figure 3.17: For question 17.

In which case will the work done by gravity be the greatest—or is the work in both cases the same? What about the work done by you as you move the block?

18 The extension of a spring of spring constant $k = 250$ N m^{-1} is 0.12 m. Calculate the elastic potential energy stored in the spring.

19 The elastic potential energy stored in a spring of spring constant $k = 380$ N m^{-1} is 1.4 J. Calculate the extension of the spring.

20 A spring of spring constant $k = 200$ N m^{-1} is slowly extended from an extension of 3.0 cm to an extension of 5.0 cm. Calculate the work done by the extending force.

21 The graph (Figure 3.18) shows how the tension force F in a spring varies with the extension x.

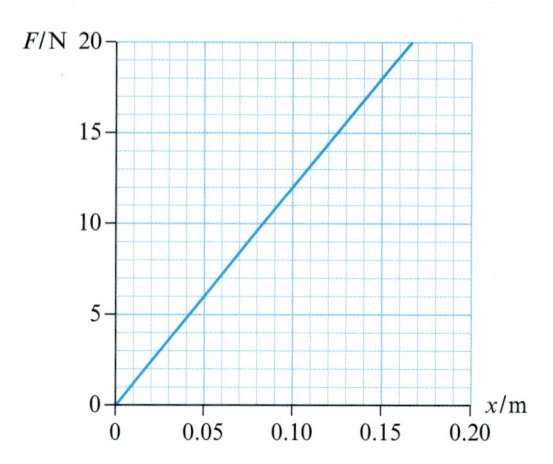

Figure 3.18: For question 21.

Calculate the work done to stretch the spring from an extension of 5.0 cm to an extension of 15 cm.

3.2 Conservation of energy

Potential energy is a property of a system, not of an individual particle. Potential energy, like kinetic energy, is a scalar quantity. Why is the quantity $E_p = mgh$ important enough or useful enough that we give it a special name? To answer this question, consider a body that falls freely under gravity along a vertical line, Figure 3.19.

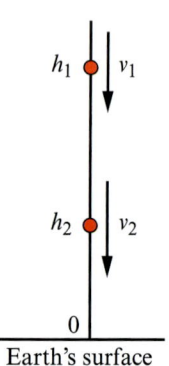

Figure 3.19: A body falling vertically increases in speed as the height decreases.

When the body is at height h_1 from the ground its speed is v_1 and when at height h_2 its speed is v_2. We know from kinematics that

$v_2^2 = v_1^2 + 2g(h_1 - h_2)$

which we may rewrite as

$\frac{1}{2}v_2^2 + gh_2 = \frac{1}{2}v_1^2 + gh_1$

Multiplying through by the mass m of the falling object we get

$\frac{1}{2}mv_2^2 + mgh_2 = \frac{1}{2}mv_1^2 + mgh_1$

This is an interesting result: each side of the equation is the sum of the kinetic energy of the falling mass and the quantity we called gravitational potential energy. The equation suggests that this sum, $E_K + E_P$, stays the same as the mass falls. So if we call this sum the **total mechanical energy** of the system, E_T, we are led to a **law of conservation of total mechanical energy**. Of course, we showed that E_T stays the same for the simple case of a mass falling freely, but this can be demonstrated for many other situations as well. This is why the concept of gravitational potential energy is useful.

So, for the system consisting of the particle and the earth, the total mechanical energy is

$E_T = E_K + E_P = \frac{1}{2}mv^2 + mgh$

Under what conditions is E_T conserved? It turns out that this happens when friction and resistance forces are absent and no other forces act on the system from outside the system. Clearly, a car travelling on a level road will come to rest when the engine is turned off. Total mechanical energy is not conserved here because of the work done by the resistance forces opposing the motion; total mechanical energy decreases. Similarly, if the driver of the car steps on the gas pedal, the car will accelerate, increasing the kinetic and hence total mechanical energy. This is because an external force has acted on the car (between the ground and the tyres), and again this external force did work, this time increasing the total mechanical energy. So we are led to this conclusion:

> **KEY POINT**
>
> If no work is done on the system from outside, the system is called **isolated** and in that case the total mechanical energy of the system does not change. We say that the total mechanical energy of the system is **conserved**.

If our system includes springs the total mechanical energy will be

$E_T = E_K + E_P + E_H = \frac{1}{2}mv^2 + mgh + \frac{1}{2}kx^2$

In the absence of external forces doing work this total mechanical energy will be conserved.

(It is important to realise that weight and spring tension are not considered external forces because their effects are included in the potential energy in the total mechanical energy of the system.)

> **CHECK YOURSELF 3**
>
> A ball starting from rest will descend the same vertical height along the paths shown in Figure 3.20. The length of the path increases from left to right.
>
> In which case will the final speed be greatest?
>
> **Figure 3.20:** For check yourself question 3.

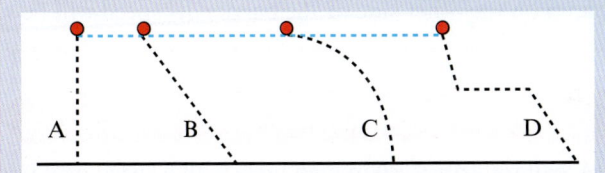

WORKED EXAMPLE 3.10

Determine the minimum speed of the mass in Figure 3.21 at the initial point such that the mass makes it over the barrier of height $h = 0.80$ m.

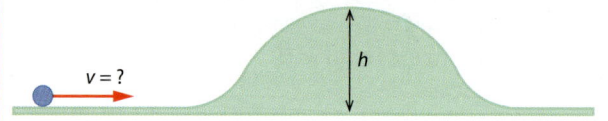

Figure 3.21: For worked example 3.10.

Answer

To make it over the barrier the mass must be able to reach the highest point. Any speed it has at the top will mean it can carry on to the other side. Therefore, at the very least, we must be able to get the ball to the highest point with zero speed.

With zero speed at the top, the total energy at the top of the barrier is $E_T = mgh$.

The total energy at the starting position is
$E_T = \frac{1}{2}mv^2$.

Equating the initial and final total energies,

$\frac{1}{2}mv^2 = mgh$

$\Rightarrow v = \sqrt{2gh}$

Thus, the initial speed must be bigger than $v = \sqrt{2gh} = \sqrt{2 \times 9.81 \times 0.80} = 3.96 \approx 4.0$ m s^{-1}.

Note that if the initial speed v of the mass is larger than 4.0 m s^{-1}, then when the mass makes it to the original level on the other side of the barrier, its speed will be v. Note also that the mass plays no role in this calculation.

WORKED EXAMPLE 3.11

A ball rolls off a 1.0 m high table with a speed of 4.0 m s^{-1}, as shown in Figure 3.22. Calculate the speed as the ball strikes the floor.

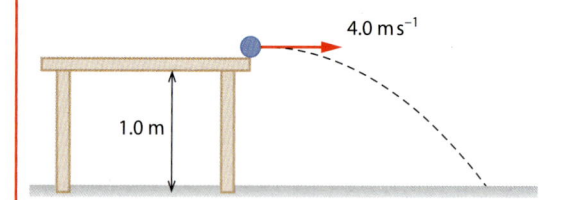

Figure 3.22: For worked example 3.11.

Answer

The total energy of the mass is conserved. As it leaves the table with speed u it has total energy given by $E_{initial} = \frac{1}{2}mu^2 + mgh$, and as it lands with speed v the total energy is $E_{final} = \frac{1}{2}mv^2$ (v is the speed we are looking for).

CONTINUED

Equating the two energies gives

$\frac{1}{2}mv^2 = \frac{1}{2}mu^2 + mgh$

$\Rightarrow v^2 = u^2 + 2gh$

$\quad v^2 = 16 + 19.62 = 35.62$

$\Rightarrow v \approx 6.0\,\text{m s}^{-1}$

Notice that if the ball was projected at an angle to the horizontal the result would be the same. Can you see why?

We mentioned earlier that the height can be measured from any horizontal surface, not just the surface of the earth. Let us see how this works in this example. Suppose first that we measure heights from a level that is 3 m *below* the surface of the earth. The total energy of the ball on the table would then be $\frac{1}{2}mu^2 + mg \times 4$. When the ball lands the total energy would be $\frac{1}{2}mv^2 + mg \times 3$. Equating the two we get

$\frac{1}{2}mu^2 + mg \times 4 = \frac{1}{2}mv^2 + mg \times 3$

$\Rightarrow \frac{1}{2}mu^2 + mg \times 1 = \frac{1}{2}mv^2$

$\Rightarrow v^2 = u^2 + 2g \times 1 = 16 + 19.62 = 35.62$

just like before. Similarly, suppose we measure heights from the level of the table. The total energy at the table is now $\frac{1}{2}mv^2 + 0$. The total energy on the ground is $\frac{1}{2}mv^2 + mg \times (-1)$ since the ground is 1 m *below* the table. Equating again,

$\frac{1}{2}mu^2 + 0 = \frac{1}{2}mv^2 + mg \times (-1)$

$\Rightarrow \frac{1}{2}mu^2 + mg \times 1 = \frac{1}{2}mv^2$

$\Rightarrow v^2 = u^2 + 2g \times 1 = 16 + 19.62 = 35.62$

again just like before. So, in using gravitational potential energy we can measure heights from any horizontal surface that is convenient.

WORKED EXAMPLE 3.12

Two identical balls are launched from a table with the same speed u (Figure 3.23). One ball is thrown vertically up and the other vertically down. The height of the table from the floor is h. Predict which of the two balls will hit the floor with the greater speed.

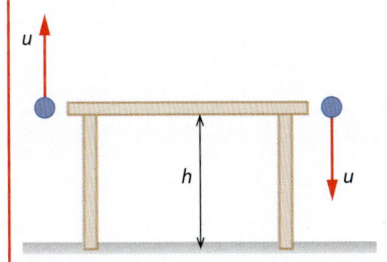

Figure 3.23: For worked example 3.12.

CONTINUED

Answer

At launch both balls have the same kinetic energy and the same potential energy. When they hit the floor their energy will be only kinetic. Hence the speeds will be identical and equal to v, where

$\frac{1}{2}mv^2 = \frac{1}{2}mu^2 + mgh$

$\Rightarrow v^2 = u^2 + 2gh$

$\Rightarrow v = \sqrt{u^2 + 2gh}$

WORKED EXAMPLE 3.13

A pendulum of length 1.0 m is released from rest with the string at an angle of 10° to the vertical. Find the speed of the mass on the end of the pendulum when it passes through its lowest position.

Answer

We measure heights from the lowest point of the pendulum (Figure 3.24). The total energy at that point is just kinetic, $E_K = \frac{1}{2}mv^2$, where v is the unknown speed.

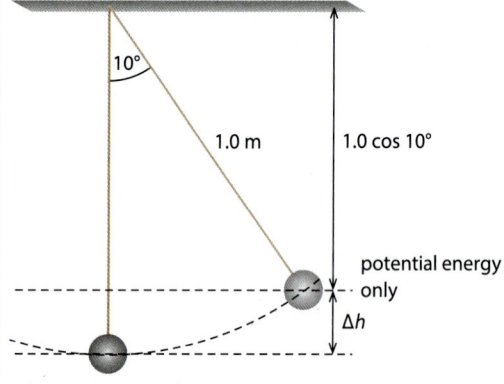

Figure 3.24: For worked example 3.13.

At the initial point, the total energy is just potential, $E_p = mg\Delta h$, where Δh is the vertical difference in height between the two positions. From the diagram,

$\Delta h = 1.0 - 1.0 \cos 10°$

$\Delta h = 0.015$ m

Equating the expressions for the total energy at the lowest point and at the start,

$\frac{1}{2}mv^2 = mg\Delta h$

$v = \sqrt{2g\Delta h}$

$v = 0.54$ m s^{-1}

Note how the mass has dropped out of the problem. (At positions other than the two shown, the mass has both kinetic and potential energy.)

3 Work, energy and power

WORKED EXAMPLE 3.14

A body of mass 4.2 kg with initial speed 5.6 m s^{-1} begins to move up an incline, as shown in Figure 3.25.

Figure 3.25: For worked example 3.14.

The body will be momentarily brought to rest after colliding with a spring of spring constant 2200 N m^{-1}. The body stops a vertical distance $h = 0.85$ m above its initial position. Determine the amount by which the spring has been compressed. Assume no frictional forces.

Answer

There are no external forces doing work, the system is isolated, and we have conservation of total mechanical energy.

Initially we have just kinetic energy, so

$E_{intial} = \frac{1}{2}mv^2 + mgh + \frac{1}{2}kx^2 =$
$\frac{1}{2} \times 4.2 \times 5.6^2 + 0 + 0 = 65.856$ J

When the body stops we have gravitational and elastic potential energies

$E_{final} = \frac{1}{2}mv^2 + mgh + \frac{1}{2}kx^2 = 0 + 4.2 \times 9.81 \times 0.85 + \frac{1}{2} \times 2200 \times x^2 = 35.02 + 1100 x^2$

Thus, equating $E_{initial}$ to E_{final} we find

$35.02 + 1100 x^2 = 65.856$

$1100 x^2 = 30.84$

$x^2 = 0.02804$

$x = 0.17$ m

What happens when external forces do work on the system?

We have seen that in the absence of external forces doing work, the total mechanical energy, E_T, of the system stays the same: we have the law of conservation of total mechanical energy. However, if there are **interactions** between the system and its surroundings (Figure 3.26) the total mechanical energy may change. These interactions mainly involve work done W_{ext} by the surroundings and/or the **transfer of thermal energy** (heat) Q, to or from the surroundings.

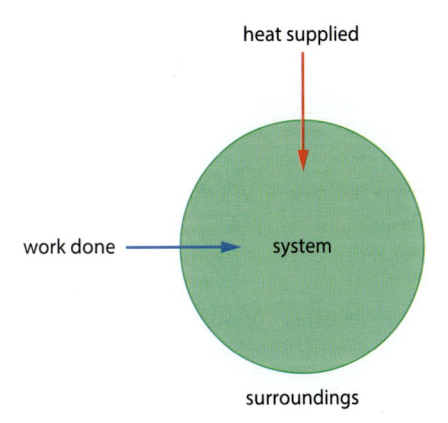

Figure 3.26: The total energy of a system may change as a result of interactions with its surroundings.

So we expect that

$\Delta E_T = W_{ext} + Q$

In this chapter we will deal with $Q = 0$ so in that case we have the relation:

$\Delta E_T = W_{ext}$

EXAM TIP

You must make sure that you do not confuse the work–kinetic energy relation $W_{net} = \Delta E_K$ with $\Delta E_T = W_{ext}$. The work–kinetic energy relation relates the net work on a system to the change in the system's kinetic energy. The other relates the work done by external forces to the change of the total energy.

WORKED EXAMPLE 3.15

A body of mass 2.0 kg (initially at rest) slides down a curved path of total length 22 m, as shown in Figure 3.27. The body starts from a vertical height of 5.0 m from the bottom. When it reaches the bottom, its speed is measured and found to equal 6.0 m s^{-1}.

a Show that there is a force resisting the motion.

b Assuming the force to have constant magnitude and opposite to the velocity, determine the magnitude of the force.

Figure 3.27: For worked example 3.15.

Answer

a We calculate the total energy initially and finally to see if energy is conserved.

At the top:

$E_{initial} = \frac{1}{2}mv^2 + mgh = 0 + 2.0 \times 9.8 \times 5.0 = 98$ J

At the bottom:

$E_{final} = \frac{1}{2}mv^2 + mgh = \frac{1}{2} \times 2.0 \times 6.0^2 + 0 = 36$ J

The total energy has decreased, which shows the presence of an external frictional force resisting the motion.

b From $\Delta E_T = W_{ext}$ we deduce that $W_{ext} = -62$ J. This is the work done by the frictional force of magnitude f.

The force acts in the opposite direction to the velocity, so

$fs \times (-1) = -62$ J

$\Rightarrow f = \frac{62}{22}$

$f = 2.8$ N

3 Work, energy and power

WORKED EXAMPLE 3.16

A mass of 5.00 kg moving up an incline with an initial velocity of 2.0 m s^{-1} is acted upon by an external force of 55 N in the direction of the velocity. The motion is opposed by a frictional force. After travelling a distance of 18 m along the incline the mass has been raised to a vertical height of 3.0 m and the velocity of the body becomes 15 m s^{-1}. Determine the magnitude of the frictional force.

Answer

The change in the total mechanical energy ΔE_T is

$$\Delta E_T = \left(\tfrac{1}{2} \times 5.0 \times 15^2 + 5.0 \times 9.81 \times 3.0\right) - \left(\tfrac{1}{2} \times 5.0 \times 2.0^2\right) = 699.7 \text{ J}$$

Let the frictional force be f. The work done on the mass by the external forces is $(55 - f) \times 18$, and so from $\Delta E_T = W_{ext}$

$(55 - f) \times 18 = 699.7$

$55 - f = \dfrac{699.7}{18}$

$55 - f = 38.87$

$f \approx 16 \text{ N}$

TEST YOUR UNDERSTANDING

22 A ball is released from rest from the top of a box along three different ramps, X, Y and Z.

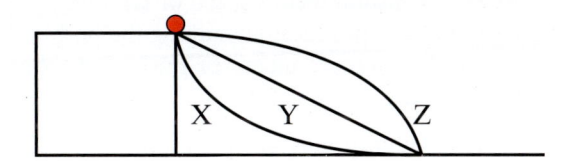

Figure 3.28: For question 22.

Along which ramp will the ball attain the greatest speed at the bottom?

23 A ball is projected from a table twice, the first time horizontally and the second time at an angle of 45° to the horizontal. The speed is the same in both cases. In which case will the ball reach the ground with the greatest speed?

24 Look at Figure 3.29.

   a Calculate the minimum initial speed v the ball must have in order to make it to position B.

   b Using the answer in **a** calculate the speed at B.

   c If the initial speed is $v = 12.0$ m s^{-1}, calculate the speed at A and B.

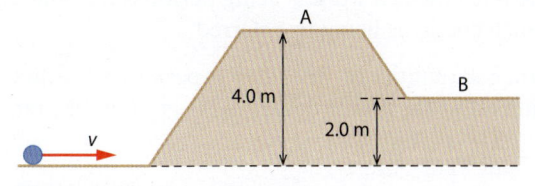

Figure 3.29: For question 24.

77

> **CONTINUED**
>
> **25** Look at Figure 3.30. The speed of the 8.0 kg mass in position A is 6.0 m s⁻¹. By the time it gets to position B, its speed is 12.0 m s⁻¹. 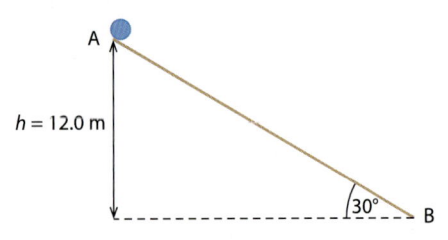
>
> **Figure 3.30:** For question 25.
>
> Estimate the frictional force opposing the motion. (The frictional force is acting along the plane.)
>
> **26** In a loop-the-loop toy, a small marble is released from rest from an initial position a height H above level ground. The radius of the loop is R. Frictional forces are negligible. 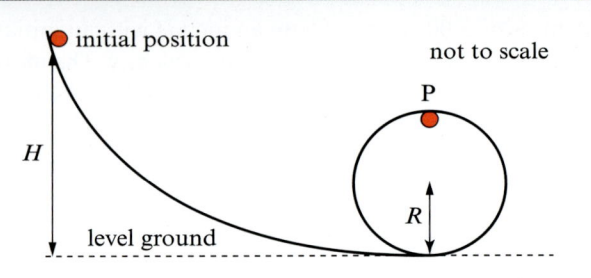
>
> **Figure 3.31:** For question 26.
>
> **a** Show that the speed of the marble at P is given by $v = \sqrt{2g(H - 2R)}$.
>
> **b** Find an expression for the normal force on the marble at P.
>
> **c** Deduce (in terms of R) the minimum value of H for which the marble will not fall off the loop.

3.3 Power and efficiency

When a machine performs work, it is important to know not only how much work is being done but also how much work is performed within a given time interval. A cyclist will perform a lot of work in a lifetime of cycling, but the same work can be performed by a powerful car engine in a much shorter time. **Power** is the rate at which work is being performed or the rate at which energy is being transferred.

When a quantity of work ΔW is performed within a time interval Δt the power developed is given by the ratio

$$P = \frac{\Delta W}{\Delta t}$$

Its unit is joules per second, and this is given the name watt (W): 1 W = 1 J s⁻¹.

Consider a constant force F, which acts on a body of mass m. The force does an amount of work $F \Delta x$ in moving the body a small distance Δx along its direction. If this work is performed in time Δt, then

$$P = \frac{F \Delta x}{\Delta t}$$

$$P = Fv$$

where v is the instantaneous speed of the body. This is the power produced in making the body move at speed v. As the speed increases, the power necessarily increases as well.

Consider an aircraft moving at constant speed on a straight-line path. If the power produced by its engines is P, and the force pushing it forward is F, then P, F and v are related by the equation above. But since the plane moves with no acceleration, the total force of air resistance must equal F. Hence the force of air resistance can be found simply from the power of the plane's engines and the constant speed with which it coasts.

> **EXAM TIP**
>
> In many questions you may be asked to find the average power developed. It can be proven that this is given by $\bar{F} \times \frac{(v + u)}{2}$, where $\bar{F}$ is the average force and u and v the initial and final speeds.

WORKED EXAMPLE 3.17

Estimate the minimum power required to lift a mass of 50.0 kg up a vertical distance of 12 m in 5.0 s.

Answer

The work done in lifting the mass is mgh:

$W = mgh = 50.0 \times 9.81 \times 12$

$W = 5.89 \times 10^3$ J

The power is therefore:

$P = \dfrac{W}{\Delta t}$

$P = \dfrac{5.89 \times 10^3}{5.0} \approx 1200$ W

This is the minimum power required. In practice, the mass has to be accelerated from rest, which will require additional work and hence more power. There will also be frictional forces to overcome adding to the power actually needed.

CHECK YOURSELF 4

A boy of mass 60 kg jumps straight up into the air from a crouching position. His centre of mass is raised by 0.50 m when he is about to lose contact with the ground. After losing contact with the ground his centre of mass is lifted an additional 0.80 m. What is the average power developed? (Assume the boy pushes against the ground with a constant force and take $g = 10$ m s^{-2}.)

Efficiency

If a machine, such as an electric motor, is used to raise a load, electrical energy must be provided to the motor. This is the input energy to the motor. The motor uses some of this energy to do the useful work of raising the load. But some of the input energy is used to overcome frictional forces and therefore gets transferred to thermal energy. So the ratio:

$\eta = \dfrac{\text{useful energy out}}{\text{actual energy in}}$ or $\dfrac{\text{useful power out}}{\text{actual power in}}$

is less than one. We call this ratio the **efficiency**, η of the machine.

Suppose that a body is being pulled up along a rough inclined plane with constant speed. The mass is 15 kg and the angle of the incline is 45°. There is a constant frictional force of 42 N opposing the motion.

The forces on the body are shown in Figure 3.32. Since the body has no acceleration, we know that

$R = mg \cos \theta = 104.1$ N

$F = mg \sin \theta + f = 104.1 + 42 = 146.1$ N

Let the force raise the mass a distance of 25 m along the plane. The work done by the force F is

$W = 146.1 \times 25$

$W = 3653$ J $\approx 3.7 \times 10^3$ J

The force effectively raised the 15 kg a vertical height of 17.7 m (that is, $25 \times \sin 45°$) and so increased the potential energy of the mass by $mgh = 2605$ J. The efficiency with which the force raised the mass is thus

efficiency $= \dfrac{2605}{3653}$

$= 0.71$

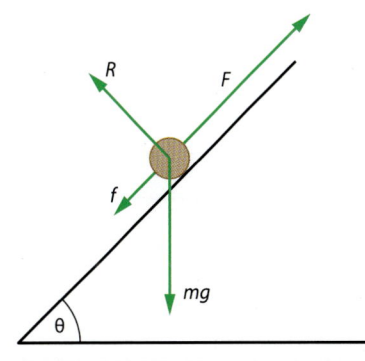

Figure 3.32: Forces on a body on an inclined plane: pulling force F, frictional force f, normal R and weight mg.

WORKED EXAMPLE 3.18

A 0.50 kg battery-operated toy train moves with constant velocity 0.30 m s^{-1} along a level track. The power of the motor in the train is 2.0 W, and the total force opposing the motion of the train is 5.0 N.

a Determine the efficiency of the train's motor.

b Assuming the efficiency and the opposing force stay the same, calculate the speed of the train as it climbs an incline of 10.0° to the horizontal.

CONTINUED

Answer

a The power delivered by the motor is 2.0 W. Since the speed is constant, the force developed by the motor is 5.0 N.

The power used in moving the train is $Fv = 5.0 \times 0.30 = 1.5$ W.

Hence the efficiency is

$\frac{\text{total power out}}{\text{total power in}} = \frac{1.5 \text{ W}}{2.0 \text{ W}} = 0.75$

The efficiency of the train's motor is 0.75 (or 75%).

b The component of the train's weight acting down the plane is $mg \sin \theta$ and the force opposing motion is 5.0 N. Since there is no acceleration (constant velocity), the net force F pushing the train up the incline is

$F = mg \sin \theta + 5.0$

$F = 0.50 \times 9.81 \times \sin 10° + 5.0$

$F = 5.852 \text{ N} \approx 5.9 \text{ N}$

Thus

efficiency = $\frac{5.852 \times v}{2.0}$

But from part **a** the efficiency is 0.75, so

$0.75 = \frac{5.852 \times v}{2.0}$

$\Rightarrow v = \frac{2.0 \times 0.75}{5.852}$

$v = 0.26 \text{ m s}^{-1}$

3.4 Energy transfers

In previous sections we saw that in a system without external forces doing work the total mechanical energy of the system stays the same; it is conserved. During a motion, the individual stores of the total energy (kinetic energy, gravitational potential energy and elastic potential energy) change, but the total energy stays the same.

Energy can be transferred from one form to another. For example, a ball rolling down an inclined plane starts with gravitational potential energy (gpe) which transfers to kinetic energy. Eventually, the ball will stop rolling because its kinetic energy is 'lost' to the surroundings as it transfers to thermal energy (and some sound).

TEST YOUR UNDERSTANDING

27 The engine of a car is developing a power of 90 kW when it is moving on a horizontal road at a constant speed of 100 km h⁻¹.

   a Estimate the total horizontal force opposing the motion of the car.

   b Assuming the opposing force stays the same, what additional power must the engine deliver for the car to continue at the same speed up an incline making an angle of 5.0° to the horizontal? The mass of the car is 1200 kg.

28 The motor of an elevator develops power at a rate of 2500 W.

   a Calculate the speed that a 1200 kg load is being raised at.

   b In practice it is found that the load is lifted more slowly than indicated by your answer to **a**. Suggest reasons why this is so.

29 A load of 50 kg is raised a vertical distance of 15 m in 125 s by a motor.

   a Estimate the power necessary for this.

   b The power supplied by the motor is 80 W. Calculate the efficiency of the motor.

   c The same motor is now used to raise a load of 100 kg the same distance. The efficiency remains the same. Estimate how long this would take.

30 The top speed of a racing car of mass 1200 kg whose engine is delivering 250 kW of power is 240 km h⁻¹. The car now moves on an uphill that makes an angle of 12° to the horizontal. Assuming the resistance force stays the same, what would the top speed of the car be?

31 A 30 kg child and a 60 kg adult both run up the same flight of stairs in the same time. Who develops more power?

A ball rising up an inclined plane does the reverse—its kinetic energy is transferred to gpe.

When a mass at the end of a compressed spring is released, the elastic potential energy transfers into kinetic, and so on.

As we move on in this course, we will encounter other forms of energy (thermal, electrical, magnetic, nuclear and so on). We will find that if we include these other forms of energy into the total energy of the system then this new total energy will always be conserved. This generalised energy conservation law has been tested in every system at every scale (from the microscopic subatomic level to the very large cosmological scale) and has never been found to be violated.

The law of conservation of energy states that energy cannot be created or destroyed—it can only be transferred from one form to another.

So a block slowing down and stopping because of friction can be described equivalently in these two ways:

Description 1: the total energy consists of just kinetic, and this is not conserved because an external force is doing work on the system.

Description 2: the frictional force did work reducing the kinetic energy of the block, but this resulted in generation of thermal energy. Including thermal energy as part of the total energy of the system means the total energy is conserved.

CHECK YOURSELF 5

A block slides down an inclined plane at constant speed. What energy transfers are taking place?

a gravitational potential energy to kinetic energy

b kinetic energy to gravitational potential energy

c kinetic energy to thermal energy

d gravitational potential energy to thermal energy

Sankey diagrams

A convenient way to represent energy transfers is by using a Sankey diagram. Each energy transfer is represented by an arrow. The arrow's width is proportional to the amount (or percentage) of energy transferred. Figure 3.33 shows a Sankey diagram for a wind turbine that produces electricity from the kinetic energy of the wind.

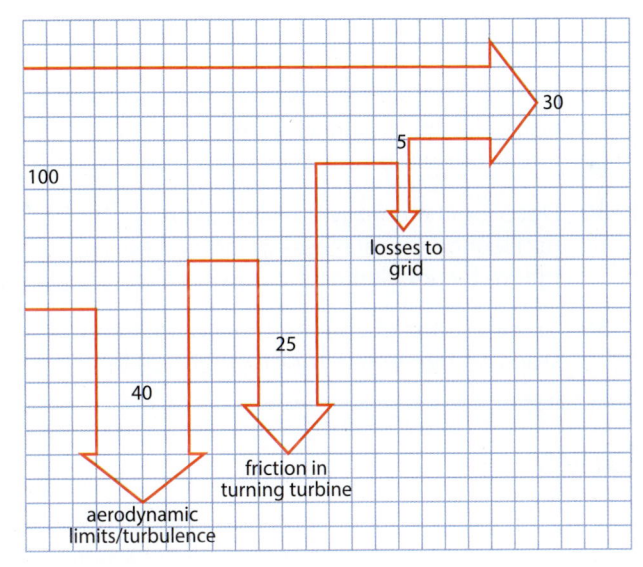

Figure 3.33: Sankey diagram for a wind turbine.

100 units of energy are coming in from the kinetic energy of the wind. The down arrows represent losses of energy, leaving a useful output for electricity production of 30 units. The efficiency of the system is then 30%.

CHECK YOURSELF 6

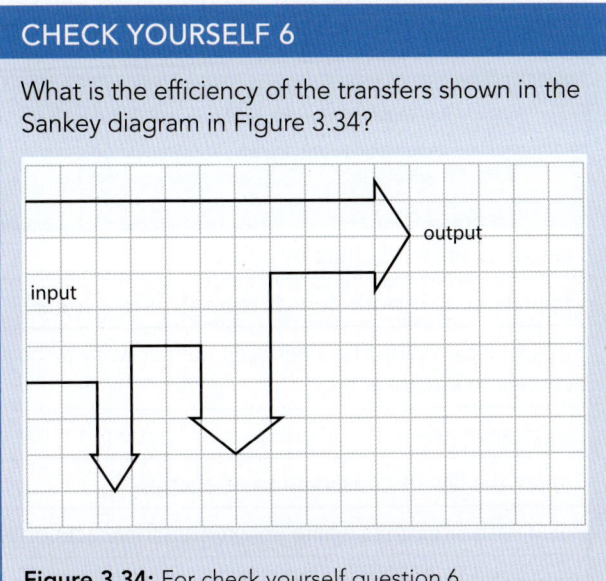

What is the efficiency of the transfers shown in the Sankey diagram in Figure 3.34?

Figure 3.34: For check yourself question 6.

TEST YOUR UNDERSTANDING

32 Describe the energy transfers in an oscillating pendulum as frictional forces bring it slowly to rest.

33 Describe the energy transfers in an oscillating horizontal mass–spring system as frictional forces bring the system slowly to rest.

34 Describe the energy transfers in an oscillating vertical mass–spring system. Ignore frictional effects.

35 An elevator starts on the ground floor and stops on the tenth floor of a high-rise building. The elevator reaches a constant speed by the time it reaches the first floor and decelerates to rest between the ninth and tenth floors. Describe the energy transfers taking place between the first and ninth floors.

36 A ball falls vertically moving at terminal velocity. Describe the energy transfers taking place.

37 A car with its engine turned off coasts down an inclined plane at constant speed. Describe the energy transfers taking place.

Links

- We will meet the law of conservation of energy in many other parts of the course. Conservation of energy is useful also in solving many kinematics questions. In Unit B, for example, we will see how conservation of energy and a few simple assumptions allow us to calculate the average temperature of the earth and how the law is applied to thermodynamics. Also how the motion of electrons inside a conductor involves collisions between the electrons and the ions which are inelastic so the electrons transfer energy to the ions. This makes the ions vibrate faster about their equilibrium positions and so the conductor gets warmer, its temperature increases.

- In Unit C we will see that conservation energy implies that the ripples in a lake created when a stone is dropped in the lake get smaller as the ripples move away. In Unit D we will see what conservation of energy has to say about planetary orbits. And in Unit E we will see that conservation of energy and Einstein's equivalence of mass and energy imply that vast amounts of energy may be released in nuclear reactions.

SELF-ASSESSMENT CHECKLIST

I am able to …	Section	Not yet	Nearly there	Ready to move on
calculate the work done by a force	3.1			
appreciate that work done is equivalent to a transfer of energy	3.1			
describe the connection between the net work done and the change in kinetic energy	3.1			
work with gravitational energy and elastic potential energy	3.1			
apply the law of conservation of energy	3.2			
deal with situations where an external force acts on the system	3.2			
understand the concept of power and efficiency and use them to solve problems	3.3			
discuss energy transfers	3.4			
use Sankey diagrams	3.4			

3 Work, energy and power

> **REFLECTION**
>
> Do you understand what is meant by the *work done by a force*? Do you know how to apply the *work-kinetic energy principle*? Do you know when *mechanical energy* is conserved? Do you know what information a graph of force versus distance gives? Can you describe the energy transfers taking place in various contexts? Can you solve problems with energy conservation?

EXAM-STYLE QUESTIONS

You can find questions in the style of IB exams in the digital coursebook.

CHECK YOURSELF ANSWERS

1. B

2. The elastic energy is four times as large and so is the kinetic energy of the ball. Hence the speed is twice as large.

3. It is the same since the vertical height is the same.

4. The boy raises his centre of mass by a total of 1.3 m and so the work done by the muscles is $mgh = 60 \times 10 \times 1.3 = 780$ J.

   After losing contact with the ground he moves up a distance of 0.80 m so his launch speed is $v = \sqrt{2gh} = 4.0$ m s^{-1}.

   His acceleration when in contact with the ground is then found from $4.0^2 = 0 + 2a \times 0.5 \Rightarrow a = 16$ m s^{-2}

   so he was in contact with the ground for $4.0 = 0 + 16 \times t \Rightarrow t = 0.25$ s.

   Hence the average power developed is $\frac{780}{0.25} = 3120 \approx 3$ kW.

   Equivalently, with an acceleration of $a = 16$ m s^{-2} the force from the ground F is found from $F - mg = ma$ and so $F = 60 \times 10 + 60 \times 16 = 1560$ N.

   The average power is then $\bar{P} = F\frac{u+v}{2} = 1560 \times \frac{0 + 4.0}{2} = 3120$ W.

5. D (kinetic energy is constant)

6. 40%

Chapter 4
Linear momentum

LEARNING OBJECTIVES

In this chapter you will learn how to:

- understand the concept of momentum
- understand the vector nature of momentum
- express Newton's second law in terms of the rate of change of momentum
- work with impulse and force–time graphs
- apply conservation of linear momentum
- work with elastic collisions, inelastic collisions and explosions
- work with two-dimensional collisions

> **GUIDING QUESTIONS**
>
> - How does Newton's second law generalise to cases of varying mass?
> - How do we use momentum conservation?

Introduction

This chapter introduces an important concept in physics: linear momentum. Newton's second law is expressed in terms of momentum. The law of conservation of linear momentum allows the prediction of outcomes in many physical situations.

4.1 Newton's second law in terms of momentum

In Chapter 2, Newton's second law was expressed as $\vec{F} = m\vec{a}$. In fact, this equation is only valid in those cases where the mass of the system remains constant. But there are plenty of situations where the mass changes, and in those situations, we must use a different version of the second law. Example situations include:

- the motion of a rocket where the mass decreases due to burnt fuel ejected away from the rocket
- sand falling on a conveyor belt
- a droplet of water falling through mist and increasing in mass.

We define **linear momentum**, $\vec{p}$, to be the product of the mass of a body and its velocity:

$$\vec{p} = m\vec{v}$$

Momentum is a vector; note that the direction of the momentum is the direction of the velocity.

Its unit is kg m s^{-1}. Because kg m s^{-1} = kg m s^{-2} s = N s, the unit of momentum is also N s.

In terms of momentum, Newton's second law is $\vec{F}_{net} = \frac{\Delta \vec{p}}{\Delta t}$: the net force on a system is equal to the rate of change of the system's momentum.

We can see that, if the mass stays constant, then this version reduces to the usual $m\vec{a}$:

$$\begin{aligned}\vec{F}_{net} &= \frac{\Delta \vec{p}}{\Delta t} = \frac{\vec{p}_F - \vec{p}_I}{\Delta t} \\ &= \frac{m\vec{v}_F - m\vec{v}_I}{\Delta t} \\ &= m\left(\frac{\vec{v}_F - \vec{v}_I}{\Delta t}\right) = m\frac{\Delta \vec{v}}{\Delta t} \\ &= m\vec{a}\end{aligned}$$

> **CHECK YOURSELF 1**
>
> A body of mass 4.0 kg moving horizontally at 8.0 m s^{-1} bounces off a vertical wall with speed 3.0 m s^{-1}.
>
> What is the magnitude of the change in the body's momentum?

> **WORKED EXAMPLE 4.1**
>
> This is not an easy worked example, but it is important to remember that you must be careful when the mass changes.
>
> A cart moves in a horizontal line with constant speed v. Rain starts to fall and the cart fills with water at a rate of σ kg s^{-1}. (This means that in 1 second, σ kg have fallen on the cart.) The cart must keep moving at constant speed. Determine the force that must be applied on the cart.
>
> **Answer**
>
> Notice that, if $F_{net} = ma$ (we drop the arrows of the vector notation) were valid, the force would have to be zero since there is no acceleration. But we need a force to act on the cart because the momentum of the cart is increasing (because the mass is).
>
> The force is $F_{net} = \frac{\Delta p}{\Delta t} = \frac{\Delta(mv)}{\Delta t} = v\frac{\Delta m}{\Delta t} = v\sigma$.
>
> So, if $\sigma = 0.20$ kg s^{-1} and $v = 3.5$ m s^{-1}, the force would have to be 0.70 N.

> **EXAM TIP**
>
> You must be careful when mass changes. Zero acceleration does not imply zero net force in this case.

WORKED EXAMPLE 4.2

A 0.50 kg ball bounces vertically off a hard surface. A graph of *velocity* against *time* is shown in Figure 4.1.

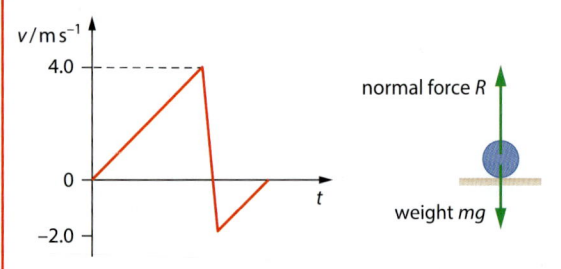

Figure 4.1: For worked example 4.2.

a Find the magnitude of the momentum change of the ball during the bounce.

b The ball stayed in contact with floor for 0.15 s. What average force did the ball exert on the floor?

Answer

a The initial momentum is $0.50 \times 4.0 = 2.0$ N s.

The final momentum is $0.50 \times (-2.0) = -1.0$ N s.

The magnitude of the change is, therefore, 3.0 N s.

b The forces on the ball during contact are its weight and the normal force from the floor:

$$F_{net} = R - mg$$
$$= \frac{\Delta p}{\Delta t}$$
$$= \frac{3.0 \text{ N s}}{0.15 \text{ s}}$$
$$= 20 \text{ N}$$

So, $R = 20 + 5.0 = 25$ N.

EXAM TIP

This is a tricky problem with lots of possibilities for error. Many students forget to include the minus sign in the rebound velocity and/or forget the weight and answer incorrectly that $R = 20$ N.

TEST YOUR UNDERSTANDING

1 The momentum of a ball increased by 12.0 N s as a result of a force that acted on the ball for 2.00 s. Find the average force on the ball.

2 A ball of mass 2.0 kg rolling on a horizontal floor with a speed 4.0 m s^{-1} hits a vertical wall. Calculate the magnitude of the change in momentum of the ball if it

   a bounces with speed 4.0 m s^{-1}

   b bounces with speed 3.0 m s^{-1}

   c sticks to the wall.

3 A ball of mass m is dropped vertically from a height h_1 and rebounds to a height h_2. The ball is in contact with the floor for a time interval of τ.

   a Show that the average net force on the ball is given by
   $$F = m \frac{\sqrt{2gh_1} + \sqrt{2gh_2}}{\tau}$$

   b If $h_1 = 8.0$ m, $h_2 = 6.0$ m, $\tau = 0.125$ s and $m = 0.250$ kg, calculate the average force exerted by the ball on the floor.

4 Water exits a horizontal pipe at a rate of 40 kg per minute with speed 9.0 m s^{-1}.

What horizontal force is needed to keep the pipe in place?

4.2 Impulse and force–time graphs

We may rearrange $\vec{F}_{net} = \dfrac{\Delta \vec{p}}{\Delta t}$ to get $\Delta \vec{p} = \vec{F}_{NET} \Delta t$.

The quantity $\vec{F}_{net} \Delta t$ is called the **impulse** of the force and is denoted by $\vec{J}$.

It is the product of the average net force and the time for which the force acts.

The impulse is also equal to the change in momentum. Notice that impulse is a vector; its direction is the same as that of the force (or the change in momentum).

$$\vec{J} = \Delta \vec{p}$$

It can also be shown that impulse is the area under the curve in a graph of *force* against *time*.

When you jump from a height of, say, 1 m, you will land on the ground with a speed of about 4.5 m s^{-1}. Assuming your mass is 60 kg your momentum just before landing will be 270 N s and will become zero after you land. From $F_{net} \Delta t = \Delta p$, this can be achieved with a small force acting for a long time or a large force acting for a short time. You will experience the large force if you do not bend your knees upon landing—keeping your knees stiff means that you will come to rest in a short time; that is, Δt will be very small and the force large (which may damage your knees).

Figure 4.2 shows three different force–time graphs. Graph **a** shows a (nonconstant) force that increases from zero, reaches a maximum value and then drops to zero again. The force acts for a time interval of about 2 ms. The impulse is the area under the curve. Without calculus we can only estimate this area by tediously counting squares: each small square has area 0.1 ms × 0.2 N = 2 × 10^{-5} N s. There are about 160 full squares under the curve, and so the impulse is 3 × 10^{-3} N s. (In this case, it is not a bad approximation to consider the shape under the curve to be a triangle but with a base of 1.3 ms so that the area is then $\frac{1}{2} \times 1.3 \times 10^{-3} \times 4 \approx 3 \times 10^{-3}$ N s.)

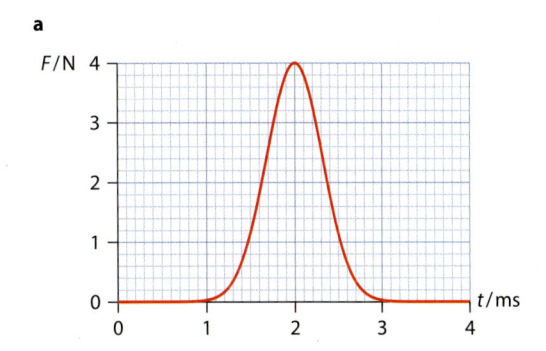

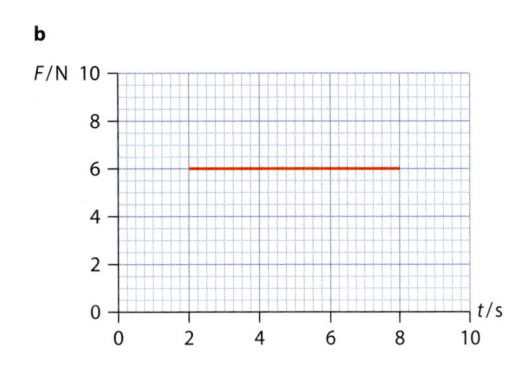

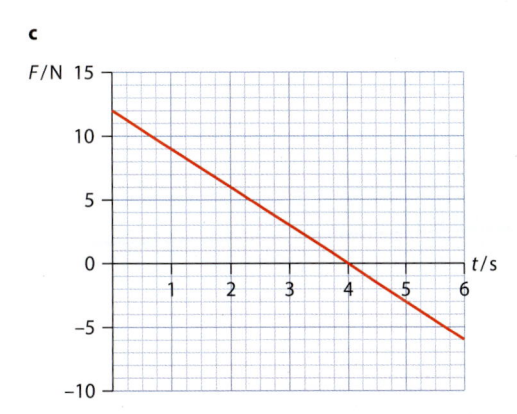

Figure 4.2: Three different force–time graphs.

In graph **b**, the force is constant. The impulse of the force is 6.0 × (8.0 − 2.0) = 36 N s. If this force were to act on a body of mass 12 kg, initially at rest, the speed of the body after the force stops acting would be found from

$\Delta p = 36$ N s

$mv - 0 = 36$ N s

$v = \dfrac{36}{12} = 3.0$ m s^{-1}

CHECK YOURSELF 2

The graph in Figure 4.3 shows the variation with time of the momentum of a body moving on a straight line.

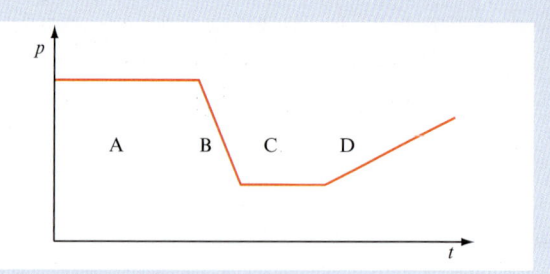

Figure 4.3: For check yourself question 2.

Identify the part of the motion where the force acting on the body has its greatest magnitude.

WORKED EXAMPLE 4.3

Consider graph c in Figure 4.2. The force acts on a body of mass 3.0 kg initially at rest.

Calculate:

a the initial acceleration of the body

b the speed at 4.0 s

c the speed at 6.0 s.

Answer

a $a = \frac{F}{m} = \frac{12}{3.0} = 4.0$ m s^{-2}.

b The impulse from 0 s to 4.0 s is the area under the graph:

$\frac{1}{2} \times 4.0 \times 12 = 24$ N s

and is equal to the change in momentum:

$mv - 0$

So, $v = \frac{24}{3.0} = 8.0$ m s^{-1}.

c The impulse from 0 s to 6.0 s is $\frac{1}{2} \times 4.0 \times 12 - \frac{1}{2} \times 2.0 \times 6.0 = 18$ N s. (Areas under the time axis are negative.)

So, the speed at 6.0 s is $v = \frac{18}{3.0} = 6.0$ m s^{-1}.

WORKED EXAMPLE 4.4

A ball of mass 0.20 kg moving at 3.6 m s^{-1} on a horizontal floor collides with a vertical wall. The ball rebounds with a speed of 3.2 m s^{-1}. The ball was in contact with the wall for 12 ms. Determine the maximum force exerted on the ball, assuming that the force depends on time according to Figure 4.4.

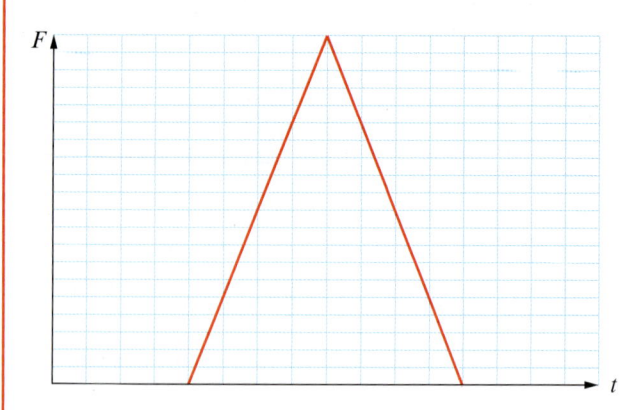

Figure 4.4: For worked example 4.4.

Answer

The change in momentum of the ball is
$0.20 \times (-3.2) - 0.20 \times 3.6 = -1.36$ N s.
The magnitude of the change is 1.36 N s. This is the area under the force–time graph.

The area is

$\frac{1}{2} \times 12 \times 10^{-3} \times F_{max}$

So:

$\frac{1}{2} \times 12 \times 10^{-3} \times F_{max} = 1.36$ N s $\Rightarrow F_{max} = 0.227 \times 10^3 \approx 2.3 \times 10^2$ N.

CHECK YOURSELF 3

A girl of mass 40 kg jumps vertically upward, lifting her centre of mass by 0.80 m after losing contact with the ground. What is the impulse she received when in contact with the ground? (Use $g = 10$ m s^{-2}.)

4 Linear momentum

Links

We have seen the application of impulse in mechanics. In Unit B the concept of impulse will be applied to show that the walls of a container exert forces on molecules and so molecules exert forces on the walls. This will explain the origin of pressure in gases.

TEST YOUR UNDERSTANDING

5 A student says that 'a large force always produces a larger impulse than a smaller force'.

Explain why the student's statement is *not* correct.

6 A time-varying force varies with time, as shown in Figure 4.5. The force acts on a body of mass 4.0 kg.

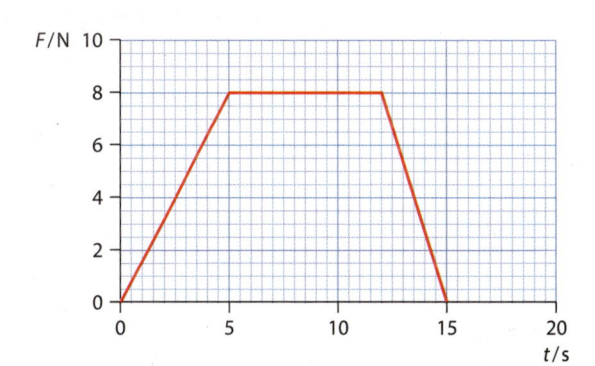

Figure 4.5: For question 6.

a Find the impulse of the force from $t = 0$ to $t = 15$ s.

b Find the speed of the mass at 15 s, assuming the initial velocity was zero.

c State the initial velocity of the body so it is brought to rest at 15 s.

7 A 0.150 kg ball moving horizontally at 3.00 m s^{-1} collides normally with a vertical wall and bounces back with the same speed.

a Calculate the impulse delivered to the ball.

b The ball was in contact with the wall for 0.125 s. Find the average force exerted by the ball on the wall.

8 A boy rides on a scooter pushing on the road with one foot with a horizontal force that depends on time, as shown in Figure 4.6. While the scooter rolls, a constant force of 25 N opposes the motion. The combined mass of the boy and scooter is 25 kg.

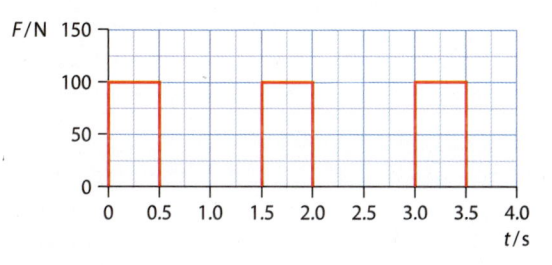

Figure 4.6: For question 8.

a Find the speed of the boy after 4.0 s, assuming he started from rest.

b Draw a graph to represent the variation of the boy's speed with time.

9 Figure 4.7 shows the variation with time of the force exerted on a ball as the ball comes into contact with a spring.

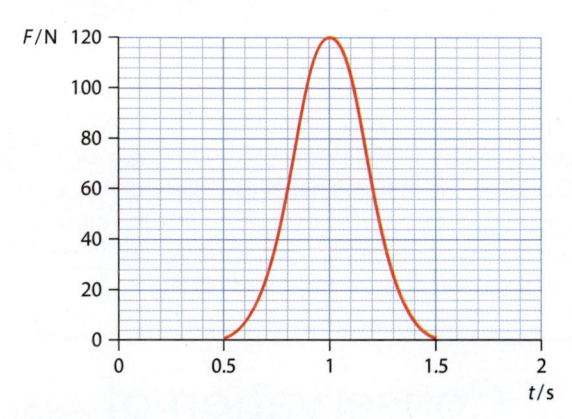

Figure 4.7: For question 9.

89

CONTINUED

a   For how long was the spring in contact with the ball?

b   Estimate the magnitude of the change in momentum of the ball.

c   What was the *average* force that was exerted on the ball?

10 Figure 4.8 shows the variation with time of the force exerted on a body of mass 4.0 kg that is initially at rest.

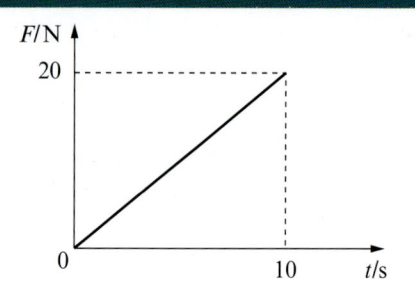

Figure 4.8: For question 10.

Calculate the average power delivered to the body during the 10 s interval.

SCIENCE IN CONTEXT

Figure 4.9: Crumple zones.

Modern cars are designed to have 'crumple zones', air bags and safety belts. Discuss how each of these features helps the safety of the passengers in the case of an accident. In Figure 4.9 the front part of the car is completely destroyed, but the passenger compartment is intact.

KEY POINT

This means that when the net force on a system is zero the momentum does not change (it stays the same); that is, it is conserved.

This is the law of **conservation of momentum**.

Notice that 'system' may refer to a single body or a collection of many different bodies. Look at Figure 4.10. Consider the blue block of mass 4.0 kg moving at speed 6.0 m s^{-1} to the right. It will collide with the red block of mass 8.0 kg that is initially at rest. Suppose that, after the collision, the bodies stick together and move as one.

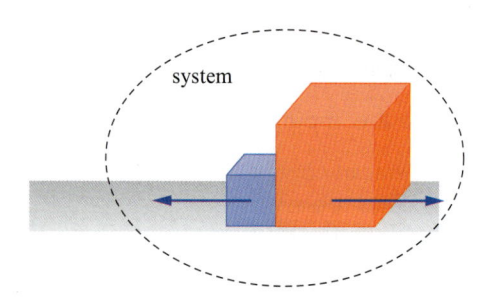

Figure 4.10: In a collision (or explosion) with no external forces acting the total momentum of the system stays the same.

4.3 Conservation of momentum

Consider a system with momentum $\vec{p}$.

The net force on the system is $\vec{F}_{net} = \frac{\Delta \vec{p}}{\Delta t}$.

If $\vec{F}_{net} = 0$, it follows that $\Delta \vec{p} = 0$.

As the blocks collide, each exerts a force on the other. The magnitude of the force on each block is the same by Newton's third law. There are no forces that come from *outside* the system (no external forces). You might say that the weights of the blocks are forces that come from the outside. That is correct, but the weights are cancelled by the normal forces from the table. So, the net external force on the system is zero. Hence we expect that the total momentum will stay the same.

The total momentum *before* the collision is

$4.0 \times 6.0 + 8.0 \times 0 = 24$ N s

The total momentum *after* the collision is $(4.0 + 8.0) \times v$ where v is the common speed of the two blocks.

So, $12v = 24 \Rightarrow v = 2.0$ m s^{-1}.

The kinetic energy before the collision is $\frac{1}{2} \times 4.0 \times 6.0^2 = 72$ J.

The kinetic energy after the collision is $\frac{1}{2} \times 12 \times 2.0^2 = 24$ J.

It appears that 48 J has been 'lost' (as other forms of energy, such as thermal energy in the blocks themselves and the surrounding air, or energy to deform the bodies during the collision and some to sound generated in the collision).

Now consider the outcome of the collision of these two blocks in which the blue block rebounds with speed 2.0 m s^{-1}, as in Figure 4.11.

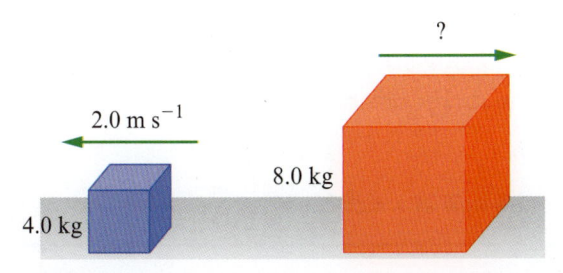

Figure 4.11: An outcome of the collision in which total kinetic energy stays the same.

What is the speed of the red block in Figure 4.11?

The total momentum before the collision is 24 N s.

The total momentum after the collision is $-4.0 \times 2.0 + 8.0 \times v$

(Note the minus sign.)

Equating the total momentum before and after the collision we find $-8.0 + 8.0 \times v = 24$.

This gives

$v = 4.0$ m s^{-1}.

The total kinetic energy after the collision is

$\frac{1}{2} \times 4.0 \times (-2.0)^2 + \frac{1}{2} \times 8.0 \times 4.0^2 = 72$ J

which is the same as the initial kinetic energy.

So, in a collision, the momentum is always conserved, but kinetic energy may or may not be conserved. There is more discussion of momentum and kinetic energy in Section 4.4.

It all depends on the system

Consider a ball that you drop from rest from a certain height. As the ball falls, its speed and momentum increase so the momentum of the ball does not stay the same, Figure 4.12.

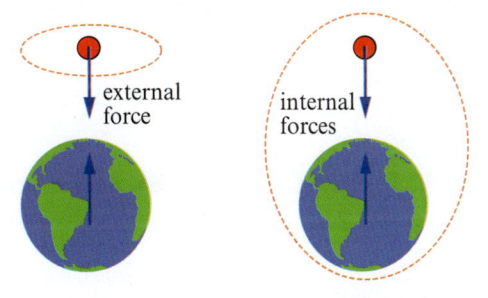

Figure 4.12: As the ball falls, an external force acts on it (its weight), increasing its momentum.

This is to be expected—there is an external force on the ball, namely its weight. So the momentum of the system that consists of just the falling ball is not conserved. If we include the earth as part of the system, then there are no external forces anymore and the total momentum will be conserved. This means that the earth moves upward a bit as the ball falls!

> **THEORY OF KNOWLEDGE**
>
> **Predicting outcomes**
>
> Physics is supposed to be able to predict outcomes. So, why is there more than one outcome in the collision of Figure 4.11?
>
> Physics does predict what happens, but more information about the nature of the colliding bodies is needed. We need to know if they are soft or hard, deformable or not, sticky or breakable, and so on. If this information is given, physics will *uniquely* predict what will happen.

EXTENSION

The rocket equation

One example of motion with varying mass is the rocket (Figure 4.13). The engines exert a force on the burnt gases pushing them out of the rocket and, by Newton's third law, the gases exert an equal and opposite force on the engines (that is, the rocket).

Figure 4.13: Exhaust gases from the booster rockets propel this space shuttle during its launch.

This is quite a complex topic and is included here only as optional material. The rocket moves with speed v. All speeds are measured by an observer at rest on the ground. The engine is turned on, and gases leave the rocket with speed u *relative to the rocket*. The initial mass of the rocket including the fuel is M. After a short time δt the rocket has ejected fuel of mass δm. The mass of the rocket is, therefore, reduced to $M - \delta m$ and its speed increased to $v + \delta v$ (see Figure 4.14).

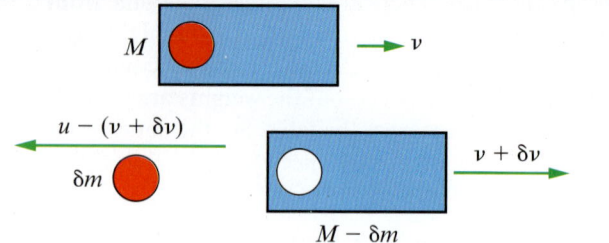

Figure 4.14: Deriving the rocket equation: The velocities are all relative to an observer 'at rest on the ground'.

Applying the law of conservation of momentum gives:

$$Mv = (M - \delta m)(v + \delta v) - \delta m(\underbrace{u - v - \delta v}_{\text{speed relative to ground}})$$

$$Mv = Mv + M\delta v - v\delta m - \delta m \delta v - u\delta m + v\delta m + \delta m \delta v$$

$$M\delta v = u\delta m$$

$$\delta v = \frac{\delta m}{M} u$$

(Note how the terms that have been written in the same colour cancel each other out.)

This gives the change in speed of the rocket as a result of gases leaving with speed u *relative to the rocket*. At time t the mass of the rocket is M. Dividing by δt and taking the limit as δt goes to zero gives the rocket differential equation

$$M\frac{dv}{dt} = \mu u$$

where μ is the rate at which mass is being ejected.

TEST YOUR UNDERSTANDING

11 A rocket in space where gravity is negligible has a mass (including fuel) of 5000 kg. It is desired to give the rocket an average acceleration of 15.0 m s^{-2} during the first second of firing the engine. The gases leave the rocket at a speed of 1500 m s^{-1} (relative to the rocket). Estimate how much fuel must be burned in that second.

4.4 Kinetic energy and momentum

We have seen that, in a collision or explosion where no external forces are present, the total momentum of the system is conserved. You can easily convince yourself that in the three collisions illustrated in Figure 4.15 momentum is conserved. The incoming body has mass 8.0 kg and the other a mass of 12 kg.

Let us examine these collisions from the point of view of energy.

In all cases the total kinetic energy before the collision is
$E_K = \frac{1}{2} \times 8 \times 10^2 = 400$ J

The total kinetic energy after the collision in each case is

case 1 $E_K = \frac{1}{2} \times 20 \times 4^2 = 160$ J

case 2 $E_K = \frac{1}{2} \times 8 \times 1^2 + \frac{1}{2} \times 12 \times 6^2 = 220$ J

case 3 $E_K = \frac{1}{2} \times 8 \times 2^2 + \frac{1}{2} \times 12 \times 8^2 = 400$ J

We observe that *whereas momentum is conserved in all cases*, kinetic energy is not.

- When kinetic energy is conserved (case 3), the collision is said to be an **elastic collision**.
- When kinetic energy is not conserved (cases 1 and 2), the collision is said to be an **inelastic collision**.

In an inelastic collision, kinetic energy is 'lost'. When the bodies stick together after a collision (case 1), the collision is said to be *totally inelastic* (or *plastic*) and, in this case, the maximum possible kinetic energy is 'lost'. (In an explosion the kinetic energy afterward is greater than the initial kinetic energy.)

The 'lost' kinetic energy is transformed into other forms of energy, such as thermal energy, deformation energy (if the bodies are permanently deformed as a result of the collision) and sound energy.

Notice that using momentum we can obtain a useful additional formula for kinetic energy:
$$E_K = \frac{1}{2}mv^2 = \frac{m^2v^2}{2m} = \frac{p^2}{2m}$$

> **CHECK YOURSELF 4**
>
> You are on a frictionless frozen lake and throw your shoes away in the same direction. Are the momentum and kinetic energy of the system consisting of you and the shoes conserved?

> **WORKED EXAMPLE 4.5**
>
> A moving body of mass m collides with a stationary body of double the mass and sticks to it. Calculate the fraction of the original kinetic energy that is lost.
>
> **Answer**
>
> The original kinetic energy is $\frac{1}{2}mv^2$, where v is the speed of the incoming mass. After the collision, the two bodies move as one with speed u that can be found from momentum conservation:
>
> $mv = (m + 2m)u \Rightarrow u = \frac{v}{3}$
>
> So, the total kinetic energy after the collision is
>
> $\frac{1}{2}(3m)\left(\frac{v}{3}\right)^2 = \frac{mv^2}{6}$
>
> So, the *lost* kinetic energy is
>
> $\frac{mv^2}{2} - \frac{mv^2}{6} = \frac{mv^2}{3}$
>
> And the fraction of the original energy that is lost is
>
> $\dfrac{\left(\frac{mv^2}{3}\right)}{\left(\frac{mv^2}{2}\right)} = \frac{2}{3}$

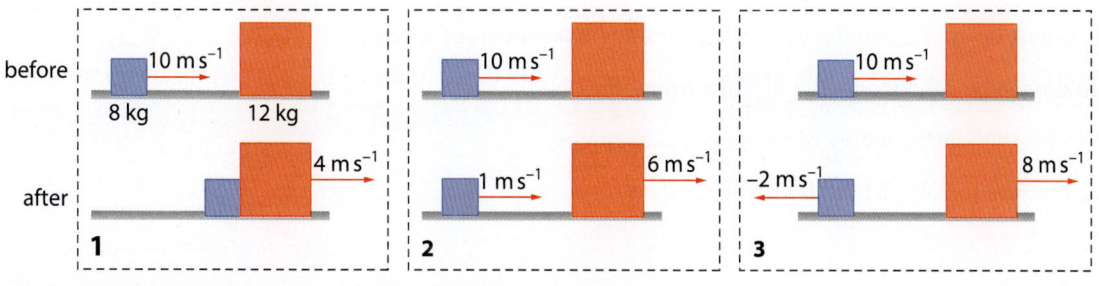

Figure 4.15: Momentum is conserved in these three collisions.

WORKED EXAMPLE 4.6

A body at rest of mass M explodes into two pieces of masses $\frac{M}{4}$ and $\frac{3M}{4}$.

Calculate the ratio of the kinetic energies of the two fragments.

Answer

It helps to use the formula for kinetic energy in terms of momentum: $E_K = \frac{p^2}{2m}$.

The total momentum before the explosion is zero, so total momentum is also zero *after* the collision. Thus, the two fragments must have *equal and opposite momenta*. Hence,

$$\frac{E_{light}}{E_{heavy}} = \frac{\left(\frac{p^2}{2M_{light}}\right)}{\left(\frac{(-p)^2}{2M_{heavy}}\right)}$$

$$= \frac{M_{heavy}}{M_{light}}$$

$$= \frac{\left(\frac{3M}{4}\right)}{\left(\frac{M}{4}\right)}$$

$$= 3$$

In an explosion, the kinetic energy increases. The increase in energy comes from the chemical energy of the explosives.

WORKED EXAMPLE 4.7

This popular exam question requires the same calculations as worked example 4.1, but it is worth doing again. Gravel falls vertically on a conveyor belt at a rate of σ kg s^{-1}, as shown in Figure 4.16.

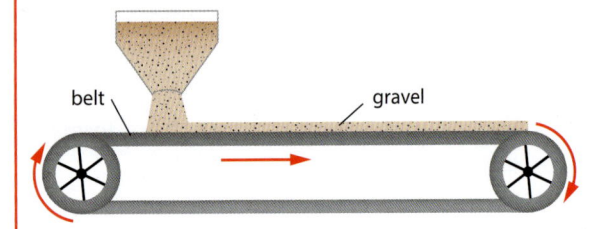

Figure 4.16: For worked example 4.7.

a Determine:

  i the force that must be applied on the belt to keep it moving at constant speed v

  ii the power that must be supplied by the motor turning the belt

  iii The rate at which the kinetic energy of the gravel is changing.

b Explain why the answers to parts **ii** and **iii** are different.

CONTINUED

Answer

a i The force is $F_{net} = \frac{\Delta p}{\Delta t} = \frac{\Delta(mv)}{\Delta t} = v\frac{\Delta m}{\Delta t} = v\sigma$.

ii The power is found from $P = Fv$ to be $P = (\sigma v)v = \sigma v^2$.

iii In 1 second the mass on the belt increases by σ kg. The kinetic energy of this mass is $E_K = \frac{1}{2}\sigma v^2$. This is the increase in kinetic energy in a time of 1 s so the rate of kinetic energy increase is $\frac{1}{2}\sigma v^2$.

b There must be a frictional force between the gravel and the belt. The gravel slides on the belt for some time until it picks up the speed of the belt. During this sliding heat is being generated. So, of the power σv^2 that is being supplied by the motor driving the belt, half goes into increasing the kinetic energy (due to the increasing mass) and the other half is wasted as heat.

More precisely, let an amount of mass Δm fall on the belt. A frictional force f will provide an acceleration $a = \frac{f}{\Delta m}$ to the mass so that over a distance d the mass will reach the speed of the belt. Thus $v^2 = 2ad = 2\frac{f}{\Delta m}d$. This says that the work done by the frictional force is $fd = \frac{1}{2}\Delta m v^2$, and so the rate at which friction dissipates energy is $\frac{1}{2}\frac{\Delta m}{\Delta t}v^2 = \frac{1}{2}\sigma v^2$.

CHECK YOURSELF 5

Water leaves a horizontal pipe of cross-sectional area 5×10^{-3} m² at a rate of 20 kg s⁻¹ and speed 15 m s⁻¹. What force keeps the pipe fixed?

TEST YOUR UNDERSTANDING

12 In a collision of two blocks, the blocks exert forces on each other. Explain why the momentum of the system consisting of the two blocks is conserved in the collision.

13 Two masses of 2.0 kg and 4.0 kg are held in place, compressing a spring between them. When they are released, the 2.0 kg mass moves away with a speed of 3.0 m s⁻¹. What was the energy stored in the spring?

14 Two masses m and M are held in place, compressing a spring between them. When they are released, m moves to the left with speed v. What is the change in momentum of M?

15 The bodies in Figure 4.17 suffer a head-on collision and stick to each other afterwards. Find their common velocity.

Figure 4.17: For question 14.

16 Two masses moving in a straight line toward each other collide as shown in Figure 4.18. Find the velocity (magnitude and direction) of the heavier mass after the collision.

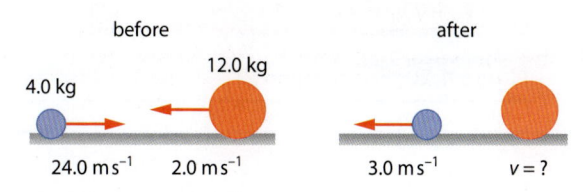

Figure 4.18: For question 15.

CONTINUED

17 A mass of 6.0 kg moving at 4.0 m s⁻¹ collides with a stationary mass of 8.0 kg and sticks to it. How much kinetic energy was 'lost' in the collision?

18 A mass of 6.0 kg moving at 14 m s⁻¹ collides head on with a stationary mass of 8.0 kg. The lighter mass rebounds with a speed of 2.0 m s⁻¹. Is this collision elastic?

19 A body of mass M breaks apart at rest into two pieces of mass $M/4$ and $3M/4$. The energy released in the break-up is Q. What is the kinetic energy carried by the lighter piece?

20 A ball of mass 0.250 kg moving on a horizontal floor collides with a vertical wall as shown in Figure 4.19. The speed of the ball before and after the collision is 4.00 m s⁻¹.

Calculate the magnitude and direction of the momentum change of the ball.

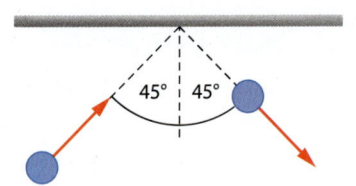

Figure 4.19: For question 19.

21 A block of mass m slides from rest down a curved wedge of mass M (Figure 4.20). The wedge is on a frictionless table. The block is released from a height h.

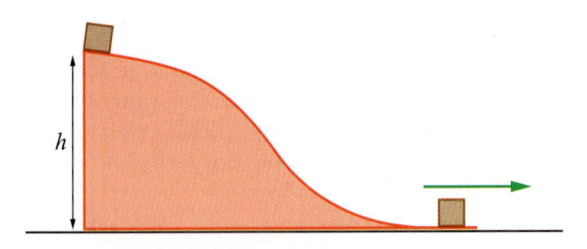

Figure 4.20: For question 21.

When the block gets on the table its speed is v.

a Determine, in terms of v, the speed with which the wedge recoils.

b Show that $v^2 = \dfrac{2gh}{1 + \frac{m}{M}}$.

22 The rotor of a drone pushes air downward with speed v at a rate of 1.80 kg per second. The mass of the drone is 1.50 kg. The drone hovers stationary in air.

a Describe the origin of the lift force on the drone.

b Calculate v while the drone hovers in air.

c Calculate the average power delivered to the air by the rotor.

d The rotor is made to rotate faster, increasing the lift force by 50%. What is the acceleration of the drone?

23 A bullet of mass 0.080 kg moving at speed v gets embedded in a block of mass 2.0 kg that hangs from a vertical string of length 1.5 m (Figure 4.21). The block and the bullet move together and stop when the string makes an angle of 34° with the vertical. What is v?

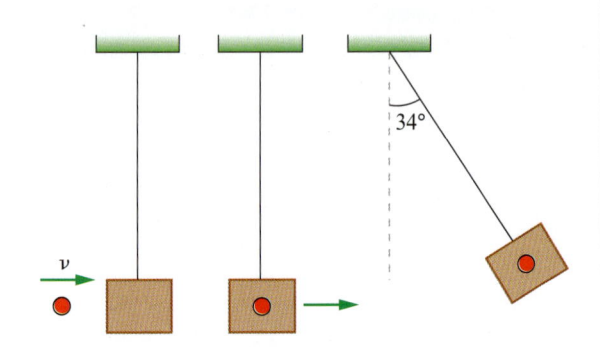

Figure 4.21: For question 23.

4.5 Two-dimensional collisions

Figure 4.22 shows a *two-dimensional* collision. The red ball collides with a stationary blue ball not exactly head on (we call this a glancing collision). As a result, the two balls move on the two-dimensional plane of the paper. We will mostly deal with situations in which one of the colliding particles is initially at rest.

The blue ball moves off with speed v in a direction making an angle θ with the x axis. The x axis was chosen to be the initial direction of motion of the red ball. The y axis is at right angles to the x axis as usual.

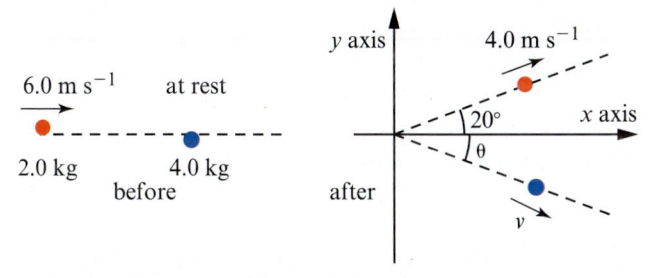

Figure 4.22: A two-dimensional collision.

Our objective is to find v and θ.

We will now find components of momentum before and after the collision along the x and y directions and demand that the *total* momentum in each direction is the same as that after the collision, i.e.

$$\underbrace{\Sigma p_x}_{\text{before}} = \underbrace{\Sigma p_x}_{\text{after}}$$

and similarly for the y direction,

$$\underbrace{\Sigma p_y}_{\text{before}} = \underbrace{\Sigma p_y}_{\text{after}}$$

Applying these equations to our collision we find

x direction: $\underbrace{2.0 \times 6.0 + 0}_{\text{total before}} = \underbrace{2.0 \times 4.0 \times \cos 20° + 4.0 \times v \times \cos\theta}_{\text{total after}}$

y direction: $\underbrace{0}_{\text{total before}} = \underbrace{2.0 \times 4.0 \times \sin 20° - 4.0 \times v \times \sin\theta}_{\text{total after}}$

These imply

$7.52 + 4.0 \times v \times \cos\theta = 12$, i.e. $4.0 \times v \times \cos\theta = 4.48$

and

$2.74 - 4.0 \times v \times \sin\theta = 0$, i.e. $4.0 \times v \times \sin\theta = 2.74$.

Dividing side by side we find $\tan\theta = \frac{2.74}{4.48} \Rightarrow \theta \approx 31°$. Having found the angle we can substitute in either of the two equations above to find $v = 1.3$ m s^{-1}.

The total kinetic energy before the collision was $\frac{1}{2} \times 2.0 \times 6.0^2 + 0 = 36$ J and after the collision is $\frac{1}{2} \times 2.0 \times 4.0^2 + \frac{1}{2} \times 4.0 \times 1.3^2 = 19$ J, so the collision was inelastic.

WORKED EXAMPLE 4.8

In the collision shown, the unknown quantities are the initial speed, w, of the red ball and the final speed, v, of the blue ball, Figure 4.23.

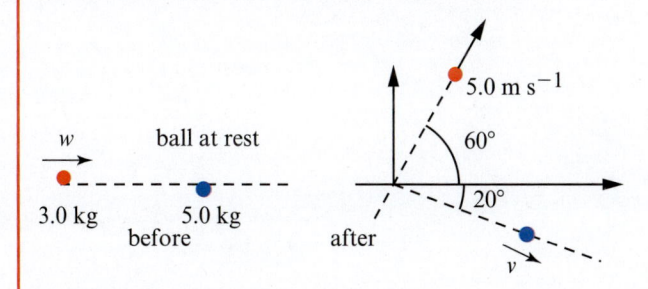

Figure 4.23: For worked example 4.8.

CONTINUED

Conservation of momentum gives

x direction: $\underbrace{3.0 \times w + 0}_{\text{total before}} = \underbrace{3.0 \times 5.0 \times \cos 60° + 5.0 \times v \times \cos 20°}_{\text{total after}}$

y direction: $\underbrace{0}_{\text{total before}} = \underbrace{3.0 \times 5.0 \times \sin 60° - 5.0 \times v \times \sin 20°}_{\text{total after}}$

These simplify to

$3.0w = 7.5 + 4.698v$

$12.990 = 1.710v$

From the second equation we find $v = 7.5965$ m s^{-1}. Substituting in the first, we find $w = 14.3961$ m s^{-1}.

We quote $w = 14$ m s^{-1} and $v = 7.6$ m s^{-1} as our answers.

WORKED EXAMPLE 4.9

The red ball has a glancing collision with a stationary blue ball of the same mass with the outcome shown (Figure 4.24).

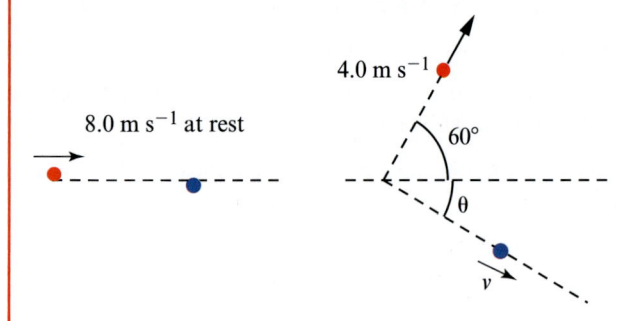

Figure 4.24: For worked example 4.9.

Calculate v and θ.

Show that the collision is elastic.

Answer

Conservation of momentum gives

x direction: $\underbrace{m \times 8.0 + 0}_{\text{total before}} = \underbrace{m \times 4.0 \times \cos 60° + m \times v \times \cos\theta}_{\text{total after}}$

y direction: $\underbrace{0}_{\text{total before}} = \underbrace{m \times 4.0 \times \sin 60° - m \times v \times \sin\theta}_{\text{total after}}$

CONTINUED

These simplify to

$8.0 = 2.0 + v\cos\theta$ i.e., $v\cos\theta = 6.0$

$2\sqrt{3} = v\sin\theta$ $v\sin\theta = 2\sqrt{3}$

Dividing side by side gives $\tan\theta = \frac{2\sqrt{3}}{6.0} = \frac{\sqrt{3}}{3} \Rightarrow \theta = 30°$. Then, $v = \frac{6.0}{\cos 30°} = \frac{6.0}{\frac{\sqrt{3}}{2}} = \frac{12}{\sqrt{3}} = 4\sqrt{3} \approx 6.9 \text{ m s}^{-1}$.

The initial kinetic energy was $E_K = \frac{1}{2}m \times 8.0^2 = 32m$. The final kinetic energy is $E_K = \frac{1}{2}m \times 4.0^2 + \frac{1}{2}m \times (4\sqrt{3})^2 = 8m + 24m = 32m$ and so the collision is elastic.

TEST YOUR UNDERSTANDING

24 In the collision in Figure 4.25, the two bodies have the same mass. What is u and what is v? Is the collision elastic? (Use exact values for sines and cosines.)

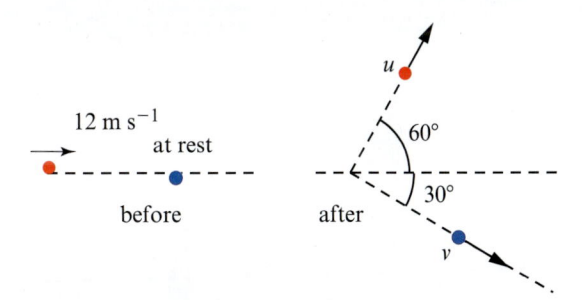

Figure 4.25: For question 24.

25 Two bodies of equal mass collide (Figure 4.26). One body has speed w, and the other is at rest. After the collision the two bodies move such that the angle between them is 90°.

    a Show that $u = w\cos\theta$ and $v = w\sin\theta$.

    b Hence show the collision is elastic.

26 What are the initial and final speeds w and u of the red particle in Figure 4.27?

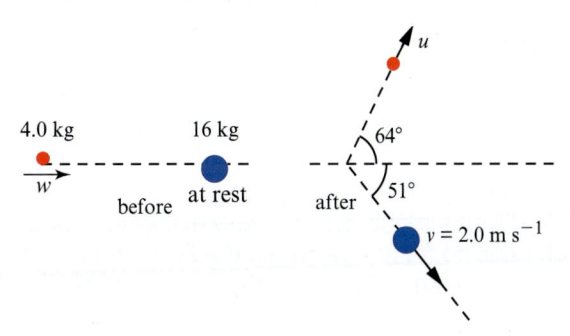

Figure 4.27: For question 26.

27 Two bodies approach each other from opposite directions and collide, Figure 4.28.

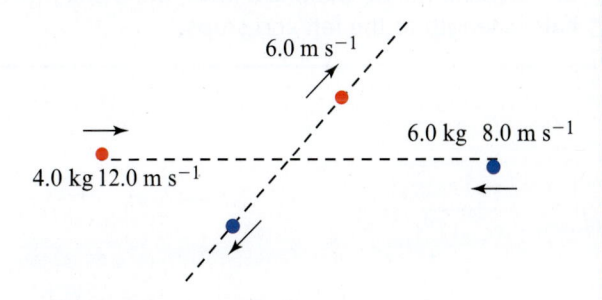

Figure 4.28: For question 27.

What is the energy lost in this collision?

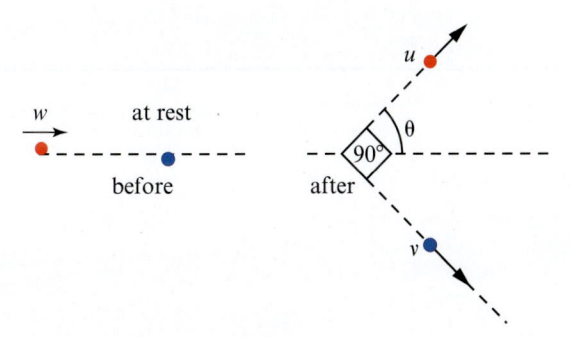

Figure 4.26: For question 25.

CONTINUED

28 Two identical bodies moving with the same speed v collide as shown in Figure 4.29 and stick together. The two bodies move together with speed $\frac{v}{2}$.

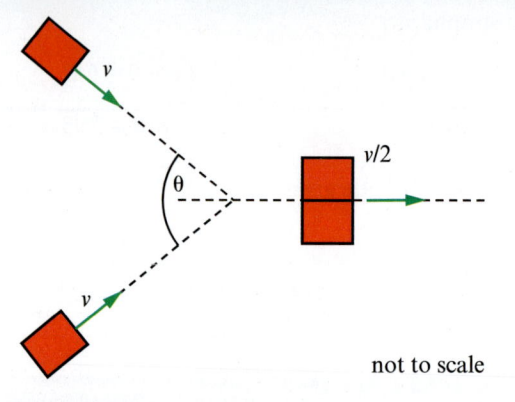

Figure 4.29: For question 28.

What is the angle θ?

NATURE OF SCIENCE

Physics and mathematics

General principles such as the conservation of momentum allow for simple and quick solutions to problems that may otherwise look complex. Consider, for example, a man of mass m who stands on a plank, also of mass m (Figure 4.30). There is no friction between the floor and the plank. The man starts walking on the plank until he gets to the other end, at which point he stops.

What happens to the plank?

The centre of mass must remain in the same place since there is no external force. So, the final position of the plank will be the one shown: the plank moves half its length to the left and stops.

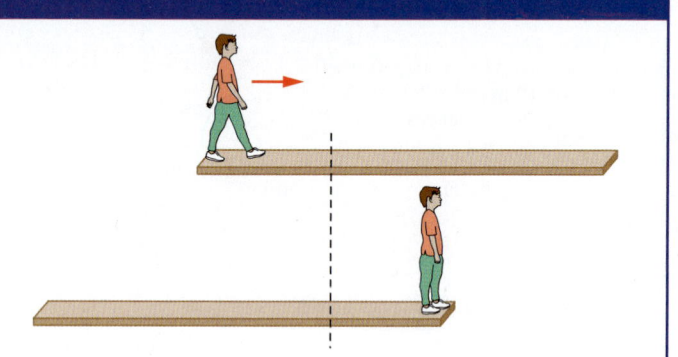

Figure 4.30: The centre of mass remains in the same place.

4 Linear momentum

SELF-ASSESSMENT CHECKLIST

I am able to …	Section	Not yet	Nearly there	Ready to move on
appreciate the vector nature of momentum	4.1			
describe that the net force on a body is the rate of change of its momentum	4.1			
define impulse	4.2			
appreciate that the area under a force–time graph is the change in momentum, which is also called impulse	4.2			
state that the law of conservation of momentum applies when the net external force on a system is zero	4.3			
apply the law of conservation of momentum in collisions and explosions	4.3			
distinguish between elastic and inelastic collisions	4.4			
to work with the relation between kinetic energy and momentum	4.4			
apply momentum conservation to 2D collisions	4.5			

REFLECTION

Can you find the change in the momentum of an object? Can you calculate the total momentum of a system? Can you apply Newton's second law in terms of momentum? Can you solve problems when mass is changing? Do you understand when momentum is conserved? Do you understand the concept of *impulse* and do you know what impulse is equal to? Do you know what information a graph of force versus time gives?

EXAM-STYLE QUESTIONS

You can find questions in the style of IB exams in the digital coursebook.

CHECK YOURSELF ANSWERS

1 $4.0 \times 3.0 - (-4.0 \times 8.0) = 44$ N s.

2 B, force is the rate of change of momentum

3 She leaves the ground with a speed found from
   $v = \sqrt{2gh} = 4.0$ m s^{-1}
   So, the impulse is
   $J = mv - 0 = 40 \times 4.0 = 160$ N s

4 Momentum is conserved but kinetic energy increases.

5 The force is equal to the rate of change of momentum of the water, which is $20 \times 15 = 300$ N.

Chapter 5
Rigid body mechanics

LEARNING OBJECTIVES

In this chapter you will learn how to:

- apply the equations of kinematics to rotational motion
- understand and apply torque
- apply the conditions of rotational and translational equilibrium
- solve problems with rotational dynamics
- apply the law of conservation of angular momentum.

5 Rigid body mechanics

> **GUIDING QUESTION**
>
> How does the physics of a point particle generalise to the case of an extended rigid body that can not only move but can also rotate about some axis?

Introduction

Up until now, when studying mechanics, we have dealt with point particles. We know that a net force applied to a point particle will accelerate the particle.

However, things change when we deal with extended bodies, such as cylinders, spheres, and so on. In these cases, forces will not only accelerate the centre of mass of the body—they may also make the body rotate.

5.1 Kinematics of rotational motion

Consider a particle that rotates around a circle about an axis through the centre. The **angular position** θ of the particle is determined by an angle (defined relative to some arbitrary reference line), Figure 5.1a. In time Δt the particle changes its angular position by sweeping an angle $\Delta \theta$, as shown in Figure 5.1b. So $\Delta \theta$ is the change in angular position and is called the **angular displacement**.

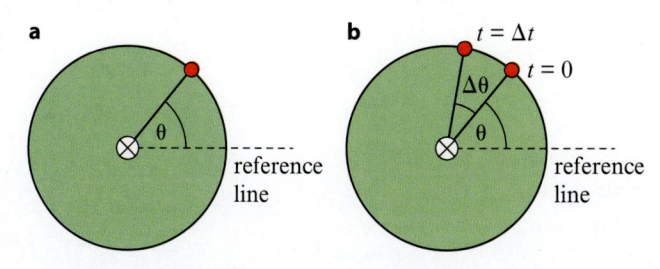

Figure 5.1: A particle that rotates about an axis that is perpendicular to the plane of the paper.

We define the average **angular velocity** of the particle to be

$$\bar{\omega} = \frac{\Delta \theta}{\Delta t}$$

and the instantaneous angular velocity to be

$$\omega = \lim_{\Delta t \to 0} \frac{\Delta \theta}{\Delta t}$$

The unit of angular velocity is rad s^{-1}.

The angular velocity will increase or decrease in the presence of angular acceleration. So, we define the average **angular acceleration** to be

$$\bar{\alpha} = \frac{\Delta \omega}{\Delta t}$$

and the instantaneous angular acceleration to be

$$\alpha = \lim_{\Delta t \to 0} \frac{\Delta \omega}{\Delta t}$$

The unit of angular acceleration is rad s^{-2}.

These definitions are analogous to definitions of linear quantities: we have a 'translation' dictionary between linear and angular quantities:

Linear quantity	Angular quantity
Position, s	Angle, θ
Linear velocity, v	Angular velocity, ω
Acceleration, a	Angular acceleration, α

Because of this correspondence between linear and angular quantities, if a formula applies to the linear quantities, a similar formula will apply to the angular quantities. In other words, we have the following relations (the subscript i refers to initial quantities at $t = 0$):

Linear quantity	Angular quantity
$\Delta s = ut + \frac{1}{2}at^2$	$\Delta \theta = \omega_i t + \frac{1}{2}\alpha t^2$
$\Delta s = \frac{u+v}{2}t$	$\Delta \theta = \frac{\omega_i + \omega_f}{2}t$
$v = u + at$	$\omega = \omega_i + \alpha t$
$v^2 = u^2 + 2a\Delta s$	$\omega^2 = \omega_i^2 + 2\alpha \Delta \theta$

We already know from Chapter 2 that the angular velocity ω and the linear velocity v are related by (Figure 5.2)

$$v = \omega r$$

where r is the radius of the circle.

A similar relation holds between angular and linear accelerations:

$$a = \alpha r$$

103

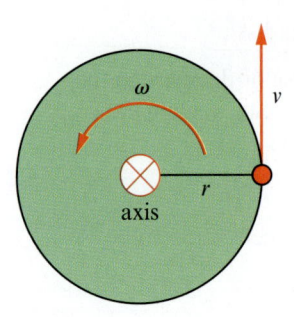

Figure 5.2: Linear and angular velocities.

Angular velocity and angular acceleration are vector quantities, but we will not make use of their vector nature in this course.

When using the formulae, always express the angle in radians (rad). Remember, 180° ≡ π rad.

So, 90° ≡ $\frac{\pi}{2}$ rad, 60° ≡ $\frac{\pi}{3}$ rad, 45° ≡ $\frac{\pi}{4}$ rad … and so on.

It is important to understand that the angular acceleration α is related to the linear acceleration a. This linear acceleration is the rate of change of speed and *is not* the centripetal acceleration of circular motion.

Similarly, whatever applies to graphs involving linear quantities also applies to graphs of angular quantities. For example:

- in a graph of angle θ against time t, the gradient (slope) is the angular velocity ω
- in a graph of angular velocity ω against time t, the gradient (slope) is the angular acceleration and the area is the angle turned (the angular displacement), $\Delta\theta$
- in a graph of angular acceleration α against time t, the area is the change in angular velocity $\Delta\omega$.

WORKED EXAMPLE 5.1

The initial angular speed of a rotating disc is 24 rad s⁻¹. The disc suffers an angular deceleration of 3.0 rad s⁻².

a Calculate how many full revolutions the disc will make before stopping.

b Determine when the disc will stop rotating.

Answer

a From $\omega^2 = \omega_i^2 + 2\alpha\Delta\theta$ we find

$0 = 24^2 + 2 \times (-3.0) \times \Delta\theta \Rightarrow$

$\Delta\theta = \frac{24^2}{2 \times 3.0} = 96$ rad

This corresponds to

$\frac{96}{2\pi} = 15.3 \approx 15$ revolutions.

b From $\omega = \omega_i + \alpha t$ we find

$0 = 24 + (-3.0)t$

$t = 8.0$ s

WORKED EXAMPLE 5.2

A wheel of radius 0.80 m is rotating about its axis with angular speed 2.5 rad s⁻¹. Find the linear speed of a point of the circumference of the wheel.

Answer

$v = \omega R = 2.5 \times 0.80 = 2.0$ m s⁻¹

WORKED EXAMPLE 5.3

A disc of radius R rotates about its axis with constant angular velocity (Figure 5.3).

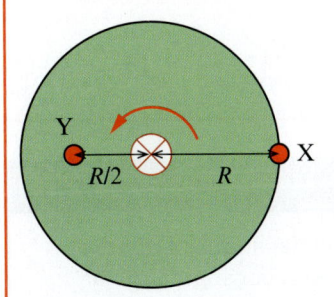

Figure 5.3: For worked example 5.3.

A point X is at the circumference of the disc and another point Y is at a distance $\frac{R}{2}$ from the axis. Calculate the ratios:

a $\dfrac{\omega_X}{\omega_Y}$

b $\dfrac{v_X}{v_Y}$.

Answer

a All points on the disc have the same angular velocity so $\dfrac{\omega_X}{\omega_Y} = 1$.

b From $v = \omega r$ we find $\dfrac{v_X}{v_Y} = \dfrac{\omega_X R}{\omega_Y \frac{R}{2}} = \dfrac{\omega R}{\omega \frac{R}{2}} = 2$.

WORKED EXAMPLE 5.4

The graph in Figure 5.4 shows the variation of the angular velocity of a rotating body. Calculate:

a the angular acceleration

b the total angle the body turned in 4.0 s.

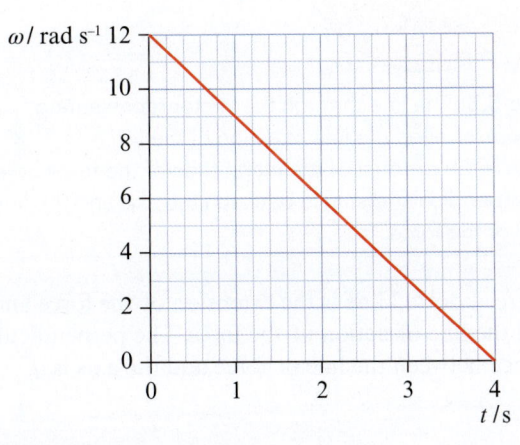

Figure 5.4: For worked example 5.4.

> **PHYSICS FOR THE IB DIPLOMA: COURSEBOOK**

> **CONTINUED**
>
> **Answer**
>
> a The angular acceleration is the gradient of the curve and so $\alpha = -3.0$ rad s^{-2}.
>
> b The angle turned is the area under the curve and so equals 24 rad.

TEST YOUR UNDERSTANDING

1 A disc has initial angular velocity 3.5 rad s^{-1} and after 5.0 s the angular velocity increases to 15 rad s^{-1}. Determine the angle though which the disc has turned in the 5.0 s.

2 A body rotates about an axis with an angular velocity of 5.0 rad s^{-1}. The angular acceleration is 2.5 rad s^{-2}. Calculate the angular velocity after the body turned through an angle of 54 rad.

3 A body rotates with an initial angular velocity of 3.2 rad s^{-1}. The angular velocity increases to 12.4 rad s^{-1} after the body has made 20 full revolutions. Calculate the angular acceleration.

4 A rotating disc has an initial angular speed of 4.0 rad s^{-1} and rotates with constant angular acceleration. After 6.0 s the disc has rotated by an angle of 35 rad. What is the angular acceleration?

5 A rod begins to rotate from rest with constant angular acceleration 1.5 rad s^{-2}.

   a What is the angular velocity after five complete revolutions?

   b Draw graphs to show the variation with time of the angular velocity and the angular position.

5.2 Rotational equilibrium and Newton's second law

Before discussing rotational equilibrium and mechanics, we need to introduce **torque**.

Torque

Torque has to do with the ability of a force to produce rotation.

Figure 5.5 shows a rigid body that is free to rotate about the axis indicated. A force F is applied at a point Q a distance r from the axis.

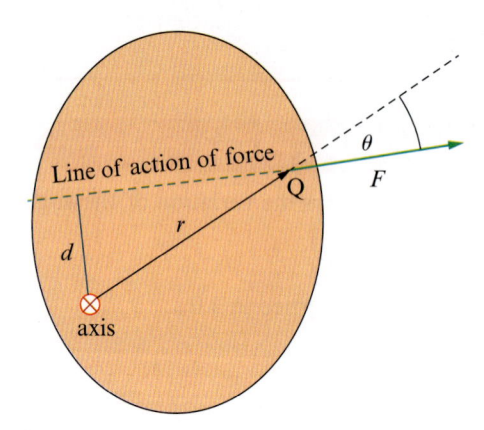

Figure 5.5: The line through the vector representing the force is called the line of action of the force. Torque is the product of the magnitude of the force times the perpendicular distance between the axis and the line of action of the force.

The green dotted line is the extension of the force and is called the line of action of the force. The perpendicular distance between the line of force and the axis is d.

106

5 Rigid body mechanics

> **KEY POINT**
>
> We define the torque τ of the force F about the axis to be the product of the force times the perpendicular distance between the line of action of the force and the axis: $\tau = Fd$.

Since the distance d is given by $d = r\sin\theta$ we also have $\tau = Fr\sin\theta$, where θ is the angle between the force and the vector from the axis to the point where the force is applied (Figure 5.6).

The unit of torque is the N m. (Although this combination of units is equivalent to the joule, we never express torque in joules.)

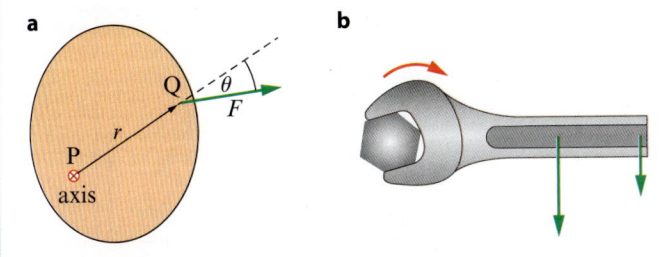

Figure 5.6: a The force tends to rotate the body about the axis in the clockwise direction. This is because the force has a torque about that axis. **b** A wrench turning a screw is a real-life application of torque. A smaller force further from the axis has the same turning effect as a larger force closer to the axis.

Notice that if the force is directed through the axis, the torque is zero (Figure 5.7). The force cannot produce a rotation in this case.

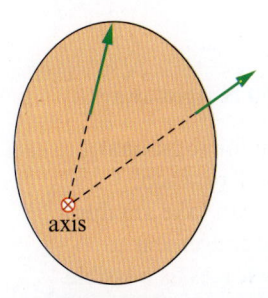

Figure 5.7: These two forces pass through the axis and so have zero torque about that axis.

> **CHECK YOURSELF 1**
>
> Look at Figure 5.8. In which diagram, a–d, is the torque of the force the greatest? The rod is 1 m long. 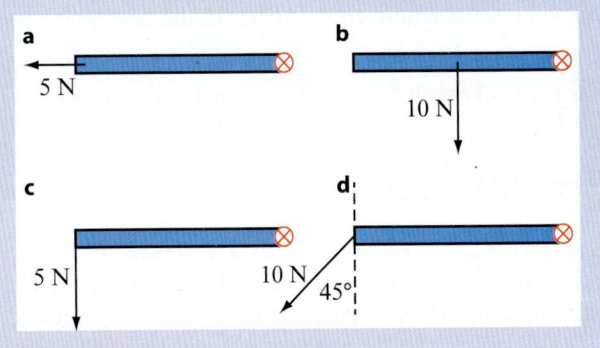
>
> **Figure 5.8:** For check yourself question 1.

> **WORKED EXAMPLE 5.5**
>
> Find the torque of the forces in the three diagrams of Figure 5.9. The length of the rod is 4 m. 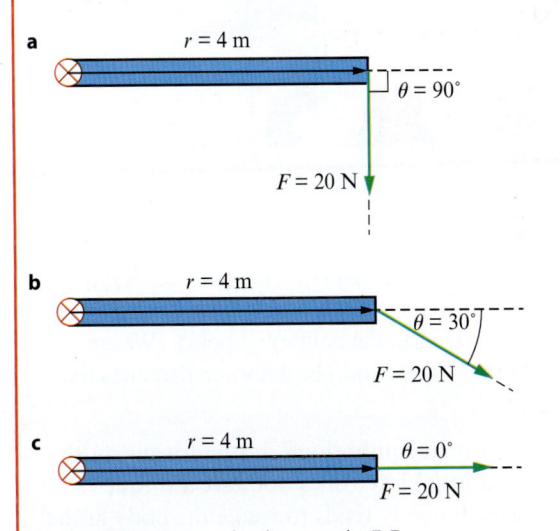
>
> **Figure 5.9:** For worked example 5.5.
>
> **Answer**
>
> a $\tau = Fr\sin\theta = 20 \times 4 \times \sin 90° = 80$ N m.
>
> b $\tau = Fr\sin\theta = 20 \times 4 \times \sin 30° = 40$ N m.
>
> c $\tau = Fr\sin\theta = 20 \times 4 \times \sin 0° = 0$. This force is directed through the axis; it cannot turn the body and has zero torque.

107

PHYSICS FOR THE IB DIPLOMA: COURSEBOOK

Torque is essential in discussing situations of equilibrium. For the case of point particles, equilibrium means that the net force is zero. For a rigid body we have to distinguish between **translational equilibrium**, when the net force of the body is zero, and **rotational equilibrium**, when the net torque of the body is zero. We will discuss equilibrium further in the next section.

In translational equilibrium, the centre of mass of the body (the point where all the mass is assumed to be located) remains at rest or moves in a straight line at constant speed.

Equilibrium

A simple example of equilibrium is a see-saw, as shown in Figure 5.10. The rod can rotate about its pivot—the point of support. How can we find the force F_2 required for equilibrium? We do not want the rod to move or to rotate. We must apply the conditions for translational and rotational equilibrium.

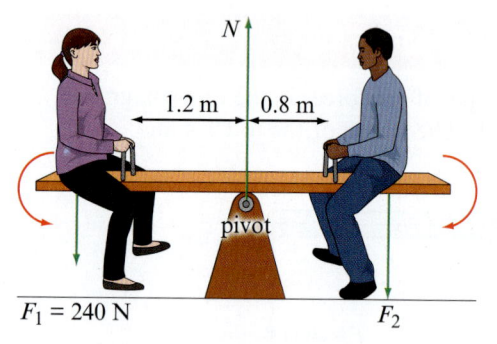

Figure 5.10: A see-saw in equilibrium.

Translational equilibrium says that the net force is zero. Apart from the two forces F_1 and F_2 we also have the normal force N on the rod from the point of support. (We are ignoring the mass of the rod.) Equilibrium demands that

$F_1 + F_2 = N$

Now, for rotational equilibrium, the net torque must be zero. The normal force does not have a torque about the axis. Force F_1 tends to rotate the body in the counterclockwise direction; force F_2 tends to rotate the body in the clockwise direction. The two forces have opposite torques. We must set these torques equal to each other to get a zero net torque. This gives

$F_1 \times 1.2 = F_2 \times 0.8$

$240 \times 1.2 = F_2 \times 0.8$

$F_2 = 360$ N

From the translational equilibrium condition we can now find

$N = 600$ N.

WORKED EXAMPLE 5.6

Figure 5.11a shows a uniform ladder of length 5.0 m resting against a vertical, frictionless wall. The other end of the ladder rests on the floor where a frictional force f prevents the ladder from slipping. The weight of the ladder is 350 N.

Calculate the minimum coefficient of static friction between the ladder and the floor so that the ladder does not slip.

The ladder makes an angle of 60° with the floor.

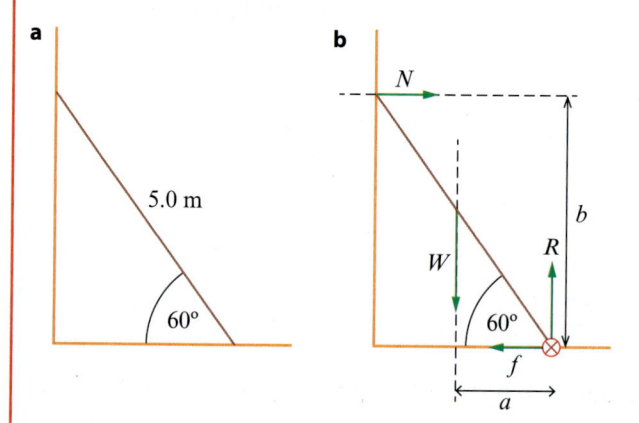

Figure 5.11: For worked example 5.6.

Answer

It is useful to first draw in the forces acting, as shown in Figure 5.11b.

Translational equilibrium demands that

$N = f$

$R = W$

Since $W = 350$ N, we find $R = 350$ N right away.

We must now apply the condition for rotational equilibrium. But what is the axis of rotation? As stated in the exam tip box, we can take anything we wish for the rotation axis. It is convenient to choose an axis such that as many forces as possible pass through. In this way their torques will be zero and we will not have to deal with them. So choosing the point where the ladder touches the floor, we have to find the torque of W and of N. The torque of N is $N \times b = N \times 5.0 \times \sin 60°$. The torque of W is $W \times a = W \times 2.5 \times \cos 60°$. The two torques are opposite so we set them equal to each other:

108

CONTINUED

$N \times 5.0 \times \sin 60° = W \times 2.5 \times \cos 60°$

$$N = \frac{W \times 2.5 \times \cos 60°}{5.0 \times \sin 60°}$$

$$= 101 \text{ N}$$

This implies that $f = 101$ N. Now $f_{max} = \mu_s R$ and so $\mu_s = \frac{f_{max}}{R} = \frac{101}{350} \approx 0.29$.

EXAM TIP

To solve a rotational equilibrium problem:

- demand that the net force is zero
- demand that the net torque is zero
- you may take torques about any axis, not just the actual axis of rotation.

Moment of inertia

Consider a rigid body that is free to rotate about some axis. Imagine splitting the body into tiny bits, each of some mass and distance from the axis. Figure 5.12 shows three of these bits—but you have to imagine the entire rigid body is covered by bits like these.

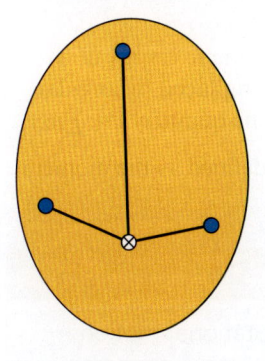

Figure 5.12: To calculate the moment of inertia we imagine splitting the entire body into tiny bits.

Each bit has mass m_i, and its distance from the axis is r_i. We multiply the mass of each bit by the distance of the bit to the axis squared and sum up for all the bits making up the body; that is, we form the quantity

$I = \sum m_i r_i^2$

which we call the **moment of inertia** of the body about the given axis.

Consider a particle of mass m that is free to rotate about an axis a distance R from the particle, as shown in Figure 5.13a.

The moment of inertia of the particle about the given axis is

$I = \sum m_i r_i^2$

But here there is just one 'bit' making up the body (the particle itself) and so the sum just has one term:

$I = mR^2$

For two particles of the same mass (Figure 5.13b) the moment of inertia is

$I = \sum m_i r_i^2 = mR^2 + mR^2 = 2mR^2$

Notice that the moment of inertia depends on the axis we choose. The same body will have different moments of inertia for different axes of rotation.

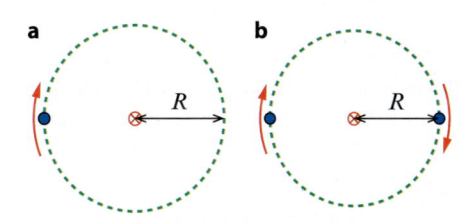

Figure 5.13: a A single particle rotating about a fixed axis. **b** Two particles moving on the same circle.

Consider a ring of radius R, as shown in Figure 5.14. We break up the ring into small bits of mass m_i. In this case, each bit has the same distance from the axis, so

$I = \sum m_i r_i^2 = \sum m_i R^2 = R^2 \sum m_i = MR^2$

where $M = \sum m_i$ is the total mass of the ring.

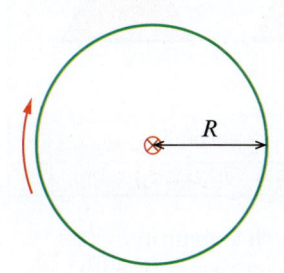

Figure 5.14: A ring rotating about a fixed axis.

PHYSICS FOR THE IB DIPLOMA: COURSEBOOK

It is not possible to find the moment of inertia of other arrangements as easily as in the previous cases. A few examples are shown with the axis of rotation indicated in Figure 5.15.

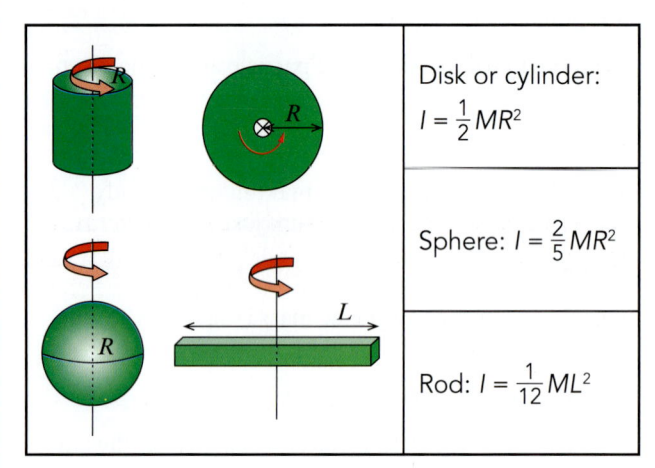

(cylinder and disk images)	Disk or cylinder: $I = \frac{1}{2}MR^2$
(sphere image)	Sphere: $I = \frac{2}{5}MR^2$
(rod image)	Rod: $I = \frac{1}{12}ML^2$

Figure 5.15: Moments of inertia of a few common shapes about the axes shown.

So we see that the moment of inertia is a quantity that depends on the mass of the body and how this mass is distributed around the rotation axis. The closer the mass is to the axis, the smaller the moment of inertia. The unit of moment of inertia is kg m².

CHECK YOURSELF 2

Look at Figure 5.16. About which axis (dashed line) is the moment of inertia of the uniform equilateral triangle the greatest?

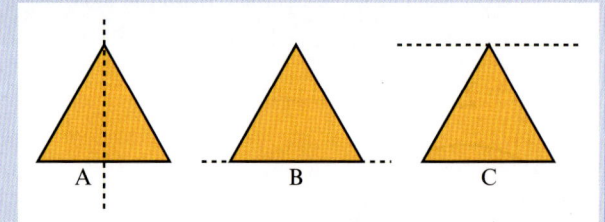

Figure 5.16: For check yourself question 2.

But why do we need to define such a quantity? Consider a body that rotates about some axis with angular speed ω and again break up the body into tiny bits, each of mass m_i, as in Figure 5.17.

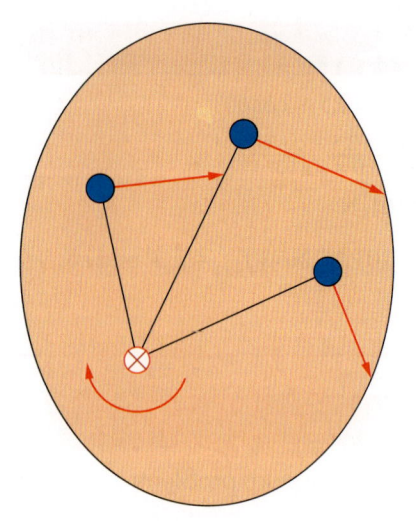

Figure 5.17: The kinetic energy of each bit of the body makes the total kinetic energy of the entire body.

The **kinetic energy of rotational motion** of the body is the sum of the kinetic energies of all the bits:

$$E_K = \frac{1}{2}m_1v_1^2 + \frac{1}{2}m_2v_2^2 + \frac{1}{2}m_3v_3^2 + \cdots$$
$$= \sum \frac{1}{2}m_iv_i^2$$

Now, each bit is at a different distance r_i from the axis of rotation, but all bits have the same angular velocity ω.

Since $v_i = \omega r_i$ we deduce that

$$E_K = \frac{1}{2}m_1\omega^2 r_1^2 + \frac{1}{2}m_2\omega^2 r_2^2 + \frac{1}{2}m_3\omega^2 r_3^2 + \cdots$$
$$= \frac{1}{2}\left(\sum m_i r_i^2\right)\omega^2$$

This is similar to the formula for kinetic energy of a point particle, but here velocity is replaced by angular velocity and mass is replaced by the quantity $I = \sum m_i r_i^2$.

This is precisely the quantity we defined as the moment of inertia of the body.

EXAM TIP

The moment of inertia is to rotational motion what mass is to linear motion.

So, for a body rotating about some axis, the kinetic energy is

$$E_K = \frac{1}{2}I\omega^2$$

where I is the moment of inertia about the rotation axis and ω is the angular velocity of the body about the (same) rotation axis.

> ### WORKED EXAMPLE 5.7
>
> A ring (moment of inertia MR^2) of mass 0.45 kg and radius 0.20 m rotates with angular velocity 5.2 rad s^{-1}. Calculate the kinetic energy of the ring.
>
> **Answer**
>
> The moment of inertia is
>
> $I = MR^2 = 0.45 \times 0.20^2 = 1.8 \times 10^{-2}$ kg m^2
>
> The kinetic energy is therefore
>
> $E_K = \frac{1}{2} I \omega^2 = \frac{1}{2} \times 1.8 \times 10^{-2} \times 5.2^2 = 0.24$ J

Rolling without slipping

When you ride a bicycle, the wheels rotate and at the same time the bicycle rolls forward.

So, consider a wheel of radius R that just rotates about its axis as in Figure 5.18a. All points on the wheel have the same angular velocity. In particular, points on the circumference have the same linear speed $v = \omega R$.

Now stop the rotation and imagine making the wheel just slide with velocity u along a horizontal floor. Every point of the wheel has a velocity u to the right.

Now imagine that the wheel moves forward as it rotates. Every point on the circumference of the wheel now has two motions:

- the motion due to the rotation
- the motion due to the translation of the wheel forward.

This means that the top point has linear velocity $v = u + \omega R$ and the bottom point a linear velocity $v = u - \omega R$.

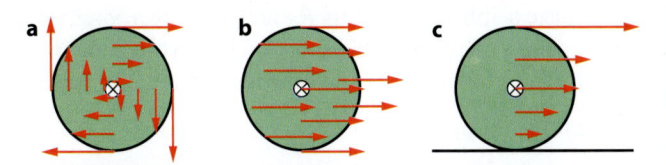

Figure 5.18: **a** A rotating disc: every point of the disc has a different linear velocity. **b** A sliding disc: every point on the disc has the same velocity. **c** A disc that rolls without slipping: the point of contact has zero velocity.

Rolling without slipping means that the centre of mass of the body has moved forward a distance of $2\pi R$ in a time equal to the period of revolution T (see Figure 5.19). (R is the distance from the centre of mass to the point of contact with the ground.)

So, $u = \frac{2\pi R}{T}$.

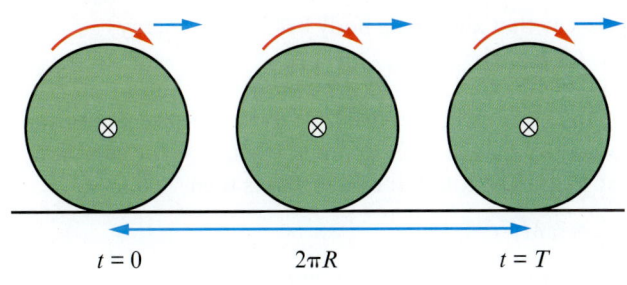

Figure 5.19: In one period, the centre of mass moves forward a distance $2\pi R$.

Since $\omega = \frac{2\pi}{T}$, it follows that $u = \omega R$; in other words, for rolling without slipping the linear speed of the centre of mass is given by ωR.

This means that the point of contact with the ground has net velocity zero (see Figure 5.20).

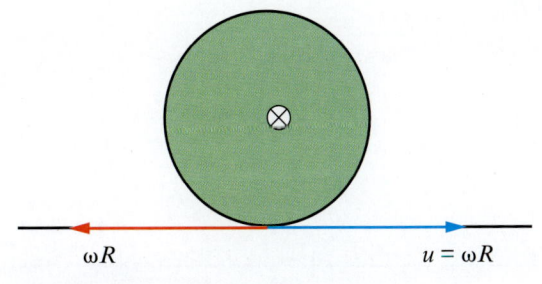

Figure 5.20: For rolling without slipping, the contact point has net velocity zero.

If we have a sphere of radius R and we apply a force on it, the centre of mass of the sphere will start to slide in the direction of the force and may also rotate.

If the force is applied

- through the centre of mass, the ball will slide but will not rotate (there is no torque to cause rotation)
- anywhere else, it will cause sliding as well as rotation.

Because angular acceleration is the rate of change of angular velocity, the condition of rolling without slipping may also be expressed in terms of angular acceleration: $a = \alpha R$.

Kinetic energy of a body that rolls without slipping

We saw that a rotating body has kinetic energy
$E_K = \frac{1}{2}I\omega^2$

If the body rolls, then we have to include the kinetic energy due to the translational motion of the centre of mass. The total kinetic energy is then
$E_K = \frac{1}{2}Mv^2 + \frac{1}{2}I\omega^2$
where v is the speed of the centre of mass.

If the centre of mass of the body is at a height h from some horizontal level then the gravitational potential energy is Mgh, and so the total mechanical energy is
$E_T = \frac{1}{2}I\omega^2 + \frac{1}{2}Mv^2 + Mgh$

In the absence of resistance forces the total energy is conserved.

If we have rolling without slipping v and ω are related by $v = \omega R$.

WORKED EXAMPLE 5.8

A cylinder of mass M and radius R (moment of inertia $I = \frac{1}{2}MR^2$) begins to roll without slipping from rest down an inclined plane (Figure 5.21).

Calculate the linear speed of the cylinder when it reaches level ground a vertical distance h lower.

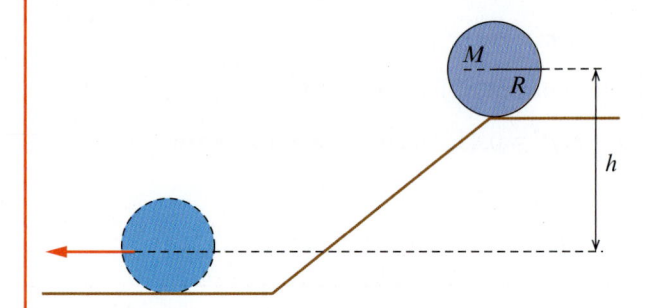

Figure 5.21: For worked example 5.8.

Answer

The initial energy is Mgh.

The energy on the horizontal level is
$E_K = \frac{1}{2}Mv^2 + \frac{1}{2}I\omega^2$.

Equating the two energies gives
$\frac{1}{2}Mv^2 + \frac{1}{2}I\omega^2 = Mgh$

The moment of inertia of the cylinder is
$I = \frac{1}{2}MR^2$

Because the cylinder rolls without slipping, $v = \omega R$ or $\omega = \frac{v}{R}$

Therefore, $\frac{1}{2}Mv^2 + \frac{1}{2}\left(\frac{1}{2}MR^2\right)\frac{v^2}{R^2} = Mgh$
$$\frac{1}{2}v^2 + \frac{1}{4}v^2 = gh$$
$$\frac{3v^2}{4} = gh$$

The linear speed is
$v = \sqrt{\frac{4gh}{3}}$

5 Rigid body mechanics

> **EXAM TIP**
>
> Notice that, if the body were a point particle, the answer for the speed would be $v = \sqrt{2gh}$, greater than the answer to worked example 5.8.

Newton's second law applied to rotational motion

When we solve problems in mechanics with rigid bodies we must apply Newton's second law to the centre of mass of the body

$F_{net} = Ma$

That is, in exactly the same way we would treat a point particle.

But we must also apply Newton's second law to the rotational motion of the body; it can be shown that this law becomes

$\tau_{net} = I\alpha$

(This is expected because torque plays the role of force and moment of inertia plays the role of mass.)

> **EXAM TIP**
>
> Moment inertia is to rotational motion what mass is to linear motion.
>
> Torque is to rotational motion what force is to linear motion.

> **THEORY OF KNOWLEDGE**
>
> Once the correspondence between linear and angular quantities is established, the formulae relating the angular quantities can be guessed from the corresponding formulae for linear quantities. The formalism is the same, and so the formulae are the same. We have seen similar connections in physics before, for example between electricity and gravitation.

We begin with an example of a sphere that rolls without slipping down an inclined plane that makes an angle θ to the horizontal. The sphere has mass M and radius R. We want to find the linear acceleration of the sphere as it comes down the plane.

Figure 5.22 shows the forces on the sphere. Notice right away that a frictional force must be present. Without one, the sphere would just slide down the plane and would not roll. (The problem would then be identical to a problem with a point mass.)

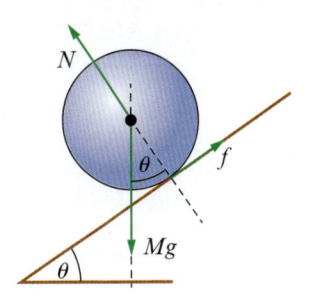

Figure 5.22: A sphere that rolls without slipping down an inclined plane. There has to be a frictional force to provide the torque for turning.

The net force on the sphere down the plane is

$Mg \sin\theta - f$

So

$F_{net} = Ma$

$Mg \sin\theta - f = Ma$ (Newton's second law for translational motion)

(We also have that $N = Mg \cos\theta$.)

The net torque about a horizontal axis through the centre of mass is fR.

N and Mg have zero torques about this axis.

The moment of inertia of a sphere about its axis is $I = \frac{2}{5} MR^2$.

So

$\tau = I\alpha$

$fR = \frac{2}{5} MR^2 \alpha$ (Newton's second law for rotational motion)

113

We assume rolling without slipping and so

$\alpha = \dfrac{a}{R}$

And our two equations become

$\begin{cases} Mg\sin\theta - f = Ma \\ fR = \dfrac{2}{5}MR^2 \dfrac{a}{R} \end{cases}$

These simplify to

$\begin{cases} Mg\sin\theta - f = Ma \\ f = \dfrac{2}{5}Ma \end{cases}$

So

$Mg\sin\theta - \dfrac{2}{5}Ma = Ma$

$\Rightarrow a = \dfrac{5g\sin\theta}{7}$

(For a body other than a sphere, the result would be $a = \dfrac{g\sin\theta}{1 + \dfrac{I}{MR^2}}$, where I is the moment of inertia about the centre of mass.)

> ### EXAM TIP
> Notice that if the body were a point particle the answer for the acceleration would be $a = g\sin\theta$ and is larger than that for the sphere (or any extended body).

Let us now calculate the speed of the ball after its centre of mass is lowered by a vertical distance h. The distance travelled down the plane is s and $h = s\sin\theta$ (see Figure 5.23).

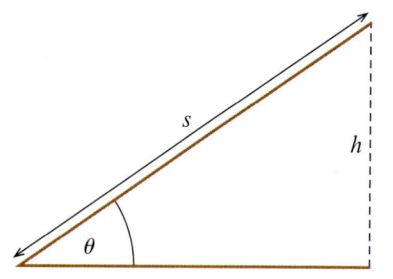

Figure 5.23: Relation between the vertical distance and the distance along the plane.

$v^2 = 2as = 2 \times \dfrac{5g\sin\theta}{7} \times s = \dfrac{10gh}{7}$

We will get the same result if we apply conservation of energy:

$\dfrac{1}{2}Mv^2 + \dfrac{1}{2}I\omega^2 = Mgh$

$\dfrac{1}{2}Mv^2 + \dfrac{1}{2}\left(\dfrac{2}{5}MR^2\right)\dfrac{v^2}{R^2} = Mgh$

$\dfrac{1}{2}v^2 + \dfrac{1}{5}v^2 = gh$

$\dfrac{7v^2}{10} = gh$

$v^2 = \dfrac{10gh}{7}$

At this point you may be wondering why we have been able to use energy conservation when there is a frictional force present. The answer is that the point of contact where the frictional force acts is not sliding; it is a point that is instantaneously at rest (as we saw earlier), and so the frictional force does not do any work and does not transfer any energy into thermal energy. Friction forces would do work, if we had rolling with slipping; but we will not consider such cases in this course.

CHECK YOURSELF 3

Figure 5.24 shows four diagrams; in each diagram, two identical, uniform spheres are joined by a rod of negligible mass. In which diagram, a–d, will the angular acceleration be the greatest? The applied forces are all the same and the distances are centre-to-centre distances.

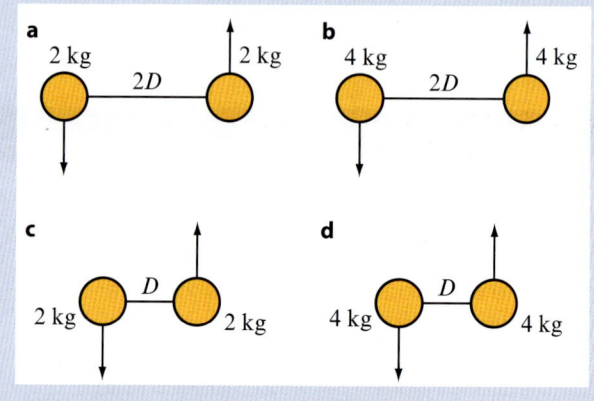

Figure 5.24: For check yourself question 3.

5 Rigid body mechanics

WORKED EXAMPLE 5.9

A block of mass m is attached to a string that goes over a cylindrical pulley (Figure 5.25).

When the block is released the pulley begins to turn as the block falls.

The mass of the pulley is M, and its radius is R. Calculate the acceleration of the block.

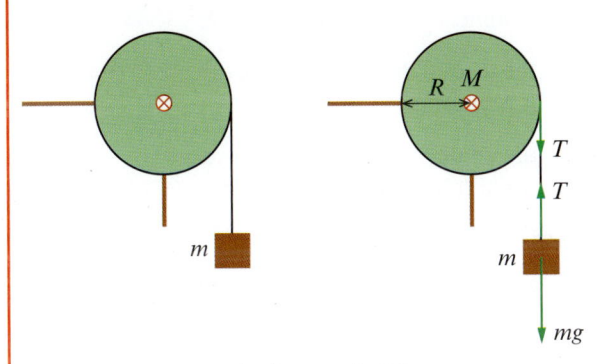

Figure 5.25: For worked example 5.9.

Answer

Applying the second law to the motion of the hanging mass,

$mg - T = ma$

Applying the second law to the rotation of the pulley gives

$TR = I\alpha$

The angular and the linear accelerations are related by $a = \alpha R$. So the two equations become

$$\begin{cases} TR = I\frac{a}{R} \\ mg - T = ma \end{cases}$$

Solve the first equation for T:

$T = \frac{Ia}{R^2} = \frac{1}{2}MR^2 \frac{a}{R^2} = \frac{1}{2}Ma$

and substitute in the second equation to get

$mg - \frac{1}{2}Ma = ma$

$mg = a(m + \frac{M}{2})$

$a = \frac{mg}{m + \frac{M}{2}}$

WORKED EXAMPLE 5.10

A snooker ball of mass M and radius R is hit horizontally at a point a distance d above the centre of mass (Figure 5.26). Determine d such that the ball rolls without slipping.

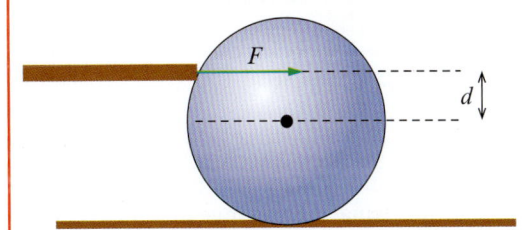

Figure 5.26: For worked example 5.10.

Answer

The torque on the ball about an axis through the centre of mass is Fd.

Therefore

$Fd = \frac{2}{5}MR^2 \alpha$

The net force on the ball is F, and so

$F = Ma$

The ball does not slip, and so the angular and the linear accelerations are related by $a = \alpha R$.

This means that we have two equations:

$$\begin{cases} Fd = \frac{2}{5}MR^2 \frac{a}{R} \\ F = Ma \end{cases}$$

Dividing side by side to get rid of F we get

$d = \frac{2}{5}R$

Work and power

Consider a constant force F that is applied on a rigid body for a time Δt. Let this force move its point of application by a distance Δs, rotating the body by an angle $\Delta\theta$ in the process. The force does work $W = F\Delta s$. But $\Delta s = R\Delta\theta$, and so the work is also given by

$W = FR\Delta\theta$

The torque of the force is $\tau = FR$ and so

$W = \tau\Delta\theta$

The familiar result from linear mechanics that the work done by the net force equals the change in kinetic energy holds here as well in the form that work done by the net torque is the change of rotational kinetic energy.

The power developed by the force is

$P = \dfrac{W}{\Delta t} = \dfrac{\tau\Delta\theta}{\Delta t}$

$P = \tau\omega$

Linear motion	Rotational motion
$F = ma$	$\tau = I\alpha$
$W = F\Delta s$	$W = \tau\Delta\theta$
$P = Fv$	$P = \tau\omega$

The formulae are direct analogues of the corresponding quantities in linear motion.

> **CHECK YOURSELF 4**
>
> A point particle slides down an inclined plane. A cylinder and a ring have the same radius and roll without slipping down the same inclined plane. All three objects have the same mass. All three start from rest at the same point on the inclined plane. Which arrives at the base of the inclined plane first and which arrives last?

> **WORKED EXAMPLE 5.11**
>
> A disc of moment of inertia 25 kg m² rotating at 320 revolutions per minute must be stopped in 12 s.
>
> a Calculate:
>
> i the work needed to stop it
>
> ii the average power developed in stopping it.
>
> b Determine:
>
> i the torque that stopped the disc (assuming it is constant).
>
> ii the angle by which the body turned while stopping.
>
> **Answer**
>
> a i The initial kinetic energy of the rotating disc is $E_K = \frac{1}{2}I\omega^2$.
>
>   We must find ω: $\omega = \dfrac{320 \times 2\pi}{60} = 33.5$ rad s⁻¹.
>
>   Hence $E_K = \frac{1}{2} \times 25 \times 33.5^2 = 1.40 \times 10^4 \approx 1.4 \times 10^4$ J.
>
>   This is the work required.
>
> ii The average power is, therefore,
>
> $P = \dfrac{1.40 \times 10^4}{12} = 1.17 \times 10^3 \approx 1.2 \times 10^3$ W.
>
> b i We can find the torque from $\tau = I\alpha = 25 \times \dfrac{33.5}{12} = 69.8 \approx 70$ N m.
>
>   But we can also use $P = \tau\omega$.
>
>   The average power involves the average angular speed, and so $\bar{P} = \tau\bar{\omega}$.
>
>   Since $\bar{\omega} = \dfrac{33.5}{2} = 16.75$ rad s⁻¹, the torque stopping the disc is $\tau = \dfrac{1.17 \times 10^3}{16.75} = 69.8 \approx 70$ N m.
>
> ii From $W = \tau\Delta\theta$, we find $\Delta\theta = \dfrac{W}{\tau} = \dfrac{1.40 \times 10^4}{69.85} \approx 200$ rad.

TEST YOUR UNDERSTANDING

6 A uniform rod of weight 450 N and length 5.0 m is supported at its ends (Figure 5.27). A block of weight 120 N is placed at a distance of 2.0 m from the left end. Calculate the force at each support.

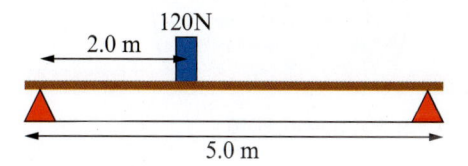

Figure 5.27: For question 6.

7 A uniform rod of mass 30 kg and length 4.0 m is supported from its left end and at a point a distance of 0.80 m from the middle as shown in Figure 5.28.

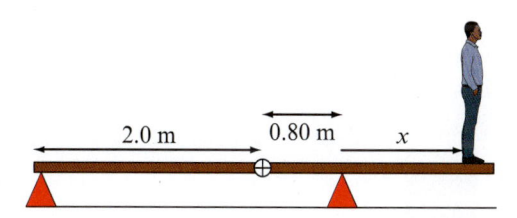

Figure 5.28: For question 7.

Calculate the largest distance x that a boy of mass 40 kg can walk to without tipping the rod over.

8 A uniform rod of length 2.0 m and weight 58 N is supported horizontally by a cable attached to a vertical wall (Figure 5.29).

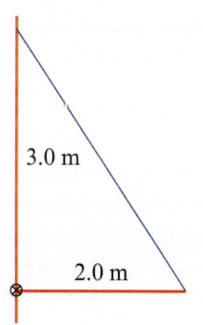

Figure 5.29: For question 8.

Calculate:

a the tension in the cable

b the magnitude and direction of the force exerted by the wall on the rod.

9 A body of moment of inertia 0.12 kg m² is uniformly accelerated from rest to an angular velocity of 24 rad s⁻¹ in 6.0 s. What is the torque that acted on the body?

10 A torque of 28 N m acts on a body of moment of inertia 3.2 kg m² for 4.0 s. The body is initially at rest.

a What is the final angular velocity?

b What is the change in the rotational kinetic energy of the body?

11 A uniform disc has radius R. A circular disc of radius r is cut away leaving a disc with a hole. The mass of the disc with the hole is M. Show that the moment of inertia of this solid about the axis shown is $\frac{1}{2}M(R^2 + r^2)$. (You do not need calculus to do this. This is an above exam level question, just for fun.)

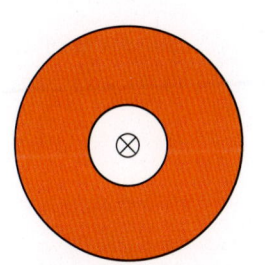

Figure 5.30: For question 11.

12 A cylinder of mass 5.0 kg and radius 0.20 m is attached to an axle through its centre of mass and parallel to its axis. A constant force of 6.5 N acts on the surface of the cylinder at right angles to the axle. Find the angular speed of the cylinder after 5.0 s.

13 A point particle, a sphere, a cylinder and a ring all have mass M. The solid bodies have the same radius R. The four bodies are released from the same height on an inclined plane. Determine the order, from least to greatest, of the speed when they reach level ground. (Assume rolling without slipping.)

117

CONTINUED

14 A disc of mass 12 kg and radius 0.35 m is spinning with angular velocity 45 rad s^{-1}.

    a Determine how many revolutions per minute (rpm) the disc is making.

    b A force is applied to the rim of the disc in a direction that is tangential to the disc's circumference. Determine the magnitude of this force if the disc is to stop spinning after 4.0 s.

    c Calculate the work done by the force in stopping the disc.

    d What is the average power developed by the force?

    e Calculate the number of revolutions made before stopping.

15 A rod of length $L = 1.20$ m is supported by a fixed support at its left end and is held horizontal (Figure 5.31).
The moment of inertia about the axis is given by $\frac{1}{3}ML^2$.

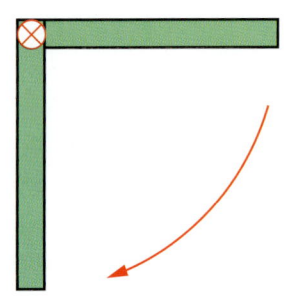

Figure 5.31: For question 15.

The rod is released from rest.

    a Calculate the initial angular acceleration of the rod.

    b State and explain whether the angular acceleration is constant in magnitude as the rod rotates.

    c Calculate the angular velocity of the rod as it moves past the vertical position.

16 A force F is applied horizontally to a cylinder of mass M and radius R as shown in Figure 5.32.

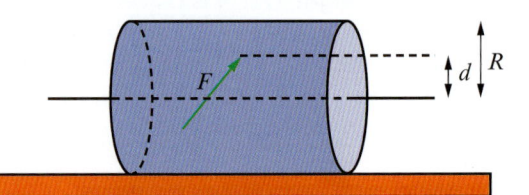

Figure 5.32: For question 16.

The force is applied at a point a distance d directly above the centre of mass of the cylinder. Determine d in terms of R such that the cylinder rolls without slipping. (The moment of inertia of a cylinder about its axis is $\frac{1}{2}MR^2$.)

17 A block of mass m hangs from the end of a string that goes over a pulley and is connected to another block of mass M that rests on a horizontal table (Figure 5.33).

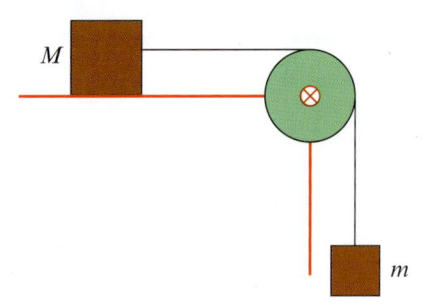

Figure 5.33: For question 17.

    a Assuming that the pulley is massless, calculate the acceleration of each block when the smaller block is released. There are no frictional forces.

    b The pulley is now assumed to have mass M and radius R. The small block is again released. The pulley turns as the blocks move. Calculate the acceleration of each block. (Hint: the tensions in each string are different.)

CONTINUED

18 The moment of inertia of a cylinder of mass M and radius R is $\frac{1}{2}MR^2$. A cylinder rolls without slipping on a horizontal surface with angular speed ω.

  a Show that the kinetic energy of the cylinder is $E_K = \frac{3}{4}M\omega^2 R^2$.

A cylinder of mass 4.0 kg and radius 0.20 m rolls without slipping on a horizontal surface with angular speed 5.0 rad s^{-1}. The cylinder then descends a vertical distance of 0.80 m along a ramp that makes an angle of 30° to the horizontal.

  b What is the final angular speed of the cylinder?

  c What is the angular acceleration of the cylinder on the ramp?

  d What is the net torque on the cylinder when on the ramp?

5.3 Angular momentum

The **angular momentum** of a rigid body of moment of inertia I that rotates about a fixed axis with angular speed ω is defined to be

$L = I\omega$

(Angular momentum is a vector.)

If the body is a point particle the angular momentum is $L = I\omega = mr^2\omega = m(\omega r)r = mvr$, an expression we will use in Unit E in relation to the Bohr model. The unit for angular momentum is kg m^2 s^{-1}. (This is equivalent to J s.)

Just as there is a relation between linear momentum and net force in particle mechanics, there is a relation between angular momentum and net torque:

$\tau_{net} = \dfrac{\Delta L}{\Delta t}$

The net torque on a body is equal to the rate of change of the angular momentum of the body.

And similarly, we have the law of **conservation of angular momentum**:

> **KEY POINT**
>
> When the net torque on a system is zero, the angular momentum is conserved; that is, it stays constant.

In Figure 5.34 the skater brings her arms closer to her body thus reducing her moment of inertia. Because there are no external torques on her body her angular momentum is conserved and so her angular speed increases.

a I large, ω small

b I small, ω large

Figure 5.34: a A skater rotates about her axis. **b** When she brings her arms in, the moment of inertia is reduced and the angular velocity increases in order to conserve angular momentum.

Rewriting the last equation as

$\Delta L = \tau_{net} \Delta t$

and calling the quantity $\tau_{net} \Delta t$ the **angular impulse** J, we see that the change in angular momentum is the angular impulse applied. This is in analogy with linear motion where $F_{net} \Delta t$ is the linear impulse applied, which in that case equals the change in linear momentum.

Linear motion	Rotational motion
$p = mv$	$L = I\omega$
$F_{net} = \frac{\Delta p}{\Delta t}$	$\tau_{net} = \frac{\Delta L}{\Delta t}$
$\Delta p = F_{net} \Delta t$	$\Delta L = \tau_{net} \Delta t$
$E_K = \frac{p^2}{2m}$	$E_K = \frac{L^2}{2I}$

You should be able to prove the last formula in the table.

CHECK YOURSELF 5

Figure 5.35 shows the elliptical path of a planet around the sun. SA = 3 SP.

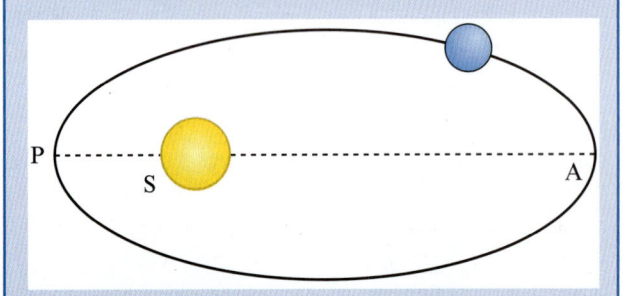

Figure 5.35: For check yourself question 5.

What is the ratio of the speed of the planet at A to that at P?

WORKED EXAMPLE 5.12

A spherical star of mass M and radius R rotates about its axis. The star explodes, ejecting mass into space. The star that is left behind has mass $\frac{M}{10}$ and radius $\frac{R}{20}$. Calculate the new angular speed of the star in terms of the original angular speed ω.

Answer

Angular momentum is conserved and so

$\frac{2}{5}MR^2\omega = \frac{2}{5}\frac{M}{10}\left(\frac{R}{20}\right)^2\omega' \Rightarrow \omega' = 10 \times 20^2 \omega = 4000\,\omega$

WORKED EXAMPLE 5.13

A horizontal disc of mass $M = 0.95$ kg and radius $R = 0.35$ m rotates about its vertical axis with angular speed 3.6 rad s^{-1}. A piece of modelling clay of mass $m = 0.30$ kg lands vertically on the disc, attaching itself at a point a distance $r = 0.25$ m from the centre. Find the new angular speed of the disc.

Answer

The moment of inertia of the disc is

$I = \frac{1}{2}MR^2 = \frac{1}{2} \times 0.95 \times 0.35^2 = 0.0582$ kg m^2

The original angular momentum of the disc is

$L_{in} = I\omega = 0.0582 \times 3.6 = 0.210$ J s

The final angular momentum is

$L_{in} = I\omega' + mr^2\omega' = (\underbrace{0.0582}_{\text{disc}} + \underbrace{0.30 \times 0.25^2}_{\text{clay}})\omega'$

Angular momentum will be conserved because there are no external torques on the disc–clay system. So

$(0.0582 + 0.30 \times 0.25^2)\,\omega' = 0.210$

$\omega' = 2.7$ rad s^{-1}

WORKED EXAMPLE 5.14

A torque of 12 N m acts on a body of moment of inertia 4.0 kg m² for 3.0 s. The body is initially at rest.

a   What is the final angular velocity of the body?

b   How many revolutions did the body make during the 3.0 s?

Answer

a   The applied angular impulse is $\tau \Delta t = 12 \times 3.0 = 36$ J s and equals the change in angular momentum. Thus $I\omega = 36$ J s and so $\omega = \frac{36}{4.0} = 9.0$ rad s⁻¹.

b   The angular acceleration of the body is

$\alpha = \frac{\tau}{I} = \frac{12}{4.0} = 3.0$ rad s⁻²

From $\omega^2 = 2\alpha\Delta\theta$ we find

$\Delta\theta = \frac{\omega^2}{2\alpha} = \frac{81}{6.0} = 13.5$ rad $\Rightarrow \frac{13.5}{2\pi} = 2.15$ revolutions

WORKED EXAMPLE 5.15

A solid object at rest explodes into two fragments X and Y of moment of inertia 8.0 kg m² and 16 kg m² respectively. Fragment X rotates with angular velocity 5.0 rad s⁻¹ about a vertical axis. The fragments just rotate with no translational motion.

a   Explain why fragment Y must also rotate about a vertical axis but in the opposite sense to that of X.

b   Calculate the angular velocity of Y.

c   Calculate the ratio $\frac{\text{rotational kinetic energy of X}}{\text{rotational kinetic energy of Y}}$.

Answer

a   The original object has zero angular momentum, and so the fragments must have equal and opposite angular momenta.

b   From $8.0 \times 5.0 = 16 \times \omega$ we find $\omega = 2.5$ rad s⁻¹.

c   Use $E_K = \frac{L^2}{2I}$ so that $\frac{\text{rotational kinetic energy of X}}{\text{rotational kinetic energy of Y}} = \frac{\frac{L^2}{2 \times 8.0}}{\frac{L^2}{2 \times 16}} = 2$.

TEST YOUR UNDERSTANDING

19 A torque of 2.8 N m acts on a body for 3.2 s. What is the change in the angular momentum of the body?

20 The angular momentum of a body changed by 24 J s in 4.0 s as a result of the action of a torque. What was the torque?

21 Two identical rods, X and Y, each of length 1.20 m and mass 2.40 kg, are made to rotate with angular velocity 4.50 rad s^{-1}, as shown in Figure 5.36.

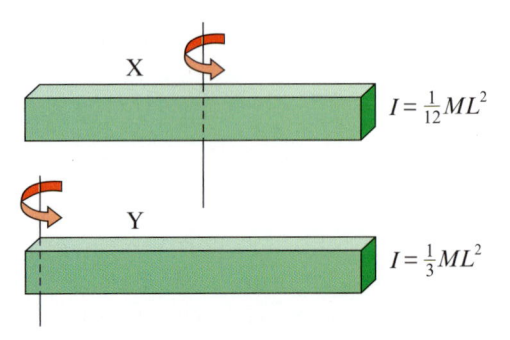

Figure 5.36: For question 21.

Calculate the kinetic energy and angular momentum of X and Y.

22 A star of mass M and radius R explodes radially symmetrically. The star is left with a mass equal to $\frac{M}{10}$ and a radius equal to $\frac{R}{50}$. Calculate the ratio of the final to the initial angular velocity of the star. ($I = \frac{2}{5}MR^2$)

23 The angular momentum of a body is 240 J s, and its rotational kinetic energy is 920 J. What is its moment of inertia?

24 A disc of moment of inertia 2.4 kg m^2 is rotating about a vertical axis through its centre with angular velocity 1.2 rad s^{-1}. A second nonrotating disc of moment of inertia 1.8 kg m^2 falls on the first disc and sticks to it as shown in Figure 5.37.

a What is the angular velocity of the two discs?

b How much kinetic energy was lost?

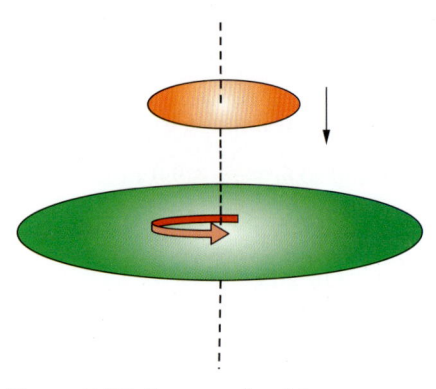

Figure 5.37: For question 24.

25 A battery-driven toy car of mass 0.18 kg is placed on a circular track that is part of a horizontal ring of moment of inertia 0.20 kg m^2 and radius 0.50 m (Figure 5.38). The ring can rotate about a vertical axis without friction.

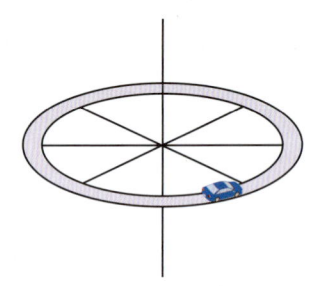

Figure 5.38: For question 25.

The car is started, and its speed relative to the ground is measured to be 0.80 m s^{-1}. Calculate the angular speed of the ring.

26 A cylinder of mass M and radius R can rotate about a horizontal axle through its centre as shown in Figure 5.39. A rope is wrapped around the cylinder, and a block of mass m hangs from the rope. The block is released from rest. The moment of inertia of the cylinder is $\frac{1}{2}MR^2$.

5 Rigid body mechanics

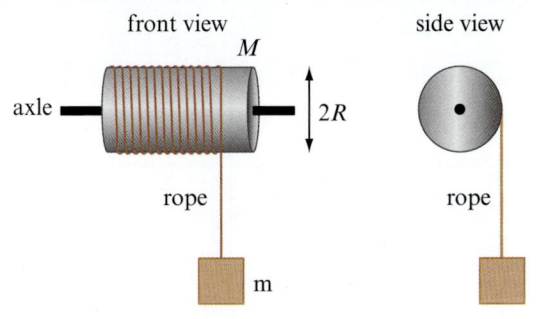

CONTINUED

Figure 5.39: For question 26.

Use the following data:

M = 4.0 kg   R = 0.20 m   m = 2.0 kg
g = 10 m s^{-2}

a Find the linear acceleration of the falling block and the angular acceleration of the cylinder.

b Calculate the tension in the string.

c Calculate the linear velocity of the block and the angular velocity of the cylinder 2.0 s after releasing the block.

d Find the change in the angular momentum of the cylinder and in the angular momentum of the block 2.0 s after releasing the block.

e What is the *net* torque on the system?

f What is the *total* angular impulse delivered to the system in 2.0 s?

NATURE OF SCIENCE

Engineers apply the laws of physics to design structures and machines that make our lives safer, more comfortable and more enjoyable. The great technological advances in energy production, food production, transportation, telecommunications, space exploration, weather prediction, medicine, the entertainment industry and myriad other cases are all the result of the application of the basic laws and principles of the sciences to practical problems.

Links

The concept of angular momentum has played a crucial role in the development of quantum theory. Bohr asserted that the angular momentum of an electron orbiting the nucleus of a hydrogen atom is an integral multiple of a basic quantity known as the Planck constant h: $mvr = n\frac{h}{2\pi}$. Using this assertion Bohr was able to show that the energy of the electron in the hydrogen atom is quantised and that only certain orbits are allowed. See Unit E.

REFLECTION

Are you confident using the equations of *rotational kinematics*? Do you understand the term *torque* and can you calculate the torque of a force? Do you understand the concept of *moment of inertia*? Can you solve problems with *Newton's second law* applied to rotational motion? Can you solve problems with energy conservation? Do you understand the term *rolling without slipping*? Can you solve problems with *angular momentum conservation*? Do you understand when angular momentum is conserved?

SELF-ASSESSMENT CHECKLIST

I am able to …	Section	Not yet	Nearly there	Ready to move on
apply the equations of rotational kinematics and exploit the analogy with linear motion	5.1			
understand and apply the concept of torque	5.2			
understand the concept of moment of inertia	5.2			
apply Newton's second law to rotational motion	5.2			
apply the law of conservation of energy in rotational motion	5.2			
understand the concept of 'rolling without slipping'	5.2			
understand the conditions under which angular momentum is conserved	5.3			
solve problems with angular momentum conservation	5.3			

EXAM-STYLE QUESTIONS

You can find questions in the style of IB exams in the digital coursebook.

CHECK YOURSELF ANSWERS

1. D; in A it is zero, in B and C it is the same (5 N m) and in D it is $5\sqrt{2}$ N m.
2. C, because more mass is away from the axis.
3. C, masses of 2 kg separated by D.
4. Point particle first, ring last. Since $a = \dfrac{g \sin\theta}{1 + \frac{I}{MR^2}}$, the point particle has acceleration $a = g \sin\theta$, the cylinder $a = \frac{2}{3} g \sin\theta$ and the ring $a = \frac{1}{2} g \sin\theta$.
5. The angular momentum of the planet is conserved, so $m v_A SA = m v_P SP$
So, $\dfrac{v_A}{v_P} = \dfrac{1}{3}$.

Chapter 6
Relativity

LEARNING OBJECTIVES

In this chapter you will learn how to:

- understand the meaning and use of the terms *reference frame* and *inertial reference frame*
- explore Galilean relativity and its transformation equations for position, time and velocity
- understand Einstein's two postulates of special relativity
- see how the postulates of special relativity lead to the Lorentz transformation equations for the same event from the point of view of two reference frames
- use the Lorentz transformation for relativistic velocity addition
- understand that the spacetime interval between two events is an invariant quantity
- use the terms proper *time interval* and *proper length*
- solve problems involving time dilation and length contraction

PHYSICS FOR THE IB DIPLOMA: COURSEBOOK

> **CONTINUED**
>
> - explore relativistic simultaneity
> - use spacetime diagrams (sometimes called Minkowski diagrams)
> - understand how muon decay experiments provide evidence for time dilation and length contraction

> **GUIDING QUESTION**
>
> What are the consequences of the constancy of the speed of light on our understanding of space and time?

Introduction

This chapter deals with the kinematic parts of the theory of special relativity introduced by Einstein in 1905. As we will see, the theory has revolutionised our traditional concepts of space and time; it leads to unexpected phenomena such as length contraction and time dilation, and it introduces the speed of light as the ultimate limiting speed for all material objects.

We will discuss the two main effects of the theory of relativity—time dilation and length contraction – and will see how muon decay experiments provided the early experimental support for the theory.

We also introduce a pictorial representation of relativistic phenomena that makes the concepts of time dilation, length contraction and simultaneity particularly transparent.

6.1 Reference frames and Lorentz transformations

In physics experiments, we (the *observers*) record the time and position at which **events** take place. To do that, we use a **reference frame**. A reference frame is a set of co-ordinate axes and a set of clocks at every point in space. If this set is *not accelerating*, the frame is called an **inertial reference frame** (see Figure 6.1).

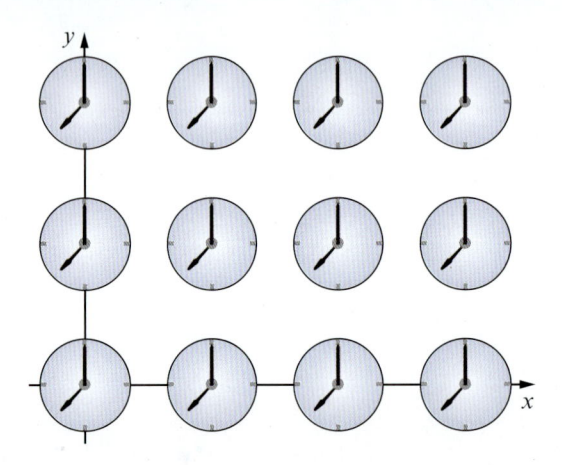

Figure 6.1: A two-dimensional reference frame. There are clocks at every point in space (only a few are shown here). All clocks are synchronised to show the same time.

> **CHECK YOURSELF 1**
>
> Which reference frames in this list are inertial frames?
>
> a A sky diver falling freely
>
> b A sky diver falling at terminal velocity
>
> c A train moving with constant speed on a straight line
>
> d A plane taking off
>
> e The earth as it rotates around the sun

If the event is a strike of a lightning, an observer will look at the reading of the clock at the point where lightning struck and record that reading as the time of the event. The co-ordinates of the strike point give the position of the event in space. In Figure 6.2, lightning strikes at time $t = 3$ s at position $x = 60$ m and $y = 0$. (We are ignoring the z co-ordinate.)

6 Relativity

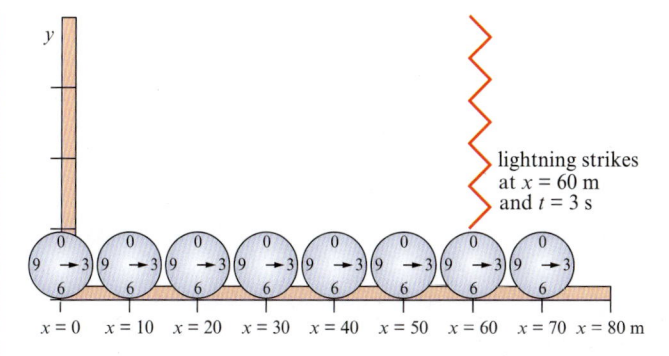

Figure 6.2: In this frame of reference the observer measures that lightning struck at time $t = 3$ s at position $x = 60$ m.

The same event can also be viewed by another observer in a different reference frame. So, consider a situation involving one observer on the ground and another who is a passenger on a train travelling at a velocity of $v = 15$ m s^{-1} relative to the ground observer, as shown in Figure 6.3.

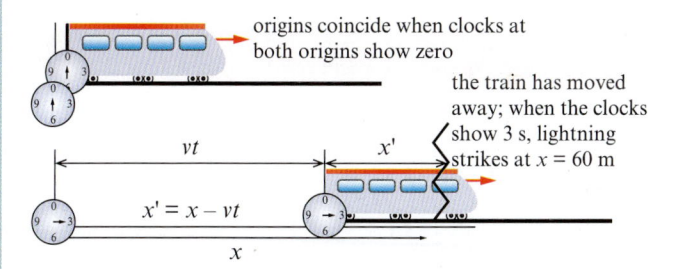

Figure 6.3: The origins of the two frames of reference coincide when clocks in both frames show zero. The origins then separate.

We can see things more clearly if we concentrate on the rulers (in metres) used by the ground and train observers. In Figure 6.4 we see the two rulers on top of each other. This happens at time zero.

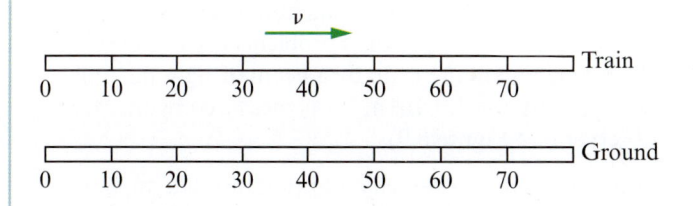

Figure 6.4: The situation at time zero.

The train moves and its ruler moves along with it. Lightning strikes at the point shown (Figure 6.5). The ground and train observers assign different co-ordinates to this event.

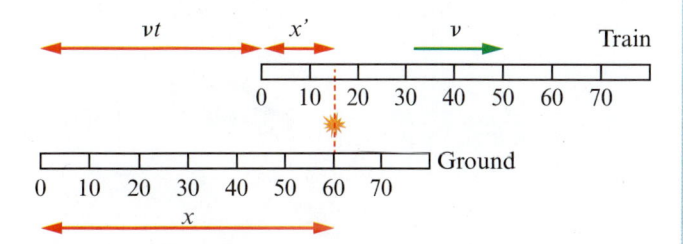

Figure 6.5: The situation at time 3 s. Clearly, $vt + x' = x$ so that $x' = x - vt$.

The ground observer uses the symbol x to denote the position of an event. The observer on the train uses the symbol x'. As shown in Figures 6.3 and 6.5, these are related by:

$x' = x - vt$

since in the time of t seconds the train moves forward a distance vt. The equation expresses the relationship between the space co-ordinates of the same event as viewed by two observers who are in relative motion. In pre-relativity physics, time was absolute; that is, all observers make the same measurements for time, so $t' = t$.

> **KEY POINT**
>
> The equations $x' = x - vt$ and $t' = t$ are two of the **Galilean transformation equations**.

Thus, to the event of Figures 6.3 and 6.5 ('lightning strikes') the ground observer assigns the co-ordinates $x = 60$ m and $t = 3$ s. The observer in the train assigns to this same event the co-ordinates $t' = 3$ s and $x' = 60 - 15 \times 3 = 15$ m.

We are assuming here what we know from everyday experience (a guide that, as we will see, may not always be reliable):

Two observers always agree on what the time co-ordinates are; in other words, time is common to both observers.

Figure 6.6 shows Galileo Galilei in an oil painting by Justus Sustermans that can be seen in the Uffizi Gallery in Florence.

Figure 6.6: Galileo Galilei (1564–1642).

Galilean relativity has an immediate consequence for the *law of addition of velocities*: consider a ball that rolls on the train floor. The train moves at 20 m s⁻¹. At time zero the ball is at the origin of the train frame, as shown in Figure 6.7.

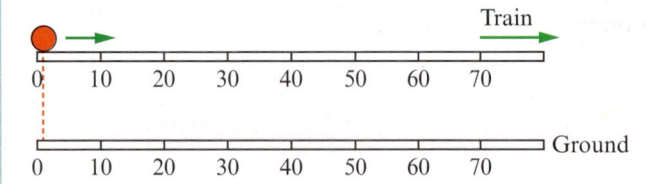

Figure 6.7: At time zero the ball is at the origin of the train frame. Its position is given by $x = x' = 0$.

Two seconds later, the train has moved forward a distance of 40 m. During this time the ball has rolled on the train floor a distance of 20 m, as shown in Figure 6.8. So the velocity of the ball for the train observer is $\frac{20}{2} = 10$ m s⁻¹.

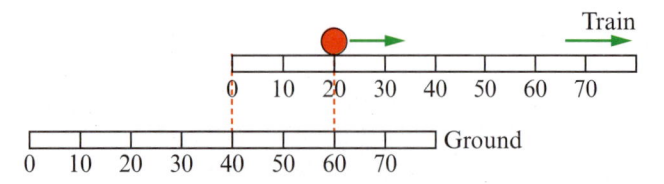

Figure 6.8: Two seconds later the ball has moved a distance of 20 m along the train floor. The train moved forward a distance of 40 m according to the ground.

The ground observer measures that the ball moved a distance of 60 m in 2 s, and for the ground observer the ball's velocity is:

$\frac{60}{2} = 30$ m s⁻¹

Notice that 30 m s⁻¹ = 20 m s⁻¹ + 10 m s⁻¹.

In general, if the train observer measures a velocity u' for the ball, the ground observer will measure a velocity $u = u' + v$, where v is the velocity of the train.

The equation $u = u' + v$ or $u' = u - v$ is the final Galilean transformation equation.

CHECK YOURSELF 2

A bird flies due south at 4 m s⁻¹. A glider flies due north at 5 m s⁻¹.

What is the velocity of the bird relative to the glider?

WORKED EXAMPLE 6.1

A ball rolls on the floor of a train at 2 m s⁻¹ towards the right (with respect to the floor). The train moves with respect to the ground:

a to the right at 12 m s⁻¹

b to the left at 12 m s⁻¹.

What is the velocity of the ball relative to the ground?

Answer

a $u = u' + v = 2 + 12 = 14$ m s⁻¹.

b $u = u' + v = 2 - 12 = -10$ m s⁻¹.

The (apparently correct) argument in the answer to worked example 6.1 presents problems if we replace the rolling ball in the train by a beam of light moving with velocity $c = 3 \times 10^8$ m s⁻¹ as measured by the train observer (see Figure 6.9).

Using the Galilean velocity addition formula implies that light would be travelling at a higher speed relative to the ground observer. At the end of the nineteenth century, considerable efforts were made to detect variations in the speed of light depending on the state of motion of the source of light. The experimental result was that no such variations were detected.

6 Relativity

Figure 6.9: An observer in the train measures the speed of light to be c. An observer on the ground would then measure a higher speed, c + v.

> **KEY POINT**
>
> *All the laws of physics are the same in all inertial frames.*

The second was new:

> **KEY POINT**
>
> *The speed of light in vacuum is the same for all inertial observers.*

Einstein had solid theoretical reasons (based on Maxwell's theory of electromagnetism) to believe that the speed of light should be the same for all inertial observers. It should not depend on the speed of its source. So, either Galileo's velocity formula was wrong or Maxwell was wrong. Einstein trusted Maxwell. Doing so meant that the equations of Galilean relativity had to be revised.

The postulates of special relativity

Einstein (Figure 6.10) based his theory of relativity on two **postulates**. The first was the old postulate of Galileo which Einstein extended to all laws of physics, not just mechanics:

Figure 6.10: Albert Einstein (1879–1955).

> **THEORY OF KNOWLEDGE**
>
> Einstein was so convinced of the constancy of the speed of light that he elevated it to one of the principles of relativity. But it was not until 1964 that conclusive experimental verification of this took place. In this experiment, at CERN, neutral pions moving at 0.99975c decayed into a pair of photons moving in different directions. The speed of the photons in both directions was measured to be c with extraordinary accuracy. The speed of light does not depend on the speed of its source. The theory of relativity has modified our fundamental ideas about space and time, ideas that went unchallenged for over two thousand years. Accepting the new ideas was not easy; the beauty of the theory of relativity lies in the amazingly simple postulates upon which it is based. It is interesting that at the time of the formulation of the theory little experimental evidence for the postulates was available. Yet, despite the simplicity of the postulates, their consequences are far reaching and have revolutionised physics.

129

These two postulates of relativity have far-reaching consequences. Einstein showed, in 1905, that, following from his two postulates, the correct equations relating measurements in the two frames are:

Galileo	Einstein	
$x' = x - vt$	$x' = \gamma(x - vt)$	$x = \gamma(x' + vt')$
$t' = t$	$t' = \gamma\left(t - \frac{v}{c^2}x\right)$	$t = \gamma\left(t' + \frac{v}{c^2}x'\right)$

where the factor γ is called the *gamma factor* and equals $\gamma = \frac{1}{\sqrt{1 - \frac{v^2}{c^2}}}$.

The first column under Einstein gives x' and t' in terms of x and t, and the second gives x and t in terms of x' and t'.

In 1890 the Dutch physicist H. Lorentz also derived these equations by demanding that the laws of electromagnetism should be the same in all inertial frames, and so these are known as *Lorentz transformations*. Einstein re-derived them from more general principles 15 years later. Notice right away that if v is very small compared to the speed of light, then $\gamma \approx 1$ and $\frac{v}{c^2}$ is negligibly small, and so the Lorentz equations reduce to the Galilean equations! In other words the effects of relativity become important only at speeds close to that of light. Notice also that these equations become meaningless for speeds equal to or greater than that of light. This is a sign that no material body can reach or exceed the speed of light.

These equations may be used to relate the co-ordinates of a *single* event in one inertial frame with those in another. We will denote with S some inertial frame. A frame that moves with speed v to the right relative to S will be called frame S'. These equations assume that when clocks in both frames show zero (i.e. $t = t' = 0$) the origins of the two frames coincide, i.e. $x = x' = 0$.

Note that $\gamma > 1$. A graph of the gamma factor against speed is shown in Figure 6.11. We see that the gamma factor is approximately 1 for velocities up to about half the speed of light but approaches infinity as the speed approaches the speed of light.

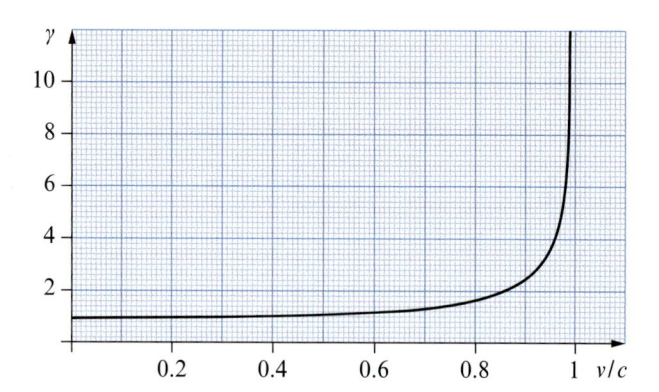

Figure 6.11: The gamma factor as a function of velocity. The value of γ stays essentially close to 1 for values of the velocity up to about half the speed of light but approaches infinity as the velocity approaches the speed of light.

CHECK YOURSELF 3

You are on an island watching the mainland some 20 km away. The instant you see light from the headlights of a car on the mainland the clock strikes midnight. Is the time co-ordinate of the event 'light is emitted from the headlights' 12 o'clock midnight?

WORKED EXAMPLE 6.2

Note: Unless stated otherwise, when clocks in both frames show zero, the origins of the two frames coincide.

Lightning strikes a point on the ground (frame S) at position $x = 3500$ m and time $t = 5.0$ s. Determine where and when the lightning struck according to a rocket that flies past the ground at speed $0.80\,c$ to the right.

Answer

This is a straightforward application of the Lorentz formulas (the gamma factor is $\gamma = \frac{1}{\sqrt{1 - 0.80^2}} = \frac{5}{3}$):

$$x' = \gamma(x - vt)$$
$$= \tfrac{5}{3}(3500 - 0.80 \times 3 \times 10^8 \times 5.0)$$
$$= -2.0 \times 10^9 \text{ m}$$

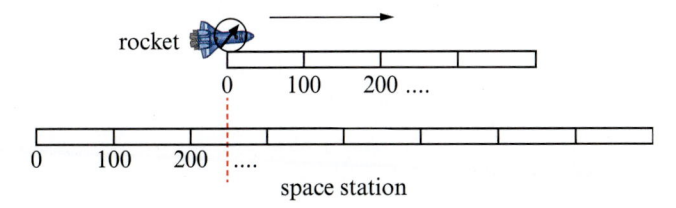

> **CONTINUED**
>
> and
>
> $t' = \gamma\left(t - \frac{vx}{c^2}\right)$
> $= \frac{5}{3}\left(5.0 - \frac{0.80 \times 3 \times 10^8 \times 3500}{(3 \times 10^8)^2}\right)$
> $= 8.3$ s
>
> The observers disagree on the co-ordinates of the event 'lightning strikes', but both are correct.
>
> However, notice that in S the quantity $c^2 t^2 - x^2$ is equal to $(3 \times 10^8 \times 5.0)^2 - 3500^2 = 2.25 \times 10^{18}$ m². In the rocket frame $c^2 t'^2 - x'^2$ is equal to $(3 \times 10^8 \times 8.3)^2 - (-2.0 \times 10^9)^2 = 2.25 \times 10^{18}$ m² which is the same value as that in S. So both observers agree that this combination of time and space co-ordinates is the same in both frames. We will understand this in the next section.

> **WORKED EXAMPLE 6.3**
>
> A rocket is moving at $0.80c$ past a space station (Figure 6.12).
>
> **a** Where is the rocket according to the space station when the rocket clock shows 0.60 μs?
>
> **b** What does the space station clock read at this position?
>
> **Figure 6.12:** For worked example 6.3.
>
> **Answer**
>
> **a** We examine the event E = rocket clock shows 0.60 μs. For this event $x' = 0$ and $t' = 0.60$ μs in the rocket frame.
>
> Hence, from the Lorentz formula:
>
> $x = \gamma(x' + vt')$
> $= \frac{5}{3}(0 + 0.80 \times 3 \times 10^8 \times 0.60 \times 10^{-6})$
> $= 240$ m
>
> **b** $t = \gamma\left(t' + \frac{vx'}{c^2}\right)$
> $= \frac{5}{3}(0.60 \times 10^{-6} + 0)$
> $= 1.0$ μs
>
> (The quantity $c^2 t^2 - x^2$ in S is equal to $(3 \times 10^8 \times 1.0 \times 10^{-6})^2 - 240^2 = 32\,400$ m². In the rocket frame $c^2 t'^2 - x'^2$ is equal to $(3 \times 10^8 \times 0.60 \times 10^{-6})^2 - 0^2 = 32\,400$ m².)

> **PHYSICS FOR THE IB DIPLOMA: COURSEBOOK**

> **EXAM TIP**
>
> It is important that you can use the Lorentz equations to go from frame S to frame S′ as well as from S′ to S.

Sometimes we will be interested in the difference in co-ordinates of a pair of events. So for events 1 and 2 we define $\Delta x' = x'_2 - x'_1$ and $\Delta t' = t'_2 - t'_1$ in S′ and $\Delta x = x_2 - x_1$ and $\Delta t = t_2 - t_1$ in S.

These differences are related by

$$\Delta x' = \gamma(\Delta x - v\Delta t); \quad \Delta t' = \gamma\left(\Delta t - \frac{v}{c^2}\Delta x\right)$$

or, in reverse,

$$\Delta x = \gamma(\Delta x' + v\Delta t'); \quad \Delta t = \gamma\left(\Delta t' + \frac{v}{c^2}\Delta x'\right)$$

WORKED EXAMPLE 6.4

Consider a rocket that moves relative to a laboratory with speed $v = 0.80\,c$ to the right, as shown in Figure 6.13. We call the inertial frame of the lab S and that of the rocket S′. The length of the rocket as measured by the rocket observers is 630 m. A photon is emitted from the back of the rocket towards the front. Calculate the time taken for the photon to reach the front end of the rocket according to observers in the rocket and in the laboratory.

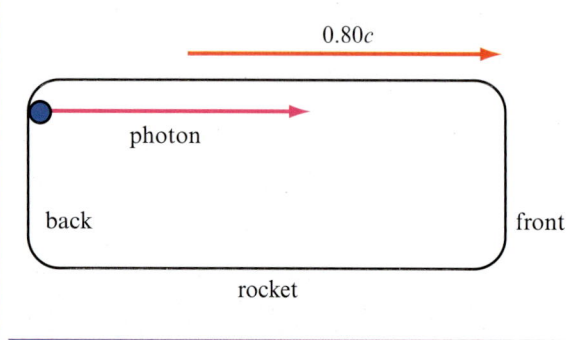

Figure 6.13: For worked example 6.4.

Answer

Event 1 is the emission of the photon. Event 2 is the arrival of the photon at the front of the rocket:

$\Delta x' = x'_{\text{arrival}} - x'_{\text{emission}} = 630$ m

This distance is covered at the speed of light, and so the time between emission and arrival (in S′) is

$\Delta t' = \frac{630}{c} = 2.1$ μs

In frame S we use

$\Delta x = \frac{5}{3}(630 + 0.80c \times 2.1 \times 10^{-6}) = 1890$ m

$\Delta t = \frac{5}{3}\left(2.1 \times 10^{-6} + \frac{0.80c \times 630}{c^2}\right) = 6.3$ μs

The spacetime interval

We have seen that observers in different inertial frames assign different space and time co-ordinates to the same events. For example, frame S assigns $(\Delta x, \Delta t)$ for the difference in co-ordinates of two events and S' assigns $(\Delta x', \Delta t')$. These are related by Lorentz transformations. Interestingly, however, there is a quantity that both observers will agree on as we have already indicated. This is called the **spacetime interval**. It is given by $(\Delta s)^2 = (c\Delta t)^2 - (\Delta x)^2$ in S. In S' the spacetime interval is $(\Delta s')^2 = (c\Delta t')^2 - (\Delta x')^2$ and it has the same value as in S (this is left as an exercise in algebra for you). In other words

$$(c\Delta t)^2 - (\Delta x)^2 = (c\Delta t')^2 - (\Delta x')^2.$$

In practice this means that if we know three of the quantities Δt, Δx, $\Delta t'$, $\Delta x'$ we can find the fourth from the spacetime interval. Consider an observer X at the origin of a frame S' that moves past a frame S with speed of $0.80c$. An observer in S measures that X turns on a light at $t = 0$ and turns it off at $t = 4.0$ s. For how long was the light on according to S'?

We know that $\Delta t = 4.0$ s, $\Delta x = 0.80c \times 4.0 = 9.6 \times 10^8$ m, $\Delta x' = 0$. Hence

$(c\Delta t)^2 - (\Delta x)^2 = (c\Delta t')^2 - (\Delta x')^2$

$(3 \times 10^8 \times 4.0)^2 - (9.6 \times 10^8)^2 = (c\Delta t')^2 - 0^2$

Hence $\Delta t' = 2.4$ s.

Of course we could get the answer with a Lorentz transformation as well:

$\Delta t' = \frac{5}{3} \times \left(4.0 - \frac{0.80c}{c^2} \times 0.80c \times 4.0\right) = 2.4$ s.

> **CHECK YOURSELF 4**
>
> A photon travels from A to B on a straight line. What is the spacetime interval for these points?

> **THEORY OF KNOWLEDGE**
>
> Note that there is no question as to which observer is right and which is wrong when it comes to measuring time intervals. Both are right. Two inertial observers moving relative to each other at constant velocity both reach valid conclusions according to the principle of relativity.

> **TEST YOUR UNDERSTANDING**
>
> 1. Give two reasons why the ground on which you stand is not an inertial reference frame. Under what approximation is it an inertial frame?
>
> 2. Imagine that you are travelling in a train at constant speed in a straight line and that you cannot look at or communicate with the outside. Think of the first experiment that comes to your mind that you could do to try to find out that you are indeed moving. Then analyse it carefully to see why it will not work.
>
> 3. Outline an experiment you might perform in a train that is accelerating along a straight line that would convince you that it is accelerating. Discuss if you could also determine the direction of the acceleration.
>
> 4. An inertial frame of reference S' moves past another inertial frame S moving to the right with speed 15 m s^{-1}. At time zero the origins of the two frames coincide.
>
>   a. A phone rings at location $x = 20$ m and $t = 5.0$ s. Determine using Galilean transformation equations the location of this event in the S' frame.
>
>   b. A ball is measured to have velocity 5.0 m s^{-1} in frame S'. Calculate the velocity of the ball in frame S.
>
> 5. An inertial frame of reference S' moves past another inertial frame S moving to the left with speed 25 m s^{-1}. At time zero the origins of the two frames coincide.
>
>   a. A phone rings at location $x' = 24$ m and $t = 5.0$ s. Determine using Galilean transformation equations the location of this event in the S frame.
>
>   b. A ball is measured to have velocity -15 m s^{-1} in frame S. Calculate the velocity of the ball in frame S'.

> **PHYSICS FOR THE IB DIPLOMA: COURSEBOOK**

> **CONTINUED**
>
> **6** A rocket moving at speed 0.80c relative to the ground emits a light signal in the direction of the velocity. What is the speed of the light signal relative to the ground according to Galileo?
>
> *In the following questions the frames S and S' have their usual meaning, i.e. S' moves past S with velocity v, and when the origins coincide clocks are set to zero. You are expected to use relativistic equations for these questions.*
>
> **7 a** Calculate the gamma factor for a speed of 0.850c and a velocity of –0.850c.
>
>   **b** Calculate the speed that gives a gamma factor of 4.00.
>
>   **c** Is there a speed that gives a gamma factor of 0.50?
>
> **8** In frame S an event E has co-ordinates (x = 600 m, t = 2.0 μs). Frame S' is moving at speed 0.75c in the positive direction. Determine the co-ordinates of E in S'.
>
> **9** An event E has co-ordinates (x' = 520 m, t' = 4.0 μs) in a frame S' that moves with velocity 0.60c relative to frame S. Determine the co-ordinates of E in S.
>
> **10** Frame S' moves with velocity 0.98c relative to S. An explosion occurs at the origin of frame S' when the clocks in S' read 6.0 μs. Calculate where and when the explosion takes place according to frame S.
>
> **11** Frame S' moves with velocity 0.60c relative to S. Calculate the reading of the clocks in frame S' as the origin of S' passes point x = 120 m.
>
> **12** Two events in frame S are such that $\Delta x = x_2 - x_1 = 1200$ m and $\Delta t = t_2 - t_1 = 6.00$ μs.
>
>   **a** Frame S' moves with velocity 0.600c relative to S. Calculate $\Delta x' = x'_2 - x'_1$ and $\Delta t' = t'_2 - t'_1$.
>
>   **b** Determine if there is another frame S" such that in this frame $\Delta t'' = 0$. Comment on your answer.
>
> **13** A rocket moving at 0.80c leaves earth towards a planet that is a distance of 24 ly from earth as measured in the earth's frame. By considering the events E_1 = rocket leaves earth and E_2 = rocket arrives at the planet, calculate the time it takes to get to the planet according to the rocket. (ly stands for 'light year'; it is the distance travelled by light in one year. 1 ly = c × year.)
>
> **14** A rocket travelling at 0.60c with respect to earth leaves earth towards a planet. After 4.0 years (as measured by the rocket clocks) a radio message is sent to earth. Calculate when it will arrive on earth as measured by:
>
>   **a** observers on earth
>
>   **b** observers on the rocket.
>
> **15** In frame S event E(arly) occurs before event L(ate). The events are separated by a time interval $\Delta t = t_L - t_E$ and a space interval $\Delta x = x_L - x_E$.
>
>   **a** If E is the event that *causes* event L to happen, explain why $\frac{\Delta x}{\Delta t} \leq c$.
>
>   **b** Is there a frame in which L occurs before E?

6.2 Effects of relativity

Time dilation

Suppose that an observer in a frame S' that moves relative to a frame S measures the time in between successive ticks of a clock. The clock is at rest in S' and so the measurement of the ticks occurs at the same place, $\Delta x' = 0$. The result of the measurement is $\Delta t'$. The observer in S will measure a time interval equal to

$$\Delta t = \gamma\left(\Delta t' + \frac{v\Delta x'}{c^2}\right)$$
$$= \gamma(\Delta t' + 0)$$
$$\Delta t = \gamma \Delta t'$$

This shows that the interval between the ticks of a clock that moves relative to the observer in S is greater than the interval measured in S' where the clock is at rest. This is known as **time dilation**. In this case, the time measured by S' is special because it represents a time interval between two events that happened at the same point in space. The clock is at rest in S' so its ticks happen at the same

6 Relativity

point in S'. Such a time interval is called **proper time interval**. (This is just a name; it is not implied that this is a more 'correct' measurement of time).

> **KEY POINT**
>
> A proper time interval is the time between two events that take place at the same point in space.

The time dilation formula is best remembered as

$$\text{time interval} = \gamma \times \text{proper time interval}$$
$$= \frac{1}{\sqrt{1-\frac{v^2}{c^2}}} \times \text{proper time interval}$$

WORKED EXAMPLE 6.5

The time interval between the ticks of a clock carried on a fast rocket is half of what observers on Earth record. Calculate the speed of the rocket relative to earth.

Answer

The rocket observers measure the proper time interval since the events 'first tick' and 'second tick' occur at the same place in the rocket frame. From the time dilation formula it follows that

$$2 = \frac{1}{\sqrt{1-\frac{v^2}{c^2}}} \Rightarrow \sqrt{1-\frac{v^2}{c^2}} = \frac{1}{2}$$
$$\Rightarrow 1 - \frac{v^2}{c^2} = \frac{1}{4}$$
$$\Rightarrow \frac{v^2}{c^2} = \frac{3}{4}$$
$$\Rightarrow v = 0.866c$$

WORKED EXAMPLE 6.6

A rocket moves past an observer in a laboratory with speed $v = 0.85c$. The observer in the laboratory measures that a radioactive isotope (which is at rest in the laboratory) has a half-life of 2.0 min. Calculate the half-life measured by the rocket observers.

Answer

We have two events here. The first is that the laboratory observer sees a container with a given mass of the radioactive isotope. The second event is that the laboratory observer sees a container with half the mass of the radioactive isotope. These events

CONTINUED

are separated by 2.0 min as far as the laboratory observer is concerned. These two events take place at the same point in space as far as the laboratory observer is concerned, and so *the laboratory observer has measured the proper time interval between these two events*. Hence the rocket observers will measure a longer half-life of time interval = $\gamma \times$ proper time interval

$$= \frac{1}{\sqrt{1-0.85^2}} \times 2.0 \text{ min}$$
$$= 3.80 \text{ min}$$

The point of this example is that you must not make the mistake of thinking that proper time intervals are measured by 'the moving' observer. There is no such thing as 'the moving' observer: the rocket observer is free to consider themselves at rest and the laboratory observer moving with velocity $v = -0.85c$.

> **SCIENCE IN CONTEXT**
>
> The Global Positioning System (GPS) depends on precisely measuring signals from satellites which move at speeds of about 4 km s^{-1}. This is a small speed compared to the speed of light. The gamma factor for this speed is greater than 1 by approximately 9×10^{-11}. In one day there are 86 400 s, so if relativity is not taken into account we would have an error of about $9 \times 10^{-11} \times 86\,400 \approx 8$ μs in clocks after one day. For signals travelling at the speed of light this would imply an uncertainty in position of about $8 \times 10^{-6} \times 3 \times 10^8 = 2400$ m. This would make the GPS worthless. (GPS also uses corrections from general relativity.)

Length contraction

Now consider a rod that is at rest in frame S'. An observer in S' measures the position of the ends of the rod, subtracts and finds a length $\Delta x' = L_0$. (Notice that since the rod is at rest, the measurement of the position of the ends can be done at different times—the rod is not going anywhere. But for the observer in S the rod is moving. So to measure its length the observer must record the position of the ends of the rod at the same time, i.e. with $\Delta t = 0$. Since $\Delta x' = \gamma(\Delta x - v\Delta t)$ where $\Delta x = L$ is the length in S, we obtain that

> **EXAM TIP**
>
> Note that it is only lengths in the direction of motion that are contracted.

$L_0 = \gamma(L - 0)$

$L = \dfrac{L_0}{\gamma}$

This shows that the rod, which moves relative to the observer in S, has a shorter length in S than the length measured S' where the rod is at rest. This is known as **length contraction**. A reference frame in which an object is at rest is called that object's **rest frame**.

> **KEY POINT**
>
> The length $\Delta x' = L_0$ is special because it is measured in a frame of reference where the rod is a rest. Such a length is called a **proper length**.

The length of an object measured by an inertial observer with respect to whom the object is at rest is called proper length. Observers with respect to whom the rod moves at speed v measure a shorter length: length $= \dfrac{\text{proper length}}{\gamma}$

> **WORKED EXAMPLE 6.7**
>
> An unmanned spacecraft leaves earth with speed $0.80c$ towards a planet that is 40 ly away as measured by earth observers. How long will the trip take according to:
>
> **a** earth clocks
>
> **b** spacecraft clocks?
>
> **Answer**
>
> **a** According to earth the time is simply
> $\dfrac{40 \text{ ly}}{0.80c} = 50 \dfrac{c \times \text{year}}{c} = 50 \text{ yr}.$
>
> **b** Leaving earth and arriving at the planet occurs at the same point according to the spacecraft so the spacecraft measures a proper time interval for the trip. Hence it takes a time of $\dfrac{50}{\gamma} = \dfrac{50}{\frac{5}{3}} = 30 \text{ yr}.$

> **CONTINUED**
>
> Equivalently we can argue that the spacecraft is at rest and the planet is coming towards the spacecraft at speed $0.80c$. The distance between earth and planet is then length contracted to $\dfrac{40}{\gamma} = \dfrac{40}{\frac{5}{3}} = 24$ ly and so 'the planet will come to the spacecraft' in a time of $\dfrac{24 \text{ ly}}{0.80c} = 30 \text{ yr}.$

> **THEORY OF KNOWLEDGE**
>
> The time dilation effect described is a 'real' effect. In the Hafele–Keating experiment, accurate atomic clocks taken for a ride aboard planes moving at ordinary speeds and then compared with similar clocks left behind show readings that are smaller by amounts consistent with the formulae of relativity. Time dilation is also a daily effect in the operation of particle accelerators. In such machines, particles are accelerated to speeds that are very close to the speed of light, and thus relativistic effects must be taken into account when designing these machines. The time dilation formula has also been verified in muon decay experiments.

Addition of velocities

Consider a frame S' that moves at constant speed v in a straight line relative to another frame S. Observers in both frames measure the velocity of an object. Observers in S' measure the velocity to be u'. Observers in S measure the velocity of the same object to be u. How are u and u' related? We saw that the Galilean answer ($u = u' + v$) cannot be correct. Einstein showed that the Lorentz equations lead to the following answer:

$u = \dfrac{u' + v}{1 + \dfrac{u'v}{c^2}}$ or, solving for u', $u' = \dfrac{u - v}{1 - \dfrac{uv}{c^2}}$

Think of frame S as the ground and the frame S' to be a rocket moving at velocity $0.80c$ relative to S. The rocket launches a missile with speed $0.50c$ relative to the rocket. This means that $v = 0.80c$ and $u' = 0.50c$. The speed of the missile relative to S is u and is given by

$$u = \frac{u' + v}{1 + \frac{u'v}{c^2}}$$

$$= \frac{0.50c + 0.80c}{1 + \frac{0.50c \times 0.80c}{c^2}}$$

$$= \frac{1.30c}{1.40}$$

$$= 0.93c$$

In Galilean relativity then answer would be $u = u' + v = 1.30c$ and so impossible. It can be easily checked that, irrespective of how close u' or v are to the speed of light, u is always less than c.

WORKED EXAMPLE 6.8

A rocket moves with speed $0.90c$ relative to the ground. A beam of light is emitted from the rocket in the forward direction. The rocket measures a speed c for the light beam. Use the velocity addition formula to show that the ground observers also measure a speed c for the light beam.

Answer

Applying the formula with $v = 0.90c$ and $u' = c$ we find

$$u = \frac{u' + v}{1 + \frac{u'v}{c^2}}$$

$$= \frac{c + 0.90c}{1 + \frac{c \times 0.90c}{c^2}}$$

$$= \frac{1.90c}{1.90}$$

$$= c$$

WORKED EXAMPLE 6.9

Two rockets move away from each other with speeds of $0.80c$ and $0.90c$ with respect to the ground, as shown in Figure 6.14. What is the velocity of rocket B as measured by rocket A?

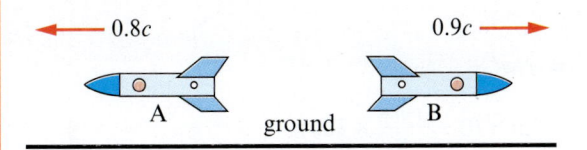

Figure 6.14: For worked example 6.9.

CONTINUED

Answer

Let us call the frame of the ground S and that of rocket A, S'. Then $v = -0.80c$. We want to find the velocity of rocket B relative to A, i.e. relative to S', so we are looking for u'. The velocity of rocket B relative to the ground (S) is $u = +0.90c$ and so

$$u' = \frac{u - v}{1 - \frac{uv}{c^2}}$$

$$= \frac{+0.90c - (-0.80c)}{1 - \frac{(0.90c)(-0.80c)}{c^2}}$$

$$= \frac{+1.70c}{1 + 0.72}$$

$$= +0.988c \approx +0.99c$$

The velocity of rocket A relative to rocket B is expected to be $-0.99c$. We can calculate this explicitly as follows: again let S be the ground frame and S' the frame of rocket B. Then $v = +0.90c$ and $u = -0.80c$. We are again looking for u' and

$$u' = \frac{u - v}{1 - \frac{uv}{c^2}}$$

$$= \frac{-0.80c - 0.90c}{1 - \frac{(-0.80c)(0.90c)}{c^2}}$$

$$\approx -0.99c$$

as expected.

Simultaneity

Another great change introduced into physics as a result of relativity is in the concept of **simultaneity**. Suppose that as usual we have frames S and S' with frame S' moving to the right with speed v relative to S. Suppose that two events take place *at the same time in frame S'*. The time interval between these two events is thus zero, $\Delta t' = 0$. What is the time interval between the same two events when measured in S? The Lorentz equations give

$$\Delta t = \gamma \left(\Delta t' + \frac{v}{c^2} \Delta x' \right)$$
$$= \gamma \frac{v}{c^2} \Delta x'$$

If $\Delta x' \neq 0$, then the events will *not* be simultaneous in other frames. On the other hand, if $\Delta x' = 0$, i.e. if the simultaneous events in S' occur at the same point in space, then they are also simultaneous in all other frames.

PHYSICS FOR THE IB DIPLOMA: COURSEBOOK

> **KEY POINT**
>
> Events that are simultaneous for one observer *and* which take place at *different points in space*, are *not* simultaneous for another observer in motion relative to the first.
>
> On the other hand, if two events are simultaneous for one observer *and* take place at the *same point in space*, they are simultaneous for all other observers as well.

Imagine an observer T is in the middle of a train carriage that is moving with constant speed to the right with respect to the train station. We are told that two light signals are emitted from the ends of the carriage at the same time as far as the observer T in the train is concerned, Figure 6.15. It is then clear that the two signals arrive at T at the same time as far as T is concerned. What does an observer G at rest on the ground say about this situation?

Figure 6.15: Light leaves A and B at the same time as far as T is concerned.

The emissions from A and B *take place at different points in space* and are simultaneous for observer T. So they will *not* be simultaneous for observer G. On the other hand the arrival of the signals at T is simultaneous for T *and happen at the same point in space* so they will also be simultaneous for G.

Which signal was emitted first according to G? From G's point of view, T is *moving away from the signal from A*. So the signal from A has a larger distance to cover to get to T. If the signals are received *at the same time*, and moved at the same speed (*c*), it must be that the one from A was emitted *before* that from B.

> **CHECK YOURSELF 5**
>
> Two observers, N and M, are at rest on the ground. M is midway between two street lights (Figure 6.16). M measures that the streetlights turn on at the same time.
>
> **Figure 6.16:** For check yourself question 5.
>
> a   Does M receive light from the two lamps at the same time?
>
> b   Do the street lights turn on at the same time according to N?
>
> c   Does N receive light from the two lamps at the same time?

> **WORKED EXAMPLE 6.10**
>
> Let us re-work the situation of Figure 6.15 quantitatively. Take the proper length of the 'train' (frame S') to be 300 m and let it move with speed $0.98c$ to the right. Determine, according to an observer on the ground (frame S), which light is emitted first and by how much.
>
> **Answer**
>
> We are told that $\Delta t' = 0$ and $\Delta x' = x'_B - x'_A = 300$ m. We want to find Δt, the time interval between the events representing the emission of light from A and B. The gamma factor is $\gamma = \frac{1}{\sqrt{1 - 0.98^2}} = 5.0$. Then
>
> $\Delta t = t_B - t_A$
>
> $= \gamma(\Delta t' + \frac{v}{c^2}\Delta x')$
>
> $= 5.0 \times (0 + \frac{0.98c}{c^2} \times 300)$
>
> $= +4.9$ μs
>
> The positive sign indicates that $t_B > t_A$, i.e. the light from A was emitted 4.9 μs *before* the light from B.

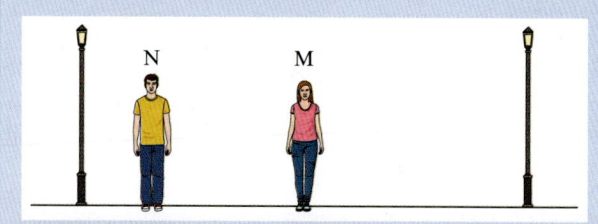

Muon decay

Muons are particles with properties similar to those of the electron except that they are more massive, are unstable and decay into electrons; they have an average lifetime of about 2.2×10^{-6} s. (The reaction is $\mu^- \rightarrow e^- + \bar{v}_e + v_\mu$.)

This is the lifetime measured when the muon is at rest—this is the proper time interval between the creation of a muon and its subsequent decay.

From the point of view of an observer in the laboratory, however, the muons are moving at high speed; the lifetime is longer because of time dilation. Consider a muon created by a source at the top of a mountain 3.0 km tall, Figure 6.17. The muon travels at $0.99c$ towards the surface of the earth.

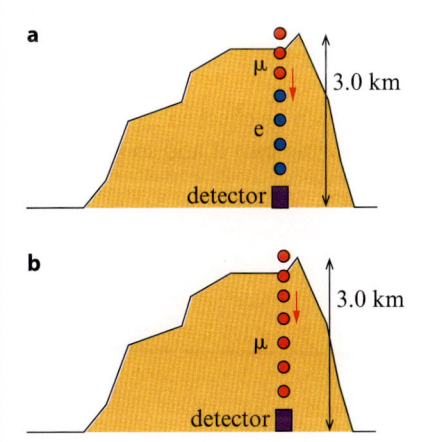

Figure 6.17: **a** Muons created at the top of the mountain would not have enough time to reach the surface as muons if relativity did not hold. **b** With relativity the muons last longer and make it to the surface before decaying.

Without the relativistic time dilation effect, the muon would have travelled a distance of only

$0.99 \times 3 \times 10^8 \times 2.2 \times 10^{-6}$ m = 0.653 km

before decaying into an electron. Thus a detector at the base of the mountain would record the arrival of electrons, not muons. But experiments show the arrival of muons at the detector. This is because the lifetime of the muon as measured by ground observers is

time interval = $\gamma \times$ proper time
$$= \frac{2.2 \times 10^{-6} \text{ s}}{\sqrt{1 - 0.99^2}}$$
$$= 1.56 \times 10^{-5} \text{ s}$$

In this time the muon travels a distance (as measured by the ground observers) of

$0.99 \times 3 \times 10^8 \times 1.56 \times 10^{-5}$ m = 4.63 km

This means that the muon reaches the surface of the earth *before* decaying.

The fact that muons do make it to the surface of the earth is evidence in support of the time dilation effect.

The muon exists as a muon for only 2.2×10^{-6} s in the muon's rest frame. So how does an observer travelling along with the muon explain the arrival of muons (and not electrons) at the surface of the earth, Figure 6.18?

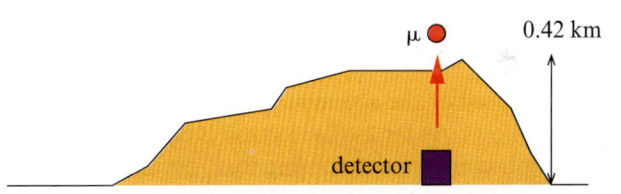

Figure 6.18: From the point of view of an observer on the muon the mountain is much shorter.

The answer is that the distance of 3.0 km measured by the observers on earth is a proper length for them but not for the observer at rest with respect to the muon. This observer claims that it is the earth that is moving upward and so measures a length-contracted distance of

$3.0 \times \sqrt{1 - 0.99^2}$ km = 0.42 km

to the surface of the earth. The earth's surface is coming up to this observer with a speed of $0.99c$ and so the time when they will meet is

$$\frac{0.42 \times 10^3}{0.99 \times 3 \times 10^8} \text{ s} = 1.4 \times 10^{-6} \text{ s}$$

that is, *before* the muon decays!

In this sense, muon decay experiments are direct confirmations of time dilation and indirect confirmations of length contraction.

PHYSICS FOR THE IB DIPLOMA: COURSEBOOK

WORKED EXAMPLE 6.11

At the Stanford Linear Accelerator (SLAC), electrons of speed $v = 0.960c$ move a distance of 3.00 km.

a Calculate how long this takes according to observers in the laboratory.

b Calculate how long this takes according to an observer travelling along with the electrons.

c Find the speed of the linear accelerator in the rest frame of the electrons.

Answer

a In the laboratory the electrons take a time of $\frac{3.00 \times 10^3}{0.960 \times 3.00 \times 10^8}$ s = 1.04×10^{-5} s

b The arrival of the electrons at the beginning and the end of the accelerator track happens at the same point in space as far as the observer travelling along with the electrons is concerned, and so that is a proper time interval. The gamma factor is $\gamma = \frac{1}{\sqrt{1-0.960^2}} = 3.571$. Thus

time interval = $\gamma \times$ proper time interval

proper time interval = $\frac{1.04 \times 10^{-5}}{3.571}$ s

$= 2.91 \times 10^{-6}$ s

c The speed of the accelerator is obviously $v = 0.960c$ in the opposite direction. But this can be checked as follows. As far as the electron is concerned, the length of the accelerator track is moving past it and so is length-contracted according to

length = $\frac{\text{proper length}}{\gamma}$

$= \frac{3.00 \text{ km}}{3.571}$

$= 0.840$ km

and so has a speed of

speed = $\frac{0.840 \times 10^3}{2.91 \times 10^{-6}}$ m s^{-1}

$= 2.89 \times 10^8$ m s^{-1}

$\approx 0.96\,c$

NATURE OF SCIENCE

General arguments apply to special cases but not the other way around.

Years before relativity was introduced by Einstein an experiment performed by Michelson and Morley gave a very puzzling result concerning the speed of light. There were frantic attempts to resolve the difficulties posed by this experiment. One attempt was to assume that moving lengths appear shorter. Similarly, Lorentz showed that if one used his Lorentz transformations equations certain difficulties with electromagnetism went away. But it was Einstein who re-derived these transformations equations from far more general principles, the postulates of relativity. By demanding that all inertial observers experience the same laws of physics and measuring the same velocity of light in vacuum the Lorentz equations emerged as the simplest linear equations that could achieve this.

TEST YOUR UNDERSTANDING

16 An earthling sits on a bench in a park eating a sandwich. It takes him 5 min to finish it according to his watch. He is being monitored by planet Zenga invaders who are passing earth at a speed of 0.90c.

    a Calculate how long the aliens reckon it takes an earthling to eat a sandwich.

    b The aliens in the spacecraft get hungry and start eating their sandwiches. It takes a Zengan 5 min to eat her sandwich according to Zengan clocks. They are actually being observed by earthlings as they fly over earth. Calculate how long it takes a Zengan to eat a sandwich according to earth clocks.

17 A cube has density ρ when the density is measured at rest. Suggest what happens to the density of the cube when it travels past you at a relativistic speed.

18 A pendulum in a fast train is found by observers on the train to have a period of 1.0 s. Calculate the period observers on a station platform would measure as the train moves past them at a speed of 0.95c.

19 A spacecraft moves past you at a speed of 0.95c, and you measure its length to be 100 m. Calculate the length you would measure if it were at rest with respect to you.

20 Two identical fast trains move parallel to each other. An observer on train A tells an observer on train B that by her measurements (i.e. A's) train A is 30 m long and train B is 28 m long.

The observer on train B takes measurements. Calculate what he will find for:

    a the speed of train A with respect to train B

    b the length of train A

    c the length of train B.

21 An unstable particle has a lifetime of 5.0×10^{-8} s as measured in its rest frame. The particle is moving in a laboratory with a speed of 0.95c with respect to the lab.

    a Calculate the lifetime of the particle according to an observer at rest in the laboratory.

    b Calculate the distance travelled by the particle before it decays, according to the observer in the laboratory.

22 The star Vega is about 50 ly away from earth. A spacecraft moving at 0.995c is heading towards Vega.

    a Calculate how long it will take the spacecraft to get to Vega according to clocks on earth.

    b The crew of the spacecraft consists of 18-year-old IB graduates. Calculate how old the graduates are (according to their clocks) when they arrive at Vega.

23 A rocket approaches a mirror on the ground at a speed of 0.90c as shown in Figure 6.19.

The distance D between the front of the rocket and the mirror is 2.4×10^{12} m, as measured by the observers on the ground, when a light signal is sent towards the mirror from the front of the rocket.

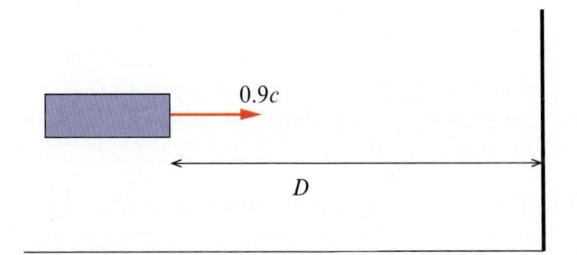

Figure 6.19: For question 23.

CONTINUED

Calculate when the reflected signal is received by the rocket as measured by:

a the observers on the ground

b the observers on the rocket.

24 Two objects move along the same straight line as shown in Figure 6.20. Their speeds are as measured by an observer on the ground.

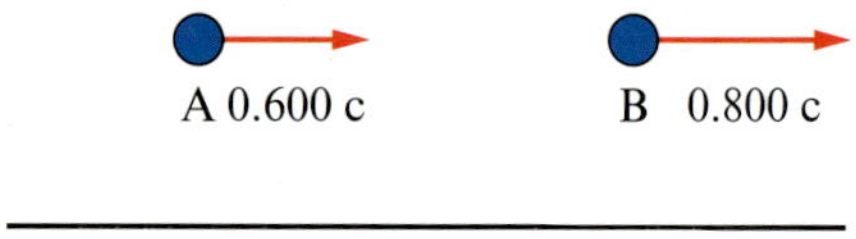

A 0.600 c   B 0.800 c

Figure 6.20: For question 24.

Find:

a the velocity of B as measured by A;

b the velocity of A as measured by B.

25 Repeat question 24 for the arrangement in Figure 6.21.

0.600 c A   B 0.800 c

Figure 6.21: For question 25.

26 A particle A moves to the right with a speed of $0.60c$ relative to the ground. A second particle B moves to the right with a speed of $0.70c$ relative to A. Calculate the speed of B relative to the ground.

27 Particle A moves to the left with a speed of $0.60c$ relative to the ground. A second particle B moves to the right with a speed of $0.70c$ relative to A. Find the speed of B relative to the ground.

28 A muon travelling at $0.95c$ covers a distance of 2.00 km (as measured by an earthbound observer) before decaying.

a Calculate the muon's lifetime as measured by the earthbound observer.

b Calculate the lifetime as measured by an observer travelling along with the muon.

29 The lifetime of the unstable pion particle is measured to be 2.6×10^{-8} s (when at rest). This particle travels a distance of 20 m in the laboratory just before decaying. Calculate its speed.

30 In frame S two light signals are emitted from the same point in space 2.0 μs apart. In frame S' the time between the emissions is measured to be 8.0 μs.

a What is the speed of S' relative to S?

b How far apart are the emission points according to S'?

31 A rocket approaches a space station. The rocket moves with velocity $0.80c$ relative to the space station. Two lights at the ends of the space station turn on at the same time according to space station observers. Which light turns on first according to rocket observers?

32 Two simultaneous events in frame S are separated by a distance $\Delta x = x_2 - x_1 = 1200$ m. Determine the time separating these two events in frame S', stating which one occurs first. S' moves past S with velocity $0.80c$.

33 A spacecraft leaves earth moving away at speed $0.60c$ relative to earth. Mandy, an astronaut, has her birthday that day. In a year's time (according to spacecraft clocks) she will have her birthday again. Her friends on earth want to celebrate by sending her a light signal. When, by earth clocks, should the light signal be sent so that it arrives at the spacecraft on Mandy's birthday?

6.3 Spacetime diagrams

We now introduce a pictorial representation of relativistic phenomena, first introduced into physics by one of Einstein's friends, H. Minkowski.

Spacetime diagrams

In Chapter 1 we saw lots of motion graphs. In particular we saw graphs of position (vertical axis) versus time (horizontal axis). In relativity it is customary to show these graphs with the axes reversed, i.e. time is plotted on the vertical axis and position on the horizontal. These are called **spacetime diagrams** (sometimes called Minkowski diagrams). For reasons we will see shortly, it is convenient to instead plot ct on the vertical axis rather than time itself. The vertical axis then also has units of length. Since the speed of light is a constant everyone agrees on, knowing the value of ct allows us to find the value of t.

Figure 6.22a shows a spacetime diagram and an event (marked by the dot). The space and time co-ordinates of the event are read from the graph in the usual way: we draw lines through the dot parallel to the axes and see where the lines intersect the axes. This event has $x = 5.0$ m and $ct = 6.0$ m giving $t = \frac{6.0}{3.0 \times 10^8} = 2.0 \times 10^{-8}$ s.

Now consider a particle that is at rest at position $x = a$, Figure 6.22b. As time goes by we may think of a sequence of events showing the position of the particle (which does not change) at different times. This sequence of events traces the blue straight line on the spacetime diagram. This is called the **worldline** of the particle. Another particle that starts from $x = 0$ at $t = 0$ and moves with constant positive velocity would have a worldline as shown in red. From the diagram:

$$\tan\theta = \frac{x}{ct} = \frac{v}{c}$$

The tangent of the angle between the worldline and the ct axis gives the speed divided by the speed of light.

This is why it is convenient to plot ct on the vertical axis: a photon moves at speed c, and so it makes an angle of $\theta = \tan^{-1}\frac{c}{c} = 45°$ to both axes. Since nothing can exceed c, the worldline of any particle will always make an angle less than 45° with the ct axis. In Figure 6.23a, the red worldline represents a particle moving to the right. The green worldline belongs to a particle moving to the left. The blue worldline is impossible since it involves a speed greater than c. Figure 6.23b shows an event E at $x = 0$ and $ct = 0$. The region coloured yellow consists of all events that can be influenced by event E. For example, E could be an explosion. We see the glass of a window shatter later on, event L. Could the event E be responsible for L?

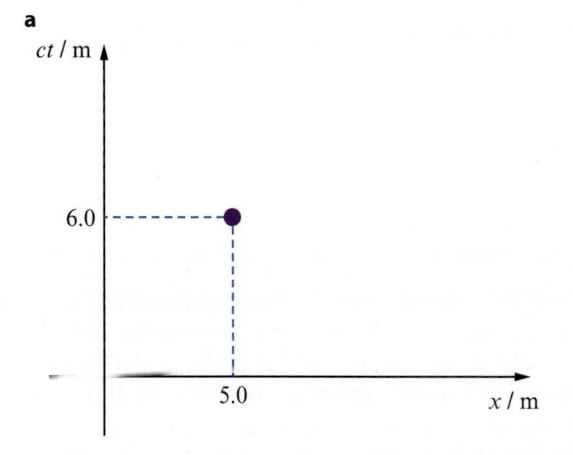

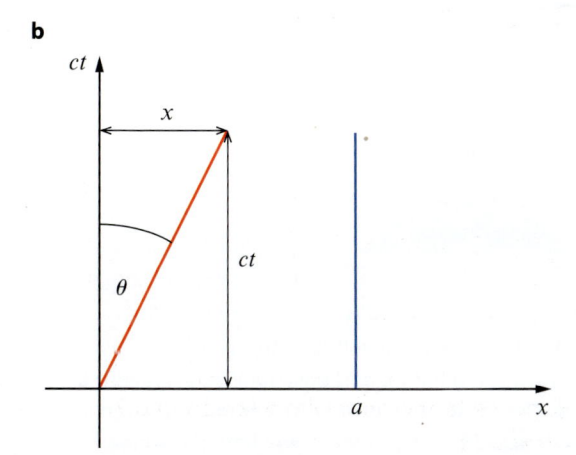

Figure 6.22: a The space and time co-ordinates of an event: $x = 5.0$ m and $ct = 6.0$ m. **b** The worldline of a particle at rest is the sequence of events showing the position of the particle at different times (blue line). A particle moving to the right has a worldline shown by the red line.

The answer is that it could if L is in the yellow region but could not if L is outside this region. The fastest a signal can travel is at the speed of light so any signal from E to L has to be within the yellow region. Similarly, events that could have influenced E are within the region coloured blue.

> **EXAM TIP**
>
> An event E can be the cause of an event L if the time separating E and L is greater than or equal to the travel time of a photon from the position of E to that of L.

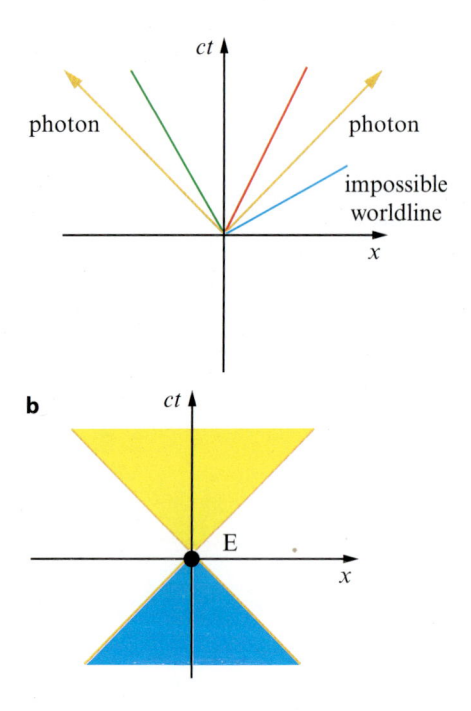

Figure 6.23: a Various worldlines. The one in blue is impossible because it corresponds to a particle moving faster than light. b Future and past light-cones. Event E could be the cause of an event if the time separation is greater or equal to the photon travel time. This means the events E could cause lie in the yellow region.

To proceed we need a small digression. In mathematics we are used to working with axes that are at right angles to each other, Figure 6.24a. But they don't have to be. The axes could be slanted, Figure 6.24b. To find the co-ordinates of a point on a diagram with slanted axes we simply draw lines parallel to the axes and see where they intersect the axes.

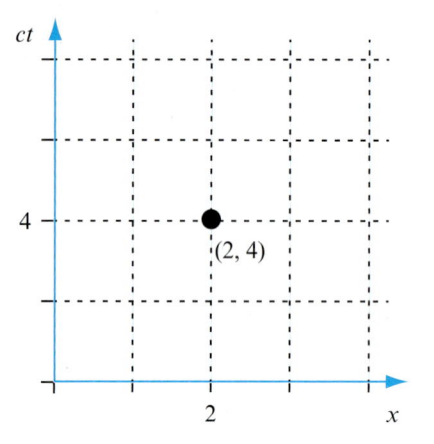

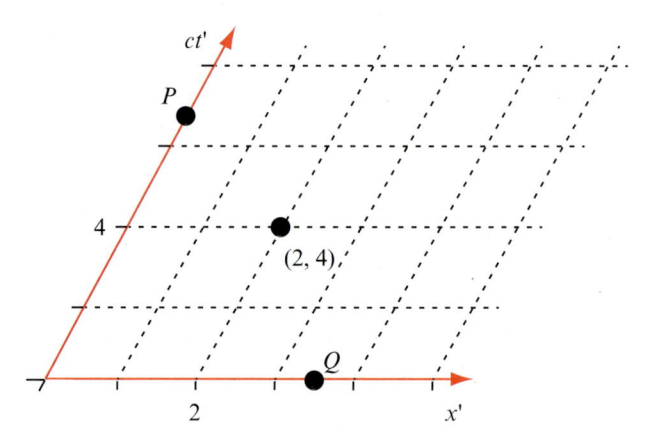

Figure 6.24: To find the co-ordinates of a point we draw lines from the point parallel to the axes and see where these lines intersect the axes.

Convince yourself that the x co-ordinate of point P and the ct co-ordinate of point Q in Figure 6.24 are both zero.

Now consider a second inertial reference frame that moves to the right with speed v. Let us assume that when clocks in both frames show zero the origins of the frames coincide. The origin of frame S' moves to the right with speed v. Therefore, the worldline of the origin of S' will make an angle $\theta = \tan^{-1}\frac{v}{c}$ with the ct axis of S. But this worldline is just the collection of all events with $x' = 0$ and so is the time axis of the frame S'. Where is the space axis? It has to make the same angle θ with the x-axis,

Figure 6.25. To see why, consider a photon emitted at the origin (yellow worldline). In the frame S' the distance travelled is L and the time taken is $ct' = L \Rightarrow t' = \frac{L}{c}$. So the speed of light in S' is $\frac{L}{t'} = c$ which is precisely what we want: the speed of light must be the same in all inertial frames. Hence the axes must be slanted as the red axes in Figure 6.25.

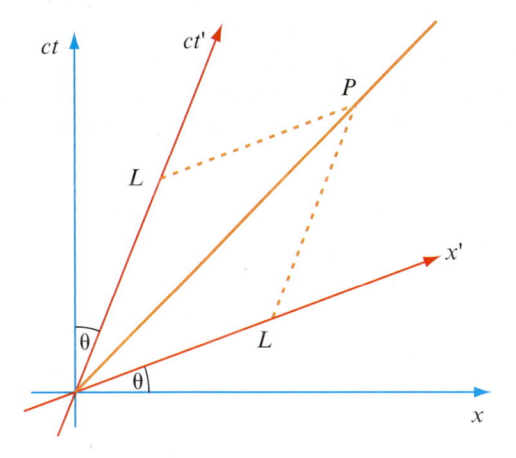

Figure 6.25: Two frames in relative velocity on the same spacetime diagram. The red axes represent a frame moving to the right.

WORKED EXAMPLE 6.12

Use the spacetime diagram in Figure 6.26 to estimate the speed of frame S' relative to frame S.

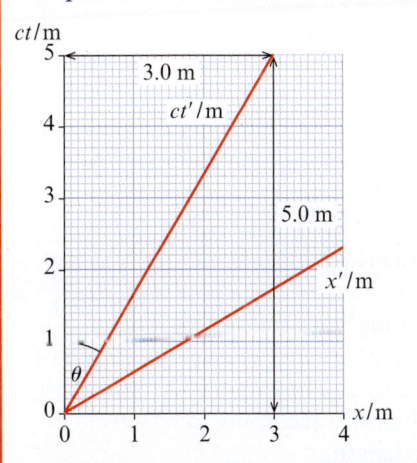

Figure 6.26: For worked example 6.12.

Answer

The tangent of the angle θ is $\tan\theta = \frac{3.0}{5.0} = 0.60$ and so $\frac{v}{c} = 0.60 \Rightarrow v = 0.60c$.

Finding the scale on the primed axes

The diagram in Figure 6.27 shows the axes of a frame S, and the red axes are the axes of a frame S' that moves with speed $0.60c$ relative to S. The important thing to notice about the red axes is that they have a different scale than those of the black axes! In other words we cannot use our ruler to find out how long a unit is on the x axis and then lay the ruler on the x' axis in order to find a length of 1. So where is the 1 on the x' axis and where is the 1 on the ct' axis?

On the x' axis we have a point with co-ordinates $x' = 1$ and $ct' = 0$. In the S frame this point has a co-ordinate that we can find using a Lorentz transformation (the gamma factor for a speed of $0.60c$ is 1.25):

$x = \gamma(x' + vt')$
$ = \gamma(1 - 0)$
$ = 1.25$

Similarly, to find the point with co-ordinates $ct' = 1$ and $x' = 0$ we use

$ct = \gamma(ct' + vcx')$
$ = \gamma(1 - 0)$
$ = 1.25$

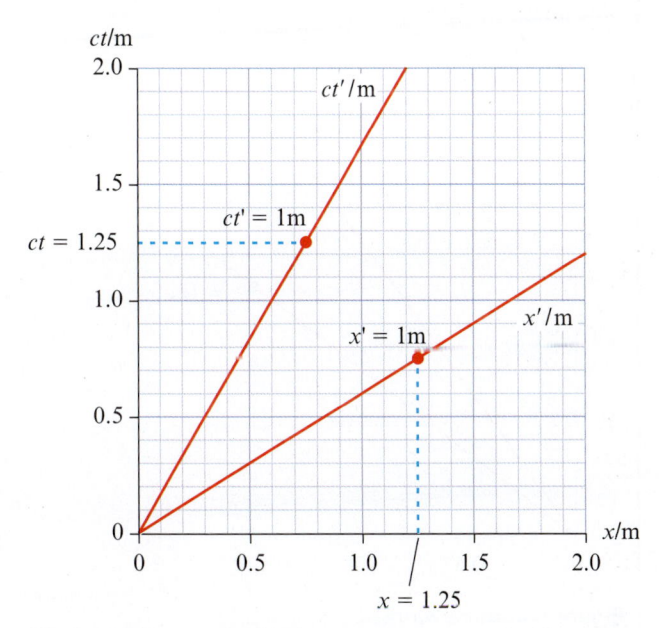

Figure 6.27

PHYSICS FOR THE IB DIPLOMA: COURSEBOOK

> **WORKED EXAMPLE 6.13**

Find the scale on the red axes in Figure 6.28a.

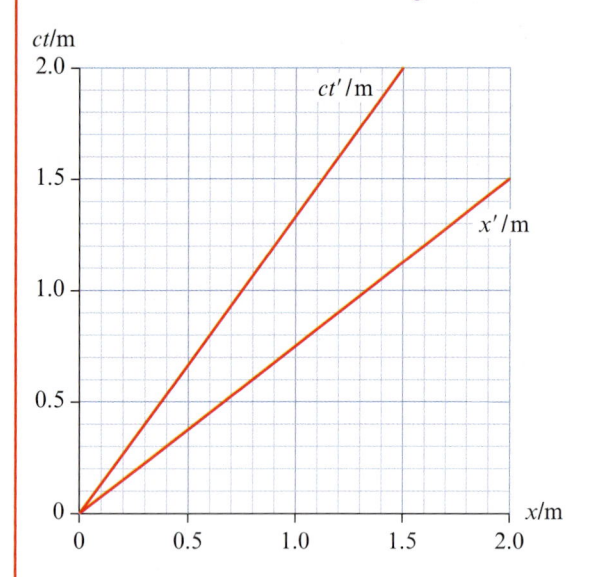

Figure 6.28a: The scale on the primed axes is different from that on the unprimed axes.

Answer

The speed of the red frame is about $0.75c$.
The gamma factor is then $\dfrac{1}{\sqrt{1 - 0.75^2}} \approx 1.5$. Where the blue lines intersect the red axes is where the '1' is.

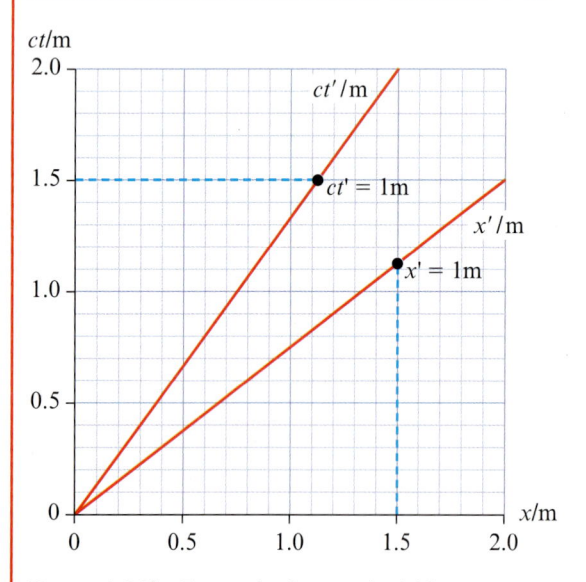

Figure 6.28b: For worked example 6.13.

Length contraction and spacetime diagrams

Spacetime diagrams show length contraction in a very clear and direct way. Imagine a rod of proper length 1 m at rest in the S' frame. This frame moves away from a frame S with some speed v. We expect that the observers in S will measure a length for the rod that will be less than 1 m. The left end of the rod is at $x' = 0$ and the other end is at $x' = 1$ m. The worldlines of the ends of the rod are shown in Figure 6.29 (red line for the left end, blue line for the right end).

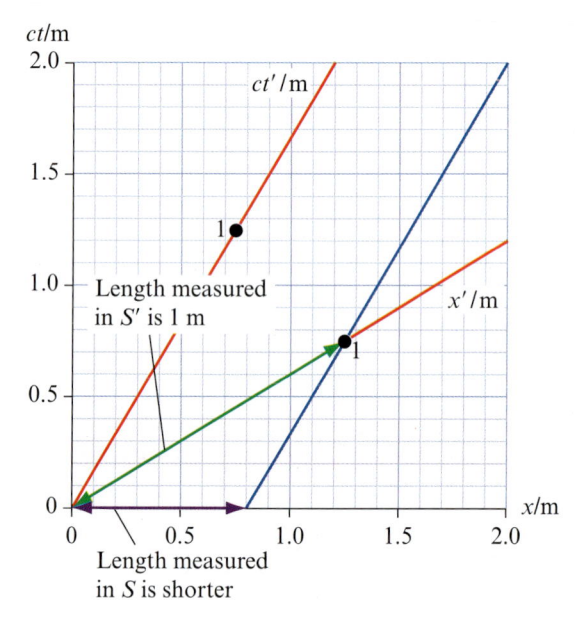

Figure 6.29: Rod at rest in S'. The observers in S' measure a length of 1 m for the rod. The blue line is the worldline of the right end of the rod. The observers in S measure a shorter length.

The worldlines of the two ends intersect the x axis at 0 and 0.8 m. These two intersection points represent the positions of the moving rod's ends *at the same time* in frame S. Their difference therefore gives the length of the rod as measured by S. The length is 0.8 m, less than 1 m. The rod which moves according to observers in S has contracted in length.

What if we had a rod of proper length 1 m at rest in the S frame which was viewed by observers in the S' frame, Figure 6.30?

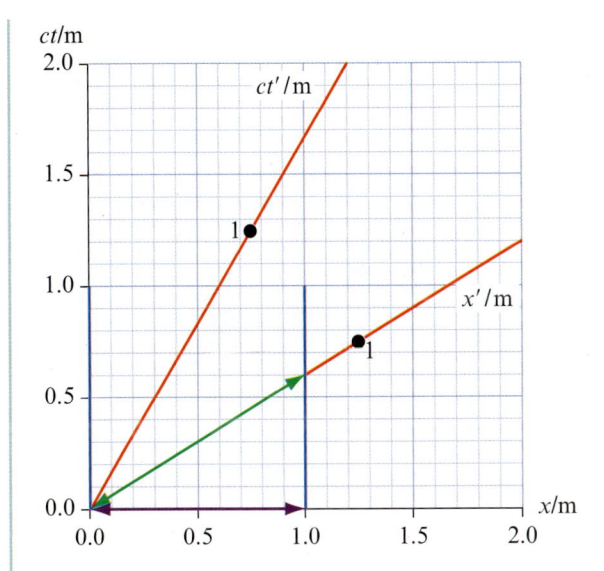

Figure 6.30: Rod at rest in S. The observers in S measure a length of 1 m for the rod. The blue lines are the worldlines of the ends of the rod. The observers in S' measure a shorter length.

> **EXAM TIP**
>
> If the rod is moving its length must be measured when the position of its ends are recorded at the same time.
>
> It is only lengths in the direction of the velocity that are contracted.

The two blue lines represent the worldlines of the ends of the rod. The worldlines of the two ends intersect the x' axis at 0 and 0.8 m. These two intersection points represent the positions of the rod's ends *at the same time* in frame S'. Their difference therefore gives the length of the rod as measured by S'. The length is 0.8 m, less than 1 m.

> **EXAM TIP**
>
> Do not be led astray by your knowledge of Euclidean geometry! The length in S' 'looks' longer. But it isn't. The scale on the two axes is not the same!

Time dilation and spacetime diagrams

Spacetime diagrams also show the phenomenon of time dilation very clearly. Figure 6.31 shows a spacetime diagram showing the standard frames S and S'. A clock at rest in the origin of S' ticks at O and then again at P. The duration of the tick is $ct' = 1$. What is the duration of the tick according to frame S? We have to draw a line parallel to the x axis through P. This intersects the S time axis at point Q. This interval is greater than 1.

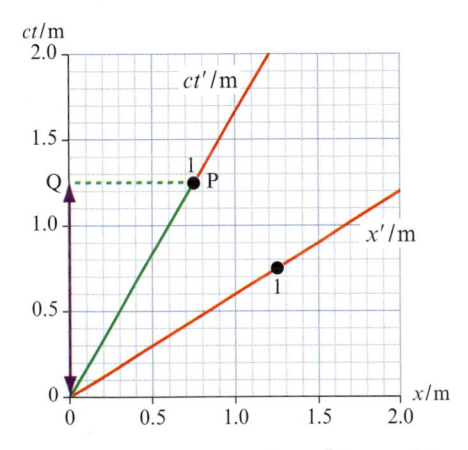

Figure 6.31: The green line is the worldline of a clock at rest in frame S'. This clock shows $ct' = 1$ at P.

Similarly, Figure 6.32 can be used to analyze a clock at rest at the origin of frame S. It ticks at O and then at P. The duration of the tick is such that $ct = 1$. From P we draw a line parallel to the axis x'. The line intersects the ct' axis at Q. The interval OQ is longer than 1.

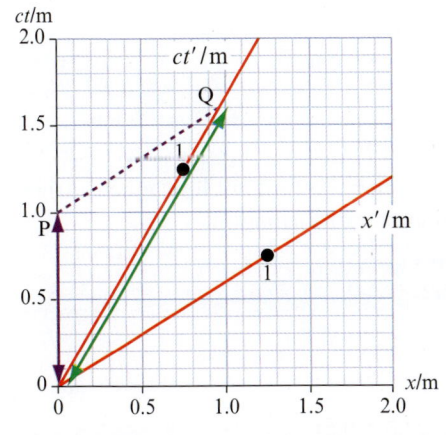

Figure 6.32: This clock shows $ct = 1$ at P.

PHYSICS FOR THE IB DIPLOMA: COURSEBOOK

> **EXAM TIP**
>
> Do not be led astray by your knowledge of Euclidean geometry! In triangle OPQ the hypotenuse is the side OP, and so it should have been the longest side of the triangle. But the geometry of spacetime diagrams is not Euclidean! The Pythagorean theorem does not hold.

Simultaneity and spacetime diagrams

Simultaneity is easy to see on spacetime diagrams. In Figure 6.33 events A and B are clearly simultaneous in frame S ($ct = 1.2$ for both).

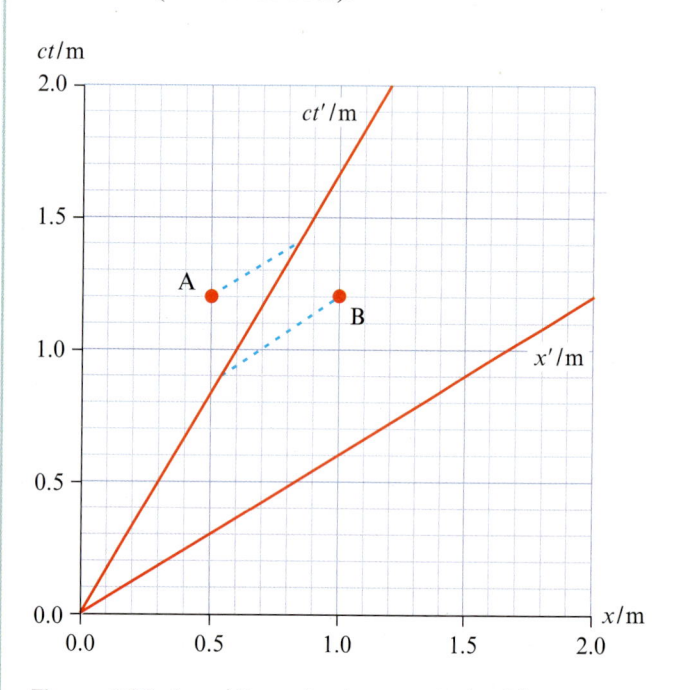

Figure 6.33: A and B are simultaneous in the S frame.

In frame S', B occurs first. To find out how much earlier B occurs use a Lorentz transformation:

$\Delta x = 1.0 - 0.5 = 0.5$ m and $\Delta t = 0$. So

$c\Delta t' = c(t'_B - t'_A)$

$\qquad = \gamma(c\Delta t - \frac{v\Delta x}{c})$

$\qquad = 1.25 \times (0 - 0.60 \times 0.5)$

$\qquad = -0.38$ m

The negative sign indicates B occurs earlier as we see from the diagram.

> **CHECK YOURSELF 6**
>
> A rocket moves past the ground. Two trees are hit by lightning the instant the rocket is halfway between the trees. The strikes happen at the same time as far the rocket is concerned. (See Figure 6.34.) 
>
> **Figure 6.34:** For check yourself question 6.
>
> Use a spacetime diagram to determine which tree is hit first according to the ground.
>
> Does light from the two strikes reach the rocket at the same time?

> **WORKED EXAMPLE 6.14**
>
> The spacetime diagram in Figure 6.35 shows a number of events. List the events from earliest to latest in each frame. 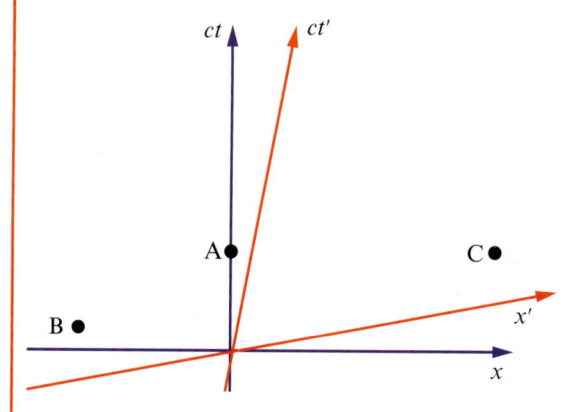
>
> **Figure 6.35:** For worked example 6.14.
>
> **Answer**
>
> In S (blue frame) events A and C are simultaneous and occur after event B. (A and C are on the same line parallel to the x axis).
>
> In S' (red frame) events B and C are simultaneous and occur before event A. (B and C are on the same line parallel to the x' axis).

6 Relativity

WORKED EXAMPLE 6.15

A spacecraft is moving away from earth at speed $0.60c$. At $ct = 0$, just as the spacecraft begins to move, a flash of light leaves a space station which is at rest 4.0 ly from earth, according to earth. Using a spacetime diagram, estimate the time the flash of light arrives at the spacecraft according to **a** earth and **b** the spacecraft.

Answer

We must draw the worldline of a photon leaving the position $x = 4.0$ ly and see where it intersects the worldline of the spacecraft. This is a time of $ct = 2.5$ ly for earth. To estimate the time for the spacecraft we must find the scale on the worldline of the spacecraft (red line). The gamma factor is 1.25. This allows us to find the '1' on the worldline of the spacecraft. The photon worldline is at 45° as shown. By measuring on the worldline we find a time of $ct' = 2.0$ ly. This is all shown on the spacetime diagram in Figure 6.36.

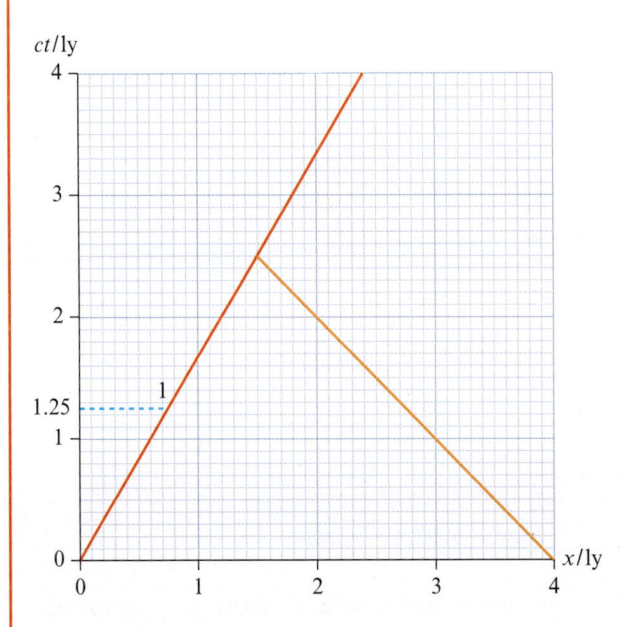

Figure 6.36: For worked example 6.15.

CHECK YOURSELF 7

Verify the conclusion of worked example 6.15 using Lorentz transformations.

WORKED EXAMPLE 6.16

Two stars, A at position −3 ly and B at position +3 ly, both explode at $ct = 0$. A spacecraft moving at velocity $+0.60c$ is at $x = 0$ when $ct = 0$. Use a spacetime diagram to determine **a** which star exploded first according to the spacecraft observers and **b** from which star explosion light reaches the spacecraft observers first.

Answer

The red lines are the axes of the spacecraft frame, Figure 6.37. By drawing lines through the events representing the explosions parallel to the space axis of the spacecraft and see where they intersect the time axis we see that B occurred first. Photon lines at 45° from A and B show that light from B arrives first.

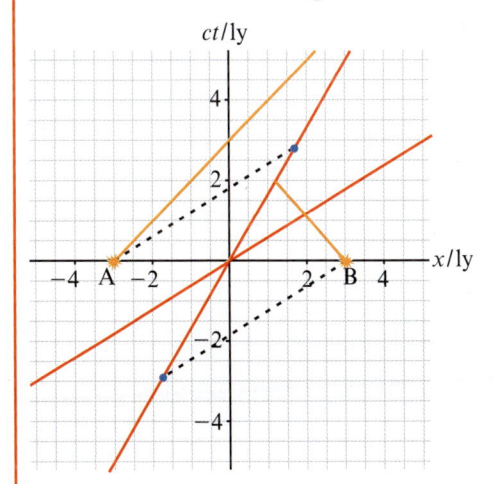

Figure 6.37: For worked example 6.16.

SCIENCE IN CONTEXT

The power of diagrams

Spacetime diagrams offer a simple and pictorial way of understanding relativity. They can be used to unambiguously resolve misunderstandings and 'paradoxes'. Their power lies in their simplicity and their clarity. In physics, the use of diagrams, as well as appropriate notation, in describing situations has always helped understanding. Spacetime diagrams are especially useful in seeing what event can or cannot cause another. Feynman diagrams are another example of this, as is the use of vectors as opposed to components.

149

PHYSICS FOR THE IB DIPLOMA: COURSEBOOK

TEST YOUR UNDERSTANDING

In the questions that follow, the spacetime diagrams represent two inertial frames. The black axes represent frame S. The red axes represent a frame S' that moves past frame S with velocity v.

34 Use the spacetime diagram (Figure 6.38) to calculate the velocity of frame S' relative to S.

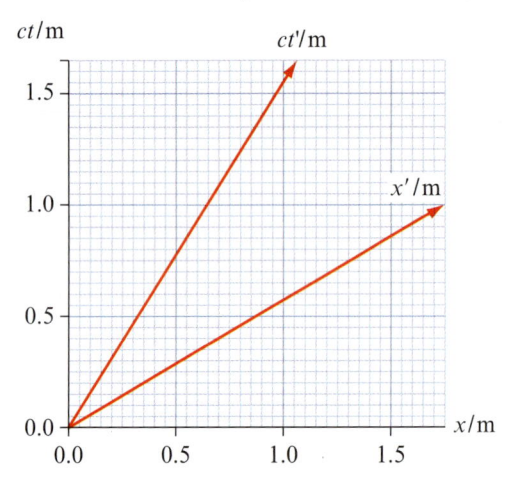

Figure 6.38: For question 34.

35 a On the spacetime diagram in Figure 6.39 draw the worldline of a particle that is:

   i at rest in frame S at $x = 1.0$ m.

   ii moving with velocity $-0.40\,c$ as measured in S and is at $x = 1.0$ m at $t = 0$.

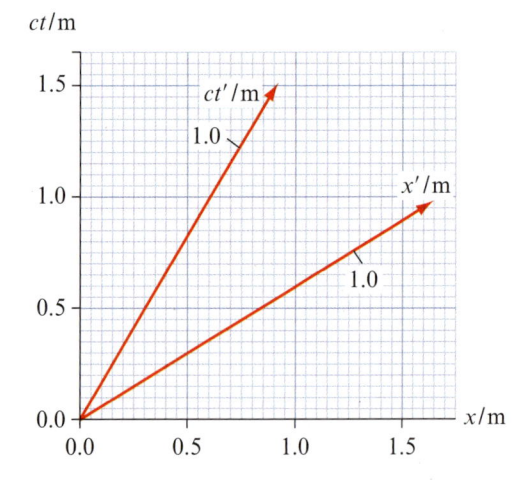

Figure 6.39: For question 35.

b A photon is emitted from position $x = 1.5$ m at $t = 0$. Use Figure 6.39 to estimate when the photon arrives at the eye of an observer at rest at the origin of frame S' according to:

   i S

   ii S'

36 a S' represents an alien attack cruise ship. Use the diagram in Figure 6.40 to determine the speed of the cruise ship relative to S.

b At $t = 0$, a laser beam moving at the speed of light is launched from $x = 2$ ly towards the cruise ship. By drawing the worldline of the laser beam, estimate the time when the beam hits the cruise ship according to:

   i S

   ii S'.

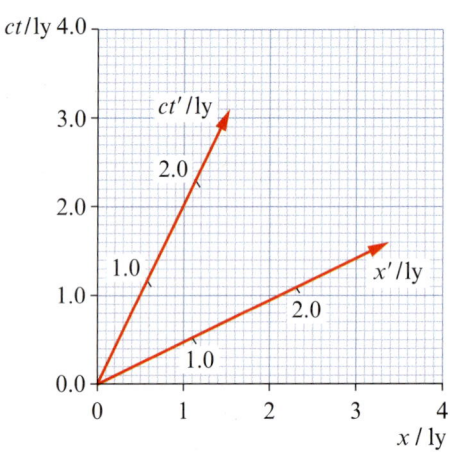

Figure 6.40: For question 36.

37 The diagram in Figure 6.41 shows two lamps at $x = \pm 0.5$ m that turn on at time zero in frame S.

CONTINUED

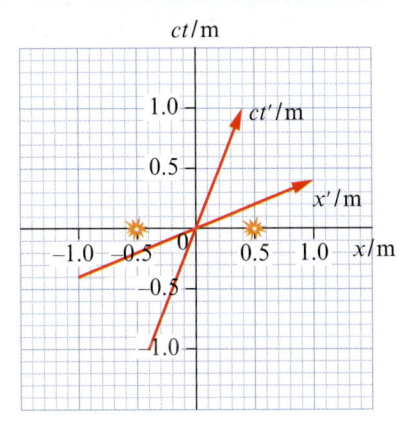

Figure 6.41: For question 37.

a Determine which lamp turns on first in frame S'.

b Draw the worldlines of the photons emitted from the two lamps towards an observer at rest at the origin of S'.

c State the lamp whose light reaches an observer at the origin of frame S' first.

38 a Look at Figure 6.42. The dashed blue line is parallel to the primed time axis and intersects the primed x axis at P. The S' frame moves with speed v relative to S. Find v and, by using Lorentz transformations, find the co-ordinates of P in the S' frame. Hence label the event with co-ordinates $x' = 1$, $ct' = 0$.

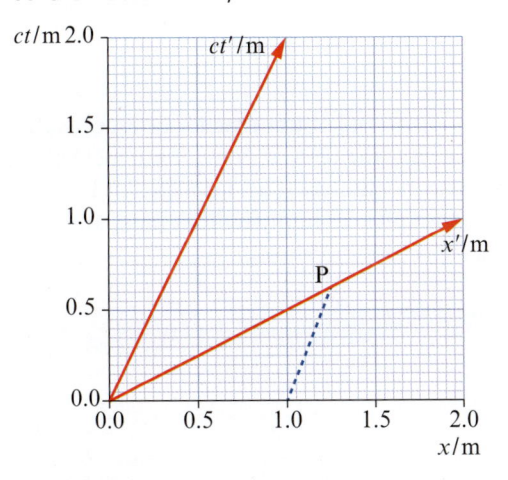

Figure 6.42: For question 38.

b Repeat part **a** where now the speed v is arbitrary to find the space co-ordinate of P. Express your answer in terms of the gamma factor.

39 By any suitable method, locate the events $(x' = 1\text{ m}, ct' = 0)$ and $(x' = 0, ct' = 1\text{ m})$ on the spacetime diagram in Figure 6.43.

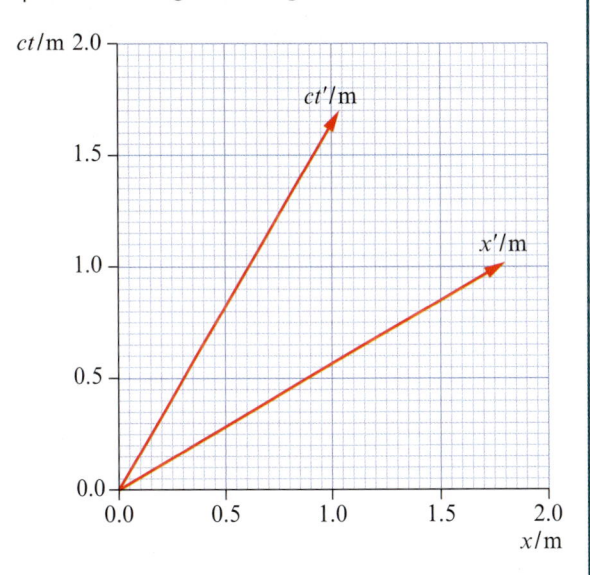

Figure 6.43: For question 39.

40 The purple line in the diagram in Figure 6.44 represents a rod of length 1.0 m at $t = 0$ as measured in the S frame.

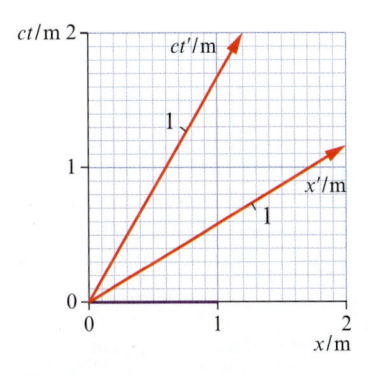

Figure 6.44: For question 40.

151

CONTINUED

a By drawing appropriate lines, show that the length of the rod measured in frame S' is less than 1 m.

b i Draw a line to represent a rod of length 1.0 m as measured in the S' frame.

   ii By drawing appropriate lines, show that the length of the rod measured in frame S is less than 1 m.

41 A clock is at rest at the origin of frame S' as shown in Figure 6.45. Its first tick occurs at $ct' = 0$. The second tick of the clock occurs at $ct' = 1$ m as measured in S'.

a Mark these events on the spacetime diagram.

b By drawing appropriate lines estimate the time in between ticks as measured in S.

42 A rocket leaves earth at speed 0.80 c on its way to a planet a distance 20 ly as measured by earth. When the rocket gets to the planet it sends a light signal to earth.

a When does the signal get to earth according to (i) earth and (ii) rocket?

b Illustrate your answers with a spacetime diagram.

c At $t = 0$, another rocket leaves the planet returning to earth with speed 0.80 c relative to earth. As the rocket sets out it sends a light signal to earth. When does the light signal arrive at earth according to (i) earth and (ii) rocket clocks?

d Illustrate your answers on a spacetime diagram.

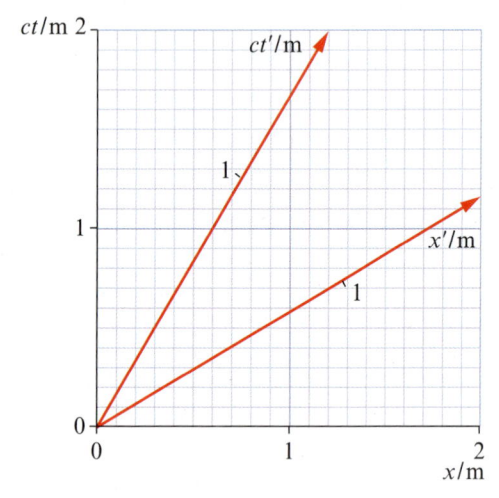

Figure 6.45: For question 41.

Links

The formulas of special relativity make no sense when the speed of a material object reaches or exceeds the speed of light. This implies that the speed of light is a limiting speed. But the laws of Newtonian mechanics say that as long as we provide energy to a body, its speed will increase indefinitely. This implies that the laws of Newtonian mechanics also need to be modified! This has serious consequences implying that mass and energy are equivalent and can be converted into each other—see Unit E.

6 Relativity

SELF-ASSESSMENT CHECKLIST

I am able to …	Section	Not yet	Nearly there	Ready to move on
understand the term *reference frame*	6.1			
work with the Galilean transformation equations	6.1			
recite the postulates of the special theory of relativity	6.1			
appreciate the constancy of the speed of light	6.1			
apply the Lorentz transformation equations	6.1			
understand the effects of time dilation and length contraction	6.2			
apply the relativistic velocity addition formula	6.2			
describe how muon decay experiments provide evidence for relativity	6.2			
understand the spacetime interval	6.3			
work with spacetime diagrams	6.3			
describe various events through spacetime diagrams	6.3			

REFLECTION

Do you understand what an *inertial reference frame* is and can you identify one? Do you understand the *postulates of relativity*? Can you apply the *Lorentz transformation* formulas? Do you understand the concepts of *time dilation* and *length contraction*? Do you understand how *muon decay* experiments provide evidence for relativity? Can you find the speed of an object from its worldline on a spacetime diagram? Can you explain time dilation using a spacetime diagram? Can you explain length contraction using a spacetime diagram?

EXAM-STYLE QUESTIONS

You can find questions in the style of IB exams in the digital coursebook.

CHECK YOURSELF ANSWERS

1. B and C because there is no acceleration.

2. 9 m s⁻¹ due south.

3. No, we have to subtract the time it took light to get to the observer.

4. If A and B are separated by a distance Δx, the time it would take the photon to get to B would be $\frac{\Delta x}{c}$. The spacetime interval is then $c^2(\Delta t)^2 - (\Delta x)^2 = c^2 \frac{(\Delta x)^2}{c^2} - (\Delta x)^2 = 0$.

5. a Yes b Yes c No

6. The spacetime diagram in Figure 6.47 shows that the left tree was hit first. Photon lines from the strikes arrive at the rocket at the same time.

7. In frame S the light will reach the spacecraft in a time t given by $0.6ct + ct = 4 \Rightarrow ct = 2.5$ ly when the spacecraft is at $x = 0.6c \times \frac{2.5}{c} = 1.5$ ly. The gamma factor is 1.25 and so $ct' = 1.25 \times (2.5 - \frac{0.6c}{c} \times 1.5) = 2.0$ ly.

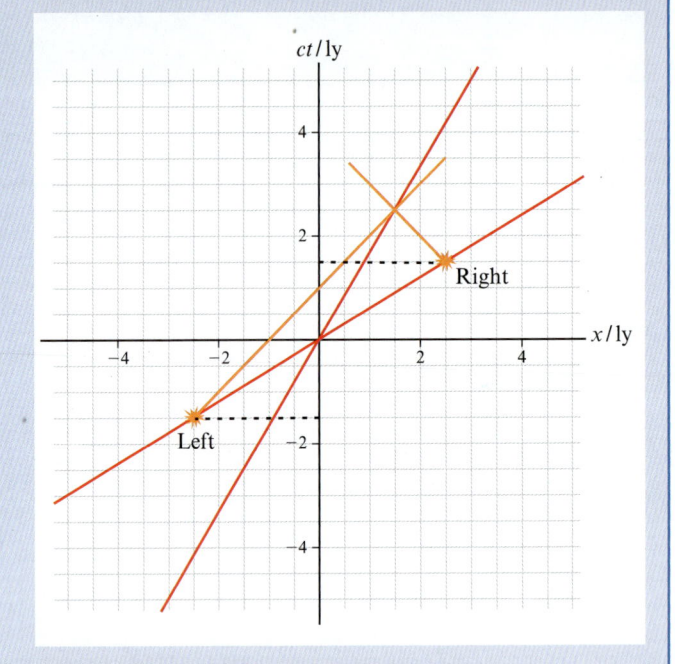

Figure 6.47: For check yourself question 6.

Unit B
The particulate nature of matter

INTRODUCTION

There is no better way to introduce this Unit than with a statement by Richard Feynman: "If, in some cataclysm, all of scientific knowledge were to be destroyed, and only one sentence passed on to the next generation of creatures, what statement would contain the most information in the fewest words? I believe it is the atomic hypothesis that *all things are made of atoms—little particles that move around in perpetual motion, attracting each other when they are a little distance apart, but repelling upon being squeezed into one another.* In that one sentence, you will see, there is an enormous amount of information about the world, if just a little imagination and thinking are applied."

As we will see, the particle model of matter will help us understand the differences between solids, liquids and gases and how phase changes occur. For a gas we will be able to relate the microscopic concept of particles into macroscopic properties such as pressure, volume and temperature and see how each of these quantities is related to particle behaviour at the microscopic level. We will also see the effect of heating on a body and the ways in which heat can be transferred from one place to another. These are topics of great practical importance; life on earth is sustained because we receive radiation from the sun.

By studying thermodynamics we will discover an astonishing limitation to how much thermal energy can be converted into mechanical work and how this is related to a special law of Physics, the second law of thermodynamics and entropy. Finally, the particle model of matter, now applied mainly to electrons allows the study of electricity and the structure of electric circuits.

Chapter 7
Thermal energy transfers

LEARNING OBJECTIVES

In this chapter you will learn how to:

- describe solids, liquids and gases in terms of atoms and molecules
- use the concept of temperature and the relation of absolute temperature to the average kinetic energy of molecules
- use the concept of internal energy
- solve problems in calorimetry using the specific heat capacities
- describe phase change and how perform calculations using the concept of specific latent heat
- describe ways by which thermal energy gets transferred from place to place
- apply the Stefan–Boltzmann and Wien laws

7 Thermal energy transfers

> **GUIDING QUESTION**
>
> What is the connection between temperature (a macroscopic concept) and the average random kinetic energy of molecules (a microscopic concept)?

Introduction

The main topic of this chapter is how thermal energy (heat) is transferred from one place to another. It also deals with what happens to a body when that body absorbs or loses thermal energy. To do this we will need to define the basic concepts of temperature, internal energy and thermal energy.

We will discuss the concept of thermal equilibrium, phase changes and basic calorimetry problems. We will pay particular attention to radiation (one of the methods of thermal energy transfer).

7.1 Particles, temperature and energy

Particles

As we look closer at matter, we discover ever-smaller structures. We find that compounds are made out of molecules, molecules are made out of atoms and atoms contain nuclei and electrons. Nuclei, in turn, contain protons and neutrons. Today it is believed that electrons do not have any substructure, but the nucleons (that is, protons and neutrons) are known to be made out of quarks. It is not known if the quarks themselves are made out of smaller particles. In thermal physics we are mostly interested in molecules, atoms and electrons – we do not need to consider any smaller structures.

In this course we will be interested in the vapour (gas), liquid and solid **states of matter**, Figure 7.1. (There are other exotic states of matter which we will not discuss in this course.)

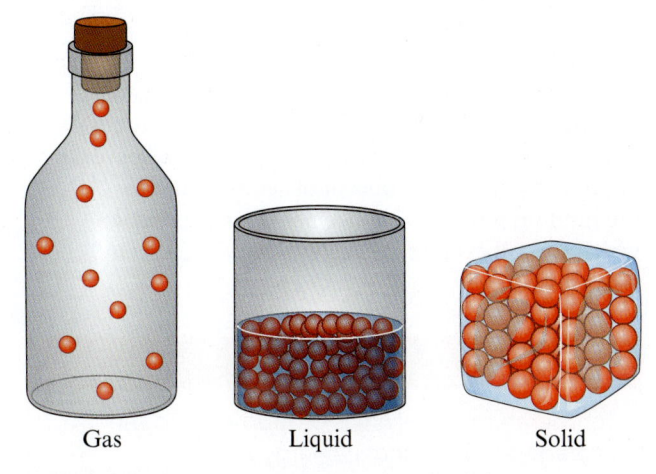

Figure 7.1: The vapour (gas), liquid and solid states of matter.

There are strong forces between particles in a solid which explains, for example, why it is difficult to break a solid apart. In liquids, the forces between the particles are weaker so particles are able to move around each other; this explains why a liquid flows and will take the shape of the container in which it is placed. However, the forces between particles in a liquid are sufficiently strong that the particles cannot move far from each other. Like solids, liquids are very nearly incompressible which suggests that the distances between the particles are similar to those in solids. In gases the forces between particles are very weak so they are essentially negligible. The only time significant forces exist between the particles is during collisions. Gases are very compressible, which is evidence that the distances between particles are large. Typically, distances between particles in gases are 10 times larger than those in solids and liquids.

This means that solids, liquids and gases also differ in density. Density, ρ, is the ratio of mass to volume $\left(\rho = \frac{M}{V}\right)$ and is measured in kg m^{-3}. Solid iron has a density of 7.8×10^3 kg m^{-3} whereas liquid iron has a density that is somewhat less, 6.9×10^3 kg m^{-3}. Gases have a much lower density: air, for example, has a density of 1.2 kg m^{-3} (but this depends on pressure and temperature as we will see). So solid and liquid densities are comparable, but gas densities are about 1000 times smaller.

Temperature

We have an intuitive concept of **temperature** as the 'coldness' or 'hotness' of a body, but it wasn't until the nineteenth century that one of the greatest discoveries in physics related the concept of temperature to the random motion of molecules. This connection, which we will explore in greater detail in Chapter 9, is expressed as:

> **KEY POINT**
>
> Temperature (in kelvin) is proportional to the average random kinetic energy of the molecules, $\bar{E}_K$.

In equation form:

$$\bar{E}_K = \frac{3}{2} k_B T$$

In this equation $k_B = 1.38 \times 10^{-23}$ J K^{-1} is a new constant in physics called the Boltzmann constant. We will work with this constant extensively in Chapter 9.

This direct proportionality between temperature and the average random kinetic energy is only true for the absolute or kelvin temperature scale. In this scale, zero is the lowest possible temperature, the **absolute zero** of temperature. Since the lowest possible value of kinetic energy is zero the lowest possible value of temperature must also be zero as $\bar{E}_K$ and T are proportional.

Many other temperature scales exist. In 1742, Anders Celsius (1701–1744) created the temperature scale that is still commonly used today and is known by his name. On the Celsius scale a value of zero degrees is assigned to the freezing point of water and a value of 100 degrees is assigned to the boiling point of water. The connection between the Celsius and Kelvin scales is:

T (in kelvin, K) = T (in degrees Celsius, °C) + 273

The lowest possible temperature on the absolute scale is zero kelvin, 0 K. On the Celsius scale the lowest possible temperature is, therefore, −273 °C.

Temperature has varied a lot in the life of the universe: at the time of the Big Bang, some 13.8 billion years ago, the temperature of the universe was about 10^{32} K. The universe has been expanding ever since, and so the temperature has been dropping. In the emptiness of space, far from stars and galaxies, its value today is only 2.7 K, Figure 7.2.

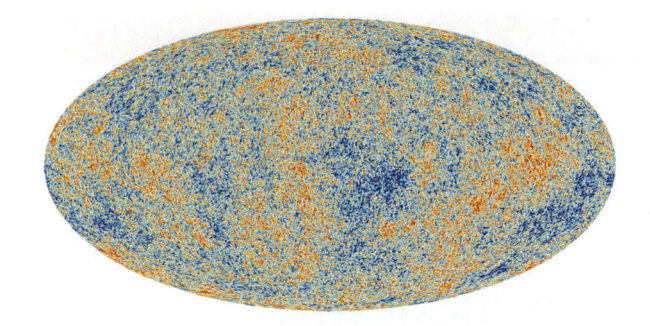

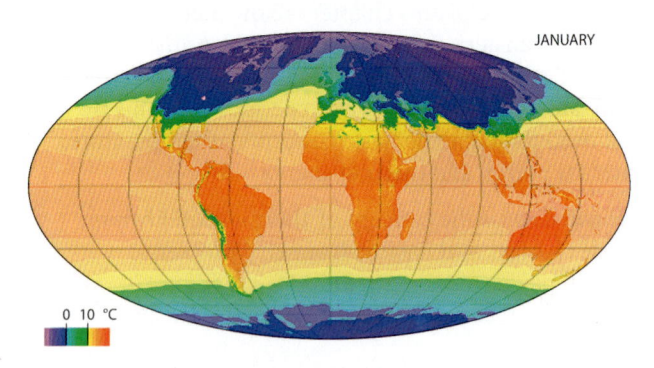

Figure 7.2: The top image shows the variation of temperature in the entire observable universe. Different colours represent tiny fluctuations about the average temperature of 2.7 K. On an entirely different scale, the lower image shows variations of the average surface temperature of the earth in January for the period 1961–1990.

> **EXAM TIP**
>
> The magnitude of a kelvin is the same as that of a degree Celsius.

The need to agree on internationally accepted units, among them those for temperature, is a good example of international collaboration to establish international systems of measurement.

> **CHECK YOURSELF 1**
>
> a What is 300 K in degrees Celsius?
>
> b What is −150 degrees Celsius in kelvin?

7 Thermal energy transfers

> **WORKED EXAMPLE 7.1**
>
> The temperature of a body increases from 320 K to 340 K. State the temperature increase in degrees Celsius.
>
> **Answer**
>
> The temperature increase in kelvin is 340 − 320 = 20 K.
>
> Since the magnitude of a kelvin is the same as that of a degree Celsius, the temperature increase is 20 °C.
>
> (Another way to look at this is to convert both temperatures to kelvin. 320 K corresponds to 320 − 273 = 47 °C and 340 K corresponds to 340 − 273 = 67 °C, giving a change of 20 °C.)

Thermal energy (heat)

When two bodies are in contact and have different temperatures, there will be a transfer of thermal energy from the hotter to the colder body. So, when a glass of cold water is placed in a warm room, thermal energy transfers from the room into the colder water until the temperature of the water becomes equal to that of its surroundings; thermal equilibrium has been reached. We say that the colder body has been 'heated'.

In other words, thermal energy is the energy that gets transferred from one body to another as a result of a temperature difference. The term heat is also used.

Internal energy

We know that there are forces between particles. For gases, these forces are very small—under reasonable conditions (low density) they are almost negligible. But forces between particles are substantial for solids. In a solid the forces between the particles can be modelled by springs joining neighbouring particles, Figure 7.3. The springs represent the bonds between the particles.

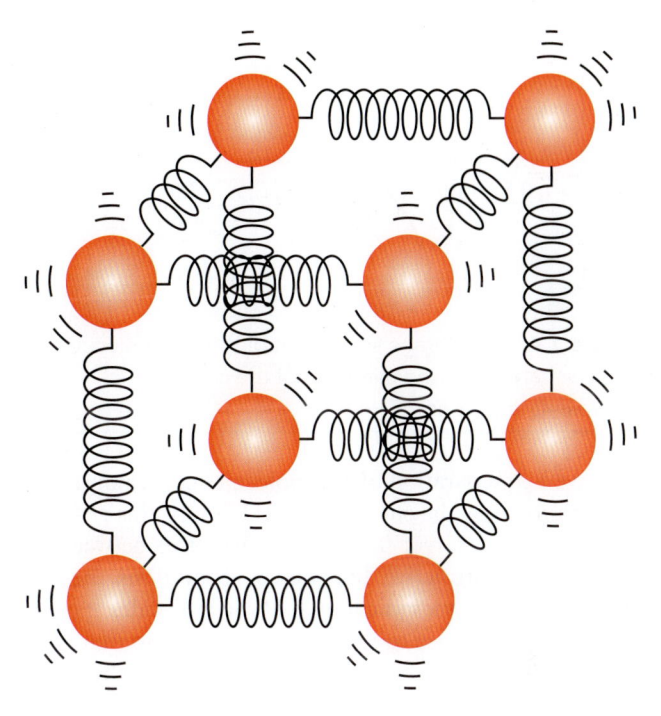

Figure 7.3: Particles in the solid phase oscillate about fixed positions but are not free to move inside the solid.

Just as we need to do work to stretch an ordinary spring (this work increases the elastic potential energy of the spring) we need to do work to increase the separation of the particles in a solid. This work goes into a new form of energy: intermolecular potential energy.

Figure 7.4 shows the intermolecular potential energy E_p of one pair of molecules as a function of the distance r separating the two molecules in a solid.

> **THEORY OF KNOWLEDGE**
>
> Heat was once thought to be a fluid (called 'caloric') that moved from body to body. The more caloric a body contained the hotter it was, and as caloric left a body the body became colder. But you can warm your hands by rubbing them together. If caloric entered your hands it must have come from another body, making it colder. But this does not happen, and so the caloric theory must be false. In the nineteenth century heat was shown to be just another form of energy.

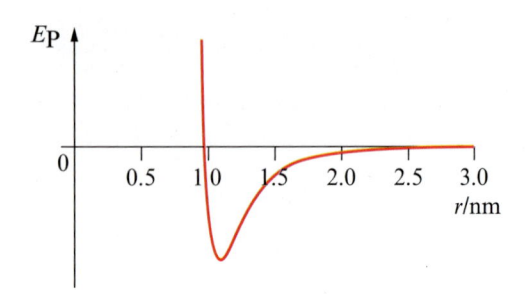

Figure 7.4: The average separation of the two molecules is the separation at the minimum of the curve, i.e. at approximately 1.2 nm.

The average separation of the molecules corresponds to the minimum of the curve, about 1.2 nm for this graph. For separations larger than 1.2 nm the forces between molecules are attractive. For smaller separations, the forces are repulsive, indicating that the molecules cannot get that close to each other. Notice also that this potential energy is negative (for separations larger than 1 nm). For a gas, the potential energy is zero. This means that in going from a solid to a liquid and then a gas, the potential energy increases.

> ### KEY POINT
>
> We define the **internal energy** of a substance as:
>
> the total random kinetic energy of the particles of a substance, plus the total intermolecular potential energy of the particles: U = total random kinetic energy + total intermolecular potential energy.

> ### CHECK YOURSELF 2
>
> Two identical containers are filled with the same quantity of gas at the same pressure and temperature. One container is at rest in a laboratory, and the other is on board a fast aircraft. A student says that the internal energy of the gas in the container on the aircraft is larger. Comment on this statement.

Energy transferred from a hot to a cold body increases the internal energy of the cold body (and decreases the internal energy of the hot body by the same amount).

The internal energy of a system can change as a result of thermal energy added or taken out but also as a result of work performed. This connection between internal energy, thermal energy and work will be explored in detail in Chapter 10.

Internal energy, thermal energy and work are three different concepts. What they have in common is that they are all measured in joules. Temperature is a measure of the random kinetic energy of a substance—not its internal energy.

TEST YOUR UNDERSTANDING

1 Explain why molecular motion stops at absolute zero. Calculate the average kinetic energy of molecules kept at 300 K.

2 Helium and neon are kept at the same temperature. How does the average kinetic energy of helium compare with that of neon? Do the molecules of neon move as fast as those of helium?

3 Distinguish between internal energy and heat.

4 A student says that a body at high temperature has more internal energy than a body at a lower temperature. What is wrong with this statement?

5 Metals expand when heated. Based on this fact, state one change to the graph of Figure 7.4 when the temperature increases.

6 Does the density of a block of copper depend on the size of the block? Does it depend on the mass of the block?

7 The density of copper is 8.9×10^3 kg m^{-3} and its molar mass is 64 g mol^{-1}. Estimate the centre-to-centre separation of two copper atoms listing the assumptions you make.

7.2 Specific heat capacity and change of phase
Calorimetry

> **KEY POINT**
>
> We define the **specific heat capacity** c of a body to be the energy required to increase the temperature of a unit mass of the body by one kelvin.

So, to increase the temperature of a body of mass m by ΔT degrees the heat Q required is:

$$Q = mc\Delta T$$

> **EXAM TIP**
>
> The term 'capacity' implies that the body somehow contains a certain amount of thermal energy, just as a water bottle contains water. This is incorrect. Heat is thermal energy 'in transit' that moves from one body into another; it is not energy contained in any one body.

Table 7.1 lists the specific heat capacity of some common substances.

Substance	c / J kg^{-1} K^{-1}
aluminium	900
lead	128
iron	440
copper	385
silver	240
water	4200
ice	2100
ethanol	2430
marble	880

Table 7.1: Specific heat capacities for several substances.

> **CHECK YOURSELF 3**
>
> Two bodies of equal mass are in thermal contact. X has temperature 0 °C and Y 100 °C. X has smaller specific heat capacity than Y. Will the final temperature of the two bodies after equilibrium is reached be less than, equal to or greater than 50 °C?

> **WORKED EXAMPLE 7.2**
>
> A quantity of heat equal to 9800 J is absorbed by a piece of iron of mass 0.50 kg and specific heat capacity 440 J kg^{-1} K^{-1}.
>
> **a** Calculate the temperature increase of the iron.
>
> **b** 9800 J of thermal energy was removed from 0.50 kg of water initially at 48 °C. The specific heat capacity of water is 4200 J kg^{-1} K^{-1}. Calculate the final temperature of the water.
>
> **Answer**
>
> **a** We need to use $Q = mc\Delta T$. This gives:
>
> $9800 = 0.50 \times 440 \times \Delta T$
>
> Solving for the change in temperature gives:
>
> $\Delta T = \frac{9800}{0.50 \times 440} = 44.6 \approx 45\,\text{K}$
>
> (Notice that we do not need to know the initial temperature of the iron to answer this question.)
>
> **b** We use $Q = mc\Delta T$ to get:
>
> $9800 = 0.50 \times 4200 \times \Delta T$
>
> Solving for the change in temperature gives:
>
> $\Delta T = \frac{9800}{0.50 \times 4200} = 4.7 \approx 5\,\text{K}$
>
> So the final temperature of the water is:
>
> $48 - 5 = 43\,°\text{C}$
>
> (Notice that the temperature changes of the iron and the water are very different. Notice also that it is unnecessary to convert between kelvin and °C since the temperature changes are the same on both scales.)

WORKED EXAMPLE 7.3

A piece of iron of mass 200 g and temperature 300 °C is dropped into 1.00 kg of water of temperature 20 °C. Predict the final equilibrium temperature of the water.

(Take c for iron as 440 J kg^{-1} K^{-1} and for water as 4200 J kg^{-1} K^{-1}.)

Answer

Let T be the final unknown temperature. The iron will also be at this temperature, so:

amount of thermal energy lost by the iron = $m_{iron} c_{iron} (300 - T)$

and

amount of thermal energy gained by the water = $m_{water} c_{water} (T - 20)$

Conservation of energy demands that thermal energy lost = thermal energy gained, so:

$m_{iron} c_{iron} (300 - T) = m_{water} c_{water} (T - 20)$

$0.200 \times 440 \times (300 - T) = 1.0 \times 4200 \times (T - 20)$

$\Rightarrow T = 25.7°C \approx 26°C$

(Note how the large specific heat capacity of water (and the larger mass) results in a small increase in the temperature of the water compared with the huge drop in the temperature of the iron.)

Change of phase

When thermal energy is absorbed by a body or transferred away from a body, the body may not necessarily change its temperature. The body may change **phase** instead. Changes of phase happen at constant temperature (Figure 7.5) and include:

- **melting**: when a solid changes to a liquid (thermal energy is transferred to the solid)
- **freezing**: when a liquid changes into a solid (thermal energy is transferred away from the liquid)
- **vaporisation** (or **boiling**): when a liquid changes into vapour (thermal energy is transferred to the liquid)
- **condensation**: when a vapour changes into a liquid (thermal energy is transferred away from the vapour).
- **evaporation**: vaporisation taking place at the surface of a liquid at any temperature

Figure 7.5: Hot lava turns into a solid upon contact with water. Thermal energy transfers from the hot lava to the cold water.

The rate of evaporation increases with increasing liquid temperature and increased surface area. It is the fastest molecules that leave the liquid surface and so the average kinetic energy of the remaining liquid molecules decreases; this means the liquid cools.

The energy supplied or removed during a phase change is called *latent* heat (because it does not result in a temperature change).

KEY POINT

Specific latent heat, L, is the energy required to change the phase of 1 kg of a substance at constant temperature and pressure.

So, the energy required to change the phase of a mass m is $Q = mL$. If the change is melting or freezing, we call it the **specific latent heat of fusion**, L_F. If the change is vaporisation or condensation then we call it **specific latent heat of vaporisation**, L_V.

7 Thermal energy transfers

Notice from Table 7.2 that the specific latent heat for vaporisation is greater than that for melting. This is because the increase in separation of the molecules is much larger when going from the liquid to the vapour phase than when going from the solid to the liquid phase. More work is needed to achieve the greater separation, and so more energy is required.

> **CHECK YOURSELF 4**
>
> Why is contact of the skin with steam at 100 °C more dangerous than contact with boiling water at 100 °C?

Substance	Specific latent heat of fusion/ kJ kg^{-1}	Melting temperature/ °C	Specific latent heat of vaporisation/ kJ kg^{-1}	Boiling temperature/ °C
water	334	0	2260	100
ethanol	109	−114	840	78
aluminium	395	660	10550	2467
lead	23	327	850	1740
copper	205	1078	2600	5190
iron	275	1540	6300	2800

Table 7.2: Specific latent heats of fusion and vaporisation together with the melting and boiling temperatures.

WORKED EXAMPLE 7.4

An ice cube of mass 25.0 g and temperature −10.0 °C is dropped into water of mass 300.0 g and temperature 20.0 °C. Calculate the final temperature.

(Specific heat capacity of ice = 2100 J kg^{-1} K^{-1}; specific latent heat of fusion of ice = 334 kJ kg^{-1}, specific heat capacity of water = 4200 J kg^{-1} K^{-1}.)

Answer

Let the final temperature be T. The water will cool down by transferring thermal energy away.

Using $Q = mc\Delta T$, the thermal energy dissipated by the water is:

$0.300 \times 4200 \times (20 - T)$

This thermal energy will be absorbed by the ice to:

- increase its temperature from −10 °C to 0 °C: the thermal energy required is $25 \times 10^{-3} \times 2100 \times 10$ J
- melt the ice cube into water at 0 °C: the thermal energy required is $25 \times 10^{-3} \times 334 \times 10^3$ J
- increase the temperature of the former ice cube from 0 °C to the final temperature T: the thermal energy required is $25 \times 10^{-3} \times 4200 \times T$.

Thus:

$0.3 \times 4200 \times (20 - T) = (25 \times 10^{-3} \times 2100 \times 10) + (25 \times 10^{-3} \times 334 \times 10^3) + (25 \times 10^{-3} \times 4200 \times T)$

Solving for T gives $T = 14$ °C.

> **PHYSICS FOR THE IB DIPLOMA: COURSEBOOK**

> **EXAM TIP**
>
> You can save yourself time and possible errors if you write this equation, as is, in the equation solver of your graphic display calculator (GDC) and ask the GDC to solve it for you.

> **WORKED EXAMPLE 7.5**
>
> A sample of 120 g of a solid initially at 20 °C is heated by a heater of constant power. The specific heat capacity of the solid is 2500 J kg^{-1} K^{-1}. The temperature of the sample varies with time as shown in Figure 7.6.
>
> Use the graph to determine:
>
> a the power of the heater
>
> b the melting temperature of the sample
>
> c the specific latent heat of fusion of the sample
>
> d the specific heat capacity of the sample in the liquid phase.

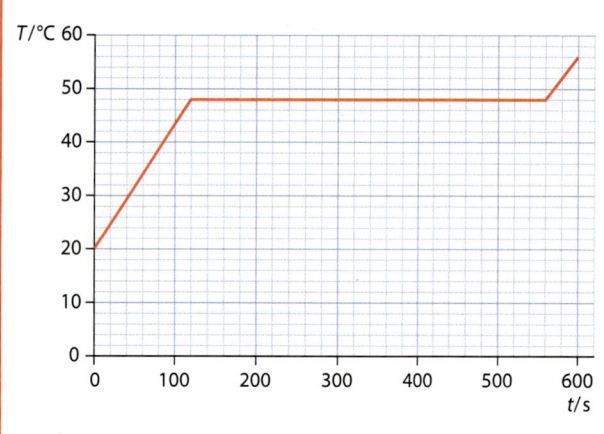

Figure 7.6: For worked example 7.5.

Answer

a It takes 120 s to raise the temperature of the solid sample from 20 °C to 48 °C.

Using $Q = mc\Delta T$, the thermal energy required is:

$0.120 \times 2500 \times (48 - 20) = 8400$ J

So the power is:

$P = \frac{Q}{t} = \frac{8400}{120} = 70$ W

> **CONTINUED**
>
> b The temperature is constant at melting, shown by the flat part of the graph, so the melting temperature is 48 °C.
>
> c The sample is melting from 120 s to 560 s, i.e. for 440 s. The thermal energy supplied during this time is therefore:
>
> $Q = Pt = 70 \times 440 = 30\,800$ J
>
> So the specific latent heat of fusion is:
>
> $L_F = \frac{Q}{m} = \frac{30\,800}{0.120} = 2.6 \times 10^5$ J kg^{-1}
>
> d The liquid increases its temperature from 48 °C to 56 °C in 40 s. In these 40 s the thermal energy provided is:
>
> $Q = Pt = 70 \times 40 = 2800$ J
>
> Using $Q = mc\Delta T$:
>
> $0.120 \times c \times (56 - 48) = 2800$ J
>
> Hence, $c = 2.9 \times 10^3$ J kg^{-1} K^{-1}.

We already mentioned that a phase change occurs at constant temperature. Ice, for example, melts at 0 °C. For a mass m of ice at 0 °C we need to supply an energy mL which turns the ice into liquid water *without a change in temperature*. How do we explain this observation? At the melting temperature, changing from a solid to a liquid means that the average distance between the molecules increases. Increasing the separation of the molecules requires work (because there are attractive forces between the molecules that need to be overcome). The thermal energy supplied increases the intermolecular potential energy (recall the graph in Figure 7.3) and not the kinetic energy of the molecules. So the temperature stays the same but the internal energy increases since the potential energy increases. It is an interesting question, of course, to ask what if anything *prevents* energy from going into kinetic energy during a phase change.

Consider thermal energy provided to melting ice and water at 0 °C. Microscopically, some thermal energy will inevitably go to a small quantity of water raising its temperature slightly above zero. This slightly warmer water is surrounded by ice and water at 0 °C, and so thermal energy will now be transferred away from this warmer water reducing its temperature back down to

0 °C. If this thermal energy is transferred to ice, it will cause the ice to melt. If thermal energy transfers back into water at 0 °C, the process repeats. The result is that more and more ice melts and the overall equilibrium temperature stays constant at 0 °C.

The method of mixtures

The electrical method described in worked example 7.5 is one method for measuring specific heat capacity and latent heat. Another method, the method of mixtures, measures the specific heat capacity of a solid as follows. A solid is put in a container of hot water and allowed time to reach a constant temperature. The temperature of the solid is thus that of the water and is recorded. The solid is then transferred into a calorimeter of known specific heat capacity and initial temperature which contains a liquid such as water (Figure 7.7). The calorimeter is insulated. The final temperature of the water is recorded after thermal equilibrium has been reached. Thermal equilibrium means that the temperatures of the bodies involved are the same.

For example, consider a mass of 0.400 kg of a solid at 80 °C that is put in a 100 g copper calorimeter containing 800 g of water at 20 °C. The final temperature of the water is measured to be 22 °C. From these values, we may deduce the specific heat capacity of the solid as follows.

Using $Q = mc\Delta T$, the amount of thermal energy (in joules) lost by the solid is:

$0.400 \times c \times (80 - 22) = 23.2c$

The amount of thermal energy gained by the calorimeter (see Table 7.1 for the value of c for copper) and the water is:

$\underbrace{0.100 \times 385 \times (22 - 20)}_{\text{calorimeter}} + \underbrace{0.800 \times 4200 \times (22 - 20)}_{\text{water}} = 6797 \text{ J}$

Equating this to the thermal energy $23.2c$ lost by the solid, we find that $c = 293$ J kg^{-1} K^{-1}.

EXAM TIP

It is likely that some thermal energy (heat) was dissipated to the surrounding air while it was being transferred. This means that the actual temperature of the solid is less than we supposed. The actual specific heat capacity is, therefore, larger than the calculated value.

The same method can be applied to measure the specific latent heat of fusion of ice. To do this, place a quantity of ice at 0 °C (the ice must therefore come from a mixture with water at 0 °C) into a calorimeter containing water at a few degrees above room temperature. Blot the ice dry before putting it into the calorimeter. The mass of the ice can be determined by weighing the calorimeter at the end of the experiment.

For example, suppose that 25.0 g of ice at 0.00 °C is placed in an aluminium calorimeter of mass 250 g containing 300 g of water at 24.0 °C. The temperature of the water is measured at regular intervals of time until the temperature reaches its minimum value of

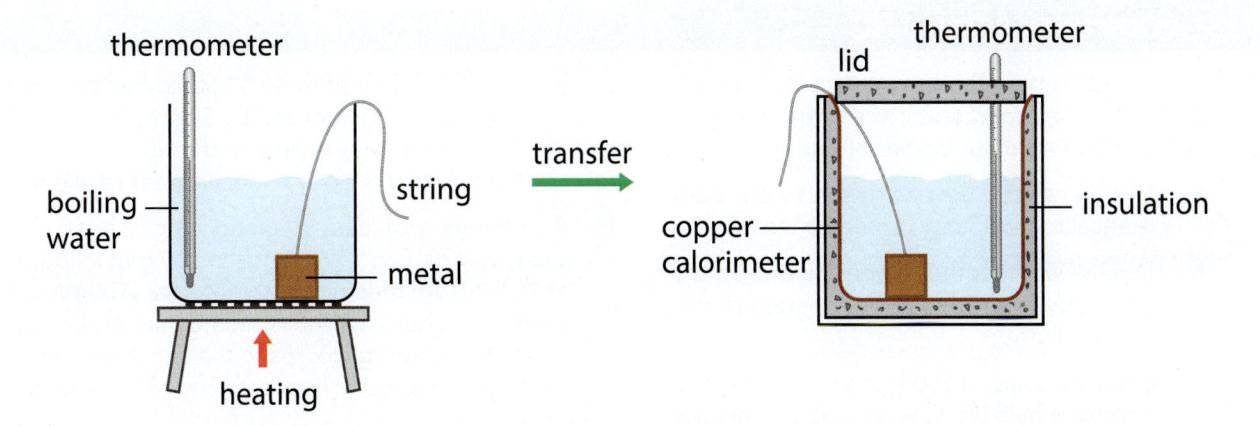

Figure 7.7: The hot metal is placed in the cold water in the calorimeter. The hot metal is removed from the container of boiling water and is quickly placed inside an insulated calorimeter containing cold water.

17.0 °C. The calorimeter and water lost thermal energy, which the ice gained.

Thermal energy transferred away from calorimeter and water:

0.250 × 900 × (24 − 17) + 0.300 × 4200 × (24 − 17) = 10 395 J

Thermal energy transferred to the ice:

$0.025 \times L_F + 0.025 \times 4200 \times 17 = 0.025 \times L_F + 1785$

Equating the two gives:

$1785 + 0.025 \times L_F = 10\,395 \Rightarrow L \approx 344$ kJ kg^{-1}.

> **NATURE OF SCIENCE**
>
> **Models change**
>
> As already mentioned, heat was once thought to be a fluid (caloric). Conservation of energy was a natural consequence of this model of heat: a body lost a certain amount of fluid and another gained it. Energy was conserved. So the concept of heat as a fluid seemed natural. But there are phenomena that cannot be explained with this simple picture. For one thing, if heat is a fluid it must have mass. So when heat leaves a body, the body must lose mass. This is not observed, so the caloric theory must be wrong. The theory has many other failings and was abandoned in the nineteenth century. A major problem is that it does not take into account the atomic theory of matter. The theory we use now is based on statistical mechanics, which uses probability theory to predict the average behaviour of very large numbers of particles.

Cooling

A hot liquid placed in colder surroundings will cool down by losing thermal energy to the surroundings until its temperature reaches that of the surroundings. Experiments show that the rate of cooling, i.e. the rate at which the temperature decreases, is proportional to the difference in temperature between the liquid and the surroundings: $\frac{\Delta T}{\Delta t} = k(T - T_s)$ where the constant k is proportional to the area of the surface of the liquid. This implies an exponential decrease of the temperature. The red curve in Figure 7.8 shows a liquid of initial temperature 40 °C which approaches the surroundings temperature of 10 °C as time goes by. The orange curve shows an identical liquid whose surface area is less than that corresponding to the red curve.

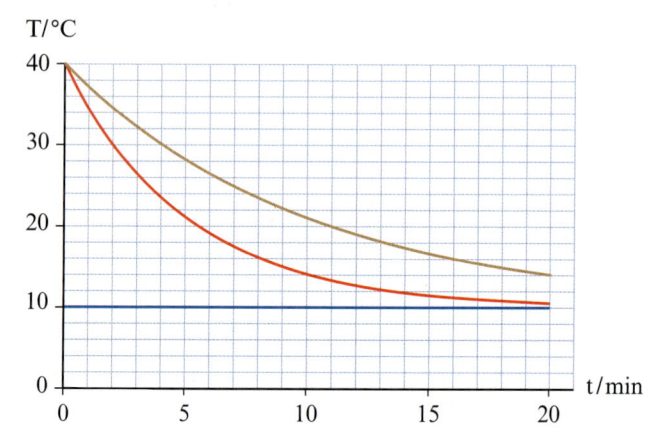

Figure 7.8: The temperature (red and orange curves) decreases exponentially, approaching the temperature of the surroundings (blue curve).

> **TEST YOUR UNDERSTANDING**
>
> **8** A hot body is brought into contact with a colder body until their temperatures are the same. Assume that no other bodies are nearby.
>
>   **a** Discuss whether the energy lost by one body is equal to the energy gained by the other.
>
>   **b** Discuss whether the temperature drop of one body is equal to the temperature rise of the other.
>
> **9** **a** A body of mass 0.150 kg has its temperature increased by 5.00 °C when 385 J of energy is provided to it. Calculate the body's specific heat capacity.
>
>   **b** Another body of mass 0.150 kg has its temperature increased by 5.00 K when 385 J of energy is provided to it. Calculate this body's specific heat capacity.
>
> **10** A calorimeter of mass 90 g and specific heat capacity 420 J kg^{-1} K^{-1} contains 310 g of a liquid at 15.0 °C. An electric heater rated at 20.0 W warms the liquid to 19.0 °C in 3.0 min. Assuming there are no energy losses to the surroundings, estimate the specific heat capacity of the liquid.

CONTINUED

11. A calorimeter for which $mc = 25$ J K^{-1} contains 140 g of a liquid. An immersion heater is used to provide energy at a rate of 40 W for a total time of 4.0 min. The temperature of the liquid increases by 15.8 °C. Calculate the specific heat capacity of the liquid. State an assumption made in reaching this result.

12. A car of mass 1360 kg descends from a hill of height 86 m at a constant speed. Assuming that all of the gravitational potential energy lost by the car goes into heating the brakes, estimate the rise in the temperature of the brakes. (It takes 16 kJ of energy to increase the temperature of the brake drums by 1 K; ignore any energy losses to the surroundings.)

13. A radiator made out of a metal of specific heat capacity 450 J kg^{-1} K^{-1} has a mass of 45.0 kg and is filled with 23.0 kg of water of specific heat capacity 4200 J kg^{-1} K^{-1}.

    a Determine the energy required to raise the temperature of the radiator–water system by 1 K.

    b If energy is provided to the radiator at the rate of 450 W, calculate how long it will take for the temperature to increase by 20.0 °C.

14. How much ice at −10 °C must be dropped into an aluminium cup containing 300 g of water at 20 °C in order for the temperature of the water to be reduced to 10 °C? The cup itself has a mass of 150 g and specific heat capacity 900 J kg^{-1} K^{-1}. Assume that no energy is lost to the surroundings.

15. The surface of a pond of area 20 m^2 is covered by ice of uniform thickness 6.0 cm. The temperature of the ice is −5.0 °C. Calculate how much energy is required to melt this amount of ice into water at 0 °C. (Take the density of ice to be 900 kg m^{-3}.)

16. Radiation from the sun falls on the frozen surface of a pond at a rate of 600 W m^{-2}. The ice temperature is 0 °C.

    a Calculate how long it will take to melt a 1.0 cm thick layer of ice. (Take the density of ice to be 900 kg m^{-3}.)

    b Suggest why the actual mass of ice that melts is less than your answer to **a**.

17. a Calculate how much energy is required to warm 1.0 kg of ice initially at −10 °C to ice at 0 °C.

    b Calculate how much energy is needed to melt the ice at 0 °C.

    c Calculate how much energy is required to further increase the temperature of the water from 0 °C to 10 °C.

18. Ice at 0 °C is added to 1.0 kg of water at 20 °C, cooling it down to 10 °C. Determine how much ice was added.

19. A quantity of 100 g of ice at 0 °C and 50 g of steam at 100 °C are added to a container that has 150 g water at 30 °C. Determine the final temperature. Ignore the container itself in your calculations.

20. Steam at 100 °C is mixed with 200 g of ice at 0 °C to produce water at 50 °C. What is the mass of steam required?

21. Two bodies (same mass and initial temperature) are dropped into two identical containers filled with water. The mass and temperature of the water in both containers is the same. The graphs in Figure 7.9 show the cooling curves of the two bodies.

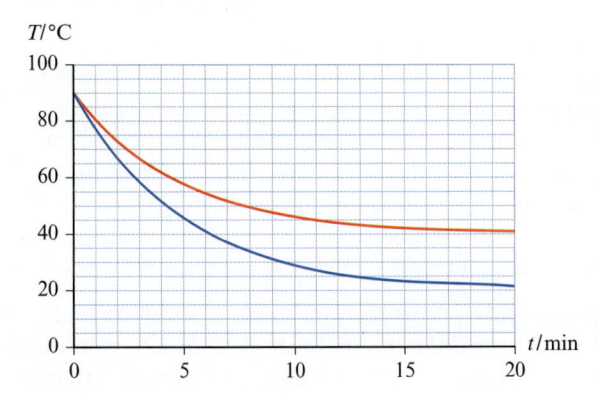

Figure 7.9: For question 21.

Which body has the higher specific heat capacity?

7.3 Thermal energy transfer

There are three distinct methods to transfer thermal energy from one place to another: conduction, convection and radiation.

Conduction

Imagine a solid with one end kept at a high temperature, as shown in Figure 7.10. The electrons at the hot end of the solid have a high average kinetic energy. This means they move a lot. The moving electrons collide with neighbouring molecules, transferring energy to them and so increasing their average kinetic energy. This means that energy is being transferred from the hot to the cold side of the solid; this is **conduction**.

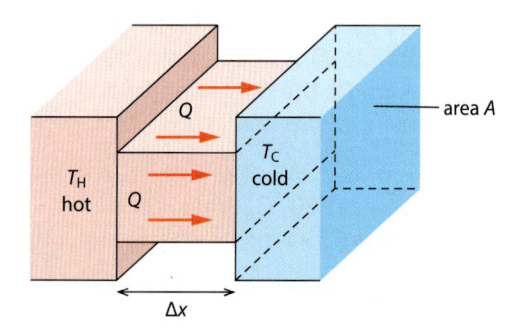

Figure 7.10: Conduction of thermal energy through a solid as a result of a temperature difference.

Collisions between electrons and molecules are the dominant way in which thermal energy is transferred by conduction, but if there are strong bonds between molecules there is another way. Molecules on the hot side of the solid vibrate about their equilibrium positions, stretching the bonds with neighbouring molecules. This stretching forces the neighbours to also begin to vibrate, and so the average kinetic energy of the neighbours increases. Energy is again transferred.

For a solid of cross-sectional area A, width Δx and temperature difference between its ends ΔT, experiments show that the rate at which energy is being transferred is:

$$\frac{\Delta Q}{\Delta t} = kA\frac{\Delta T}{\Delta x}$$

where k is called the conductivity and depends on the nature of the substance. Referring to Figure 7.10, $\Delta T = T_H - T_C$.

> **CHECK YOURSELF 5**
>
> Figure 7.11 shows the cross sections of three walls made of the same material and of thicknesses L, $2L$ and $4L$. Thermal energy transfers from left to right through the same cross sectional area. In which case is the rate of transfer of thermal energy the greatest? 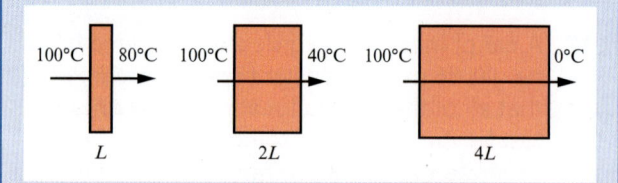
>
> Figure 7.11: For check yourself question 5.

> **WORKED EXAMPLE 7.6**
>
> Two rods of different materials but of the same cross sectional area and length are joined as shown. The thermal conductivities are shown in Figure 7.12. 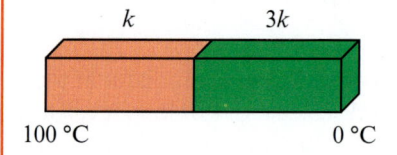
>
> Figure 7.12: For worked example 7.6.
>
> The left end is kept at constant temperature of 100 °C and the right end at a constant temperature 0 °C. What is the temperature at the point where the rods are joined?
>
> **Answer**
>
> Let us call the temperature at the joining point T. Then the rate at which thermal energy transfers in the left rod is $kA\frac{100-T}{L}$ and in the right rod it is $(3k)A\frac{T-0}{L}$. The two rates must be equal by energy conservation. Hence
>
> $$kA\frac{100-T}{L} = (3k)A\frac{T-0}{L}$$
> $$100 - T = 3T$$
> $$T = 25\,°C$$

Convection

Convection is a method of energy transfer that applies mainly to fluids, i.e. gases and liquids. If you put a pan of water on a stove, the water at the bottom of the pan is heated by conduction. As it gets hotter the water expands, it gets less dense and so rises to the top. In this way thermal energy from the bottom of the pan is transferred to the top. Similarly, air over a hot radiator in a room is heated, expands and rises, transferring warm air to the rest of the room. Colder air takes the place of the air that rose and the process repeats, creating **convection currents**. In other words convection is due to differences in density. Convection is responsible for winds in the atmosphere and for ocean currents.

Radiation

Both conduction and convection require a material medium through which thermal energy is to be transferred. The third method of thermal energy transfer, **radiation**, does not. Energy from the sun has been warming the earth for billions of years. This energy arrives at earth as radiation having travelled through the vacuum of space at the speed of light.

Stefan–Boltzmann law

One of the great advances in physics in the nineteenth century was the discovery that all bodies that are kept at some absolute (kelvin) temperature T radiate energy in the form of electromagnetic waves. This is radiation created by oscillating electric charges in the atoms of the body. The power radiated by a body is governed by the **Stefan–Boltzmann law** (obtained experimentally by J. Stefan and deduced theoretically by L. Boltzmann).

> **KEY POINT**
>
> The power radiated by a black body depends on its surface area A and the absolute temperature of the surface T and is given by $P = \sigma A T^4$. The constant σ is the Stefan–Boltzmann constant and equals $\sigma = 5.67 \times 10^{-8}$ W m^{-2} K^{-4}.

The power radiated per unit area of the body, the radiated **intensity**, is then $\frac{P}{A} = \sigma T^4$.

Strictly, this applies to a theoretical body called a **black body**. This is a perfect radiator as well as a perfect absorber. A black body will absorb all the radiation falling upon it, reflecting none. A black body at low temperature radiates very little, and since it absorbs all the radiation falling on it, it looks black. At high temperature it radiates a lot and looks very bright. A very good example of this is a piece of charcoal: dark when cold, glowing orange-red when hot. (In Chapter 8 we will see how the Stefan–Boltzmann law is modified to apply to real bodies as well.)

Links

Light incident on a shiny metallic surface will reflect with little light being absorbed. Light incident on glass will pass through the glass with very little being absorbed. So why does a black body absorb all the radiation incident on it, transmitting none and reflecting none? The incident light is an electromagnetic wave and so contains an electric field (see Sections 13.3 and 18.1). This field will set electrons in a surface oscillating. In the case of glass, the electrons are very tightly bound to their atoms and so cannot oscillate much. The light just goes through. In the case of the metal, there are lots of free electrons. The electric field makes them oscillate a lot which means they are accelerated. But accelerated charges radiate electromagnetic waves, and this is the reflected light. In a black body, the electric field also accelerates electrons which gain energy, but before they have a chance to radiate they collide with atoms giving them their kinetic energy. The incident radiation has been absorbed and the temperature of the body increases. As the temperature increases more and more the vibrations of the atoms get larger and larger. Now, the collisions between atoms and electrons are very violent and give electrons massive accelerations. The electrons now radiate; the body is emitting black body radiation.

Figure 7.13 shows three black-body spectra emitted from the same surface at three different temperatures of the surface ($T = 273$ K, 320 K and 350 K). We see that with increasing temperature, the peak of the curve occurs at lower wavelengths and the height of the peak increases. The quantity B plotted on the vertical axis is the power emitted per unit area per unit wavelength and so has units of $(W\,m^{-2})\,m^{-1} = W\,m^{-3}$. It is called spectral intensity. The area under the graph is the radiated intensity, σT^4.

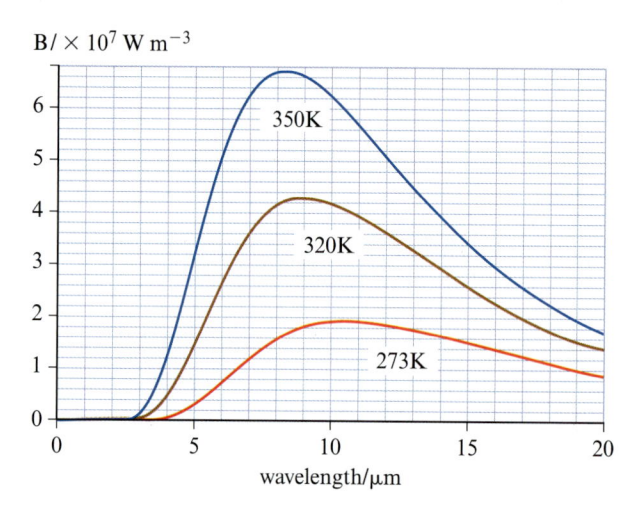

Figure 7.13: Black-body spectra for a body at the three temperatures shown. Notice that as the temperature increases the peak gets higher and the wavelength at the peak shifts to the left.

The energy radiated is electromagnetic radiation and is distributed over an infinite range of wavelengths. The peak of the spectrum corresponds to a specific wavelength λ_{max}, Figure 7.14, called the **peak wavelength**.

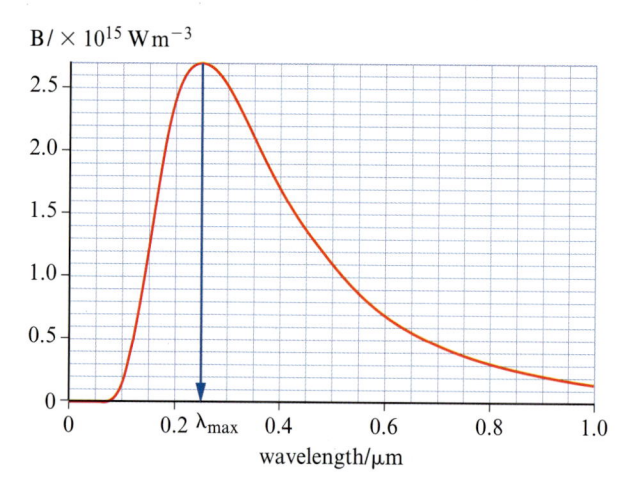

Figure 7.14: For this graph, the peak wavelength is 0.25×10^{-6} m.

Wien's law

The peak wavelength λ_0 depends on temperature according to **Wien's law**.

Wien's law states that $\lambda_{max} T = 2.90 \times 10^{-3}$ K m.

So, for the graph of Figure 7.14, the temperature is
$T = \frac{2.90 \times 10^{-3}}{0.25 \times 10^{-6}} = 11600 \approx 1.2 \times 10^4$ K.

> **EXAM TIP**
>
> Increasing the temperature shifts the peak wavelength to the left and makes the curve taller.

> **CHECK YOURSELF 6**
>
> The area of the body in Figure 7.14 is doubled. How does the graph change?

> **WORKED EXAMPLE 7.7**
>
> A human body has temperature 37 °C, the average earth surface temperature is 288 K and the temperature of the sun is 5800 K. In each case, calculate the peak wavelength of the emitted radiation.
>
> **Answer**
>
> We just have to apply Wien's law, $\lambda_{max} T = 2.90 \times 10^{-3}$ K m, and make sure we use kelvins in each case. So:
>
> human body: $\lambda_{max} = \frac{2.90 \times 10^{-3}}{273 + 37} \approx 9 \times 10^{-6}$ m, an infrared wavelength
>
> earth surface: $\lambda_{max} = \frac{2.90 \times 10^{-3}}{288} \approx 1 \times 10^{-5}$ m, an infrared wavelength
>
> sun: $\lambda_{max} = \frac{2.90 \times 10^{-3}}{5800} \approx 5 \times 10^{-7}$ m, which is a visible wavelength.

WORKED EXAMPLE 7.8

By what factor does the power emitted by a black body increase when the temperature is increased from 100 °C to 200 °C?

Answer

The temperature in kelvin increases from 373 K to 473 K. Since the emitted power is proportional to the fourth power of the temperature, power will increase by a factor:

$$\left(\frac{473}{373}\right)^4 = 2.59$$

EXAM TIP

Make sure the temperature is in kelvin.

TEST YOUR UNDERSTANDING

22 Describe what is meant by
   a conduction
   b convection.

23 Half the floor of a room is covered by marble tiles and the other half by a carpet. Why does walking barefoot feel colder on the marble tiles?

24 For most people, walking in 20 °C weather would be considered comfortable but swimming in 20 °C water would be uncomfortable. Suggest a reason for this.

25 A pan of water placed on a stove comes to a boil. Discuss how thermal energy is transferred from the stove to the surface of the water.

26 How does blowing over a hot cup of coffee help the coffee cool down?

27 The road over a bridge freezes before the road on the ground. Suggest why this happens.

28 Suggest whether there is any point in using a ceiling fan in winter.

CONTINUED

29 You stand on land by the sea on a hot summer day. Why is there a breeze from the sea towards the land?

30 By what method does a spacecraft in the vacuum of space 'lose' thermal energy?

31 A cylindrical solid tube is made out of two smaller tubes, X and Y, of different material. X and Y have the same length and cross-sectional area. The tube is used to conduct energy from a hot to a cold reservoir (see Figure 7.15).

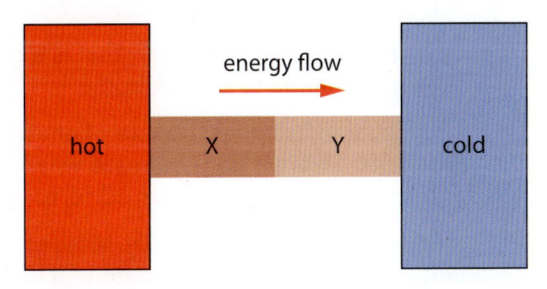

Figure 7.15: For question 31.

State and explain whether the following are equal or not:

   a the rates of transfer of energy through X and through Y
   b the temperature differences across X and across Y.

32 In the previous problem the temperatures of the hot and cold reservoirs are constant at 80 °C and 20 °C respectively. The thermal conductivity of X is k and that of Y is $2k$. Calculate the temperature where X and Y join.

33 The temperature of a room in winter is kept constant at 24 °C by using a heater. The room is separated from the outside, where the temperature is −5.0 °C, by a wall of area 12 m² and thickness 0.20 m. The material of the wall has a thermal conductivity of 0.15 W m⁻¹ K⁻¹. Estimate the power of the heater.

CONTINUED

34 A cylindrical metallic rod has radius 1.0 cm and length 25 cm. One end of the rod is placed into a large chunk of ice at 0 °C and the other in boiling water at 100 °C. The thermal conductivity of the rod is 350 W m^{-1} K^{-1}. Estimate how long it will take to melt 1 g of ice. It takes about 334 J to melt 1 g of ice at 0 °C.

35 Calculate the ratio of the power radiated per unit area from two black bodies at temperatures 900 K and 300 K.

36 a State what you understand by the term *black body*.

  b Give an example of a body that is a good approximation to a black body.

  c By what factor does the rate of emitted radiation from a body increase when the temperature is raised from 50 °C to 100 °C?

37 A star radiates like a black body. Most of the energy is emitted at a wavelength of 410 nm. What is the surface temperature of the star?

38 Star X has peak wavelength 480 nm and star Y has peak wavelength 560 nm. Which star has the higher surface temperature?

39 The surface area and kelvin temperature of a black body are both doubled. By what factor do:

  a the radiated power

  b the radiated intensity

  increase?

40 A sphere of radius R and a cube of side R radiate like black bodies. The sphere and the cube are at the same temperature. Which body loses more energy per second?

41 The graph (Figure 7.16) shows a black-body spectrum.

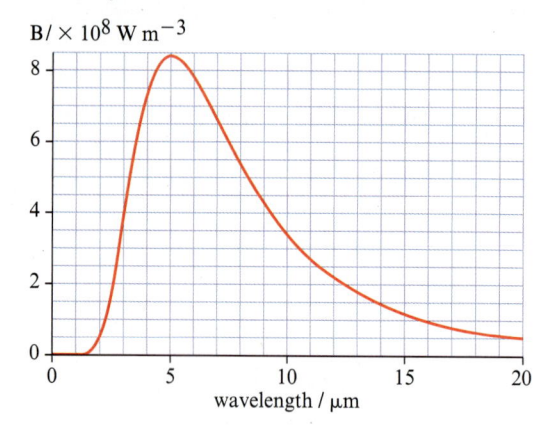

Figure 7.16: For question 41.

  a Determine the temperature of the black body.

  b The kelvin temperature of the black body in **a** is doubled. What is the peak wavelength?

  c The area of the body in **a** is reduced, but the temperature stays the same as that found in **a**. Draw a graph to show the new black-body spectrum.
  (**Hint:** what does the area represent?)

42 The graph (Figure 7.17) shows the black-body spectrum of the sun plotted for the range of visible wavelengths only.

  a Find the surface temperature of the sun.

  b Do you agree with the statement that the color of the sun is white?

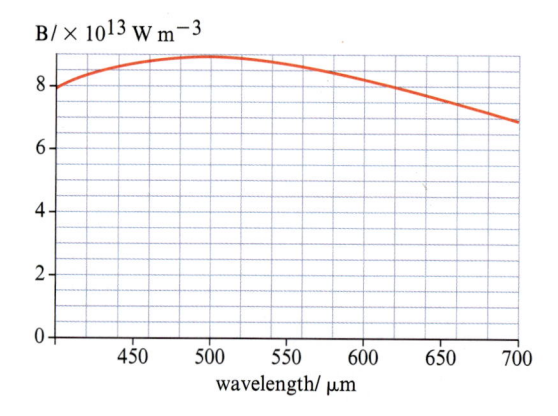

Figure 7.17: For question 42

Luminosity and apparent brightness

In an example of lack of economy of symbols and terms, the quantity $I = \frac{P}{4\pi d^2}$ is called **apparent brightness** by astronomers and is given the symbol b.
Thus, apparent brightness is the power received per unit area of the detector. Astronomers also call the total power radiated by a star **luminosity**, L and so in astronomy we have:

$$b = \frac{L}{4\pi d^2}$$

Luminosity is a major characteristic of a star. As we saw when we discussed black-body radiation, stars are excellent approximations to a black body and so the luminosity of a star is given by the Stefan–Boltzmann law:

$$L = \sigma A T^4$$

where $\sigma = 5.67 \times 10^{-8}$ W m^{-2} K^{-4} is the Stefan–Boltzmann constant, A is the surface area of the star and T its surface temperature in kelvin.

Now, two stars of the same luminosity will not appear equally bright when observed from earth if they are at different distances from earth. Apparent brightness is a measure of how bright a star actually appears.

By combining the formula for luminosity with that of apparent brightness we see that

$$b = \frac{\sigma A T^4}{4\pi d^2}$$

Apparent brightness is easily measured (with a charge-coupled device, or CCD). If we also know the luminosity then we can determine the distance.

WORKED EXAMPLE 7.9

The apparent brightness of a star is 3.4×10^{-8} W m^{-2} and its luminosity is 5.1×10^{28} W.
What is its distance?

Answer

$b = \frac{L}{4\pi d^2} \Rightarrow d = \sqrt{\frac{L}{4\pi b}}$

Therefore:

$d = \sqrt{\frac{5.1 \times 10^{28}}{4\pi \times 3.4 \times 10^{-8}}} = 3.5 \times 10^{17}$ m

WORKED EXAMPLE 7.10

a The radius of star A is three times that of star B and its temperature is double that of B. Find the ratio of the luminosity of A to that of B.

b The stars in **a** have the same apparent brightness when viewed from earth. Calculate the ratio of their distances.

Answer

a $\frac{L_A}{L_B} = \frac{\sigma 4\pi R_A^2 T_A^4}{\sigma 4\pi R_B^2 T_B^4}$

$= \frac{R_A^2 T_A^4}{R_B^2 T_B^4}$

$= \frac{(3 R_B)^2 (2 T_B)^4}{R_B^2 T_B^4}$

$= 3^2 \times 2^4 = 144$

b $\frac{b_A}{b_B} = 1$

$1 = \frac{\left(\frac{L_A}{4\pi d_A^2}\right)}{\left(\frac{L_B}{4\pi d_B^2}\right)}$

$1 = \left(\frac{L_A}{L_B}\right)\left(\frac{d_B^2}{d_A^2}\right)$

$\Rightarrow \frac{d_A}{d_B} = \sqrt{\frac{L_A}{L_B}} = \sqrt{144} = 12$

WORKED EXAMPLE 7.11

The apparent brightness of a star is 6.4×10^{-8} W m^{-2}. Its distance is 15 ly (1 ly $= 9.46 \times 10^{15}$ m). Find its luminosity.

Answer

We use $b = \frac{L}{4\pi d^2}$ to find

$L = b 4\pi d^2$

$= \left(6.4 \times 10^{-8} \frac{W}{m^2}\right) \times 4\pi \times (15 \times 9.46 \times 10^{15})^2 \, m^2$

$= 1.62 \times 10^{28}$ W $\approx 1.6 \times 10^{28}$ W

> **WORKED EXAMPLE 7.12**

A star has half the sun's surface temperature and 400 times its luminosity. Estimate the ratio of the star's radius to that of the sun. (The symbol ⊙ refers to the sun.)

Answer

We have that:

$$400 = \frac{L}{L_\odot} = \frac{\sigma 4\pi R^2 T^4}{\sigma 4\pi R_\odot^2 T_\odot^4}$$

$$= \frac{R^2 (T_\odot/2)^4}{R_\odot^2 T_\odot^4}$$

$$= \frac{R^2}{R_\odot^2 \, 16}$$

$$\frac{R^2}{R_\odot^2 \, 16} = 400$$

$$\frac{R^2}{R_\odot^2} = 16 \times 400 \quad \Rightarrow \quad R = 80\, R_\odot$$

Links

We have learned about the particle nature of matter, i.e. atoms and molecules. This poses the obvious question of what the nature of matter really is. What other particles do we discover as we go deeper and deeper into atoms? The production of steam through the boiling of water made the steam engine possible. In a similar way, pressurized steam created by using the energy produced in fission reactions makes the production of electricity possible by rotating a coil in a magnetic field. The concept of a black body made possible our understanding of how stars radiate through application of the Stefan–Boltzmann law.

TEST YOUR UNDERSTANDING

43 The luminosity of a star is 4.5×10^{28} W and its distance from earth is 8.3×10^{17} m. Calculate the apparent brightness of the star.

44 The luminosity of the sun is 3.9×10^{26} W and its distance from earth is 1.5×10^{11} m. Calculate the apparent brightness of the sun.

45 The light from a star a distance of 6.6×10^{17} m away is received on earth with an apparent brightness of 3.0×10^{-8} W m^{-2}. Calculate the luminosity of the star.

46 The apparent brightness of a star is 8.4×10^{-10} W m^{-2} and its luminosity is 6.2×10^{32} W. Calculate the distance to the star.

47 Two stars are the same distance from earth, and their apparent brightnesses are 9.0×10^{-12} W m^{-2} (star A) and 3.0×10^{-13} W m^{-2} (star B). Calculate the ratio of the luminosity of star A to that of star B.

48 Two stars, A and B, have the same size, but A has a temperature that is four times larger than that of B.

  a Estimate how much more energy per second A radiates.

  b The apparent brightness of the two stars is the same; determine the ratio of the distance of B to that of A.

49 Two stars have the same luminosity. Star A has a surface temperature of 5000 K, and star B a temperature of 10 000 K.

  a Suggest which is the larger star and by how much.

  b The apparent brightness of A is double that of B; calculate the ratio of the distance of A to that of B.

50 Star A has apparent brightness 8.0×10^{-13} W m^{-2} and its distance is 120 ly. Star B has apparent brightness 2.0×10^{-15} W m^{-2} and its distance is 150 ly. The two stars have the same size. Calculate the ratio of the temperature of star A to that of star B.

51 Take the surface temperature of our sun to be 6000 K and its luminosity to be 3.9×10^{26} W. Find, in terms of the solar radius, the radius of a star with:

  a temperature 4000 K and luminosity 5.2×10^{28} W

  b temperature 9250 K and luminosity 4.7×10^{27} W.

52 Two stars, X and Y, have the same apparent brightness and temperature. The distance to X is double the distance to Y. What is the ratio of radii $\frac{R_X}{R_Y}$?

53 a Describe how the colour of the light from a star can be used to determine the surface temperature of the star.

  b A star appears blue and another appears red. Which is hotter?

54 Stars A and B emit most of their light at wavelengths of 650 nm and 480 nm, respectively. Star A has twice the radius of star B. Find the ratio of the luminosity of star A to that of star B.

SELF-ASSESSMENT CHECKLIST

I am able to …	Section	Not yet	Nearly there	Ready to move on
understand the connection between temperature and average kinetic energy of molecules	7.1			
understand the concept of intermolecular potential energy	7.1			
distinguish between the concepts of temperature, thermal energy and internal energy	7.1			
solve problems in calorimetry	7.2			
explain why temperature stays the same during a phase change	7.2			
understand the ways by which thermal energy can be transferred	7.3			
apply the Stefan–Boltzmann and Wien laws	7.3			
solve problems with luminosity and apparent brightness	7.3			

REFLECTION

Are you comfortable with the concepts of *heat* and *internal energy*? Can you compare the internal energy of equal masses of a solid, a liquid and a gas at the same temperature? Can you solve *calorimetry problems*? Can you explain why the temperature stays constant during a *phase change*? Can you describe the three methods of *heat transfer*? Can you work with *luminosity* and *apparent brightness*?

EXAM-STYLE QUESTIONS

You can find questions in the style of IB exams in the digital coursebook.

CHECK YOURSELF ANSWERS

1   a 27 °C.   b 123 K.

2   The student is not correct. Internal energy includes the random kinetic energy of the molecules, and that is determined only by temperature. The velocity of the plane does not affect the random kinetic energy of the molecules. The internal energies of the two containers are the same.

3   Above 50 °C. The high specific heat capacity of Y implies its temperature will not change by much.

4   Steam will release its enormous latent heat of vaporization as it condenses into water.

5   The one with the largest value of $\frac{\Delta T}{L}$ (the middle diagram)

6   It will stay the same. Doubling the area doubles the emitted power, but the vertical axis measures the spectral intensity B, which is power *per unit area* per unit wavelength so B will not change.

Chapter 8
The greenhouse effect

LEARNING OBJECTIVES

In this chapter you will learn how to:

- calculate the average intensity of radiation received by earth
- understand the definitions of albedo and emissivity
- calculate the equilibrium temperature of the earth
- understand the greenhouse effect
- understand the mechanism through which greenhouse gases absorb radiation emitted from the surface of earth
- appreciate that human activities related to the burning of fossil fuels leads to the enhanced greenhouse effect.

PHYSICS FOR THE IB DIPLOMA: COURSEBOOK

> **GUIDING QUESTION**
>
> What is the mechanism by which the earth maintains a constant average temperature?

> **KEY POINT**
>
> Albedo is the ratio $\alpha = \dfrac{\text{total reflected power}}{\text{total incident power}}$.
>
> Albedo has no unit.

Introduction

An important application of the black-body radiation law is to the energy balance of the earth. The earth receives energy from the sun but also partly reflects and partly radiates this energy back into space. This keeps the average earth temperature roughly constant. This phenomenon allows life on earth to be sustained—so it is an important area of study.

8.1 Radiation from real bodies

Black bodies are idealized bodies. Real bodies radiate according to the modified Stefan–Boltzmann law: $P = e\sigma A T^4$. The constant e is known as the **emissivity** of the surface. Its value is between 0 and 1; the value $e = 1$ corresponds to the idealized black body.

Emissivity is the ratio of the power per unit area radiated by a body to the power per unit area radiated by a black body of the same temperature.

> **KEY POINT**
>
> The power radiated per unit area is called (radiated) intensity and so equals $I = e\sigma T^4$.
>
> The unit of intensity is $W\,m^{-2}$.

Unlike a black body that absorbs all the radiation incident on it, reflecting none, a real body will reflect some of the incident radiation. The ratio of the reflected intensity (or power) to the incident intensity (or power) is called the **albedo** of the body.

For a body that can only absorb or reflect (i.e. it cannot *transmit*) the emissivity and albedo are related by $e + \alpha = 1$.

Consider a body of emissivity e and surface temperature T whose surroundings have a temperature T_s. The surroundings may be assumed to be a black body. The body radiates an intensity $e\sigma T^4$. The surroundings radiate an intensity σT_S^4. Of this intensity the body will *reflect* a fraction $\alpha \sigma T_S^4$ and so will *absorb* a fraction $(1-\alpha)\sigma T_S^4$, i.e. $e\sigma T_S^4$. The *net intensity* for the body is then $I_{net} = e\sigma T^4 - e\sigma T_S^4$. Thus the rate at which energy leaves the body (the power) of surface area A is

$$P_{net} = e\sigma A(T^4 - T_S^4)$$

At equilibrium no net power leaves the body and so $T = T_s$, as we might expect. Table 8.1 gives values for the emissivity of various surfaces.

Surface	Emissivity
black body	1
ocean water	0.8
ice	0.1
dry land	0.7
land with vegetation	0.6

Table 8.1: Emissivity of various surfaces.

Figure 8.1 shows the variation of the spectral intensity B with wavelength λ from various different surfaces kept at the same temperature (300 K). The difference in the curves is due to the different emissivities ($e = 1.0$, 0.8 and 0.2). The curves are identical apart from an overall factor that shrinks the height of the curve as the emissivity decreases. The peak wavelength is the same for all three curves because the temperature is the same.

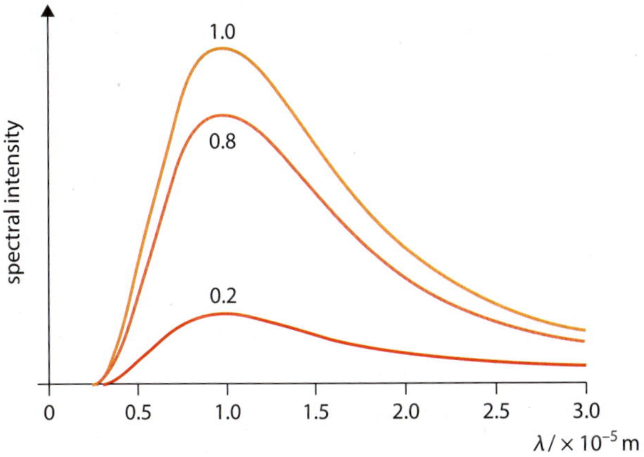

8 The greenhouse effect

Figure 8.1: The spectra of three bodies with different emissivities at the same temperature (300 K). The vertical axis shows spectral intensity.

CHECK YOURSELF 1

The kelvin temperature and radius of a spherical black body are both doubled. By what factor does **a** the radiated power and **b** the radiated intensity increase?

WORKED EXAMPLE 8.1

The emissivity of the naked human body may be taken to be $e = 0.90$. Assuming a body temperature of 37 °C and a body surface area of 1.60 m², calculate the total amount of energy lost by the body when exposed to a temperature of 0.0 °C for 30 minutes.

Answer

The net power lost is the difference between the power emitted by the body and the power received. Let the body temperature be T_1 and the temperature of the surroundings be T_2. Then:

$P_{net} = e\sigma A(T_1^4 - T_2^4)$

Substituting the values from the question:

$P_{net} = 0.90 \times 5.67 \times 10^{-8} \times 1.60 \times (310^4 - 273^4)$

$P_{net} = 301$ W

CONTINUED

So the energy lost in time t seconds is:

$E = P_{net} t$

$E = 301 \times 30 \times 60$

$E = 5.4 \times 10^5$ J

(What does this mean for the human body? For the purposes of an estimate, assume that the body has mass 60 kg and is made out of water, with specific heat capacity $c = 4200$ J kg⁻¹ K⁻¹. This energy loss would result in a drop in body temperature of $\Delta T = \frac{5.4 \times 10^5}{60 \times 4200} = 2.1$ K.)

The solar constant

The sun may be considered to radiate as a black body. The sun emits a total power $P = 3.9 \times 10^{26}$ W. The average earth–sun distance is $d = 1.50 \times 10^{11}$ m. Imagine a sphere of radius d centred at the sun. The power of the sun is distributed over the area of this sphere ($4\pi d^2$) and so the power per unit area, i.e. the **intensity**, *received* by earth is:

$I = \frac{P}{4\pi d^2}$

We generalise the definition of intensity given earlier to:

KEY POINT

Intensity is the power of radiation *received* or *emitted* per unit area. Its unit is W m⁻².

Substituting the numerical values for our sun gives:

$I = \frac{3.9 \times 10^{26}}{4\pi(1.50 \times 10^{11})^2} = 1379 \approx 1400$ W m⁻².

This is called the **solar constant**, S. It is the intensity of the solar radiation at the top of the earth's atmosphere. $S \approx 1400$ W m⁻².

The radius of the sun is 7.0×10^8 m. The intensity *emitted* by the sun is

$I = \frac{3.9 \times 10^{26}}{4\pi(7.0 \times 10^8)^2} = 6.3 \times 10^7$ W m⁻².

PHYSICS FOR THE IB DIPLOMA: COURSEBOOK

TEST YOUR UNDERSTANDING

1 The graph (Figure 8.2) shows the variation with wavelength of the spectral intensity of radiation emitted by two bodies of identical shape and size.

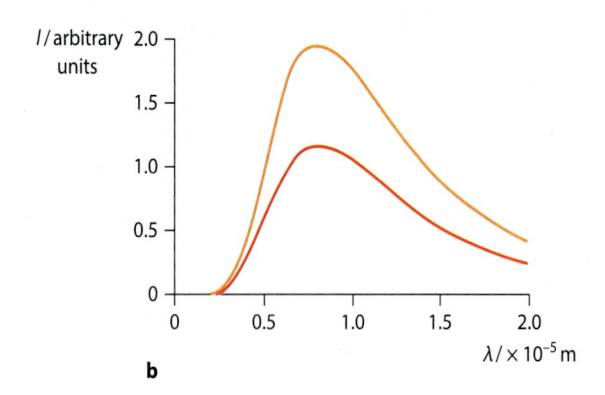

Figure 8.2: For question 1.

    a Explain why the temperature of the two bodies is the same.

    b The upper line corresponds to a black body. Calculate the emissivity of the other body.

2 The total power radiated by a surface of area 5.00 km² and emissivity 0.800 is 1.35×10^9 W. Assume that the surface radiates into a vacuum at temperature 0 K. Calculate the temperature of the surface.

3 A sphere of emissivity 0.80 has radius 0.50 m and temperature 27 °C. The temperature of the surroundings is 57 °C. At what rate does the body emit radiation and at what rate does it absorb radiation?

4 A sphere of emissivity 0.70 has radius 0.60 m and temperature 300 K. The temperature of the surroundings is assumed to be 0 K.

    a What is the intensity of the emitted radiation?

    b What is the intensity of the received radiation at a distance of 2.2 m from the centre of the sphere?

5   a Define the term *intensity* in the context of radiation.

    b Estimate the net intensity of radiation of a naked human body of surface area 1.60 m², temperature 37 °C and emissivity 0.90 assuming black-body surroundings at −15 °C.

8.2 Energy balance of the earth

Figure 8.3 shows radiation from the sun reaching the earth. The sun is so far away that the rays arrive essentially parallel. The radiation that reaches the earth has to go through the area of a disc of radius R where R is the radius of the earth. The intensity of the incident radiation is called the solar constant S. The power going through the disc is then

$P = S\pi R^2$

EXAM TIP

The solar constant S is intensity. Intensity is power per unit area so $P = SA$.

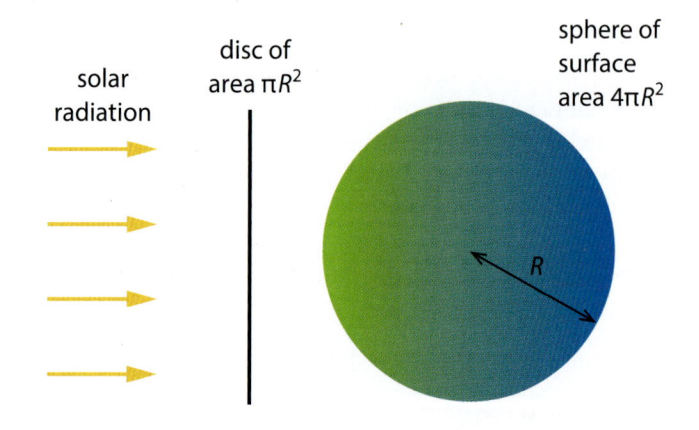

Figure 8.3: The radiation reaching the earth must first go through a disc of area πR^2, where R is the radius of the earth.

8 The greenhouse effect

Clearly, the earth's surface receives radiation during the day when it faces the sun. But if we want to define a night and day average of the incident intensity, I_{av}, we must divide the power through the disc ($S\pi R^2$) by the total surface area of the earth ($4\pi R^2$) to get

$$\frac{S\pi R^2}{4\pi R^2} = \frac{S}{4}$$

> **EXAM TIP**
>
> You must be able to justify the factor of 4 in the average intensity received by earth.

The albedo of the earth is α, and so a fraction $\alpha\frac{S}{4}$ is reflected, leaving an average intensity reaching the earth surface of:

$$I_{av} = (1 - \alpha)\frac{S}{4}$$

Because the average albedo of earth is about 0.30, this amounts to $\frac{0.7 \times 1400}{4} = 245 \text{ W m}^{-2}$.

In other words, at any moment of the day or night, anywhere on earth, 1 m² of the surface may be thought to receive 245 J of energy every second.

We are interested in the equilibrium temperature of the earth. This is the temperature attained by the earth when the energy input to the earth is equal to the energy output by the earth (Figure 8.4).

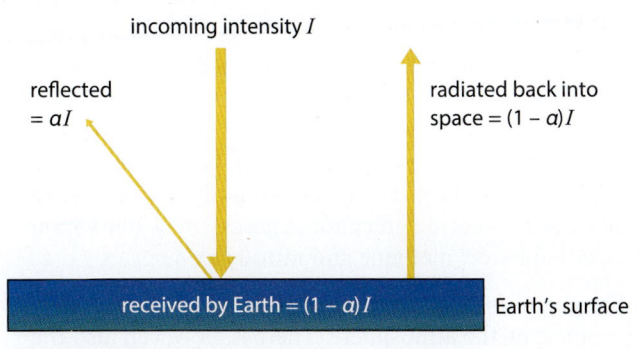

Figure 8.4: Energy diagram showing energy transfers in a model without an atmosphere. Note that the energy in equals the energy out.

The next worked example introduces a first glimpse of an **energy balance equation**, leading to an estimate of the equilibrium temperature of the earth.

> **WORKED EXAMPLE 8.2**
>
> Assume that the earth's surface has a fixed temperature T and that it radiates as a black body. The average incoming solar radiation reaching the surface has intensity $I_{av} = (1 - \alpha)\frac{S}{4} = 245 \text{ W m}^{-2}$. (The albedo of 0.30 is provided by the atmosphere, but all other effects of the atmosphere are ignored.)
>
> a Write down an equation expressing the fact that the intensity received by the earth equals the intensity radiated by the earth into space (an energy balance equation).
>
> b Solve the equation to calculate the equilibrium earth temperature.
>
> c Comment on your answer.
>
> **Answer**
>
> a The average intensity reaching the surface is:
>
> $$I_{av} = (1 - \alpha)\frac{S}{4} = 245 \text{ W m}^{-2}$$
>
> The intensity radiated is:
>
> $$I_{out} = \sigma T^4$$
>
> (Here we are assuming that the earth is a black body, so $e = 1$ and the surrounding space is taken to have a temperature of 0 K.)
>
> Equating the incident and outgoing intensities we get:
>
> $$245 = \sigma T^4$$
>
> b Solving the equation, we find:
>
> $$T = \sqrt[4]{\frac{245}{5.67 \times 10^{-8}}} = 256 \text{ K}$$
>
> This temperature is $-17\ °C$.

181

> **PHYSICS FOR THE IB DIPLOMA: COURSEBOOK**

CONTINUED

c It is perhaps surprising that this extremely simple model has given an answer that is not off by orders of magnitude! But a temperature of 256 K is 32 K lower than the earth's average temperature of 288 K, and so obviously the model is too simplistic. One reason this model is too simple is precisely because we have not taken into account the fact that not all the power radiated by the earth actually escapes. Some of the power is absorbed by the gases in the atmosphere and is re-radiated in all directions including back down to the earth's surface, causing further warming that we have neglected to take into account. In other words, this model neglects the greenhouse effect. This simple model also points to the general fact that increasing the albedo (more energy reflected) results in lower temperatures.

The model used in Worked example 2.2 assumes that the *surface* of the earth behaves as a black body ($e = 1$ and $\alpha = 0$) but that the atmosphere does not ($\alpha = 0.30$). Another drawback of the simple model is that it is essentially a zero-dimensional model. The earth is treated as a point without interactions between the surface and the atmosphere. (Latent heat flows, thermal energy flow in oceans through currents and thermal energy transfer between the surface and the atmosphere due to temperature differences between the two are all ignored.) Realistic models must take all these factors (and many others) into account and so are very complex.

The albedo of the earth varies which is why we use an average value. The variations depend on whether an area is covered by many or few clouds, latitude (high latitudes include more snow and ice coverage, $\alpha = 0.80$), on whether one is over deserts ($\alpha = 0.40$), forests ($\alpha = 0.14$) or deep ocean water ($\alpha = 0.06$) and so on.

CHECK YOURSELF 2

In the simple example of worked example 8.2, would you expect the average temperature of the earth to increase or decrease if the albedo were to increase?

The greenhouse effect

The earth's surface radiates as all bodies do. But the earth's surface is at an average temperature of 288 K and using Wien's law, we find that the peak wavelength at which this energy is radiated is an infrared wavelength. Unlike visible light wavelengths, which pass through the atmosphere mainly unobstructed, infrared radiation is strongly absorbed by various gases in the atmosphere, the so-called **greenhouse gases**. This radiation is in turn re-radiated by these gases in all directions. This means that some of this radiation is received by the earth's surface again, causing additional warming (Figure 8.5).

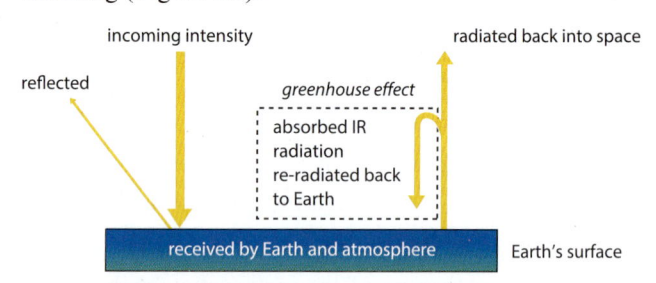

Figure 8.5: A simplified energy transfer diagram to illustrate the greenhouse effect.

This is radiation that would be lost in space were it not for the greenhouse gases. Without this **greenhouse effect**, the earth's temperature would be 32 K lower than what it is now.

The greenhouse effect may be described as the warming of the earth caused by infrared radiation, emitted by the earth's surface, which is absorbed by various gases in the earth's atmosphere and is then partly re-radiated towards the surface. The gases primarily responsible for this absorption (the greenhouse gases) are water vapour, carbon dioxide, methane and nitrous oxide.

The greenhouse effect is a natural consequence of the presence of the atmosphere. There is, however, also the **enhanced greenhouse effect**. This refers to additional warming due to increased quantities of the greenhouse gases in the atmosphere. The increases in the gas concentrations are due to human activity and are closely related to the burning of fossil fuels.

8 The greenhouse effect

Greenhouse gas	Natural sources	Anthropogenic sources
H_2O	evaporation of water from oceans, rivers and lakes	irrigation
CO_2	forest fires, volcanic eruptions, evaporation of water from oceans	burning fossil fuels in power plants, cars, airplanes, burning forests
CH_4	wetlands, oceans, lakes and rivers, termites	flooded rice fields, farm animals, processing of coal, natural gas and oil, burning biomass
N_2O	forests, oceans, soil and grasslands	burning fossil fuels, manufacture of cement, fertilisers, deforestation (reduction of nitrogen fixation in plants)

Table 8.2: Sources of greenhouse gases.

Greenhouse gases in the atmosphere have natural as well as human-made (anthropogenic) origins (Table 8.2). Along with these sources of the greenhouse gases, we have 'sinks' as well, that is to say, mechanisms that reduce these concentrations. For example, carbon dioxide is absorbed by plants during photosynthesis; it is also dissolved in oceans.

Mechanism of photon absorption

As with atoms, the energy of molecules is discrete; molecules have energy levels as we will see in Chapter 21. The difference in energy between molecular energy levels is the energy of an infrared photon. This means that infrared photons travelling through greenhouse gases will be absorbed. The gas molecules that have absorbed the photons will now be excited to higher energy levels. But the molecules prefer to be in low-energy states, and so they will immediately make a transition to a lower-energy state by emitting the photons they absorbed. But these photons are not all emitted outwards into space. Some are emitted back towards the earth, thereby warming the earth's surface (Figure 8.6).

There is an alternative way to explain photon absorption by the greenhouse gases. This makes use of the concept of resonance, which we will discuss further in Chapter 15. All systems have their own natural frequency of oscillation. For example, a pendulum oscillates back and forth with a frequency that depends on the length of the string to which it is attached. Suppose we exert a force on the pendulum by pushing it at regular intervals of time. How will the pendulum respond to this external force? It turns out

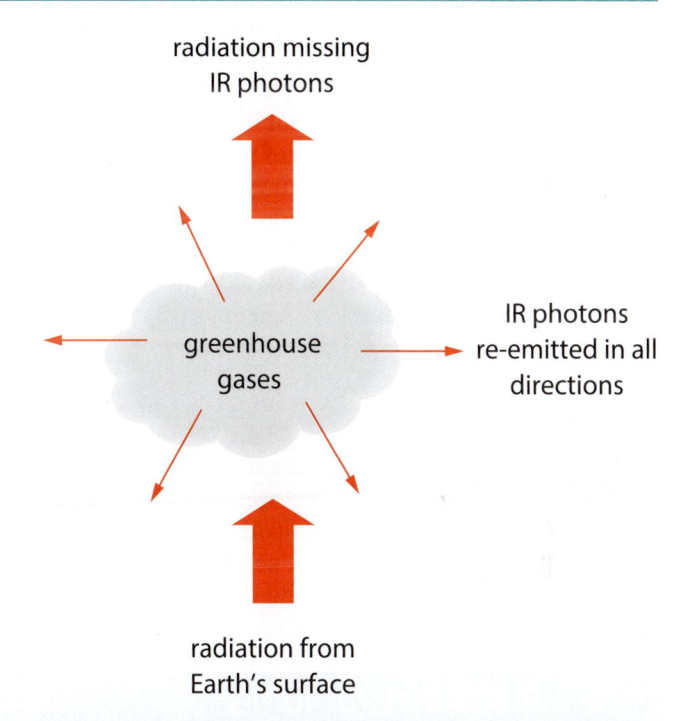

Figure 8.6: Greenhouse gases absorb infrared (IR) photons and re-radiate them in all directions.

that the amplitude of the oscillations (how far out the pendulum swings to the sides) will be large only when the frequency with which the external force is applied is equal to the natural frequency of the pendulum. When this happens we have resonance. In the case of the greenhouse gases the natural frequency is the frequency of the photons the greenhouse gases can absorb. Resonance is achieved when the photons emitted by the earth's surface have the same frequency as the natural frequency. In that case, photons will be absorbed.

PHYSICS FOR THE IB DIPLOMA: COURSEBOOK

WORKED EXAMPLE 8.3

One consequence of warming of the earth is that more water will evaporate from the oceans. Predict whether this fact alone will tend to increase the temperature of the earth further or whether it will tend to reduce it.

Answer

Evaporating means that energy must be transferred to water to turn it into vapour, and so this energy will have to come from the surroundings, reducing the temperature. Further, there will be more cloud cover, so more solar radiation will be reflected back into space, further reducing temperatures. This is an example of negative feedback: the temperature increases for some reason, but the effect of this increase is a tendency of the temperature to decrease and not increase further. (There is, however, another factor of positive feedback that will tend to increase temperatures: evaporating water means that the carbon dioxide that was dissolved in the water will now return to the atmosphere!) To decide the overall effect, detailed calculations are necessary. (Negative feedback wins in this case.)

THEORY OF KNOWLEDGE

To reach reliable predictions about climate change and its consequences, very complex and time-consuming modelling is required. Even before models are constructed we need accurate and reliable data to be the input to the models. Models for climate behaviour are complex because of the very large number of parameters involved, the interdependence of these parameters on various kinds of feedback effects and the sensitivity of the equations on the initial values of the parameters. This makes predictions somewhat less reliable than we would like. This gives ammunition to some politicians not to accept the reality of climate change. Advances in computing power, the availability of more data and further testing and debate on the various models will improve our ability to predict climate change more accurately in the future, and this will hopefully force governments into action so as to limit the damage caused by climate change.

Links

Climate change is an instance where many scientific disciplines come into play. To understand how the greenhouse gases absorb infrared radiation we need to understand atomic physics (Chapter 21), to understand how they radiate we need to understand the Stefan–Boltzmann law (Chapters 7 and 8) and to understand how energy is exchanged between the surface and the atmosphere we need the methods of heat transfer (Chapter 7). We also need atmospheric physics to tell us how clouds are formed and how they move, and finally we need sophisticated computer code to model all the complex interactions taking place.

TEST YOUR UNDERSTANDING

6   A surface *absorbs* 120 W m^{-2} of radiation and reflects 30 W m^{-2}. What is the albedo of the surface?

7   The following data are available for a climate model of a planet in equilibrium (Figure 8.7):

Incident intensity on planet	340 W m^{-2}
Incident intensity on surface	160 W m^{-2}
Intensity reflected from cloud	75 W m^{-2}
Intensity reflected from surface	30 W m^{-2}

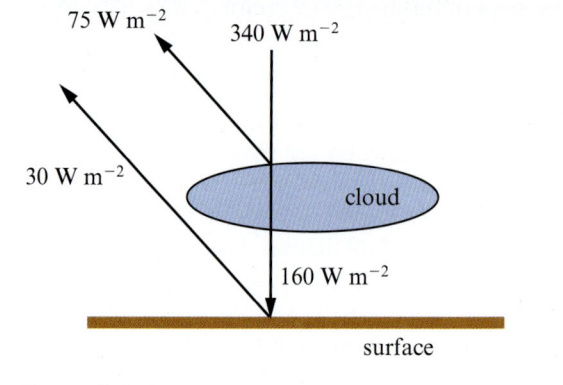

Figure 8.7: For question 7.

CONTINUED

  a What is the albedo of the cloud?
  b What is the albedo of the surface?
  c What is the albedo of the planet?
  d What is the intensity absorbed by the cloud?
  e What is the total radiated intensity into space?

8 The following data are available for a climate model of the earth in equilibrium (Figure 8.8):

Solar intensity	180 W m^{-2}
Intensity of greenhouse gases radiation	320 W m^{-2}
Convection currents	85 W m^{-2}

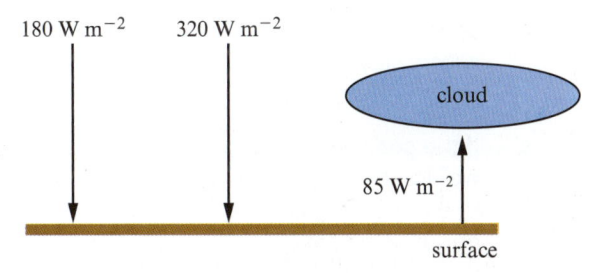

Figure 8.8: For question 8.

What is the intensity radiated by the surface?

9 Construct an energy flow diagram for an energy-balanced model of a planet with the following data:

The whole planet is in equilibrium and so is the surface (S) by itself and the cloud and atmosphere system (CAS) by itself.

Incoming solar intensity	100 W m^{-2}
Incoming solar intensity absorbed by CAS	23 W m^{-2}
Intensity reflected by CAS	23 W m^{-2}
Intensity reflected by S	7.0 W m^{-2}
Intensity radiated by CAS into space	58 W m^{-2}
Intensity radiated by S	116 W m^{-2}
Convection currents and latent heat into CAS from S	29 W m^{-2}

Use your diagram to find the following intensities:

  a Solar intensity absorbed by surface
  b The radiation emitted by the surface that escapes into space
  c The radiation emitted by the surface that gets absorbed by CAS
  d The radiation emitted by CAS back down to the surface

  and

  e Calculate the albedo of the surface.

10 A researcher uses the following data for a simple climatic model of a planet without an atmosphere: incident solar radiation = 350 W m^{-2}, absorbed solar radiation = 250 W m^{-2}.

  a Make an energy transfer diagram for these data.
  b Determine the average albedo for the planet that is to be used in the modelling.
  c Determine the intensity of the outgoing long-wave radiation.
  d Estimate the temperature of the planet according to this model, assuming a constant planet temperature. Take the emissivity of the surface to be 1 minus the albedo in **b**.

11 The present equilibrium temperature of the earth is 288 K. An increase in greenhouse gas concentrations in the atmosphere will lead to a new and higher equilibrium temperature of the earth. Carefully explain why. (Use the Stefan–Boltzmann law.)

12 The distance d between the sun and the earth is increasing very slowly. This means the earth's average temperature T will go down. The fraction of the power radiated by the sun that is received on earth is proportional to $\frac{1}{d^2}$; the power radiated by the earth is proportional to T^4.

CONTINUED

    a Deduce the dependence of the temperature T of the earth on the distance d.

    b Hence estimate the expected drop in temperature if the distance increases by 1.0%. Take the average temperature of the earth to be 288 K.

    c Can you think of a reason why the sun–earth distance might be increasing?

    d The distance is actually increasing at a rate of 1.5 cm per year. This distance is now 1.5×10^{11} m. After how many years will the distance increase by 1%?

13 Assume that the planet Venus has a circular orbit around the sun with orbit radius 1.08×10^{11} m. The albedo of the planet is 0.75.

    a Show that the solar constant at the position of Venus is about 2.6 kW m^{-2}.

    b Estimate the equilibrium temperature of Venus.

    c The surface temperature of Venus varies from 710 K to 760 K. What can we conclude about the atmosphere of Venus?

    d Mercury is closer to the sun than Venus but has a lower average surface temperature and a huge variation (700 K to 100 K) between day and night temperature. What can we conclude about the atmosphere of Mercury?

14 A body radiates energy at a rate (power) P.

    a Deduce that the intensity of this radiation at distance d from the body is given by:
$$I = \frac{P}{4\pi d^2}$$

    b State *one* assumption made in deriving this result.

15 **a** Define the term *albedo*.

    b State *three* factors that the albedo of earth depends on.

    c State what is meant by the *greenhouse effect*.

    d State the main greenhouse gases in the earth's atmosphere, and for each give *one* natural and *one* human-made source.

16 Outline the main ways in which the surface of the earth transfers thermal energy to the atmosphere and to space.

17 **a** Compare the albedo of a subtropical, warm, dry land with that of a tropical ocean.

    b Suggest mechanisms through which the subtropical land and the tropical ocean transfer thermal energy to the atmosphere.

    c If the sea level were to increase, sea water would cover dry land. Suggest *one* change in the regional climate that might come about as a result.

18 Evaporation is a method of thermal energy loss. Explain whether you would expect this method to be more significant for a tropical ocean or an arctic ocean.

19 It is estimated that a change of albedo by 0.01 will result in a 1 °C temperature change. A large area of the earth consists of 60% water and 40% land. Calculate the expected change in temperature if melting ice causes a change in the proportion of the area covered by water from 60% to 70%. Take the albedo of dry land to be 0.30 and that of water to be 0.10.

8 The greenhouse effect

SELF-ASSESSMENT CHECKLIST

I am able to …	Section	Not yet	Nearly there	Ready to move on
apply the Stefan–Boltzmann radiation law	8.1			
determine the temperature of a radiating body from its spectrum curve	8.1			
understand the concepts of emissivity and albedo	8.1			
perform simple energy balance calculations	8.2			
explain why the average solar constant is $\frac{S}{4}$	8.2			
appreciate the greenhouse effect	8.2			
describe the mechanism of photon absorption	8.2			

REFLECTION

Can you explain the *greenhouse effect*? Can you calculate the *equilibrium temperature* of a body? Can you describe the mechanism by which greenhouse gases absorb infrared radiation?

EXAM-STYLE QUESTIONS

You can find questions in the style of IB exams in the digital coursebook.

CHECK YOURSELF ANSWERS

1. a. The area increases by a factor of 4 and so the power increases by $4 \times 2^4 = 64$.

   b. The intensity depends on temperature so it increases by 16.

2. From $\sigma T^4 = (1 - \alpha)\frac{S}{4}$ an increase in albedo reduces the temperature.

Chapter 9
The gas laws

LEARNING OBJECTIVES

In this chapter you will learn how to:

- use the concepts of the mole, the molar mass and the Avogadro constant
- solve problems using moles, molar masses and the Avogadro constant
- use the concept of pressure
- solve problems using the equation of state of an ideal gas
- understand the assumptions behind the kinetic model of an ideal gas
- understand the connection between average kinetic energy of molecules and the kelvin temperature
- recognise the conditions under which a real gas may be described by the ideal gas law.

9 The gas laws

> **GUIDING QUESTIONS**
>
> - How can the macroscopic behaviour of gases be explained in terms of the motion of molecules?
> - What is the origin of pressure in a gas?

Introduction

This chapter introduces the equation that relates the pressure, volume, absolute temperature and number of moles of an ideal gas: the equation of state of an ideal gas.

By applying ideas of mechanics to the motion of molecules, we can derive a formula that relates the pressure of a gas to its density and root mean square speed of the molecules. Combining this equation with the equation of state results in one of the jewels of nineteenth-century physics—that the average kinetic energy of molecules is directly proportional to the absolute temperature.

9.1 Moles, molar mass and the Avogadro constant

According to the new definitions of SI units, one **mole** of any substance contains as many particles as atoms in 12 g of carbon-12; this is exactly $6.02214076 \times 10^{23}$ particles. This number is known as the **Avogadro constant**, N_A, and is one of the fundamental constants of physics.

What we mean by 'particle' depends on the substance; it can be a single atom or a molecule. For example, the particles in carbon are single atoms, the particles in hydrogen gas (H_2) are diatomic molecules and the particles in carbon dioxide gas (CO_2) are triatomic molecules.

So, one mole of carbon, one mole of H_2 and one mole of CO_2 all contain 6.02×10^{23} particles.

	Number of particles	Consisting of
One mole of carbon	6.02×10^{23}	6.02×10^{23} atoms of carbon
One mole of H_2	6.02×10^{23}	$2 \times 6.02 \times 10^{23}$ hydrogen atoms
One mole of CO_2	6.02×10^{23}	6.02×10^{23} carbon atoms and $2 \times 6.02 \times 10^{23}$ oxygen atoms

Table 9.1

If a substance contains N particles then the number of moles n is:

$$n = \frac{N}{N_A}$$

> **KEY POINT**
>
> The **molar mass** of a substance is the mass, in grams, of one mole of the substance.
> The unit of molar mass is g mol^{-1}.

For the element $^A_Z X$ (which contains Z protons, A protons and neutrons and Z electrons) the molar mass is *approximately* A g mol^{-1}. So, for example, the molar mass of $^4_2 He$ is 4 g mol^{-1} and that of $^{238}_{92} U$ is 238 g mol^{-1}.

The number of moles in a quantity of m grams of a substance with molar mass μ is then $n = \frac{m}{\mu}$.

> **CHECK YOURSELF 1**
>
> a Which has more atoms: 5 moles of $^4_2 He$ or 1 mole of $^{20}_{10} Ne$?
>
> b Which has more atoms: 1 kg of $^4_2 He$ or 1 kg of $^{238}_{92} U$?
>
> c Which atom is heavier: an atom of $^4_2 He$ or an atom of $^{238}_{92} U$?

189

PHYSICS FOR THE IB DIPLOMA: COURSEBOOK

WORKED EXAMPLE 9.1

a Estimate the number of atoms of gold in 1.0 kg of gold ($^{197}_{79}$Au).

b Calculate the mass of an atom of gold.

Answer

a The molar mass of gold is 197 g mol^{-1}. So 1000 g of gold (= 1 kg) contains $\frac{1000}{197} \approx 5.1$ mol. One mole contains 6.02×10^{23} atoms, so the number of atoms in 1 kg of gold is

$6.02 \times 10^{23} \times 5.1 = 3 \times 10^{24}$.

b One mole of gold has a mass of 197 g and contains N_A, atoms. Hence the mass of one atom is

$\frac{197 \times 10^{-3}}{6.02 \times 10^{23}} = 3.3 \times 10^{-25}$ kg.

WORKED EXAMPLE 9.2

Calculate how many grams of scandium, $^{45}_{21}$Sc, contain the same number of particles as 8.0 g of argon, $^{40}_{18}$Ar.

Answer

The molar mass of argon is 40 g mol^{-1}, so a quantity of 8.0 g of argon corresponds to $\frac{8.0}{40} = 0.20$ mol. Thus, we need 0.20 mol of scandium. This corresponds to $0.20 \times 45 = 9.0$ g.

WORKED EXAMPLE 9.3

Estimate the number of water molecules in an ordinary glass of water. The molar mass of water is 18 g mol^{-1}.

Answer

A glass contains about 200 cm^3 of water, which has a mass of 200 g. So the glass contains $\frac{200}{18} \approx 11$ mol or $6.02 \times 10^{23} \times 11 \approx 7 \times 10^{24}$ molecules of water.

TEST YOUR UNDERSTANDING

1 How many tyres are there in one mole of Ferraris?

2 Calculate the number of *molecules* in 28 g of hydrogen gas (H$_2$, molar mass 2.0 g mol^{-1}).

3 A substance has a molar mass of 28 g mol^{-1}. How many moles of the substance are there in 12 g of the substance?

4 Calculate the number of moles in 6.0 g of helium gas (molar mass 4.0 g mol^{-1}).

5 Determine the number of moles in a sample of a gas that contains 2.0×10^{24} molecules.

6 A substance has a molar mass of 32 g mol^{-1}. What is the mass in grams of 3 moles of the substance?

7 A sample contains 3.0×10^{24} molecules. The molar mass of the sample is 12 g mol^{-1}. What is the mass of the sample?

8 Determine the mass in grams of carbon (molar mass 12 g mol^{-1}) that contains as many molecules as 21 g of krypton (molar mass 84 g mol^{-1}).

9 The molar mass of helium is 4.0 g mol^{-1}. Calculate the mass of a helium atom.

9.2 Ideal gases

Pressure

Pressure is defined as the normal force applied per unit area. In Figure 9.1a the force is normal to the area A, so the pressure is:

$$P = \frac{F}{A}$$

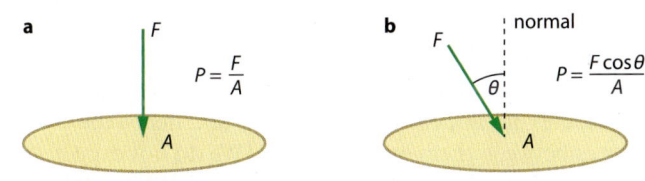

Figure 9.1: Pressure is the normal force per unit area.

The force in Figure 9.1b acts at an angle θ, so the pressure on the area A is given by the expression:

$$P = \frac{F \cos \theta}{A}$$

The unit of pressure is newton per square metre, $N\,m^{-2}$, also known as the pascal, Pa.

Another commonly used non-SI unit is the **atmosphere**, atm, which is equal to 1.013×10^5 Pa.

Figure 9.2 shows a molecule that collides with a container wall. The momentum normal to the wall before the collision is $mv \cos \theta$. After the collision momentum normal to the wall is $-mv \cos \theta$. So the change in momentum has magnitude $2mv \cos \theta$. The fact that the momentum of the molecule has changed means that a force acted on the molecule (from the wall). By Newton's third law, therefore, the molecule exerted on the wall an equal and opposite force. Taking into account the forces due to all the molecules colliding with the walls results in a force, and hence pressure, on the walls.

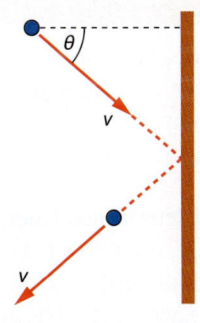

Figure 9.2: A molecule has its momentum changed when it collides with a wall. A force is exerted on the molecule, and so the molecule exerts an equal and opposite force on the wall.

> **EXAM TIP**
>
> You must be able to give an explanation of pressure in terms of molecules colliding with the container walls.

WORKED EXAMPLE 9.4

A solid cylinder of density 8.0×10^3 kg m^{-3} has height $h = 25$ cm (see Figure 9.3).

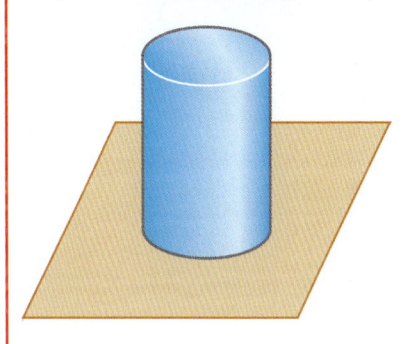

Figure 9.3: For worked example 9.4.

What is the pressure exerted by the cylinder on the horizontal surface on which it rests?

Answer

The surface exerts a normal force on the cylinder equal to the weight of the cylinder, and so the cylinder exerts the same force on the surface.

The weight of the cylinder is:

$$W = mg = \rho V g = 8.0 \times 10^3 \times A \times 0.25 \times 9.8 \text{ N}$$

where A is the area of the base and ρ is the density.

This weight acts on an area A so the pressure is:

$$P = \frac{8.0 \times 10^3 \times A \times 0.25 \times 9.8}{A} = 2.0 \times 10^4 \text{ Pa}$$

PHYSICS FOR THE IB DIPLOMA: COURSEBOOK

> **CHECK YOURSELF 2**
>
> Two solid cylinders made of the same material rest on a horizontal surface (see Figure 9.4). Which cylinder exerts the greater pressure?
>
> **Figure 9.4:** For check yourself question 2.
>
> a   The taller cylinder
> b   The shorter cylinder
> c   The heavier cylinder
> d   The lighter cylinder

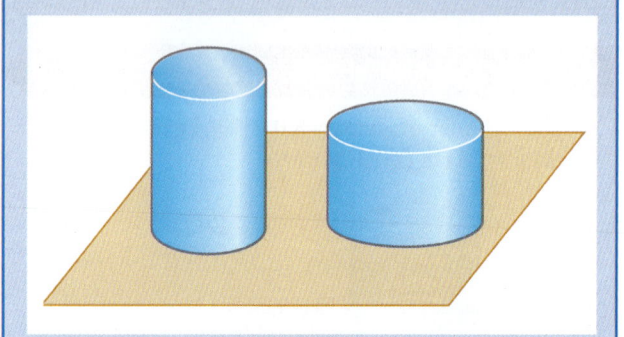

The ideal gas

An **ideal gas** is a theoretical model of a gas. It helps us to understand the behaviour of **real gases**. We assume that an ideal gas obeys the following:

- The molecules are point particles, each with negligible volume.
- The molecules obey the laws of mechanics.
- There are no forces between the molecules except when the molecules collide.
- The duration of a collision is negligible compared to the time between collisions.
- The collisions of the molecules with each other and with the container walls are elastic.
- Molecules have a range of speeds and move randomly.

> **EXAM TIP**
>
> You must be able to recall and describe a few of these assumptions in an exam.

An ideal gas (unlike real gases) cannot be liquefied or solidified. You should be able to see how some of these assumptions may not be obeyed by a real gas. For example, there will always be forces between molecules of a real gas, not just when the molecules are in contact. In general, we expect that a real gas will behave like an ideal gas when the density is low (so that molecules are not close to each other and hence the forces between them are negligible). We do not expect ideal gas behaviour at high densities (molecules will be too close to each other and will exert forces on each other). Similarly, we do not expect ideal gas behaviour from a real gas at very low temperature because the gas will then become a liquid or even a solid! We also do not want *very* high temperatures. At very high temperatures collisions between molecules may not be elastic as some energy may be transferred to electrons in atoms forcing them to make transitions to higher energy levels (see Chapter 21).

> **KEY POINT**
>
> A real gas may be approximated by an ideal gas when the density is low and the temperature moderate.

(*Low* and *moderate* are vague words because we have to compare them with something else! The interested reader may want to research this further.)

> **EXAM TIP**
>
> A real gas may be approximated by an ideal gas at low density which is equivalent to low pressure and moderate temperature.

The **state of a gas** is determined when we know the values of the pressure, the volume, the temperature and the number of moles present. The parameters P, V, T and n are related to each other. The equation relating them is called the equation of state or the ideal gas law. Our objective is to discover the equation of state for a gas. To do this a number of simple experiments can be performed as described in the following sections.

9 The gas laws

The pressure–volume law (Boyle–Mariotte law)

The equipment shown in Figure 9.5 can be used to investigate the relationship between pressure and volume of a fixed quantity of gas that is kept at constant temperature.

The pump forces oil to move higher, decreasing the volume of the air trapped in the tube above the oil. A pressure gauge reads the pressure of the trapped air, and so the relationship between pressure and volume may be investigated. The changes in pressure and volume must take place slowly so that the temperature stays the same.

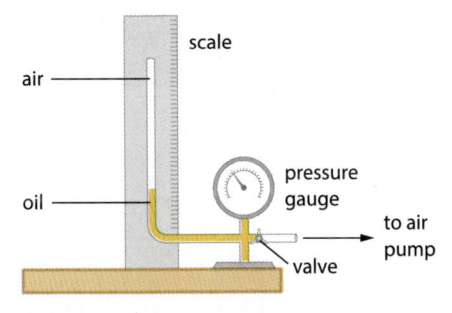

Figure 9.5: Apparatus for investigating the pressure–volume law. The pump forces oil to move up the tube, decreasing the volume of air.

The results of a typical experiment are shown in Figure 9.6. We have plotted *pressure* against the *inverse of the volume* and obtained a straight line through the origin.

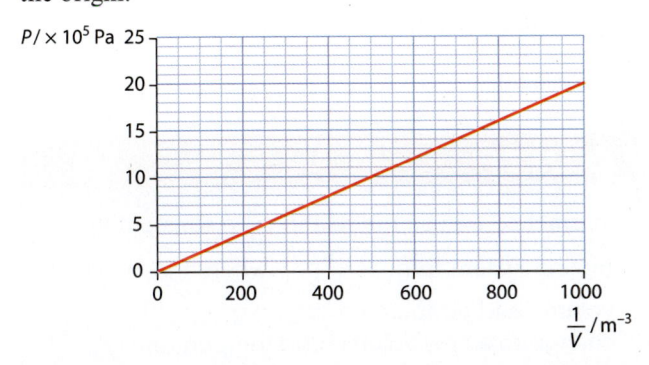

Figure 9.6: Graph of *pressure* against *inverse volume* at constant temperature.

This implies that at constant temperature and with a fixed quantity of gas, pressure is inversely proportional to volume, that is:

$P \propto \frac{1}{V}$ or $PV = $ constant

Figure 9.7 shows the same data now plotted as *pressure* against *volume*.

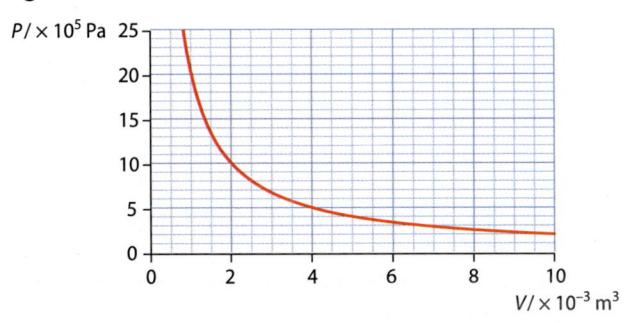

Figure 9.7: The relationship between pressure and volume at constant temperature for a fixed quantity of a gas. The product PV is the same for all points on the curve.

The curve in the pressure–volume diagram is known as an **isothermal curve**: the temperature at all points on the curve is the same.

> **EXAM TIP**
>
> In practice we use the relation $PV = $ constant in the equivalent form $P_1V_1 = P_2V_2$ when the initial pressure and volume (P_1, V_1) change to a new pressure and volume (P_2, V_2) at constant temperature.

> **WORKED EXAMPLE 9.5**
>
> The pressure of a fixed quantity of gas is 2.0 atm and its volume is 0.90 dm³. The pressure is increased to 6.0 atm at constant temperature. Determine the new volume.
>
> **Answer**
>
> Use $P_1V_1 = P_2V_2$.
>
> Substituting the known values we have:
>
> $2.0 \times 0.90 = 6.0 \times V$
>
> $V = 0.30$ dm³

The volume–temperature law (Charles' law)

The dependence of volume on temperature of a fixed quantity of gas kept at constant pressure can be investigated with the apparatus shown in Figure 9.8. Air is trapped in a thin capillary tube that is immersed

193

in heated water. The air is trapped by a thin thread of very concentrated sulfuric acid. The thread is exposed to the atmosphere, and so the pressure of the trapped air is constant.

It is found that the volume increases uniformly with temperature. The striking fact is that when the straight line is extended backwards it always crosses the temperature axis at −273 °C, as in Figure 9.9. This suggests that there exists a minimum possible temperature, namely −273 °C. (With a real gas the experiment cannot be conducted at very low temperatures since the gas would liquefy—hence the dotted line.

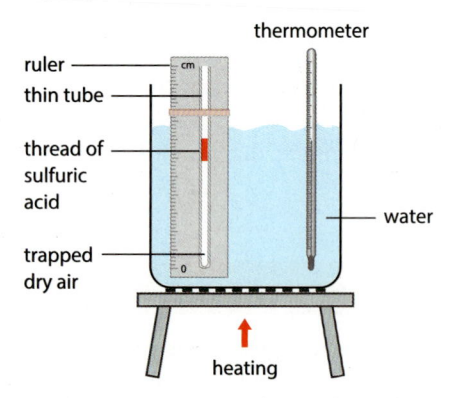

Figure 9.8: Apparatus for verifying the volume–temperature law.

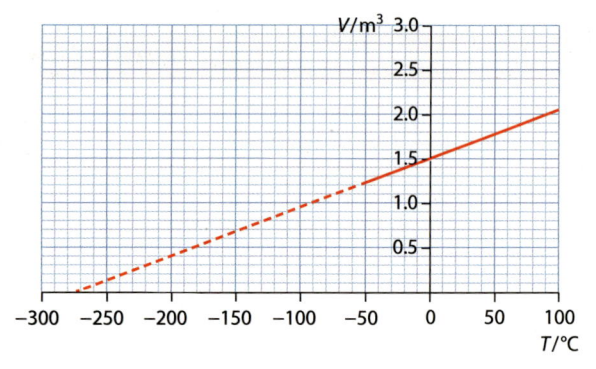

Figure 9.9: When the graph of *volume* against *temperature* is extended backwards the line intersects the temperature axis at −273 °C.

If this same experiment is repeated with a different quantity of gas, or a gas at a different constant pressure, the result is the same. In each case, the straight-line graph of *volume* against *temperature* crosses the temperature axis at −273 °C (Figure 9.10). In Figure 9.11, the same graphs are drawn using the Kelvin temperature scale.

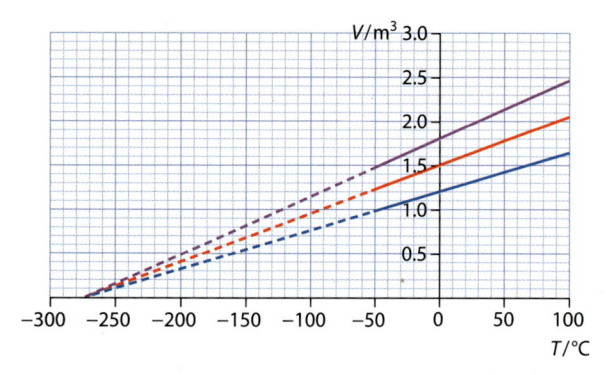

Figure 9.10: When the graph of *volume* against *temperature* is extended backwards, all the lines intersect the temperature axis at the same point.

When the temperature is expressed in kelvin we obtain the graphs of Figure 9.11.

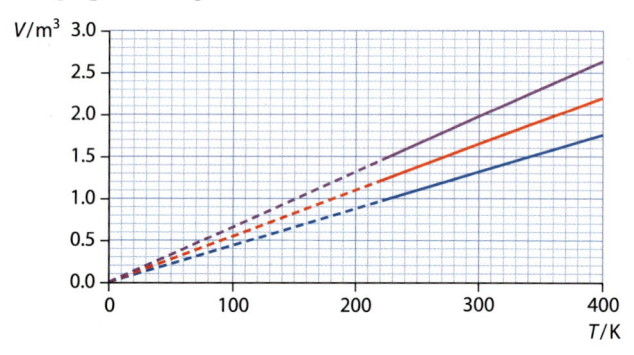

Figure 9.11: When temperature is expressed in kelvin, the lines start at zero temperature.

When the temperature is expressed in kelvin, this experiment implies that at constant pressure:

$$\frac{V}{T} = \text{constant}$$

EXAM TIP

In practice we use the relation $\frac{V}{T}$ = constant in the equivalent form as $\frac{V_1}{T_1} = \frac{V_2}{T_2}$ where the initial volume and temperature of the gas (V_1, T_1) change to a new volume and temperature (V_2, T_2) at constant pressure.

9 The gas laws

WORKED EXAMPLE 9.6

A gas expands at constant pressure from an original volume of 2.0 m³ at 22 °C to a volume of 4.0 m³. Calculate the new temperature.

Answer

Substituting in $\frac{V_1}{T_1} = \frac{V_2}{T_2}$ it follows that:

$\frac{2.0}{295} = \frac{4.0}{T}$

$\Rightarrow T = 590$ K or 317 °C

Note that we converted the original temperature into kelvin. (It is very easy to forget this conversion and get the incorrect answer of 44 °C.)

The pressure–temperature law (Gay-Lussac's law)

What remains now is to investigate the dependence of pressure on temperature of a fixed quantity of gas in a fixed volume. This can be done with the apparatus shown in Figure 9.12. The gas container is surrounded by water whose temperature can be changed. A pressure gauge measures the pressure of the gas. We find that pressure increases uniformly with increasing temperature, as shown by the graph in Figure 9.13.

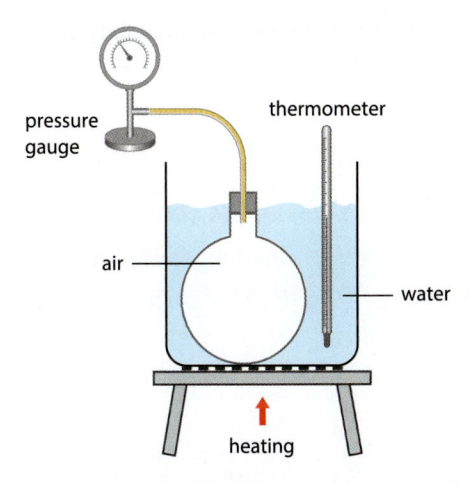

Figure 9.12: Investigating the pressure–temperature law.

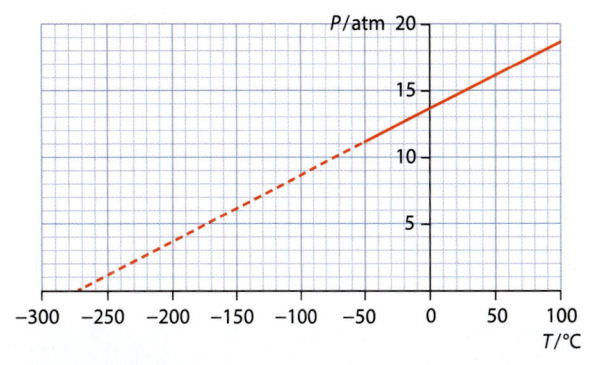

Figure 9.13: The graph of *pressure* against *temperature* is a straight line that, when extended backwards, again intersects the temperature axis at −273 °C.

For quantities of gases containing different numbers of moles at different volumes the results are the same, as shown in Figure 9.14. When the temperature is expressed in kelvin, the straight lines all pass through the origin (Figure 9.15).

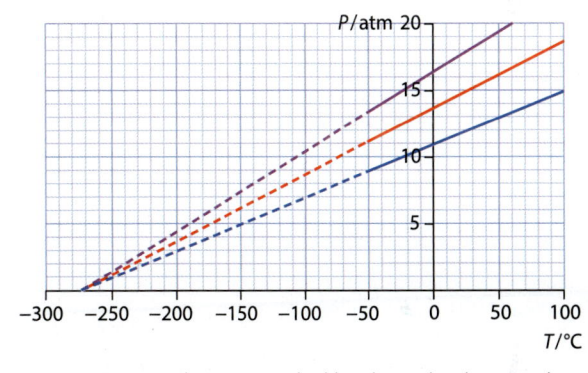

Figure 9.14: When extended backwards, the graphs of *pressure* against *temperature* for three different quantities of gas all intersect the temperature axis at the same point.

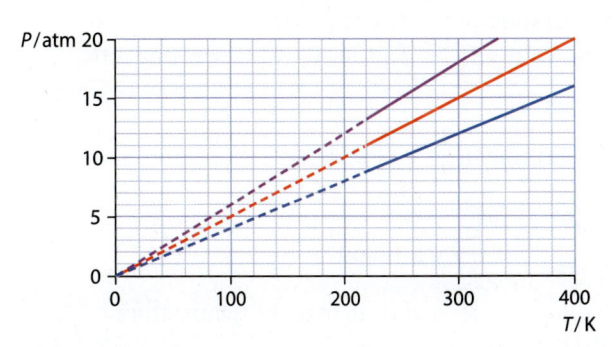

Figure 9.15: If temperature is expressed in kelvin, the lines start at zero temperature.

When the temperature is expressed in kelvin, this experiment implies that at constant volume:

$\frac{P}{T}$ = constant

195

> **PHYSICS FOR THE IB DIPLOMA: COURSEBOOK**

EXAM TIP

In practice we use the relation $\frac{P}{T}$ = constant in the equivalent form $\frac{P_1}{T_1} = \frac{P_2}{T_2}$ where the initial pressure and temperature of the gas (P_1, T_1) change to a new pressure and temperature (P_2, T_2) at constant volume. (Remember, T is in kelvin.)

CHECK YOURSELF 3

The graph (Figure 9.16) shows the variation with kelvin temperature of the pressure of equal quantities of two gases at different volume.

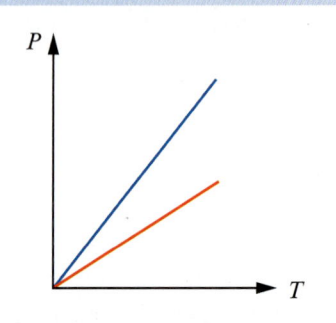

Figure 9.16: For check yourself question 3.

Which gas has the smaller volume?

WORKED EXAMPLE 9.7

A gas in a container of fixed volume is heated from a temperature of 37 °C and pressure 3.0×10^5 Pa to a temperature of 87 °C. Calculate the new pressure.

Answer

Substituting in $\frac{P_1}{T_1} = \frac{P_2}{T_2}$ we have:

$$\frac{3.0 \times 10^5}{310} = \frac{P}{360}$$

$$\Rightarrow \quad P = 3.5 \times 10^5 \text{ Pa}$$

(Notice that we had to change the temperature into kelvin.)

The ideal gas law

If we combine the results of the three preceding experiments, we find that:

$\frac{PV}{T}$ = constant

What is the value of the constant? To determine that, we repeat all of the preceding experiments, this time using different quantities of the gas. We discover that the constant in the last equation is proportional to the number of moles n of the gas in question:

$\frac{PV}{T} = n \times$ constant

We can now measure the pressure, temperature, volume and number of moles for a large number of different gases and calculate the value of $\frac{PV}{nT}$.

We find that this constant has the same value for all gases—it is a universal constant. We call this the **gas constant** R.

It has the numerical value $R = 8.31$ J K^{-1} mol^{-1}.

Thus, finally, the **ideal gas law** (also known as the equation of state) is:

$PV = RnT$

(Remember that temperature must always be in kelvin.)

In Section 9.3 we will see the importance of a new constant of physics, the **Boltzmann constant**:

$k_B = \frac{R}{N_A} = \frac{8.31}{6.02 \times 10^{23}} = 1.38 \times 10^{-23}$ J K^{-1}

In terms of this constant the equation of state may also written as $PV = R\frac{N}{N_A}T = Nk_B T$.

EXAM TIP

Since $R = \frac{PV}{nT}$, in practice we use the equation of state in the form $\frac{P_1 V_1}{n_1 T_1} = \frac{P_2 V_2}{n_2 T_2}$ when a gas changes from values (P_1, V_1, n_1, T_1) to (P_2, V_2, n_2, T_2).

9 The gas laws

WORKED EXAMPLE 9.8

Estimate how many molecules there are in a gas of temperature 320 K, volume 0.025 m³ and pressure 4.8×10^5 Pa.

Answer

The number is:

$$N = \frac{PV}{k_B T}$$

$$N = \frac{4.8 \times 10^5 \times 0.025}{1.38 \times 10^{-23} \times 320} = 2.7 \times 10^{24}.$$

WORKED EXAMPLE 9.9

A container of hydrogen of volume 0.10 m³ and temperature 25 °C contains 3.2×10^{23} molecules.

Calculate the pressure in the container.

Answer

$$P = \frac{Nk_B T}{V} = \frac{3.2 \times 10^{23} \times 1.38 \times 10^{-23} \times 298}{0.10}$$

$$= 1.3 \times 10^4 \, \text{Pa}$$

WORKED EXAMPLE 9.10

A fixed quantity of gas of volume 3.0×10^{-3} m³, pressure 3.0×10^5 Pa and temperature 300 K expands to a volume of 4.0×10^{-3} m³ and a pressure of 6.0×10^5 Pa. Calculate the new temperature of the gas.

Answer

Use $\frac{P_1 V_1}{n_1 T_1} = \frac{P_2 V_2}{n_2 T_2}$ with $n_1 = n_2$ to get:

$$\frac{3.0 \times 10^5 \times 3.0 \times 10^{-3}}{300} = \frac{6.0 \times 10^5 \times 4.0 \times 10^{-3}}{T}$$

Solving for T gives $T = 800$ K.

WORKED EXAMPLE 9.11

Figure 9.17 shows two isothermal curves for equal quantities of two ideal gases. State and explain which gas is at the higher temperature.

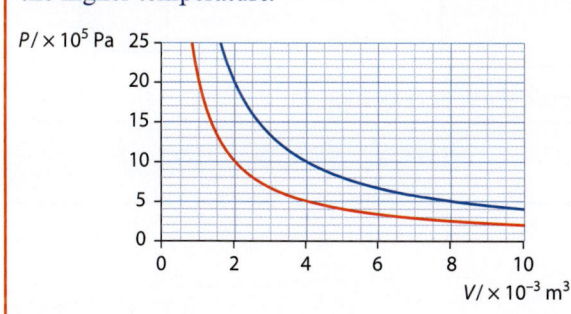

Figure 9.17: Two isothermal curves for equal quantities of two gases.

PHYSICS FOR THE IB DIPLOMA: COURSEBOOK

CONTINUED

Answer

Draw a vertical line that intersects the two isothermals at two points. At these points both gases have the same volume and n is the same.

So, for these points $\frac{P}{T}$ is constant. The point on the blue curve has higher pressure, so it must have the higher temperature.

TEST YOUR UNDERSTANDING

10 A sealed bottle contains air at 22.0 °C and a pressure of 12.0×10^5 Pa. The temperature is raised to 120.0 °C. Calculate the new pressure.

11 A gas has pressure 8.2×10^6 Pa and volume 2.3×10^{-3} m³. The pressure is reduced to 4.5×10^6 Pa at constant temperature. Calculate the new volume of the gas.

12 A mass of 12.0 kg of helium is required to fill a bottle of volume 5.00×10^{-3} m³ at a temperature of 20.0 °C. Determine the pressure in helium.

13 Determine the mass of carbon dioxide (molar mass 44 g mol⁻¹) required to fill a tank of volume 12.0×10^{-3} m³ at a temperature of 20.0 °C and a pressure of 4.00 atm.

14 A flask of volume 300.0×10^{-6} m³ contains air at a pressure of 5.00×10^5 Pa and a temperature of 27.0 °C. The flask loses molecules at a rate of 3.00×10^{19} per second. Estimate how long it takes for the pressure in the flask to fall to half its original value. (Assume that the temperature of the air remains constant during this time.)

15 The point marked in Figure 9.18 represents the state of a fixed quantity of ideal gas in a container with a movable piston. The temperature of the gas in the state shown is 600 K. Copy the diagram. Indicate on the diagram the point representing the new state of the gas after the following separate changes.

a The volume doubles at constant temperature.

b The volume doubles at constant pressure.

c The pressure halves at constant volume.

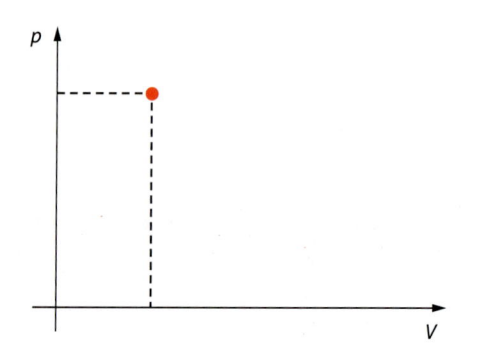

Figure 9.18: For question 15.

16 Two ideal gases are kept at the same temperature in two containers separated by a valve, as shown in Figure 9.19. Estimate the pressure when the valve is opened. (The temperature stays the same.)

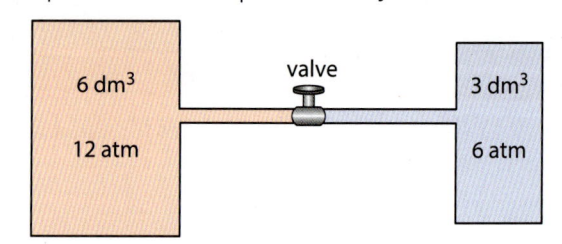

Figure 9.19: For question 16.

9 The gas laws

CONTINUED

17 Figure 9.20 shows a cylinder in a vacuum, which has a movable, frictionless piston at the top. An ideal gas is kept in the cylinder. The piston is at a distance of 0.500 m from the bottom of the cylinder and the volume of the cylinder is 0.050 m³. The weight on top of the cylinder has a mass of 10.0 kg. The temperature of the gas is 19.0 °C.

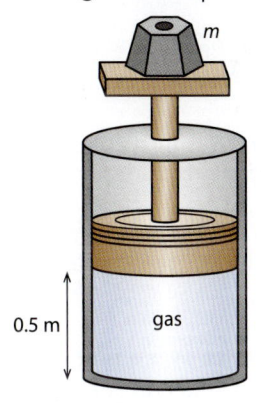

Figure 9.20: For question 17.

  a Calculate the pressure of the gas.
  b Determine how many molecules there are in the gas.
  c The temperature is increased to 152 °C. Calculate the new volume of the gas.

18 The molar mass of a gas is 28 g mol⁻¹. A container holds 2.00 mol of this gas at 0.00 °C and a pressure of 1.00×10^5 Pa. Determine the mass and volume of the gas.

19 A balloon has a volume of 404 m³ and is filled with helium of mass 70.0 kg. The temperature inside the balloon is 17.0 °C. Determine the pressure inside the balloon.

20 A flask has a volume of 5.0×10^{-4} m³ and contains air at a temperature of 300 K and a pressure of 150 kPa.

  a Calculate the number of moles of air in the flask.
  b Determine the number of molecules in the flask.
  c Estimate the mass of air in the flask. You may take the molar mass of air to be 29 g mol⁻¹.

21 The molar mass of helium is 4.00 g mol⁻¹.

  a Calculate the volume of 1.0 mol of helium at standard temperature and pressure (stp), i.e. at T = 273 K, P = 1.0×10^5 Pa.
  b Determine the density of helium at stp.

22 a A gas is heated at constant volume. Give a qualitative reason why the pressure increases.

  b A gas is heated at constant pressure. Give a qualitative reason why the volume increases.

9.3 The Boltzmann equation

The molecules of a gas move about randomly with a range of speeds. The graph in Figure 9.21 shows the distribution of speeds for oxygen molecules kept at two different temperatures: the blue curve is at 100 K and the red curve at 300 K. The vertical axis shows the fraction of molecules having a given speed v. You will not be examined on this graph but knowing a few of its features helps a lot in understanding how gases behave.

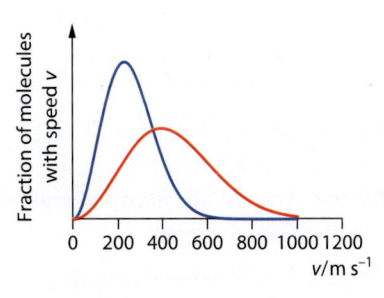

Figure 9.21: The distribution of speeds at two different temperatures.

199

We see that there is a speed that corresponds to the peak of the curve. For the blue curve this is about 200 m s^{-1} and for the red curve it is 400 m s^{-1}. The speed at the peak represents the most probable speed that would be found if you picked a molecule at random. One other speed is important:

The root mean square (rms) speed c, is the square root of the average of the squares of the speeds of the molecules; that is:

$$c = \sqrt{\frac{v_1^2 + v_2^2 + v_3^2 + \cdots + v_N^2}{N}}$$

Why do we bother to work with an rms speed? Consider the *average kinetic energy* for the N molecules, which is given by:

$$\overline{E}_K = \frac{\frac{1}{2}mv_1^2 + \frac{1}{2}mv_2^2 + \frac{1}{2}mv_3^2 + \cdots + \frac{1}{2}mv_N^2}{N}$$

$$= \frac{1}{2}m\left(\frac{v_1^2 + v_2^2 + v_3^2 + \cdots + v_N^2}{N}\right)$$

$$= \frac{1}{2}mc^2$$

So we see that the average kinetic energy involves the rms speed. These two speeds (most probable and rms speed as well as the average speed) are all different but numerically close to each other. So, even though it is not technically correct, we may assume that all three speeds mean the same thing and we will use the symbol c for all of them.

WORKED EXAMPLE 9.12

A flask contains a gas at a temperature of 300 K. An identical flask is aboard a fast-moving aircraft. The temperature inside the aircraft is 300 K. Suggest how the rms speeds of the two gases compare.

Answer

The temperature of the gas depends on the random motion of the molecules and not on any additional uniform motion imposed on the gas as a result of the motion of the container. The speeds are the same.

We will now show that the pressure of a gas can be written as $P = \frac{1}{3}\rho c^2$, where c stands for the rms speed and ρ is the density of the gas. You do not need to recall the proof of this equation for exam purposes.

Figure 9.22 shows a molecule of mass m moving with horizontal velocity v_x. The molecule collides with the walls elastically.

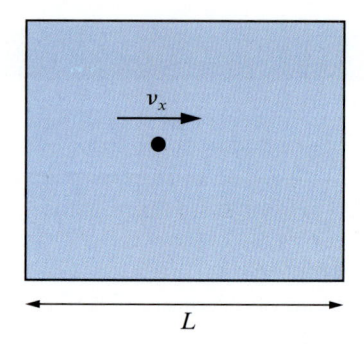

Figure 9.22: A molecule moves back and forth between the walls exerting a force at every collision.

The magnitude of the impulse during a collision with the right wall is:

$$J = mv_x - (-mv_x) = 2mv_x$$

The molecule will hit the right wall again after a time:

$$T = \frac{2L}{v}$$

We need to find the average force over a time interval long compared to T, say a time interval NT, where N is large. In this interval the total impulse is NJ and so the average force is $\frac{NJ}{NT}$ i.e. $\frac{J}{T}$.

$$\frac{J}{T} = \frac{2mv_x}{\frac{2L}{v}} = \frac{mv_x^2}{L}$$

The pressure from one molecule is then (we assume the container is a cube):

$$P_1 = \frac{\frac{mv_x^2}{L}}{L^2} = \frac{mv_x^2}{L^3} = \frac{mv_x^2}{V}$$

There are N molecules in the container so the total pressure becomes:

$$P = \frac{mv_{1x}^2}{V} + \frac{mv_{2x}^2}{V} + \cdots + \frac{mv_{Nx}^2}{V} = \frac{m}{V}(v_{1x}^2 + v_{2x}^2 + \cdots + v_{Nx}^2).$$

The average of the squares of the x components of velocity is:

$$\overline{v_x^2} = \frac{v_{1x}^2 + v_{2x}^2 + \cdots + v_{Nx}^2}{N}$$

and so $P = \frac{mN}{V}\overline{v_x^2}$.

By symmetry, $\overline{v_x^2} = \overline{v_y^2} = \overline{v_z^2}$ (all directions are equivalent)

And since $\overline{v_x^2} + \overline{v_y^2} + \overline{v_z^2} = c^2$, it follows that $\overline{v_x^2} = \frac{c^2}{3}$.

Hence the pressure is:

$$P = \frac{1}{3}\frac{Nmc^2}{V}$$

But Nm is the total mass M of the gas and so finally we get $\left(\rho = \frac{M}{V}\right)$:

$P = \frac{1}{3}\rho c^2$

Pressure is related to the rms speed and the density of the gas.

Links

Notice how the ideas we studied in Chapter 4 are also heavily used here but in a different context.

We get a very interesting result if we combine this equation with the ideal gas law. In what follows, N stands for the number of molecules and m for the mass of one molecule. Start with the ideal gas law:

$PV = Nk_B T$

replace pressure with $P = \frac{1}{3}\rho c^2$ to get:

$\left(\frac{1}{3}\rho c^2\right)V = Nk_B T$

replace density with $\frac{mass}{volume}$ to get:

$\frac{1}{3}\frac{(Nm)c^2 V}{V} = Nk_B T$

multiply both sides by $\frac{3}{2}$ to get:

$\frac{1}{2}mc^2 = \frac{3}{2}k_B T$

(Recall that the Boltzmann constant is $k_B = \frac{R}{N_A} = \frac{8.31}{6.02 \times 10^{23}} = 1.38 \times 10^{-23} \text{ J K}^{-1}$.)

The last equation states that the average random kinetic energy of the particles is directly proportional to the kelvin temperature:

$\bar{E}_K = \frac{3}{2}k_B T$

This exceptional equation relates a microscopic quantity, the average kinetic energy of molecules, to a macroscopic quantity, temperature. It also says that at $T = 0$, all molecular motion stops.

CHECK YOURSELF 4

When the volume of a fixed quantity of an ideal gas is decreased at constant temperature, the pressure will increase. Three reasons are proposed for this increase:

a the molecules collide with each other more frequently

b the molecules collide with the walls more frequently

c the molecules are moving faster on average

Which is/are the correct reason(s) for the pressure increase?

Using this equation we can find an expression for the internal energy of an ideal gas. Remember that the internal energy of an ideal gas consists only of the random kinetic energy of its molecules and zero potential energy. Suppose that the gas has N molecules. Then, since the average kinetic energy is $\frac{3}{2}k_B T$, the total random kinetic energy, i.e. the internal energy U, is:

$U = \frac{3}{2}Nk_B T$

But recall that $k_B = \frac{R}{N_A}$, so that another expression is:

$U = \frac{3}{2}nRT$

Yet another expression comes from using the ideal gas law, $PV = nRT$, which gives:

$U = \frac{3}{2}PV$

EXAM TIP

You must be able to obtain an expression for the internal energy of an ideal gas.

CHECK YOURSELF 5

Which has a greater internal energy: 40 g of helium (molar mass 4 g mol^{-1}) or 40 g of argon (molar mass 40 g mol^{-1})? Both gases are at the same temperature.

WORKED EXAMPLE 9.13

The kelvin temperature of a gas is doubled. By what factor does the average speed increase?

Answer

From $\frac{1}{2}mc^2 = \frac{3}{2}k_B T$ we find that when T is doubled then c^2 will double, so c itself will increase by a factor of $\sqrt{2}$.

WORKED EXAMPLE 9.14

Calculate the ratio of the average speed of helium (molar mass 4.0 g mol⁻¹) to argon (molar mass 40 g mol⁻¹) atoms when both gases are at the same temperature.

Answer

Since the temperature is the same for both gases, using $\frac{1}{2}mc^2 = \frac{3}{2}k_B T$ we find that:

$\frac{1}{2}m_{He}c_{He}^2 = \frac{1}{2}m_{Ar}c_{Ar}^2$ and so $\frac{c_{He}^2}{c_{Ar}^2} = \frac{m_{Ar}}{m_{He}}$

So, we need to find the ratio of the masses of the molecules.

One mole of helium has a mass of 4 g so one molecule has a mass (in grams) of $\frac{4}{N_A}$.

Similarly, the mass in grams of an argon molecule is $\frac{40}{N_A}$.

So, $\frac{c_{He}^2}{c_{Ar}^2} = \frac{\frac{40}{N_A}}{\frac{4}{N_A}} = 10 \Rightarrow \frac{c_{He}}{c_{Ar}} = \sqrt{10} \approx 3.2$

WORKED EXAMPLE 9.15

Calculate the average speed of helium ($^4_2$He) atoms at a temperature of −15 °C.

Answer

We use $\frac{1}{2}mc^2 = \frac{3}{2}k_B T$.

First we need to find the mass m of a helium atom. One mole of helium has a mass of 4.0 g so the mass of one molecule is given by:

$m = \frac{4.0}{N_A} = \frac{4.0}{6.02 \times 10^{23}} = 6.64 \times 10^{-24}$ g $= 6.64 \times 10^{-27}$ kg

Now remember to convert the temperature into kelvin: 273 − 15 = 258 K.

So we have:

$\frac{1}{2} \times 6.64 \times 10^{-27} \times c^2 = \frac{3}{2} \times 1.38 \times 10^{-23} \times 258$

This gives $c^2 = 1.61 \times 10^6$ and so $c = 1.3 \times 10^3$ m s⁻¹.

NATURE OF SCIENCE

Models must be correct but also simple

Boyle thought that a gas consists of particles joined by springs. Newton thought that a gas consists of particles that exert repulsive forces on each other. Bernoulli thought that a gas is a collection of a very large number of particles that exert forces on each other only when they collide. All three could explain why a gas exerts a pressure on its container, but Bernoulli's picture is the simplest. We assume that the ordinary laws of mechanics apply to the individual particles making up the gas. Even though the laws apply to each individual particle, we cannot observe or analyse each particle individually since there are so many of them. By concentrating on average behaviours of the whole gas and using probability and statistics, physicists developed a new field of physics known as statistical mechanics. This has had enormous success in advancing our understanding of gases and other systems, including where the approximation to an ideal gas breaks down.

TEST YOUR UNDERSTANDING

23. Helium has molar mass 4 g mol⁻¹ and neon has molar mass 20 g mol⁻¹. The helium and neon are kept in the same container. What is the ratio of:

    a the average kinetic energies of molecules $\dfrac{\bar{E}_{He}}{\bar{E}_{Ne}}$

    b the average rms speeds of molecules $\dfrac{c_{He}}{c_{Ne}}$?

24. The density of an ideal gas is 1.35 kg m⁻³. The temperature in kelvin and the pressure are both doubled. What happens to the density of the gas?

25. A gas is kept at pressure 2.8×10^5 Pa. The density of the gas is 1.2 kg m⁻³. What is the rms speed of the molecules?

26. The pressure and the volume of a fixed mass of an ideal gas are both doubled.

    a What happens to the rms speed of the molecules?

    b What happens to the internal energy?

27. A fixed mass of an ideal gas is compressed to half its volume at constant pressure.

    a What happens to the rms speed of the molecules?

    b What happens to the internal energy?

28. A fixed mass of an ideal gas is compressed to half its volume at constant temperature. Explain what happens to the rms speed of the molecules by using:

    a $P = \dfrac{1}{3}\rho c^2$

    b $\bar{E}_K = \dfrac{3}{2}k_B T$.

29. Calculate the rms speed of krypton atoms at a temperature of 350 K. The molar mass of krypton is 84 g mol⁻¹.

30. Show that the rms speed of molecules of a gas of molar mass M (expressed in kg mol⁻¹) kept at a temperature T is given by $c = \sqrt{\dfrac{3RT}{M}}$.

31. Krypton (molar mass 84 g mol⁻¹) is kept at 300 K. At what temperature would xenon (molar mass 132 g mol⁻¹) have the same rms speed as krypton?

32. Calculate the internal energy of a gas kept at pressure 1.3×10^5 Pa and volume 0.25 m³.

SELF-ASSESSMENT CHECKLIST

I am able to …	Section	Not yet	Nearly there	Ready to move on
work with moles, molar mass, Avogadro's number and number of molecules	9.1			
calculate the mass of a molecule given the molar mass	9.1			
be aware of the origin of pressure in a gas	9.2			
solve problems with the ideal gas law in various situations	9.2			
appreciate the quantitative relationship between the average random kinetic energy of molecules and the absolute temperature	9.3			
calculate the internal energy of an ideal gas	9.3			
calculate the internal energy of an ideal gas	9.3			

PHYSICS FOR THE IB DIPLOMA: COURSEBOOK

> **REFLECTION**
>
> Are you comfortable with the terms *mole* and *Avogadro's number*? Do you know the assumptions behind the kinetic model of an *ideal gas*? Do you understand the origin of *pressure* in a gas? Can you solve problems using the *gas laws*? Do you understand the connection between kelvin temperature and *average random kinetic energy*? Do you understand the conditions under which a *real gas* behaves as an ideal gas?

EXAM-STYLE QUESTIONS

You can find questions in the style of IB exams in the digital coursebook.

CHECK YOURSELF ANSWERS

1. a 5 mol of helium.

   b 1 kg of helium has 1000/4 moles whereas 1 kg of uranium has 1000/238 moles. Hence helium has more atoms.

   c 1 mol of each element has the same number of atoms, but the mole of uranium weighs more. So an atom of uranium is heavier.

2. $P = \dfrac{W}{A} = \dfrac{\rho V g}{A} = \dfrac{\rho A h g}{A} = \rho h g$.

   So, the cylinder with the greater height exerts the greater pressure.

3. Draw a vertical line that will intersect the two straight lines. These points have the same temperature. The blue line has higher pressure and so smaller volume by the Boyle–Mariotte law.

   Alternatively from $PV = nRT$ we get $P = \dfrac{nR}{V} T$ so the gradient of a P–T graph is $\dfrac{nR}{V}$. The blue curve has larger gradient and so smaller volume.

4. b is the correct answer.

   a is a correct statement, but it does not explain why the pressure increases.

   c is wrong since T = constant.

5. From $U = \dfrac{3}{2} nRT$, helium, having more moles (10 versus 1 for argon), has higher internal energy.

Chapter 10
Thermodynamics

LEARNING OBJECTIVES

In this chapter you will learn how to:

- calculate changes in the internal energy of an ideal gas
- calculate work done in thermodynamics
- apply the first law of thermodynamics
- use the first law to understand thermodynamic processes
- identify and understand isovolumetric, isobaric, isothermal and adiabatic processes
- apply the concept of entropy
- understand a statistical interpretation of entropy
- understand the second law of thermodynamics in terms of entropy
- calculate work done by a heat engine
- understand why the Carnot cycle is the most efficient cycle for given operating temperatures

PHYSICS FOR THE IB DIPLOMA: COURSEBOOK

> **GUIDING QUESTIONS**
>
> - How does the law of conservation of energy apply to thermodynamic systems?
> - Is there a limit to how much thermal energy can be converted to mechanical work?

Introduction

Thermodynamics deals with the relationships between heat, work, temperature and energy.

The first law of thermodynamics states that the amount of thermal energy given to a system is used to increase that system's internal energy and to do work.

The second law of thermodynamics places limitations on how much thermal energy can actually be transferred into mechanical work.

10.1 Internal energy

This chapter deals with how we apply the law of conservation of energy to thermodynamics. To do so, we must first discuss the concept of **internal energy**, how we calculate work done in thermodynamics and discuss various processes using pressure–volume diagrams and equations.

In Chapter 7 we defined the internal energy of a gas as the total random kinetic energy of the particles of the gas plus the potential energy associated with the intermolecular forces. If the gas is ideal, the intermolecular forces are assumed to be strictly zero, and the internal energy of the gas is just the total random kinetic energy of the particles of the gas. We have seen that the average kinetic energy of the particles is given by:

$$\bar{E}_K = \tfrac{3}{2} k_B T$$

where $k_B = \frac{R}{N_A} = 1.38 \times 10^{-23}$ J K^{-1} is the Boltzmann constant.

It follows that the internal energy U of an ideal gas with N particles is given by $N\bar{E}_K$; that is:

$$U = \tfrac{3}{2} N k_B T$$

This formula shows that the internal energy of an ideal gas is directly proportional to the (kelvin) temperature. Since $k_B = \frac{R}{N_A}$ and $PV = nRT$, we also have that:

$$U = \tfrac{3}{2} nRT = \tfrac{3}{2} PV$$

where $n = \frac{N}{N_A}$ is the number of moles.

> **EXAM TIP**
>
> You must know the equivalent ways of expressing internal energy.

> **EXAM TIP**
>
> Throughout this chapter we deal with monatomic gases.

The *change* in internal energy is thus given by the formulae:

$$\Delta U = \tfrac{3}{2} N k_B \Delta T = \tfrac{3}{2} n R \Delta T = \tfrac{3}{2} \underbrace{P \Delta V}_{\text{if } P = \text{const}}$$

$$= \tfrac{3}{2} \underbrace{V \Delta P}_{\text{if } V = \text{const}}$$

> **CHECK YOURSELF 1**
>
> A fixed quantity of an ideal gas at pressure 6.0×10^5 Pa and volume 3.0×10^{-3} m^3 undergoes a change to pressure 9.0×10^5 Pa and volume 2.0×10^{-3} m^3. What is the change in the internal energy of the gas?

Systems and processes

In thermodynamics we often deal with *systems*; this means the complete set of objects under consideration. Thus, a gas in a container is a system, as is a certain mass of ice in a glass. What is not in the system is the *surroundings* of the system. Heat can enter or leave a system depending on its temperature relative to that of the surroundings, as shown in Figure 10.1.

10 Thermodynamics

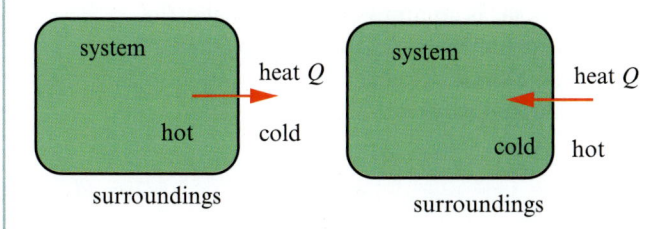

Figure 10.1: A system and its surroundings.

In a **closed system** mass cannot enter or leave the system. In an **isolated system**, no energy or mass can enter or leave the system. If all the parameters defining the system are given, we speak of the system being in a particular *state*. For example, a fixed quantity of an ideal gas is specified if its pressure, volume and temperature are specified. Any process that changes the state of a system is called a *thermodynamic process*. Thus, heating a gas may result in changed pressure, temperature or volume and is thus a thermodynamic process. Doing work on the gas by compressing it is another thermodynamic process.

Internal energy is a property of the particular state of the system under consideration, and for this reason internal energy is called a state function. Thus, if two equal quantities of an ideal gas originally in different states are brought to the same state (i.e. same pressure, volume and temperature), they will have the same internal energy irrespective of what the original state was and how the gas was brought to that final state. By contrast, heat and work are not state functions. Heat and work are related to *changes* in the state of the system, not to the state itself.

Process	Description	Equation
Isothermal	Temperature stays constant	$P_1 V_1 = P_2 V_2$
Isobaric	Pressure stays constant	$\dfrac{V_1}{T_1} = \dfrac{V_2}{T_2}$
Isovolumetric	Volume stays constant	$\dfrac{P_1}{T_1} = \dfrac{P_2}{T_2}$
Adiabatic	No heat enters or leaves the system	$P_1 V_1^{5/3} = P_2 V_2^{5/3}$

Table 10.1: A few thermodynamic processes.

In this course we will be mainly interested in four different types of thermodynamic processes. These are defined in Table 10.1. We have seen all the equations before except that for the adiabatic process which we will discuss shortly.

Pressure–volume diagrams

Changes in a gas may be conveniently shown on pressure–volume diagrams. Examples of isovolumetric (red) and isobaric (blue) processes are shown in Figure 10.2.

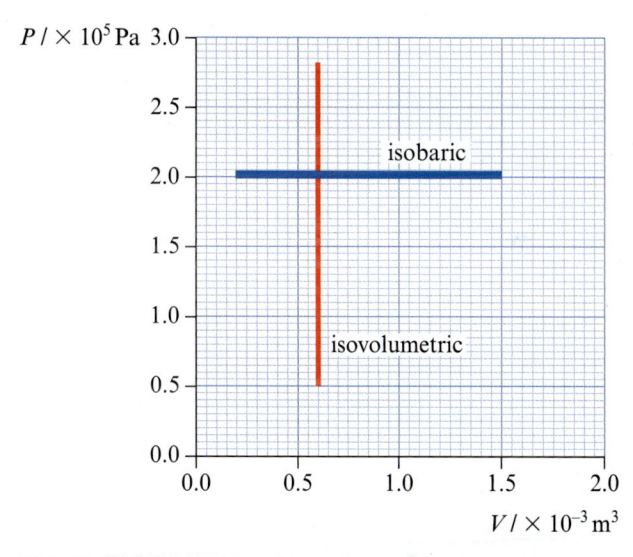

Figure 10.2: Isobaric and isovolumetric processes

The adiabatic equation

In an adiabatic process no heat enters or leaves the system. It can be shown that if the state of a fixed quantity of an ideal gas is changed adiabatically from pressure P_1 and volume V_1 to pressure P_2 and volume V_2 we have that

$$P_1 V_1^{\tfrac{5}{3}} = P_2 V_2^{\tfrac{5}{3}}$$

i.e. during an adiabatic process

$$PV^{\tfrac{5}{3}} = \text{constant} = c_1$$

This means that in an adiabatic change the temperature also changes. From the ideal gas law we have that $\dfrac{PV}{T} = \text{constant} = c_2$. Solving this for pressure we get

$P = \dfrac{c_2 T}{V}$, and substituting this in the adiabatic law $\left(\dfrac{c_2 T}{V}\right) V^{\frac{5}{3}} = c_1$; that is:

$TV^{\frac{2}{3}} = $ constant or $T_1 V_1^{\frac{2}{3}} = T_2 V_2^{\frac{2}{3}}$.

So, when a gas is compressed adiabatically, the temperature increases. An everyday example of this is pumping a bicycle tire: the valve gets very hot. This will be explained shortly.

WORKED EXAMPLE 10.1

An ideal gas expands adiabatically from a state with pressure 5.00×10^5 Pa, volume 2.20×10^{-3} m³ and temperature 485 K to a new volume of 3.80×10^{-3} m³. Calculate the new pressure and temperature of the gas.

Answer

From $P_1 V_1^{\frac{5}{3}} = P_2 V_2^{\frac{5}{3}}$ we find:

$5.00 \times 10^5 \times (2.20 \times 10^{-3})^{\frac{5}{3}} = P_2 \times (3.80 \times 10^{-3})^{\frac{5}{3}}$

$P_2 = \dfrac{5.00 \times 10^5 \times (2.20 \times 10^{-3})^{\frac{5}{3}}}{(3.80 \times 10^{-3})^{\frac{5}{3}}} = 5.00 \times 10^5 \times \left(\dfrac{2.20 \times 10^{-3}}{3.80 \times 10^{-3}}\right)^{\frac{5}{3}} = 5.00 \times 10^5 \times \left(\dfrac{2.20}{3.80}\right)^{\frac{5}{3}}$

$= 2.01 \times 10^5$ Pa

To find the new temperature we may use $T_1 V_1^{\frac{2}{3}} = T_2 V_2^{\frac{2}{3}}$, but it is simpler to use the ideal gas law and write

$\dfrac{P_1 V_1}{T_1} = \dfrac{P_2 V_2}{T_2}$

so that:

$\dfrac{5.00 \times 10^5 \times 2.20 \times 10^{-3}}{485} = \dfrac{2.01 \times 10^5 \times 3.80 \times 10^{-3}}{T_2}$

$T_2 = \dfrac{2.01 \times 10^5 \times 3.80 \times 10^{-3} \times 485}{5.00 \times 10^5 \times 2.20 \times 10^{-3}}$

$= 337$ K

An adiabatic expansion on a pressure volume diagram is steeper than an isothermal.
Figure 10.3a shows an isothermal (blue) and an adiabatic (red) *expansion* of the same gas from a common state.
Figure 10.3b shows an isothermal and adiabatic *compression* of the same gas from a common state.

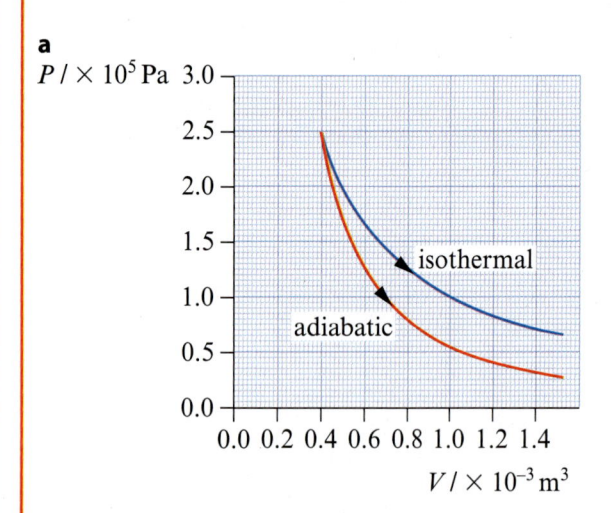

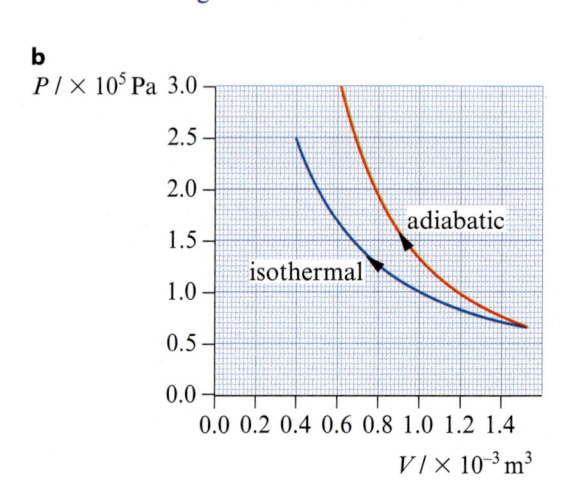

Figure 10.3: a Isothermal and adiabatic expansions form the same state. **b** Isothermal and adiabatic compressions from the same state. In both cases the adiabatic curve is steeper.

10 Thermodynamics

CONTINUED

Isothermal processes are slow (to allow time for the temperature to equalize and stay constant) while adiabatic processes are fast (so there is no time for heat to be exchanged).

We know that temperature increases in an adiabatic compression. We will be able to understand this when we learn about the first law of thermodynamics. But we can also understand it in terms of molecular motion: imagine a gas in a container with a piston; the gas is compressed so the piston moves inwards. The process is adiabatic so the piston has to move fast. Molecules colliding with the inward moving piston will bounce back with *increased* speed. The average kinetic energy of the molecules will increase and so the temperature has to increase.

CHECK YOURSELF 2

Consider Figure 10.3b and look at the point on each curve corresponding to a volume of 1.0×10^{-3} m³. Explain using the graph why the point on the adiabatic has a higher temperature.

Work done on or by a gas

Consider a quantity of a gas in a container with a frictionless, movable piston, Figure 10.4. If the piston is to stay in place a force from the outside has to be applied to counterbalance the force due to the pressure of the gas. Let us now compress the gas by pushing the piston in with a very slightly greater force.

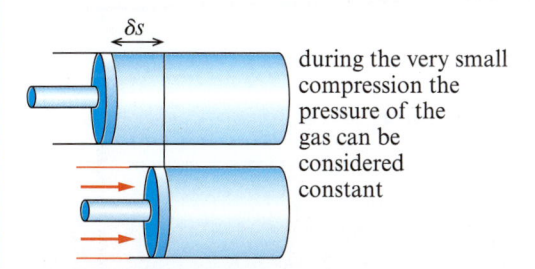

Figure 10.4: When the piston is pushed in by a small amount, work is being done *on* the gas.

If the pressure in the gas initially is P, and the cross-sectional area of the piston is A, then the force with which one must push is PA. If the pressure stays constant, the force is constant and so we may use the result from mechanics that work is force times distance moved in the direction of the force. The piston moves a distance Δs, so the work done is

$W = F \Delta s$

$ = PA \Delta s$

But $A \Delta s$ is change in the volume of the gas, ΔV. The same result holds if, instead, the piston is moved outwards by the gas as it expands.

KEY POINT

The work done when the volume of the gas is changed by ΔV at constant pressure is $W = P \Delta V$.

Figure 10.5 shows that the work done is the area under the isobaric curve; the area is a rectangle of base ΔV and height P. The work done in this case is

$W = 1.5 \times 10^5 \times (1.6 \times 10^{-3} - 0.4 \times 10^{-3}) = 180$ J.

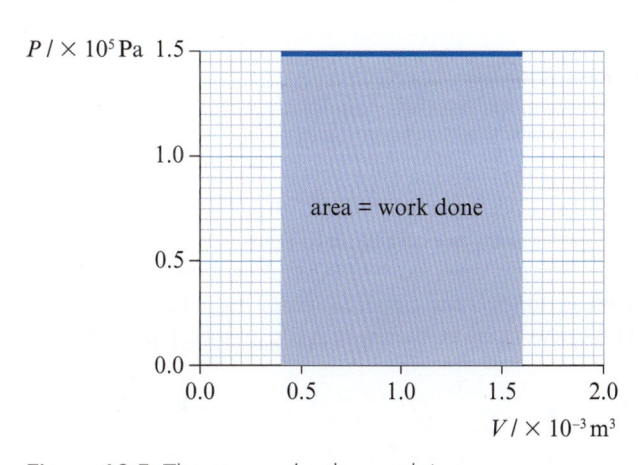

Figure 10.5: The area under the graph in a pressure-volume diagram gives the work done.

What if the pressure changes? Then the force is not constant and we have to do what we did in mechanics: the work done is the area under the curve in a force–distance graph. Here the corresponding result is the area under the pressure–volume graph.

> **PHYSICS FOR THE IB DIPLOMA: COURSEBOOK**

> **KEY POINT**
>
> The work done when the gas expands by an arbitrary amount is the area under the graph in the pressure–volume diagram.

> **CHECK YOURSELF 3**
>
> An ideal gas has a constant volume 5.0×10^{-3} m³. It is heated so that the pressure increases from 2.0×10^5 Pa to 6.0×10^5 Pa. What is the work done?

In Figure 10.6 we have to calculate the area of the trapezium:

$$W = \frac{(1.4 + 2.6) \times 10^5}{2} \times 1.2 \times 10^{-3} = 240 \text{ J}$$

> **WORKED EXAMPLE 10.2**
>
> A gas is compressed at constant pressure 2.00×10^5 Pa from a volume of 2.00 m³ to a volume of 1.75 m³.
>
> **a** Find the work done.
>
>   The temperature was initially 240.0 °C.
>
> **b** Calculate the final temperature of the gas in °C.
>
> **Answer**
>
> **a** Since the compression takes place under constant pressure, the work done is
>
> $P \times$ change in volume $= 2.00 \times 10^5$ Pa $\times 0.25$ m³
> $= 5.0 \times 10^4$ J
>
> **b** The final temperature is found from
>
> $\frac{V}{T}$ = constant
>
>   that is,
>
> $\frac{2.00}{513} = \frac{1.75}{T}$
>
>   giving
>
> $T = 449$ K $= 176$ °C.

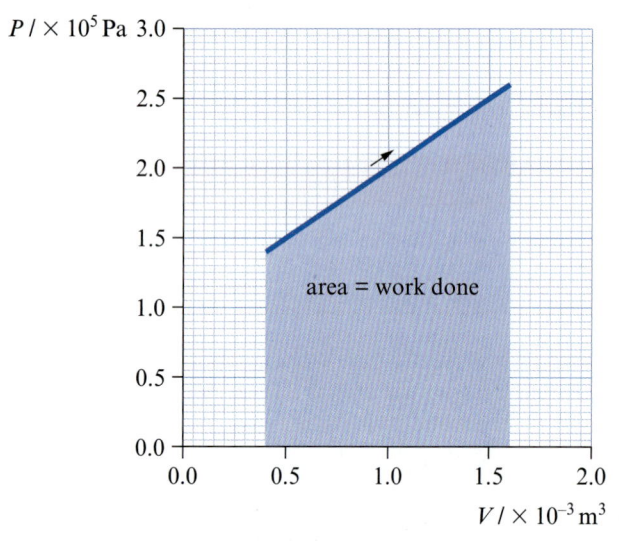

Figure 10.6: The work done is found from the area under the curve in the pressure–volume diagram.

The pressure–volume diagrams in Figure 10.7 show an ideal gas that starts expanding from state A to state B and is then compressed back to state A along a different path. The gas does work in expanding from A to B, but work is done *on* the gas in compressing it back to A. The *net* work done therefore is the area of the loop.

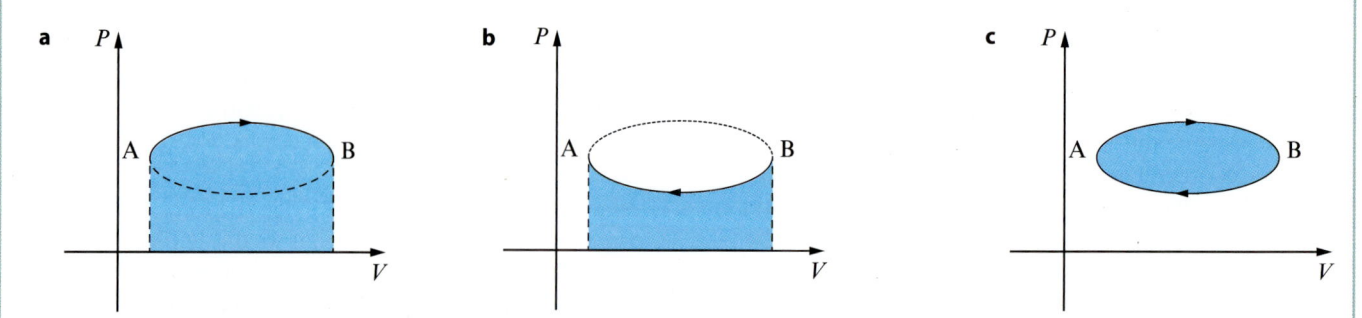

Figure 10.7: For a closed loop in a pressure–volume diagram, the work done is the area of the loop.

TEST YOUR UNDERSTANDING

1. Why are isothermal processes slow and adiabatic processes fast?

2. Using ideas on molecular motion explain why in an adiabatic expansion of an ideal gas the temperature drops.

3. An ideal gas expands adiabatically from a state with pressure 8.1×10^5 Pa and volume 2.5×10^{-3} m^3 to a state of volume 4.6×10^{-3} m^3. Calculate the new pressure of the gas.

4. An ideal gas expands adiabatically from a state with volume 2.8×10^{-3} m^3 and temperature 560 K to a state of volume 4.8×10^{-3} m^3. Calculate the new temperature of the gas.

5. A gas expands at a constant pressure of 5.4×10^5 Pa from a volume of 3.6×10^{-3} m^3 to a volume of 4.3×10^{-3} m^3. Calculate the work done by the gas.

6. A gas is compressed isothermally from a given state to final volume V. An amount of work W is done on the gas. If instead the gas was compressed adiabatically from the same state to a state of volume V, would the work done on the gas be equal to, greater than or less than W?

7. An ideal gas expands isothermally from pressure P and volume V to volume 2V. Sketch this change on a pressure–volume diagram. An equal quantity of an ideal gas at pressure P and volume V expands adiabatically to a volume 2V. Sketch this change on the same axes. Determine in which case the work done by the gas larger.

10.2 The first law of thermodynamics

When an amount of heat Q is given to a gas, the gas will absorb that energy and use it to change its internal energy and/or to do work. Conservation of energy demands that

$Q = \Delta U + W$

where ΔU is the change in internal energy and W is the work done. This formula goes with certain conventions that you must know:

$Q > 0$ means heat is supplied to the system; $Q < 0$ means heat is removed

$\Delta U > 0$ means the internal energy and temperature increase; $\Delta U < 0$ means U and T decrease

$W > 0$ means that the work is done by the gas as it expands; $W < 0$ means that the work is done on the gas by compressing it.

> **EXAM TIP**
>
> The conventions of signs in the first law are crucial.

> **EXAM TIP**
>
> The first law is just the law of conservation of energy applied to thermodynamics.

> **CHECK YOURSELF 4**
>
> An amount of work equal to 250 J is done on a gas, compressing it, and 250 J of thermal energy is removed from the gas.
>
> Did the temperature of the gas increase, decrease or stay the same?

> **PHYSICS FOR THE IB DIPLOMA: COURSEBOOK**

WORKED EXAMPLE 10.3

An ideal gas in a container with a piston expands isothermally. Energy $Q = 2.0 \times 10^5$ J is transferred to the gas. Calculate the work done by the gas.

Answer

The process is isothermal so we know that T = constant; it follows that $\Delta U = 0$ and since

$Q = \Delta U + W$

we must have

$W = Q$

So, the work done by the gas in this case is equal to the energy supplied to it: 2.0×10^5 J.

WORKED EXAMPLE 10.4

An ideal gas expands adiabatically.

a Explain why the temperature will decrease.

b Use your answer in **a** to explain why the adiabatic curve of an ideal gas expanding from a given state is steeper than the corresponding isothermal curve.

Answer

a Using the first law $Q = \Delta U + W$, we have that $Q = 0$ because the process is adiabatic. Hence

$0 = \Delta U + W$

from which we find $\Delta U = -W$. The gas expands; it is the gas that does the work so $W > 0$. Therefore $\Delta U < 0$.

That is, the internal energy and thus temperature decreases. Similarly, if the gas is compressed adiabatically, the temperature will increase.

b This explains why the adiabatic curve starting from a point on the pressure–volume diagram is steeper than the isothermal curve starting from that same point (see Figure 10.3). Consider an adiabatic and an isothermal process, both starting from the same point and bringing the gas to the same (expanded) final volume. Since the adiabatic process will reduce the temperature and the isothermal process will not, it follows that the pressure of the final state after the adiabatic expansion will be lower than the pressure of the state reached by the isothermal expansion. Hence, the adiabatic curve must be steeper.

WORKED EXAMPLE 10.5

An ideal gas with initial volume 0.100 m³ is compressed at constant pressure 3.00×10^6 Pa to a volume of 0.080 m³. Find:

a the work done on the gas

b the heat energy transferred.

Answer

a The work done is:

$W = P \times \Delta V = 3.00 \times 10^6 \times (0.080 - 0.100) = -6.00 \times 10^4$ J

(The work is negative because the gas is being compressed, work is being done on the gas.)

b From the first law:

$Q = \Delta U + W$

So, to find the energy transferred we must first find the change in the internal energy of the gas. Here the pressure is constant so:

$\Delta U = \frac{3}{2} P \Delta V$

$= \frac{3}{2}(-6.00 \times 10^4)$

$= -9.00 \times 10^4$ J

Finally

$Q = -9.00 \times 10^4 - 6.00 \times 10^4$

$= -1.50 \times 10^5$ J

The negative sign in Q means that this energy was transferred *away* from the gas.

WORKED EXAMPLE 10.6

Figure 10.8 is a pressure–volume diagram showing two adiabatics, an isovolumetric and an isobaric process making up a loop ABCDA for an ideal gas.

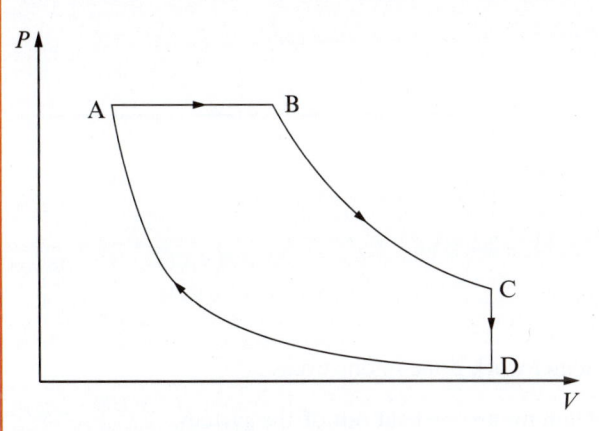

Figure 10.8: For worked example 10.6.

CONTINUED

a Determine along which legs energy is supplied (Q_{in}) to the gas or removed (Q_{out}) from the gas.

b Find the relation between Q_{in}, Q_{out} and the net work done in the loop.

Answer

a There is no energy transferred along the adiabatics BC and DA. Along AB, work is done *by* the gas so that $W > 0$ and $\Delta U > 0$ since the temperature at B is higher than that at A. Hence $Q > 0$ and energy is supplied to the gas. Along CD, $W = 0$ (the volume does not change) and $\Delta U < 0$ because the temperature at D is lower than that at C. Hence $Q < 0$ and energy is transferred away from the gas.

b Applying the first law for the total change A → A, we see that $\Delta U = 0$ so

$$Q_{in} + 0 - Q_{out} + 0 = 0 + W_{net}$$

$$W_{net} = Q_{in} - Q_{out}$$

(W_{net} is the area of the loop.)

WORKED EXAMPLE 10.7

The loop ABCA in Figure 10.9 consists of an isobaric, an isovolumetric and an isothermal process for a fixed quantity of an ideal gas.

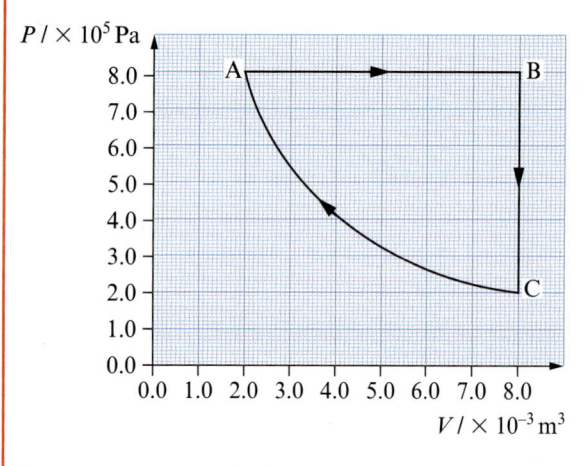

Figure 10.9: For worked example 10.7.

a The temperature of the gas at A is 320 K. Calculate:

  i the temperature at B

  ii the energy transferred from A to B

  iii the energy transferred from B to C.

b The work done on the gas from C to A is 2.2 kJ. Calculate the net work done in one cycle.

c Verify that the net work done is equal to the heat into the system minus the heat out of the system.

CONTINUED

Answer

a i The temperature at B is found from
$$\frac{V_A}{T_A} = \frac{V_B}{T_B}$$
that is,
$$\frac{2.0 \times 10^{-3}}{320} = \frac{8.0 \times 10^{-3}}{T_B}$$
$$\Rightarrow T_B = 1280 \approx 1300 \text{ K}$$

ii The work done by the gas as it expands from A to B is
$$W_{AB} = P_A \Delta V$$
$$= 8.0 \times 10^5 \times (8.0 \times 10^{-3} - 2.0 \times 10^{-3})$$
$$= 4800 \text{ J} = 4.8 \text{ kJ}$$

From the first law, $Q_{AB} = \Delta U_{AB} + W_{AB}$, so we need to find the change in internal energy. Since pressure is constant, $\Delta U = \frac{3}{2} P \Delta V = \frac{3}{2} \times 4.8 \times 10^3 = 7.2 \times 10^3 \text{ J}$. Hence $Q_{AB} = 4.8 + 7.2 = +12$ kJ.

iii $Q_{BC} = \Delta U_{BC}$ since $W = 0$ for the change from B to C (the volume is constant). The magnitude of the temperature change from B to C is the same as that from A to B, so the changes in internal energy have the same magnitude (but opposite sign). Therefore $Q_{BC} = -7.2$ kJ.

b The net work is therefore $4.8 - 2.2 = 2.6$ kJ.

c The heat in is 12 kJ. The heat out is 7.2 kJ along BC and 2.2 kJ along CA.

Therefore $Q_{in} - Q_{out} = 12 - (7.2 + 2.2) = 2.6 \text{ kJ} = W_{net}$.

TEST YOUR UNDERSTANDING

8 The pressure of an ideal gas is halved at constant volume. Was thermal energy added or removed from the gas?

9 A quantity of energy Q is supplied to three ideal gases, X, Y and Z. Gas X absorbs Q isothermally, gas Y isovolumetrically and gas Z isobarically. Complete Table 10.2 by inserting the words *positive*, *zero* or *negative* for the work done W, the change in internal energy ΔU and the temperature change ΔT of each gas.

	W	ΔU	ΔT
X			
Y			
Z			

Table 10.2

CONTINUED

10 An ideal gas is compressed adiabatically.

    a Use the first law of thermodynamics to state and explain the change, if any, in the temperature of the gas.

    b Explain your answer to part **a** by referring to the motion of molecules.

11 An ideal gas is kept at constant pressure 6.00×10^6 Pa. Its initial temperature is 300 K. The gas expands at constant pressure from a volume of 0.200 m³ to a volume of 0.600 m³. Calculate

    a the work done by the gas

    b the temperature of the gas at the new volume

    c the energy taken out of or put into the gas.

12 Does the addition of heat Q to a system always result in an increase in the internal energy of the system? Explain.

13 In an isothermal expansion of an ideal gas the work done is 3 kJ. Is the heat energy exchanged less than, equal to or greater than 3 kJ?

14 A gas expands doing 500 J of work. 500 J of heat are added to the gas. Does the temperature of the gas increase, stay the same or decrease?

15 A gas is compressed adiabatically with 500 J of work done on the gas. What is the change in the internal energy of the gas?

16 An ideal gas undergoes a change from state P to state Q as shown in Figure 10.10. (The temperature is in kelvin.) For this change, state and explain:

    a whether work is done on the gas or by the gas

    b whether energy is supplied to the gas or taken out of the gas.

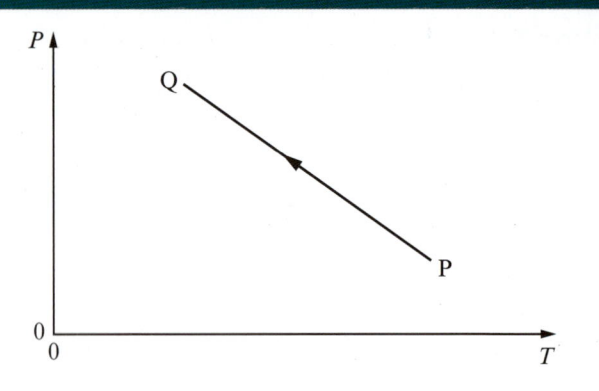

Figure 10.10: For question 16.

17 Two ideal gases, X and Y, have the same pressure, volume and temperature. The same quantity of heat is supplied to both gases. Gas X absorbs the thermal energy at constant volume whereas gas Y absorbs the thermal energy at constant pressure. State and explain which of the two gases will have the highest final temperature.

18 Two ideal gases, X and Y, have the same pressure, volume and temperature. Thermal energy is supplied to both gases. Gas X absorbs the thermal energy at constant volume whereas gas Y absorbs the thermal energy at constant pressure. The increase in temperature of both gases is the same. State and explain which of the two gases received the largest quantity of energy.

19 An ideal gas changes its state from state A to state B along two different paths I and II as shown in Figure 10.11.

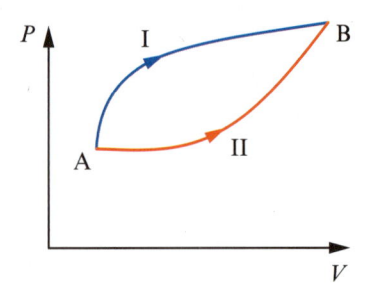

Figure 10.11: For question 19.

In which case is the heat supplied larger?

CONTINUED

20 An ideal gas changes its state from state A to state B along two different paths I and II as shown in Figure 10.12.

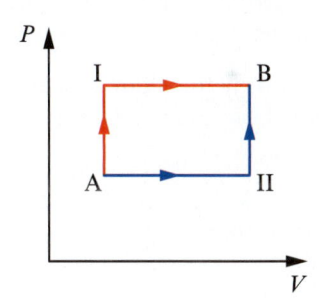

Figure 10.12: For question 20.

In which case is the thermal energy supplied larger?

21 An ideal gas changes its state from state A to state B along two different paths I and II as shown in Figure 10.13.

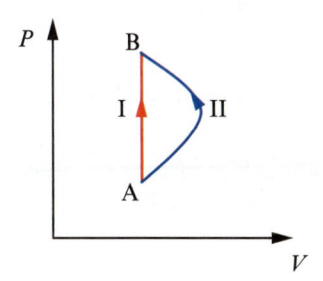

Figure 10.13: For question 21.

In which case is the thermal energy supplied larger?

22 The *molar specific heat capacity* of an ideal gas is defined as the amount of energy required to change the temperature of one mole of a gas by one kelvin. When n moles of gas absorb energy Q at constant pressure, $Q = nc_p\Delta T$ where c_p is the molar specific heat capacity at constant pressure.

When n moles of gas absorb energy Q at constant volume, $Q = nc_v\Delta T$ where c_v is the molar specific heat capacity at constant volume.

Use the first law of thermodynamics to show that $c_p - c_v = R$, where R is the universal gas constant.

23 A fixed mass of an ideal gas is taken through a cycle ABCA as shown in Figure 10.14.

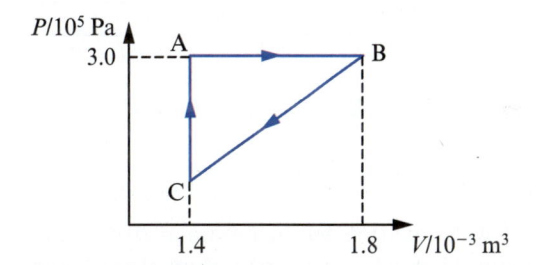

Figure 10.14: For question 23.

a Show that during the change A → B the energy supplied to the gas is 300 J.

b During the change B → C the amount of work done is 100 J and the energy transferred is 490 J. Calculate the change in the internal energy of the gas during the change B → C.

c Deduce the area of the triangle in the diagram.

d Hence deduce the pressure at C.

e Determine the energy transferred during the change C → A.

> **CONTINUED**
>
> **24** Consider the loop ABCDA shown in Figure 10.15. The temperature at A is 400.
>
> [Figure: P-V diagram showing rectangular loop ABCDA. P axis in $\times 10^5$ Pa from 0 to 4; V axis in $\times 10^{-3}$ m³ from 0 to 0.4. A at (0.1, 4), B at (0.4, 4), C at (0.4, 2), D at (0.1, 2).]
>
> **Figure 10.15:** for question 24
>
> Calculate:
>
> **a** the temperature at points B, C and D
>
> **b** the change in internal energy along each of the four legs of the cycle
>
> **c** the amount of energy transferred to and transferred away from the gas along each leg
>
> **d** the ratio of net work done to total thermal energy into the system.

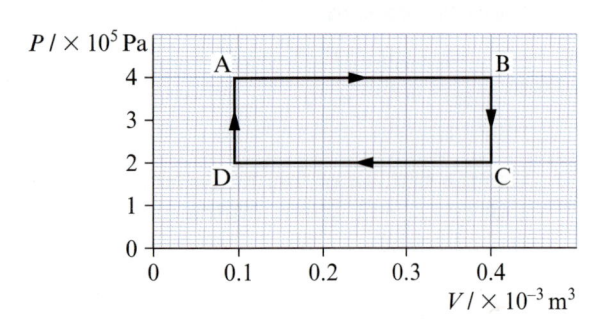

10.3 The second law of thermodynamics

A glass of water at 10 °C left in a room at 20 °C will warm up until it reaches the temperature of the room. But the reverse never happens—if it did, the cold water would lose thermal energy, making it colder, and the room would become warmer.

What law of physics prevents this reverse process from happening? It is *not* the first law of thermodynamics; the reverse process *is* consistent with the first law.

It is forbidden by a special law of physics—the second law of thermodynamics. This law involves a new concept, that of **entropy**. We loosely refer to entropy as a measure of the disorder of a system.

But what is disorder?

- A gas is more disordered than a solid at the same temperature because its atoms move about randomly whereas those of the solid are regularly arranged—we know less about the position of the gas atoms.
- Blue paint mixed together in a container with red paint is more disordered than a layer of red paint on top of a layer of blue paint.
- A Rubik's cube is ordered when each face has the same colour but quickly becomes disordered when faces are turned and colours scramble.

Systems, left on their own, evolve so as to increase disorder. If we plant rows of plants with fixed distances from plant to plant we will have an ordered system. After a few years, seeds produced by the plants will fall to the ground and create new plants. The new plants will be in random positions, with no rows and no fixed distances from plant to plant. The system will evolve into a disordered state. As we will see in the next section, this is because a disordered state is more likely than an ordered state.

Even though we will not define entropy precisely we will define the change in entropy, ΔS, to be:

$$\Delta S = \frac{Q}{T}$$

where Q is a quantity of heat given to or removed from the system at a temperature T (in kelvin). The unit of entropy is J K^{-1}.

When heat is given to the system, $Q > 0$ and entropy increases. When heat is removed, $Q < 0$ and entropy decreases. For a reversible process that returns the system to its original state, $\Delta S = 0$. One such reversible process is the isothermal expansion of a gas and the subsequent isothermal compression back to the initial state. Since the expansion and compression are isothermal, leaving the temperature constant, we may write

$$\Delta S_1 = +\frac{|Q|}{T}$$

during expansion and

$$\Delta S_2 = -\frac{|Q|}{T}$$

during compression. (The gas receives thermal energy upon expanding and discards thermal energy upon compressing.) The net entropy change is thus zero.

> **EXAM TIP**
>
> The formula $\Delta S = \frac{Q}{T}$ must be used with great care. Strictly, it applies when a quantity of heat enters or leaves a system without appreciably changing the temperature. If temperature changes, calculus is required to evaluate $\Delta S = \int \frac{dQ}{T}$, which is not part of this course.

Let us apply the expression for ΔS given above to the case of the flow of heat between a hot body at temperature T_h and a cold body at temperature T_c (Figure 10.16a). If a quantity of heat Q flows from the hot to the cold body (as we know will happen), the total entropy change of the Universe is:

$$\Delta S = -\frac{Q}{T_h} + \frac{Q}{T_c}$$
$$= Q\left(\frac{1}{T_c} - \frac{1}{T_h}\right)$$
$$\Rightarrow \Delta S > 0$$

(the temperature of each body is assumed unchanged during this small exchange of thermal energy). The entropy of the system has increased, and so this is what we expect to happen. The reverse process (Figure 10.16b) does not happen. It corresponds to a net decrease in the entropy of the Universe:

$$\Delta S = \frac{Q}{T_h} - \frac{Q}{T_c}$$
$$= Q\left(\frac{1}{T_h} - \frac{1}{T_c}\right)$$
$$\Rightarrow \Delta S < 0$$

a hot cold

here entropy increases

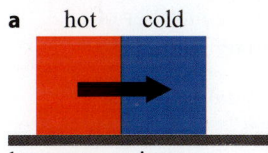

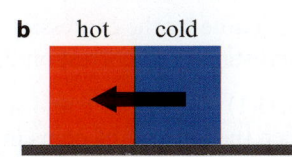

b hot cold

here entropy decreases–hence this process does not happen

Figure 10.16: a When thermal energy flows from a hot to a cold body, the entropy of the universe increases. **b** If the reverse were to happen without any performance of work, the entropy would decrease.

Similarly, when energy is given to a solid at its melting temperature, the solid will use that energy to turn into a liquid at the same temperature. The entropy formula again shows that the entropy increases as the solid absorbs the latent heat of fusion.

This allows us to state the second law of thermodynamics in its general form involving entropy:

> **KEY POINT**
>
> The entropy of an isolated system never decreases. Entropy increases in realistic irreversible processes and stays the same in theoretical, idealized, reversible processes.

There are other equivalent formulations of the second law:

One, proposed by Rudolf Clausius, states that it is impossible for heat to flow from a cold to a warmer body without the performance of work.

And another, proposed by William Thomson (first Baron Kelvin), states that it impossible for a device *working in a cycle* to change all the heat extracted from a hot reservoir into mechanical work.

> **CHECK YOURSELF 5**
>
> An ideal gas expands adiabatically, doubling its volume.
>
> During this expansion did the entropy of the gas increase, decrease or stay the same?

PHYSICS FOR THE IB DIPLOMA: COURSEBOOK

WORKED EXAMPLE 10.8

An ideal gas in state A can reach state B at constant volume and state C at constant pressure, Figure 10.17. The temperatures at B and C are the same. Determine which process results in the greatest entropy change.

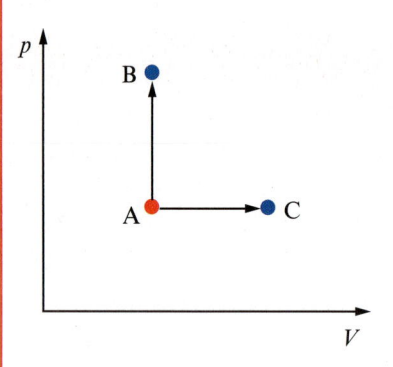

Figure 10.17: For worked example 10.8.

Answer

Since the temperatures at B and C are the same the change in internal energy for both paths is the same. The path to B involves zero work done, but the path to C involves positive work done by the gas. Hence Q is greater for the path to C and so is the entropy change.

WORKED EXAMPLE 10.9

A metallic sphere of mass 0.50 kg, specific heat capacity 480 J kg^{-1} K^{-1} and temperature 90 °C is dropped into a very large quantity of water at 10 °C. After some time the temperature of the sphere becomes 10 °C. The temperature of the water does not change appreciably because the mass of the water is large. The entropy of the sphere *decreases* by 60 J K^{-1}. Explain how this observation is consistent with the second law of thermodynamics.

Answer

The heat that enters the water is $\Delta Q = mc\Delta T = 0.50 \times 480 \times 80 = 1.92 \times 10^4$ J. This happens at a constant temperature of 283 K and so the entropy change of the water is an *increase* of $\frac{\Delta Q}{T} = \frac{1.92 \times 10^4}{283}$ = 68 J K^{-1}. The overall entropy of the Universe therefore increased by 8 J K^{-1}, consistently with the second law.

A statistical view of entropy—a simple model

Suppose we want to arrange four coins along a line. Each coin can show heads (H) or tails (T) on its top face. One arrangement is that all coins show heads. Another is that two show heads and two show tails and so on.

The possibilities are summarised in Table 10.3.

Number of H	Possible arrangements	Number of arrangements
0	TTTT	1
1	HTTT, THTT, TTHT, TTTH	4
2	HHTT, TTHH, HTHT, THTH, HTTH, THHT	6
3	HHHT, HHTH, HTHH, THHH	4
4	HHHH	1
Total		$2^4 = 16$

Table 10.3: The possible arrangements of four coins.

Our system is the set of coins. The system can be described by the number of heads that appear.

Since this number can be anything from 0 to 4 we say that our system is described by five macrostates.

To each macrostate correspond microstates, the number of different arrangements of coins which give the same macrostate.

We denote by the expression $\Omega(H)$ the number of microstates that correspond to a macrostate H.

So, $\Omega(1) = 4$, $\Omega(2) = 6$ and so on. What happens when the number of coins increases?

Table 10.4 shows the situation for 10 coins.

Number of H	Number of arrangements
0	1
1	10
2	45
3	120
4	210
5	252
6	210
7	120
8	45
9	10
10	1
Total	$2^{10} = 1024$

Table 10.4: The number of possible arrangements of 10 coins.

Here $\Omega(2) = 45$, $\Omega(5) = 252$, and so on.

The mathematicians among you should have recognised that the numbers of microstates are binomial coefficients. For example, $\Omega(2) = {}^{10}C_2 = \frac{10!}{2! \times 8!} = 45$.

Suppose we arrange the 10 coins randomly and ask for the probability of obtaining the state H = 1.

The answer is $\frac{10}{1024} \approx 0.0098$.

The probability for the state H = 5 is $\frac{252}{1024} \approx 0.25$ and so it is far more likely than the state with H = 1.

What happens if we increase the number of coins even further? Table 10.5 shows the situation with 100 coins.

Number of H	Number of arrangements
0	1
1	100
2	4950
⋮	⋮
40	1.4×10^{28}
45	6.1×10^{28}
50	1.0×10^{29}
55	6.1×10^{28}
60	1.4×10^{28}
⋮	⋮
98	4950
99	100
100	1
Total	$2^{100} \approx 1.27 \times 10^{30}$

Table 10.5: The number of possible arrangements of 100 coins.

From Figure 10.18 we see that the probability for the state H = 1 is negligibly small. The most likely outcomes of a random throw of 100 coins would be about equal numbers of H and T. It *is possible* that the outcome might be H = 1 but it is *highly unlikely*.

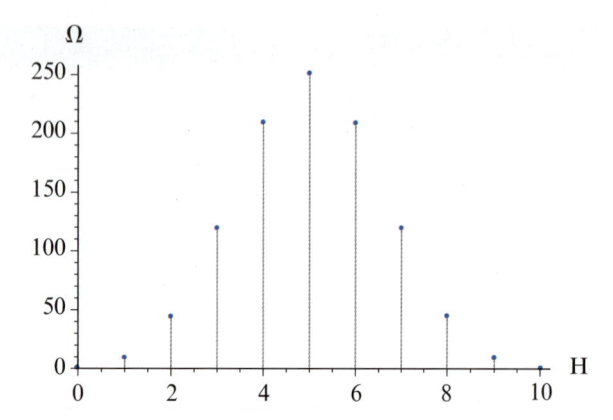

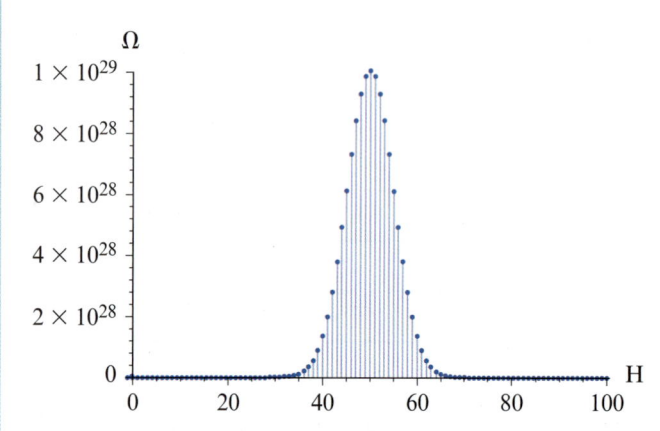

Figure 10.18: The variation of the number of microstates with the number of heads for 10 and 100 coins.

This situation becomes much more pronounced as we let the number of coins increase and become, say 10^{23}, a number close to Avogadro's number (the number of particles in a mole).

We define a quantity called the entropy, S, of a given macrostate of the system as:

$$S = k_B \ln \Omega$$

where k_B is the Boltzmann constant and Ω is the number of possible microstates of the system.

We see that the states which are likely to occur have large entropy. We can now see the connection between entropy and disorder. The likely states are also the more disordered ones. The system of 10 coins with 5H and 5T is more disordered than the system where all 10 coins show H. There are many ways (252 ways) to get the system with 5H and 5T but only one to get it with 10H. Entropy is a measure of disorder.

The change in entropy in going from a state with H = 45 to the most likely state H = 50 is $\Delta S = 1.38 \times 10^{-23} \times \ln(1.0 \times 10^{29}) - 1.38 \times 10^{-23} \times \ln(6.1 \times 10^{28}) \approx 7 \times 10^{-24}$ J K^{-1}. There is an increase in entropy. Going the reverse way from H = 50 to H = 45 would imply a decrease in entropy.

Real systems

The ideas developed in the last section also apply to actual physical systems, for example a gas. Here, too, we have macrostates (determined for example by the total energy of the gas), and for each macrostate we have many microstates. (To actually calculate the number of microstates for a real system such as a gas is beyond the level of this course.) If the number of microstates is Ω we again define the entropy of the system to be $S = k_B \ln \Omega$.

> **CHECK YOURSELF 6**
>
> What is the largest entropy of a system of six coins?

WORKED EXAMPLE 10.10

Refer to Table 10.5.

a What is the probability of obtaining the state with H = 1?

b Suppose you throw 100 coins every second. After how much time would you expect to get the outcome of H = 1?

Answer

a The probability is $p = \dfrac{100}{1.27 \times 10^{30}} \approx 7.9 \times 10^{-29}$.

b To get H = 1 we must throw the 100 coins N times such that $Np = 1$. Thus, $N = \dfrac{1}{p} = 1.27 \times 10^{28}$.
Since it takes 1 s to throw the coins, the time is 1.27×10^{28} s or about 10^{20} years. (This is a long time! The age of the universe is about 10^{17} s.)

THEORY OF KNOWLEDGE

The entropy of the universe increases, and we are led from ordered to less ordered and more chaotic situations. But the world around us is full of examples of systems that evolve from highly disordered to very ordered forms (and hence forms with less entropy). Life itself evolved from simple microorganisms to the complex forms we see today. A small quantity of water freezing leads to the highly structured, ordered (and beautiful) snowflakes. For this to happen, energy has been exchanged with the surroundings in such a way that the systems evolved into highly ordered, complex forms. However, the decrease in entropy in these systems is accompanied by a larger increase in the entropy of the surroundings, leading to an overall increase in the entropy of the universe.

The nature of time has always mystified scientist and nonscientists alike. The fact that there appears to be a connection between the direction from past to future (the arrow of time) and thermodynamics is a fascinating and not well understood aspect of the second law.

The laws of mechanics do not distinguish the arrow of time: a film of billiard balls colliding with each other does not look strange if run backwards. So why do the same laws when applied to very many particles in a gas, say, show a preference for one direction of time, the one leading to increased entropy and more disorder? The answer has to do with the fact that the system is led to a more disordered, higher entropy state because this state is the vastly more likely state; the result of the very many random collisions among the particles of the gas.

Entropy in thermodynamics may be defined as $S = k \ln \Omega$ where k is Boltzmann's constant and Ω is the number of ways in which a particular macroscopic state of a system may be realised. It is quite extraordinary that this formula of thermodynamics has featured extensively in Claude Shannon's theory of information, a crucial part of modern telecommunications theory.

TEST YOUR UNDERSTANDING

25 Explain why in an isothermal compression of an ideal gas the entropy of the gas decreases. Why does this decrease in entropy of the gas not violate the second law of thermodynamics?

26 In an isothermal expansion of an ideal gas all the thermal energy supplied is used to perform work. Doesn't this violate the second law of thermodynamics?

27 In an isothermal expansion of an ideal gas the entropy of the gas increases. How do we understand this increase in entropy in terms of microstates?

28 In an adiabatic expansion you would expect the entropy to increase since the volume increases, thus increasing disorder. What accounts for the fact that the entropy change is zero?

29 Could you cool down your kitchen by keeping the refrigerator door open?

30 Calculate the change in entropy of 25 g of ice at 0 °C that melts into water at 0 °C. Take the specific latent heat of fusion of ice to be 334 kJ kg^{-1}.

31 Two very large bodies at 0 °C and 100 °C are brought into thermal contact. Calculate the overall change in entropy when an amount of heat of 50 J leaves the hot body and enters the cold body.

32 A 15 g ice cube at 0 °C is dropped into a *very large* container of water at 20 °C. Take the specific latent heat of fusion of ice to be 334 kJ kg^{-1} and the specific heat capacity of water to be 4200 J kg^{-1} K^{-1}.

   a Calculate the change in entropy of the ice after all the ice has turned into water at 0 °C.

   b The 15 g of water at 0 °C will eventually reach 20 °C. During this process the entropy of the 15 g of water increases by 4.5 J K^{-1}. Calculate the overall change in entropy of the ice and the water after equilibrium is reached.

10.4 Heat engines

It is possible (and easy) to transfer mechanical energy to thermal energy: just think of a car when the brakes are applied. Some of the car's kinetic energy is transferred to thermal energy in the brake pads (the temperature of the brake pads increases). All of the mechanical energy can be transferred to thermal energy in this way. Is the reverse possible? In other words, can we transfer thermal energy to mechanical energy with 100% efficiency? Thermodynamics says that this is not possible, as we will see.

A **heat engine** is a device that transfers thermal energy to mechanical or electrical energy, which can then be used to do mechanical work.

A schematic example is shown in Figure 10.19.

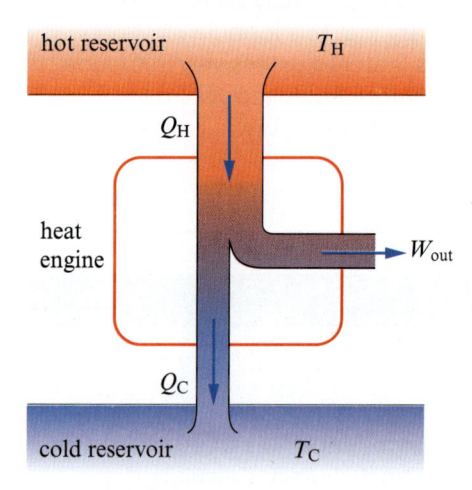

Figure 10.19: In a heat engine, energy flowing from the hot to the cold reservoir may be used to perform mechanical work.

A very simple attempt at a 'heat engine' can be illustrated by the pressure–volume diagram of an isothermal expansion, Figure 10.20.

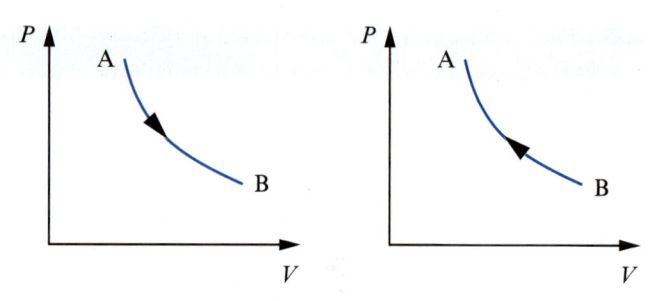

Figure 10.20: a A gas expanding isothermally transferring thermal energy which can be used to do mechanical work. **b** The process is reversed, bringing the system back to its original state.

The gas is in contact with a hot reservoir (a source of thermal energy). The temperature of the source is ever so slightly higher than that of the gas and so thermal energy gets transferred to the gas that expands doing work. This is what we want: the transfer of thermal energy can be used to do mechanical work. But this is a useless engine! An engine needs to be used over and over again to keep producing work continuously. If the engine is a water pump that needs to pump water out of flooded house, we want it to work over and over again until all the water is out. So the engine must work in a cycle: we must somehow bring the state of the gas at B in Figure 10.20a back to the original state at A so we can repeat the process. One way of doing this is to reverse the expansion of that in Figure 10.20a, leading to Figure 10.20b. But this is useless too: we would have to do the same work compressing the gas as the gas did for us as it expanded. The net work in this 'cycle' would be zero! Figure 10.21 shows a better version of a useful cycle.

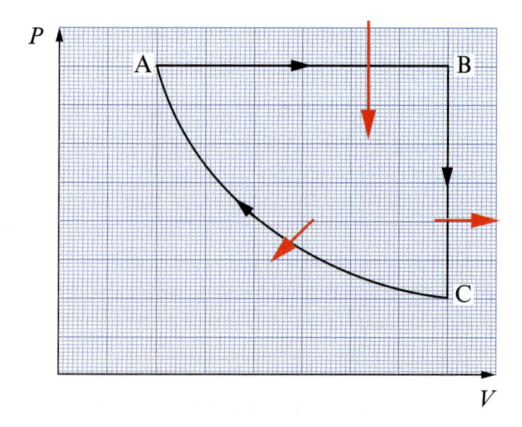

Figure 10.21: A cycle on a P–V diagram for a heat engine.

A hot reservoir (a source of thermal energy) at temperature T_H transfers heat into the engine. The hot reservoir could be a fire created by burning a fuel. Think of the engine as a gas in a cylinder with a piston. From A to B, the gas expands pushing the piston out, and this can be exploited to do mechanical work by, for example, raising a load, Figure 10.22. (The 'load' could be the mass of water that we want to pump out of the flooded house.) At B the load is removed. From B to C the gas is allowed to cool down to its original temperature at constant volume. A 'pin' can lock the piston in place, keeping the volume constant. From B to C, heat is removed from the gas and is rejected into a sink of temperature T_C. The sink could be the surroundings of the engine. An external force now compresses the gas isothermally from C back to the original state at A. Heat again leaves the gas and goes into the sink at temperature T_C. The external force did less work than the gas did upon expanding, so we achieved a net work out of this engine. The net work done is the heat in, Q_H, minus the heat out, Q_C. Figure 10.22 shows the process just described in pictures.

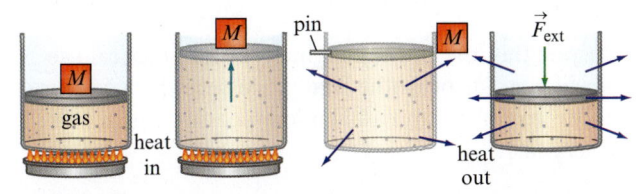

Figure 10.22: The hot reservoir provides heat to the gas which expands, raising a load. The load is removed, and the gas is allowed to cool at constant volume. Heat is released to the surroundings. An external force compresses the gas back to its original state. The process can then repeat so that the transfer of thermal energy can be used to do mechanical work.

The **efficiency** of a heat engine is:

$$\eta = \frac{\text{useful work}}{\text{input energy}}$$

Here the input energy is Q_H and so,

$$\eta = \frac{W}{Q_H} = \frac{Q_H - Q_C}{Q_H} = 1 - \frac{Q_C}{Q_H}.$$

CHECK YOURSELF 7

A heat engine has efficiency 0.40. The heat entering the engine from the hot reservoir is 500 J.

How much heat is rejected?

WORKED EXAMPLE 10.11

A heat engine has efficiency 0.20. The heat rejected into the cold reservoir is 800 J. What is the useful work done by the engine?

Answer

From $0.20 = 1 - \frac{800}{Q_H}$ we find $Q_H = 1000$ J. Hence $W = 200$ J.

A refrigerator, Figure 10.23, is another type heat engine in which the performance of mechanical work extracts heat from the cold reservoir and deposits it in the hot reservoir. (The food that is to be kept cool is the cold reservoir.)

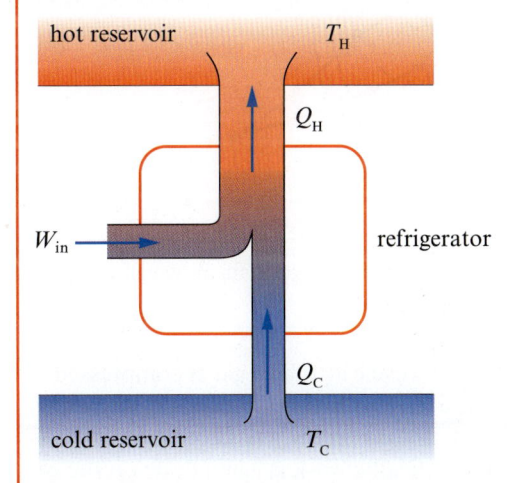

Figure 10.23: In a refrigerator mechanical work is used to extract heat from a cold reservoir and deposit it in the hot reservoir.

Note that it impossible to operate this refrigerator without the performance of work! If that were possible we would have a situation where heat is transferred from a cold to a warmer body, and as we have seen this would violate the second law of thermodynamics.

The Carnot cycle

In 1824 the French engineer Sadi Carnot investigated the question of how the transfer of thermal energy can be used to do mechanical work in the most efficient way. He asked if there was a limit to how efficient an engine can be. Carnot showed that there is.

Figure 10.24 shows the **Carnot cycle** that he investigated. It consists of two isothermals and two adiabatic curves.

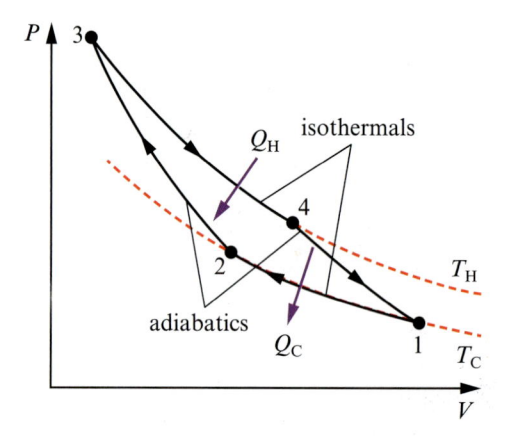

Figure 10.24: The Carnot cycle consists of two isothermals and two adiabatics.

The engine starts its cycle at 1. The gas is compressed isothermally until 2. During this stage heat Q_C leaves the gas and work is done on the gas. From 2 to 3 it is compressed adiabatically; work is again done on the gas. From 3 to 4 the gas expands isothermally receiving heat Q_H from a hot reservoir; work is done by the gas. From 4 to 1 the gas expands adiabatically; work is done by the gas. The net work done by the engine is therefore

$$W = Q_H - Q_C$$

The temperature along the isothermal $3 \to 4$ is T_H and along the lower isothermal $1 \to 2$ is T_C. The total change in entropy of the engine is

$$\Delta S = \Delta S_{12} + \Delta S_{23} + \Delta S_{34} + \Delta S_{41}$$

But the stages $2 \to 3$ and $4 \to 1$ are adiabatics: $Q = 0$ and so there is no change in entropy during the adiabatic stages. Along $3 \to 4$, $\Delta S_{34} = \frac{Q_H}{T_H}$ and along $1 \to 2$, $\Delta S_{12} = -\frac{Q_C}{T_C}$. Because the process starts and ends at A and because entropy is state function, the total entropy change is zero:

$0 = \frac{Q_H}{T_H} - \frac{Q_C}{T_C}$ which implies that $\frac{Q_C}{Q_H} = \frac{T_C}{T_H}$.

As we saw earlier the efficiency is $\eta = 1 - \frac{Q_C}{Q_H}$.

But for the Carnot engine $\frac{Q_C}{Q_H} = \frac{T_C}{T_H}$ so we find the Carnot efficiency to be:

$$\eta_C = 1 - \frac{T_C}{T_H}$$

Carnot's engine must have an efficiency less than 100%. It would be 100% in the impossible cases of either $T_C = 0$ or $T_H = \infty$.

The importance of the Carnot engine is that no engine is more efficient than the Carnot engine operating between the same temperatures. It can be shown that this follows from the second law of thermodynamics.

(Despite this, the Carnot engine is of no practical use since it consists of isothermal processes, which are very slow to complete, and adiabatic processes, which must be very fast.)

CHECK YOURSELF 8

A heat engine removes 100 J from the hot reservoir at 600 K and rejects 30 J of energy into the cold reservoir at 400 K. Is this possible?

THEORY OF KNOWLEDGE

The argument presented in the extension material is almost like a geometrical proof argument or a logic argument. This is another way of seeing that the second law is a very special law of physics!

10 Thermodynamics

EXTENSION

To see why no engine can have a higher efficiency than the Carnot efficiency, consider a hypothetical such engine connected to a refrigerator running on a Carnot cycle, Figure 10.25.

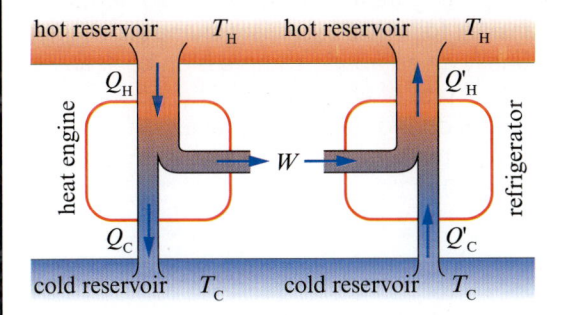

Figure 10.25: A hypothetical high efficiency engine connected to a Carnot refrigerator.

The work output (W) of the heat engine is work input (W) in the Carnot refrigerator. If the Carnot refrigerator ran as a heat engine its efficiency would be $\frac{W}{Q'_H}$. Now if we assume that the engine on the left has greater efficiency that the Carnot efficiency then

$$\frac{W}{Q_H} > \frac{W}{Q'_H}$$

This implies that $Q'_H > Q_H$. This means that $Q'_H - Q_H > 0$. Since $W = Q_H - Q_C = Q'_H - Q'_C$ it means that $Q'_C - Q_C = Q'_H - Q_H = Q$. The combination has the effect of transferring heat $Q > 0$ from the cold to the hot reservoir without performance of work. This violates the second law. So the assumption of an engine with better efficiency than the Carnot efficiency must be false.

NATURE OF SCIENCE

The second law of thermodynamics stands out as a special law of physics. A law such as the conservation of energy places restrictions on what can and cannot happen: A 1.0 kg ball with total energy 10 J cannot jump over a barrier that is higher than 1.0 m; therefore such an event is completely forbidden (in classical physics). The second law says that certain processes do not happen not because they *really* are impossible but because they are so highly unlikely so as to be impossible for all practical purposes. It is quite amazing that Carnot was able to reach his conclusions about the limitations on the efficiencies on heat engines before the concept of entropy was discovered and before the first law of thermodynamics. The connection of the second law with probability and the number of microstates that realise a particular macroscopic state make this law a truly special law of physics. However, many physicists are not happy with the probabilistic interpretation of entropy and the second law. Recent work appears to have interpreted the second law not in terms of what is likely and unlikely but in terms of deeper quantum mechanical principles such as quantum entanglement. See the article *Physicists Rewrite the Fundamental Law That Leads to Disorder*, in Quanta magazine, May 27, 2022.

Links

The idea of the 'heat death' of the universe goes back to Kelvin. If we could consider the universe as a closed system to which the laws of thermodynamics could be applied, then as the universe gets older and older we are driven to a state of ever increasing entropy and disorder. As we approach thermodynamic equilibrium temperature differences disappear. With no energy differences there can be no transfer of energy and no work done. The universe would be an uninteresting and boring place in which nothing happens. Estimates give us a time of about 10^{100} years until we get there, which is a very long time. Not everyone agrees with this reasoning, arguing that it is by no means clear if the laws of thermodynamics can be applied to the universe as a whole or whether the concept of entropy as a whole has any meaning when it is applied to the whole universe. For a heretical view of how this eternal boredom can be avoided, see the article *Time without an end*, by Freeman Dyson in *Rev. Mod. Phys. 51, 447*.

TEST YOUR UNDERSTANDING

33 Figure 10.26 shows the cycles of three engines.

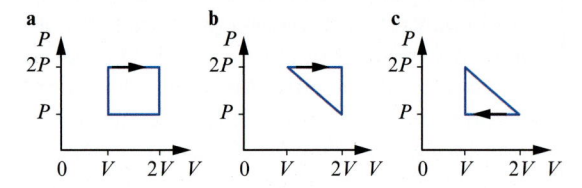

Figure 10.26: For question 33.

Rank the engines in order of increasing efficiency.

34 Explain whether you should invest money in a revolutionary new design of a heat engine that claims to operate between temperatures of 300 K and 500 K with an efficiency of 0.42.

35 Figure 10.27 shows three heat engines. Which are possible and which are impossible?

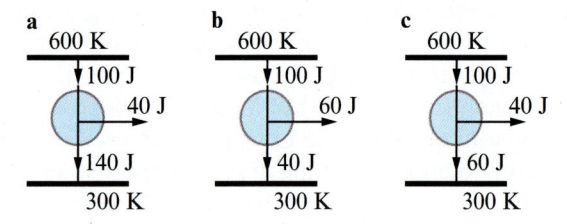

Figure 10.27: For question 35.

36 Figure 10.28 shows the thermodynamic cycle of a heat engine working with an ideal gas. A quantity of thermal energy is provided to the gas.

  a Identify the part of the cycle where this energy is absorbed.

  b Calculate the efficiency of this engine.

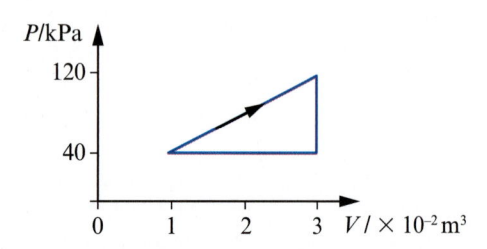

Figure 10.28: For question 36.

37 a State the second law of thermodynamics.

  b Explain, by reference to a Carnot engine, why a heat engine operating in a cycle must reject energy into the surroundings.

38 The graph (Figure 10.29) shows an isothermal expansion, followed by an isovolumetric change and finally an adiabatic compression back to the initial state of an ideal gas. The work done by the gas during the isothermal expansion is 900 J, and the temperature of the isothermal curve is 300 K.

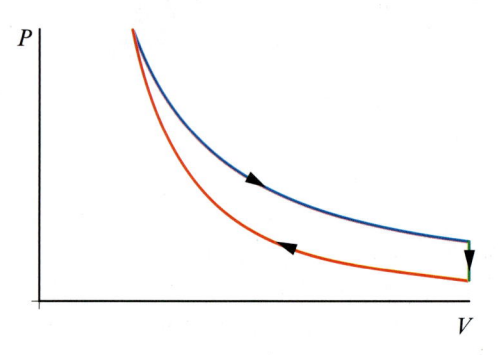

Figure 10.29: For question 38.

What is the entropy change of the gas during:

  a the isothermal expansion?

  b the isovolumetric change?

39 Figure 10.30 shows a cycle ABCDA of an ideal gas. Curves AB and CD are adiabatic.

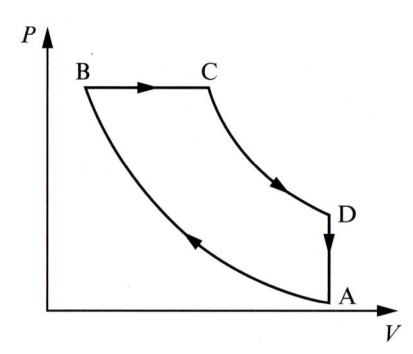

Figure 10.30: For question 39.

CONTINUED

a State what is meant by an adiabatic curve.

b State the name of the processes BC and DA.

c Determine along which stage heat is given to the gas.

d Along DA the pressure drops from 4.0×10^6 Pa to 1.4×10^6 Pa. The volume along DA is 8.6×10^{-3} m³. The efficiency of the engine is 0.36. Calculate:

  i the heat taken out of the gas

  ii the heat given to the gas

  iii the area of the loop ABCDA.

40 Figure 10.31 shows the isothermal compression of an ideal gas from state 1 of volume V_1 to state 2 of volume V_2.

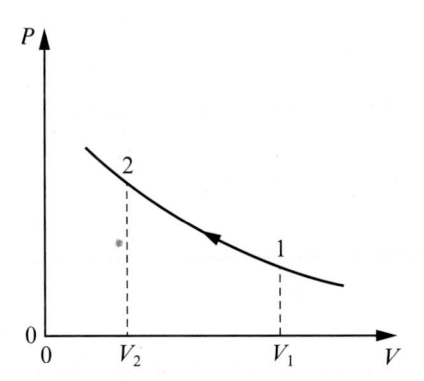

Figure 10.31: For question 40.

a On the axes in the figure draw a curve to show the adiabatic compression of the same gas from state 1 to a state of volume V_2.

b Explain in which case the work done on the gas is the largest.

c The temperature of the gas in state 1 is 300 K. The work done on the gas during the isothermal compression is 25 kJ. Determine the change in entropy of the gas during the isothermal compression.

41 A heat engine has an efficiency of 0.25. In one cycle, 300 J of work is performed.

a What is the heat input to the engine?

b How much heat is expelled to the cold reservoir?

42 A Carnot engine has an efficiency of 0.30. The engine receives 900 J of energy from a hot reservoir at 600 K.

a How much heat is expelled to the cold reservoir?

b What is the temperature of the cold reservoir?

43 An isothermal compression is said to be a reversible process.

a What is the change in the entropy of the universe during a reversible isothermal compression?

b How is the answer to part **a** reconciled with the fact that the entropy of the gas decreases?

c Suggest why for this reversible process the temperature of the surroundings must be infinitesimally lower than that of the gas.

d Hence deduce why the isothermal compression must be conducted very slowly.

SELF-ASSESSMENT CHECKLIST

I am able to …	Section	Not yet	Nearly there	Ready to move on
calculate changes in the internal energy of an ideal gas	10.1			
work with adiabatic, isothermal, isovolumetric and isobaric processes	10.1			
calculate work done in thermodynamics	10.1			
apply the first law of thermodynamics	10.2			
use the first law to understand thermodynamic processes	10.2			
understand the concept of entropy	10.3			
give a description of the statistical interpretation of entropy	10.3			
state the second law of thermodynamics in terms of entropy	10.3			
calculate work done by a heat engine	10.4			
explain why the Carnot cycle is the most efficient cycle for given operating temperatures	10.4			

REFLECTION

Do you understand the terms *isothermal*, *adiabatic*, *isovolumetric* and *isobaric*? Can you solve problems with the *adiabatic law*? Can you calculate the work done during a change in an ideal gas? Can you solve problems with the *first law of thermodynamics*? Do you have a reasonable understanding of *entropy*? Can you state the *second law of thermodynamics*? Do you understand the *Carnot cycle*?

EXAM-STYLE QUESTIONS

You can find questions in the style of IB exams in the digital coursebook.

CHECK YOURSELF ANSWERS

1. The change is an isothermal change and so $\Delta U = 0$.

2. The point on the adiabatic has the same volume as that on the isothermal but greater pressure. Hence from $\frac{P_1}{T_1} = \frac{P_2}{T_2}$, it has higher temperature.

3. The work done is zero since the volume does not change.

4. $\Delta U = Q - W = -250 - (-250) = 0$.
   So the temperature stays the same.

5. It stays the same since no heat is exchanged.

6. The largest entropy belongs to the state with 3H and 3T. For this state $\Omega = 20$ and so $S = k \ln \Omega = 1.38 \times 10^{-23} \times \ln 20 = 4.1 \times 10^{-23}$ J K^{-1}.

7. The useful work is $0.40 \times 500 = 200$ J so the heat rejected is 300 J.

8. The efficiency of this engine is 70%. A Carnot engine operating between the same temperatures would have efficiency $1 - 400/600 = 0.33$ or 33% (it is lower, and so is impossible).

Chapter 11
Current and circuits

LEARNING OBJECTIVES

In this chapter you will learn how to:

- calculate current, potential difference and power dissipated in circuit components
- understand how current in a circuit component generates thermal energy
- define and understand electric resistance
- describe Ohm's law
- understand the factors that affect resistance
- combine resistors
- analyse an electric circuit
- distinguish between emf and terminal potential difference
- work with potential divider circuits

> **PHYSICS FOR THE IB DIPLOMA: COURSEBOOK**

> **GUIDING QUESTION**
>
> How do we analyse an electric circuit?

Introduction

We have seen that the particle model of matter helps us understand the properties of gases and the phenomena of phase changes. To do that, we had to look at matter at a molecular and atomic level.

If we look even closer, we find that atoms are made of nuclei surrounded by electrons. Nuclei and electrons share a property called electric charge.

Nuclei carry positive charge, and electrons have a negative charge. The unit of electric charge is the coulomb, symbol C; the charge on an electron is -1.6×10^{-19} C, and its mass is 9.1×10^{-31} kg.

Like energy, charge is conserved; in any process, the total charge before is the same as the total charge after.

In a metal, most of the electrons are attached to particular nuclei; these electrons can only move around their respective nuclei. But some electrons are only loosely attached to nuclei and are free to move throughout the volume of the metal; these are called free electrons. Because nuclei are much heavier than electrons, they cannot move—they are fixed in a lattice of positive charges. This chapter deals with what happens when free electrons are forced to move in the same direction in an electric circuit.

11.1 Potential difference, current and resistance

Potential difference

In Chapter 18 we will learn that there are electric forces between electric charges. The electric force is repulsive for same sign charges and attractive for opposite sign charges. So if we want to move a positive charge q closer to another positive charge, work must be done. If the work done in moving a charge q from A to B is W, the ratio $\frac{W}{q}$ is defined to be the **potential difference** between points A and B (Figure 11.1).

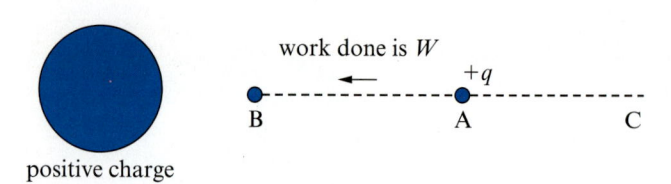

Figure 11.1: The potential difference between points A and B is the work done to move the charge from A to B divided by q. If the charge q is released at A it will accelerate to the right, gaining kinetic energy.

Conversely, if the charge at A is released, the electric force will push it away and the charge will gain kinetic energy. At point C the kinetic energy gained will be equal to qV where now V is the potential difference between points A and C.

> **KEY POINT**
>
> The potential difference V between two points is the work done per unit charge to move a point charge from one point to the other:
>
> $V = \frac{W}{q}$
>
> The unit of potential difference is the volt, V, and $1\text{ V} = 1\text{ J C}^{-1}$.

> **WORKED EXAMPLE 11.1**
>
> The work done in moving a charge of 2.0 μC between two points in an electric field is 1.50×10^{-4} J. Determine the potential difference between the two points.
>
> **Answer**
>
> From the definition, the potential difference is:
>
> $V = \frac{W}{q}$
>
> $V = \frac{1.50 \times 10^{-4}}{2.0 \times 10^{-6}}$
>
> $V = 75$ V

WORKED EXAMPLE 11.2

An electron is accelerated from rest through a potential difference of 75 V. What is the speed acquired by the electron?

Answer

From $V = \frac{W}{q}$ we find $W = qV$.

This work goes into the increase in kinetic energy, so we use the magnitude of the electron charge:

$W = 1.6 \times 10^{-19} \times 75 = 1.2 \times 10^{-17}$ J

Hence: $\frac{1}{2}mv^2 = 1.2 \times 10^{-17}$ J

and so $v = \sqrt{\frac{2 \times 1.2 \times 10^{-17}}{9.1 \times 10^{-31}}} = 5.1 \times 10^6$ m s^{-1}.

Electric current

Materials with many free electrons per unit volume are called **conductors** (such as metals).

In **insulators** (such as plastics) the number of free electrons per unit volume is very small.

In metals we have of order 10^{28} free electrons per metre cubed. These 'free' electrons move randomly, much like gas molecules in a container. They do so at high speeds, of order 10^5 m s^{-1}. During this random motion, as many electrons move in one direction as in another (Figure 11.2) and so no charge is transferred in any one direction.

a

'free' electrons

atom with electron cloud

b

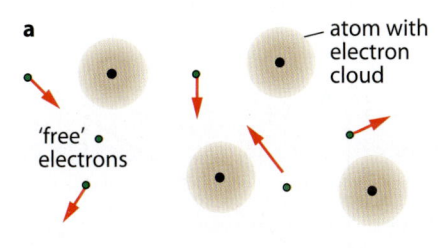

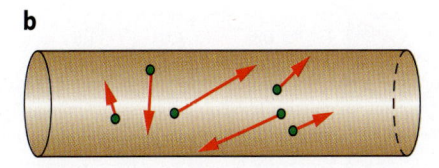

Figure 11.2: a The free electrons are not attached to any one particular atom. **b** The random electron motion does not carry net charge in any direction.

To transfer charge, the electrons have to move in the *same direction*. This motion of electrons in the same direction is known as a **direct current (dc)**.

Links

The same materials that are good conductors of thermal energy are also good conductors of electricity. This suggests that the mechanisms of thermal energy and charge transfer are similar; they both involve electrons.

KEY POINT

We define electric current I in a wire as the rate of flow of charge through the cross-sectional area of a conductor:

$I = \frac{\Delta q}{\Delta t}$

The unit of electric current is the ampere (A), which is a flow of one coulomb of charge per second (1 A = 1 C s^{-1}).

CHECK YOURSELF 1

A current of 1 A is established in a conductor.

How many electrons move through the cross-sectional area of the conductor in 1 s?

To make the electrons move in the same direction requires a source of potential difference. One way to do this is to connect the conductor to a cell or a battery as will be explained later on.

WORKED EXAMPLE 11.3

Light is incident on a metallic plate. As a result, electrons are emitted from the surface at a rate of 2.6×10^{15} per second. What is the current leaving the surface?

Answer

The charge carried away from the surface in 1 s is $2.6 \times 10^{15} \times 1.6 \times 10^{-19} = 4.2 \times 10^{-4}$ C. Hence the current is 4.2×10^{-4} A.

Electric resistance

When a given potential difference is established at the ends of a conductor, an electric current will be established in the conductor. The size of the current depends on a property of the conductor called its **electric resistance**.

> **KEY POINT**
>
> The electric resistance R of a conductor is defined as the potential difference V across its ends divided by the current I through it:
>
> $R = \dfrac{V}{I}$
>
> The unit of electric resistance is the volt per ampere which is called the ohm, Ω.

> **EXAM TIP**
>
> You must be able to turn the equation $R = \dfrac{V}{I}$ into $V = IR$ or $I = \dfrac{V}{R}$ instantly.

> **WORKED EXAMPLE 11.4**
>
> The potential difference across a conductor is 4.0 V. The resistance is 16 Ω.
>
> What is the current through the conductor?
>
> **Answer**
>
> From $R = \dfrac{V}{I}$ we find $I = \dfrac{V}{R} = \dfrac{4.0}{16} = 0.25$ A.

The electric resistance of conducting wires is very small, so it is a good approximation to ignore this resistance. Conducting wires are represented by thin line segments in diagrams. Conductors whose resistance cannot be neglected are denoted by boxes and are called resistors (Figure 11.3).

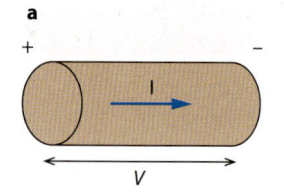

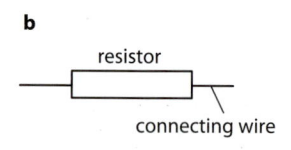

Figure 11.3: a The potential difference V across the ends of the conductor creates an electric field within the conductor that forces a current I through the conductor. **b** How we represent a resistor and connecting wires in a circuit diagram.

In 1826, the German scientist Georg Ohm (1789–1854) discovered that when the temperature of most metallic conductors is kept constant, the current through the conductor is proportional to the potential difference across it:

$I \propto V$

This statement is known as **Ohm's law**.

Materials that obey Ohm's law have a constant resistance at constant temperature. For these ohmic materials, a graph of I against V gives a straight line through the origin (Figure 11.4).

A filament light bulb will obey Ohm's law as long as the current through it is small. As the current is increased, the temperature of the filament increases and so does the resistance (Figure 11.5).

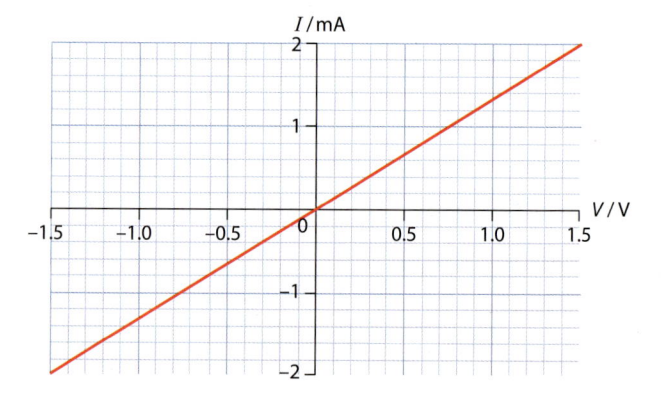

Figure 11.4: The current–potential difference graph for a material that obeys Ohm's law.

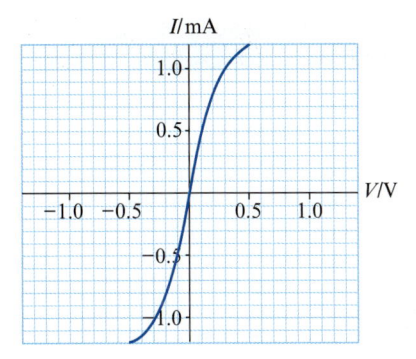

Figure 11.5: The current–potential difference graph for a filament lamp; the resistance increases as the voltage increases.

In the graph for the ohmic material, no matter which point on the graph we choose (say the one with voltage 1.2 V and current 1.6 mA), the resistance is always the same:

$$R = \frac{1.2}{1.6 \times 10^{-3}} = 750 \, \Omega$$

However, looking at the graph in Figure 11.5 (the lamp filament), we see that at a voltage of 0.2 V the current is 0.8 mA and so the resistance is:

$$R = \frac{0.2}{0.8 \times 10^{-3}} = 250 \, \Omega$$

At a voltage of 0.3 V the current is 1.0 mA and the resistance is:

$$R = \frac{0.3}{1.0 \times 10^{-3}} = 300 \, \Omega$$

We see that as the current in the filament increases the resistance increases, so Ohm's law is not obeyed. This is a nonohmic device.

Two other common components with variable resistance include **light dependent resistors (LDRs)** and **thermistors**. The resistance of an LDR decreases as the intensity of light falling on it increases. The resistance of an NTC type thermistor decreases as the ambient temperature increases. Later on we will meet another component: the potentiometer.

Experiments show that three factors affect the resistance of a conductor kept at constant temperature. They are:

- the nature of the material
- the length of the conductor
- the cross-sectional area of the conductor.

It is found that the electric resistance R of a conductor (at fixed temperature) is proportional to its length L and inversely proportional to the cross-sectional area A:

$$R = \rho \frac{L}{A}$$

The constant ρ is called **resistivity** and depends on the material of the conductor and the temperature. The unit of resistivity is $\Omega \, m$.

CHECK YOURSELF 2

The length and radius of a cylindrical conductor are both doubled. What happens to the resistance of the conductor?

A microscopic view of resistance

Electrons moving through a metal suffer collisions with the atoms of the metal. The collisions are inelastic which means the electrons lose energy which the atoms of the wire gain. Thus the atoms in the wire vibrate about their equilibrium positions with increased kinetic energy. We know from Chapter 7 that an increase in the random kinetic energy of molecules implies an increase in the temperature of the wire. This explains the heating effect of a current in a conductor.

The increased vibration of atoms means that we have an increased probability of collision between an electron and an atom. This means that the average speed of the electrons is reduced so the rate of flow of charge, i.e. the current, is reduced. This implies that resistance increases $\left(R = \frac{V}{I}\right)$. In other words, in most metallic conductors, an increase in temperature leads to an increase in resistance.

WORKED EXAMPLE 11.5

The resistivity of copper is $1.68 \times 10^{-8} \, \Omega \, m$. Calculate the length of a copper wire of diameter 4.00 mm that has a resistance of 5.00 Ω.

Answer

We use $R = \rho \frac{L}{A}$ to get $L = \frac{RA}{\rho}$ and so:

$$L = \frac{5.00 \times \pi \times (2.00 \times 10^{-3})^2}{1.68 \times 10^{-8}}$$

$$L = 3739 \, m$$

The length of copper wire is about 3.74 km.

EXAM TIP

Do not confuse diameter with radius.

TEST YOUR UNDERSTANDING

1. The work done in moving a charge of 5.0 nC across two points is 240 nJ. What is the potential difference between the points?

2. An alpha particle has twice the charge of a proton and 4 times its mass. An alpha particle and a proton are accelerated from rest by a potential difference of 250 V. What are the ratios $\frac{\text{kinetic energy of alpha particle}}{\text{kinetic energy of proton}}$ and $\frac{\text{speed of alpha particle}}{\text{speed of proton}}$?

3. The current in a wire is 2.0 A. How many electrons move through the cross-sectional area of a wire in a time of 5 s?

4. The current in a wire is I. The charge of an electron is e. How many electrons go through the cross-sectional area of the wire in 1 s?

5. The current in a device obeying Ohm's law is 1.5 A when connected to a source of potential difference 6.0 V. What will the potential difference across the same device be when the current is 3.5 A?

6. The current through a resistor obeying Ohm's law is 0.80 A when the potential difference across the resistor is 240 V. What current would we have when the potential difference is decreased to 160 V?

7. Electrons are moving in a metallic wire of cross-sectional area A. There are n free electrons per unit volume. The charge on one electron is e and the average speed of the electrons is v.

   a Show that an expression for the electric current is $I = nAve$.

   b Estimate the magnitude of the drift speed in a wire that carries a current of 1 A. The wire has radius 2 mm, and the number of electrons per unit volume (the number density) of free electrons is $n = 10^{28}$ m^{-3}.

   c Figure 11.6 shows electric current that flows in a conductor of variable cross-sectional area. State and explain whether the electron drift speed at B is smaller than, equal to, or greater than that at A.

   Figure 11.6: For question 7.

8. a Why does the passage of current in a conductor result in heating of the conductor?

   b Why does the resistance of a metallic conductor increase when the temperature increases?

9. The graph (Figure 11.7) shows the current–voltage characteristics of a device.

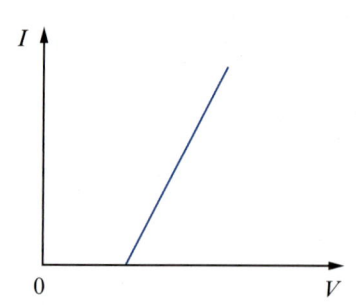

   Figure 11.7: For question 9.

   By finding how the resistance varies as the voltage increases, explain why the device does not obey Ohm's law.

CONTINUED

10 Figure 11.8 shows a light-dependent resistor connected to an ohmic resistor. The intensity of light increases. The current stays the same. What happens to the reading of the voltmeter?

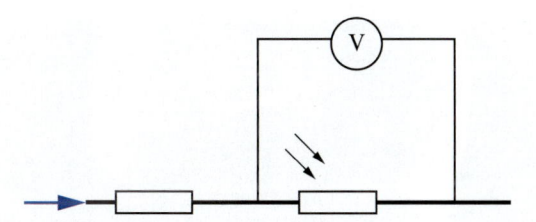

Figure 11.8: For question 10.

11 A filament lamp is most likely to burn out when it is turned on rather than when it is turned off. What could be the reason for this?

12 The graphs (Figure 11.9) show the current as a function of voltage across the same piece of metal wire which is kept at two different temperatures.

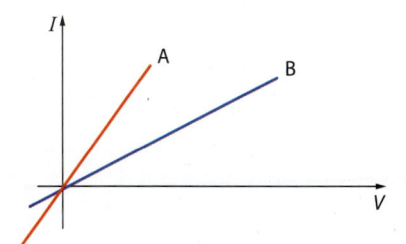

Figure 11.9: For question 12.

  a Discuss whether the wire obeys Ohm's law.

  b Suggest which of the two lines on the graph corresponds to the higher temperature.

13 A cylindrical copper wire has resistance R. The wire is melted and a new wire of double the length is made out of all the available material. What is the resistance of the new wire?

14 A conductor has the shape of a rectangular block of size 10 cm × 20 cm × 40 cm as shown in Figure 11.10.

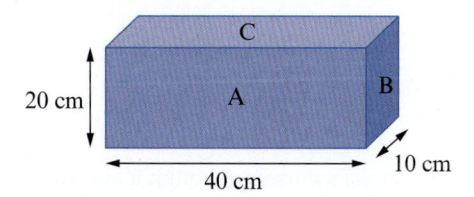

Figure 11.10: For question 14.

A potential difference is established across opposite faces of the block.
In which case is the smallest current established in the block?

15 The resistivity of a metal wire is 2.5×10^{-8} Ω m. The radius of the wire is 0.25 mm, and its length is 2.2 m. What is the resistance of the wire?

16 What happens to the resistance of a cylindrical wire if the length and the radius are both tripled?

17 The resistivity of a metal wire is 1.7×10^{-8} Ω m. The radius of the wire is 0.30 mm, and its resistance is 5.0 Ω. What is its length?

18 The resistivity of a metal wire is 5.6×10^{-8} Ω m. The length of the wire is 3.5 km, and its resistance is 4.0 Ω. What is its radius?

19 Two copper wires X and Y have the same resistance. X has double the length of Y. What is the ratio $\frac{\text{radius of X}}{\text{radius of Y}}$?

11.2 Voltage, power and emf

Voltage

The defining equation for resistance, $R = \frac{V}{I}$, can be rearranged in terms of the potential difference V:

$V = IR$

This says that if there is a current through a conductor that has resistance, i.e. a resistor, then there must be a potential difference across the ends of that resistor. The term **voltage** is commonly used for potential difference.

Figure 11.11 shows part of a circuit. The current is 5.0 A and the resistance is 15 Ω. The voltage across the resistor is given by $V = IR = 5.0 \times 15 = 75$ V. The resistance between B and C is zero, so the voltage across B and C is zero.

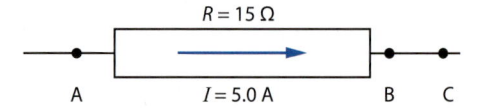

Figure 11.11: There is a voltage across points A and B and zero voltage across B and C.

Electric power

We saw that whenever an electric charge q is moved between two points that have a potential difference V, work is done. This work is given by $W = qV$.

Consider a resistor with a potential difference V across its ends. Since power is the rate of doing work, the power P dissipated in the resistor in moving a charge q across it in time t is:

$P = \frac{\text{work done}}{\text{time taken}}$

$P = \frac{qV}{t}$

But $\frac{q}{t}$ is the current I in the resistor, so the **electric power** is given by:

$P = IV$

This power manifests itself in thermal energy and/or work performed by an electrical device.

We can use $R = \frac{V}{I}$ to rewrite the formula for power in equivalent ways:

$P = IV = RI^2 = \frac{V^2}{R}$

In a filament lamp electrical energy is transferred to light and thermal energy (Figure 11.12).

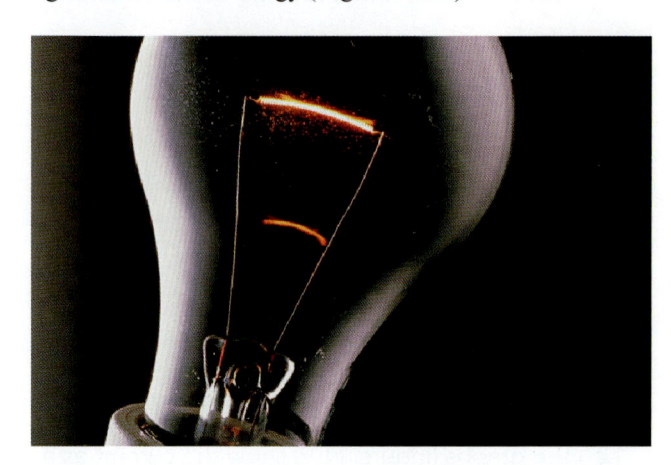

Figure 11.12: The metal filament in a light bulb glows as the current passes through it. It is also very hot. This shows that electrical energy is transferred to both thermal energy and light energy.

> ### CHECK YOURSELF 3
>
> The power dissipated in a resistor of constant resistance is 32 W when a potential difference of 12 V is established at its ends.
>
> What is the dissipated power when the potential difference is increased to 15 V?

> ### WORKED EXAMPLE 11.6
>
> A resistor of resistance 12 Ω has a current of 2.0 A flowing through it. How much energy is generated in the resistor in one minute?
>
> **Answer**
>
> The power generated in the resistor is:
>
> $P = RI^2$
>
> $P = 12 \times 4 = 48$ W
>
> Thus, in one minute (60 s) the energy E generated is:
>
> $E = 48 \times 60 \text{ J} = 2.9 \times 10^3$ J

Electrical devices are usually rated according to the power they use. A light bulb rated as 60 W at 220 V means that it will dissipate 60 W when a potential difference of 220 V is applied across its ends. If the potential difference across its ends is anything other than 220 V, the power dissipated will be different from 60 W.

> **WORKED EXAMPLE 11.7**
>
> A light bulb rated as 60 W at 220 V has a potential difference of 110 V across its ends. Find the power dissipated in this light bulb.
>
> **Answer**
>
> Let R be the resistance of the light bulb and P the power we want to find. Assuming R stays constant (so that it is the same when 220 V or 110 V are applied to its ends), we have:
>
> $P = \frac{110^2}{R}$ and $60 = \frac{220^2}{R}$
>
> Dividing the first equation by the second, we find:
>
> $\frac{P}{60} = \frac{110^2}{220^2}$
>
> This gives $P = 15$ W.

> **EXAM TIP**
>
> The power of the light bulb is 60 W only when the voltage across it is 220 V.
>
> If we change the voltage, we will change the power.

Electromotive force (emf)

In an electric circuit, the simplest source of potential difference is a cell or a battery (a battery is a collection of cells). The potential difference is created by chemical reactions inside the cell, Figure 11.13a. The chemicals also create a resistance inside the cell, an **internal resistance**. In such a cell the source of energy is chemical. In solar cells (photovoltaic cells) the source energy is the solar energy radiated by the sun.

When the cell is connected to an external circuit, Figure 11.13b, electrons flow into the cell from the positive terminal and enter the circuit from the negative terminal. By convention the electric current is taken to be in a direction opposite to the electron flow.

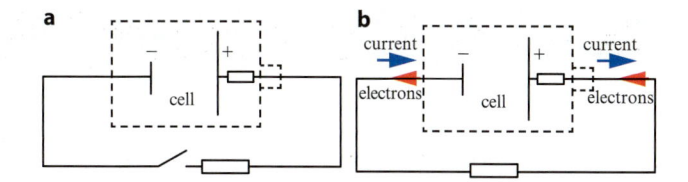

Figure 11.13: a Chemical reactions maintain a potential difference across the terminal of the cell. **b** When the cell is connected to an external circuit, electrons flow into the battery from the positive terminal and exit into the circuit from the negative terminal. By convention, the current is said to flow in the opposite direction.

A simple mechanical model of a cell involves the following idea. Suppose that in Figure **11.13a** you had a 'conveyor belt' that moved electrons from the right terminal of the cell to the left. This would make the right terminal positively charged and the left terminal negatively charged. This would continue until there is enough negative charge on the negative plate to repel any new electrons from arriving there. There is now a potential difference across the terminals. In a real cell, chemical reactions play the role of this imaginary 'conveyor belt'.

> **KEY POINT**
>
> The **electromotive force (emf)** ε (of a cell or battery) is the work done per unit charge in moving charge from one terminal of the battery to the other. The unit of emf is the volt, V.
>
> $\varepsilon = \text{emf} = \frac{W}{q}$

(In batteries, the work done is chemical work. In general, in defining emf, the work done is always nonelectrical.)

By conservation of energy, this work is also equal to the work done W in moving charge q around the circuit. If we divide both numerator and denominator by time, we may also obtain the very convenient fact:

$\varepsilon = \text{emf} = \frac{P}{I}$

So, to find the *total* power dissipated in a circuit all we have to do is multiply the emf by the current leaving the cell or battery.

This formula is very useful when discussing circuits, as you will see later.

TEST YOUR UNDERSTANDING

20
 a What is the resistance per unit length of copper wire (resistivity = 1.7×10^{-8} Ω m) of radius 4.0 mm?

 b A current of 7.5 A is sent down a copper wire of radius 4.0 mm.
 How much power is dissipated in a length of 150 km of the wire (Figure 11.14)?

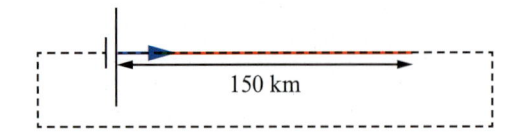

Figure 11.14: For question 20.

 c What is the potential difference at the ends of the 150 km long wire?

21 The heating element of an electric kettle dissipates 1.1 kW of power when connected to a source of potential difference 230 V. Calculate the resistance of the heating element.

22 The filament of a lamp rated as 60 W at 120 V has resistivity 3.6×10^{-7} Ω m.

 a Calculate the resistance of the lamp when it is connected to a source of 120 V.

 b The radius of the filament is 0.042 mm. Determine its length.

 c Referring to your answer to part **b**, suggest how the filament can fit within the light bulb.

23 The graph (Figure 11.15) shows how the resistance R of a device varies with applied voltage V for a range of voltages.

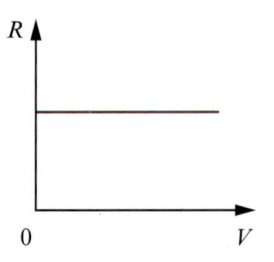

Figure 11.15: For question 23.

Sketch a graph to show how the current varies with applied voltage.

24 The graph (Figure 11.16) shows how the resistance R of a device varies with applied voltage V.

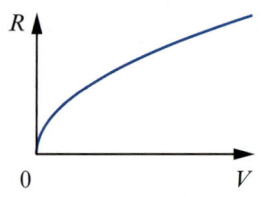

Figure 11.16: For question 24.

Sketch a graph to show how the current varies with applied voltage.

25 Figure 11.17 shows two resistors with a current of 2.0 A in the wire.

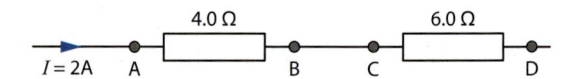

Figure 11.17: For question 25.

 a Calculate the potential difference across each resistor.

 b State the potential difference between points B and C and points A and D.

26 A device is rated 60 W at 120 V. What is the current in the device?

27 The power dissipated in a resistor is 12 W when the potential difference across it is 6.0 V. What power would be dissipated if the potential difference becomes 9.0 V?

28 The power dissipated in a resistor is 4.0 W. What would the dissipated power be if the resistance of the resistor is halved and the potential difference across it stays the same?

29 The power dissipated in a resistor is 32 W. What would the dissipated power be if the resistance of the resistor and the potential difference across it are both doubled?

> **CONTINUED**
>
> **30** In a circuit the emf of the cell is 6.0 V and the current leaving the cell is 2.5 A. What is the total power dissipated in the circuit?
>
> **31** A charge of 12 C is moved around a circuit. The work done is 48 J. What is the emf of the source?

11.3 Resistors in electric circuits

Simple circuits

We have so far defined emf, voltage, resistance, current and power dissipated in a resistor. We are now ready to put all these ideas together and discuss the main topic of this chapter—electric circuits.

These circuits include cells and batteries, connecting wires, ammeters (to measure current) and voltmeters (to measure voltage) and various resistors. The symbols used for these circuit components are shown in Table 11.1.

Symbol	Component name
	connecting wire
	cell
	battery of cells
	resistor
	dc power supply
	ac power supply
	junction of conductors
	crossing conductors (no connection)
	lamp
	voltmeter

Symbol	Component name
	ammeter
	switch
	galvanometer
	potentiometer
	variable resistor
	heating element
	Light dependent resistor (LDR)
	Thermistor

Table 11.1: Names of electrical components and their circuit symbols.

We start with the circuit shown in Figure 11.18. The cell is assumed to have zero internal resistance. The current enters the circuit from the positive terminal of the cell. The direction of the current is shown by the blue arrow. The terminals of the cell are directly connected to the ends of the resistor (there is no intervening internal resistor). Therefore, the potential difference at the ends of the resistor is 12 V. Using the definition of resistance we write $R = \frac{V}{I}$.

Substituting values gives $24 = \frac{12}{I}$, and rearranging gives $I = \frac{12}{24} = 0.5$.

So, the current I in the circuit is 0.5 A.

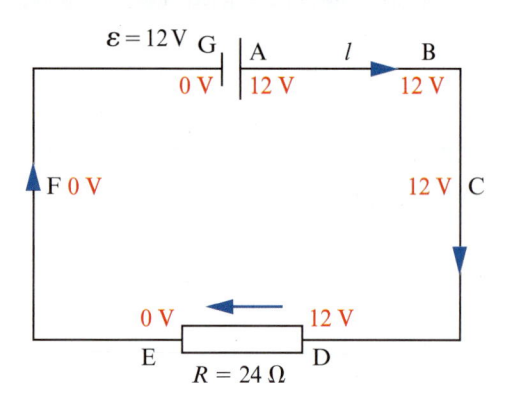

Figure 11.18: A simple one-loop circuit with one cell with negligible internal resistance and one resistor.

A very useful and convenient way to understand circuits is to think in terms of a quantity called potential rather than potential difference. We will not define potential but will assume that if a cell has an emf ε then we can assign zero potential to the negative terminal and potential ε to the positive terminal. As we follow the current in the circuit starting from the positive terminal the rule is that the potential stays unchanged unless we come to a resistance. This is why points B, C and D have potential 12 V. The potential difference between B and C or D is then zero. If we now follow the circuit starting from G, the negative terminal, to F and then E we again see that the potential stays the same, i.e. 0 V, until we reach the resistor at E. So we see that the potential difference across the resistor is 12 V. So as we go through the resistor in the direction of the current the potential *drops*.

Resistors

Resistors in series

Consider the circuit in Figure 11.19 that contains two resistors. The resistors are connected in **series** which means the wire joining the two does is a single wire without any junctions. The two resistors take the same current. What is this current?

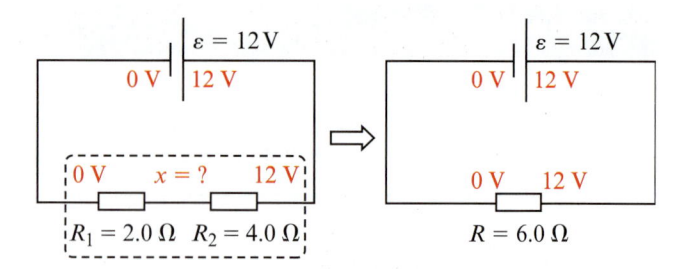

Figure 11.19: Finding the total resistance of the circuit.

Notice that the potential between the resistors is unknown. If we call it x, then the *potential difference* across R_2 is $12 - x$ and the potential difference across R_1 is $x - 0$.

But, if we add these potential differences, we get 12 V, in other words, the emf of the circuit.

So, if we call the voltage across R_1, V_1 and the voltage across R_2, V_2 we have $V_1 + V_2 = 12$.

But $V_1 = IR_1$ and $V_2 = IR_2$, so $IR_1 + IR_2 = 12$.

In other words, $2.0I + 4.0I = 12$, so the current is 2.0 A.

Can we generalise so we can find the answer faster?

From $IR_1 + IR_2 = 12$ we find $I = \dfrac{12}{R_1 + R_2}$.

This is the same answer we would get if we replaced the two resistors in the dotted box by a single resistor of value $R_1 + R_2$.

In other words, there is an equivalent circuit that replaces the given circuit with a circuit with only one resistor of value $R_1 + R_2$. This is called the total resistance of the original circuit with two resistors.

But the equivalent circuit with just one resistor is very easy. We immediately find $I = 2.0$ A. Having found the current, we can find the voltages across each resistor:

- across the 2.0 Ω it is $2.0 \times 2.0 = 4.0$ V
- across the 4.0 Ω it is $2.0 \times 4.0 = 8.0$ V.

The sum of the voltages is the emf as expected. (The *potential* in between the two resistors is, therefore, 4.0 V.)

> **EXAM TIP**
>
> The voltages across all resistors in series add up to the emf of the source.

For any number of resistors in series, the total resistance is their sum: $R_T = R_1 + R_2 + R_3 + \cdots$.

Adding resistors in series increases the total resistance.

> ### CHECK YOURSELF 4
>
> A circuit contains two resistors connected in series. A third resistor is added in series to the other two. What happens to the current in the circuit?

Figure 11.20 shows a circuit with three resistors $R_1 = 2.0\ \Omega$, $R_2 = 6.0\ \Omega$ and $R_3 = 4.0\ \Omega$ in series.

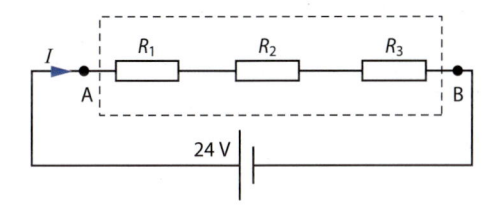

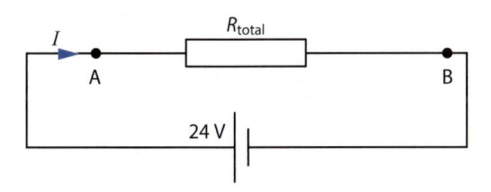

Figure 11.20: The top circuit is replaced by the equivalent circuit containing just one resistor.

We replace the three resistors by the equivalent resistor of $R_T = 2.0 + 6.0 + 4.0 = 12\ \Omega$. The current through the equivalent resistor is found as follows:

$$R = \frac{V}{I}$$

$$\Rightarrow I = \frac{V}{R} = \frac{24}{12} = 2.0\ \text{A}$$

This current, therefore, is also the current that enters the dotted box. In other words, it is the current in each of the three resistors of the original circuit. We may thus deduce that the voltages across each of the three resistors are:

$V_1 = IR_1 = 4.0\ \text{V}$

$V_2 = IR_2 = 12\ \text{V}$

$V_3 = IR_3 = 8.0\ \text{V}$

Notice that the sum of the voltages equals the emf of the cell.

WORKED EXAMPLE 11.8

What is the voltage across each resistor in Figure 11.21?

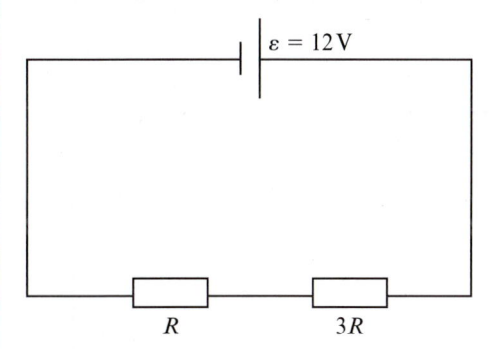

Figure 11.21: For worked example 11.8.

Answer

Method 1

The two voltages must add up to 12 V. The voltage across $3R$ will be three times larger, so the voltages are 3 V and 9 V.

Method 2

The total resistance for the circuit is $4R$.

Hence the current is $I = \frac{12}{4R} = \frac{3}{R}$

The voltage across R is $V = IR = \frac{3}{R} \times R = 3$ V.

The voltage across $3R$ is $V = I(3R) = \frac{3}{R} \times 3R = 9$ V.

WORKED EXAMPLE 11.9

In the circuit in Figure 11.22, the intensity of light incident on the LDR is increased. What will happen to the potential difference across the LDR?

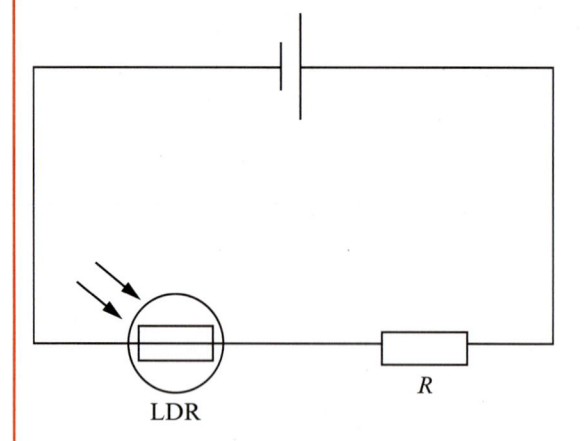

Figure 11.22: For worked example 11.9.

Answer

The sum of the potential differences across the LDR and R is the emf. The resistance of the LDR will decrease and so the current in the circuit will increase. Hence the potential difference across R will increase and so that across the LDR will decrease.

Resistors in parallel

Consider now part of another circuit, in which the current splits into three other currents that flow in three resistors, as shown in Figure 11.23 The current that enters the junction at A must equal the current that leaves the junction at B, by the law of conservation of charge. The left ends of the three resistors are connected at the same point and the same is true for the right ends. This means that three resistors have the same potential difference across them. This is called a **parallel connection**. We must then have that:

$$I = I_1 + I_2 + I_3$$

This is again a consequence of charge conservation. The current entering the junction is I and the currents leaving the junction are I_1, I_2 and I_3. Whatever charge enters the junction must exit the junction and so the sum of the currents into a junction equals the sum of the currents leaving the junction.

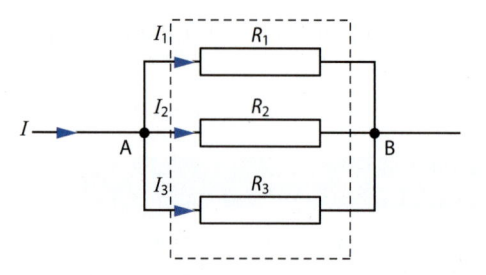

Figure 11.23: Three resistors connected in parallel.

Let V be the common potential difference across the resistors. Then:

$$I_1 = \frac{V}{R_1}, I_2 = \frac{V}{R_2} \text{ and } I_3 = \frac{V}{R_3}$$

and so:

$$I = \frac{V}{R_1} + \frac{V}{R_2} + \frac{V}{R_3}$$

$$I = V\left(\frac{1}{R_1} + \frac{1}{R_2} + \frac{1}{R_3}\right)$$

If we replace the three resistors in the dotted box with a single resistor R_T, the potential difference across it would be V and the current through it would be I. Thus:

$$I = \frac{V}{R_T}$$

Comparing with the last equation, we find:

$$\frac{1}{R_T} = \frac{1}{R_1} + \frac{1}{R_2} + \frac{1}{R_3}$$

The formula shows that the total resistance is *smaller* than any of the individual resistances being added.

We have thus learned how to replace resistors that are connected in series or parallel by a single resistor in each case, thus greatly simplifying the circuit.

EXAM TIP

Adding resistors in series increases the total resistance of a circuit (and so decreases the current leaving the battery). Adding resistors in parallel decreases the total resistance of the circuit (and so increases the current leaving the battery).

CHECK YOURSELF 5

The total resistance of three identical resistors is 1 Ω when they are connected in parallel. What is the total resistance when they are connected in series?

> **WORKED EXAMPLE 11.10**
>
> In the part of the circuit shown in Figure 11.24 the current is 3.0 A.
>
> What is the current in each resistor? 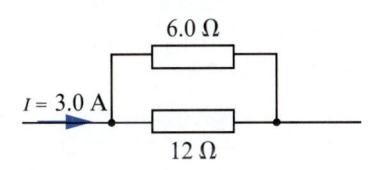
>
> **Figure 11.24:** For worked example 11.10.
>
> **Answer**
>
> **Method 1**
>
> The total resistance is found from $\frac{1}{R_T} = \frac{1}{6.0} + \frac{1}{12} = \frac{1}{4.0}$.
>
> So, $R_T = 4.0\ \Omega$.
>
> Hence the common potential difference across the two resistors is:
>
> $V = IR_T = 3.0 \times 4.0 = 12$ V
>
> And the currents are:
>
> $I_1 = \frac{12}{6.0} = 2.0$ A (top) and $I_2 = \frac{12}{12} = 1.0$ A (bottom).
>
> **Method 2**
>
> The two resistors are connected in parallel so they have the same potential difference across them.
>
> The potential difference across the top resistor is $6.0I_1$ and that across the lower resistor is $12I_2$.
>
> Hence $6.0I_1 = 12I_2 \Rightarrow I_1 = 2I_2$.
>
> (The smaller resistor gets more current.)
>
> But also, $I_1 + I_2 = 3.0$ A, so $I_1 = 2.0$ A and $I_2 = 1.0$ A.

Resistors in series and parallel

A typical circuit will contain both parallel and series connections. In Figure 11.25, the two top resistors are in series. They are equivalent to a single resistor of 8.0 Ω. This resistor and the 24 Ω resistor are in parallel, so together they are equivalent to a single resistor of:

$\frac{1}{R_T} = \frac{1}{8.0} + \frac{1}{24} = \frac{1}{6}$

$\Rightarrow R_T = 6.0\ \Omega$

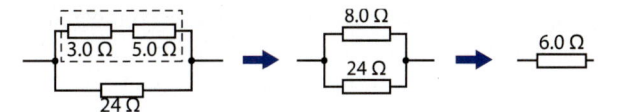

Figure 11.25: Part of a circuit with both series and parallel connections.

Consider now Figure 11.26. The two top 6.0 Ω resistors are in series, so they are equivalent to a 12 Ω resistor. This, in turn, is in parallel with the other 6.0 Ω resistor, so the left block is equivalent to:

$\frac{1}{R_T} = \frac{1}{12} + \frac{1}{6.0} = \frac{1}{4}$

$\Rightarrow R_T = 4.0\ \Omega$

Let us go to the right block. The lower 12 Ω and the 24 Ω resistors are in series, so they are equivalent to 36 Ω. This is in parallel with the top 12 Ω, so the equivalent resistor of the right block is:

$\frac{1}{R_T} = \frac{1}{36} + \frac{1}{12} = \frac{1}{9}$

$\Rightarrow R_T = 9.0\ \Omega$

The overall resistance is thus:

$4.0 + 9.0 = 13\ \Omega$

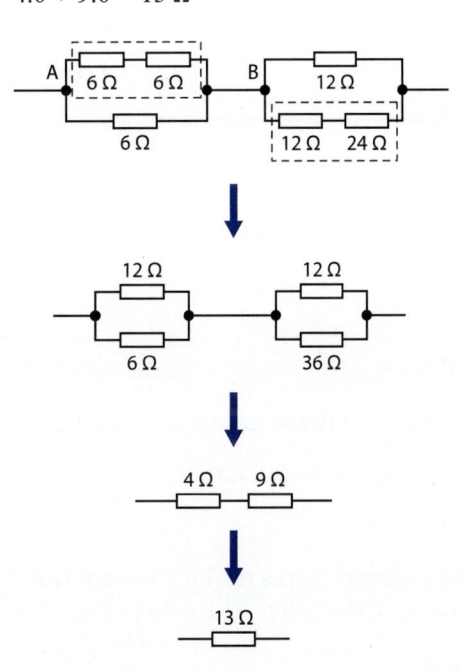

Figure 11.26: A complicated part of a circuit containing many parallel and series connections.

245

Suppose now that this part of the circuit is connected to a source of emf 156 V (and negligible internal resistance). The current that leaves the source is:

$$I = \frac{156}{13} = 12\text{ A}$$

When it arrives at point A, it will split into two parts. Let the current in the top part be I_1 and that in the bottom part I_2. We have $I_1 + I_2 = 12$ A. We also have that $12I_1 = 6I_2$, since the top and bottom resistors of the block beginning at point A are in parallel and so have the same potential difference across them. Thus, $I_1 = 4.0$ A and $I_2 = 8.0$ A. Similarly, in the block beginning at point B the top current is 9.0 A and the bottom current is 3.0 A.

> ### CHECK YOURSELF 6
>
> Two identical resistors are connected in series to a cell of negligible internal resistance. The total power dissipated is 16 W.
>
> What is the power dissipated when the two resistors are connected to the same cell in parallel?

WORKED EXAMPLE 11.11

a Determine the total resistance of the circuit shown in Figure 11.27.

b Hence calculate the current and power dissipated in each of the resistors.

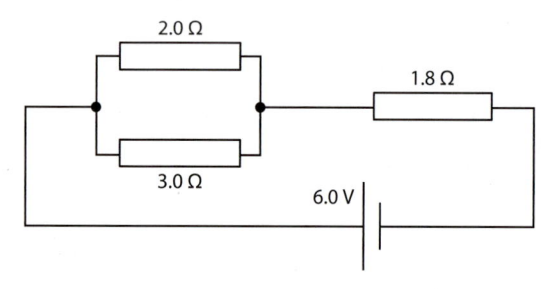

Figure 11.27: For worked example 11.11.

Answer

a The resistors of 2.0 Ω and 3.0 Ω are connected in parallel and are equivalent to a single resistor of resistance R that may be found from:

$$\frac{1}{R} = \frac{1}{2} + \frac{1}{3} = \frac{5}{6}$$

$$\Rightarrow R = \frac{6}{5} = 1.2\text{ Ω}$$

In turn, this is in series with the resistance of 1.8 Ω, so the total equivalent circuit resistance is $1.8 + 1.2 = 3.0$ Ω.

b The current that leaves the cell is thus:

$$I = \frac{6.0}{3.0} = 2.0\text{ A}$$

The potential difference across the 1.8 Ω resistor is $V = 1.8 \times 2.0 = 3.6$ V, leading to a potential difference across the two parallel resistors of $V = 6.0 - 3.6 = 2.4$ V. Thus the current in the 2 Ω resistor is:

$$I = \frac{2.4}{2.0} = 1.2\text{ A}$$

This leads to power dissipated of:

$$P = RI^2 = 2.0 \times 1.2^2 = 2.9\text{ W}$$

or $P = \frac{V^2}{R} = \frac{2.4^2}{2.0} = 2.9\text{ W}$

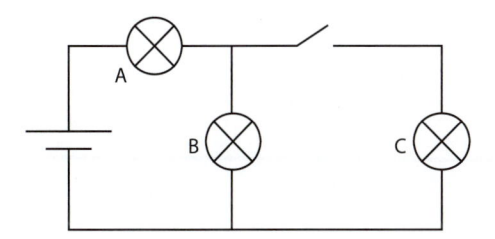

> **CONTINUED**
>
> or $P = VI = 2.4 \times 1.2 = 2.9$ W
>
> For the 3 Ω resistor:
>
> $I = \frac{2.4}{3.0} = 0.80$ A
>
> which leads to power dissipated of $P = RI^2 = 3.0 \times 0.80^2 = 1.9$ W.
>
> The power in the 1.8 Ω resistor is $P = RI^2 = 1.8 \times 2.0^2 = 7.2$ W.
>
> (The total power is $2.9 + 1.9 + 7.2 = 12$ W and equals emf × current = $6.0 \times 2.0 = 12$ W as expected.)

> **WORKED EXAMPLE 11.12**
>
> In the circuit of Figure 11.28 the three lamps are identical and may be assumed to have a constant resistance. Discuss what happens to the brightness of:
>
> **a** lamp A
>
> **b** lamp B
>
> when the switch is closed.
>
> (Take 'brightness' to mean the same as power dissipated.)
>
> **Figure 11.28:** For worked example 11.12.
>
> **Answer**
>
> **a** When the switch is closed the total resistance of the circuit decreases because we have a parallel connection for lamps B and C. Hence the current through A increases and the brightness increases.
>
> **b** Method 1
>
> With the switch open, A and B are connected in series and have the same resistance, so the potential difference across A and across B is $\frac{\varepsilon}{2}$ (half the emf of the cell).
>
> This means that A and B are equally bright. When the switch is closed, B and C have a total resistance that is half that of A. So, the potential difference across A is double that across B.
>
> This means that:
>
> - the potential difference across A is $\frac{2\varepsilon}{3}$
> - the potential difference across B is $\frac{\varepsilon}{3}$.

> ## CONTINUED

So, A increases in brightness and B gets dimmer.

Method 2 (a mathematical answer)

Let the emf of the cell be ε and the resistance of each lamp be R.

Before the switch is closed, A and B take equal current $\frac{\varepsilon}{2R}$ and so are equally bright (the total resistance is $2R$).

When the switch is closed, the total resistance of the circuit changes and so the current changes as well. The new total resistance is $\frac{3R}{2}$ (lamps B and C in parallel and the result in series with A) so the total current is now $\frac{2\varepsilon}{3R}$, larger than before.

The current in A is greater and so the power (that is, the brightness) is greater than before.

The current of $\frac{2\varepsilon}{3R}$ is divided equally between B and C.

B now takes a current $\frac{\varepsilon}{3R}$, which is smaller than before.

So, B is dimmer.

WORKED EXAMPLE 11.13

Look at Figure 11.29. Determine the current in the 2.0 Ω resistor and the potential difference across the two marked points, A and B, when the switch is:

a open

b closed.

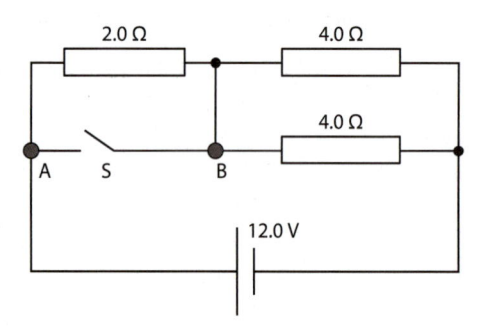

Figure 11.29: For worked example 11.13.

Answer

a When the switch is open, the total resistance is 4.0 Ω, so the total current is 3.0 A.

The potential difference across the 2.0 Ω resistor is $2.0 \times 3.0 = 6.0$ V.

The potential difference across points A and B is the same as that across the 2.0 Ω resistor (= 6.0 V).

b When the switch is closed, no current flows through the 2.0 Ω resistor, since the current takes the path through the switch, which offers no resistance. (The 2.0 Ω resistor has been 'shorted out'.)

11 Current and circuits

CONTINUED

The resistance of the circuit is then 2.0 Ω and the current leaving the cell is 6.0 A.

The potential difference across points A and B is now zero. (There is current flowing from A to B, but the resistance from A to B is zero, hence the potential difference is $I \times R = 6.0 \times 0 = 0$ V.)

WORKED EXAMPLE 11.14

Four lamps each of constant resistance 60 Ω are connected as shown in Figure 11.30.

a Determine the power in each lamp.

b Lamp A burns out. Calculate the power in each lamp and the potential difference across the burnt-out lamp.

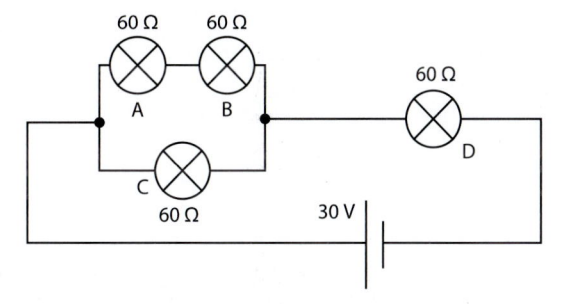

Figure 11.30: For worked example 11.14.

Answer

a We know the resistance of each lamp, so to find the power we need to find the current in each lamp.

Lamps A and B are connected in series so they are equivalent to one resistor of value $R_{AB} = 60 + 60 = 120$ Ω. This is connected in parallel to C, giving a total resistance of:

$$\frac{1}{R_{ABC}} = \frac{1}{120} + \frac{1}{60}$$

$$\frac{1}{R_{ABC}} = \frac{1}{40}$$

$\Rightarrow R_{ABC} = 40$ Ω

Finally, this is in series with D, giving a total circuit resistance of:

$R_T = 40 + 60 = 100$ Ω

The current leaving the cell is thus:

$I = \frac{30}{100} = 0.30$ A

The current through A and B is 0.10 A, and that through C is 0.20 A. The current through D is 0.30 A.

So, the power in each lamp is:

$P_A = P_B$

$P_A = 60 \times (0.10)^2 = 0.6$ W

CONTINUED

$P_C = 60 \times (0.20)^2 = 2.4$ W

$P_D = 60 \times (0.30)^2 = 5.4$ W

b With lamp A burnt out, the circuit is as shown in Figure 11.31.

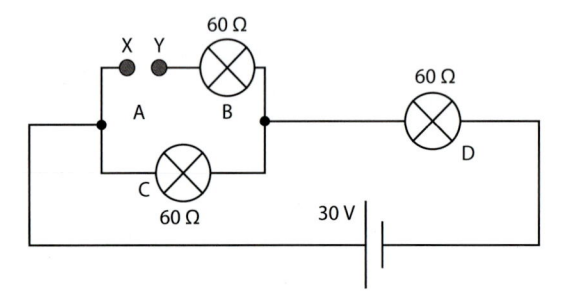

Figure 11.31: For worked example 11.14 part b.

Lamp B gets no current, so we are left with only C and D connected in series, giving a total resistance of:

$R_T = 60 + 60 = 120$ Ω

The current is:

$I = \frac{30}{120} = 0.25$ A.

The power in C and D is:

$P_C = P_D = 60 \times (0.25)^2 = 3.8$ W

We see that D becomes dimmer and C brighter.

The potential difference across lamp C is:

$V = IR$

$V = 0.25 \times 60$

$V = 15$ V

Lamp B takes no current, so the potential difference across it is zero. The potential difference across points X and Y is the same as that across lamp C (= 15 V).

TEST YOUR UNDERSTANDING

32 A wire has resistance R. The wire is cut into two pieces of equal length. The two pieces are connected in parallel. What is the resistance of the combination?

33 A wire has resistance R. The wire is cut into two pieces. One piece has twice the length of the other. The two pieces are connected in parallel. What is the resistance of the combination?

34 Determine the total resistance for each of the circuit parts in Figure 11.32.

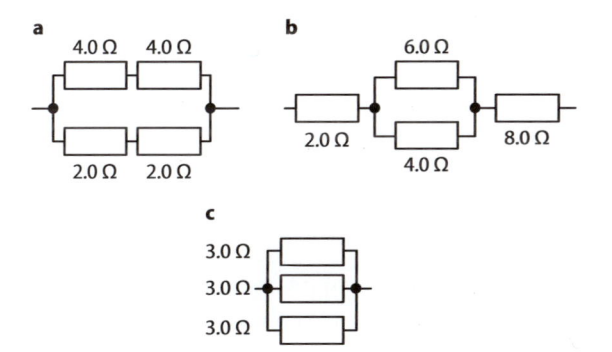

a 4.0 Ω, 4.0 Ω, 2.0 Ω, 2.0 Ω

b 6.0 Ω, 2.0 Ω, 8.0 Ω, 4.0 Ω

c 3.0 Ω, 3.0 Ω, 3.0 Ω

Figure 11.32: For question 34.

35 Six identical resistors each of resistance R are connected as shown in Figure 11.33. The total resistance is 11 Ω.

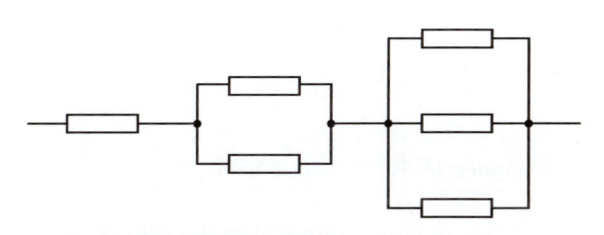

Figure 11.33: For question 35.

a What is the value of R?

b For mathematicians only: if the pattern of resistors shown in the figure were to continue forever by adding 4 and 5 (and so on) parallel resistors, would it make sense to ask for the total resistance?

36 Another problem for mathematicians: what is the total resistance between X and Y in the arrangement that extends forever, shown in Figure 11.34? Each resistance is 1.0 Ω.

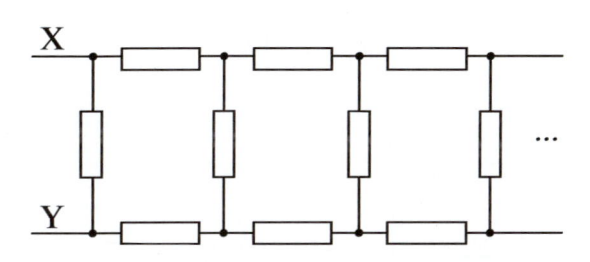

Figure 11.34: For question 36.

37 Look at Figure 11.35. What is the resistance between points X and Y?

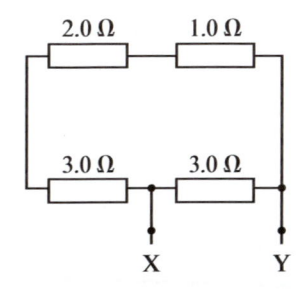

Figure 11.35: For question 37.

38 In the circuit shown in Figure 11.36, the cell has emf ε and negligible internal resistance. Derive an expression for the voltage V_1 across resistor R_1 and the voltage V_2 across resistor R_2.

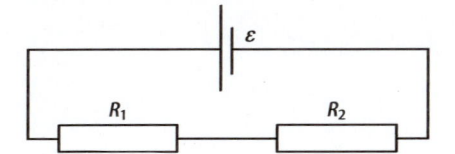

Figure 11.36: For question 38.

CONTINUED

39 Look at Figure 11.37. The cell has negligible internal resistance and emf 9.0 V.

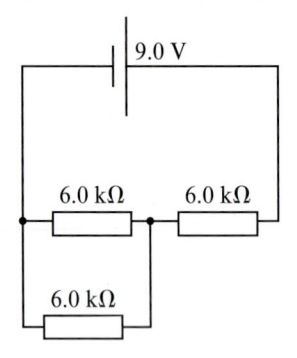

Figure 11.37: For question 39.

What is the current in each resistor?

40 For the potential divider circuit (Figure 11.38), state *one* change in R_1 and *one* change in R_2 so that when both changes are made V_{out} will definitely increase.

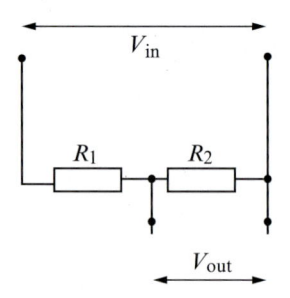

Figure 11.38: For question 40.

41 Three identical lamps are connected to a cell of negligible internal resistance as shown in Figure 11.39.

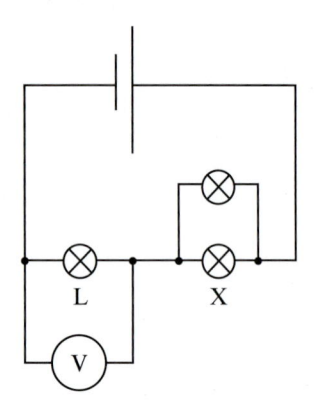

Figure 11.39: For question 41.

Lamp X burns out. What happens to the voltage across lamp L?

42 Three identical lamps are connected to a cell of negligible internal resistance as shown in Figure 11.40.

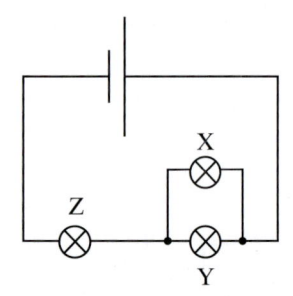

Figure 11.40: For question 42.

A fourth lamp, identical to the others, is connected in parallel to the lamps X and Y. What happens to the brightness of lamp Z?

CONTINUED

43 Figure 11.41 shows a simple circuit with three identical lamps.

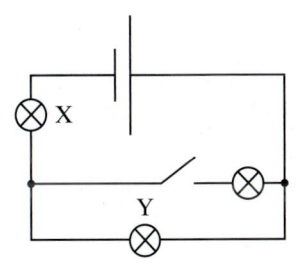

Figure 11.41: For question 43.

a The total power dissipated in the circuit when the switch is open is P. The internal resistance of the cell is negligible. What is the total power dissipated when the switch is closed?

b What happens to the brightness of the lamps X and Y when the switch is closed?

44 Look in Figure 11.42. The emf of the cell is 24 V and its internal resistance is negligible. The voltmeter reads zero. What is the resistance of resistor X?

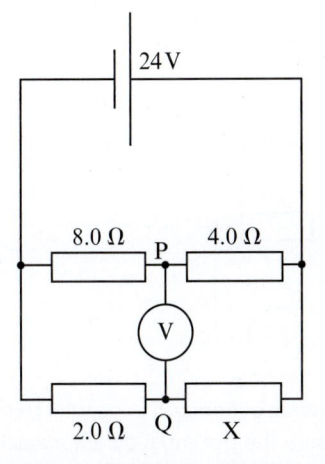

Figure 11.42: For question 44.

45 Look at Figure 11.43. All cells and resistors are identical. All cells have zero internal resistance.

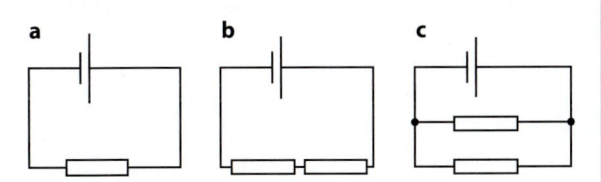

Figure 11.43: For question 45.

The power dissipated in circuit a is P. What is the power dissipated in circuits b and c?

46 Look at Figure 11.44.

The graph shows the I–V characteristics of two resistors, X and Y.

Circuit A shows the resistors X and Y connected in parallel to a cell of emf 1.5 V and negligible internal resistance. Circuit B shows the resistors X and Y connected in series to the same cell.

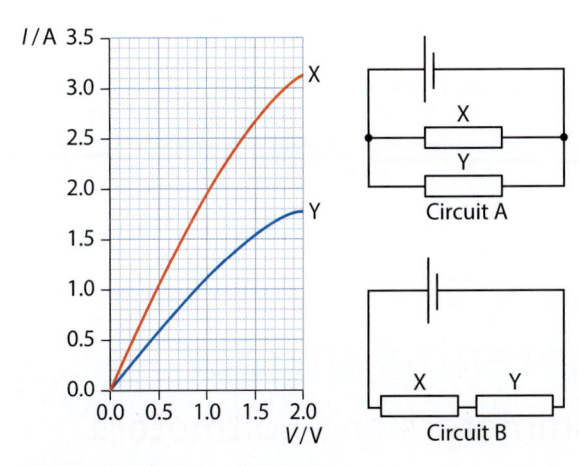

Figure 11.44: For question 46.

a Calculate the total current leaving the cell in circuit A.

b Estimate the total current leaving the cell in circuit B.

> **CONTINUED**
>
> **47** Look at Figure 11.45. A cell of emf 3.00 V is connected to two filament lamps and an ohmic resistor R. The I–V characteristics of X and Y are shown in the graph.
>
> **a** The current in X is 0.15 A. Find the current in Y.
>
> **b** Determine the resistance R.
>
> **c** The filament of Y breaks.
>
> State, without calculation, the effect of this on the current leaving the cell.
>
> **d** Hence, suggest the effect on the resistance of X.
>
> **Figure 11.45:** For question 47.

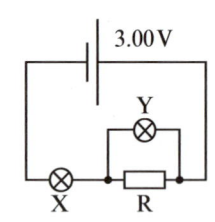

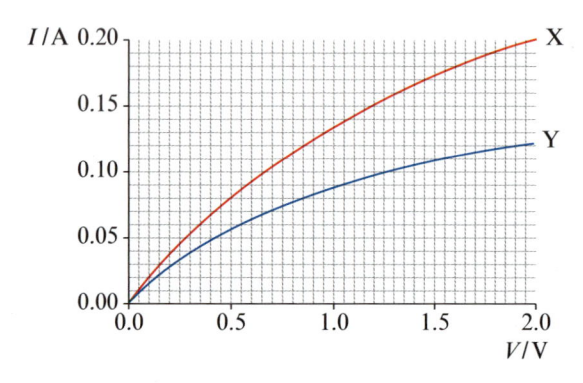

11.4 Terminal potential difference and the potential divider

Ammeters and voltmeters

The current through a resistor is measured by an instrument called an **ammeter**, which is connected in series to the resistor as shown in Figure 11.46.

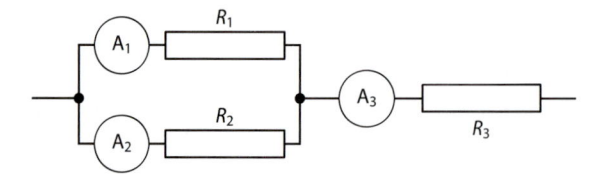

Figure 11.46: An ammeter measures the current in the resistor connected in series to it.

The ammeter itself has a small electric resistance. An **ideal ammeter** has zero resistance. The potential difference across a resistor is measured with a **voltmeter** connected in parallel to the resistor (Figure 11.47).

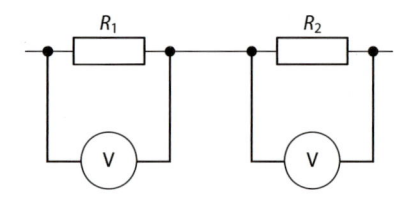

Figure 11.47: A voltmeter is connected in parallel to the device we want to measure the potential difference across.

An **ideal voltmeter** has infinite resistance, which means that it takes no current when it is connected to a resistor. Real voltmeters have very high resistance. Unless otherwise stated, ammeters and voltmeters will be assumed to be ideal.

Thus, to measure the potential difference across and current through a resistor, the arrangement shown in Figure 11.48 is used.

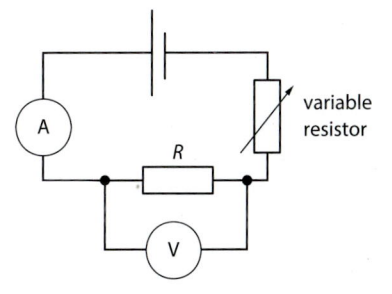

Figure 11.48: The correct arrangement for measuring the current through and potential difference across a resistor. The variable resistor allows the current in the resistor R to be varied so as to collect lots of data for current and voltage.

WORKED EXAMPLE 11.15

In the circuit in Figure 11.49, the emf of the cell is 9.00 V and the internal resistance is assumed negligible. A nonideal voltmeter whose resistance is 500 kΩ is connected in parallel to a resistor of 500 kΩ.

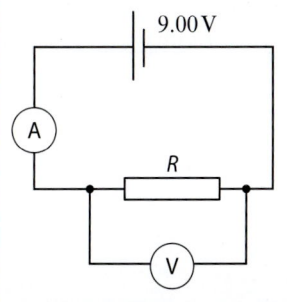

Figure 11.49: For worked example 11.15.

a Determine the reading of the (ideal) ammeter.

b A student is shown the circuit and assumes, incorrectly, that the voltmeter is ideal. Estimate the resistance the student would calculate if he were to use the current found in **a**.

c The resistance R is changed to one of 50 Ω. What resistance would a student measure if she assumes the voltmeter is ideal?

CONTINUED

Answer

a Since the two 500 kΩ resistances are in parallel, the total resistance of the circuit is found from:

$$\frac{1}{R} = \frac{1}{500} + \frac{1}{500} = \frac{1}{250}$$

$$\Rightarrow R = 250 \text{ k}\Omega$$

Using $I = \frac{V}{R}$, the current that leaves the cell is:

$$I = \frac{9.0}{250 \times 10^3} = 3.6 \times 10^{-5} \text{ A}$$

$$I = 36 \text{ μA}$$

This is the reading of the ammeter in the circuit.

b The reading of the voltmeter is 9.0 V. If the student assumes the voltmeter is ideal, he or she would conclude that the current in the resistor is 36 μA. He or she would then calculate that:

$$R = \frac{V}{I} = \frac{9.0 \text{ V}}{36 \text{ μA}} = 250 \text{ k}\Omega \text{ and would get the wrong}$$

answer for the resistance. The percent error is

$$\left|\frac{\text{measured} - \text{true}}{\text{true}}\right| \times 100\% = \left|\frac{250 - 500}{500}\right| \times 100\% = 50\%$$

c The total resistance of the circuit is now found from:

$$\frac{1}{R} = \frac{1}{500 \times 10^3} + \frac{1}{50} \Rightarrow R = 49.9995 \approx 50 \text{ }\Omega$$

This is what we would have if the voltmeter were ideal. The student will measure the correct resistance at 50 Ω. The voltmeter behaves as an ideal voltmeter if its resistance is much larger than the other resistances in the circuit.

PHYSICS FOR THE IB DIPLOMA: COURSEBOOK

WORKED EXAMPLE 11.16

A student constructs the circuit shown in Figure 11.50 and incorrectly places an ideal voltmeter in series to the resistor.

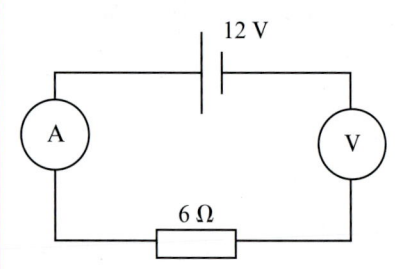

Figure 11.50: For worked example 11.16.

What is the reading of the ammeter, and what is the reading of the voltmeter?

Answer

The voltmeter has infinite resistance so the total resistance of the circuit is infinite. Hence the current is zero. Since there is no current, there is no voltage drop across the ammeter and no voltage drop across the resistor, and so the voltmeter will read 12 V.

WORKED EXAMPLE 11.17

The graph (Figure 11.51a) shows the I–V characteristics of an ohmic resistor and a filament lamp. The lamp and the resistor are connected in series to a cell of emf 2.7 V and negligible internal resistance (Figure 11.51b).

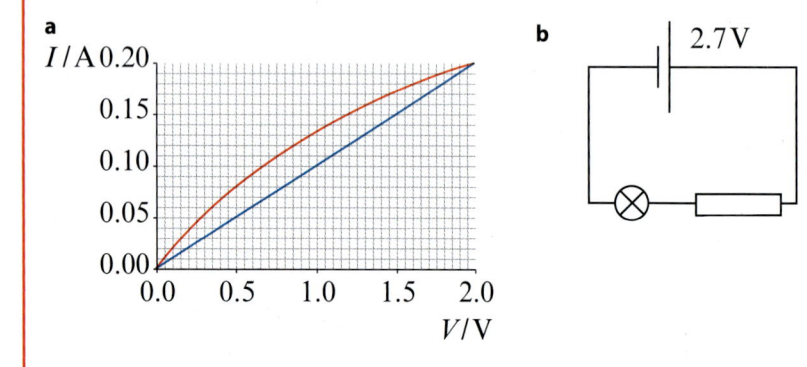

Figure 11.51: For worked example 11.17.

What is the total power dissipated in the circuit?

Answer

The lamp and the resistor take the same current so we must look at horizontal lines in the graph (which correspond to the same current in the lamp and the resistor), find the corresponding voltages and see if they add up to 2.7 V. This is a trial and error method. Trying a few cases we see that a current of 0.15 A corresponds to a voltage of 1.2 V across the lamp and 1.5 V across the resistor, so this is the right choice. The total power is then $\varepsilon I = 2.7 \times 0.15 = 0.40$ W.

Terminal potential difference

In all the examples we have considered so far, the cell or battery was assumed to be ideal. In reality, some energy is always dissipated inside the cell or the battery which implies that cells and batteries have an internal resistance, the yellow box in Figure 11.52. What would a voltmeter read if it is connected across the terminals of a battery?

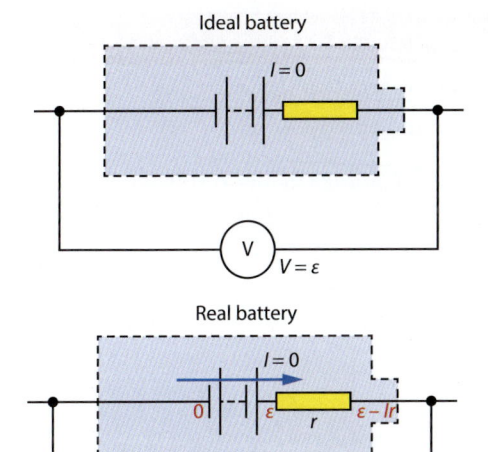

Figure 11.52: The potential difference across the terminals of a battery is equal to the emf when there is no current in the circuit. It is less than the emf when there is current.

If the current through the battery is zero, then there is zero potential difference across the internal resistance and the voltmeter would measure the emf of the battery. If there is current I through the battery then there is a potential difference Ir across the internal resistance. The internal resistance drops the potential from ε to $\varepsilon - Ir$ and so the voltmeter would read

$$V = \varepsilon - Ir$$

This confirms that when the current is zero ($I = 0$), $V = \varepsilon$.

CHECK YOURSELF 7

A cell with emf 6.0 V and internal resistance 0.50 Ω is connected in series to an external resistor of resistance 2.5 Ω. What is the power dissipated in:

a the cell

b the external resistor?

WORKED EXAMPLE 11.18

The potential difference across the terminals of a battery is 9.6 V when the current is 1.2 A and 9.0 V when the current is 1.5 A. Determine the emf of the battery and the internal resistance.

Answer

We need to use $V = \varepsilon - Ir$ twice:

$9.6 = \varepsilon - 1.2r$

$9.0 = \varepsilon - 1.5r$

Subtracting, we get $0.6 = 0.3r$ and so $r = 2.0$ Ω. Hence $\varepsilon = 12$ V.

WORKED EXAMPLE 11.19

A cell is connected to a variable resistor (Figure 11.53a). As the resistance is varied the terminal voltage and the current in the circuit are measured. The graph (Figure 11.53b) shows how the potential difference across the terminals of a cell varies with the current leaving the cell.

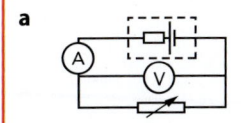

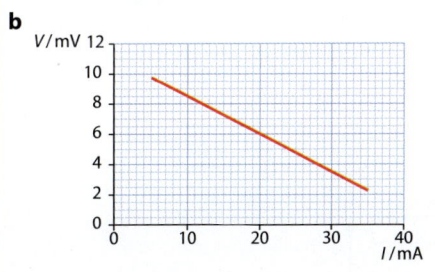

Figure 11.53: For worked example 11.19.

Determine the emf of the cell and its internal resistance.

Answer

We again need to use $V = \varepsilon - Ir$, from which we deduce that the emf is the vertical intercept and the internal resistance the negative of the gradient of the graph. Extending the straight line we find an intercept of 11 mV, which is the emf, and a (negative) gradient of 0.25 Ω, which is the internal resistance.

Potential dividers

The circuit in Figure 11.54a shows a potential divider (which is also known as a potentiometer). XY is usually a wire of fixed length, and S (the slider) can be attached to any point of the wire (with a crocodile clip, for example). It can be used to investigate, for example, the current–voltage characteristic of some device denoted by resistance R. This complicated-looking circuit is simply equivalent to the circuit in Figure 11.54b. In this circuit, the resistance R_1 is the resistance of the wire from end X to the slider S, and R_2 is the resistance of the wire from S to end Y. The current that leaves the cell splits at point M. Part of the current goes from M to N, and the rest goes into the device with resistance R. The right end of the resistance R (the slider) can be connected to any point on the wire XY.

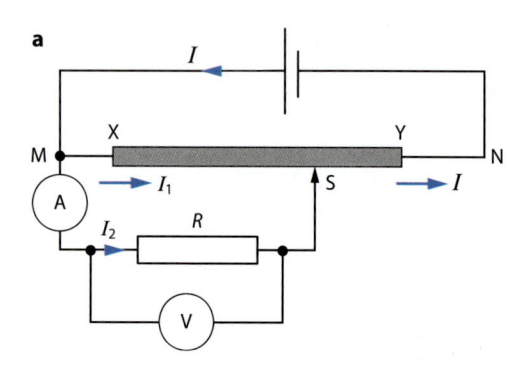

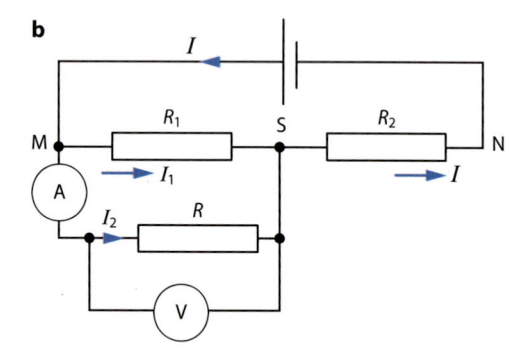

By varying where the slider S connects to XY, different potential differences and currents are obtained for the device R. One advantage of the potential divider is that now the potential difference across the resistor can be varied from a minimum of zero volts, when the slider S is placed at X, to a maximum of ε, the emf of the battery (assuming zero internal resistance), by connecting the slider S to point Y.

> ### WORKED EXAMPLE 11.20
>
> Look at Figure 11.55. The cell has negligible internal resistance and emf 18 V.
>
> What is the range of readings of the voltmeter as the slider is moved from X to Y? 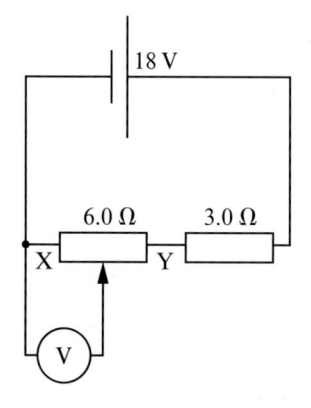
>
> **Figure 11.55:** For worked example 11.20.
>
> **Answer**
>
> The current leaving the cell is 2.0 A.
>
> So the potential difference across the 6.0 Ω resistor is 12 V.
>
> At X the voltmeter will read 0 V and at Y 12 V so the range is 0 to 12 V.

Figure 11.54: a This circuit uses a potential divider. The voltage and current in the device with resistance R can be varied by varying the point where the slider S is attached to the variable resistor. **b** The potential divider circuit is equivalent to this simpler-looking circuit.

11 Current and circuits

NATURE OF SCIENCE

In 1825 in England, Peter Barlow proposed a law explaining how wires conducted electricity. His careful experiments using a constant voltage showed good agreement, and his theory was accepted. At about the same time in Germany, Georg Ohm proposed a different law backed up by experimental evidence using a range of voltages. The experimental approach to science was not popular in Germany, and Ohm's findings were rejected. It was not until 1841 that the value of his work was recognised, first in England and later in Germany. In modern science, before research findings are published they are reviewed by other scientists working in the same area (peer review). This would have shown the errors in Barlow's work and given Ohm recognition sooner.

TEST YOUR UNDERSTANDING

48 A cell has emf 6.0 V. When connected to an external 5.0 Ω resistor the current leaving the cell is 1.0 A.

   a   What is the internal resistance of the cell?

   b   What is the terminal potential difference?

49 The terminal potential difference across a cell is 5.8 V when the current leaving the cell is 0.50 A. When the current is 0.60 A the terminal potential difference is 5.7 V.

   a   What is the internal resistance of the cell?

   b   What is the emf of the cell?

50 A cell of emf 6.0 V and internal resistance 2.0 Ω is connected to an external variable resistor R.

   a   By making a graph (on your graphics calculator) of the power dissipated in R against R (or otherwise) determine the value of R for which the power dissipated is a maximum.

   b   Estimate this maximum power.

51 A voltmeter is connected across the terminals of a cell. An ammeter is inserted as shown in Figure 11.56.

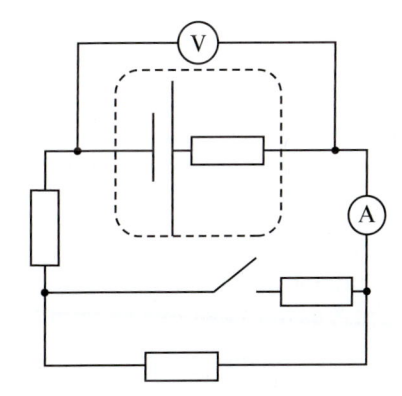

Figure 11.56: For question 51.

   a   What happens to the readings of the ammeter and of the voltmeter when the switch is closed?

   b   How do the answers to part **a** change, if at all, if the cell had zero internal resistance?

CONTINUED

52 Figure 11.57 shows a potential divider (potentiometer). The cell has negligible internal resistance and emf 12 V.

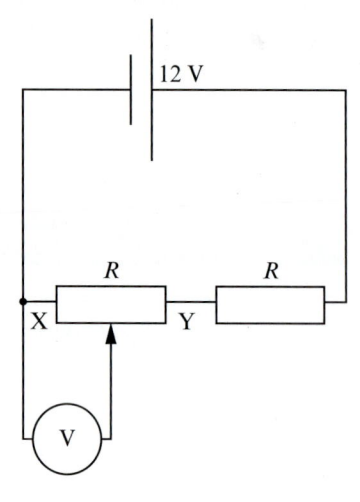

Figure 11.57: For question 52.

a What is the reading of the voltmeter when the slider is connected to **i** X and **ii** Y?

b Sketch a graph to show how the reading of the voltmeter varies with the distance d from point X as the slider moves from X to Y.

53 The circuit in Figure 11.58 has a variable resistor; its resistance can be varied from 0 to 6.0 Ω. The cell has emf 9.0 V and negligible internal resistance.

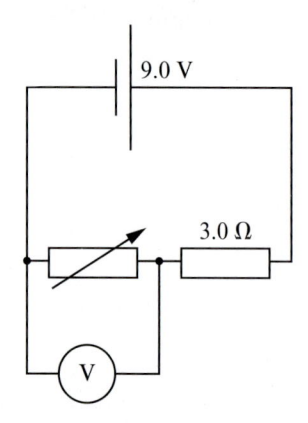

Figure 11.58: For question 53.

a What is the range of readings of the voltmeter?

b How does the answer to part **a** change, if at all, if the cell had an internal resistance of 1.0 Ω?

54 A source supplies electrical power to a device D at a distance of 2.0 km. The device operates properly at 120 V and current 25 A. The connecting wires have a resistance per unit length of 4.0 Ω km^{-1} (Figure 11.59).

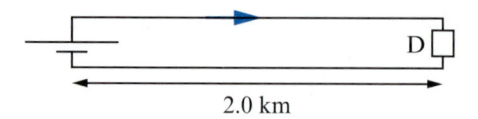

Figure 11.59: For question 54.

a What is the minimum emf required at the source?

b What fraction of the power produced by the source gets wasted in the connecting wires?

55 Look at Figure 11.60. In both circuits, the cell has emf 6.0 V and an internal resistance 2.0 Ω. The external resistance is 3.0 Ω.

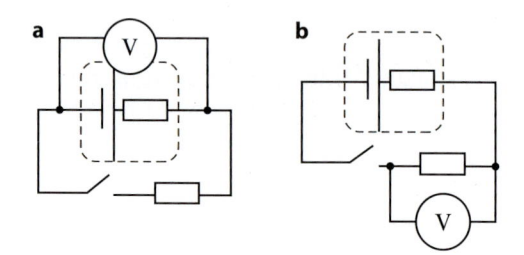

Figure 11.60: For question 55.

What is the reading of the voltmeters in circuits A and B:

a when the switch is open?

b when the switch is closed?

11 Current and circuits

Links

The microscopic–macroscopic connection

If you are plumber, do you need to know the molecular structure of water to help you in your work? The flow of water in pipes is a macroscopic phenomenon whereas the detailed molecular structure of water is microscopic. We have a vast difference in scales of length in the two cases. In very many phenomena the presence of two different scales means that the detailed physics operating at one scale does not affect the physics at the other. This is also the case with current: it was possible to give detailed descriptions of the behaviour of current in circuits long before it was discovered that current is electrons moving in the same direction. (However, the most complicated problems in physics are those in which the physics at one length scale does affect the physics at the other scale.)

SELF-ASSESSMENT CHECKLIST

I am able to …	Section	Not yet	Nearly there	Ready to move on
calculate current, potential difference and resistance	11.1			
explain how current in a circuit component generates thermal energy	11.1			
define and understand electric resistance	11.1			
describe Ohm's law	11.1			
describe the factors that affect resistance	11.1			
define emf and calculate power dissipated	11.2			
find the total resistance of a combination of resistors	11.3			
analyse an electric circuit	11.3			
distinguish between emf and terminal potential difference	11.4			
work with potential divider circuits	11.4			

REFLECTION

Do you understand the concept of *potential difference*? Do you understand the concept of *electric current*? Can you define *electrical resistance*? Do you understand *Ohm's law*? Can you find the *total resistance* of a set of resistors connected in series and in parallel? Can you solve a simple electrical circuit? Do you understand the difference between *emf* and *terminal potential difference*? Are you comfortable with *potential divider* circuits?

EXAM-STYLE QUESTIONS

You can find questions in the style of IB exams in the digital coursebook.

CHECK YOURSELF ANSWERS

1. The charge transferred is 1 C which corresponds to $\frac{1}{1.6 \times 10^{-19}} = 6.2 \times 10^{18}$ electrons.

2. $R = \rho \frac{L}{A}$. L is doubled; the radius is doubled so the area increases by 4. Hence the new resistance is $R' = \rho \frac{2L}{4A} = \frac{R}{2}$.

3. $P = \frac{V^2}{R}$
   So, $32 = \frac{12^2}{R} \Rightarrow R = \frac{12^2}{32}$
   The new power is:
   $P' = \frac{V^2}{R} = \frac{15^2}{\left(\frac{12^2}{32}\right)} = \frac{15^2}{12^2} \times 32 = \frac{5^2}{4^2} \times 32 = 50$ W.

4. The total resistance increases so the current decreases.

5. We are told that $\frac{1}{R} + \frac{1}{R} + \frac{1}{R} = \frac{1}{1}$ which means that $R = 3\,\Omega$. So the series connection would give a total resistance of 9 Ω.

6. The total resistance in the series connection is $2R$. In the parallel connection it is $\frac{R}{2}$. Since resistance is reduced by 4 the power will go up by 4 $\left(\text{since } P = \frac{V^2}{R}\right)$ and so the new power will be 64 W.

7. The total resistance of the circuit is 6.0 Ω and so the current is $I = \frac{6.0}{3.0} = 2.0$ A.

   a. The power dissipated in the cell is $P = rI^2 = 0.50 \times 2.0^2 = 2.0$ W.

   b. The power in the external resistor is $P = RI^2 = 2.5 \times 2.0^2 = 10$ W. (The total power is $P = \varepsilon I = 6.0 \times 2.0 = 12$ W (= 10 + 2.0) as expected.)

Unit C
Wave behaviour

INTRODUCTION

In Topic B we discussed one of the great models of Physics, the particle model. In this topic we will meet another great model of Physics, the wave model. Wave behaviour can be found everywhere in nature and is responsible for spectacular phenomena such as the blue colour of the sky and the colours of the rainbow. It is also involved in terrifying phenomena such as earthquakes and tsunamis. Wave behaviour helps us understand the sound from a violin or a flute. Light itself was shown to be a wave in one of the greatest unifications ever made in Physics, Maxwell's electromagnetic theory in the second half of the 19th century.

We will see that, basic to any wave motion is the concept of an oscillation, the back and forth motion such as that of a swing hanging from a tree or the motion of an atom in a metal rod that has been hit on one end. The need to understand wave motion in terms of oscillations led to the development of an enormous field in Mathematics called Fourier analysis. There have been many instances where the need to understand a particular physical phenomenon led to the development of entire branches of Mathematics. Calculus is the obvious example with Fourier analysis a close second.

We will meet many phenomena associated with waves but the one that will stand out will be that of interference: two waves meeting at a point may re-enforce each other or completely cancel each other out. Interference has no analogue in the particle model and so its presence is the revealing sign of wave behavior. So it came as a great surprise in the beginning of the 20th century that electrons also show interference phenomena, implying that electrons have a dual wave—particle nature. That realisation was the beginning of the revolution of quantum theory. We will discuss a few of these ideas in Topic E.

Chapter 12
Simple harmonic motion

LEARNING OBJECTIVES

In this chapter you will learn how to:

- identify the conditions under which simple harmonic oscillations take place
- identify and use the concepts of period, frequency, amplitude and displacement
- analyse simple harmonic oscillations graphically
- identify the connection between angular frequency and period
- describe the energy transfers taking place in oscillations and analyse them graphically

12 Simple harmonic motion

CONTINUED

- use the equations that describe simple harmonic motion
- understand the concept of phase angle and phase difference
- use the quantitative approach to energy in simple harmonic motion.

GUIDING QUESTION

Why are simple harmonic oscillations the basis for understanding all oscillations and all wave motion?

Introduction

This chapter deals with one of the most common phenomena in physics: oscillations.

What do airplane wings, suspension bridges, skyscrapers, tree branches, car suspension systems and atoms all have in common? They all oscillate about some equilibrium position.

These diverse phenomena can be analysed by first understanding a basic kind of oscillation called simple harmonic motion. Understanding oscillations is also the first step in understanding the behavior of waves.

12.1 Simple harmonic oscillations

Oscillations refer to back and forth motion that repeats. A typical example of an oscillation is provided by the simple pendulum, i.e. a mass attached to a vertical string. When the mass is displaced slightly sideways and then released, the mass begins to oscillate. In an oscillation the motion is periodic, i.e. repetitive, and the body moves back and forth around an **equilibrium position**.

Two important characteristic of oscillatory motion, shown in Figures 12.1a and 12.1b, are:

- the **period**, T, which is the time taken to complete one full oscillation

- the **amplitude** of the oscillation, which is the maximum **displacement** away from the equilibrium position.

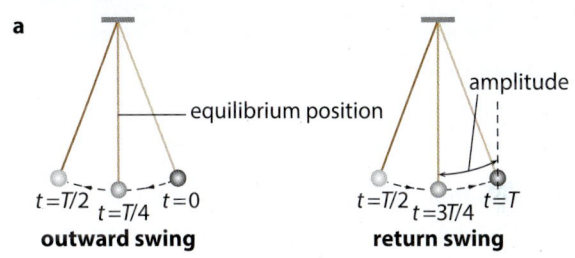

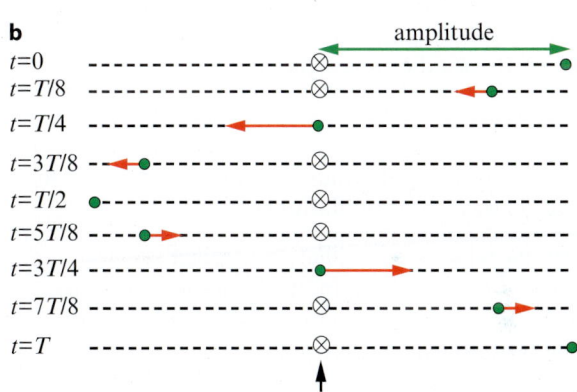

Figure 12.1: **a** A full oscillation lasts for one period. At the end of a time interval equal to one period T, the system is in the same state as the state it started from. **b** The red arrows represent velocities.

The **frequency** f of the oscillations is the number of oscillations per second. The unit of frequency is the inverse second, s^{-1}, and is called the hertz (Hz).

Since we have one oscillation in a time equal to the period T, the number of oscillations in 1 s is $\frac{1}{T}$ and so:

$$f = \frac{1}{T}.$$

> **PHYSICS FOR THE IB DIPLOMA: COURSEBOOK**

> **CHECK YOURSELF 1**
>
> A particle performs oscillations completing five full oscillations in 4 s. What is the period and frequency of the oscillations?

It can be shown that the period of a pendulum only depends on the length of the string and not the mass of the bob. It is given by:

$T = 2\pi\sqrt{\frac{L}{g}}$

> **CHECK YOURSELF 2**
>
> The length of a pendulum is increased by a factor of 4. By what factor does the period change?

In real life examples of oscillations can be found everywhere including the motion of a diving board as a diver prepares to dive, a tight guitar string that is set in motion by plucking the string, or a skyscraper under the action of the wind or an earthquake.

For a system to oscillate it is necessary to have a restoring force, i.e. a force that tends to bring the system back towards its equilibrium position when the system is displaced away from equilibrium.

A very special kind of oscillation is called **simple harmonic motion (SHM)**. In SHM, the acceleration is proportional to and opposite to the displacement. Mathematically, these two conditions can be stated as
$a \propto -x$ or $a = -\omega^2 x$

(Since $F = ma$, this is equivalent to saying that the restoring force is also proportional to and opposite to the displacement.)

The constant ω is known as the angular frequency and is related to the period T by the relation $\omega = \frac{2\pi}{T}$. Since $f = \frac{1}{T}$ we also have that $\omega = 2\pi f$. Angular frequency is measured in radians per second.

A simple system that undergoes simple harmonic oscillations is that of a block attached to a horizontal spring on a frictionless table. The top diagram in Figure 12.2 shows the equilibrium position of the system: the spring has its natural length.

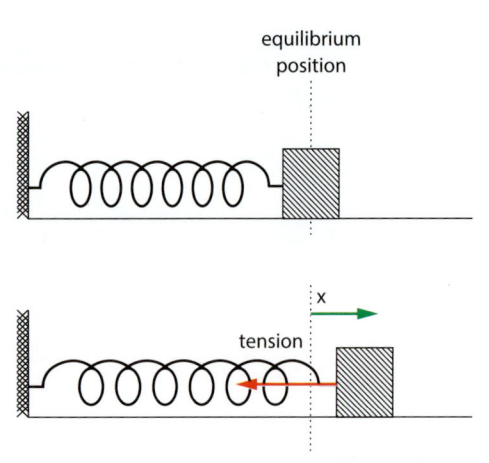

Figure 12.2: The mass–spring system. The net force on the body is proportional to the displacement and opposite in direction.

In the lower diagram the block has been displaced by an amount x away from the equilibrium position. A tension force of magnitude kx develops in the spring directed opposite to the displacement; this is the net force on the block. By Newton's second law we then have

$ma = -kx$

The minus sign is there because the force is opposite to the displacement x.

This means that the acceleration is $a = -\frac{k}{m}x$. Comparing with $a = -\omega^2 x$ we see that for this case $\omega^2 = \frac{k}{m}$ and so the period is

$T = \frac{2\pi}{\omega} = \frac{2\pi}{\sqrt{\frac{k}{m}}} = 2\pi\sqrt{\frac{m}{k}}$

> **CHECK YOURSELF 3**
>
> The mass at the end of a spring oscillates with period T. What will be the period if the mass is halved and the spring constant is doubled?

Displacement–time graphs

Figure 12.3 shows two of the many possible graphs to describe the displacement of an object performing simple harmonic oscillations. In mathematics, cosine and sine functions are called harmonic functions, which is why these oscillations are called harmonic.

12 Simple harmonic motion

We see that even though the amplitude changed, the period stayed the same. This is another characteristic of SHM.

In SHM

- the period does not depend on amplitude
- the amplitude stays constant as time goes on.

Let us have another look at Figure 12.3a. What can we say about the velocity in this oscillation? We know that velocity is the gradient of a displacement–time graph. So we can say something about velocity by looking at the gradient of the graph Figure 12.3a at each point. At $t = 0$ the gradient is zero, so the velocity is also zero. As t increases the gradient becomes negative and at $t = 1.0$ s it becomes zero again. The gradient has its largest magnitude at $t = 0.5$ s. From $t = 1.0$ s to $t = 2.0$ s the gradient is positive. Its magnitude is largest at $t = 1.5$ s. Figure 12.5a shows the velocity plotted against time. Figure 12.5b does the same for the displacement in Figure 12.3b.

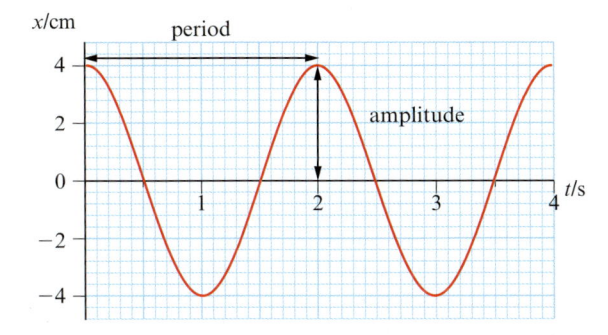

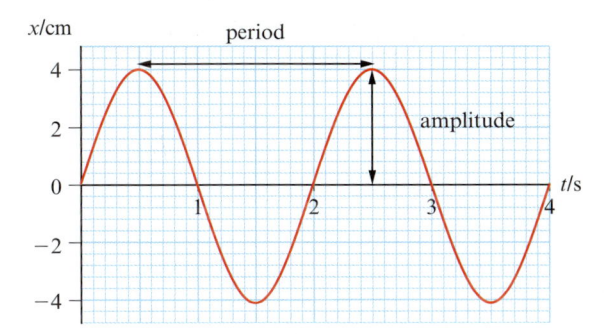

Figure 12.3: The variation of displacement with time in SHM. Two possibilities include **a** a cosine or **b** a sine depending on when the clock is started, i.e. what the initial position and velocity are.

What can we tell from these graphs? The maximum extension past equilibrium is 4.0 cm so this is the amplitude of the motion. One full oscillation takes 2.0 s so this is the period of the motion. The frequency is $f = \frac{1}{T} = 0.50$ Hz. Notice that the amplitude stays constant as time goes on: this is a characteristic of SHM.

In Figure 12.3 the amplitude was 4.0 cm. What would happen if the amplitude was 2.0 cm? The answer is shown by the blue curve in Figure 12.4 where we have also shown the curve in 12.3a for comparison.

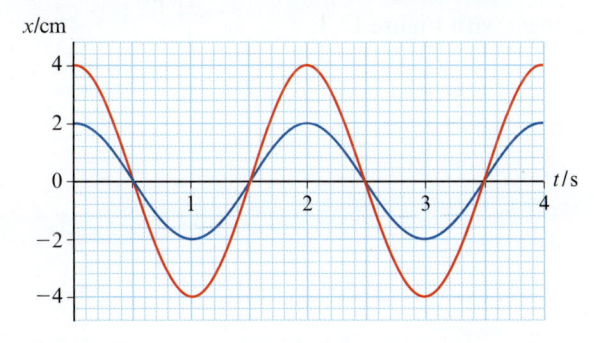

Figure 12.4: The blue curve has a smaller amplitude but the same period.

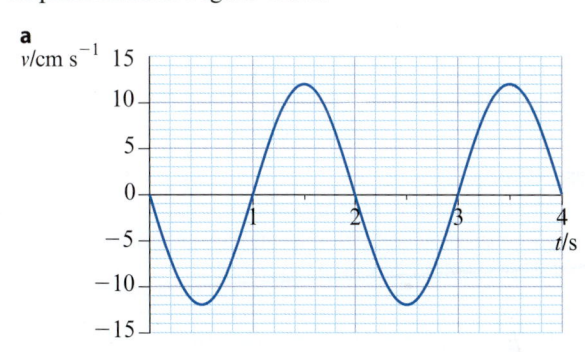

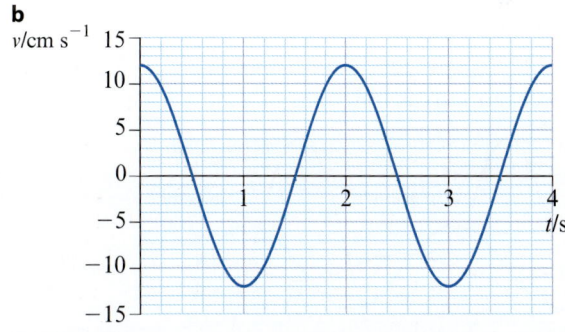

Figure 12.5: a The variation of velocity v with time t in SHM for the displacement graph of Figure 12.3a. **b** The variation of velocity v with time t in SHM for the displacement graph of Figure 12.3b.

In the same way, we can get information about acceleration by looking at the gradient of the velocity–time graph. But it is much simpler to recall that $a \propto -x$. This means that the acceleration–time graph has the opposite shape to the displacement–time graph—the peaks on the displacement–time graph become troughs on the acceleration–time graph (of course the scale on the vertical axis will be different). This is shown in Figure 12.6.

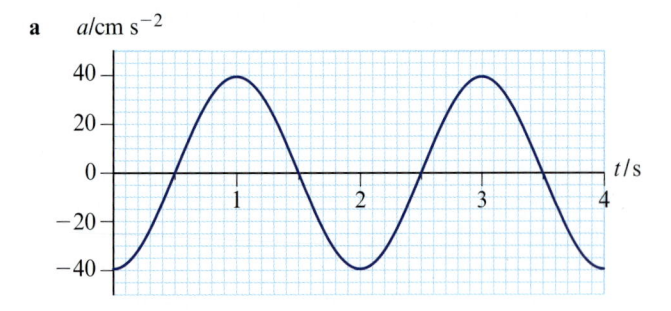

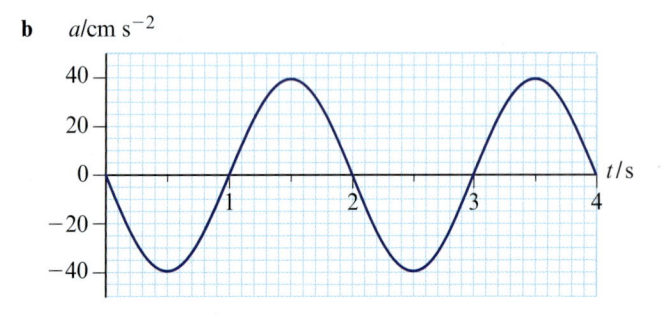

a $a/\text{cm s}^{-2}$

b $a/\text{cm s}^{-2}$

Figure 12.6: a The variation of acceleration a with time t in SHM for the displacement graph of Figure 12.3a. **b** The variation of acceleration a with time t in SHM for the displacement graph of Figure 12.3b.

Since $F = ma$, a graph of force versus time would have the same shape as the graph in Figure 12.6.

Figure 12.7 shows all three (displacement, velocity and acceleration) as functions of time.

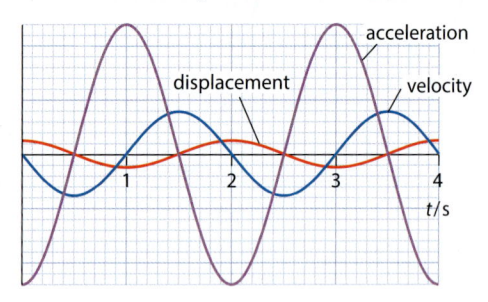

Figure 12.7: The variation with time of displacement, velocity and acceleration in SHM on the same axes.

Acceleration–displacement graph

Since the acceleration is proportional to and opposite to the displacement a graph of acceleration versus displacement gives a straight line through the origin with a negative slope, as shown in Figure 12.8. The graph corresponds to the motion in Figure 12.3.

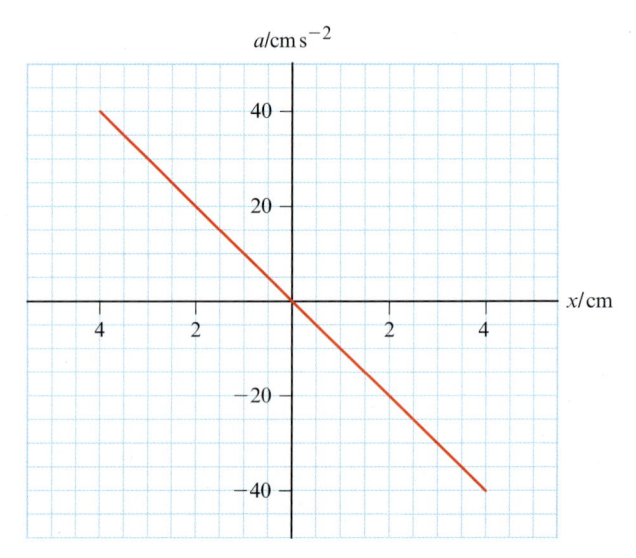

Figure 12.8: The graph of acceleration a versus displacement x is a straight line through the origin with a negative slope.

(Since $F = ma$, a graph of force versus displacement would have the same shape as the graph in Figure 12.8.)

Since $a = -\omega^2 x$, the gradient (slope) of the acceleration versus displacement graph is $-\omega^2$. The gradient of the graph in Figure 12.8 is $-\omega^2 = \frac{-40 - 40}{4.0 - (-4.0)} = -10 \text{ s}^{-2}$, $\omega = \sqrt{10}$ rad s^{-1} and so the period is $T = \frac{2\pi}{\sqrt{10}} \approx 2.0$ s in agreement with Figure 12.3.

12 Simple harmonic motion

WORKED EXAMPLE 12.1

State and explain whether graphs I, II and III in Figure 12.9 represent simple harmonic oscillations.

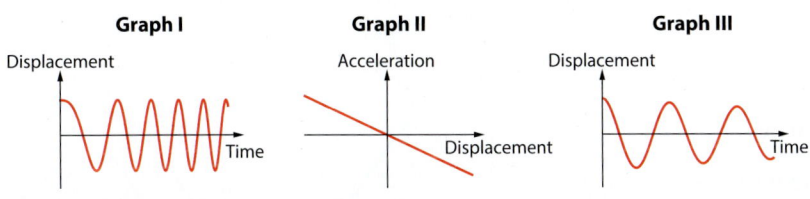

Figure 12.9: For worked example 12.1.

Answer

Graph I does not show SHM, since the period does not stay constant as time goes on. Graph II does, since the acceleration is proportional and opposite to the displacement (straight-line graph through origin with negative slope). Graph III does not, since the amplitude does not stay constant.

CHECK YOURSELF 4

Figure 12.10 shows the standard representation of SHM. The red arrows represent velocity.

On a copy of the diagram, put blue arrows at each step to represent acceleration.

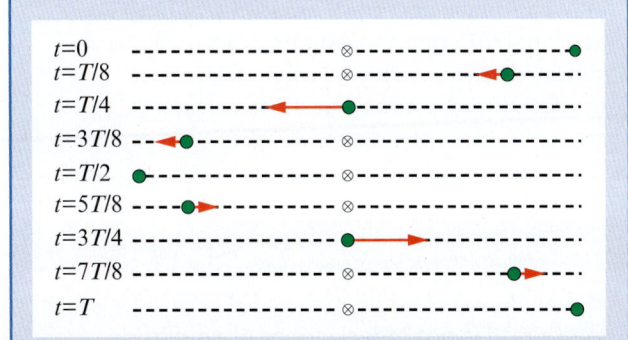

Figure 12.10: For check yourself 4.

WORKED EXAMPLE 12.2

The graph in Figure 12.11 shows the variation with time of the displacement of a particle from a fixed equilibrium position.

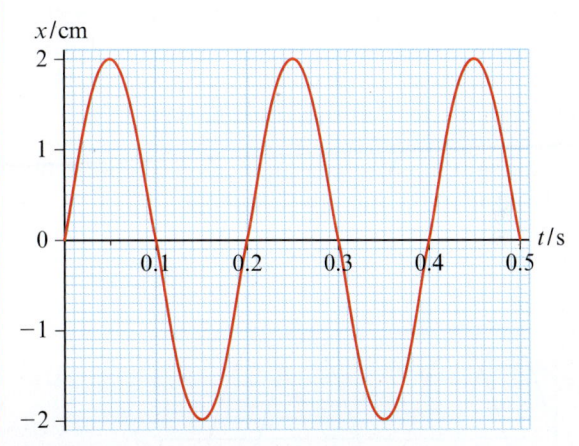

Figure 12.11: Graph showing the variation with time of the displacement of a particle performing SHM.

a Use the graph to determine the period of the motion.

b On a copy of the graph, mark:

  i   a point where the velocity is zero (label this with the letter Z)

  ii a point where the velocity is positive and has the largest magnitude (label this with the letter V)

269

PHYSICS FOR THE IB DIPLOMA: COURSEBOOK

CONTINUED

    iii a point where the acceleration is positive and has the largest magnitude (label this with the letter A).

Answer

a The period is read off the graph as $T = 0.20$ s.

b i The velocity is zero at any point where the displacement is at a maximum or a minimum.

   ii For example at $t = 0$ s, 0.20 s or $t = 0.40$ s.

   iii For example at $t = 0.15$ s, 0.35 s.

Phase difference

Figure 12.12 shows two harmonic oscillations. They have the same amplitude and period so are in fact identical. So why do the graphs look different? The reason is that the observer who is observing the oscillations started the stopwatch at different times; they started it when the displacement was zero for the blue curve and when the displacement was −1.0 cm for the red curve. We say there is a **phase difference** between the two oscillations. Phase difference, $\Delta\varphi$, is an angle and is given by: $\Delta\phi = \frac{\Delta t}{T} \times 2\pi$ (in radians)

where the shift Δt is the separation in time between two neighbouring peaks and T is the period.

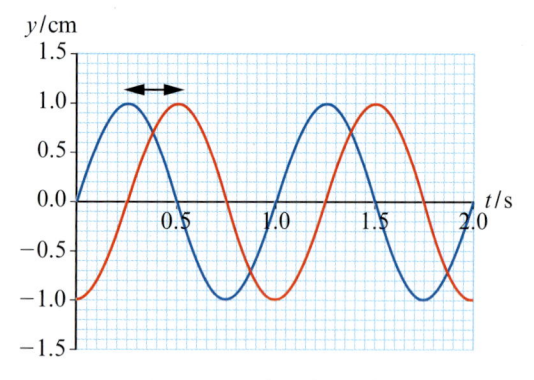

Figure 12.12: Two graphs of simple harmonic oscillations with a phase difference between them.

In Figure 12.12, two neighbouring peaks are separated by 0.25 s and the period is 1.0 s. The phase difference is then $\Delta\phi = \frac{\Delta t}{T} \times 2\pi = \frac{0.25}{1.0} \times 2\pi = \frac{\pi}{2}$.

CHECK YOURSELF 5

What is the phase difference between the two oscillations shown in Figure 12.13?

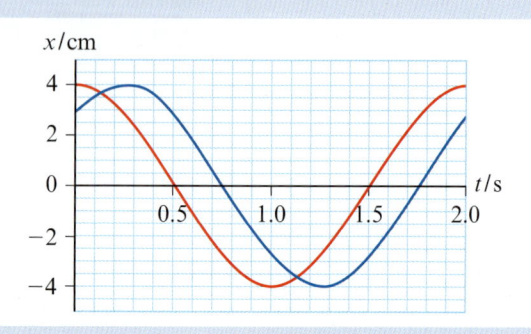

Figure 12.13: For check yourself question 5.

SCIENCE IN CONTEXT

The measurement of time depends on regular oscillations. In early time-keeping devices the oscillations were mechanical, for example the swinging of a pendulum. Now they are electrical oscillations in electronic circuits. The need for internationally accepted measures of time is essential for communications, travel, electricity supply and practically all other aspects of modern life. Time is what these devices measure, but nobody knows what time *really* is!

NATURE OF SCIENCE

In real life we observe many oscillations for which the period is not independent of amplitude, for example the waving of a branch in the wind or the bouncing of a ball released above the ground. These do not obey the simple SHM equations in this section. But the general principles of physics we have met in this section govern many oscillations in the world about us, from water waves in the deep ocean to the vibration of a car's suspension system. The idea of the simple harmonic oscillator and the mathematics of SHM give physicists powerful tools to describe all periodic oscillations.

12 Simple harmonic motion

Links

In Chapters 13–16 we will see that simple harmonic oscillations are the key for understanding waves. When a mechanical wave travels through a medium the particles of the medium will oscillate about their equilibrium positions with simple harmonic motion. The frequency of the oscillations is the frequency of the wave.

TEST YOUR UNDERSTANDING

1. State what is meant by:
   a. an oscillation
   b. a simple harmonic oscillation.

2. A ball goes back and forth along a horizontal floor, bouncing off two vertical walls. No resistance forces are present. Suggest whether this motion is simple harmonic.

3. A ball keeps bouncing vertically off the floor. No resistance forces are present. Suggest whether this motion is simple harmonic.

4. Figure 12.14 shows the variation with displacement of the acceleration of a particle that is performing oscillations.

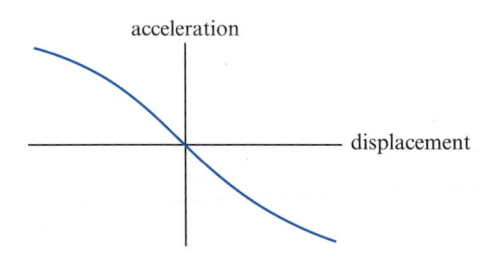

   Figure 12.14: For question 4.

   Explain:
   a. how it is known that the particle is performing oscillations
   b. why the oscillations are not simple harmonic
   c. why the oscillations *are* simple harmonic for small amplitudes.

5. What is the length of a pendulum of period 1.0 s?

6. The length of the metallic thread of a pendulum increases by 4.0% due to a temperature increase. By what percentage does the period of the pendulum change? (Use ideas of propagation of uncertainties.)

7. A mass is performing simple harmonic oscillations at the end of a spring of spring constant 240 Nm^{-1}. The period of oscillation is 1.2 s. What is the mass?

8. In a spacecraft in orbit, everything feels weightless. How could an astronaut measure her mass?

9. A student investigates the pendulum equation $T = 2\pi\sqrt{\frac{L}{g}}$.
   a. He plots T on the vertical axis. What variable should he plot on the horizontal axis in order to get a straight line?
   b. What would the gradient be?
   c. Another student plots T^2 on the vertical axis. What variable should she plot on the horizontal axis in order to get a straight line?
   d. What would the gradient be?

10. Look at Figure 12.15.
    a. What is the phase difference between the two oscillations?
    b. What is the angular frequency of each oscillation?
    c. What is the acceleration of a point on the blue curve at $t = 1$ s?

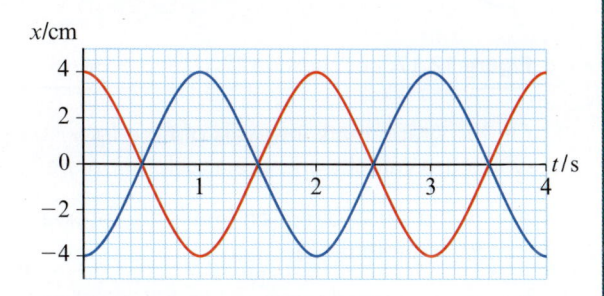

    Figure 12.15: For question 10.

CONTINUED

11 The graph (Figure 12.16) shows the variation with time of the position of a particle executing SHM.

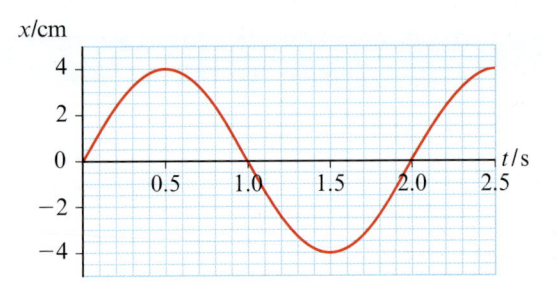

Figure 12.16: For question 11.

a State a time at which

  i the velocity is zero

  ii the velocity is positive and a maximum

  iii the acceleration is zero

  iv the acceleration is positive and a maximum.

b Calculate the frequency and angular frequency of oscillations.

12 Figure 12.17 shows part of the graph of the variation with time of the displacement of a particle executing SHM.

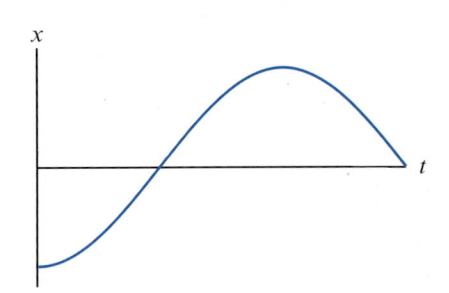

Figure 12.17: For question 12.

On the graph mark intervals of time for which the velocity and the acceleration are:

a in the same direction (mark this interval with the letter S)

b in opposite directions (mark this interval with the letter O).

13 The graph (Figure 12.18) shows the variation with time of the velocity of a particle in SHM.

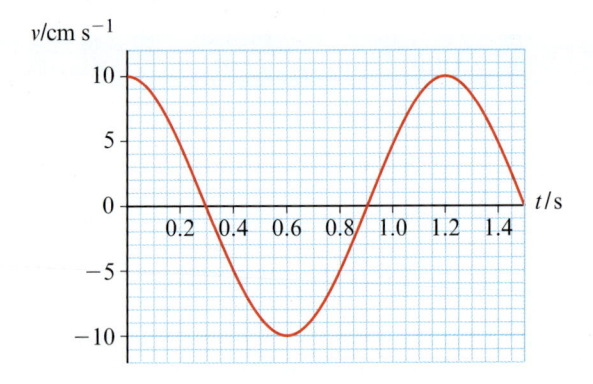

Figure 12.18: For question 13.

a Estimate to one significant figure the amplitude of the *displacement*, explaining your reasoning.

b Mark with the letter M a point where the acceleration is positive and a maximum.

c Mark with the letter E a point where the particle is passing through the equilibrium position.

d At $t = 1.0$ s, is the displacement positive, negative or zero?

14 The graph (Figure 12.19) shows the variation with displacement of the acceleration of a particle.

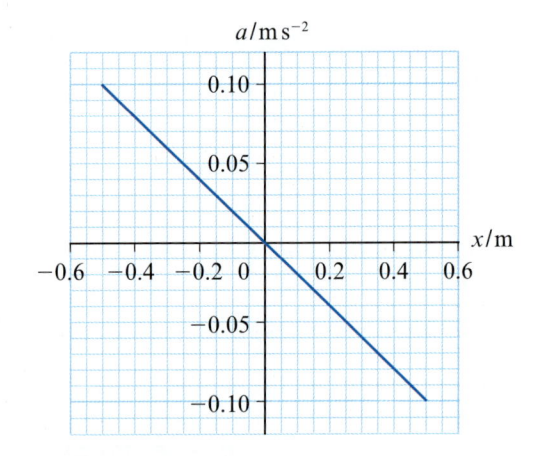

Figure 12.19: For question 14.

> **CONTINUED**
>
> a Explain why the motion is SHM.
>
> b Mark with the letter V a point on the graph where the speed is a maximum.
>
> c Determine the period of the motion.
>
> d The mass of the oscillating body is 0.15 kg. Calculate the restoring force when the displacement is −0.20 m.
>
> e How would the graph change if the amplitude of oscillations is halved?

12.2 Details of simple harmonic motion

This section is a quantitative discussion of SHM. We saw that SHM takes place whenever the acceleration is opposite to and proportional to the displacement. We can express this mathematically as

$a = -\omega^2 x$

We learned in the previous chapter that the angular frequency ω is related to the period T by $\omega = \frac{2\pi}{T}$.

What is the equation that gives the displacement as a function of time? Using calculus, it can be shown that the defining equation $a = -\omega^2 x$ implies that the displacement x is given by the formula

$x = x_0 \sin(\omega t + \phi)$

where ϕ is called the **phase angle** and x_0 is the amplitude.

The phase angle has to do with the position and velocity of the particle at zero time. In other words, it has to do with when you start the stopwatch as you observe the oscillations. So, the same oscillation may be described by $x_1 = x_0 \sin(\omega t + \phi_1)$ or $x_2 = x_0 \sin(\omega t + \phi_2)$.

The phase difference $\Delta\phi$ we defined in Section 12.1 is simply $\Delta\phi = |\phi_1 - \varphi_2|$.

> **CHECK YOURSELF 6**
>
> In a SHM the amplitude of oscillations is 0.20 m and the period is 1.5 s.
>
> a What is the initial displacement if the phase angle is:
>
>   i zero
>
>   ii $\frac{\pi}{2}$?
>
> b Write down the equation for displacement in the case of a phase angle of $\frac{\pi}{2}$ in its simplest form.

From $x = x_0 \sin(\omega t + \phi)$ and again using calculus, we can find the velocity and the acceleration. The results are:

$v = \omega x_0 \cos(\omega t + \phi)$

$a = -\omega^2 x_0 \sin(\omega t + \phi)$

Notice that the last equation says $a = -\omega^2 x$ as it should be. These equations imply that the maximum values of velocity and acceleration are:

$v_{max} = \omega x_0$

$a_{max} = \omega^2 x_0$

> **CHECK YOURSELF 7**
>
> In a simple harmonic oscillation the displacement is given by $x = 15 \sin\left(\frac{\pi t}{3}\right)$ where t is in seconds. What are the angular frequency and period for this motion?

WORKED EXAMPLE 12.3

The graph of Figure 12.20 shows the variation with displacement x of the acceleration a of a particle.

a Explain why the oscillations are simple harmonic.

b Determine the period of oscillation.

c Determine the maximum speed and acceleration in this motion.

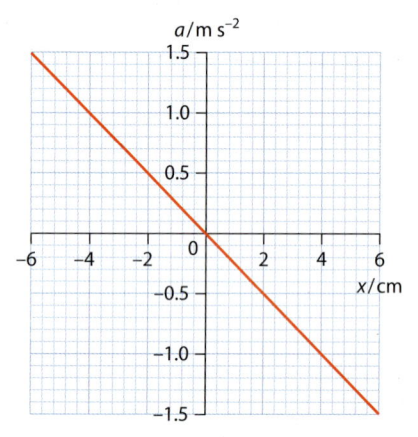

Figure 12.20: For worked example 12.3.

Answer

a The oscillations are simple harmonic because the acceleration is proportional to displacement (straight-line graph through the origin) and opposite to it (negative gradient). So it fits the defining equation $a = -\omega^2 x$.

b The gradient of the line in the graph is $-\omega^2$. From the graph the gradient is:

$$-\omega^2 = \frac{-3.0 \text{ m s}^{-2}}{0.12 \text{ m}}$$

$$\omega^2 = 25 \text{ s}^{-2}$$

$$\omega = 5.0 \text{ rad s}^{-1}.$$

Hence the period is:

$$T = \frac{2\pi}{\omega} = \frac{2\pi}{5.0} \approx 1.3 \text{ s}.$$

c The maximum speed is ωx_0, i.e. $5.0 \times 0.06 = 0.30 \text{ m s}^{-1}$. The maximum acceleration is $\omega^2 x_0$, i.e. $25 \times 0.06 = 1.5 \text{ m s}^{-2}$.

EXAM TIP

Watch the unit conversion. The amplitude is read from the graph as 0.06 m.

WORKED EXAMPLE 12.4

A particle undergoes SHM with amplitude 4.0 mm and frequency 0.32 Hz. At $t = 0$, the displacement is 4.0 mm.

a Write down the equation giving the displacement and velocity for this motion.

b Calculate the velocity when the displacement is 2.0 mm for the first time.

Answer

a We start with $x = x_0 \sin(\omega t + \phi)$.

We are told that at time zero $4.0 = 4.0 \sin(0 + \phi)$

So the phase angle is $\frac{\pi}{2}$.

Hence $x = 4.0 \sin\left(\omega t + \frac{\pi}{2}\right) = 4.0 \cos(\omega t)$.

We have been given frequency f so the angular frequency ω is:

$\omega = 2\pi f = 2\pi \times 0.32 = 2.01 \approx 2.0 \text{ rad s}^{-1}$.

So the equation for the displacement is:

$x = 4.0 \cos(2.0t)$

where t is in seconds and x is in millimetres.

The equation for the velocity is:

$v = \omega x_0 \cos(\omega t + \phi) = 8.0 \cos\left(2.0t + \frac{\pi}{2}\right)$
$= -8.0 \sin(2.0t)$.

b From $x = 4.0 \cos(2.0t)$ we find $2.0 = 4.0 \cos(2.0t)$ and so $\cos(2.0t) = \frac{1}{2}$. This means that $2.0t = \frac{\pi}{3} \Rightarrow t = 0.5236$ s. At this time the velocity is
$v = -8.0 \sin(2.0 \times 0.5236) = -6.9 \text{ mm s}^{-1}$.

(Make sure your calculator is set in radians.)

12 Simple harmonic motion

WORKED EXAMPLE 12.5

The graph of Figure 12.21 shows the displacement of a particle from a fixed equilibrium position.

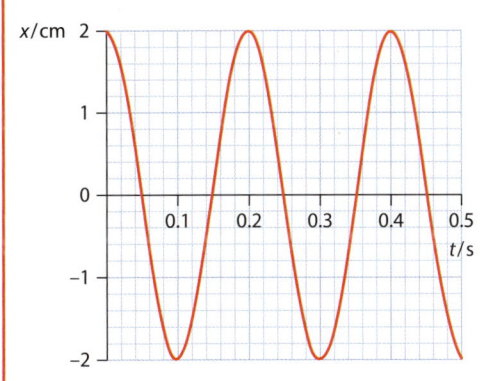

Figure 12.21: For worked example 12.5.

a Use the graph to determine:

  i the period of the motion

  ii the maximum velocity of the particle during an oscillation

  iii the maximum acceleration experienced by the particle.

b On a copy of the diagram, mark:

  i a point where the velocity is zero (label this with the letter Z)

CONTINUED

  ii a point where the velocity is positive and has the largest magnitude (label this with the letter V)

  iii a point where the acceleration is positive and has the largest magnitude (label this with the letter A).

Answer

a i The period is read off the graph as $T = 0.20$ s.

Since $T = \frac{2\pi}{\omega}$ we have that:

$\omega = \frac{2\pi}{T} = 31.4 \approx 31$ rad s^{-1}

  ii The maximum velocity is then:

$v_{max} = \omega x_0 = 31.4 \times 0.020 = 0.63$ m s^{-1}

  iii The maximum acceleration is found from:

$a_{max} = \omega^2 x_0 = 31.4^2 \times 0.020 = 20$ m s^{-2}

b i The velocity is zero at any point where the displacement is at a maximum or a minimum.

  ii For example at $t = 0.15$ s.

  iii For example at $t = 0.10$ s or $t = 0.30$ s.

CHECK YOURSELF 8

In a simple harmonic oscillation the maximum speed is 4.0 m s^{-1} and the maximum acceleration is 8.0 m s^{-2}. What is the period?

TEST YOUR UNDERSTANDING

15 The restoring force depends on displacement from equilibrium x through

- $F = k^2 x$
- $F = -k^2 \sin x$
- $F = k^2 \frac{x}{x-1}$
- $F = (1 - e^{k^2 x})$.

  a Explain why none of these gives rise to simple harmonic oscillation.

  b For students who know about MacLaurin series: are any of these simple harmonic for small amplitude?

16 A 2.0 kg block is connected to two springs. Each spring has spring constant $k = 120$ N m^{-1}. The springs have their natural length.

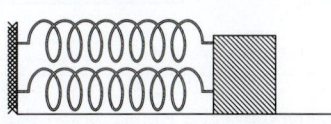

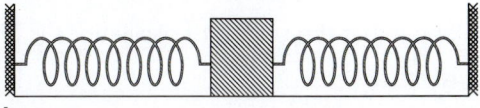

Figure 12.22: For question 16.

CONTINUED

a The springs are connected as in part **a** of Figure 12.22. Calculate the period of the oscillations of this block when it is displaced from its equilibrium position and then released.

b The springs are now connected as in part **b** of the diagram. State and explain whether the period changes.

17 In a SHM the maximum velocity is 12 m s^{-1} and the maximum acceleration is 48 m s^{-2}. What is:

a the period of oscillations

b the amplitude of oscillations?

18 In simple harmonic motion $x = x_0 \sin(\omega t + \phi)$ and $v = \omega x_0 \cos(\omega t + \phi)$.

a Using the identity $\sin^2 \theta + \cos^2 \theta = 1$ for $\theta = \omega t + \phi$, show that $v^2 = \omega^2(x_0^2 - x^2)$.

b The maximum speed in a simple harmonic oscillation is v. What is the speed when the displacement is half the amplitude?

19 Figure 12.23a shows a rectangular solid of mass M floating in a liquid of density ρ. The cross sectional area of the solid is A. In Figure 12.23b the block has been pushed downward by a distance x.

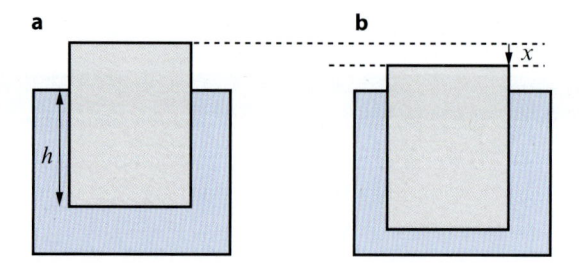

Figure 12.23: For question 19.

a Show that SHM will take place when the block is released.

b Show that the period of oscillations is given by $T = 2\pi \sqrt{\dfrac{M}{\rho g A}}$.

20 Figure 12.24 shows a simple pendulum of length L. The mass of the bob is m.

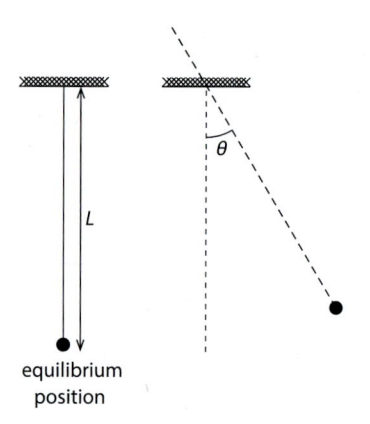

Figure 12.24: For question 20.

a Draw the forces on the bob when the pendulum has been displaced by an angle θ to the vertical.

b Show that the acceleration of the bob in this position is $a = -g \sin \theta$.

c The displacement x of the bob is the length of the arc subtended by the angle θ and $x = L\theta$.

Explain why for very small angles in radians the acceleration is approximately $a = -\dfrac{g}{L}x$.

d Hence deduce that the period of oscillations is given by $T = 2\pi \sqrt{\dfrac{L}{g}}$.

21 A point undergoes SHM oscillations with amplitude 5.0 cm and period 0.25 s. Calculate, for this point,

a the maximum speed

b the maximum acceleration.

22 The displacement, in metres, in a simple harmonic motion is given by $x = 6.0 \sin\left(\dfrac{2t}{3} + \dfrac{\pi}{5}\right)$ where t is in seconds. What are the angular frequency and period?

CONTINUED

23 The displacement of a particle executing SHM is given by $x = 5\sin(2\pi t)$ where x is in millimetres and t is in seconds. Calculate:

  a the initial displacement of the particle

  b the period of the oscillations

  c the displacement at $t = 1.2$ s

  d the time at which the displacement first becomes -2.0 mm.

24 A particle undergoes SHM oscillations such that the displacement, in cm, is given by $x = 12 \sin\left(\frac{\pi t}{2}\right)$, where time is in seconds. Calculate, for this particle, when the displacement is 6.0 cm:

  a the velocity

  b the acceleration.

25 a Write down an equation for the displacement of a particle undergoing SHM with amplitude 8.0 cm and frequency 14 Hz, assuming that at $t = 0$ the displacement is 8.0 cm and the particle is at rest.

  b Find the displacement, velocity and acceleration of this particle at a time of 0.025 s.

26 A point on a guitar string oscillates in SHM with an amplitude of 5.0 mm and a frequency of 460 Hz. Determine the maximum velocity and acceleration of this point.

27 A guitar string, whose two ends are fixed, oscillates as shown in Figure 12.25.

Figure 12.25: For question 27.

The vertical displacement of a point on the string a distance x from the left end is given by $y = 6.0\cos(1040\pi t)\sin(\pi x)$, where y is in millimetres, x is in metres and t is in seconds. Use this expression to:

  a deduce that all points on the string execute SHM with a common frequency and common phase, and determine the common frequency

  b deduce that different points on the string have different amplitudes

  c determine the maximum amplitude of oscillation

  d calculate the length L of the string

  e calculate the amplitude of oscillation of the point on the string where $x = \frac{L}{4}$.

28 Figure 12.26 shows the variation with time t of the velocity v of a particle executing SHM.

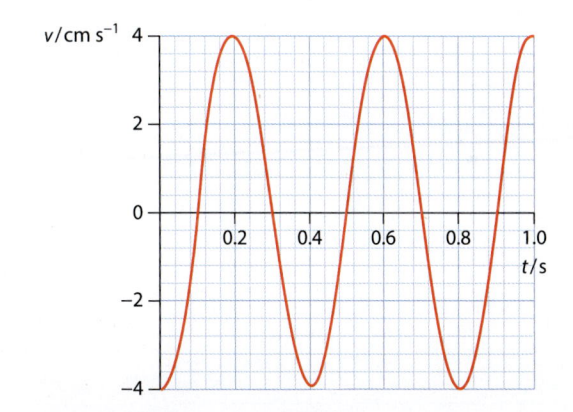

Figure 12.26: For question 28.

  a Estimate the area under the curve from 0.10 s to 0.30 s.

  b What does this area represent?

CONTINUED

29 Figure 12.27 shows the variation with time t of the displacement x of a particle executing SHM.

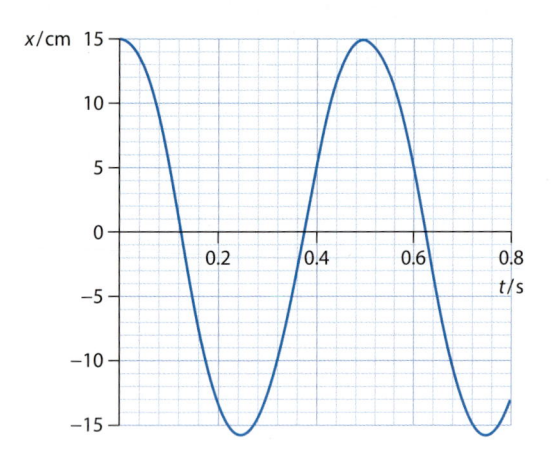

Figure 12.27: For question 29.

Draw a graph to show the variation with displacement x of the acceleration a of the particle (put numbers on the axes).

30 A body of mass 0.120 kg is placed on a horizontal plate. The plate oscillates vertically in SHM making five oscillations per second (see Figure 12.28).

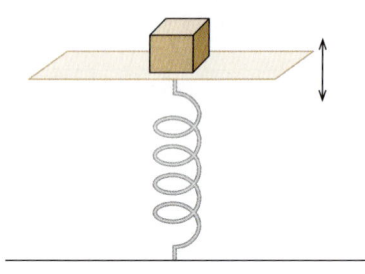

Figure 12.28: For question 30.

a Determine the largest possible amplitude of oscillations such that the body never loses contact with the plate.

b Calculate the normal reaction force on the body at the lowest point of the oscillations when the amplitude has the value found in **a**.

31 What is the phase angle for each of the two simple harmonic oscillations shown in Figure 12.29?

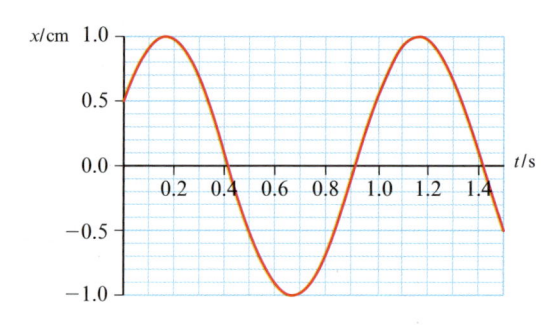

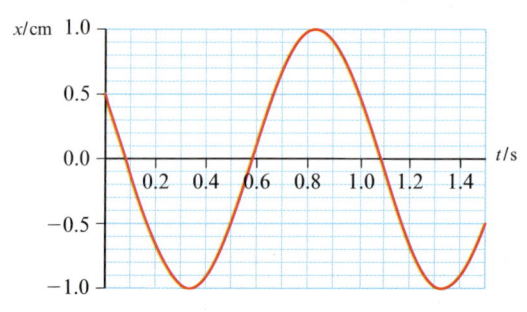

Figure 12.29: For question 31.

32 Show that the phase angle is given by the formula $\varphi = \arctan \frac{\omega x(0)}{v(0)}$ where $x(0)$ and $v(0)$ are the displacement and velocity at time zero.

33 Consider a particle that rotates counterclockwise around a circle of radius R with constant angular speed ω. At time zero, the particle is in the position shown, making an angle φ with the positive x-axis.

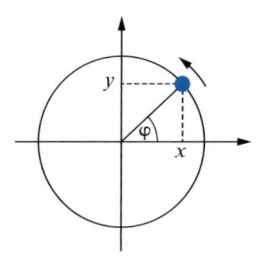

Figure 12.30: For question 33.

Show that the x and y coordinates of the particle perform simple harmonic oscillations.

12.3 Energy in simple harmonic motion

Kinetic and potential energy

Consider again a particle at the end of a horizontal spring. Let the extension of the spring be x at a particular instant of time, and let the velocity of the particle be v at that time. The system has elastic potential energy and kinetic energy. Figure 12.31 shows how these energies vary with displacement. These shapes are parabolic. The total energy E_T of the system is then:

$$E_T = E_P + E_K$$

In the absence of frictional and other resistance forces, this total energy is conserved, and so E = constant.

The maximum velocity is achieved when $x = 0$, i.e. as the mass moves past its equilibrium position. Here there is no extension, so the elastic potential energy is zero. At the extremes of the motion, $x = \pm A$ and $v = 0$, so the kinetic energy is zero. Thus at $x = \pm A$ the system has elastic potential energy only, and at $x = 0$ it has kinetic energy only. At intermediate points the system has both forms of energy: elastic potential energy and kinetic energy. During an oscillation, we therefore have transfers from one form of energy into another.

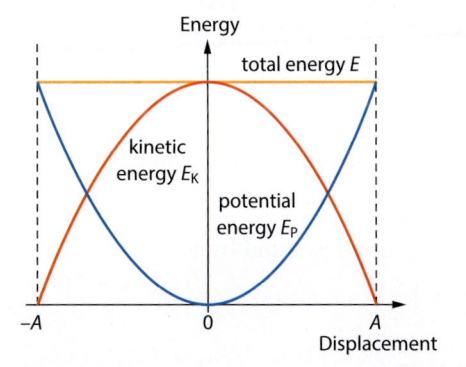

Figure 12.31: Graphs showing the variation with displacement of the potential energy and kinetic energy of a particle on a spring. The total energy is a horizontal straight line. The graphs are parabolas.

CHECK YOURSELF 9

Figure 12.32 shows the variation with displacement of the potential energy of a particle in SHM.

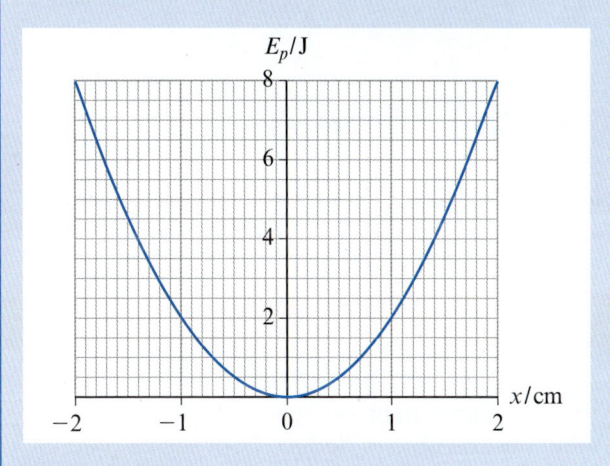

Figure 12.32: For check yourself question 9.

What is the kinetic energy when the displacement is 1.0 cm?

The variation of the kinetic and potential energies with time is a bit more complicated.

Suppose that we have a SHM where the displacement versus time graph is that of Figure 12.33.

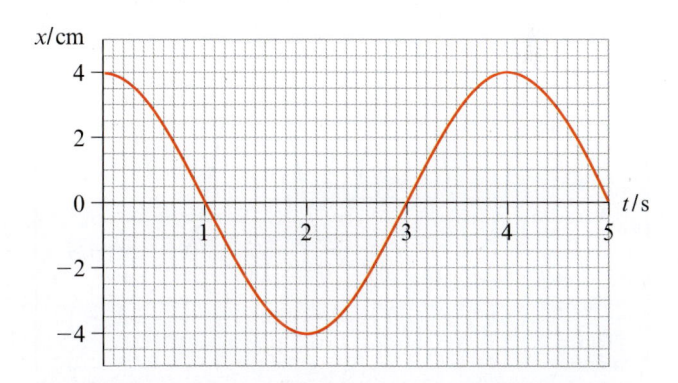

Figure 12.33: Displacement versus time graph.

We see that the speed will be zero at the following times: 0 s, 2 s and 4 s. The speed will be maximum at times: 1 s, 3 s and 5 s. So a graph of kinetic energy versus time will look like the red curve in Figure 12.34. The potential energy is maximum when the displacement is maximum or minimum, i.e. at times 0 s, 2, s and 4 s and zero when the displacement is zero, i.e. at times 1 s, 3 s and 5 s. This gives the blue curve in Figure 12.34.

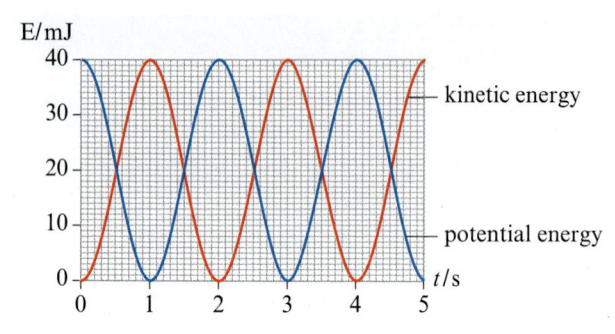

Figure 12.34: Variation of kinetic and potential energies with time.

> **EXAM TIP**
>
> The graphs above are specific to the displacement graph of Figure 12.33! You must be able to deduce from such a graph that the period of oscillations is 4 s.

> **CHECK YOURSELF 10**
>
> Figure 12.35 shows the variation with time of the kinetic energy of a particle in SHM. 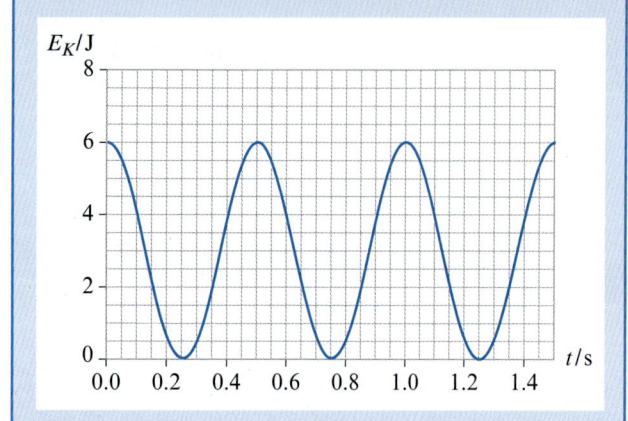
>
> **Figure 12.35:** For check yourself question 10.
>
> Draw the corresponding displacement versus time graph. (No numbers are necessary on the displacement axis.)

> **WORKED EXAMPLE 12.6**
>
> The graph in Figure 12.36 shows the variation with displacement of the kinetic energy of a particle of mass 0.40 kg performing SHM at the end of a spring. 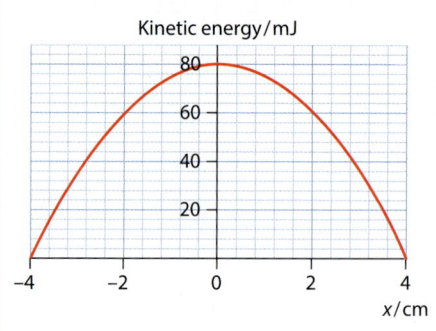
>
> **Figure 12.36:** Graph showing the variation with displacement of the kinetic energy of a particle.
>
> a Use the graph to determine:
>
>   i the total energy of the particle
>
>   ii the maximum speed of the particle
>
>   iii the amplitude of the motion
>
>   iv the potential energy when the displacement is 2.0 cm.
>
> b On a copy of the axes, draw the variation with displacement of the potential energy of the particle.
>
> **Answer**
>
> a i The total energy is equal to the maximum kinetic energy, i.e. 80 mJ.
>
>   ii The maximum speed is found from:
>
> $$\tfrac{1}{2} m v_{max}^2 = E_{max}$$
>
> $$v_{max}^2 = \frac{2 E_{max}}{m}$$
>
> $$v_{max} = \sqrt{\frac{2 \times 80 \times 10^{-3}}{0.40}}$$
>
> $$= 0.63 \text{ m s}^{-1}$$
>
>   iii The amplitude is 4.0 cm.
>
>   iv When $x = 2.0$ cm, the kinetic energy is 60 mJ and so the potential energy is 20 mJ.
>
> b The graph is a parabola like the blue curve in Figure 12.31.

12.4 More about energy in SHM

In SHM we know that the displacement is given by $x = x_0 \sin(\omega t + \phi)$ and the velocity by $v = \omega x_0 \cos(\omega t + \phi)$. The kinetic energy is then given by

$$E_K = \tfrac{1}{2} mv^2 = \tfrac{1}{2} m\omega^2 x_0^2 \cos^2(\omega t + \phi)$$

This can be rewritten as

$$E_K = \tfrac{1}{2} m\omega^2 x_0^2 (1 - \sin^2(\omega t + \phi))$$

$$E_K = \tfrac{1}{2} m\omega^2 x_0^2 - \tfrac{1}{2} m\omega^2 x^2.$$

The maximum kinetic energy is then $\tfrac{1}{2} m\omega^2 x_0^2$, and so this must also be the total energy of the system:

$$E_T = \tfrac{1}{2} m\omega^2 x_0^2$$

The total energy is the sum of the potential and kinetic energies:

$$E_T = E_P + E_K$$

Therefore

$$E_P = \tfrac{1}{2} m\omega^2 x_0^2 - \left(\tfrac{1}{2} m\omega^2 x_0^2 - \tfrac{1}{2} m\omega^2 x^2 \right)$$

$$E_P = \tfrac{1}{2} m\omega^2 x^2$$

KEY POINT

In SHM the energies are $E_P = \tfrac{1}{2} m\omega^2 x^2$, $E_K = \tfrac{1}{2} m\omega^2 (x_0^2 - x^2)$ and $E_T = \tfrac{1}{2} m\omega^2 x_0^2$.

Since $E_K = \tfrac{1}{2} mv^2$, we find a very useful formula for velocity in terms of displacement:

$$v = \pm \omega \sqrt{x_0^2 - x^2}$$

The plus or minus sign is needed because for any given displacement x, the particle may be going one way or the opposite way. This equation allows us to see that at the extremes of the motion, $x = \pm x_0$, and so $v = 0$ as we expect. This formula allows for a much simpler solution to a problem such as problem 24 in the previous chapter. Using the data for that problem the velocity is simply

$$v = \pm \omega \sqrt{x_0^2 - x^2} = \pm \tfrac{\pi}{2} \sqrt{0.12^2 - 0.06^2} = \pm 0.16 \text{ m s}^{-1}.$$

WORKED EXAMPLE 12.7

The graph of Figure 12.37 shows the variation with the square of the displacement (x^2) of the potential energy E_P of a particle of mass 40 g that is executing SHM. Using the graph, determine:

a the period of oscillation

b the maximum speed of the particle during an oscillation.

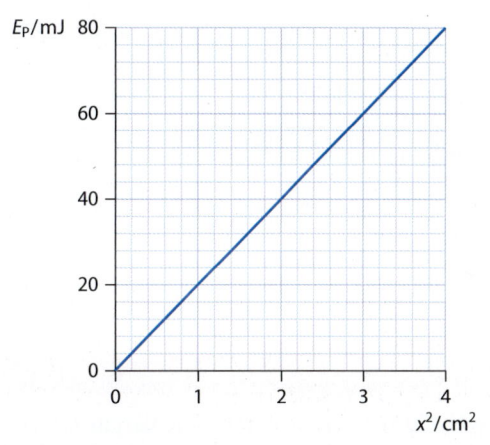

Figure 12.37: For worked example 12.7.

Answer

a The maximum potential energy is $E_P = \tfrac{1}{2} m\omega^2 x_0^2$.

From the graph, the maximum potential energy is 80 mJ ($= 8.0 \times 10^{-2}$ J) and the amplitude is $\sqrt{4.0 \text{ cm}^2} = 2.0$ cm ($= 2.0 \times 10^{-2}$ m).

The mass of the particle is 0.040 kg, so:

$$80 \times 10^{-3} = \tfrac{1}{2} \times 0.040 \times \omega^2 \times x_0^2$$

Rearranging:

$$\omega^2 = \frac{2 \times 80 \times 10^{-3}}{0.040 \times (2.00 \times 10^{-2})^2}$$

$$\omega^2 = 10^4 \text{ s}^{-2}$$

$$\omega = 10^2 \text{ rad s}^{-1}$$

The period is $T = \tfrac{2\pi}{\omega}$, so:

$$T = \tfrac{2\pi}{10^2} = 0.063 \text{ s}$$

b The maximum speed is found from:

$$v_{max} = \omega x_0 = 100 \times 2.00 \times 10^{-2} = 2.00 \text{ m s}^{-1}$$

WORKED EXAMPLE 12.8

In SHM the maximum speed is 4.0 m s^{-1} and the maximum acceleration is 35 m s^{-2}. Determine:

a the period of the motion

b the amplitude of oscillations.

Answer

a $v_{max} = \omega x_0$ and $a_{max} = \omega^2 x_0$

So, $\dfrac{a_{max}}{v_{max}} = \dfrac{\omega^2 x_0}{\omega x_0} = \omega$

Hence, $\omega = \dfrac{35}{4.0} = 8.75$ s^{-1}

The period is $T = \dfrac{2\pi}{\omega} = \dfrac{2\pi}{8.75} \approx 0.72$ s.

b From $v_{max} = \omega x_0$ we find $4.0 = 8.75 \times x_0$

So, $x_0 = \dfrac{4.0}{8.75} = 0.46$ m.

WORKED EXAMPLE 12.9

The graph of Figure 12.38 shows the variation with time t of the kinetic energy E_K of a particle of mass 0.25 kg that is undergoing SHM.

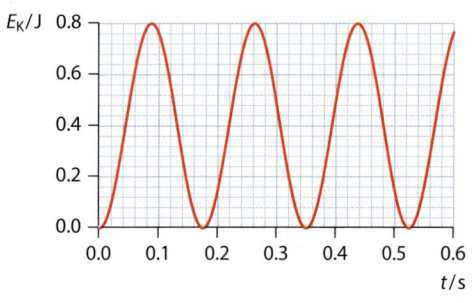

Figure 12.38: For worked example 12.9.

For this motion, determine:

a the period

b the amplitude

c the kinetic energy when the displacement is 0.080 m.

CONTINUED

Answer

a At $t = 0$ the kinetic energy is zero, meaning that the particle is at one extreme of the oscillation. It is zero again at about 0.175 s when it is at the other end. To find the period the particle has to return to its original position and that happens at 0.35 s, so $T = 0.35$ s.

b The angular frequency is found from $\omega = \dfrac{2\pi}{T}$:

$\omega = \dfrac{2\pi}{0.35} = 17.95 \approx 18$ rad s^{-1}

The maximum kinetic energy is given by $E_{Kmax} = \dfrac{1}{2} m\omega^2 x_0^2$ and so:

$0.80 = \dfrac{1}{2} \times 0.25 \times 17.95^2 \times x_0^2$

Rearranging:

$x_0 = \sqrt{\dfrac{2 \times 0.80}{0.25 \times 17.95^2}} = 0.141 \approx 0.14$ m

c We know the displacement so use a formula that gives kinetic energy in terms of displacement:

$E_K = \dfrac{1}{2} m\omega^2 (x_0^2 - x^2)$

This gives:

$E_K = \dfrac{1}{2} \times 0.25 \times 17.95^2 (0.141^2 - 0.080^2) = 0.54$ J

EXAM TIP

It is important to understand how to find the period from this graph.

12 Simple harmonic motion

NATURE OF SCIENCE

The complex can be understood in terms of the simple.

The equation for SHM can be solved in terms of simple sine and cosine functions. These simple solutions help physicists to visualise how an oscillator behaves. Although real oscillations are very complex, a powerful mathematical machinery called Fourier analysis allows the decomposition of complex oscillations, sounds, noise and waves in general, in terms of sines and cosines. Energy exchange in oscillating electrical circuits is modelled using this type of analysis. Therefore the simple descriptions used in this topic can also be used in more complex problems as well.

TEST YOUR UNDERSTANDING

34 Figure 12.39 shows the variation with displacement x of the acceleration a of a body of mass 0.150 kg.

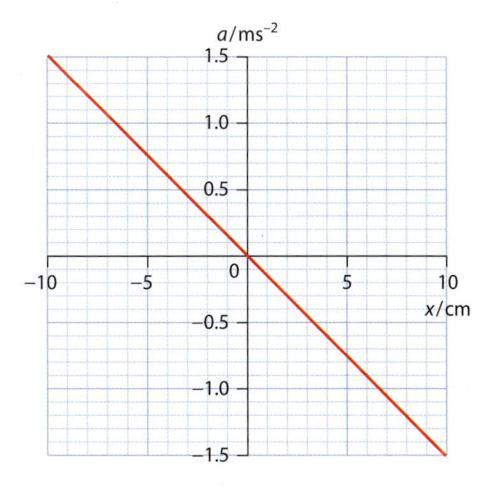

Figure 12.39: For question 34.

a Use the graph to explain why the motion of the body is SHM.

Determine the following:

b the period of the motion

c the maximum velocity of the body during an oscillation

d the maximum net force exerted on the body

e the total energy of the body.

35 Figure 12.40 shows the variation with time of the kinetic energy of a particle that is undergoing simple harmonic oscillations.

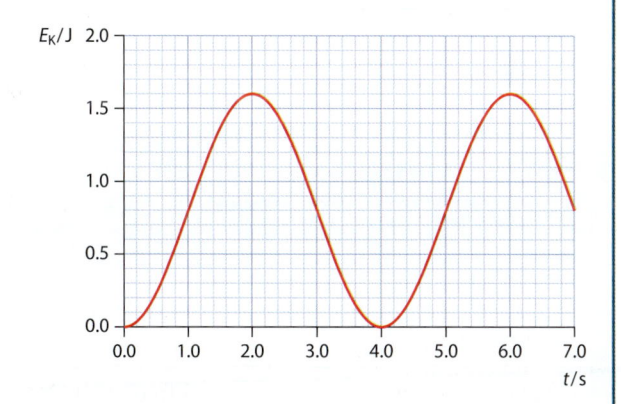

Figure 12.40: For question 35.

a Use the graph to determine the period of oscillation.

b Draw a graph to show the variation with time of the potential energy.

c What is the potential energy at

    i 1.0 s

    ii 2.0 s?

36 In a SHM the amplitude of oscillations is 15 cm and the period is 2.0 s. The mass of the particle is 0.12 kg.

a What is the potential energy when the displacement is 9.0 cm?

b What is the kinetic energy when the displacement is 6.0 cm?

283

CONTINUED

37 The total energy of a body executing SHM is 18 J. The amplitude of oscillations is 12 cm. What is the potential energy of the body when a chevron is needed by 37 displacement is 8.0 cm?

38 The total energy of a body executing SHM is 12 J. The amplitude of oscillations is 8.0 cm. What is the kinetic energy of the body when the displacement is 4.0 cm?

39 The total energy of a particle in SHM is 8.0 J. The amplitude of the motion is 5.0 cm. What is the displacement when the kinetic energy is 6.0 J?

40 A point undergoes SHM oscillations with period 1.5 s. The speed when the displacement is 4.0 cm is 18 cms^{-1}. Determine the amplitude of the oscillations.

41 At a particular displacement x in a SHM, the potential energy equals the kinetic energy. The amplitude of the motion is 4.2 cm. What is x?

SELF-ASSESSMENT CHECKLIST

I am able to ...	Section	Not yet	Nearly there	Ready to move on
identify the conditions under which simple harmonic oscillations will take place	12.1			
determine the amplitude, period and frequency graphically	12.1			
describe how velocity and acceleration vary during an oscillation	12.1			
explain the energy transformations taking place in simple harmonic oscillations	12.3			
understand the concept of phase difference	12.1			
use the equation for displacement	12.2			
understand the meaning of the phase angle	12.2			
write down equations for the velocity and acceleration given the formula for displacement	12.2			
solve problems using the equations for simple harmonic motion	12.2			
solve problems with kinetic energy and potential energy quantitatively	12.3			

12 Simple harmonic motion

> **REFLECTION**
>
> Can you state the necessary conditions for simple harmonic oscillations to take place? Can you find the period of oscillations from a graph of acceleration versus displacement? Can you describe the energy transfers in simple harmonic oscillations?
>
> Do you understand the equations for displacement, velocity and acceleration in simple harmonic motion? Are you comfortable with the term *phase angle*? Can you solve problems using the equations for simple harmonic oscillations?

EXAM-STYLE QUESTIONS

You can find questions in the style of IB exams in the digital coursebook.

CHECK YOURSELF ANSWERS

1. The period is 0.80 s and the frequency is 1.25 Hz.

2. It will increase by the square root of 4, i.e. 2.

3. It will decrease by the square root of 4, i.e. 2.

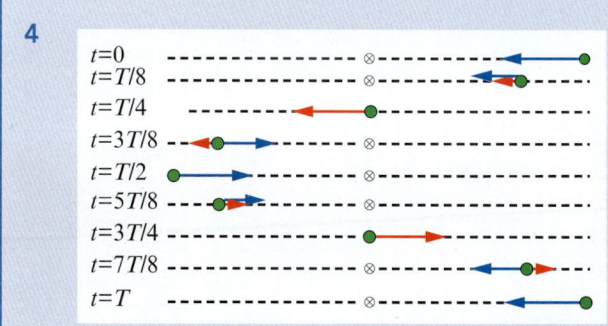

4.
   (diagram showing positions and velocity vectors at $t=0, T/8, T/4, 3T/8, T/2, 5T/8, 3T/4, 7T/8, T$)

5. The shift is 0.25 s and the period is 2.0 s so the phase difference is $\phi = \frac{\text{shift}}{T} \times 2\pi = \frac{0.25}{2.0} \times 2\pi = \frac{\pi}{4}$ or 45°.

6. **a** i Zero   ii 0.20 m

   b $x = 0.20 \sin\left(\frac{2\pi}{1.5}t + \frac{\pi}{2}\right)$

   $= 0.20 \sin\left(\frac{4\pi}{3}t + \frac{\pi}{2}\right) = 0.20 \cos\left(\frac{4\pi}{3}t\right)$.

7. Comparing with $x = x_0 \sin(\omega t)$ we find $\omega = \frac{\pi}{3}$ and $T = \frac{2\pi}{\omega} = \frac{2\pi}{\frac{\pi}{3}} = 6.0$ s.

8. $v_{max} = \omega x_0$ and $a_{max} = \omega^2 x_0$ so $\frac{a_{max}}{v_{max}} = \frac{\omega^2 x_0}{\omega x_0} = \omega = \frac{2\pi}{T}$. So $T = 2\pi \frac{v_{max}}{a_{max}} = 2\pi \times \frac{4.0}{8.0} = 3.1$ s.

9. The potential energy is 2.0 J and the total energy is 8.0 J so the kinetic energy is 6.0 J.

10. A sine graph as shown, or a negative sine graph with period 1 s.

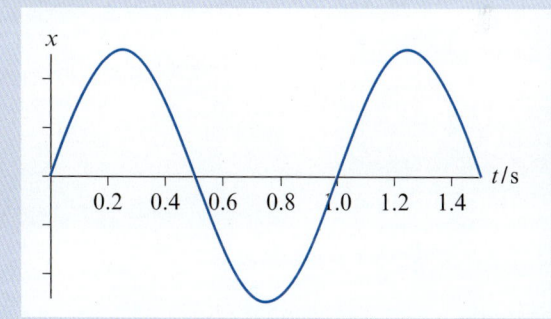

    (graph of x vs t/s showing sinusoidal curve with zero crossings at 0.4, 0.8, 1.2)

Chapter 13
The wave model

LEARNING OBJECTIVES

In this chapter you will learn how to:

- describe waves and wave motion
- identify wavelength, frequency and period from graphs of *displacement* against *distance* or *time*
- solve problems with wavelength, frequency, period and wave speed
- describe the motion of a particle in a medium through which a wave travels
- describe the difference between transverse and longitudinal waves
- understand the nature of electromagnetic waves
- understand the nature of sound waves.

13 The wave model

> **GUIDING QUESTIONS**
>
> - What is a wave?
> - How do waves transfer energy?
> - What is oscillating in an electromagnetic wave?

Introduction

This section introduces waves and wave motion.

What do these things have in common?

- the sounds we hear
- the warmth we feel from the sun
- the motion of electrons inside atoms.

Answer: we can analyse them all in the same way—by using the language and physics of waves.

There are four main classes of waves: mechanical waves (such as sound and waves on strings), electromagnetic waves (such as light), gravitational waves, and matter waves (such as electron motion in atoms).

13.1 Mechanical pulses and waves

If we take the free end of a taut, horizontal rope and we give it a sudden up and down jerk, a *pulse* will be produced that will travel down the length of the rope at a certain speed (Figure 13.1).

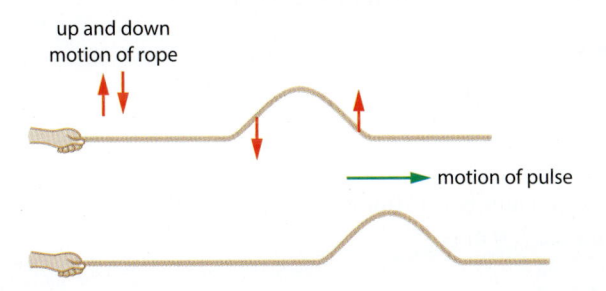

Figure 13.1: A pulse on a taut rope. The rope itself moves up and down. What moves to the right is the pulse.

The upward force due to the hand forces a section of the rope to move up. Because of the tension in the rope, this section pulls the section in front of it upwards. In this way the pulse moves forward. In the meantime the hand has moved down, forcing sections of the rope to return to their horizontal equilibrium position. Neighbouring sections again do the same because of the tension in the rope. If the motion of the hand holding the free end is continuous then a **mechanical wave** is established on the rope. Figure 13.2 shows two full waves travelling down the length of the rope.

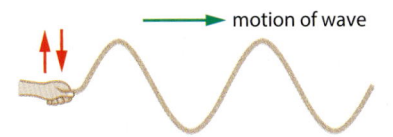

Figure 13.2: A continuous wave travelling along the rope.

Now if the right end of the rope is attached to a body that is free to move, the body will move when the wave gets to it. This means that the wave transfers energy and momentum.

> **KEY POINT**
>
> A mechanical wave is a disturbance that travels in a medium through oscillations of the particles of the medium. A wave transfers energy and momentum. The direction of propagation of the wave is the direction of energy transfer.

How does a wave transfer energy? As we will learn in the next chapter, when a wave travels in a medium the particles of the medium perform simple harmonic oscillations about their equilibrium positions. In Chapter 12.1 we learned that in simple harmonic motion we have kinetic and elastic potential energy. This energy has to be supplied by the source that creates the wave. Suppose that the source provides an amount of energy E in order to produce one full wave. This happens in a time equal to one period. In the next period the source has to provide an additional amount E and so on. In this way, as the wave progresses, energy is carried along by the wave, flowing from the source through the medium in the direction of propagation of the wave. It follows that the speed at which energy is being transferred is the speed of the wave.

Figure 13.3 shows one full wave.

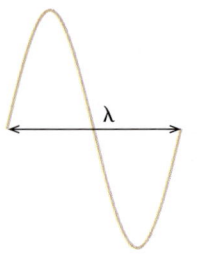

Figure 13.3: One full wave.

The length of one full wave is known as the **wavelength**, λ.

It is also the distance from crest to crest or trough to trough (Figure 13.4). (A crest is the highest point on the wave and a trough the lowest.)

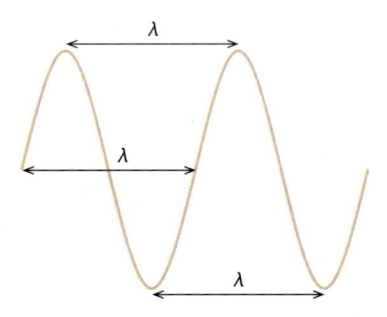

Figure 13.4: Three distances that all give the wavelength.

The time to create one full wave is known as the **period** of the wave, T.

Frequency, f, is the number of full waves created in 1 s. $f = \frac{1}{T}$.

If the period of wave is $T = 0.25$ s, for example, then the number of full waves produced in one second is 4.

Suppose we have a wave on a rope, of wavelength λ, period T and frequency f. Figure 13.5 shows the rope at time zero when we have not yet produced any waves, and at time T where we have produced one full wave. The wave has moved a distance equal to one wavelength in a time equal to one period and so the speed of the wave is:

$$v = \frac{\text{distance for one full wave}}{\text{time for one full wave}} = \frac{\lambda}{T}$$

Since $f = \frac{1}{T}$ we also have that:

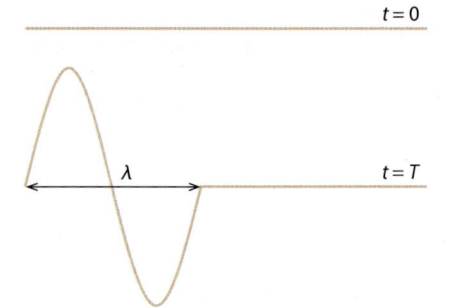

$$v = f\lambda$$

Figure 13.5: In a time of one period, the wave has moved forward a distance of one wavelength. The speed of the wave depends only on the properties of the medium and not on how it is produced.

KEY POINT

The speed of a wave is determined only by the properties of the medium and not on how the wave is produced.

CHECK YOURSELF 1

A wave travels in a medium with speed v and wavelength λ. The frequency of the wave is doubled. What happens to the speed of the wave and its wavelength?

WORKED EXAMPLE 13.1

A sound wave of frequency 450 Hz is emitted from A and travels towards B, a distance of 150 m away. How many full waves fit in the distance from A to B? (Take the speed of sound to be 340 m s^{-1}.)

Answer

The wavelength is:

$\lambda = \frac{340}{450} = 0.756$ m

Thus the number of full waves that fit in the distance 150 m is:

$N = \frac{150}{0.756}$

$N = 198$ full wavelengths.

WORKED EXAMPLE 13.2

The noise of thunder is heard 3 s after the flash of lightning. How far away is the place where lightning struck? (Take the speed of sound to be 340 m s^{-1}.)

Answer

Light travels so fast that we can assume that lightning struck exactly when we see the flash of light.

If thunder is heard 3 s later, it means that it took 3 s for sound to cover the unknown distance, d. Thus:

$d = vt$

$d = 340 \times 3$

$d = 1020$ m.

WORKED EXAMPLE 13.3

Water wave crests in a lake are 5.0 m apart and pass by an anchored boat every 2.0 s. What is the speed of the water waves?

Answer

Use $v = f\lambda$. The wavelength is 5.0 m and the period is 2.0 s. So:

$v = \dfrac{5.0}{2.0}$

$v = 2.5$ m s^{-1}.

TEST YOUR UNDERSTANDING

1. In football stadiums fans often create a 'wave'. Suggest factors that determine the speed of the 'wave'.

2. A number of dominoes are stood next to each other along a straight line. A small push is given to the first domino, and one by one the dominoes fall over.

   a. Outline how this is an example of wave motion.

   b. Suggest how the speed of the wave pulse could be increased.

   c. Design an experiment in which this problem can be investigated.

3. Draw a labelled diagram to explain the terms:
   - wavelength
   - period
   - amplitude
   - crest
   - trough.

4. Calculate the frequency of light (speed 3.0 × 10^8 m s^{-1}) of wavelength 656 nm.

5. Calculate the wavelength that corresponds to a sound frequency of:

   a. 256 Hz

   b. 25 kHz.

   (Take the speed of sound to be 330 m s^{-1}.)

> **CONTINUED**
>
> **6** A boy shouts towards a vertical cliff a distance of 250 m away and 1.5 s later hears an echo. What is an estimate of the speed of sound from these data?
>
> **7** A sound wave (speed 330 m s^{-1}) and a light wave (speed 3.0 × 10^8 m s^{-1}) have the same wavelength. What is the ratio of the light to the sound frequency?

13.2 Transverse and longitudinal waves

Transverse waves

How do the particles of a medium move when there is a wave in the medium? We will now see the connection between simple harmonic motion (SHM) and wave motion: as a wave propagates through a medium, the particles of the medium perform SHM with a frequency that is the same as that of the wave.

In transverse waves the particles of the medium perform simple harmonic oscillations in a direction at right angles to the direction of energy transfer.

> **KEY POINT**
>
> A wave is **transverse** if the displacement of the particles of the medium is at *right angles* to the direction of energy transfer.

The diagram in Figure 13.6 shows three particles in the medium (the rope). The wave moves from left to right. The wave is transverse which means that the particles are moving along the double headed arrows as the wave progresses.

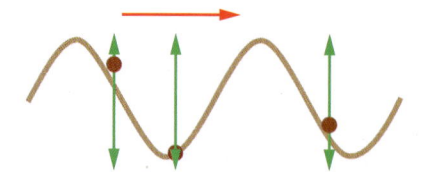

Figure 13.6: Particles in the medium move strictly at right angles to the direction of energy transfer.

To understand precisely how the particles in the medium move as the wave propagates through the medium consider Figure 13.7. Think of each graph as a photograph of the rope. Photographs are taken every 0.5 ms. Something is shaking the left end of the rope, creating the waves. Concentrate on just one particle in the medium, point Q. At $t = 0$, it happens to be at a crest. As we expect, this point will perform oscillations along a line at right angles to the direction of energy transfer. So at 0.5 ms the particle is a bit lower, but always along the vertical dotted line. After 3 ms the particle is back at its initial position so this must be the period of this wave.

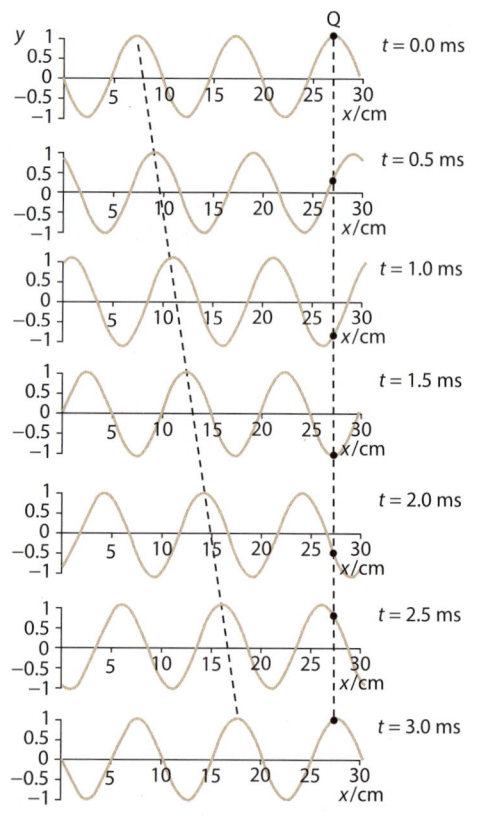

Figure 13.7: Snapshots of a rope every 0.5 ms. Particles of the rope move along vertical lines. What moves forward is the position of crests (and troughs).

In Figure 13.7, look also at the crest at $x = 7.5$ cm at $t = 0$. The wavelength is 10 cm (obtained from any one of the graphs). As time passes, the position of the crest shifts to the right. After one period, it has moved to position $x = 17.5$ cm. The distance covered by the crest is 10 cm and equals the wavelength as it should. The speed of the wave is then $v = \frac{\lambda}{T} = \frac{0.10}{3.0 \times 10^{-3}} = 33$ m s^{-1}.

A very simple way to determine where a particle will be when a wave moves through the medium is the following: the blue curve in Figure 13.8 shows the wave at some instant. Four points on the wave have been marked (dark blue circles). Where will these points be an instant later? We know they will move along the vertical dotted lines. Now draw a copy of the blue wave, make it dashed and place it on the diagram but *shifted a bit forward* (because the wave moves to the right). This will tell us the new positions of the particles (light blue circles).

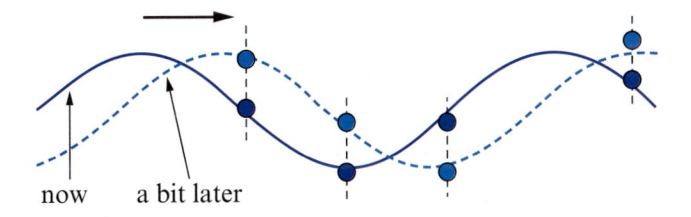

Figure 13.8: How medium particles move when a transverse wave propagates.

A snapshot of the wave shows the displacement of the rope along its length at the moment the picture was taken. In the same way a graph of the displacement of the wave as a function of position, i.e. distance from the left end of the rope, gives the displacement at each point on the rope at a specific point in time (Figure 13.9).

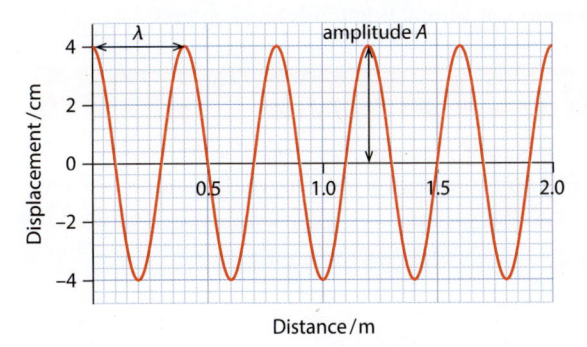

Figure 13.9: A graph of displacement versus position tells us the displacement of any point on the rope at a specific moment in time.

We get two important pieces of information from a displacement–distance graph. The first is the **amplitude** of the wave (that is, the largest displacement). The second is the wavelength.

> **EXAM TIP**
>
> It is a common mistake to think that the amplitude is the crest to trough distance.

For the wave of Figure 13.9 the amplitude is 4.0 cm. The wavelength is 0.40 m. This graph also tells us that at the point on the string that is 0.10 m from the rope's left end the displacement is zero at that specific instant of time. At that same instant of time at a point 1.0 m from the left end the displacement is −4.0 cm, etc. Thus, a graph of displacement versus position is like a photograph or a snapshot of the rope taken at a particular time. If we take a second photograph of the string some time later, the rope will look different because the wave has moved in the meantime.

There is a second type of graph that we may use to describe waves. This is a graph of displacement versus time: we imagine looking at *one specific point on the rope* and observe how the displacement of that point varies with time. So, for example, Figure 13.10 shows the variation with time of a specific point on a rope as the wave of Figure 13.9 travels down the length of the rope.

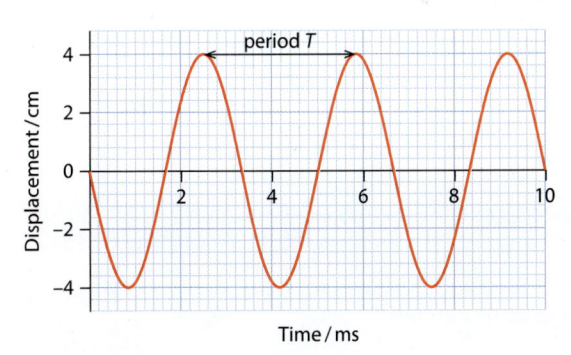

Figure 13.10: The same wave as in Figure 13.9 now showing the variation of the displacement of a specific point with time.

We get two important pieces of information from a displacement–time graph: the first is the amplitude of the wave and the second is the period.

PHYSICS FOR THE IB DIPLOMA: COURSEBOOK

> **EXAM TIP**
>
> To find the period from Figure 13.10, it is safer to count three loops so that three periods are 10 ms. Also, make sure to check carefully the units on the axes—in this example time is in ms, not seconds.

We already know the amplitude: it is 4.0 cm. The period is 3.33 ms. So the frequency is $\frac{1}{3.33 \times 10^{-3}}$ = 300 Hz.

The speed of this wave is therefore $v = f\lambda = 0.40 \times 300 = 120$ m s^{-1}.

(Now suppose that we are told that Figure 13.10 shows the displacement of the point at $x = 0.10$ m (call it P). And suppose that the graph of Figure 13.9 is a snapshot of the wave at 0.0 ms. Which way is the wave travelling? Go to Figure 13.9 and find $x = 0.10$ m: if you shift the wave slightly to the left (i.e. if the wave moves left) P gets a negative displacement. If you shift it to the right (i.e. if the wave moves right) P gets a positive displacement. Which is correct? Refer to Figure 13.10: immediately after $t = 0.0$ ms the displacement becomes negative. So the wave is travelling to the left.)

> **CHECK YOURSELF 2**
>
> Figure 13.11 shows, at a particular instant, a transverse wave travelling towards the left. A point in the medium is marked.
>
> **Figure 13.11:** For check yourself question 2.
>
> What is the direction of velocity of the marked particle at this instant?

> **WORKED EXAMPLE 13.4**
>
> A transverse wave of amplitude 2.0 cm, wavelength 0.40 m and frequency 350 Hz propagates on a string.
>
> a What is the average velocity of a point on the string during one period?
>
> b What is the average speed of a point on the string during one period?
>
> c What is the ratio $\frac{\text{wave speed}}{\text{speed in (b)}}$?
>
> **Answer**
>
> a During one period any point on the string will have a displacement of zero so the average velocity will be zero.
>
> b During one period any point on the string will move a distance equal to 4 times the amplitude, i.e. 8.0 cm. The period is $T = \frac{1}{350} = 0.002857$ s. Hence the average speed is $\bar{v} = \frac{0.080}{0.002857} = 28$ m s^{-1}.
>
> c The wave speed is $v = 350 \times 0.40 = 140$ m s^{-1}, hence the ratio is $\frac{140}{28} = 5.0$.

Longitudinal waves

Imagine that you push the left end of a slinky in and out as in Figure 13.12. The coils of the slinky move in a direction that is parallel to that of the wave. As the hand moves to the right it forces coils to move forward, causing a compression (coils crowd together). As the hand moves to the left, coils right in front of it also move left, causing an expansion or rarefaction (coils move apart).

> **KEY POINT**
>
> A wave is **longitudinal** if the displacement is parallel to the direction of energy transfer.

13 The wave model

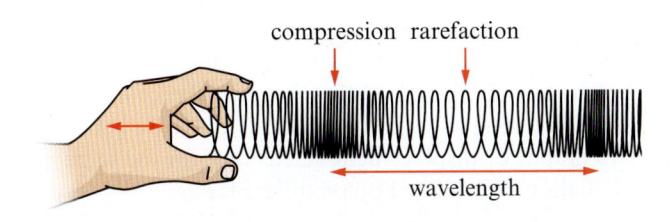

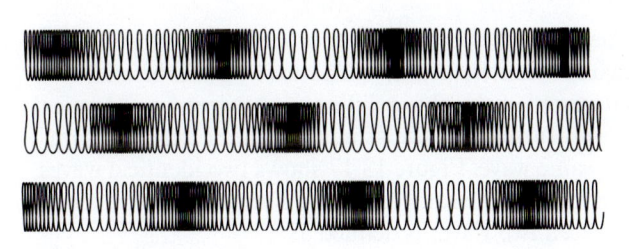

Figure 13.12: A longitudinal wave in which the medium moves parallel to the direction of energy transfer.

Sound waves are longitudinal waves that can travel in gases and liquids as well as in solids. A sound wave consists of a series of compressions and rarefactions in the medium in which it is travelling. Figure 13.13 shows the compressions and rarefactions produced in the air by a loudspeaker.

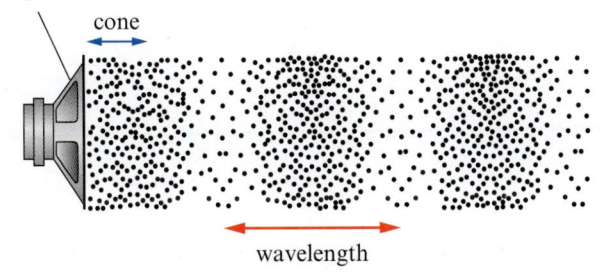

Figure 13.13: A vibrating loudspeaker cone produces compressions and rarefactions. These compressions and expansions move through air as a wave called sound.

As with transverse waves, we can plot a graph of displacement versus distance along the wave. The graph in Figure 13.14 shows the displacement y of the molecules against distance x at some instant of time. Positive displacement means motion to the right and negative displacement motion to the left. The red arrows represent the displacement of the molecules. Molecules at $x = 0$, 2.0 cm and 4.0 cm have not moved ($y = 0$); those between $x = 0$ and 2.0 cm and between $x = 4.0$ cm and 5.0 cm have moved to the right ($y > 0$); and those between $x = 2.0$ cm and 4.0 cm have moved to the left ($y < 0$).

Below the graph in Figure 13.14 is a row of the medium molecules shown in their equilibrium positions; these are the positions of the molecules when no wave travels in the medium. The row below shows their positions when the wave is present.

The molecule at $x = 2.0$ cm is, therefore, at the centre of a **compression** (a region of higher than normal density), while that at $x = 4.0$ cm is at the centre of a **rarefaction** (a region of lower than normal density).

> **EXAM TIP**
>
> You cannot tell whether a wave is transverse or longitudinal by looking at displacement–distance or displacement–time graphs. The graphs look the same for both.

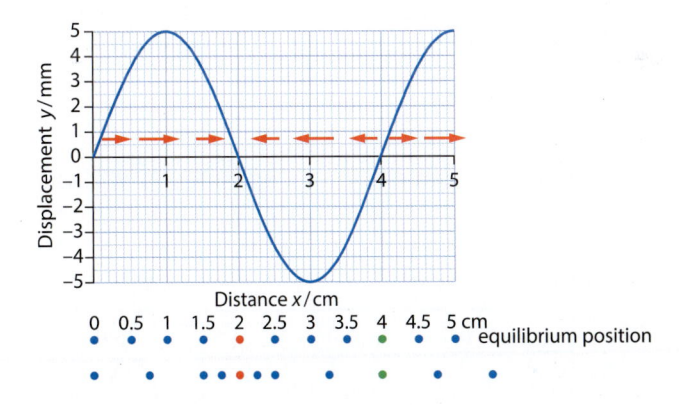

Figure 13.14: Molecules to the left of that at $x = 2.0$ cm move to the right, while the neighbours to the right move left. This means that the region at $x = 2.0$ cm is the centre of a compression. At $x = 4.0$ cm we have the centre of a rarefaction.

Since a compression is a region where molecules crowd together, the pressure and density of the medium in a compression is higher than normal. To give an idea of the differences in pressure involved, a sound of frequency 1000 Hz can be heard by the human ear when the pressure of air at the eardrum exceeds atmospheric pressure by just 20 μPa. (Normal atmospheric pressure is 10^5 Pa.) The amplitude of oscillations for air molecules under these conditions is about 10^{-11} m, or a tenth of the diameter of the hydrogen atom! In a rarefaction the reverse is true, with the molecules moving farther apart so that the density and pressure are a bit less than normal.

293

CHECK YOURSELF 3

Figure 13.15 shows, at a particular instant, a longitudinal wave travelling towards the left. A point in the medium is marked.

Figure 13.15: For check yourself question 3.

What is the direction of velocity of the marked particle at this instant?

WORKED EXAMPLE 13.5

The solid line in Figure 13.16 shows a wave travelling to the right and the dashed line shows the wave 5.0 ms later (the period of the wave is longer than 5.0 ms).

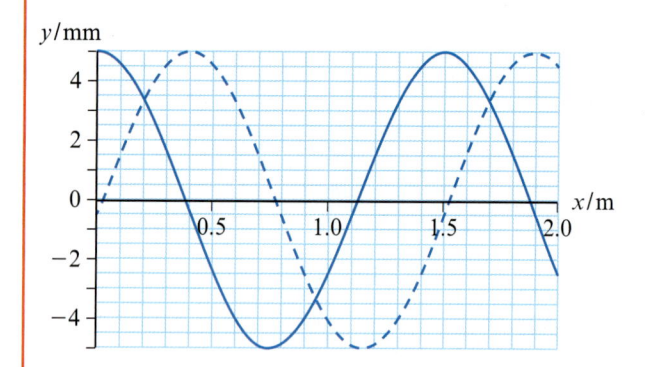

Figure 13.16: For worked example 13.5.

Determine the speed and frequency of the wave.

Answer

In 5.0 ms crests moved forward 0.40 m and so the speed is $v = \frac{0.40}{5.0 \times 10^{-3}} = 80 \text{ m s}^{-1}$.

The wavelength is 1.5 m and so the frequency is $f = \frac{80}{1.5} \approx 53 \text{ Hz}$.

Phase difference

In Chapter 12 we defined the phase difference in the context of simple harmonic motion. There we had two graphs of displacement versus time for the same oscillation. We defined phase difference as

$$\Delta\phi = 2\pi \frac{\Delta t}{T}$$

where T is the period and Δt is the time separating two consecutive peaks. With waves we will be mainly interested in the phase difference between two identical waves travelling in the same medium or two points on the same wave. Figure 13.17 shows two identical waves travelling in the same medium. The phase difference between two waves is defined as

$$\Delta\phi = 2\pi \frac{\Delta x}{\lambda}$$

where Δx is the distance between consecutive peaks of the waves and λ is the wavelength. For the waves in Figure 13.17 we find a phase difference of

$$\Delta\phi = 2\pi \frac{1.0}{4.0} = \frac{\pi}{2}$$

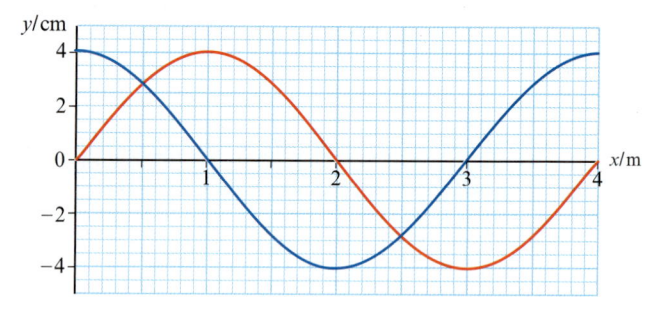

Figure 13.17: Two identical waves in the same medium with a phase difference.

The same formula can also be used to find the phase difference between two different points on the *same* wave. In that case Δx is the distance between the two points. So consider the blue wave in Figure 13.17. The phase difference between the point at $x = 0$ and the point at $x = 2$ cm is $\Delta\phi = 2\pi \frac{2.0}{4.0} = \pi$. We can see that the phase difference increases as we move away from $x = 0$. By the time we get one wavelength away, at $x = 4$ cm, the phase difference is $\Delta\phi = 2\pi \frac{4.0}{4.0} = 2\pi$, i.e. no difference at all since phase difference is an angle. (This holds for travelling waves; we will see a *different* behaviour of phase difference when we discuss standing waves in Chapter 15.)

13 The wave model

> **NATURE OF SCIENCE**
>
> Careful observations of the vibrations of a plucked violin string led the Swiss mathematician Daniel Bernoulli to find a way to describe the oscillation using mathematics. This was a simple setting—a single string fixed at both ends—and led to a simple solution. Scientists found similar patterns in more complex oscillations and waves in the natural world, but also differences in the way that waves propagated. By looking for trends and discrepancies in their models for different waves produced under different conditions, scientists developed wave equations that apply across many areas of physics.

TEST YOUR UNDERSTANDING

8 Figure 13.18 shows three points on a string on which a transverse wave propagates to the right.

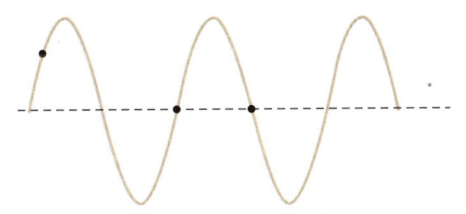

Figure 13.18: For question 8.

a What do you understand by the term transverse wave?

b Indicate how these three points will move in the next instant of time.

c How would your answers change if the wave were moving to the left?

9 The graph (Figure 13.19) shows, at an instant of time, a longitudinal wave travelling to the right. Displacements to the right are positive.

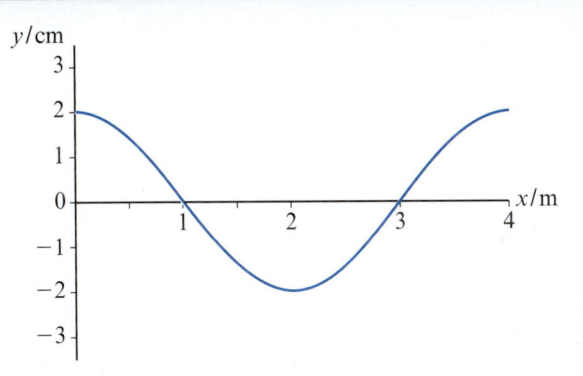

Figure 13.19: For question 9.

a What do you understand by the term longitudinal wave?

b On the graph, draw arrows to represent the velocity of points in the medium whose equilibrium positions are at $x = 1.0$ m and $x = 3.0$ m.

PHYSICS FOR THE IB DIPLOMA: COURSEBOOK

CONTINUED

10 Figure 13.20 shows a piece of cork floating on the surface of water when a wave travels through the water to the right. What is the shape of the water surface half a wave period later? What is the position of the cork then?

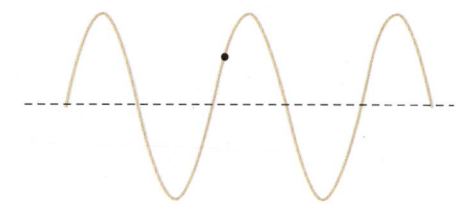

Figure 13.20: For question 10.

11 The solid graph of Figure 13.21 shows the variation with distance of the displacement of a wave travelling to the right. The dashed graph shows the same wave 1.25 ms later.

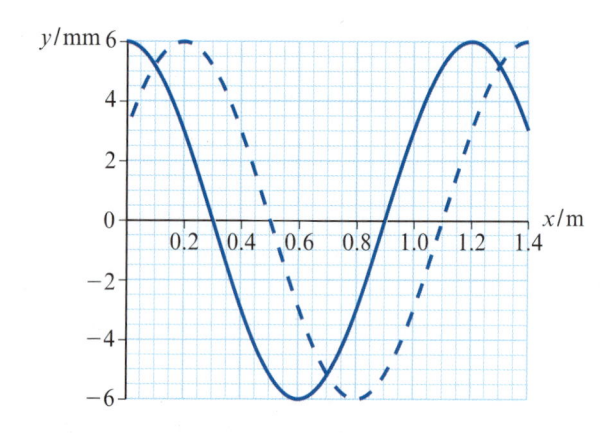

Figure 13.21: For question 11.

Determine, for this wave:

a the speed

b the frequency.

12 Two waves are emitted from the same point and arrive at an observer 4.2 s apart. The waves have speeds 3.4 km s^{-1} and 8.0 km s^{-1}. How far away was the emission point?

13 Figure 13.22 shows a transverse wave at a particular instant of time. The wave is travelling to the right.

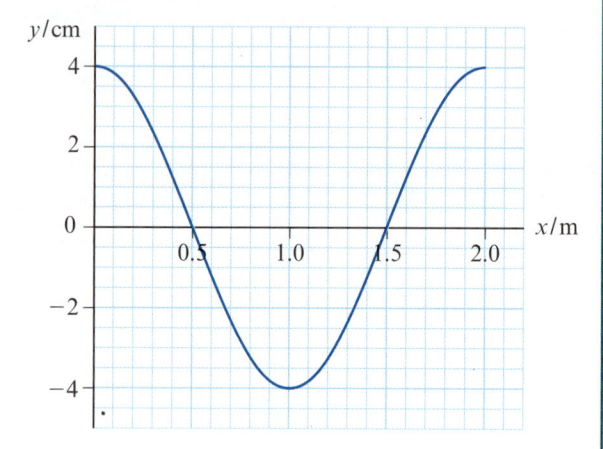

Figure 13.22: For question 13.

At this instant, for the particle in the medium whose equilibrium position is at $x = 0.50$ m,

a Explain why the speed is a maximum.

b Draw an arrow on the graph to indicate the direction of the velocity.

c State the value of the acceleration.

d Label one point whose acceleration is positive and maximum.

e What is the phase difference between the points at $x = 0.5$ m and $x = 1.5$ m?

14 Figure 13.23a shows the displacement d of the particles in a medium against position x when a longitudinal wave pulse travels through the medium from left to right with speed 2.0 cm s^{-1}. This is the displacement at $t = 0$.

Figure 13.23b shows a line of nine molecules separated by 1.0 cm. The positions shown are the equilibrium positions of the molecules when no wave travels in the medium.

296

CONTINUED

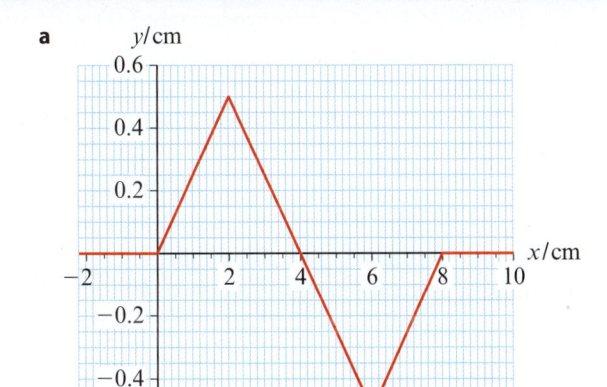

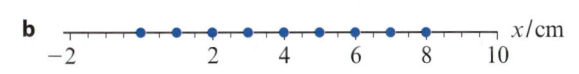

Figure 13.23: For question 14.

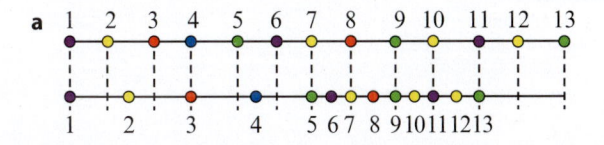

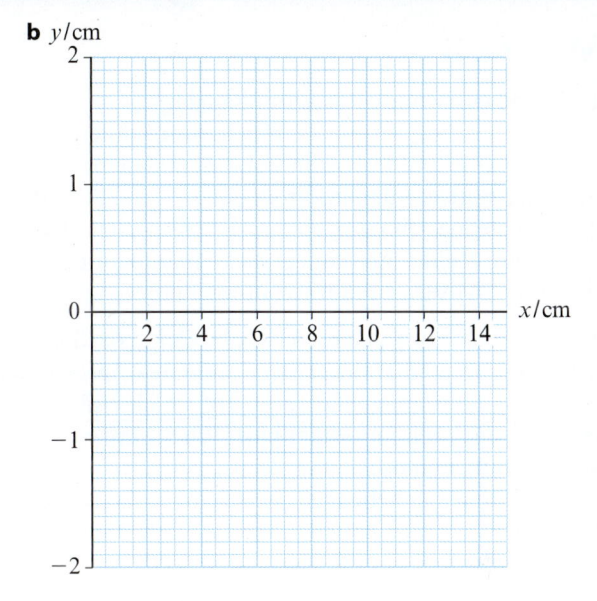

Figure 13.24: For question 15.

a State what is meant by a *longitudinal wave pulse*.

b i Copy the horizontal axis from Figure 13.23b. Immediately below the copied axis draw another line to show the position of these molecules at $t = 0$.

   ii Indicate on the diagram the position of a compression.

c i Repeat **b i** to show the position of these molecules at $t = 2.0$ s.

   ii Comment on the position of the compression at 2.0 s.

15 Figure 13.24a shows the equilibrium positions of molecules in a medium, numbered 1 to 13. At equilibrium they are separated by 1 cm. A wave pulse travels through a medium.

Figure 13.24a also shows the positions of the 13 molecules at $t = 0$. The equilibrium position of the first molecule is at $x = 0$.

a Copy the axes (Figure 13.24b) and draw the shape of the pulse at $t = 0$. Take displacements to the right to be positive.

b The pulse moves to the right with speed 20 cm s^{-1}. On the same axes draw the shape of the pulse at $t = 0.1$ s.

16 Figure 13.25 shows the variation with distance x of the displacement y of air molecules as a sound wave travels to the right through air.

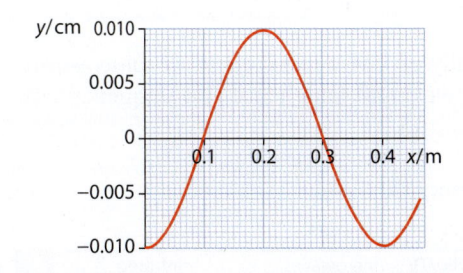

Figure 13.25: For question 16.

Positive displacement means motion to the right. The speed of sound in air is 340 m s^{-1}.

a Determine the frequency of the sound wave.

b State a distance x at which **i** a compression and **ii** a rarefaction occurs.

13.3 Electromagnetic waves

Each and every one of us is irradiated by **electromagnetic (EM) waves** from a lots of different sources: radio and television stations, mobile phones and base station antennas, from doctors' and dentists' X-ray machines, the sun, computer screens, light bulbs and so on. Unlike mechanical waves that require a medium, EM waves can travel in vacuum.

It was the towering achievement of J.C. Maxwell in the mid-1800s to predict the existence of a new, special kind of wave—electromagnetic waves—of which visible light is a very small but important part. What Maxwell showed is that an oscillating electric field produces an oscillating magnetic field (see Chapters 18–20) such that the two are at right angles to each other and both propagate in space at the speed of light (Figure 13.26).

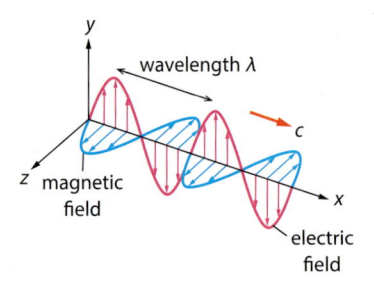

Figure 13.26: An EM wave propagating along the direction of the x-axis. The electric and magnetic fields are in phase, i.e. they have matching crests, troughs and zeroes. The two fields are at right angles to each other at all times.

What all EM waves have in common is that they move at the speed of light in a vacuum. That speed is (exactly) $c = 299\,792\,458 \text{ m s}^{-1}$ or approximately $3.00 \times 10^8 \text{ m s}^{-1}$. According to Einstein's relativity theory this is the limiting speed for anything moving through space. Maxwell's theory predicts that the speed of light is not affected by the speed of its source—a very curious fact. Einstein used this fact as one of the building blocks of his theory of relativity.

Since both the electric and the magnetic field making up the EM wave are at right angles to the direction of energy transfer of the wave, EM waves are transverse.

Electromagnetic waves are produced when electric charges accelerate or during transitions in molecular, atomic or nuclear energy levels (see Chapters 21–25).

CHECK YOURSELF 4

State two differences between an electromagnetic wave and a sound wave.

WORKED EXAMPLE 13.6

A radio station emits at a frequency of 90.8 MHz. What is the wavelength of the waves emitted?

Answer

The waves emitted are electromagnetic waves and move at the speed of light ($3 \times 10^8 \text{ m s}^{-1}$). Therefore, from $c = f\lambda$ we find $\lambda = 3.3$ m.

The huge family of EM waves consists of many waves of different wavelength (and hence also frequency), as shown in Figure 13.27.

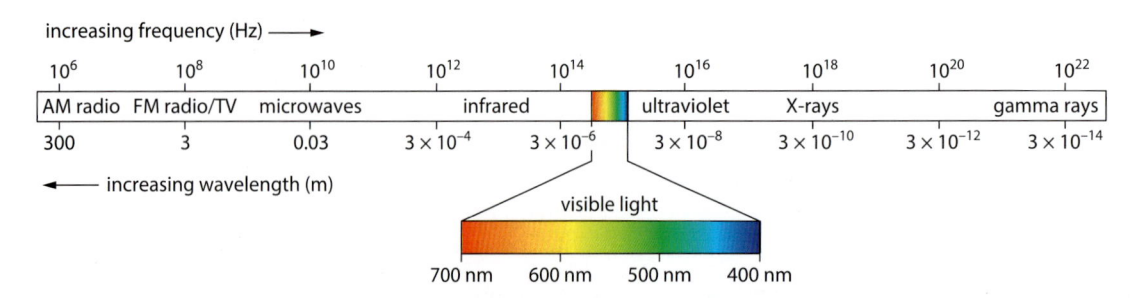

Figure 13.27: The electromagnetic spectrum.

13 The wave model

Links

In mechanical waves a medium is always required for the wave to propagate through. In that case the displacement of the wave is the actual displacement of the particles of the medium which perform simple harmonic oscillations about their equilibrium positions. By definition, then, a mechanical wave cannot travel in vacuum. An electromagnetic wave can because the displacement in this case is not that of a material object but rather the oscillation of something much more abstract: a field. Specifically, electric and magnetic fields. We will discuss fields in detail in Unit D.

TEST YOUR UNDERSTANDING

17 Give *one* example that shows that EM waves carry energy.

18 Explain why we call EM waves transverse.

19 Recall Wien's law from Chapter 7.3. The universe is filled with EM waves at a temperature of 2.7 K. What part of the EM spectrum do these waves belong to?

20 The distance between the earth and the sun is 1.5×10^{11} m. How long does light take to travel to earth from the sun?

13.4 Waves extension

Gravitational waves

Einstein presented his general theory of relativity in 1915. This was a revolutionary theory that replaced Newton's theory of gravitation and predicts and explains new phenomena that Newton's theory cannot. The basic ingredient of the theory is that the presence of matter curves the space in which the matter finds itself. One prediction of the theory is that a new kind of wave should exist: gravitational or gravity waves. (The history around gravity waves, including Einstein's own involvement in it, is absolutely fascinating, and you may want to find out more about it.) These waves would be generated whenever very large masses such as neutron stars and black holes collide with each other. Like electromagnetic waves, gravity waves are transverse and travel at the speed of light. The passage of a gravity wave through space distorts space, stretching and compressing it. So if a gravity wave were to travel into the plane of this paper where a ring is placed, the ring would oscillate as shown in Figure 13.28.

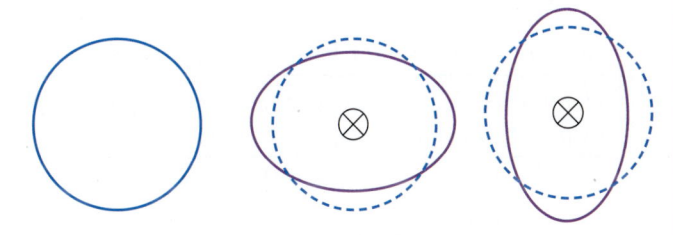

Figure 13.28: A gravity wave moving into the page would make a ring oscillate as shown.

The scale in the diagram is greatly exaggerated. The displacement in either direction for a 1 m diameter ring is typically of the order of 10^{-21} m! This explains why it has been so difficult to detect these waves. Success came in 2015 by LIGO (the Laser Interferometry Gravitational wave Observatory) in the United States. The group detected gravity waves that originated in the collision of two black holes of mass 29 and 36 solar masses some 1.3 billion light years away. Indirect evidence for gravity waves was observed earlier, in 1974, by Hulse and Taylor in the study of a binary pulsar star system: the two stars orbiting each other were losing energy by radiating gravity waves and so their period of revolution around each other was changing; this was measured. The change in period was consistent with gravity waves being emitted.

Matter waves

Quantum theory demands that all particles have wave properties. The waves corresponding to particles are called matter waves. These are waves of probability: the displacement of the wave is related to the probability of finding a particle near a particular position. Details about these waves can be found in Chapters 21–25.

PHYSICS FOR THE IB DIPLOMA: COURSEBOOK

SELF-ASSESSMENT CHECKLIST

I am able to …	Section	Not yet	Nearly there	Ready to move on
explain what a wave is	13.1			
solve problems with the basic wave equation $v = f\lambda$	13.1			
identify wavelength, frequency and period from graphs of displacement against distance or time	13.2			
describe the motion of a particle in a medium through which a wave travels	13.2			
understand the difference between transverse and longitudinal waves	13.2			
describe the nature of a sound wave	13.2			
describe what an electromagnetic wave is	13.3			

REFLECTION

Can you describe what a *travelling wave* is? Do you know what information a graph of displacement versus distance gives? Do you know what information a graph of displacement versus time gives? Do you understand the connection between wave motion and simple harmonic oscillations? Do you understand the difference between a *transverse* and a *longitudinal* wave? Can you predict the displacement from equilibrium of a particle in a medium when a wave travels through? Can you describe an *electromagnetic wave*?

EXAM-STYLE QUESTIONS

You can find questions in the style of IB exams in the digital coursebook.

CHECK YOURSELF ANSWERS

1. The medium is the same so the speed is unchanged. If frequency doubles the wavelength halves.
2. Vertically up.
3. To the right.
4. EM waves can travel in vacuum; sound cannot. EM waves are transverse; sound is longitudinal.

Chapter 14
Wave phenomena

LEARNING OBJECTIVES

In this chapter you will learn how to:
- identify wavefronts and rays
- apply the laws of reflection and refraction
- apply the principle of superposition
- qualitatively describe diffraction, the spreading of a wave through openings and past obstacles
- understand the phenomenon of interference from two sources
- understand Young's two-slit experiment
- identify the effect of the slit width and of the wavelength on the single slit diffraction pattern

> **CONTINUED**
>
> > describe how the single-slit diffraction pattern modulates the two-slit intensity pattern
> >
> > describe the changes in the interference pattern as the number of slits increases
> >
> > solve problems with the diffraction grating equation

> **GUIDING QUESTION**
>
> What do interference and diffraction tell us about the nature of light?

Introduction

This chapter introduces the basic phenomena identified with waves: reflection, refraction, diffraction, superposition and interference.

We shall see behavior that we are not used to from mechanics:

Two tennis balls colliding cannot pass through each other; they will bounce. But two waves *can* pass through each other.

Two tennis balls cannot meet at a point and disappear; but two waves can.

In the AHL section of this chapter, we will discuss the spreading of a wave through a slit and study the effect of the slit width on the interference pattern of many slits.

14.1 Reflection and refraction

This section deals with ways to describe waves and the phenomena of reflection and refraction.

Wavefronts and rays

Imagine waves on the surface of water approaching the shore (Figure 14.1). These waves are propagating in a horizontal direction. Imagine planes going through the crests of the waves; the planes will be normal to the direction of the wave. These planes are called **wavefronts**. Lines at right angles to the wavefronts show the direction of wave propagation—these are called **rays**.

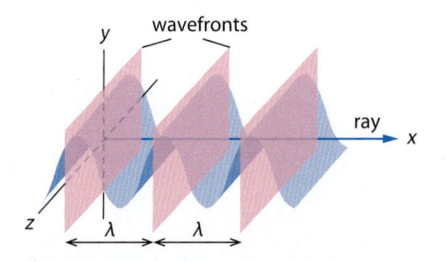

Figure 14.1: Surfaces through crests and normal to the direction of energy propagation of the wave are called wavefronts. Rays are mathematical lines perpendicular to the wavefronts and give the direction of energy transfer.

Now imagine the waves on the surface of water caused by a stone dropped in a pool of water. These waves radiate out across the water surface from the point of impact. In this case the wavefronts are cylindrical surfaces (Figure 14.2a).

A point source emits waves in all directions. The wavefronts from a point source are spherical (Figure 14.2b).

14 Wave phenomena

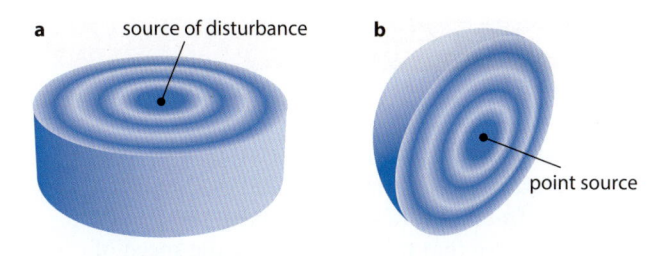

Figure 14.2: Example of cylindrical and spherical wavefronts. **a** The cylinders go through the crests and are normal to the plane of the paper. **b** The wavefronts from a point source radiate in all directions. For clarity, only half of each spherical wavefront is shown.

Reflection

This is an everyday phenomenon: you can see your reflection in a mirror, and the reflection of the blue sky in sea water makes the water look blue.

The **law of reflection** states that the angle of incidence i (angle between the ray and the normal to the reflecting surface at the point of incidence) is equal to the angle of reflection r (angle between the normal and the reflected ray).

The reflected and incident rays and the normal to the surface lie on the same plane, called the plane of incidence.

The ray diagrams in Figure 14.3 illustrate reflection from a plane surface.

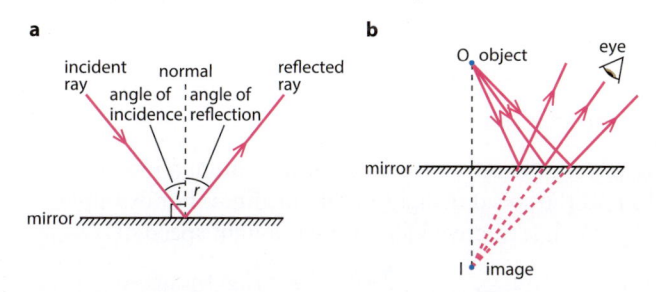

Figure 14.3: a Reflection at a plane (flat) surface. **b** The position of an image seen in a plane mirror.

Reflection takes place when the reflecting surface is sufficiently smooth. This means that the wavelength of the incident wave has to be larger than the size of any irregularities of the surface. The wavelength of the reflected waves is the same as that of the incident wave.

Refraction

Light travels with a velocity of 3.0×10^8 m s^{-1} in a vacuum. In all other media, the velocity of light is smaller. Refraction is the phenomenon of the passage of light or any other wave from one medium into another where it has a different speed. Refraction changes the direction of the incident ray (unless the incident ray is normal to the boundary of the two media).

When a ray strikes an interface between two media, there is both reflection and refraction. The top three diagrams in Figure 14.4 show the case when a wave enters a medium where the speed of the wave is lower. In this case the ray bends towards the normal. The parts of the wavefronts that have reached the interface are shown in blue. The lower three diagram show the reverse case where the wave enters a medium where the speed is higher. The ray bends away from the normal.

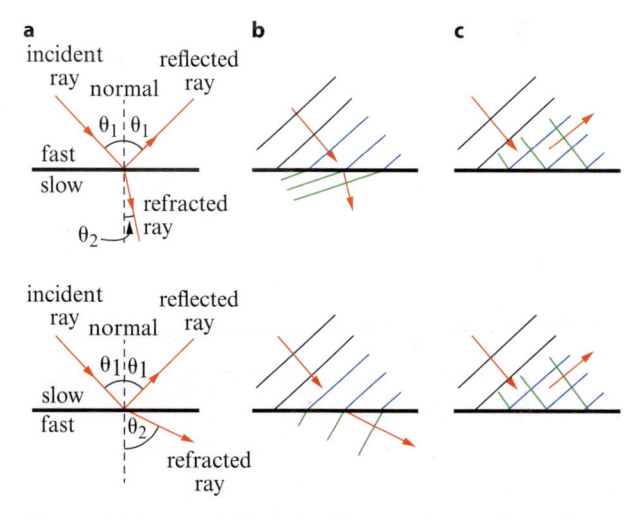

Figure 14.4: A ray of light incident on the interface of two media partly reflects and partly refracts. The top three diagrams show the case of a wave that enters a medium where the speed is lower. In the lower three diagrams the wave enters a medium where the wave speed is higher. **a** Ray diagram. **b** Wavefront diagram for refraction. **c** Wavefront diagram for reflection. The angle between a ray and the normal is the same as that between a wavefront and the surface.

The frequency cannot change as the wave moves into the second medium: imagine an observer right at the boundary of the two media. The frequency can be found from the number of wavefronts that cross the interface per second. This number is the same for both media. So, since the frequency does not change but the speed does, it follows that in refraction the wavelength changes.

303

> **CHECK YOURSELF 1**
>
> Light of wavelength 656 nm in air enters glass where the speed of light is 2.0×10^8 m s^{-1}. What is the wavelength of the light in glass?

WORKED EXAMPLE 14.1

Light of wavelength 686 nm in air enters water where the speed of light is 2.3×10^8 m s^{-1}, making an angle of 40° with the normal. Determine:

a if the angle of refraction will be greater or smaller than 40°

b the wavelength of light in water.

Explain your working.

Answer

a The wave has a lower speed in water so the ray will bend towards the normal so the angle of refraction will be less than 40°.

b The frequency in air is $f = \frac{c}{\lambda}$ where λ is the wavelength in air. The frequency in water is the same. Therefore $\frac{c}{\lambda} = \frac{c_w}{\lambda_w}$ and so $\lambda_w = \frac{c_w}{c}\lambda = \frac{2.3 \times 10^8}{3.0 \times 10^8} \times 686 = 526$ nm.

WORKED EXAMPLE 14.2

The paths of rays of red and violet light passing through a glass prism are as shown in Figure 14.5.

Discuss what can be deduced about the speed of light in glass for red and violet light.

Figure 14.5: For worked example 14.2.

CONTINUED

Answer

Considering the first refraction when the rays first enter the glass, we see that violet makes a smaller angle of refraction (draw the normal at the point of incidence to see that this is so). Hence the speed of light for violet in glass must be less than that for red.

Snell's law

There is a relation between the angle of incidence and the angle of refraction known as Snell's law. It states that (see Figure 14.4)

$$\frac{\sin \theta_1}{c_1} = \frac{\sin \theta_2}{c_2}$$

where c_1 is the speed of the wave in medium 1 and c_2 that in medium 2. So revisiting worked example 14.1, the angle of refraction is found from:

$$\frac{\sin 40°}{3.0 \times 10^8} = \frac{\sin \theta_2}{2.3 \times 10^8} \Rightarrow \sin \theta_2 = \frac{2.3 \times 10^8}{3.0 \times 10^8} \times \sin 40° = 0.493 \Rightarrow \theta_2 \approx 30°$$

If we multiply both sides of Snell's equation by c, the speed of light in vacuum, we get

$$\frac{c}{c_1}\sin \theta_1 = \frac{c}{c_2}\sin \theta_2$$

We then define the ratio $\frac{c}{c_1}$ to be the refractive index n_1 of medium 1 and $\frac{c}{c_2}$ to be the refractive index n_2 of medium 2. So, in terms of the refractive indices Snell's law for light can be written as

$$n_1 \sin \theta_1 = n_2 \sin \theta_2$$

Knowing the refractive index of a medium allows us to find the speed of light in that medium. For example, glass with refractive index 1.5 has a light speed of

$$1.5 = \frac{3.0 \times 10^8}{c_{glass}} \Rightarrow c_{glass} = \frac{3.0 \times 10^8}{1.5} = 2.0 \times 10^8 \text{ m s}^{-1}.$$

Consider light of wavelength $\lambda = 600$ nm in air that enters glass of refractive index 1.5. The frequency will stay the same but the speed will change and so the wavelength will change as well:

$$f = \frac{c}{\lambda} = \frac{c_{glass}}{\lambda_{glass}}$$

This can be rewritten as

$$\frac{c}{c_{glass}} = \frac{\lambda}{\lambda_{glass}}, \text{ i.e. } n_{glass} = \frac{\lambda}{\lambda_{glass}} \text{ and so } \lambda_{glass} = \frac{\lambda}{n_{glass}} = \frac{600}{1.5} = 400 \text{ nm}.$$

14 Wave phenomena

SCIENCE IN CONTEXT

Total internal reflection

An interesting phenomenon occurs when a wave moving in an optically dense medium arrives at the interface with a less dense medium, for example light in water reaching the boundary with air. Some light is reflected at the boundary and some light is refracted. As shown in Figure 14.6a, the angle of refraction is greater than the angle of incidence. As the angle of incidence increases the angle of refraction eventually reaches 90°, as shown in Figure 14.6b. The angle of incidence for which the angle of refraction is 90° is called the critical angle.

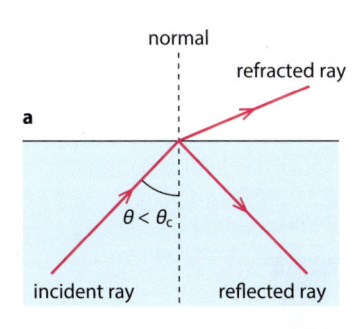

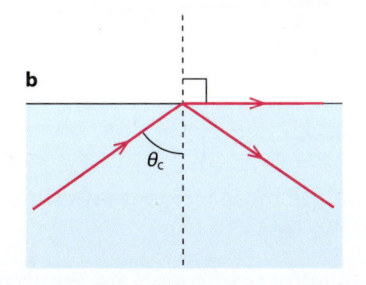

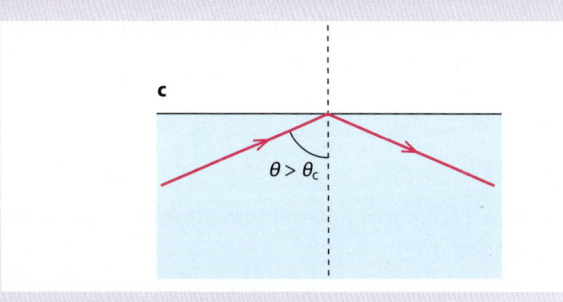

Figure 14.6: Total internal reflection occurs when the angle of incidence is greater than the critical angle.

As shown in Figure 14.6c there is no refracted ray when the angle of incidence is greater than the critical angle; there is just the reflected ray, and so we call this phenomenon **total internal reflection**.

One of the great modern applications of total internal reflection is the propagation of digital signals carrying coded information securely in optical fibres. The signal stays within the core, as shown in Figure 14.7. This means that the signal can travel large distances without much loss of energy and so does not require frequent amplification. The signal suffers little distortion which means the transmitted signal is of high quality.

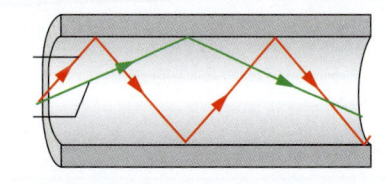

Figure 14.7: Laser light carrying coded information travels down the length of the optical fibre in a sequence of total internal reflections.

THEORY OF KNOWLEDGE

It can be shown that the path followed by light as it moves from one medium into another is such so as to minimize the time taken. In other words, light follows a path of *least time*. This principle was formulated in 1662 by Pierre Fermat. The principle was developed further by Joseph Louis Lagrange in the eighteenth century and has led to a new formulation of classical mechanics that could be used to describe quantum theory two centuries later. The principle of least time immediately raised the question: how does light "know" what is the path of least time without sampling the time taken for all other paths? The resolution of this conundrum came later when it was firmly established that light is a wave.

PHYSICS FOR THE IB DIPLOMA: COURSEBOOK

TEST YOUR UNDERSTANDING

1. In the context of wave motion, explain, with the aid of a diagram, the terms:

    a wavefront

    b ray.

2. Figure 14.8 shows planar wavefronts incident on a surface.

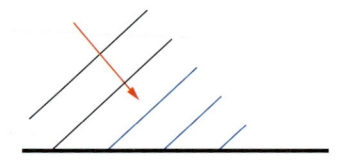

    Figure 14.8: For question 2.

    Complete the wavefronts in blue to show reflected wavefronts. (Keep the length of the wavefront the same as the wavefronts in black.)

3. Figure 14.9 shows planar wavefronts incident on the boundary of two media. The wave speed in each medium is shown.

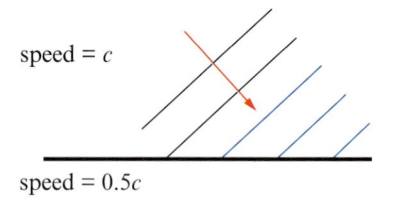

    speed = c

    speed = $0.5c$

    Figure 14.9: For question 3.

    Complete the wavefronts in blue to show refracted wavefronts. (Keep the length of the wavefront the same as the wavefronts in black.)

4. Figure 14.10 shows planar wavefronts incident on the boundary of two media. The wave speed in each medium is shown.

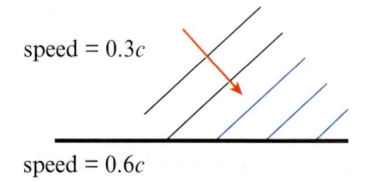

    speed = $0.3c$

    speed = $0.6c$

    Figure 14.10: For question 4.

    Complete the wavefronts in blue to show refracted wavefronts. (Keep the length of the wavefront the same as the wavefronts in black.)

    Figure 14.11 shows rays of light going through a converging lens.

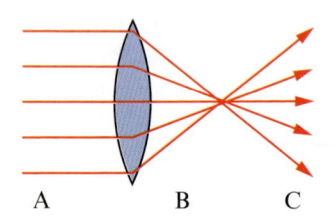

    A B C

    Figure 14.11: For question 5.

5. Draw a wavefront in each region A, B and C.

6. Figure 14.12 shows wavefronts after they have gone through a diverging lens.

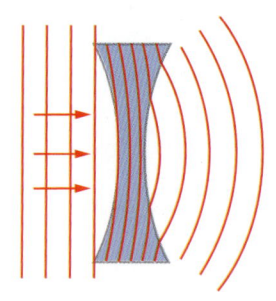

    Figure 14.12: For question 6.

    Continue the three incident rays shown to the right of the lens.

7. Plane wavefronts of sound are approaching land from the sea, as shown in Figure 14.13.

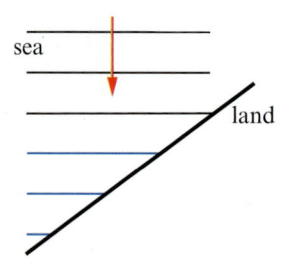

    sea

    land

    Figure 14.13: For question 7.

CONTINUED

On a hot summer day, the temperature over land is greater than the temperature over the water. Suggest how the wavefronts in blue move over land. Explain your reasoning.

8 Light of frequency 6.0×10^{14} Hz is emitted from point A and is directed towards point B a distance of 3.0 m away. The light will travel 1.5 m in a vacuum and 1.5 m in glass where the speed of light is 2.0×10^8 m s^{-1}. (See Figure 14.14.)

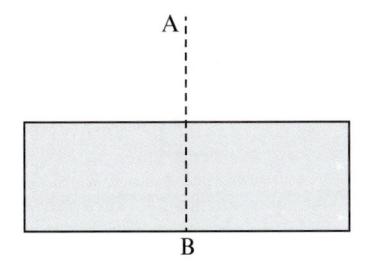

Figure 14.14: For question 8.

a Determine how long it will take light to get to **B**.

b Calculate how many full waves fit in the space between **A** and **B**.

c Draw three wavefronts in the vacuum and three in the glass.

9 Figure 14.15 shows an electromagnetic wave travelling in a vacuum until x = 2.

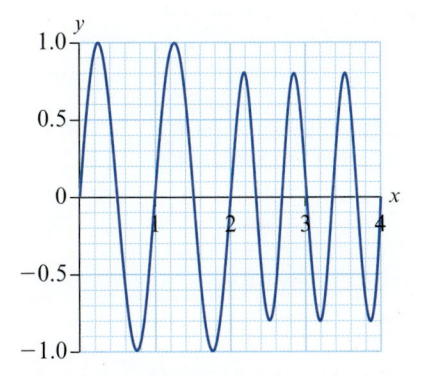

Figure 14.15: For question 9.

At x = 2 the wave enters a new medium. What is the speed of light in the new medium? (Units on both axes are arbitrary.)

10 Describe what is meant by total internal reflection. Describe one application of total internal reflection.

11 A ray of light of wavelength 680 nm is travelling in a medium X where the refractive index is 1.20 and enters a medium Y of refractive index 1.80. The ray makes an angle of 35° with the normal at the boundary. Calculate:

a the angle of refraction

b the wavelength of the light in Y.

c A ray moving in Y enters X making an angle of 32° with the normal. What is the angle of refraction?

d What is the critical angle for a ray moving from Y to X?

12 A ray of light is incident on a rectangular block of glass of refractive index 1.45 at an angle of 40°, as shown in Figure 14.16.

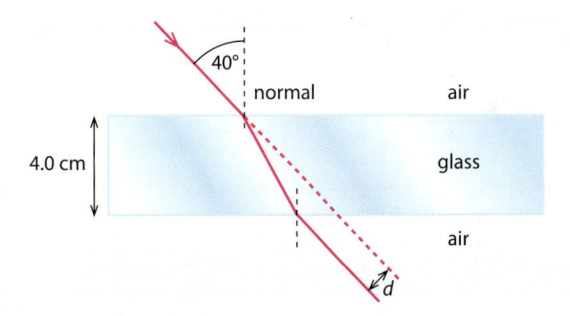

Figure 14.16: For question 12.

The thickness of the block is 4.00 cm.

a Explain why the ray that exits the glass is parallel to the initial ray incident on the glass.

b Calculate the distance d by which the ray gets deviated.

14.2 The principle of superposition

Suppose that two pulses are produced in the same rope and are travelling towards each other from opposite ends. Something amazing happens when the two pulses meet. Figure 14.17 shows what happens in a sequence of pictures. For simplicity we have drawn idealised square pulses.

a

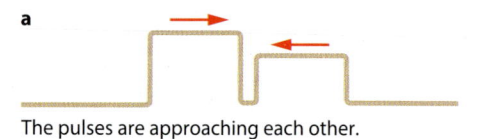

The pulses are approaching each other.

b

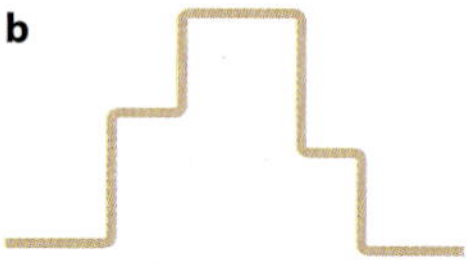

The pulses are beginning to overlap.

c

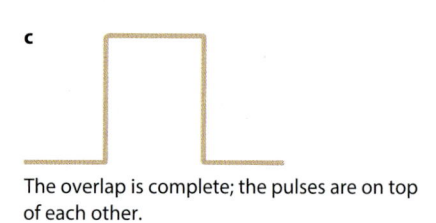

The overlap is complete; the pulses are on top of each other.

d

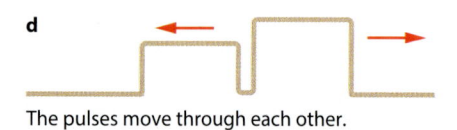

The pulses move through each other.

Figure 14.17: The superposition of two positive pulses.

The disturbance gets bigger when the two pulses meet, but subsequently the two pulses simply 'go through each other' with no 'memory' of what happened. You should contrast this with what happens in the motion of material particles: when two balls collide they bounce off each other.

What happens when two (or more) pulses meet at some point in space is described by the **principle of superposition**.

The principle of superposition states that when two or more waves of the same type arrive at a given point in space at the same time, the displacement of the medium at that point is the *algebraic* sum of the individual displacements.

So, if y_1 and y_2 are individual displacements, then the total displacement has the value:

$y = y_1 + y_2$

Note the word 'algebraic'. This means that if one pulse is 'up' and the other is 'down', then the resulting displacement is the difference of the individual pulses.

Let us look at Figure 14.17b in detail. The two pulses are partially overlapping—Figure 14.18 shows both of them separately (the pulse moving toward the right is drawn in dark blue and the one moving to the left in pale blue). Adding the two pulses according to the principle of superposition gives the shape in Figure 14.18.

Figure 14.18: The situation in Figure 14.17b analysed.

Figure 14.19 shows the superposition of a positive and a negative pulse on the same rope. In Figure 14.19a the positive and negative pulses are approaching each other. In Figure 14.19b the positive and negative pulses momentarily cancel each other out when they totally overlap. The pulses move through each other, and Figure 14.19c shows the positive and negative pulses continuing along the rope.

a

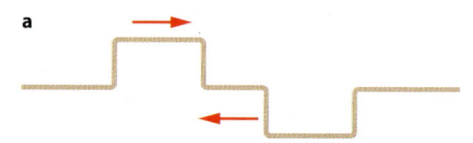

Positive and negative pulses are approaching each other.

b

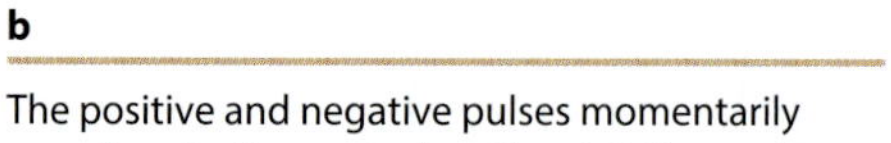

The positive and negative pulses momentarily cancel each other out when they totally overlap.

c

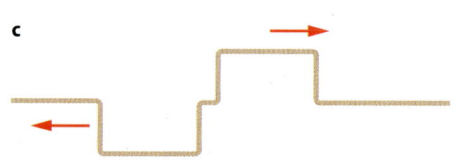

The positive and negative pulses move through each other.

Figure 14.19: The superposition of a positive and a negative pulse.

14 Wave phenomena

> **CHECK YOURSELF 2**
>
> Two identical pulses move towards each other with speed 7.5 cm s^{-1}. Figure 14.20 shows the pulses at $t = 0$. 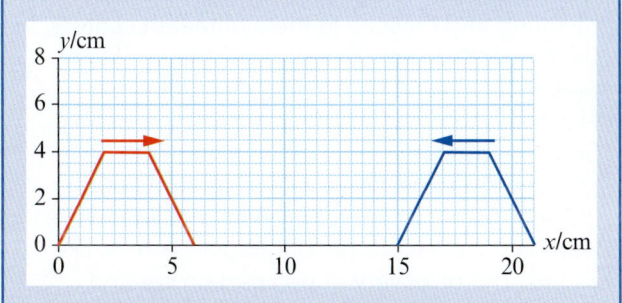
>
> Figure 14.20: For check yourself question 2.
>
> a After what time will the pulses completely overlap?
>
> b Copy Figure 14.20 and add the shape of the pulses at the instant of complete overlap.

Links

Let us consider a simple problem in mechanics. A particle of mass m moving with speed v collides head on with another heavier particle of mass M that is at rest. Applying the laws of conservation of energy and momentum, we can find the velocities of both particles after the collision. Calling the velocity of m, u and that of M, w we find $u = -\frac{M-m}{M+m}v$ and $w = \frac{2m}{M+m}v$. The light particle bounces back and the heavy particle starts moving to the right. But there is another solution with $u = v$ and $w = 0$. In mechanics we reject this solution because it implies that m goes through M leaving M at rest. But the equations are clever. This is what happens with pulses and waves; they go through each other. The equations of mechanics are general enough to allow for this possibility as well.

Reflection of pulses

What happens when a pulse created in a rope with one end fixed approaches that fixed end? Consider the pulse of Figure 14.21a. The instant the pulse hits the fixed end, the rope attempts to move the fixed end upward: that is, it exerts an upward force on the fixed end. By Newton's third law, the wall will then exert an equal but opposite force on the rope. This means that a displacement will be created in the rope that will be negative and will start moving towards the left.

The pulse has been reflected by the wall and has been *inverted*. This is the same as saying that the wave experiences a phase change of 180° when reflected.

If the end of the rope is not fixed but free to move (imagine that the end of the rope is now tied to a ring that can slide up and down a vertical pole), the situation is different (Figure 14.21b). As the pulse arrives at the ring it pulls it upwards. Eventually the ring falls back down and in so doing creates a pulse moving to the left that is not inverted; that is, there is no phase change.

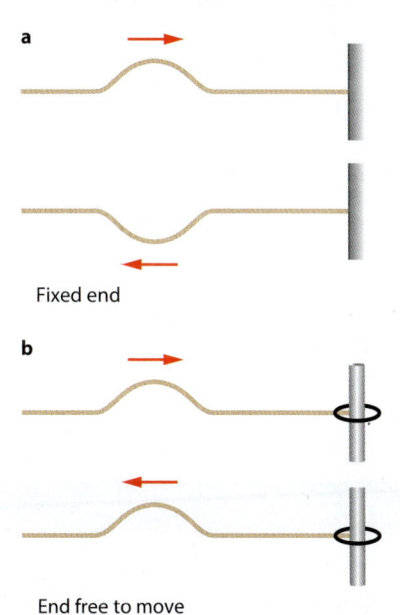

Figure 14.21: Reflection of a pulse from **a** a fixed end and **b** a free end. Notice the inversion in the case of the fixed end.

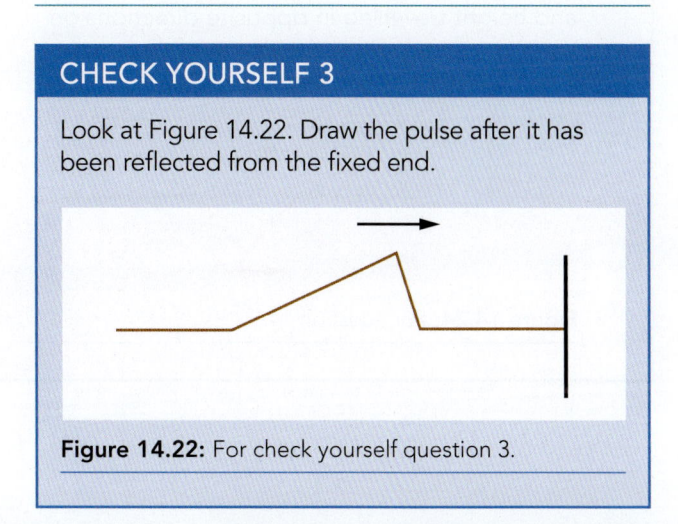

> **CHECK YOURSELF 3**
>
> Look at Figure 14.22. Draw the pulse after it has been reflected from the fixed end.
>
> Figure 14.22: For check yourself question 3.

WORKED EXAMPLE 14.3

Use the results about pulses reflecting from fixed and free ends to predict what happens when:

a a pulse in a heavy rope encounters a light rope (Figure 14.23a)

b a pulse in a light rope encounters a heavy rope (Figure 14.23b).

Figure 14.23: For worked example 14.3.

Answer

a With the light rope to the right, the situation is similar to a pulse in a rope approaching a free end. So the reflected pulse will not be inverted.

b With the heavy rope to the right, the situation is similar to a pulse in a rope approaching a fixed end. So the reflected pulse will be inverted.

Notice that in both cases, there will be a pulse transmitted into the rope to the right.

NATURE OF SCIENCE

Particles or a wave?

The early nineteenth century saw a revival of the wave approach to light, mainly due to the work of Young and Fresnel. In the eighteenth century, the Newtonian view of a particle nature of light prevailed, making research in directions that Newton would not 'approve' almost impossible. So the early researchers of the nineteenth century had to be brave as well as ingenious! It is interesting to note, however, that light waves were first thought to be longitudinal waves, like sound. The discovery of polarisation created enormous difficulties for the supporters of the wave theory because it could not be understood in terms of a longitudinal wave theory of light. It was Young who finally suggested that light was a transverse wave (an idea which Maxwell took much further when he proposed that light was an electromagnetic wave). So the phenomenon of polarisation that helps Monarch butterflies, bees and ants navigate (it may even have helped the Vikings reach Vinland, i.e. North America) is the phenomenon that for the first time introduced light as a transverse wave in physics.

TEST YOUR UNDERSTANDING

13 In Figure 14.19b the two pulses completely cancelled each other out. What happened to the energy carried by each pulse?

14 Figure 14.24 shows two pulses of equal width and height travelling in opposite directions on the same string. Draw the shape of the string when the pulses completely overlap.

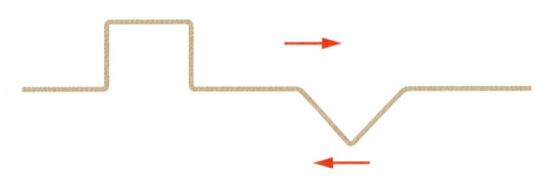

Figure 14.24: For question 14.

15 Figure 14.25 shows two pulses of equal width and height travelling in opposite directions on the same string.
Draw the shape of the string when the pulses completely overlap.

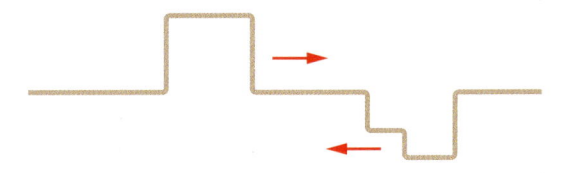

Figure 14.25: For question 15.

CONTINUED

16 The wave pulses shown in Figure 14.26 travel at 1 cm s^{-1}, and both have width 2 cm. The heights are indicated on the diagram. In each case, draw the shape of the resulting pulse according to the principle of superposition at times $t = 0.5$ s, $t = 1.0$ s and $t = 1.5$ s. Take $t = 0$ s to be the time when the pulses are about to meet each other.

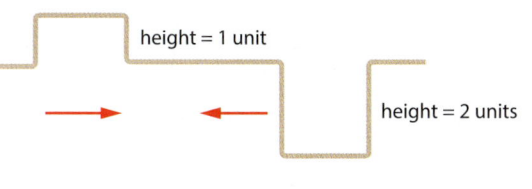

Figure 14.26: For question 16.

17 Two pulses are simultaneously generated on a string. The graph (Figure 14.27) shows the variation of displacement y with distance x. Draw the actual shape of the string.

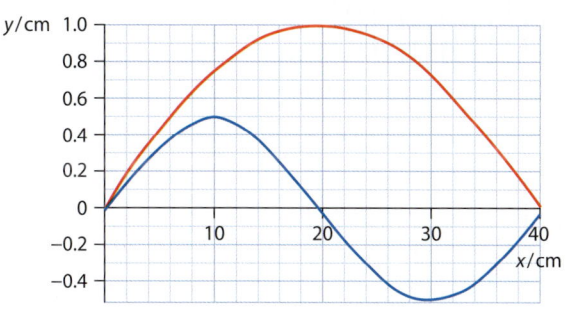

Figure 14.27: For question 17.

14.3 Diffraction and interference

The spreading of a wave as it goes past an obstacle or through an aperture is called **diffraction**. Let us consider a plane wave of wavelength λ moving towards an aperture (Figure 14.28). What will the wavefronts look like after the wave has gone through the aperture? The answer depends on the size of the wavelength compared to the size of the aperture.

In Figure 14.28a the wavelength is small compared to the aperture, so there is little diffraction. In Figure 14.28b the wavelength is similar to the aperture, so there is a lot of diffraction.

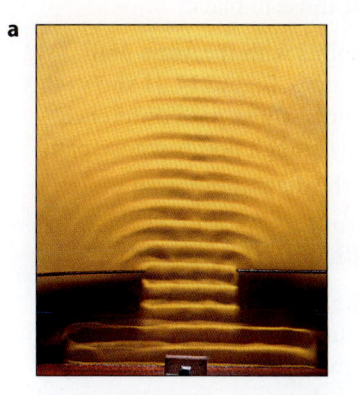

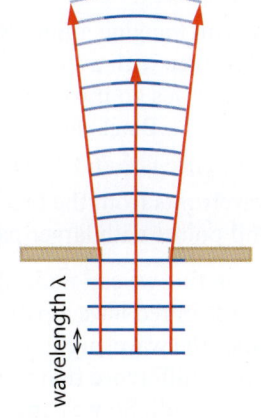

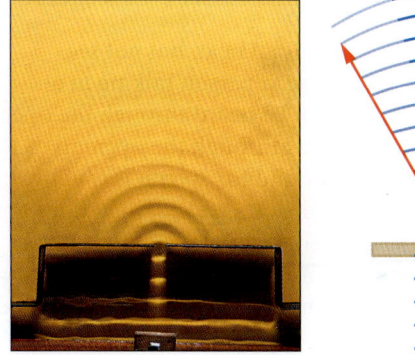

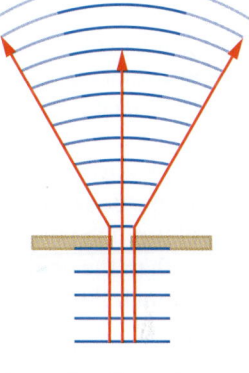

Figure 14.28: Waves in a ripple tank passing through an aperture, demonstrating the principle of diffraction.
a When these waves pass through a large aperture they change shape and form flattened concentric waves centred on the aperture. The amount by which the waves change shape depends on the size of the aperture. Diffraction is greatest when the aperture size is similar to the wavelength. This is seen in **b**, where waves of the same wavelength are passing through a smaller aperture.

> **EXAM TIP**
>
> When you draw diffraction diagrams, make sure that you do not change the distance between the wavefronts.

311

Figure 14.29 shows diffraction around obstacles.

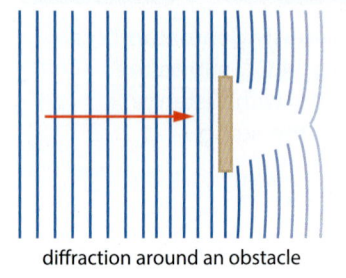

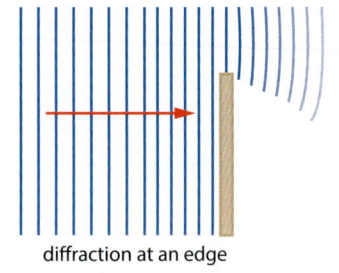

Figure 14.29: Diffraction around obstacles.

Diffraction explains why we can hear, but not see, around corners. For example, a person talking in a corridor outside a room can be heard through the open door because sound diffracts through the opening of the door—the wavelength of sound for speech is roughly the same as the door size. On the other hand, light does not diffract through the door since its wavelength is much smaller than the opening of the door. Hence we can hear through the open door, even though we cannot see the speaker.

Double-source interference

When two identical waves meet at the same point in space, the principle of superposition states that the resulting wave has a displacement that is the sum of the individual displacements. This results in a phenomenon called **interference**: the resulting amplitude can be anything from zero to twice the amplitude of one of the waves. All waves show interference.

Consider two identical sources S_1 and S_2 (Figure 14.30). Wavefronts from the two sources meet at various points. The waves from both sources have the same speed, wavelength, frequency and amplitude. Let us focus on point P. Point P is a distance from source S_1 equal to 2λ and a distance of 3λ from S_2. The **path difference** is the difference in distance of the point from the two sources, $\Delta r = |S_1P - S_2P|$. For P, the path difference is equal to λ. All the points marked red in Figure 14.15 have a path difference that is one wavelength, λ. At point P the waves from both sources arrive as crests. At point Q (the path difference is still λ) the waves arrive as troughs.

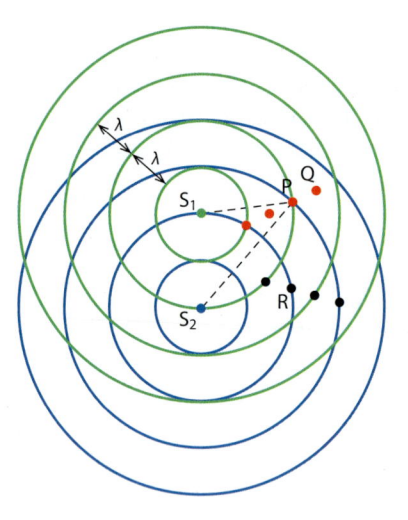

Figure 14.30: Wavefronts from two sources meet and interfere.

In either case, when the individual waves are added (as the principle of superposition says) the resulting wave will have the same wavelength, frequency and speed as the individual waves but double the amplitude. This is true for all the points in red.

Now look at the points marked in black on Figure 14.30. The path difference for all of these points is $\Delta r = \frac{\lambda}{2}$. At point R, the wave from source S_2 arrives as a crest but the wave from S_1 arrives as a trough. When the two waves are added the resulting wave has amplitude zero—the waves cancel each other out and vanish! This is true for all the points in black. We say there is **constructive interference** for the points in red and **destructive interference** for those in black.

We can imagine joining points with the same path difference with a smooth curve. Figure 14.31 shows this. Red curves go through points whose path difference is 0, λ, 2λ. Black curves go through points whose path difference is $\frac{\lambda}{2}$ and $\frac{3\lambda}{2}$. (If the diagram showed more wavefronts from the two sources, we would be able to find points with larger path differences.)

From this we can make the general observation that points in red have a path difference that is an integer times the wavelength, whereas points in black have a path difference that is a half-integer times the wavelength. So we conclude that:

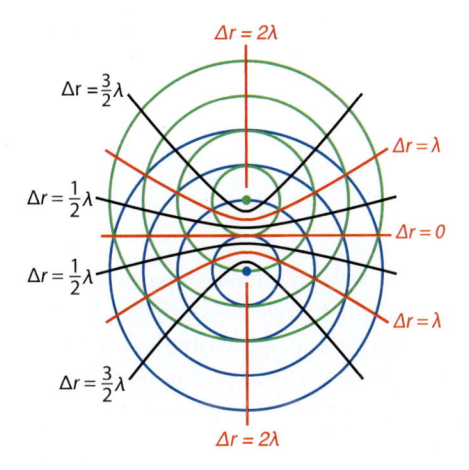

Figure 14.31: Curves in red join points where the path difference is an integral multiple of the wavelength. Curves in black join points with a path difference that is a half integral multiple of the wavelength. (The curves are hyperbolas.)

Constructive interference occurs when the path difference:

$|S_1P - S_2P| = n\lambda$ with $n = 0, 1, 2, 3, \ldots$

Destructive interference occurs when the path difference:

$|S_1P - S_2P| = \left(n + \frac{1}{2}\right)\lambda$ with $n = 0, 1, 2, 3, \ldots$

So, constructive interference occurs when the waves are in phase (meaning the waves meet crest to crest and trough to trough), and destructive interference occurs when they are exactly out of phase (meaning the waves meet crest to trough)—see Figure 14.32.

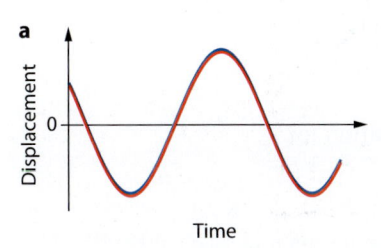

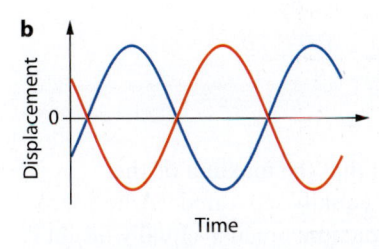

Figure 14.32: Displacement–time curves for waves that interfere **a** constructively and **b** destructively.

> **WORKED EXAMPLE 14.4**
>
> Identical waves leaving two sources arrive at point P. Point P is 12 m from the first source and 16.5 m from the second. The waves from both sources have a wavelength of 3.0 m.
>
> State and explain what is observed at P.
>
> **Answer**
>
> The path difference is 16.5 − 12 = 4.5 m.
>
> Dividing the path difference by the wavelength $\frac{4.5}{3.0} = 1.5$; in other words, the path difference is a half-integral multiple of the wavelength so there is destructive interference.

If the path difference is anything other than an integral or half-integral multiple of the wavelength, then the resultant amplitude of the wave at P will be some value between zero and $2A$, where A is the amplitude of one of the waves.

When sound waves from two sources interfere, points of constructive interference are points of high intensity of sound. Points of destructive interference are points of no sound at all. If the waves involved are light waves, constructive interference produces points of bright light, and destructive interference results in points of darkness. Complete destructive interference takes place only when the two waves have equal amplitudes.

Young's two-slit experiment

Interference for light was first demonstrated in 1801 by Thomas Young, an English polymath who also came very close to deciphering hieroglyphics. This experiment definitively established the wave nature of light. Figure 14.33 shows plane wavefronts of light approaching two extremely thin, parallel, vertical slits. Because of diffraction, the wavefronts spread out from each slit. Wavefronts from the slits arrive on a screen and interfere. At those points on the screen where the path difference is an integral multiple of the wavelength of light constructive interference takes place. The screen looks bright at those points, marked on the diagram as $n = 0, \pm 1, \ldots$. The value of n indicates that the path difference is $n\lambda$. At other points where the path difference is a half-integral multiple of λ, the screen looks dark: we have destructive interference.

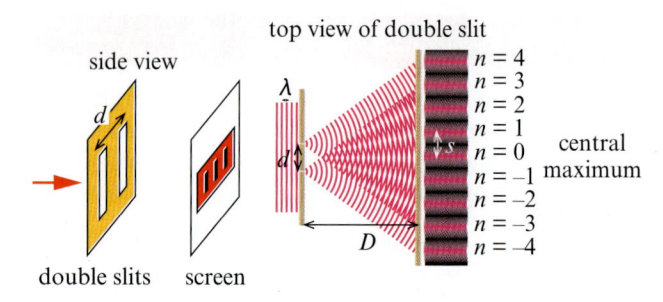

Figure 14.33: Double-slit interference for light. The fringe spacing s is also marked.

Figure 14.34a shows two rays which have diffracted through each slit and meet at point P on the screen. The diagram is not to scale: the distance between the slits, d, is only a fraction of a millimetre and the distance to the screen is about a metre. This means that these rays are almost parallel as shown in Figure 14.19b. (The two angles labelled θ are equal because they have their sides mutually perpendicular). Using this diagram we see that the path difference is the distance S_2Z.

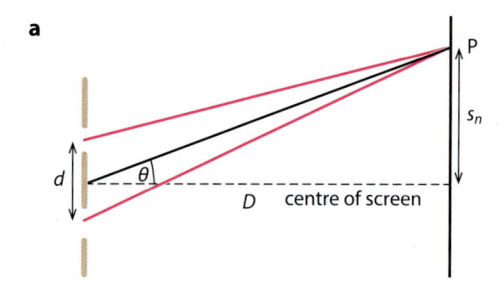

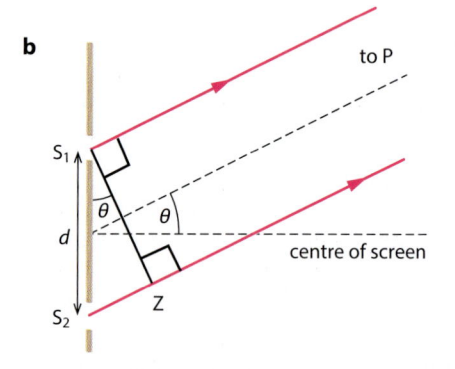

Figure 14.34: The geometry of Young's double-slit experiment. **a** The nth maximum at P is a distance s_n from the centre of the screen. **b** Using geometry to find the path difference.

Using trigonometry, the distance S_2Z, which is the path difference, is equal to $d \sin\theta$. Here, d is the separation of the two slits. This gives the conditions necessary for constructive and destructive interference at P.

For constructive interference: $d \sin\theta = n\lambda$

For destructive interference: $d \sin\theta = \left(n + \frac{1}{2}\right)\lambda$

$n = 0, \pm 1, \pm 2, \ldots$

Because the distance d is very small in comparison to the distance to the screen, the angle θ is quite small, so $\sin\theta$ is small. This means we can approximate $\sin\theta$ by $\tan\theta$. You can check on your calculator that, for small angles θ in radians, it is an excellent approximation that $\sin\theta \approx \tan\theta \approx \theta$.

The derivation that follows is not important—you should know the result. The angle θ is zero for the position directly opposite the slits, where we find the central maximum. Here $n = 0$ (Figure 14.34). The angle θ increases for each successive maximum moving away from the central maximum.

From Figure 14.34 we deduce that:

$$\tan\theta = \frac{s_n}{D}$$

where D is the distance of the slits from the screen and s_n is the distance of the point P from the middle point of the screen.

Using the small angle approximation, we have:

$$\tan\theta \approx \sin\theta$$

$$\Rightarrow s_n = D\sin\theta$$

The condition for constructive interference is $d \sin\theta = n\lambda$, so:

$$\sin\theta = \frac{n\lambda}{d}$$

Substituting in the equation for s_n:

$$s_n = \frac{n\lambda D}{d}$$

The linear separation on a screen of *two consecutive maxima*, s, is thus:

$$s = s_{n+1} - s_n = (n+1)\frac{\lambda D}{d} - \frac{n\lambda D}{d} = \frac{\lambda D}{d}$$

$$s = \frac{\lambda D}{d}$$

This last formula shows that the maxima of the interference pattern are equally separated. (Additional work shows that these maxima are also equally bright if the slit width is negligibly small.)

Notice that the waves arriving at the two slits originate from the same source and so the phase difference between them does not change with time. We say that the waves are **coherent**. If the light originated from two separate sources, such as two flashlights, the phase difference between the two sources would be very rapidly changing. There would be an interference pattern, but the maxima and minima would be changing places so fast that we would see the average of many different interference patterns, i.e. uniform illumination on a screen and no fringes.

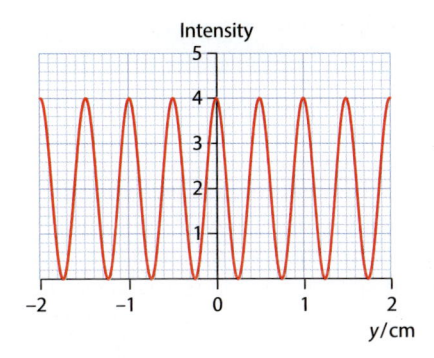

Figure 14.35: The intensity pattern for two slits of negligible width. The horizontal axis label y refers to the distance from the centre of the screen.

> ### CHECK YOURSELF 4
>
> Red light and blue light are incident on two narrow slits. Bright and dark fringes are formed on a screen beyond the slits. In which case is the fringe separation greater?

WORKED EXAMPLE 14.5

In a Young's two-slit experiment, a source of light of unknown wavelength is used to illuminate two very narrow slits a distance of 0.150 mm apart. On a screen at a distance of 1.30 m from the slits, bright spots are observed separated by a distance of 4.95 mm. What is the wavelength of light being used?

Answer

Use the equation $s = \frac{\lambda D}{d}$.

Rearranging to make λ the subject, and substituting the values from the question, we get:

$$\lambda = \frac{sd}{D}$$
$$= \frac{4.95 \times 10^{-3} \times 1.50 \times 10^{-4}}{1.30}$$
$$= 5.71 \times 10^{-7} \text{ m}$$

The wavelength of the light is 571 nm.

In Figure 14.35, the units on the vertical axis are arbitrary. An intensity of one unit corresponds to the intensity from only one slit. At points of constructive interference the amplitude is double that of just one wave. Since intensity is proportional to the square of the amplitude, the intensity is four times as large.

WORKED EXAMPLE 14.6

Use the graph in Figure 14.35 for this question. In a double-slit interference experiment the two slits are separated by a distance of 4.2×10^{-4} m and the screen is 3.8 m from the slits.

a Determine the wavelength of light used in this experiment.

b Suggest the effect on the separation of the fringes of decreasing the wavelength of light.

c State the feature of the graph that enables you to deduce that the slit width is negligible.

Answer

a Reading from the graph, the separation of the bright fringes is 0.50 cm.

   Applying $s = \frac{\lambda D}{d}$ gives:

   $$\lambda = \frac{ds}{D}$$
   $$= \frac{4.2 \times 10^{-4} \times 0.50 \times 10^{-2}}{3.8}$$
   $$= 5.5 \times 10^{-7} \text{ m}$$

b From the separation formula we see that if we decrease the wavelength the separation decreases.

c The intensity of the side fringes is equal to the intensity of the central fringe.

EXAM TIP

'Check the units!'

NATURE OF SCIENCE

Competing theories and progress in science

In 1817 Augustin-Jean Fresnel published a new wave theory of light. The mathematician Siméon Poisson favoured the particle theory of light and worked out that Fresnel's theory predicted the presence of a bright spot in the shadow of a circular object, which he believed was impossible. François Arago, a supporter of Fresnel, was able to show by experiment that there was indeed a bright spot in the centre of the shadow. In further support of his theory, Fresnel was able to show that the polarisation of light could only be explained if light was a transverse wave. The wave theory then took precedence until new evidence showed that light could behave as both a wave and a particle.

TEST YOUR UNDERSTANDING

18 Planar waves of wavelength 1.0 cm approach an aperture whose opening is also 1.0 cm. Draw the wavefronts of this wave as they emerge through the aperture.

19 Repeat question 18 for waves of wavelength 1.0 mm approaching an aperture of size 10 cm.

20 Two speakers 16 m apart emit sound waves in phase of wavelength 0.80 m. Point P is a distance 9.0 m from the left speaker. (See Figure 14.36.)

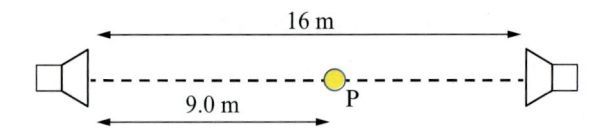

Figure 14.36: For question 20.

What is observed at P?

21 Two speakers emit sound waves in phase of wavelength 2.0 m, as shown in Figure 14.37.

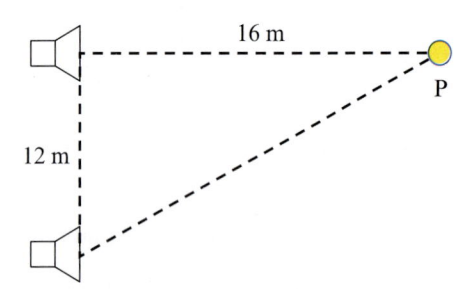

Figure 14.37: For question 21.

a Explain what will be heard at point P.
b The wavelength of the waves is changed to 1.6 m. Explain what will be observed at P now.

22 A sound wave of wavelength 24 cm enters a tube as shown in Figure 14.38. The wave splits at A and recombines at B.

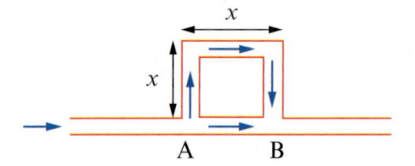

Figure 14.38: For question 22.

No sound is heard from the other end of the tube. What is the smallest possible distance x?

23 Figure 14.39 shows wavefronts emitted from two identical sources.

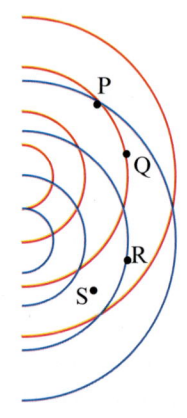

Figure 14.39: For question 23.

State and explain what will be observed at points P, Q, R and S.

CONTINUED

24 Figure 14.40 shows wavefronts emitted from two identical sources. An observer walks along the dotted line from P to Q.

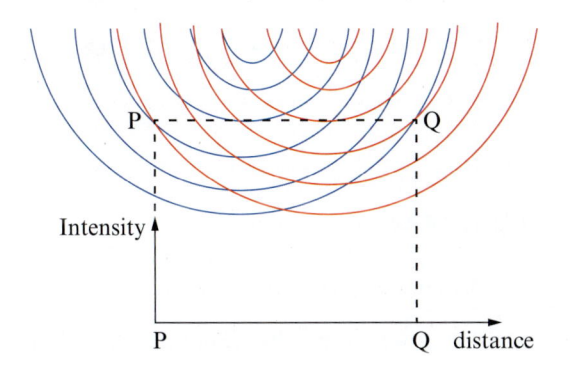

Figure 14.40: For question 24.

On the axes, draw a sketch graph to show how the intensity of sound heard by the observer varies with distance from P.

25 A radio station antenna, R, emits radio waves of wavelength 1600 m which reach a house, H, directly and after reflecting from a mountain, M, behind the house (see Figure 14.41). The reception at the house is very poor. Estimate the shortest possible distance between the house and the mountain. (The wave reflected from the mountain will undergo a phase change by π.)

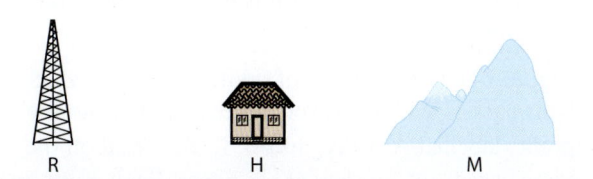

Figure 14.41: For question 25.

26 In a Young's two-slit experiment, we have destructive interference at a point P on a screen. Where did the energy each of the waves carried to P go?

27 In a Young's two-slit experiment, a coherent source of light of wavelength 680 nm is used to illuminate two very narrow slits a distance of 0.12 mm apart. A screen is placed at a distance of 1.50 m from the slits. Calculate the separation of two successive bright spots.

28 Explain why two identical flashlights pointing light at the same spot on a screen will never produce an observable interference pattern.

29 In a Young's two-slit experiment it is found that an nth-order maximum for a wavelength of 680.0 nm coincides with the $(n + 1)$th maximum of light of wavelength 510.0 nm. Determine n.

30 The graph (Figure 14.42) shows the intensity pattern from a two-slit interference experiment.

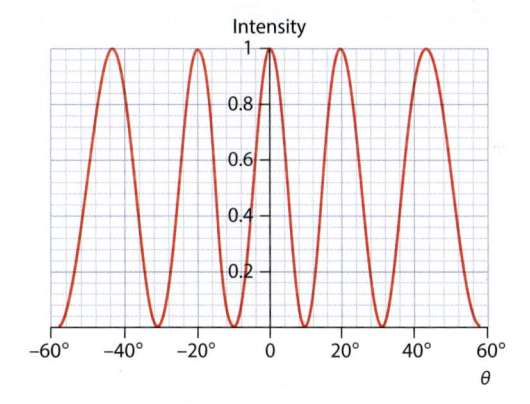

Figure 14.42: For question 30.

a Determine the separation of the slits in terms of the wavelength of light used.

b Suggest how the pattern in **a** changes if the slit separation is halved.

31 Light is incident normally on two narrow parallel slits a distance of 1.00 mm apart. A screen is placed a distance of 1.2 m from the slits. The distance on the screen between the central maximum and the centre of the $n = 4$ bright spot is measured to be 3.1 mm.

a Determine the wavelength of light.

b This experiment is repeated in water. Suggest how the distance of 3.1 mm would change, if at all.

CONTINUED

32 Figure 14.43 shows two radio sources 3.0 m apart that emit identical waves, in phase, of wavelength 0.60 m.

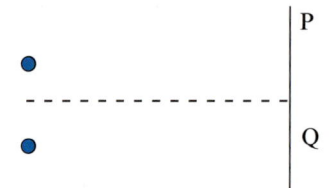

Figure 14.43: For question 32.

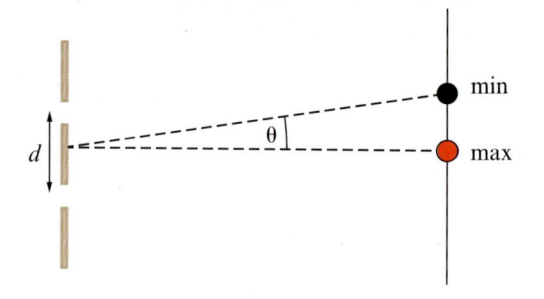

Figure 14.44: For question 33.

a A sensor is moved along the line PQ. How many maxima will the sensor record?

b How many maxima would be recorded if the sensor moved in a full circle around the sources?

33 In a two-slit experiment the angular separation θ of the central maximum and the first minimum is 0.012 rad. The wavelength of light used is 656 nm. (See Figure 14.44.)

a What is the slit separation d?

b What would be the effect on the angular separation θ, if any, if d is made smaller?

34 In a two-slit experiment the screen is 1.20 m from the slits and the slit separation is 0.150 mm. The distance on the screen between the first minimum and the fourth minimum is 12.6 mm. What is the wavelength of light used in the experiment?

14.4 Single-slit diffraction

This section deals in detail with the problem of single-slit diffraction and the effect of slit width on the interference pattern produced. An interference pattern is produced because light originating from one part of the slit interferes with light from all the other parts of the slit.

Diffraction by a single rectangular slit

As we saw in Section 14.3 when a wave of wavelength λ is incident on an aperture whose opening size is b, an important wave phenomenon called diffraction takes place where the wave spreads out past the aperture. The amount of diffraction is appreciable if the wavelength is of the same order of magnitude as the opening or bigger, $λ ≥ b$. However, diffraction is negligible if the wavelength is much smaller than the opening size, $λ << b$.

Figure 14.45 shows a slit of width b through which light passes. When a wavefront reaches the slit, the points labelled A_1 to A_5 and B_1 to B_5 are all on the same wavefront, so they are in phase. Each point on the wavefront acts as a source of waves. These waves are also in phase, so they can interfere. We see the result of the interference on a screen placed a large distance away.

14 Wave phenomena

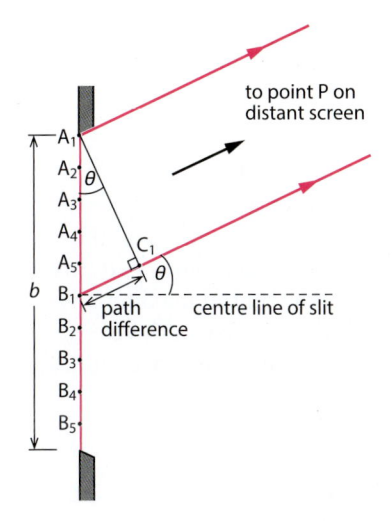

Figure 14.45: For a narrow slit each point on the wavefront entering the slit acts as a source of waves. The result of interference between waves depends on the path difference.

In Figure 14.45 we see rays from A_1 and B_1 travelling at an angle θ relative to the centre line of the slit. The interference between the waves is seen at point P on the screen. The wave from A_1 travels a slightly different distance to reach the screen than the wave from B_1. The interference seen at P depends on this path difference. From the diagram, the path difference for the waves from A_1 and B_1 equals the distance B_1C_1. Since P is far away, lines A_1P and B_1P are approximately parallel, so triangle $A_1B_1C_1$ is approximately right angled and angle $B_1A_1C_1$ equals θ. We see that the distance A_1B_1 is equal to $\frac{b}{2}$, so:

path difference = $B_1C_1 = \frac{b}{2}\sin\theta$

If the path difference is half a wavelength, the two waves will destructively interfere when they get to P. But we have only considered waves from A_1 and B_1. What about waves from A_2 and B_2?

Figure 14.46 shows that for P a long way from the slit, the rays from A_1, A_2, B_1 and B_2 are all parallel. The points are all equally spaced along the slit so $A_1B_1 = A_2B_2$. Triangles $A_1B_1C_1$ and $A_2B_2C_2$ are both right-angled and angle $B_1A_1C_1$ = angle $B_2A_2C_2$. The triangles are therefore congruent, so the path difference B_1C_1 is equal to the path difference B_2C_2.

Thus, if we get zero wave at P from the first pair of points, we will get the same from the second pair as well. For every point on the upper half of the slit there is a corresponding point on the lower half, so we see that all the points on the wavefront will result in complete destructive interference if the first pair results in destructive interference.

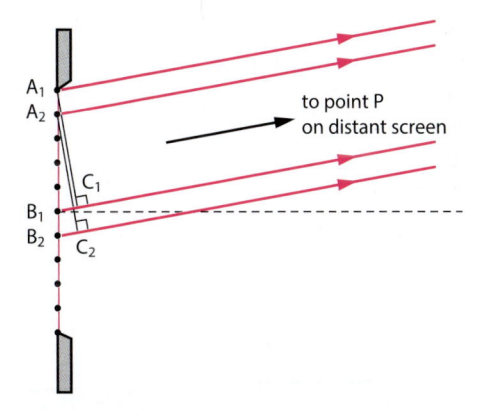

Figure 14.46: Triangles $A_1C_1B_1$ and $A_2C_2B_2$ are congruent.

The path difference between waves arriving at P from A_1 and B_1 is $\frac{b}{2}\sin\theta$.

This means that we get a minimum at P if:

$\frac{b}{2}\sin\theta = \frac{\lambda}{2}$

$\Rightarrow b\sin\theta = \lambda$

(By similar arguments we can show that we get additional minima whenever $b\sin\theta = n\lambda$, $n = 1, 2, 3, \ldots$, but we will not deal with those.)

Since the angle is small (in radians) we may approximate $\sin\theta \approx \theta$ and we have the approximate formula for the angle of the first diffraction minimum:

$\theta = \frac{\lambda}{b}$

WORKED EXAMPLE 14.7

The first diffraction minimum using a single slit of opening 2.0 µm is at an angle of 12.5°. What is the wavelength of the light used?

Answer

From $\theta = \frac{\lambda}{b}$ we get $\lambda = b\theta$.

We must, however, use the angle in radians:

$12.5° = 12.5 \times \frac{\pi}{180} = 0.218$ radians. (Here, the angle is at the limit of what may be considered a "small" angle.)

And so $\lambda = 2.0 \times 10^{-6} \times 0.218 = 4.4 \times 10^{-7}$ m.

Intensity in single slit diffraction

The intensity of light observed on a screen some distance from the slit is shown in Figure 14.47 for red light with slit opening $b = 1.4 \times 10^{-5}$ m.

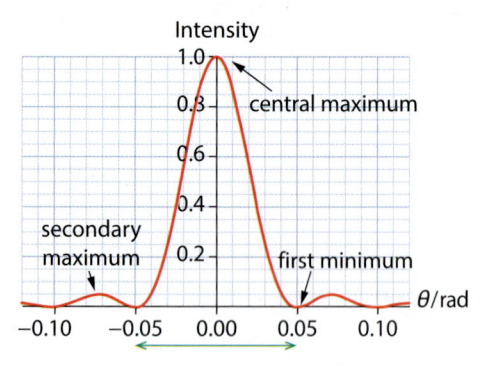

Figure 14.47: The single-slit intensity pattern for red light and slit width 1.4×10^{-5} m.

The intensity of the first secondary maximum is only about 4.5% of the intensity at the central maximum. The units on the vertical axis are arbitrary.

We see that the first minimum occurs at $\theta = 0.05$ rad.

Since $\theta = \frac{\lambda}{b}$, we may deduce the wavelength of the light used:

$\lambda = b\theta = 1.4 \times 10^{-5} \times 0.05 = 7.0 \times 10^{-7}$ m

The double arrow measures the angular width of the central maximum.

It equals $\frac{2\lambda}{b}$ or 0.10 rad in this case.

Blue light has a shorter wavelength and so with blue light the first minimum occurs at smaller angle, as shown in Figure 14.48.

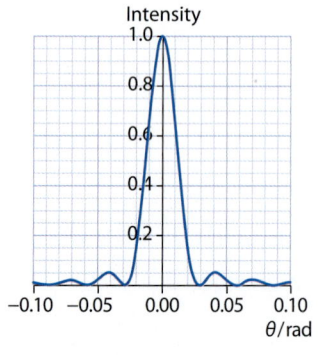

Figure 14.48: The single-slit intensity pattern for blue light and slit width 1.4×10^{-5} m.

If we increase the slit width, more light goes through so the intensity will increase and the angular width will decrease.

The discussion above applies to **monochromatic light** (light of one specific wavelength). When white light is incident on a slit there will be a separate diffraction pattern observed for each wavelength making up the white light. Figure 14.49 shows the combined patterns due to just four wavelengths. The central maximum is white since all the colours produce maxima there. But as we move away from the centre the fringes appear coloured with blue showing up first.

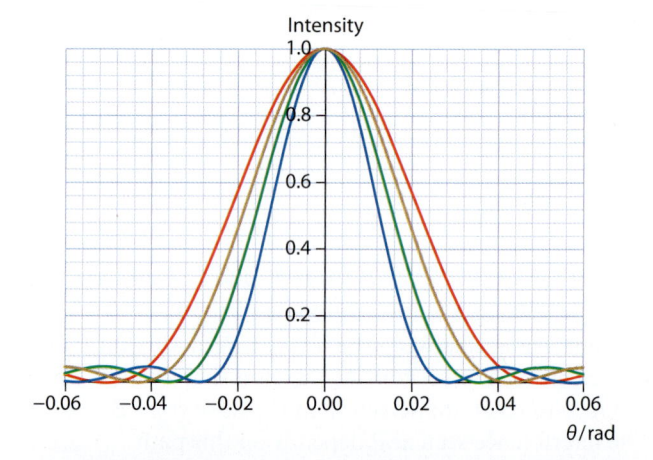

Figure 14.49: The single-slit intensity pattern for white light. The central bright spot is white but the rest of the pattern is coloured. As we move to larger angles we see blue first and finally red.

Links

Diffraction and interference are the defining phenomena of wave behaviour. Anything that diffracts or interferes must be a wave. In Chapter 22 we will see that electrons diffract and interfere so electrons must have a wave nature as well as a particle nature.

14 Wave phenomena

> **NATURE OF SCIENCE**
>
> The interference patterns seen in diffraction through a single slit provide evidence of the wave nature of light. The pattern we see is very different from the simple geometrical shadow expected if light consisted of particles. In this section, you have seen how summing the different waves leads to the pattern observed and how the width of the slit affects the intensity pattern. In a similar way, the waves diffracted around objects can be summed. Figure 14.50 shows the result of diffraction of light around a small circular object. There is a bright spot at the centre of the disc, where a particle model of light would predict darkness! It was this spot, predicted by Fresnel's wave theory and observed by François Arago, that led to the acceptance of the wave theory in the nineteenth century (the debate between Fresnel and Poisson was described previously in this chapter). This is an example of how theory can be used to predict what should be observed. This can then be tested by experiment to give a result supporting the theory. The bright spot in the centre is now called Fresnel's spot or Arago's spot.
>
> **Figure 14.50: a** The Fresnel spot. **b** The intensity of light as a function of horizontal distance showing the peak in the middle of the disc.

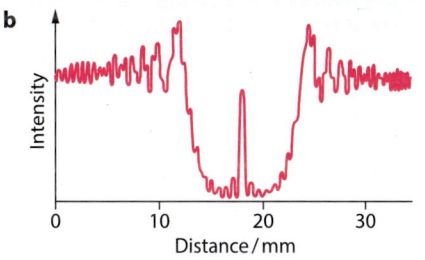

Effect of the slit width on the two-slit intensity pattern

We know that if the slit width is negligibly small the intensity pattern in the two-slit experiment has peaks of equal intensity, as shown in blue in Figure 14.51. Also shown on the same graph in red is the single slit diffraction pattern for a slit whose width is not negligible. How is the two-slit intensity pattern modified when the slits have a non-zero width?

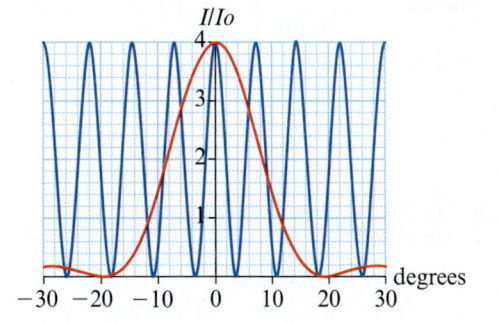

Figure 14.51: The blue curve is the two-slit intensity pattern in the case of negligible slit width. The red curve is the single slit diffraction pattern.

The effect of the slit width is that the red curve becomes the envelope of the blue curve, i.e. the blue curve is pushed under the red curve. We say that the single slit diffraction pattern modulates the two-slit pattern so that the intensity is given by the blue curve in Figure 14.52.

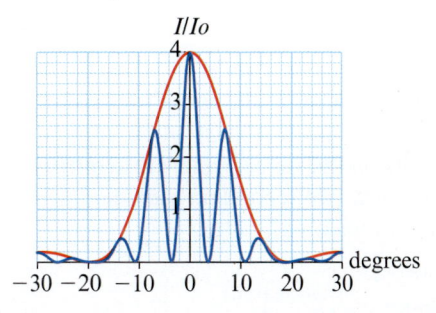

Figure 14.52: The two-slit intensity pattern (in blue) when the slit width is not negligible.

> **CHECK YOURSELF 5**
>
> In a two-slit experiment the slit separation is d and the slit width is $b = \frac{d}{3}$. Explain why the third order maximum of the two-slit interference pattern will not be observed.

PHYSICS FOR THE IB DIPLOMA: COURSEBOOK

TEST YOUR UNDERSTANDING

35 A single slit of width 1.50 μm is illuminated with light of wavelength 500.0 nm. Determine the angular width of the central maximum.

36 In a single-slit diffraction experiment the slit width is 0.12 mm and the wavelength of the light used is 6.00×10^{-7} m. Calculate the linear width of the central maximum on a screen 2.00 m from the slit.

37 The intensity pattern for single-slit diffraction is shown in Figure 14.53. (The vertical units are arbitrary.) The wavelength of the light used is λ.

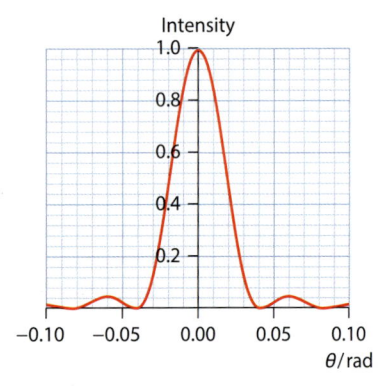

Figure 14.53: For question 37.

a Find the width of the slit b in terms of λ.

b On a copy of the axes draw a graph to show how intensity varies with diffraction angle for a slit with:

   i width $\frac{b}{2}$ and wavelength λ

   ii width $\frac{b}{2}$ and wavelength $\frac{\lambda}{2}$.

(You do not need numbers on the intensity axis.)

38 Two very narrow, parallel slits separated by a distance of 1.4×10^{-5} m are illuminated by coherent, monochromatic light of wavelength 7.0×10^{-7} m.

a Describe what is meant by *coherent* and *monochromatic* light.

b Draw a graph to show how the intensity of light observed on a screen far from the slits varies with angle assuming the slit width is negligible.

c By drawing another graph on the same axes, illustrate the effect on the intensity distribution of using slits of width 4.7×10^{-6} m.

14.5 Multiple slits

As the number of slits increases, the interference pattern increases in complexity. Consider the case of four slits. The intensity pattern is shown in Figure 14.54. In the following graphs units on the vertical axis are arbitrary. We see that there are now two secondary maxima in-between the primary maxima.

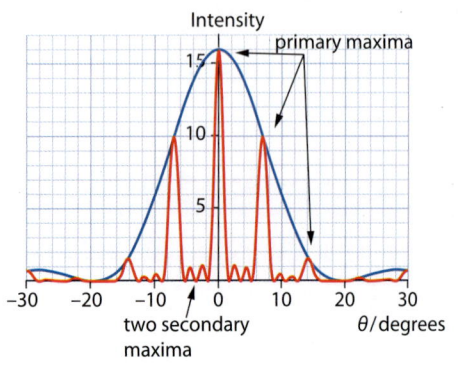

Figure 14.54: Intensity pattern for four slits.

Figure 14.55 shows the case of six slits. There are now four secondary maxima between primary maxima. As the number of slits increases the secondary maxima become unimportant. (With N slits, there are $N - 2$ secondary maxima. The intensity of the central maximum is N^2 times the intensity of just one slit by itself.)

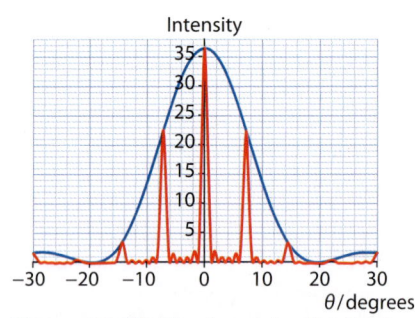

Figure 14.55: The intensity distribution for six slits. Note how the width of the maxima decreases but their position stays the same. Note also how the relative importance of the secondary maxima decreases with increasing slit number.

Figure 14.56 shows the case with 20 slits. The secondary maxima have all but disappeared. We also observe that as the number of slits increases, the width of the primary maxima decreases; the bright fringes become very sharp and easily identifiable.

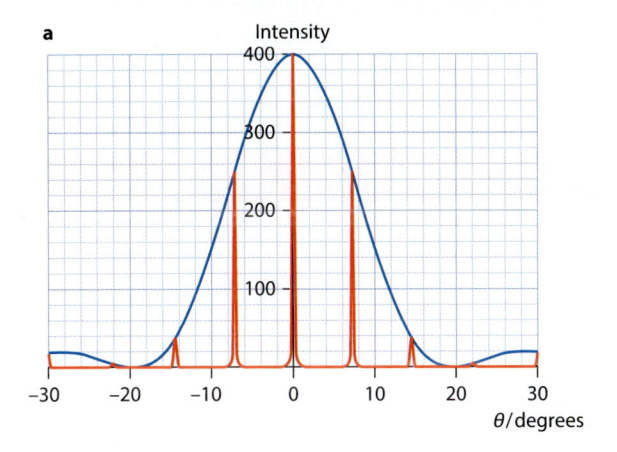

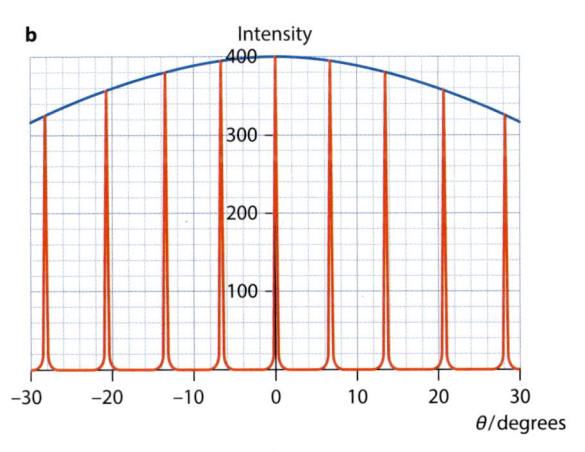

Figure 14.56: **a** The intensity distribution for 20 slits. The secondary maxima are completely unimportant and the primary maxima are very narrow. In **b** the slit width is much smaller so that the single-slit diffraction pattern is very wide. The primary maxima now have roughly the same intensity.

Notice that the slit separation d and the slit width b have been kept the same in all graphs from Figure 14.52 to Figure 14.56a.

So, in summary, we observe that as the number of slits increases:

- The primary maxima are observed at the same angles
- The primary maxima get narrower and brighter
- The secondary maxima become unimportant.

> **WORKED EXAMPLE 14.8**
>
> Look at Figure 14.56a which shows the intensity pattern for 20 slits. Verify that the slit width is three times the wavelength and determine the separation of two consecutive slits in terms of the wavelength.
>
> **Answer**
>
> The minimum of the single-slit diffraction pattern (the blue curve) is about 19° ≈ 0.33 rad.
>
> Using the approximate single-slit diffraction formula $\theta \approx \frac{\lambda}{b}$ we deduce that:
>
> $b \approx \frac{\lambda}{\theta} = \frac{\lambda}{0.33} \approx 3\lambda$
>
> So the slit width is three times the wavelength, as claimed previously.
>
> The first primary maximum away from the central is at θ = 7°. Since:
>
> $d \sin \theta = 1 \times \lambda$
>
> $\Rightarrow d = \frac{\lambda}{\sin 7°} \approx 8\lambda$

The diffraction grating

The **diffraction grating** is an important device in spectroscopy (the analysis of light). It is mainly used to measure the wavelength of light. A diffraction grating consists of a large number of parallel slits of very small width. Instead of actual slits, modern gratings consist of a transparent slide on which rulings or grooves have been precisely cut.

The advantage of a large number of slits is that the maxima in the interference pattern are sharp and bright and can easily be distinguished from their neighbours (Figure 14.57). These bright fringes are called 'lines'. Because the fringes are very narrow the measurement of their separation is more accurate.

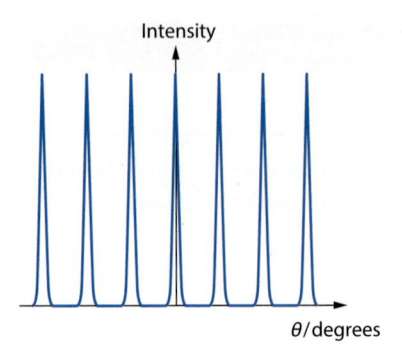

Figure 14.57: The intensity distribution for a diffraction grating. The maxima have roughly the same intensity and are very narrow.

The maxima of the pattern are observed at angles that can be found by an argument similar to that for just two slits: Figure 14.58 shows the path difference (in light blue) between rays leaving the slits. The smallest path difference is δ: that between the top two rays. By similar triangles, any other path difference is an integral multiple of δ. So if δ is an integral multiple of λ, all other path differences will also be an integral multiple of λ. But $\delta = d\sin\theta$. Hence the condition for constructive interference is:

$d\sin\theta = n\lambda, \quad n = 0, \pm 1, \pm 2 \ldots$

In practice, a diffraction grating is stated by its manufacturer to have 'x lines per millimetre'. This means that the separation of the slits is $d = \frac{1}{x}$ mm. So a diffraction grating with 600 lines per mm corresponds to a slit separation of $d = 1.67 \times 10^{-6}$ m. A maximum observed at say $n = 2$ is called the second order maximum, that at $n = 3$ is called the third order maximum and so on.

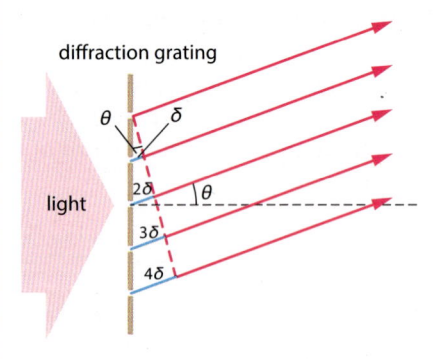

Figure 14.58: The path difference between any two rays is an integral multiple of the smallest path difference δ between the top two rays. The red dashed line is normal to the rays, which makes the angle between this line and the grating θ.

CHECK YOURSELF 6

Light consisting of two wavelengths, 400 nm and 500 nm, is incident on a diffraction grating.

Find the order (other than the zero order) of the 400 nm wavelength that coincides with an order of the 500 nm wavelength.

WORKED EXAMPLE 14.9

Light of wavelength 680 nm falls normally on a diffraction grating that has 600 lines per mm.

a What is the angle separating the first order ($n = 1$) from the second ($n = 2$)?

b How many maxima can be seen?

Answer

a The separation between slits is:

$d = \frac{1}{600} \times 10^{-3}$ m

With $n = 1$ we find: ($\sin\theta = \frac{n\lambda}{d}$)

$\sin\theta = 1 \times (680 \times 10^{-9}) \times (600 \times 10^{3})$

$\quad\quad = 0.408$

Hence $\theta = 24.1°$.

For $n = 2$ we find $\theta = 54.7°$. The angle separating the two is therefore 30.6°.

b The largest θ can get is 90° and so $\frac{1}{600} \times 10^{-3} \times 1 = n \times 680 \times 10^{-9}$, giving $n = 2.45$.

Since n is an integer we must take $n = 2$ as the highest order that can be observed, i.e. 5 in total, 2 on each side plus the central maximum.

Figure 14.59 shows what happens when white light is incident on a diffraction grating.

In each order, the white light breaks up into its component wavelengths (only three colours are shown here for clarity) except of course for the $n = 0$ order which appears white. In Figure 14.59a the orders are well separated. In Figure 14.59b the $n = 1$ and $n = 2$ orders are beginning to overlap (see problems at the end of this chapter).

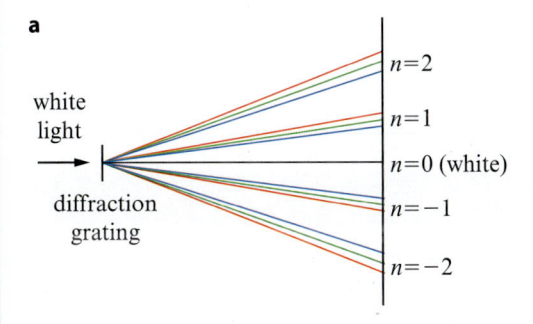

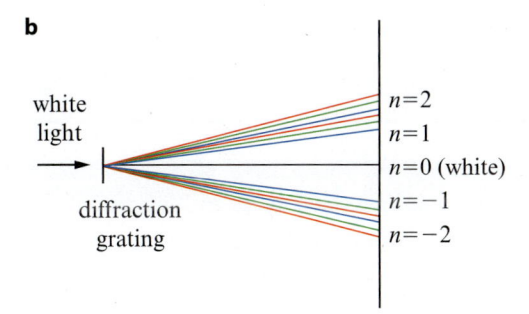

Figure 14.59: a Well separated orders for all wavelengths. b The first and second orders are beginning to overlap.

NATURE OF SCIENCE

Curiosity and serendipity

The shimmering colours of a peacock's tail feathers, the colours inside the paua shell and the glistening surface of a golden stag beetle's coat are all examples of iridescence in nature. Similar colours are seen in soap bubbles and oil films. Curious as to what caused these beautiful colours and effects in nature, scientists speculated on different mechanisms. One suggestion was that the surface pigments of iridescent feathers appeared to reflect different colours when viewed from different angles.

Another suggestion was that the colours were formed as a result of the structure of the surface, not anything to do with the pigments. With the acceptance of the wave theory of light, scientists in the late nineteenth century developed a theory of interference in thin films that could explain these colours. Developments in microscopy meant that finer and finer structure could be seen, and using an electron microscope in the twentieth century it was possible to see complex thin-film structures in iridescent bird feathers.

Figure 14.60: The iridescent 'eye' of a peacock's tail feather.

CONTINUED

In 1817 Joseph Fraunhofer accidentally produced a thin film coating when he left nitric acid on a polished glass surface. Experimenting with different glasses, he was able to produce a surface with the same vivid colours seen in soap bubbles. When he observed the same colours appearing as a coating of alcohol evaporated from a polished metal surface, he concluded that such colours would appear in any transparent thin film. This was the start of the technology of thin films, developed in the twentieth century to make optical coatings for glass.

TEST YOUR UNDERSTANDING

39 a Draw a graph to show the variation with angle of the intensity of light observed on a screen some distance from two very narrow, parallel slits when coherent monochromatic light falls on the slits.

  b Describe how the graph you drew in **a** changes when:

   i the number of slits increases but their separation stays the same

   ii the number of slits stays at two but their separation decreases.

40 A diffraction grating with 400 lines per mm is illuminated normally with light of wavelength 620 nm.

  a Determine the angle of the first order maximum.

  b Determine the largest order that can be seen with this grating and this wavelength.

41 A diffraction grating has 300 lines per mm. Light consisting of two wavelengths, 500 nm and 600 nm, is incident normally on the diffraction grating. What is the angle separating the second order maxima for each wavelength?

42 A diffraction grating has 150 lines per mm. Light consisting of two wavelengths, 400 nm and 500 nm, is incident normally on a diffraction grating. What is the smallest angle for which maxima of the two wavelengths coincide?

43 A diffraction grating produces two consecutive maxima at angles 17.46° and 23.58° with a wavelength of 656 nm. How many lines per mm does the grating have?

44 Light (with wavelengths in the range of 400 nm to 700 nm) is incident normally on a diffraction grating with 400 lines per mm.

  a Show that there are only seven maxima in which all wavelengths are present.

  b What is the largest wavelength present in the fourth order?

45 In a multiple slit arrangement the slit width is 1.20×10^{-6} m. The $n = 4$ interference maximum is missing. What is the separation of the slits?

46 Light containing wavelengths in the range 420 nm to 630 nm is incident normally on a diffraction grating with 160 lines per mm. What is the smallest angle at which there is overlap between consecutive orders?

47 A diffraction grating has 300 lines per mm. Visible light (400 nm to 700 nm) is incident normally on the grating.

  a What is the highest order for which all wavelengths are present?

  b What is the angular width of the order in part **a**?

14 Wave phenomena

SELF-ASSESSMENT CHECKLIST

I am able to …	Section	Not yet	Nearly there	Ready to move on
understand refraction using wavefronts and rays	14.1			
understand and apply the principle of superposition	14.2			
understand the meaning of diffraction and the role of the wavelength	14.3			
understand what is meant by interference	14.3			
solve interference problems with two sources	14.3			
draw the single slit diffraction pattern	14.4			
calculate the angle of the first minimum of the single slit diffraction pattern	14.4			
understand the effect of single slit diffraction of the two-slit interference pattern	14.4			
explain qualitatively what happens when the number of slits increases	14.5			
solve problems with the diffraction grating equation	14.5			

REFLECTION

Can you describe a wave through *wavefronts* and *rays*? Do you know how to apply Snell's law? Do you understand what is meant by *superposition* and do you know how to apply it? Do you understand what is meant by *diffraction* and *interference*? Do you understand the concept of *path difference*? Can you solve problems with two-slit interference?

Do you understand *single slit diffraction*? Can you describe the effect of slit width on the *two slit interference pattern*? Can you describe the effect of increasing the number of slits? Can you solve problems on the *diffraction grating*?

EXAM-STYLE QUESTIONS

You can find questions in the style of IB exams in the digital coursebook.

CHECK YOURSELF ANSWERS

1. $\dfrac{3.0 \times 10^8}{656 \times 10^{-9}} = \dfrac{2.0 \times 10^8}{\lambda} \Rightarrow \lambda = 437$ nm.

2. a 1.0 s

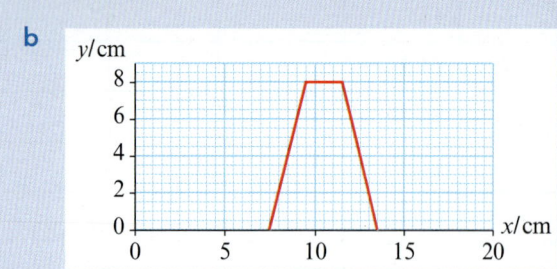

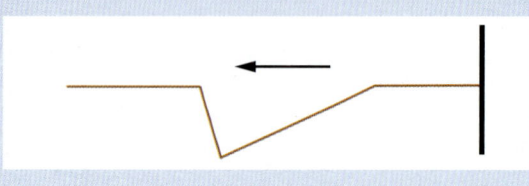

   b *(graph: y/cm vs x/cm, trapezoidal pulse peaking at 8 cm between x ≈ 7 and 12 cm)*

3. *(diagram showing wave refraction at boundary)*

4. For red light because red has larger wavelength.

5. The third order maximum is expected at an angle given by $\sin\theta = \dfrac{3\lambda}{d}$ or approximately $\theta \approx \dfrac{3\lambda}{d}$ since angles are small. The first minimum of the single slit pattern is at $\theta \approx \dfrac{\lambda}{b} = \dfrac{\lambda}{\left(\frac{d}{3}\right)} = \dfrac{3\lambda}{d}$, i.e. at the same angle and so the intensity there is zero.

6. From $d\sin\theta = n\lambda$ we find $n \times 400 = m \times 500$. The smallest integers satisfying this equation are $n = 5$, $m = 4$.

Chapter 15
Standing waves and resonance

LEARNING OBJECTIVES

In this chapter you will learn how to:

- explain the formation of standing waves using superposition
- explain the differences between standing waves and travelling waves
- describe nodes and antinodes
- work with standing waves on strings and in pipes
- solve problems with standing waves on strings and in pipes
- understand the effect of damping on the oscillations of a system
- identify how a system responds as the frequency of an external force varies
- recognize the importance of resonance.

PHYSICS FOR THE IB DIPLOMA: COURSEBOOK

> **GUIDING QUESTION**
>
> How is a standing wave different from a travelling wave?

Introduction

A special wave is formed when two identical waves travelling in opposite directions meet and interfere. The result is a standing (or stationary) wave: a wave in which the crests stay in the same place.

Wind and string musical instruments work because of standing waves.

An oscillating system that is subject to frictional forces will lose energy, and the amplitude of oscillations will decrease; we have damping. The response of an oscillating to an external periodic force depends on the relation between the natural frequency of the system and the frequency of the external force.

When these two frequencies are equal we have resonance, and the system responds by showing oscillations with large amplitude.

15.1 Standing waves

When two waves of the same speed, wavelength and amplitude travelling in opposite directions meet, a **standing wave** is formed. According to the principle of superposition, the resulting wave has a displacement that is the sum of the displacements of the two **travelling waves**.

Figure 15.1 shows a red travelling wave moving to the left and an identical blue travelling wave moving to the right. Both waves travel on the same string. The graphs show the displacement due to each wave every one-twentieth of a period as a function of distance from the left end of the string. The wave shown in the thick purple line is the sum of the two and therefore shows the actual shape of the string. In the first diagram the waves are on top of each other.

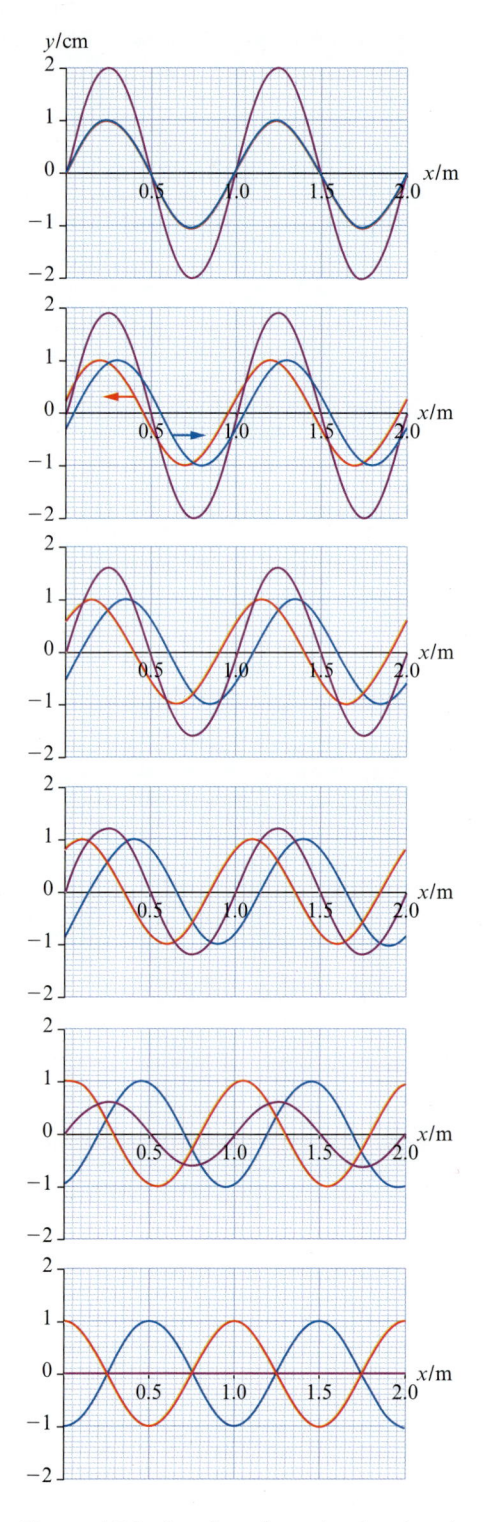

Figure 15.1: A series of graphs showing the superposition of two identical travelling waves moving in opposite directions. The wave in blue travels to the right, and the wave in red travels to the left.

In the top graph, at $t = 0$, the two travelling waves are on top of each other, and so the resultant wave has its maximum displacement at this time. At this instant the amplitude is twice the amplitude of one of the travelling waves.

In the following graphs the waves are moving apart and the amplitude of the purple wave decreases. In the last graph, a quarter of a period later, the two waves meet crest to trough and the resulting wave is zero: the entire string is flat at that particular instant of time.

Notice the following features that are characteristic of standing waves.

- The position of crests and troughs of the purple wave in each graph are always at the same position $x = 0.25$ m, 0.75 m, 1.25 m and 1.75 m. They do not move right or left as they do in the case of travelling waves.

- There are some points on the string where, as a result of destructive interference between the two waves, the displacement is *always* zero. We call these points **nodes**. The distance between two consecutive nodes is half a wavelength. In Figure 15.1 the nodes are at $x = 0$, 0.50 m, 1.0 m, 1.5 m and 2.0 m.

- Half-way between nodes are points where, as a result of constructive interference, the displacement gets as large as possible. These points are called **antinodes**. Note that the nodes always have zero displacement whereas the antinodes are at maximum displacement for an instant of time only. In Figure 15.1 the antinodes are at $x = 0.25$ m, 0.75 m, 1.25 m and 1.75 m.

- The amplitude of oscillation is different at different points on the string.

- A standing wave does not transfer energy: it consists of two travelling waves that transfer energy in opposite directions so the standing wave itself transfers no energy.

- The ends of a standing wave are either nodes or antinodes. These 'boundary' or 'end conditions' determine the possible wavelength of the wave as we will see.

> **CHECK YOURSELF 1**
>
> All points on a standing wave have the same:
>
> a   amplitude
>
> b   average speed
>
> c   frequency
>
> d   displacement

> **EXAM TIP**
>
> You must be able to explain the formation of a standing wave in terms of the superposition of two oppositely moving travelling waves.

How do we create standing waves in practice? We will examine two cases: standing waves on strings and in pipes.

> **TEST YOUR UNDERSTANDING**
>
> 1   Describe what is meant by a standing wave.
>
> 2   Outline how a standing wave is formed.
>
> 3   List ways in which a standing wave differs from a travelling wave.
>
> 4   In the context of standing waves describe what is meant by:
>
>   a   node
>
>   b   antinode
>
>   c   wave speed.

15.2 Standing waves on strings

Take a string of length L, tighten it and keep both ends fixed by attaching one end to a clamp and the other end to an oscillator. (The point on the string that is attached to the oscillator does not move relative to the oscillator so we have a node there.) In this case the end conditions are node–node. The oscillator creates travelling waves that move towards the fixed end of the string. The waves reflect at the fixed end, and so at any one time there are two identical travelling waves on the string travelling in opposite directions. As we saw, this is the condition for a standing wave to form. However, for the standing wave to fit on the string the right frequency has to be used, as we will see (see worked example 15.1). Different standing wave patterns will be established on the string depending on the frequency used. Figure 15.2 shows four possibilities. In the top diagram we see one loop, with two nodes and one antinode. This is the standing wave with the longest wavelength (and the lowest frequency): it is called the **first harmonic**. The higher **harmonics** have more loops, and the wavelength decreases and the frequency increases, as shown in the lower part of Figure 15.2. In the figure, the symbol n stands for the number of the harmonic so that, for example, $n = 3$ indicates the third harmonic.

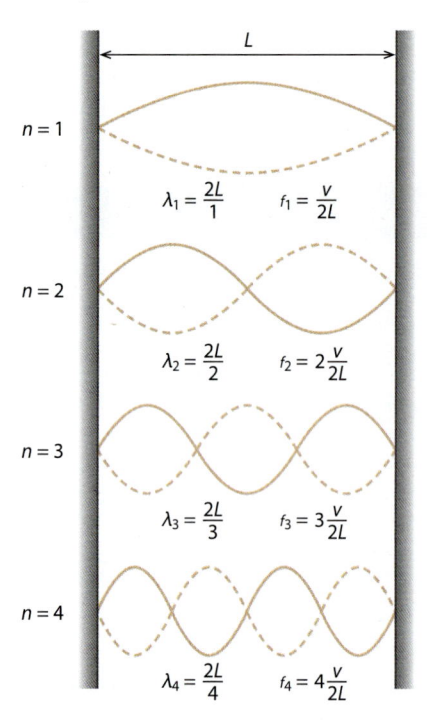

Figure 15.2: Standing waves on a string with both ends fixed. The first four harmonics are shown. (The oscillator is not shown.)

It is important to realise that, for each harmonic, there is a definite relationship between the wavelength and the length of the string.

Remember that the distance between two consecutive nodes is half a wavelength. So for the first harmonic we have:

$\frac{\lambda_1}{2} = L \Rightarrow \lambda_1 = 2L = \frac{2L}{1}$

For the second harmonic:

$2 \times \frac{\lambda_2}{2} = L \Rightarrow \lambda_2 = L = \frac{2L}{2}$

For the third harmonic:

$3 \times \frac{\lambda_3}{2} = L \Rightarrow \lambda_3 = \frac{2L}{3}$

In general, we find that the wavelengths satisfy:

$\lambda_n = \frac{2L}{n}$, $n = 1,2,3,4...$

Figure 15.2 also gives the frequencies of the harmonics using the equation $f = \frac{v}{\lambda}$, where v is the speed of the travelling waves making up the standing wave and λ the wavelength of the harmonic. The first harmonic has the lowest frequency. Notice the important fact that all harmonics have frequencies that are integral multiples of the first harmonic frequency.

WORKED EXAMPLE 15.1

The speed for waves on a string of length 1.20 m is 140 m s^{-1}.

At what frequency should the oscillator be set so that the string vibrates in the first harmonic?

Answer

The wavelength in the first harmonic is twice the length of the string (1.20 × 2 = 2.40 m).

The required frequency is, therefore:

$f = \frac{v}{\lambda} = \frac{140}{2.40} \approx 58$ Hz

Figure 15.3 shows successive positions of the string for the first harmonic. This diagram shows that different points on the standing wave oscillate with different amplitudes. The figure shows the shape of the string at different times (seven times in this case). There is an antinode midway between the two nodes.

15 Standing waves and resonance

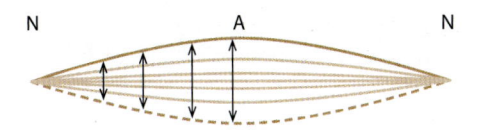

Figure 15.3: Different points on the string have different amplitudes.

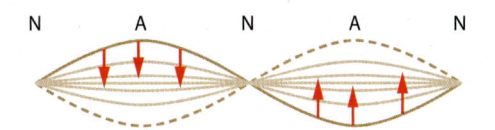

Figure 15.4: Points within consecutive nodes have velocity in the same direction. Points in the next loop have opposite velocity directions.

Figure 15.5 shows an actual string vibrating in the second harmonic.

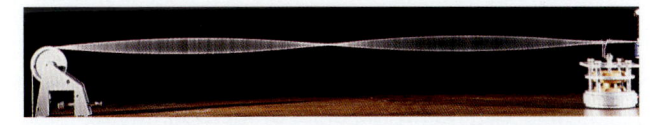

Figure 15.5: This string vibrates in the second harmonic.

> **CHECK YOURSELF 2**
>
> In Figure 15.3, which point on the string has the largest average speed in the course of one period?

Figure 15.4 shows how the string oscillates in its second harmonic. Here we have three nodes and two antinodes. The arrows represent the velocity vectors of points on the string. Notice that the direction of the velocity is the same for points within the same loop. We say that points within the same loop oscillate in phase. In the next loop the velocities are also in the same direction but opposite to those in the previous loop. We say there is a 180° phase difference between points in one loop and points in the next loop.

> **CHECK YOURSELF 3**
>
> In Figure 15.5 the tension in the string is increased, doubling the speed of the wave. The frequency of the oscillator and the length of the string are unchanged. What is the shape of the new standing wave?

WORKED EXAMPLE 15.2

A standing wave is set up on a string with both ends fixed. The frequency of the first harmonic is 150 Hz. The speed of the wave on the string is 240 m s^{-1} and the speed of sound in air is 340 m s^{-1}.

Calculate:

a the length of the string

b the wavelength of the sound produced.

Answer

a The wavelength is given by:

$\lambda_1 = \frac{240}{150} = 1.6$ m

The wavelength of the first harmonic is $2L$ and so $L = 0.80$ m.

b The sound will have the same frequency as that of the standing wave, i.e. 150 Hz. The wavelength of the sound is thus:

$\lambda = \frac{340}{150} \approx 2.3$ m

333

PHYSICS FOR THE IB DIPLOMA: COURSEBOOK

TEST YOUR UNDERSTANDING

5   a   Describe how you would arrange for a string that is kept under tension, with both ends fixed, to vibrate in its second harmonic mode.

   b   Draw the shape of the string when it is vibrating in its second harmonic mode.

6   A string is held under tension, with both ends fixed, and has a first harmonic frequency of 250 Hz. The speed of a transverse wave on a sting is given by $v = \sqrt{\frac{T}{\mu}}$ where T is the tension.

   a   By finding the units of the quantity μ, identify μ.

   b   The tension in the string is doubled. Predict the new frequency of the first harmonic.

7   Strings X and Y have both ends fixed. The speed of transverse waves in X is double that in Y, and the length of X is half that of Y. Determine the ratio of the frequency of the first harmonic in X to that in Y.

8   The wave velocity of a transverse wave on a string of length 0.500 m is 225 m s^{-1}.

   a   Determine the frequency of the first harmonic of a standing wave on this string when both ends are kept fixed.

   b   Calculate the wavelength of the sound produced in air by the oscillating string in part **a**. (Take the speed of sound in air to be 340 m s^{-1}.)

9   The velocity of a transverse wave on a string is 122 m s^{-1}. The string has both ends fixed, and a standing wave of frequency 512 Hz is established on the string. What is the distance between consecutive nodes?

10   A string has both ends fixed. A particular harmonic has frequency 340 Hz. The next harmonic has frequency 425 Hz. What is the frequency of the first harmonic?

11   A string has both ends fixed and oscillates in the first harmonic. The amplitude in the middle of the string is 5.0 mm and the frequency of the harmonic is 480 Hz. What is the average speed of a point in the middle of the string during one full oscillation?

15.3 Standing waves in pipes

The standing waves discussed so far in this chapter apply to string musical instruments such as guitars and violins. But standing waves can also be produced within pipes which can have open or closed ends. These standing waves apply to wind instruments such as flutes and clarinets.

Consider a pipe of length L that is open at both ends; that is, the end conditions are antinode–antinode (Figure 15.6). A flute is an example of this. A travelling wave sent down the pipe will reflect from the ends (even though they are open—you may want to look further into this), and we again have the condition for the formation of a standing wave, namely two waves travelling in opposite directions.

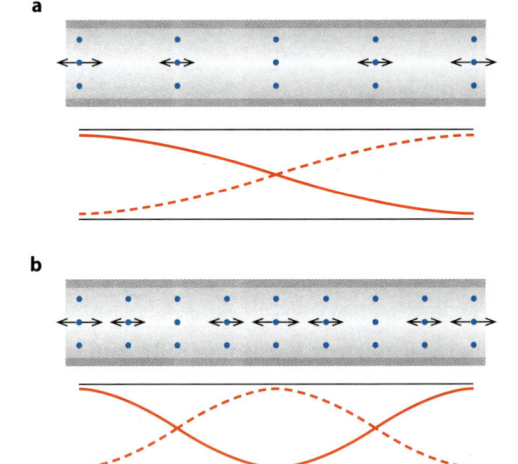

Figure 15.6: a A pipe with both ends open has two antinodes at the open ends and a node in the middle. **b** The second harmonic in an open pipe.

15 Standing waves and resonance

The top part of Figure 15.6a represents the first harmonic in a pipe with open ends. The dots represent molecules of air in the pipe. The double-headed arrows show how far these molecules oscillate back and forth (the amplitude of the oscillations). We see that the molecules at the ends oscillate the most: they are at antinodes. The molecules in the middle of the pipe do not oscillate at all: they are at a node. We have antinodes at the open ends, and there is a node in the middle. The lower diagram is how we normally represent the standing wave in the pipe—you must understand that it represents what the top diagram shows. Figure 15.6b represents the second harmonic.

> **EXAM TIP**
>
> You must be able to explain how molecules move in a longitudinal standing wave such as one in a pipe.

Note that these diagrams also give the harmonics for the case of a string with both ends free. (Imagine a vertical string.)

The case of a pipe with both ends closed (which is not very useful) is similar to that of a string with ends fixed: Figure 15.7 shows the first and second harmonics.

The wavelength for pipes with both ends closed or both ends open is:

$\lambda_n = \frac{2L}{n}$, $n = 1, 2, 3, 4, \ldots$

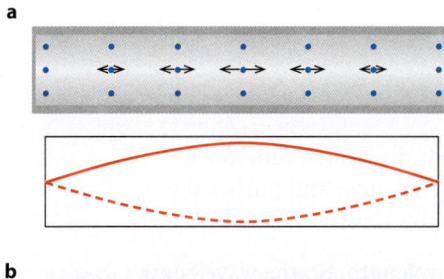

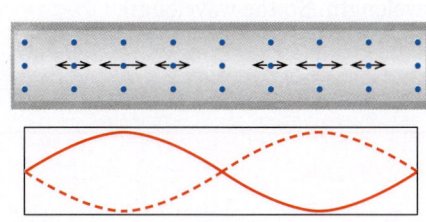

Figure 15.7: The first and second harmonics for a pipe with both ends closed.

We consider finally the case of a pipe with one closed and one open end (in other words, end conditions node–antinode). This could apply to clarinets and some organ pipes. The closed end will be a node and the open end an antinode.

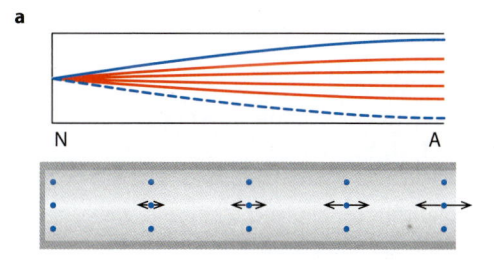

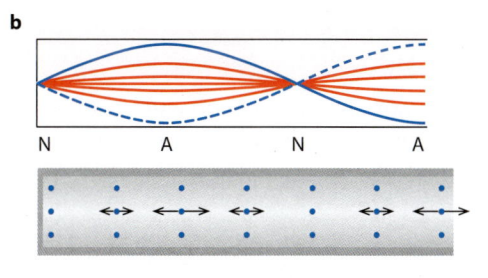

Figure 15.8: The first two harmonics in a pipe with one open and one closed end.

Figure 15.8 shows the first two harmonics. The distance between a node and an antinode is a quarter of a wavelength, and so the wavelength of the first harmonic is given by:

$1 \times \frac{\lambda_1}{4} = L \Rightarrow \lambda_1 = 4L = \frac{4L}{1}$

The wavelength of the next harmonic is:

$3 \times \frac{\lambda_3}{4} = L \Rightarrow \lambda_3 = \frac{4L}{3}$

Notice that only 'odd' harmonics are present. In general, the allowed wavelengths are:

$\lambda_n = \frac{4L}{n}$, $n = 1, 3, 5, \ldots$

This formula also gives the wavelength for the case of a string with one fixed and one free end.

Table 15.1 summarises the relationships for standing waves in strings and pipes.

335

String of length L	Both ends fixed or both free: $\lambda_n = \frac{2L}{n}$ $n = 1, 2, 3, 4, \ldots$
	One end fixed, the other free: $\lambda_n = \frac{4L}{n}$ $n = 1, 3, 5, \ldots$
Pipe of length L	Both ends open or both closed: $\lambda_n = \frac{2L}{n}$ $n = 1, 2, 3, 4, \ldots$
	One end closed, the other open: $\lambda_n = \frac{4L}{n}$ $n = 1, 3, 5, \ldots$

Table 15.1: Wavelengths for allowed harmonics for standing waves in strings and pipes.

> **CHECK YOURSELF 4**
>
> In a pipe with one end closed and the other open, a particular harmonic has frequency 126 Hz. The next harmonic has frequency 210 Hz. What is the frequency of the first harmonic in this pipe?

WORKED EXAMPLE 15.3

A pipe X has one open and one closed end. Another pipe Y has both ends open. The first harmonic in both pipes has the same wavelength. Determine the ratio of the length of X to the length of Y.

Answer

In X the wavelength is $\lambda = 4L_x$ and in Y, $\lambda = 2L_y$. Hence:

$4L_x = 2L_y \Rightarrow \frac{L_x}{L_y} = \frac{1}{2}$.

WORKED EXAMPLE 15.4

A source of sound of frequency 2100 Hz is placed at the open end of a tube. The other end of the tube is closed. Powder is sprinkled inside the tube. When the source is turned on it is observed that the powder collects in heaps a distance of 8.0 cm apart.

a Explain this observation.

b Use this information to estimate the speed of sound.

Answer

a A standing wave is established inside the tube since the travelling waves from the source superpose with the reflected waves from the closed end. At the antinodes air oscillates the most and pushes the powder right and left. The powder collects at the nodes where the air does not move.

b The heaps collect at the nodes, and the distance between nodes is half a wavelength. So the wavelength is 16 cm. The speed of sound is then:

$v = f\lambda = 2100 \times 0.16 = 336 \approx 340 \text{ m s}^{-1}$

WORKED EXAMPLE 15.5

A tube with both ends open is placed inside a container of water, Figure 15.9. When a tuning fork above the tube is sounded, a loud sound comes out of the tube. The shortest length of the column of air for which this happens is L. The frequency of the tuning fork is 486 Hz, and the speed of sound is 340 m s^{-1}.

a Determine the length L.

b Predict the least distance by which the tube must be raised for another loud sound to be heard from the tube when the same tuning fork is sounding.

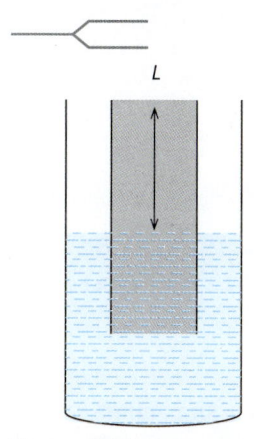

Figure 15.9: For worked example 15.5.

Answer

a Since the air column length L is the least possible for a standing wave to form, the standing wave must be in its first harmonic. The water surface makes the lower end of the tube closed so the wavelength is $4L$. The wavelength is given by:

$\lambda = \frac{340}{486} = 0.6996 \approx 0.700$ m

and so:

$L = \frac{0.6996}{4} = 0.1749 \approx 0.175$ m

b The length of the air column in the tube must be increased so that the next harmonic can fit. The wavelength must be the same as before (since the tuning fork is the same). In Figure 15.10 we show the original standing wave in blue and the new one in red. It is clear from the diagram that the extra length needed is half a wavelength, that is, 0.35 m.

CONTINUED

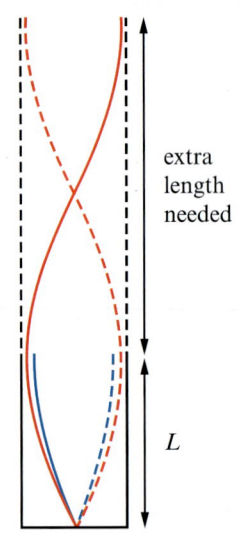

Figure 15.10: For worked example 15.5 part b.

Alternatively, you can argue that since the wavelength must be the same as before, the new air column length for the next harmonic is given by:

$\frac{4L'}{3} = 0.700$ m

So $L' = 0.525$ m.

The tube must be raised by $0.525 - 0.175 = 0.35$ m.

CHECK YOURSELF 5

The top end of a vertical string is attached to an oscillator. The lower end is free. The speed of a transverse wave on the string is 24 m s^{-1}.
When the oscillator is set to a frequency of 5.0 Hz the string oscillates in the first harmonic mode. What is the length of the string?

NATURE OF SCIENCE

Physics is universal

The universality of physics is evident almost everywhere including in the theory of standing waves. From the time of Pythagoras onwards philosophers and scientists have used mathematics to model the formation of standing waves on strings and in pipes. The theory that we have developed here applies to simple vibrating strings and air columns, but it can be used to give detailed accounts of the formation of musical sound in instruments as well as the stability of buildings shaken by earthquakes.

TEST YOUR UNDERSTANDING

12 A pipe has one end closed and the other open. A particular harmonic has frequency 300 Hz. The next harmonic has frequency 420 Hz. What is the frequency of the first harmonic?

13 Draw the standing wave representing the third harmonic standing wave in a tube with one closed and one open end.

14 A glass tube is closed at one end. The air column it contains has a length that can be varied between 0.50 m and 1.20 m. A tuning fork of frequency 425 Hz is sounded at the top of the tube. Predict the lengths of the air column at which loud sounds would be heard from the tube. (Take the speed of sound to be 340 m s^{-1}.)

15 A glass tube with one end open and the other end closed is used in an experiment to determine the speed of sound. A tuning fork of frequency 427 Hz is used, and a loud sound is heard when the air column has length equal to 20.0 cm.

    a Calculate the speed of sound.

    b Predict the next length of air column when a loud sound will again be heard.

16 Figure 15.11 shows a standing wave in a pipe. The red curve represents the standing wave at $t = 0$. The blue curve represents the standing wave at time $t = T/10$, where T is the period. What is the direction of the velocity at $t = T/10$ of a molecule of air whose equilibrium position is at:

    a point P

    b point Q?

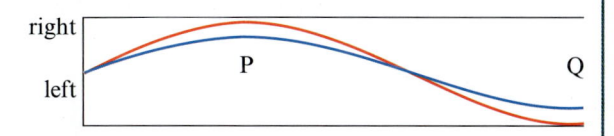

Figure 15.11: For question 16.

17 A tube has both ends open. When a tuning fork is sounded next to one of the ends of the pipe, a loud sound comes out of the tube. The shortest length of the tube for which this happens is L. The frequency of the tuning fork is 586 Hz, and the speed of sound is 340 m s^{-1}.

    a Determine the length L.

    b Predict the least distance by which the tube must be lengthened for another loud sound to be heard from the tube when the same tuning fork is sounding.

18 A pipe with both ends open has two consecutive harmonics of frequencies 300 Hz and 360 Hz. Take the speed of sound to be 340 m s^{-1}.

    a Suggest which harmonics are excited in the pipe.

    b Determine the length of the pipe.

19 A pipe X has both ends open and a pipe Y has one open and one closed end. The second harmonic in X has the same frequency as the first harmonic in Y. Calculate the ratio of the length of pipe X to that of pipe Y.

> **CONTINUED**

20 Consider a string with both ends fixed. A standing wave in the second harmonic is established on the string, as shown in Figure 15.12. The speed of the wave is 180 m s⁻¹.

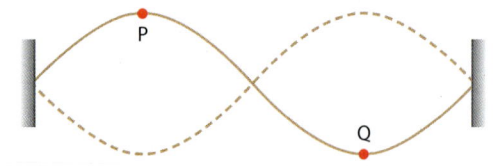

Figure 15.12: For question 20.

   a Explain the meaning of *wave speed* in the context of standing waves.

   b Consider the vibrations of two points on the string, P and Q. The displacement of point P is given by the equation $y = 5.0 \cos(45\pi t)$, where y is in millimetres and t is in seconds. Calculate the length of the string.

   c State the phase difference between the oscillation of point P and that of point Q. Hence write down the equation giving the displacement of point Q.

21 A horizontal aluminium rod of length 1.2 m is hit sharply with a hammer. The hammer rebounds from the rod 0.37 ms later.

   a Explain why the hammer rebounds.

   b Calculate the speed of sound in aluminium.

   c The hammer created a longitudinal standing wave in the rod. Estimate the frequency of the sound wave by assuming that the rod vibrates in the first harmonic.

15.4 Resonance and damping

We now examine the effect of resistance forces and other externally applied forces on an oscillating system.

Oscillations and damping

In Chapter 12 we saw examples of systems performing oscillations. Those were free oscillations, i.e. oscillations without loss of energy and without externally applied forces. In this case the amplitude of oscillations stays constant. In this chapter we will examine the effects of the presence of such forces. If the forces resist the motion we will have **damping**; in other words, loss of energy in an oscillating system.

In light damping the amplitude of oscillation decreases slowly with time and eventually becomes zero; the oscillations stop, Figure 15.13. The amplitude decreases exponentially (dotted blue line).

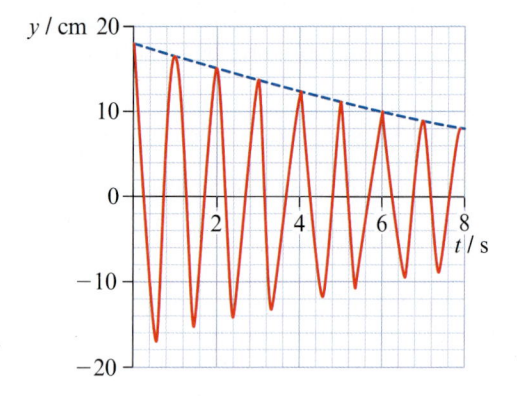

Figure 15.13: In damped oscillations the amplitude is decreasing with time exponentially.

Driven oscillations and resonance

We will now examine qualitatively the effect of an externally applied force F on a system that is free to oscillate with frequency f_0. This is called the **natural frequency** of the system. The force F will be assumed to vary periodically with time with frequency f_D, called the **driving frequency**, for example $F = F_0 \cos(2\pi f_D t)$. The oscillations that take place in this case are called forced or **driven oscillations**.

15 Standing waves and resonance

As an example consider a pendulum of length L that hangs vertically as in Figure 15.14. The point of support is made to oscillate with some frequency f_D. How does the pendulum react to this force?

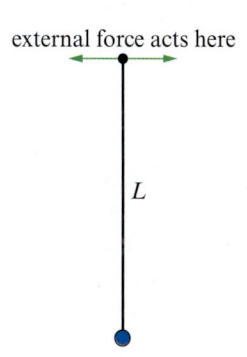

Figure 15.14: Forced oscillations: the point of support is acted upon by a periodic force that makes the point of support vibrate.

In general, after the external force is first applied, the system *will eventually switch to oscillations with a frequency equal to the driving frequency f_D*. This is true both when the system is initially at rest and when it is oscillating at its own frequency before the force is applied. In the absence of damping, the amplitude of oscillations approaches infinity as the driving frequency approaches the natural frequency, Figure 15.15. This is impossible; it shows that we have to take damping into account.

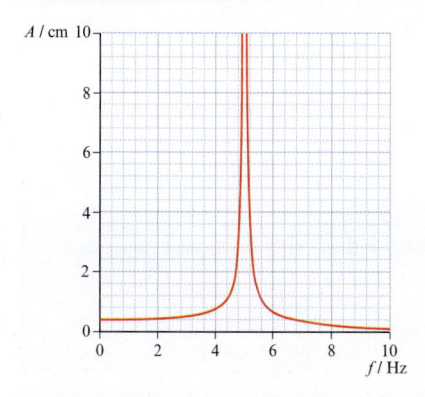

Figure 15.15: Graph showing the variation with driving frequency of the amplitude of driven SHM when the system is driven by an external periodic force and no damping. The natural frequency is 5 Hz here.

The amplitude of the oscillations will depend on f_D and the amount of damping. A detailed analysis produces the graph in 15.16 showing how the amplitude of oscillation of a system with natural frequency f_0 varies as it is subjected to a periodic force of frequency f_D. The degree of damping increases as we move from the top curve down.

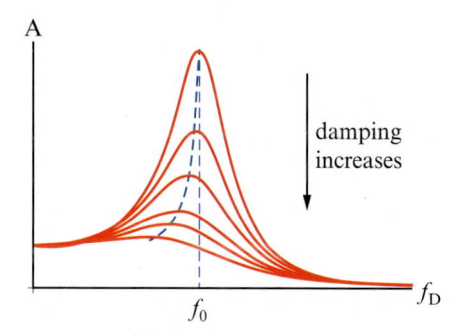

Figure 15.16: Graph showing the variation with driving frequency of the amplitude of oscillations when the system is driven by an external periodic force. For very small damping, the peak occurs at a frequency very close to the natural frequency. As the damping increases, the peak occurs at a frequency less than f_0, as indicated by the dark dashed curve.

The general features of the graph in Figure 15.16 are as follows:

- For very small damping, the peak of the curve occurs very close to the natural frequency of the system, f_0. In other words, when the driving frequency is equal to the natural frequency the amplitude of oscillations is a maximum. This condition is called **resonance**. Resonance has been experienced by anyone trying to push a swing: even a small force exerted on the swing at the right time intervals results in large oscillations of the swing.

- As the amount of damping increases, the peak shifts to lower frequencies and becomes wider and shorter. In other words, with large damping the amplitude is a maximum when the driving frequency is slightly less than the natural frequency.

- At very low frequencies, the amplitude is essentially constant, and at high frequencies the amplitude goes to zero.

In all cases the system oscillates at the driven frequency.

We distinguish three cases in the amount of damping, Figure 15.17. In light damping the system returns to equilibrium after many oscillations of decreasing amplitude. In critical damping, the system returns to equilibrium in the shortest possible time without performing oscillations. Finally, in the heavy or overdamped case the system returns to equilibrium after a very long time without performing oscillations.

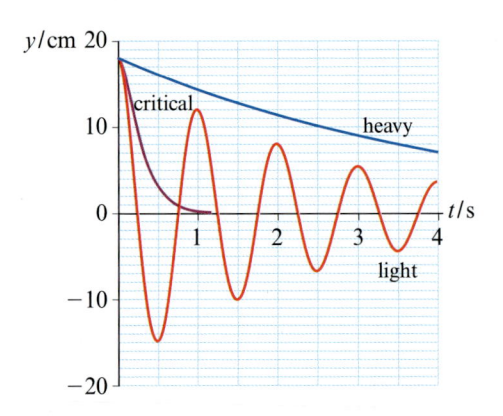

Figure 15.17: Light, critical and heavy damping.

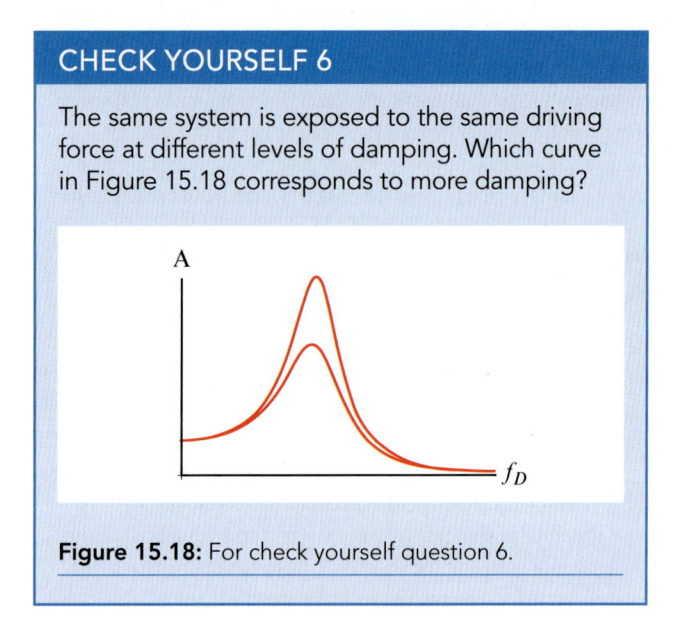

> ### CHECK YOURSELF 6
>
> The same system is exposed to the same driving force at different levels of damping. Which curve in Figure 15.18 corresponds to more damping?
>
> **Figure 15.18:** For check yourself question 6.

Resonance can be disastrous: we do not want an aircraft wing to resonate, nor is it good for a building or a bridge to be set into resonance by an earthquake or the wind, Figure 15.19.

Figure 15.19: The Tacoma Narrows Bridge in Washington State in the United States oscillating before collapsing in 1940, a victim of resonance.

Resonance can be irritating if the car in which you drive is set into resonance by bumps on the road or by a poorly tuned engine. But resonance can also be a good thing: resonance is used by a microwave oven to warm food; and your radio uses resonance to tune into one specific station and not another.

Links

- The fact that greenhouse gases in the atmosphere absorb infrared radiation emitted by the earth's surface is an example of resonance: the frequency of the infrared photons matches the natural frequency of the greenhouse gases. The natural frequency in this case is the frequency of the photons the gases can emit.

- In damped driven oscillations, energy is being dissipated and so the driving force must provide the energy needed to keep the amplitude constant. Application of the law of energy conservation gives the interesting result that the power supplied by the driving force is a maximum when the frequency of the driving force is exactly equal to the natural frequency of the system. So resonance can also be understood as the condition under which the power supplied is a maximum.

> ### CHECK YOURSELF 7
>
> In driven damped oscillations, the maximum amplitude occurs when the driving frequency:
>
> a   is equal to the natural frequency of the system
>
> b   is slightly greater than the natural frequency of the system
>
> c   is slightly smaller than the natural frequency of the system
>
> d   approaches zero.

15 Standing waves and resonance

NATURE OF SCIENCE

The phenomenon of resonance is ubiquitous in physics and engineering: microwave ovens emit electromagnetic radiation in the microwave region at wavelengths that match the vibration wavelengths of water molecules so they can be absorbed and warm food; in a technique known as MRI in medicine, resonance is used to force absorption of radio frequency radiation by protons in the body that is exposed to a magnetic field making possible superior images of body organs and cellular functions; detailed studies are necessary in any structure in order to avoid the structure coming into resonance with a variety of sources that might create catastrophic large amplitude oscillations.

TEST YOUR UNDERSTANDING

22 a In the context of oscillations, state what is meant by damping.

   b Distinguish between free and driven oscillations.

23 State what is meant by resonance.

24 If you walk at one step a second holding a cup of water (diameter 8 cm) the water will spill out of the cup. Use this information to estimate the speed of the waves in water.

25 Figure 15.20 shows the variation of the displacement of a system performing oscillations.

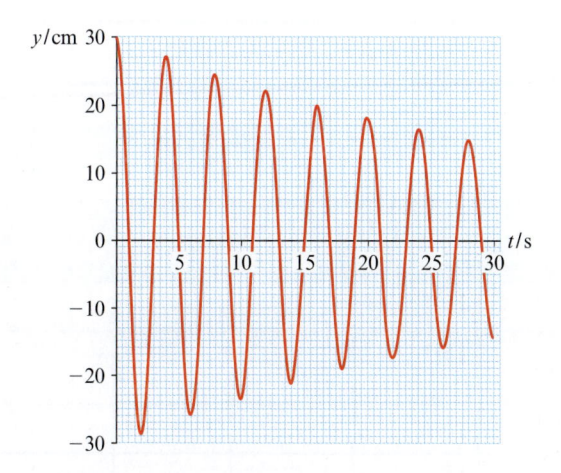

Figure 15.20: For question 25.

   a Determine the frequency of oscillations.

   b Draw a sketch graph to show the variation with time of the energy of the system (no numbers required on the axes).

   c The amount of damping increases. State and explain the effect of this on the graph.

26 a State the conditions that must be satisfied for simple harmonic oscillations to take place.

   b Draw a graph of displacement versus time for a particle undergoing lightly damped simple harmonic oscillations.

   c A system has natural frequency f_0. A periodic force of variable frequency f acts on the system.

   Copy the axes from Figure 15.21.

   Draw graphs to show the variation with f of the amplitude of oscillation of the system for:

   i   light damping

   ii heavy damping.

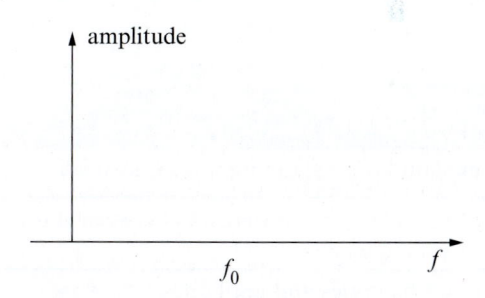

Figure 15.21: For question 26c.

27 a At what frequency should a 2.0 m long pendulum be pushed in order to achieve large oscillations?

   b Are there any other frequencies which will achieve large oscillations?

CONTINUED

28 Figure 15.22 shows a set of weights of mass 0.50 kg hanging at the end of a spring of spring constant 220 N m^{-1}. The other end of the spring is attached to an oscillator. The oscillations are very slightly damped.

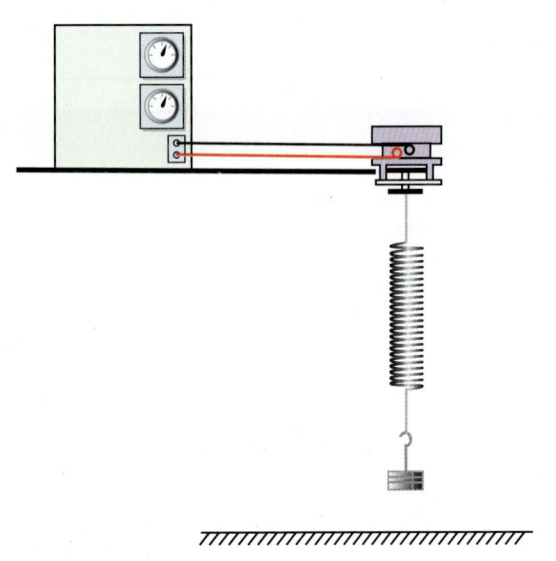

Figure 15.22: For question 28.

a At what frequency must the oscillator be set in order to achieve large amplitude oscillations of the weights?

b What happens to the frequency in part **a** if the damping increases?

29 Describe a situation where resonance is desirable and one where it is not.

30 Distinguish between light, critical and heavy damping. Suggest how the oscillations in the shock absorbers of a car should be damped.

SELF-ASSESSMENT CHECKLIST

I am able to …	Section	Not yet	Nearly there	Ready to move on
explain how a standing wave is formed	15.1			
state and explain differences between standing waves and travelling waves	15.1			
describe nodes and antinodes	15.1			
calculate the wavelength of a standing wave knowing the length of a string	15.2			
solve problems with standing waves on strings	15.2			
calculate the wavelength of a standing wave knowing the length of a pipe	15.3			
solve problems with standing waves in pipes	15.3			

15 Standing waves and resonance

CONTINUED

I am able to ...	Section	Not yet	Nearly there	Ready to move on
describe the effect of damping on the oscillations of a system	15.4			
describe how a system responds as the frequency of an external force varies	15.4			
appreciate the importance of resonance	15.4			

REFLECTION

Can you describe how a *standing wave* is formed? Do you know the differences between a travelling wave and a standing wave? Can you determine the wavelength of waves on strings and in pipes in terms of the length of the string or pipe? Do you know what is meant by *resonance* and *resonant frequency*? Do you know what is meant by *damping*? Do you know the effect of increased damping on the resonant frequency?

EXAM-STYLE QUESTIONS

You can find questions in the style of IB exams in the digital coursebook.

CHECK YOURSELF ANSWERS

1 All points have the same frequency, C.

2 The point in the middle since the point there moves the largest distance in one period.

3 The speed doubles and the frequency stays the same so the wavelength doubles. The string will now have just one loop, the first harmonic.

4 The wavelength is given by $\lambda = \frac{4L}{n}$ where n is odd and so the frequency is $f = \frac{c}{\lambda} = \frac{c}{4L} n$.

So, $126 = \frac{c}{4L} n$ and $210 = \frac{c}{4L}(n+2)$.

This gives $\frac{210}{126} = \frac{\frac{c}{4L}(n+2)}{\frac{c}{4L}n} = \frac{n+2}{n}$.

Thus, $\frac{5}{3} = \frac{n+2}{n} \Rightarrow 5n = 3n + 6$ and so $n = 3$.

This means $126 = f_1 \times 3 \Rightarrow f_1 = 42$ Hz.

Alternatively, you can argue as follows:

The frequencies are given by $f = \frac{c}{4L} n$ with n odd.

So, two consecutive harmonics differ in frequency by the constant amount $\frac{c}{2L}$ = 210 − 126 = 84 Hz.

Hence the first harmonic has frequency 126 − 84 = 42 Hz.

Yet another way to solve this is that the difference in frequency of two consecutive harmonics in the pipe is double the first harmonic frequency and so the answer is half of 84 Hz or 42 Hz.

And, finally, another way is to find the greatest common factor of 210 = {210, 70, 42, 30,...}, and 126 = {126, 42, 25.2, ...} i.e. 42 Hz.

5 The wavelength is $4L$ where L is the length of the string. Thus, $24 = 5.0 \times 4L \Rightarrow L = 1.2$ m. (This is a simplistic answer; this is worth investigating as an IA perhaps.)

6 The lower curve.

7 From the discussion in the text, the answer is C.

345

> Chapter 16
The Doppler effect

LEARNING OBJECTIVES

In this chapter you will learn how to:

- explain the shift in observed frequency through wavefront diagrams
- solve problems involving wavelength shifts and frequency using the approximate Doppler equations

> apply the Doppler equations for sound for moving sources or moving observers.

16 The Doppler effect

> **GUIDING QUESTION**
>
> Why does the frequency change when there is relative motion between source and observer?

Introduction

This section looks at the Doppler effect: the change in the observed frequency of a wave when there is relative motion between the source and the observer. The Doppler effect is a fundamental wave phenomenon with many applications. The phenomenon applies to all waves, but only sound and light waves are considered here.

16.1 The Doppler effect at low speeds

If you stand by the edge of a road and a car moving at high speed approaches you will hear a high-pitched sound. The instant the car moves past you, the frequency of the sound will drop abruptly and will stay low as the car moves away from you: this is the **Doppler effect**. It is more pronounced if the car going by is a Formula 1 racing car!

The Doppler effect is the change in the observed frequency of a wave when there is relative motion between the source and the observer.

We can explain most aspects of the Doppler effect using wavefront diagrams. Consider first a source of sound, S, that is stationary in still air. The source emits spherical wavefronts of frequency, f. (See Figure 16.1).

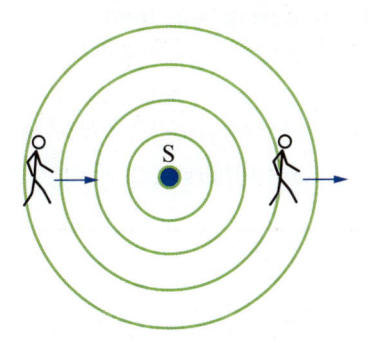

Figure 16.1: The wavefronts emitted by a stationary source are concentric. The common centre is the position of the source.

This means that f wavefronts are emitted per second. An observer who moves towards the stationary source will meet one wavefront after the other more frequently and so will measure a higher frequency of sound than f. The distance between the wavefronts does not change and so the moving observer will measure the same wavelength of sound as the source. Similarly, if the observer moves away from the source, then he or she will meet wavefronts less frequently and so will measure a frequency lower than f. The wavelength will be the same as that measured by the source.

If it is the source that is moving, then the wavefronts will look like those in Figure 16.2.

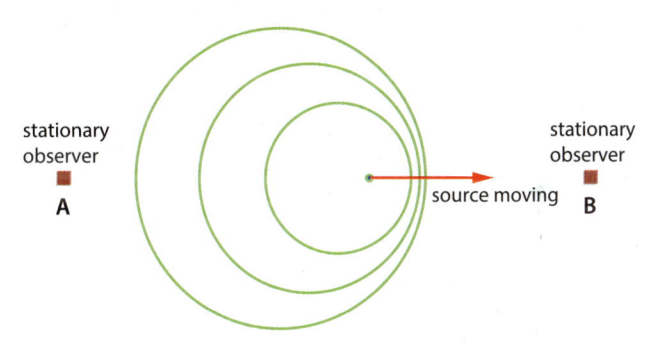

Figure 16.2: A source is moving away from a stationary observer A and is approaching the stationary observer B.

How do we understand this diagram? The large wavefront was emitted first. The position of the source when this wavefront was emitted was at the centre of this wavefront. The second wavefront was emitted later, and in this time the position of the source moved to the right. So this wavefront has its centre shifted to the right, and similarly for the third wavefront.

The diagram shows that the wavefronts between the source and observer B are getting closer to each other. This means that observer B will meet them more frequently, i.e. he or she will measure a frequency *higher* than f. Because of the bunching of the wavefronts the wavelength measured will be less than the wavelength measured by the source. For observer A, the wavefronts are further apart, and the frequency measured by this observer will be less than f. The wavelength measured is larger than that at the source because the wavefronts are further apart. These are the main features of the Doppler effect for sound.

> **PHYSICS FOR THE IB DIPLOMA: COURSEBOOK**

> **EXAM TIP**
>
> A common mistake is to confuse frequency with intensity (or loudness) of the sound. As a source approaches at constant speed, the intensity keeps increasing because the source is getting closer. The frequency observed has a *constant* value, higher than the frequency emitted.

The Doppler effect for light

The Doppler effect also applies to light. In the case in which the speed of the source or the observer is *small* compared to the speed of light, the approximate Doppler formula is:

$$\frac{\Delta f}{f} \approx \frac{v}{c}$$

In this formula v is the speed of the source or the observer, c is the speed of light and f is the emitted frequency. Then Δf gives the change in the observed frequency.

(Note that this approximate formula may also be used for sound provided the speed of the source or the observer is small compared to the speed of sound.)

Since $c = f\lambda$ it also follows that:

$$\frac{\Delta \lambda}{\lambda} \approx \frac{v}{c}$$

In this formula v is the speed of the source or the observer, c is the speed of light and λ is the emitted wavelength. Then $\Delta \lambda$ gives the change in the observed wavelength.

(This may also be used for sound but only for the case of a moving source. As we saw earlier, a moving observer will measure the same wavelength as that emitted.)

Remember that if the source of light approaches, then the frequency increases and the wavelength decreases. When the wavelength decreases we say we have a **blue-shift**. If the source of light moves away then the frequency decreases and the wavelength increases. In this case we speak of a **red-shift**.

Light from distant galaxies measured on earth shows a red-shift, i.e. it is longer than the wavelength emitted. This means that the galaxies are moving *away* from us. This great discovery in 1929 is convincing evidence for an expanding universe, a universe where galaxies get further apart from each other.

> **CHECK YOURSELF 1**
>
> A source emitting sound at 500 Hz and an observer are both moving towards the right as shown in Figure 16.3. Both have speed 10 m s^{-1}. The speed of sound is 340 m s^{-1}.
>
> What is the frequency heard by the observer?
>
> **Figure 16.3:** For check yourself question 1.

> **WORKED EXAMPLE 16.1**
>
> Hydrogen atoms in a distant galaxy emit light of wavelength 656 nm. The light received on earth is measured to have a wavelength of 689 nm.
>
> State whether the galaxy is approaching the earth or moving away, and calculate the speed of the galaxy.
>
> **Answer**
>
> The received wavelength is longer than that emitted, and so the galaxy is moving away from earth (we have a red-shift). Using $\Delta \lambda \approx \frac{v}{c}\lambda$ we get:
>
> $$v = \frac{c\Delta\lambda}{\lambda}$$
>
> $$v = \frac{3.00 \times 10^8 \times (689 - 656)}{656} = 1.5 \times 10^7 \text{ m s}^{-1}$$

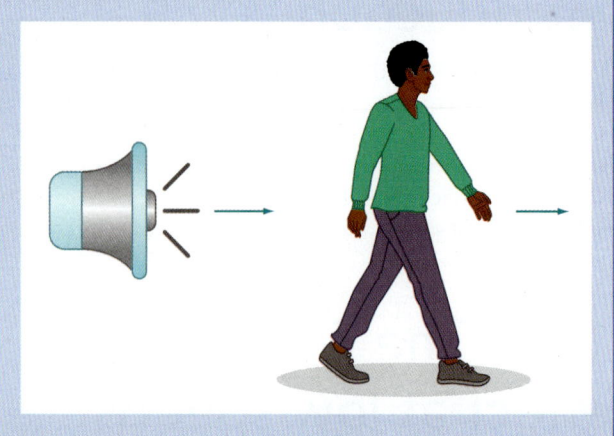

16 The Doppler effect

SCIENCE IN CONTEXT

The Doppler effect was first proposed to explain changes in the wavelength of light from binary stars as they rotate around each other. The effect also explains the change in pitch that occurs when a fast-moving source of sound passes by. Applying the theory to different types of waves in different areas of physics has led to hand-held radar guns to check for speeding vehicles and improvements in weather forecasting using the Doppler shift in radio waves reflected from moving cloud systems. But the striking application is in medicine, where Doppler imaging techniques are now routinely used to measure the speed of flow of blood cells in an artery, to monitor heart functions and examine the development of a fetus.

NATURE OF SCIENCE

Christian Doppler (1803–1853) proposed the effect that now bears his name in 1842. It was not immediately accepted. An "experiment" of musicians playing horns on a moving train platform in 1845 provided some support for his theory for sound, but the effect for light was severely attacked by a colleague of Doppler at the Austrian Academy of Sciences. Dejected and sick with tuberculosis, Doppler resigned his position and left for Venice where he died a few months later. Definitive verification of Doppler's ideas came in 1868 and 1872, long after Doppler's death, when astronomers measured the shift of spectral lines from stars.

Doppler would have greatly enjoyed knowing that the expansion of the universe, discovered by Edwin Hubble (1889–1953), was made by applying Doppler's red-shift formula. Observers on earth who measure the light emitted by galaxies find that the wavelength is longer than that emitted. The galaxies must be moving away.

But there would be another twist in the story. The modern view based on Einstein's general theory of relativity is that space in between galaxies is being stretched. This stretching makes all distances, including wavelengths, get larger. Yet the Doppler effect remains as a simple, intuitive if not completely correct description of what is actually going on, which gives the right answer for galaxies that are not too far away.

Links

The formula for the Doppler shift for light given previously is only approximate and is valid if the speed of the source or receiver is small compared to the speed of light. Things change drastically when this condition is not satisfied. In that case special relativity has to be used because clocks 'in motion' tick at a different rate compared to those 'at rest' (Chapter 6). This results in a more complicated formula for the Doppler shift. In the nonrelativistic Doppler effect it is the velocity along the line of sight between source and observer that is important. In relativity there is a new effect involving the component of velocity at right angles to the line of sight. This *transverse* Doppler effect, predicted by relativity, was one of the early tests of Einstein's theory.

TEST YOUR UNDERSTANDING

1. Explain the Doppler effect by drawing appropriate wavefront diagrams for:
   a. a stationary source and a moving observer
   b. a moving source and a stationary observer.

2. Calculate the speed of a galaxy emitting light of wavelength 5.48×10^{-7} m which when received on earth is measured to have a wavelength of 5.65×10^{-7} m.

3. A story told by Feynman tells of a man who appeared in front of a judge, accused of running a red traffic light. The man's defense was that due to the Doppler effect the red light appeared green as he was approaching it. The judge, who knew physics, accepted the man's defense but fined him very heavily anyway. Why?

4. Light from a nearby galaxy is emitted at a wavelength of 657 nm and is observed on earth at a wavelength of 654 nm.
   a. Deduce the speed of this galaxy.
   b. State what, precisely, can be deduced about the direction of the velocity of this galaxy.

5. The sun rotates about its axis with a period of 24.5 days at the equator. The radius of the sun is 7.00×10^8 m. Discuss the shifts in wavelength of light emitted from the sun's equator and received on earth. Assume that the sun emits monochromatic light of wavelength 5.00×10^{-7} m.

6. In a binary star system, two stars orbit a common point and move so that they are always in diametrically opposite positions. Light from both stars reaches an observer on earth. Assume that both stars emit light of wavelength 6.58×10^{-7} m.

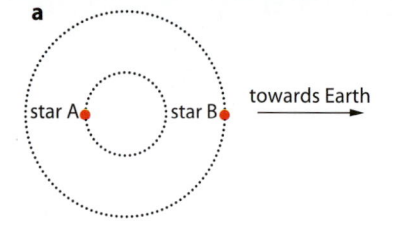

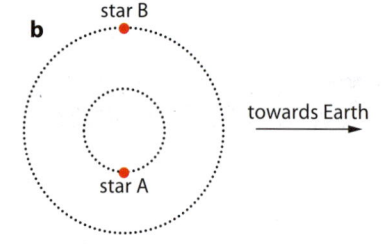

Figure 16.4: For question 6.

   a. When the stars are in the position shown in Figure 16.4a, the observer on earth measures a wavelength of light of 6.58×10^{-7} m from both stars. Explain why there is no Doppler shift in this case. (We ignore effects of special relativity.)
   b. When the stars are in the position shown in Figure 16.4b, the observer on earth measures two wavelengths in the received light, 6.50×10^{-7} m and 6.70×10^{-7} m. Determine the speed of each of the stars.

7. Ultrasound of frequency 5.000 MHz reflected from red blood cells moving in an artery is found to show a frequency shift of 2.4 kHz. The speed of ultrasound in blood is $v = 1500$ m s^{-1}.

   a. Explain why the appropriate formula for the frequency shift is $\frac{\Delta f}{f} = \frac{2u}{v}$, where u is the speed of the blood cells.
   b. Estimate the speed of the blood cells.
   c. In practice, a range of frequency shifts is observed. Explain this observation.

16.2 The Doppler effect for sound

Moving source and stationary observer

To derive a formula relating the emitted and observed frequencies, look at the situation in Figure 16.5.

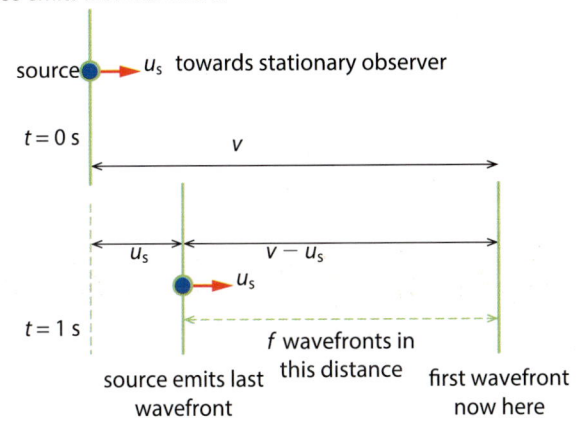

Figure 16.5: Determining the Doppler frequency.

The source emits sound of frequency f and wavelength λ. The sound has speed v in still air. So, in one second, the source will emit f wavefronts.

The source is moving with speed u_s towards the observer. So, in one second, the source will move a distance equal to u_s towards the stationary observer.

The movement of the source means that these f wavefronts are all within a distance of $v - u_s$. The stationary observer will, therefore, measure a wavelength λ' (separation of wavefronts) equal to:

$$\lambda' = \frac{v - u_s}{f}$$

The frequency f' measured by the stationary observer is then:

$$f' = \frac{v}{\lambda'} = \frac{v}{\frac{v - u_s}{f}}$$

In other words:

$$f' = f\left(\frac{v}{v - u_s}\right) \text{ (Source moving towards stationary observer.)}$$

A similar calculation gives:

$$f' = f\left(\frac{v}{v + u_s}\right) \text{ (Source moving away from stationary observer.)}$$

> **EXAM TIP**
>
> Notice that the speed of the wave measured by the observer is still v despite the fact the source moves. The speed of a wave is determined by the properties of the medium. This is still air for both source and observer, and both measure the same speed, v.

As the source approaches, the stationary observer thus measures a higher frequency than that emitted by the source. The wavelength measured by the observer will be shorter than the wavelength measured at the source. You can see this clearly from the wavefront diagram of Figure 16.2: the distance between the wavefronts in front of the source is smaller than that in Figure 16.1.

Using the basic wave formula $v = f\lambda = f'\lambda'$ we find

$$\lambda' = \frac{v}{f'} = \frac{v}{f\frac{v}{v - u_s}}$$

$$\lambda' = \frac{v}{f}\left(1 - \frac{u_s}{v}\right)$$

$$\lambda' = \lambda\left(1 - \frac{u_s}{v}\right) \text{ (Source moving towards stationary observer.)}$$

And similarly:

$$\lambda' = \lambda\left(1 + \frac{u_s}{v}\right) \text{ (Source moving away from stationary observer.)}$$

> **CHECK YOURSELF 2**
>
> A source of sound approaches a stationary observer at speed 40 m s^{-1}. The speed of sound is 340 m s^{-1}.
>
> What is the ratio $\frac{\text{wavelength observed}}{\text{wavelength emitted}}$?

351

WORKED EXAMPLE 16.2

The siren of a car moving at 28.0 m s^{-1} emits sound of frequency 1250 Hz. The car is directed towards a stationary observer X and moves away from an observer Y. Calculate the frequency and wavelength of sound observed by X and Y. The speed of sound in still air is 340 m s^{-1}.

Answer

We need to use the formula for a moving source; this is:

$$f' = f \frac{v}{v \pm u_s}$$

It can be difficult to decide whether the sign in the denominator should be plus or minus. The easy way to figure this out is to realise that if the source is approaching observer X we expect an increase in frequency. This means we need to use the minus sign to make the denominator smaller and so get a larger frequency. So substituting the values for X:

$$f' = 1250 \times \frac{340}{340 - 28} = 1362 \approx 1360 \text{ Hz.}$$

Remember that the speed of the sound is still v. To find the wavelength measured by X we use the relationship between speed, frequency and wavelength:

$$\lambda' = \frac{340}{1362} \approx 0.25 \text{ m}$$

For Y:

$$f' = 1250 \times \frac{340}{340 + 28} = 1155 \approx 1150 \text{ Hz and}$$

$$\lambda' = \frac{340}{1155} \approx 0.29 \text{ m}$$

Stationary source and moving observer

In the case of a stationary source and a moving observer we may argue as follows. First, let us consider the case of the observer moving towards the source. The observer who moves with speed u_o with respect to the source may claim that he is at rest and that it is the source that approaches him with speed u_o. But the air is also coming towards the observer with speed u_o and so the observer will measure a higher wave speed, $v + u_o$.

EXAM TIP

The speed of sound relative to the observer is no longer v. The medium has changed. For the source the medium is still air. For the observer the medium is moving air.

We can now apply the same equations as for a source moving towards the observer, and so the frequency measured by the observer is:

$$f' = f \frac{v + u_o}{v + u_o - u_o}$$

$$f' = f \left(\frac{v + u_o}{v} \right) \text{ (Observer moving towards source.)}$$

Similarly:

$$f' = f \left(\frac{v - u_o}{v} \right) \text{ (Observer moving away from source.)}$$

EXAM TIP

The IB data booklet has the formulae for frequency.

There is no need to remember the formulas for wavelength—just use the relationship:

$$\text{wavelength} = \frac{\text{wave speed}}{\text{frequency}}$$

WORKED EXAMPLE 16.3

An observer runs towards a stationary source with speed u_o. Show that the wavelength measured by the observer will be the same as that measured by the source (as we expect from the analysis with wavefront diagrams).

Answer

We need to use the formulas for a moving observer; this is:

$$f' = f \left(\frac{v + u_o}{v} \right)$$

Then

$$\lambda' = \frac{v + u_o}{f'}$$

$$\lambda' = \frac{v + u_o}{f \left(\frac{v + u_o}{v} \right)}$$

$$\lambda' = \frac{v}{f} = \lambda.$$

16 The Doppler effect

> **CHECK YOURSELF 3**
>
> A source moving at 40 m s^{-1} emitting sound of frequency 500 Hz approaches a stationary observer. The frequency heard by the observer will be $f' = 500 \times \left(\dfrac{340}{340-40}\right) = 567$ Hz.
>
> What frequency would an observer hear if she was moving at 40 m s^{-1} towards a stationary source of frequency 500 Hz?

WORKED EXAMPLE 16.4

A train sounding a 0.500 kHz horn is moving at a constant speed of 25 m s^{-1}. The train approaches and then moves away from an observer at the train station. Sketch a graph to show how the frequency heard by the observer varies with time. (Assume that the train goes past the observer at $t = 10$ s and take the speed of sound to be 340 m s^{-1}.)

Answer

As the train approaches the constant frequency observed is:

$$f' = f\left(\dfrac{v}{v - u_s}\right) = 500 \times \dfrac{340}{340 - 25} = 540 \text{ Hz}$$

As it moves away, the constant frequency is:

$$f' = f\left(\dfrac{v}{v + u_s}\right) = 500 \times \dfrac{340}{340 + 25} = 466 \text{ Hz}$$

This leads to the graph in Figure 16.6, showing the sudden drop in frequency at 10 s.

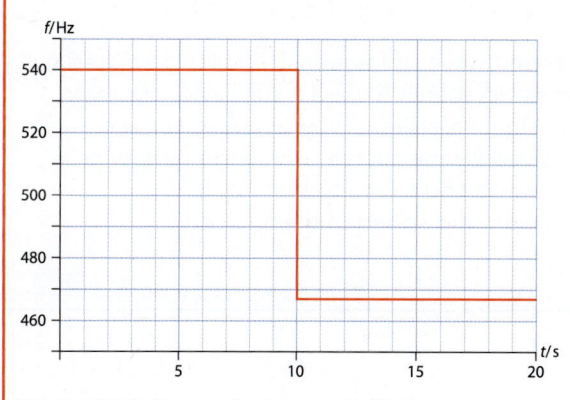

Figure 16.6: For worked example 16.4.

(This is an idealised graph with sharp corners. A realistic graph would be smooth.)

WORKED EXAMPLE 16.5

A sound wave of frequency 15.0 kHz is emitted towards an approaching car. The wave is reflected from the car and is then received back at the emitter at a frequency of 16.1 kHz.

Calculate the velocity of the car. (Take the speed of sound to be 340 m s^{-1}.)

Answer

The car is approaching the emitter so the frequency it receives is:

$$f_1 = 15.0 \times \dfrac{340 + u}{340} \text{ kHz}$$

where u is the unknown car speed.

The car now acts as an emitter of a wave of this frequency (f_1), and the original emitter will act as the new receiver.

So, the frequency received (16.1 kHz) from the approaching car is:

$$16.1 = \left(15.0 \times \dfrac{340 + u}{340}\right) \times \dfrac{340}{340 - u}$$

$$\Rightarrow \dfrac{16.1}{15.0} = \dfrac{340 + u}{340 - u}$$

$$\dfrac{340 + u}{340 - u} = 1.073$$

Solving for u (easiest done using the solver of your graphics calculator): $u = 12$ m s^{-1}.

TEST YOUR UNDERSTANDING

Take the speed of sound in still air to be 340 m s^{-1}.

8. We define the Doppler effect as the shift in observed frequency when there is relative motion between the source and the observer. Could we replace wavelength for frequency in this definition?

9. Explain, with the help of diagrams, the Doppler effect. Show clearly the cases of a source that:

   a. moves towards a stationary observer

   b. goes away from a stationary observer, as well the case of a moving observer.

10. A source approaches a stationary observer at 40 m s^{-1} emitting sound of frequency 500 Hz.

    a. Determine the frequency the observer measures.

    b. Calculate the wavelength of the sound as measured by

        i. the source

        ii. the observer.

11. A source is moving away from a stationary observer at 32 m s^{-1} emitting sound of frequency 480 Hz.

    a. Determine the frequency the observer measures.

    b. Calculate the wavelength of the sound as measured by:

        i. the source

        ii. the observer.

12. A sound wave of frequency 512 Hz is emitted by a stationary source toward an observer who is moving away at 12 m s^{-1}.

    a. Determine the frequency the observer measures.

    b. Calculate the wavelength of the sound as measured by:

        i. the source

        ii. the observer.

13. A sound wave of frequency 628 Hz is emitted by a stationary source toward an observer who is approaching at 25 m s^{-1}.

    a. Determine the frequency the observer measures.

    b. Calculate the wavelength of the sound as measured by:

        i. the source

        ii. the observer.

14. A source of sound is directed at an approaching car. The sound is reflected by the car and is received back at the source. Carefully explain what changes in frequency the observer at the source will detect.

15. A sound wave of frequency 500 Hz is emitted by a stationary source toward a receding observer. The signal is reflected by the observer and received by the source, where the frequency is measured and found to be 480 Hz. Calculate the speed of the observer.

16. A sound wave of frequency 500 Hz is emitted by a moving source toward a stationary observer. The signal is reflected by the observer and received by the source, where the frequency is measured and found to be 512 Hz. Calculate the speed of the source.

CONTINUED

17 A train emitting sound of frequency 800 Hz has speed 40 m s^{-1} when far from a train station. The train decelerates at 2.0 m s^{-2} as it approaches the train station and stops at $t = 20$ s at the train station next to the observer.

Sketch a graph to show the variation with time of the frequency heard by an observer at the train station. (See Figure 16.7.)

Figure 16.7: For question 17.

18 Consider the general case when both the source and the observer move towards each other. Let u_s be the velocity of the source and u_o that of the observer. In the frame of reference in which the observer is at rest, the waves appear to move with velocity $v + u_o$ and the source appears to move with velocity $u_s + u_o$. Show that the frequency received by the observer is:

$$f_o = f_s \frac{c + v_o}{c - v_s}.$$

SELF-ASSESSMENT CHECKLIST

I am able to ...	Section	Not yet	Nearly there	Ready to move on
explain the Doppler effect through wavefront diagrams	16.1			
apply the approximate Doppler formula for light	16.1			
solve problems using the Doppler formulae for sound	16.2			

REFLECTION

Can you explain the *Doppler effect* through wavefront diagrams? Can you apply the approximate formulas for the Doppler shift?

Can you apply the formulas for the Doppler effect for sound including the effect on wavelength?

EXAM-STYLE QUESTIONS

You can find questions in the style of IB exams in the digital coursebook.

CHECK YOURSELF ANSWERS

1. 500 Hz. There is no relative motion between source and observer so no Doppler effect.

2. From $\lambda' = \lambda\left(1 - \frac{u_s}{v}\right)$ we find $\frac{\lambda'}{\lambda} = 1 - \frac{u_s}{v} = 1 - \frac{40}{340} = 0.89$.

3. From $f' = f\left(\frac{v + u_o}{v}\right)$ we find $f' = 500 \times \left(\frac{340 + 40}{340}\right) = 559$ Hz.

Unit D
Fields

INTRODUCTION

The introduction of fields created a mechanism for 'action at a distance'. A mass creates a gravitational field around it at every point in space. An electric charge creates an electric field. A mass placed at some point in space "reacts" to the existence of the gravitational field by experiencing a gravitational force and similarly an electric charge experiences an electric force in the presence of an electric field. Maxwell, in his synthesis of electric and magnetic phenomena in the 19th century (one of the greatest unifications of knowledge in the history of science) wrote down the equations that describe the behaviour of electric and magnetic fields. It was a straightforward consequence of these equations that energy and momentum are carried by these fields in the form of electromagnetic waves propagating at the speed of light. If a charge were to suddenly appear, an electric field would be established in space at the speed of light. The 'information' about the existence of the charge is carried by electromagnetic waves travelling through vacuum at the speed of light. It is similarly believed that gravitational waves carry the 'information' about the existence of mass.

The idea of a field started as a classical concept but has found a smooth passage into quantum theory as well, at least for fields other than the gravitational field. According to Einstein, the presence of mass curves space-time. Another mass that finds itself in this curved space-time will follow a path of least length (in space-time). This geometric interpretation of gravity is unique to gravity which perhaps explains why the transition from the classical to the quantum field, while very successful for electromagnetic and other phenomena, has not been met with the same success for the gravitational field. Hence physicists have looked elsewhere for solutions to these problems, focusing on the idea that the elementary constituents of matter may not be point-like particles as field theory suggests but tiny one dimensional objects known as strings.

Chapter 17
Gravitation

LEARNING OBJECTIVES

In this chapter you will learn how to:

- apply Newton's law of gravitation
- apply the concept of gravitational field strength
- use Kepler's three laws of planetary motion
- apply Newton's law of gravitation to orbiting bodies
- understand how Kepler's laws follow from Newton's law of gravitation and the laws of mechanics

> understand the concepts of gravitational potential energy and gravitational potential

> derive an expression for the total energy of a body in a gravitational field

> solve problems on orbital motion

> calculate the escape speed from any point in a gravitational field

> recognize the effects of a frictional force (viscous drag) on a satellite's orbit radius and speed

17 Gravitation

> **GUIDING QUESTION**
>
> What does the law of gravitation imply for the motion of a falling apple and a celestial body?

Introduction

In this chapter we will discuss one of the fundamental laws of physics: **Newton's law of gravitation**.

We will apply it to the motion of bodies such as satellites and planets that orbit a fixed body.

We will see that the three laws of planetary motion deduced by Kepler are a direct consequence of Newton's laws.

In the AHL material, we will examine the details of motion in a gravitational field.

17.1 Newton's law of gravitation

Newton's second law implies that, whenever a particle moves with acceleration, a net force must be acting on it.

You may have heard the story about Newton sitting under an apple tree. A falling apple made him think about the nature of gravitation.

The apple, falling freely under gravity, would have been accelerating at $9.8\,\mathrm{m\,s^{-2}}$. It would have experienced a net force in the direction of the acceleration. This force is what we call the 'weight' of the apple.

Similarly, a planet that orbits around the sun also experiences acceleration, and thus a force is acting on it.

Newton hypothesised that the force responsible for the falling apple is the same kind of force as that acting on a planet as it moves around the sun.

> **KEY POINT**
>
> Newton proposed that the attractive force of gravitation between two **point masses** (idealised bodies with no physical size) is given by the formula:
>
> $F = G\dfrac{M_1 M_2}{r^2}$
>
> where M_1 and M_2 are the masses of the bodies, r is the distance between them and G is a constant. It has the value $G = 6.67 \times 10^{-11}\,\mathrm{N\,m^2\,kg^{-2}}$. The direction of the force is along the line joining the two masses.

This formula applies to point masses, but it can also be applied to any two bodies provided the distance between them is very large compared to the physical size of the bodies. In addition, Newton proved that for bodies that are spherical and of uniform density, one can assume that the entire mass of the body is concentrated at its centre—so in this case, the body acts as if it were a point mass. The distance r in the formula is the centre-to-centre separation of the spherical bodies.

> **THEORY OF KNOWLEDGE**
>
> **Deterministic system**
>
> The laws of mechanics, along with Newton's law of gravitation, are the basis of classical physics. They describe a perfectly *deterministic* system. This means that if we know the positions and velocities of the particles in a system at some instant of time, then the future positions and velocities of the particles can be predicted with absolute certainty. Since the beginning of the twentieth century we have known that this is not true in many cases. In situations normally associated with 'chaos' the sensitivity of the system to the initial conditions is such that it is not possible to make accurate predictions of the future state.

Figure 17.1 shows the gravitational force between two masses. The gravitational force is always attractive. The magnitude of the force on each mass is the same. This follows both from the formula as well as from Newton's third law.

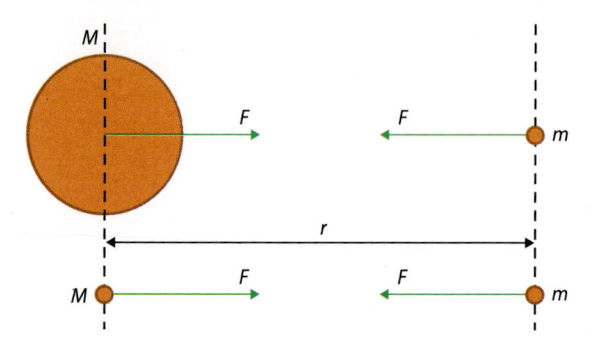

Figure 17.1: The mass of the spherical body to the left can be thought to be concentrated at its centre.

> ### CHECK YOURSELF 1
>
> The distance between two point masses is tripled. What happens to the force between the two masses?

> ### WORKED EXAMPLE 17.1
>
> The average distance between the earth and the sun is 1.5×10^{11} m.
>
> The mass of the earth is 6.0×10^{24} kg.
>
> The mass of the sun is 2.0×10^{30} kg.
>
> a Estimate the force between the sun and the earth.
>
> b What is the acceleration experienced by earth?
>
> **Answer**
>
> a Substituting these values into the formula $F = \frac{GM_1 M_2}{r^2}$ gives:
>
> $F = \frac{(6.67 \times 10^{-11}) \times (6.0 \times 10^{24}) \times (2.0 \times 10^{30})}{(1.5 \times 10^{11})^2}$
>
> $= 3.6 \times 10^{22}$ N
>
> b acceleration of the earth $= \frac{F}{M_E}$
>
> $= \frac{3.6 \times 10^{22}}{6.0 \times 10^{24}}$
>
> $= 6.0 \times 10^{-3}$ m s^{-2}

Gravitational field strength

For hundreds of years, many physicists and philosophers—including Newton—have wondered how a mass 'knows' about the presence of another mass nearby that will attract it. By the nineteenth century, physicists had developed the idea of a 'field'. This provided a (partial) answer to the question.

A mass M is said to create a **gravitational field** in the space around it. This means that, when another mass is placed at some distance from M, it 'feels' the gravitational field in the form of a gravitational force.

> ### KEY POINT
>
> The **gravitational field strength**, at a certain point, is the gravitational force per unit mass experienced by a small point mass m placed at that point:
>
> $g = \frac{F}{m}$
>
> The unit of gravitational field strength is N kg^{-1} (equivalent to m s^{-2}). It is a vector quantity.

Turning this around, we find that the gravitational force on a point mass m is $F = mg$. But this is the expression we previously called the weight of the mass m.

So, we learn that the gravitational field strength is the same as the acceleration of free fall.

The force experienced by a small point mass m placed at distance r from a (spherical) mass M is:

$F = G\frac{Mm}{r^2}$

So the gravitational field strength $\left(\frac{F}{m}\right)$ of the spherical mass M is:

$g = \frac{GM}{r^2}$

> ### THEORY OF KNOWLEDGE
>
> **Law of gravitation**
>
> Where did the law of gravitation come from? Not just from Newton's great intuition but also from the knowledge obtained earlier by Kepler, that planets move around the sun with a period that is proportional to the $\frac{3}{2}$ power of the average orbit radius. To get such a law, the force of gravitation had to be an inverse square law.

17 Gravitation

> **CHECK YOURSELF 2**
>
> The gravitational field strength on the surface of a planet is g. A satellite orbits the planet at a height from the surface equal to the radius of the planet.
>
> What is the magnitude of the acceleration of the satellite?

The direction of the gravitational field strength at some point is given by the direction of the force a point mass would experience if placed at that point. The gravitational field strength around a single point or spherical mass is **radial**, which means that it points towards the centre of the mass creating the field. This is illustrated in Figure 17.2. This field is not uniform—the field lines get farther apart with increasing distance from the point mass, showing that the magnitude of g decreases as we move away from M.

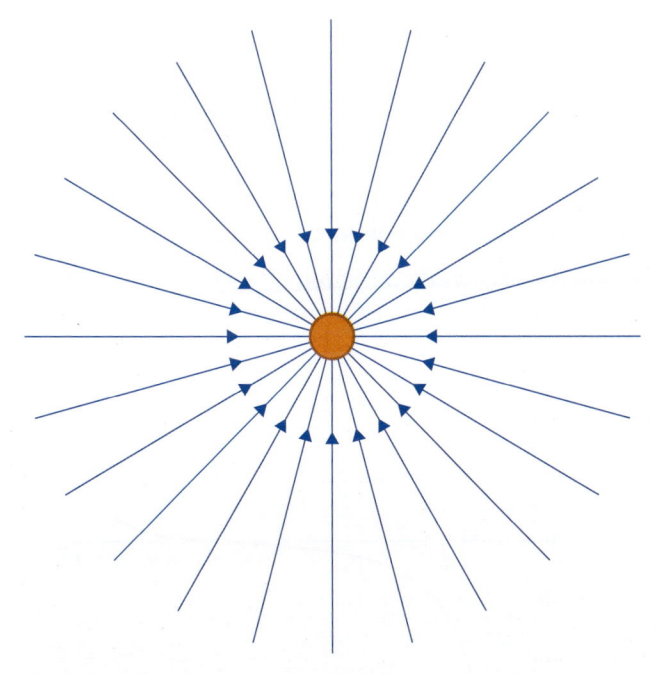

Figure 17.2: The gravitational field around a point (or spherical) mass is radial.

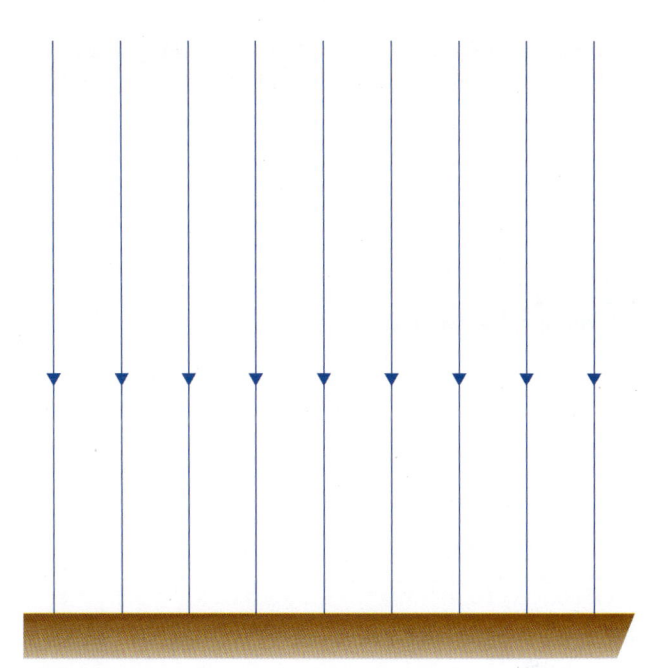

Figure 17.3: The gravitational field above a flat mass is uniform.

> **CHECK YOURSELF 3**
>
> The gravitational field strength at a point P in a gravitational field is 15 N kg^{-1}. A point mass of 0.40 kg is placed at P.
>
> What is the gravitational force on the mass?

> **WORKED EXAMPLE 17.2**
>
> The distance between two bodies is doubled.
>
> Predict what will happen to the gravitational force between them.
>
> **Answer**
>
> Since the force is inversely proportional to the square of the separation, doubling the separation decreases the force by a factor of $2^2 = 4$.

By contrast, Figure 17.3 shows a field with constant gravitational field strength. Here the field lines are equally spaced and parallel. The assumption of constant acceleration of free fall (which we used for projectile motion in Chapters 1–4) corresponds to this case.

WORKED EXAMPLE 17.3

Determine the acceleration of free fall (the gravitational field strength) on a planet 10 times as massive as the earth and with a radius 20 times as large.

Answer

From $g = \dfrac{GM}{r^2}$ we find:

$$g = \dfrac{G(10M_E)}{(20r_E)^2}$$

$$g = \dfrac{10GM_E}{400 r_E^2}$$

$$g = \dfrac{1}{40}\dfrac{GM_E}{r_E^2}$$

$$g = \dfrac{1}{40}g_E \approx 0.25 \text{ m s}^{-2}$$

EXAM TIP

For this type of problem write the formula for g and then replace mass and radius in terms of those for earth. It is a common mistake to forget to square the factor of 20 in the denominator.

WORKED EXAMPLE 17.4

Calculate the acceleration of free fall at a height of 300 km from the surface of the earth (the earth's radius, R_E, is 6.4×10^6 m and its mass is 6.0×10^{24} kg).

Answer

The acceleration of free fall is the same as the gravitational field strength. At height h from the surface:

$$g = \dfrac{GM_E}{(R_E + h)^2}$$

where $R_E = 6.4 \times 10^6$ m is the radius of the earth. We can now put the numbers in:

$$g = \dfrac{6.67 \times 10^{-11} \times 6.0 \times 10^{24}}{(6.7 \times 10^6)^2}$$

$$g \approx 9 \text{ N kg}^{-1}$$

EXAM TIP

Notice the addition of the height to the radius of the earth.

Figure 17.4 shows two spherical masses M and m a distance d apart. We want to find the gravitational field strength at a point in between the two masses, on the line joining them (Figure 17.4).

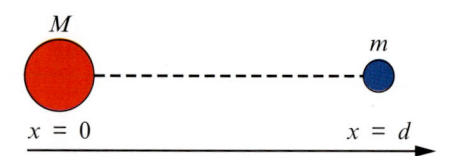

Figure 17.4

At a point that is a distance x from the centre of the larger mass the net gravitational field strength is:

$$g = -\dfrac{GM}{x^2} + \dfrac{Gm}{(d-x)^2}$$

This is because the large mass creates a gravitational field $\dfrac{GM}{x^2}$ directed to the left and the small mass a gravitational field $\dfrac{Gm}{(d-x)^2}$ directed to the right.

A negative sign indicates a field pointing to the left and a positive sign a field pointing to the right.

Figure 17.5 shows the variation of g with $\dfrac{x}{d}$. What is the ratio $\dfrac{M}{m}$?

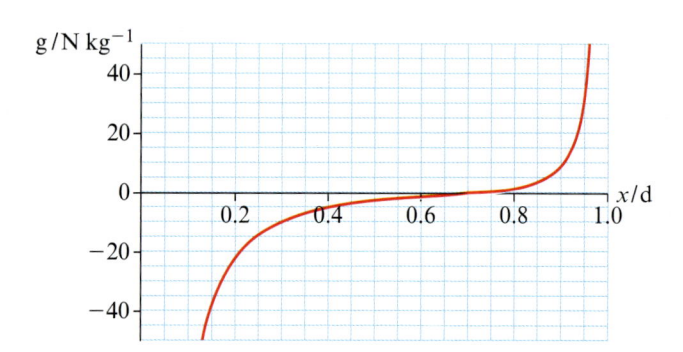

Figure 17.5: The variation of g with distance from the large mass.

We see that at $\dfrac{x}{d} = 0.75$, $g = 0$.

This means:

$$-\dfrac{GM}{0.75^2} + \dfrac{Gm}{0.25^2} = 0$$

And so:

$\frac{M}{m} = \frac{0.75^2}{0.25^2} = 9$

Orbital motion

Figure 17.6 shows a particle of mass m orbiting a larger body of mass M in a circular orbit of radius r. To maintain a constant orbit there must be no frictional forces, so the only force on the particle is the force of gravitation, $F = \frac{GMm}{r^2}$.

This force provides the centripetal force on the particle. Therefore:

$\frac{mv^2}{r} = \frac{GMm}{r^2}$

Cancelling the mass m and a factor of r, this leads to:

$v = \sqrt{\frac{GM}{r}}$

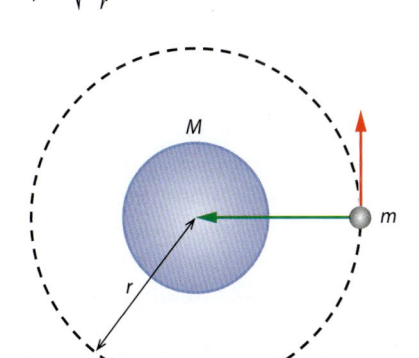

Figure 17.6: A particle of mass m orbiting a larger body of mass M in a circular orbit of radius r.

This gives the speed in a circular orbit of radius r. Notice that the closer the satellite is to the surface, the higher the speed. But we know that $v = \frac{2\pi r}{T}$, where T is the period of revolution (that is, the time to complete one full revolution). Squaring $v = \frac{2\pi r}{T}$ and equating the two expressions for v^2, we deduce that:

$\frac{4\pi^2 r^2}{T^2} = \frac{GM}{r}$

$\Rightarrow T^2 = \frac{4\pi^2 r^3}{GM}$

This shows that the period of planets going around the sun is proportional to the $\frac{3}{2}$ power of the orbit radius. Newton knew this from Kepler's discoveries (see next section), so he knew that his choice of inverse distance squared in the law of gravitation was reasonable.

Kepler's laws of planetary motion

Newton wrote down his law of gravitation in 1687. Between 1609 and 1619, the astronomer Johannes Kepler analysed the observations on the motion of planets made by the astronomer Tycho Brahe. Kepler's spectacular achievement was to discover the three laws that govern the motion of the planets around the sun.

Kepler's first law states that planets move on ellipses with the sun at one of the foci of the ellipse. (See Figure 17.7).

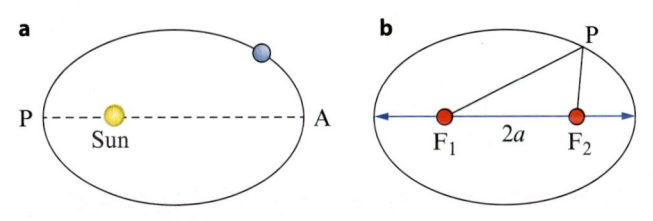

Figure 17.7: a The orbits of planets are elliptical. **b** The ellipse has two special points on its long axis, called the foci. The sum of the distances of any point on the ellipse from each of the foci is a constant.

The length of the long axis of the ellipse (the major axis) is called $2a$. This length is important for Kepler's third law.

Kepler's second law states that the line joining a planet and the sun sweeps equal areas in equal times. (See Figure 17.8.)

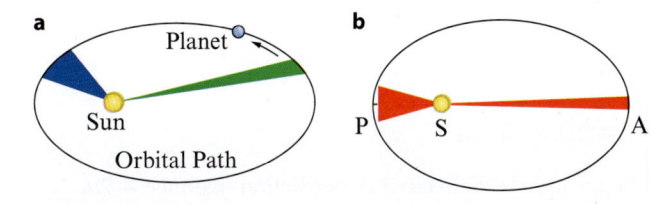

Figure 17.8: a In equal times, the line joining the planet to the sun sweeps out equal areas. **b** The special case when the planet is at perihelion (P) and aphelion (A).

Figure 17.8b shows the planet at its closest (perihelion) and furthest (aphelion) from the sun. We approximate the areas swept by the planet when at P and A by the red triangles. In equal times the areas are the same. The area of the left triangle is $\frac{1}{2}$ base × height = $\frac{1}{2} v_P t \times$ SP. The right triangle area is similarly $\frac{1}{2} v_A t \times$ SA. Equating the areas gives $\frac{1}{2} v_P t \times$ SP $= \frac{1}{2} v_A t \times$ SA and so $\frac{v_P}{v_A} = \frac{SA}{SP}$. This shows that the planet moves fastest at perihelion.

Kepler's third law states that the period of revolution of a planet around the sun is proportional to the $\frac{3}{2}$ power of the semi-major axis of the ellipse (the length a in Figure 17.7). More precisely:

$$T^2 = \frac{4\pi^2 a^3}{GM}$$

For a circular orbit of radius r, r and a are the same.

Newton knew of Kepler's discoveries. He realised that a force of attraction between two bodies that varied as $F \sim \frac{1}{r^2}$ would lead to elliptical or circular closed orbits (Kepler's first law). He also knew that such a law would lead to Kepler's third law. And finally by applying the law of conservation of angular momentum he could derive Kepler's second law. The fact that Newton's laws lead to the empirical laws discovered by Kepler was solid evidence that Newton was right about his law of gravitation.

WORKED EXAMPLE 17.5

Halley's comet has a period of about 75 years. The perihelion distance (when it is closest to the sun) is 8.8×10^{10} m. Find the distance between the comet and the sun when the comet is at aphelion (furthest from the sun) and calculate the ratio of the perihelion to aphelion speed.

Answer

From $T^2 = \frac{4\pi^2 a^3}{GM}$ we find:

$$a = \left(\frac{GMT^2}{4\pi^2}\right)^{\frac{1}{3}}$$

$$= \left(\frac{6.67 \times 10^{-11} \times 2.0 \times 10^{30} \times (75 \times 365 \times 24 \times 3600)^2}{4\pi^2}\right)^{\frac{1}{3}}$$

$$= 2.7 \times 10^{12} \text{ m}$$

Since aphelion distance + perihelion distance = $2a$, it follows that the aphelion distance is 5.3×10^{12} m.

The perihelion to aphelion speed ratio is then $\frac{5.3 \times 10^{12}}{8.8 \times 10^{10}} \approx 60$.

CHECK YOURSELF 4

Why are comets such a rare sight?

Links

The prediction of the orbits of the planets was the crowning achievement of the Newtonian theory, so much so that soon after electrons were discovered, one of the first models of the atom was a miniature planetary system with electrons orbiting the nucleus of the atom in circular orbits. That was the Rutherford model which was soon replaced by the Bohr model which also had the electrons in circular orbits. So strong was the influence of the Newtonian planetary model that Sommerfeld modified the Bohr model to include elliptical electron orbits. But this reliance on the old ideas had to stop when new phenomena were observed that required a radically new approach to the whole subject.

NATURE OF SCIENCE

Predictions versus understanding

Combining the laws of mechanics with the law of gravitation enables scientists to predict with great accuracy the orbits of spacecraft, planets and comets. But to what degree do they enable an understanding of why planets, for example, move the way they do? In ancient times, Ptolemy was also able to predict the motion of planets with exceptional precision. In what sense is the Newtonian approach 'better'? Ptolemy's approach was specific to planets and could not be generalised to other examples of motion, whereas the Newtonian approach can. Ptolemy's method gives no explanation of the observed motions whereas Newton 'explains' the motion in terms of one single universal concept, that of a gravitational force that depends in a specific way on mass and separation. In this sense the Newtonian approach is superior and represents progress in science. But there are limits to the degree to which one demands 'understanding': the obvious question for Newton would be, 'Why is there a force between two masses?' Newton could not answer this question.

TEST YOUR UNDERSTANDING

Unless stated otherwise, take the radius and mass of the earth to be 6.4×10^6 m and 6.0×10^{24} kg, respectively.

1. Calculate the gravitational force between:
   a. the earth and the moon (distance between earth and moon = 3.8×10^5 km; moon's mass = 7.3×10^{22} kg)
   b. a proton and an electron separated by 10^{-10} m (mass of proton = 1.67×10^{-27} kg; mass of electron = 9.11×10^{-31} kg).

2. A mass m is placed at the centre of a thin, hollow, spherical shell of mass M and radius r, as shown in Figure 17.9a.

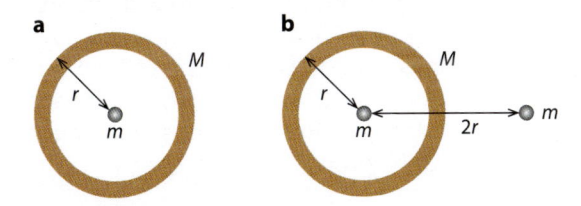

Figure 17.9: For question 2.

   a. Determine the gravitational force the mass m experiences.
   b. Determine the gravitational force m exerts on M.

   A second mass m is now placed a distance of $2r$ from the centre of the shell, as shown in Figure 17.9b.

   c. Determine the gravitational force the mass inside the shell experiences.
   d. Suggest what gravitational force is experienced by the mass outside the shell.

3. Stars A and B have the same mass, and the radius of star A is nine times larger than the radius of star B. Calculate the ratio of the gravitational field strength on star A to that on star B.

4. Planet A has a mass that is twice as large as the mass of planet B and a radius that is twice as large as the radius of planet B. Calculate the ratio of the gravitational field strength on planet A to that on planet B.

5. Stars A and B have the same density, and star A is 27 times more massive than star B. Calculate the ratio of the gravitational field strength on star A to that on star B.

6. A star explodes and loses half its mass. Its radius becomes half as large. Determine the new gravitational field strength on the surface of the star in terms of the original one.

7. The mass of the moon is about 81 times less than that of the earth. Estimate the fraction of the distance from the earth to the moon where the gravitational field strength is zero. (Take into account the earth and the moon only.)

8. Figure 17.10 shows point P is halfway between the centres of two equal spherical masses that are separated by a distance of 2×10^9 m. Calculate the gravitational field strength at point P and state the direction of the gravitational field strength at point Q.

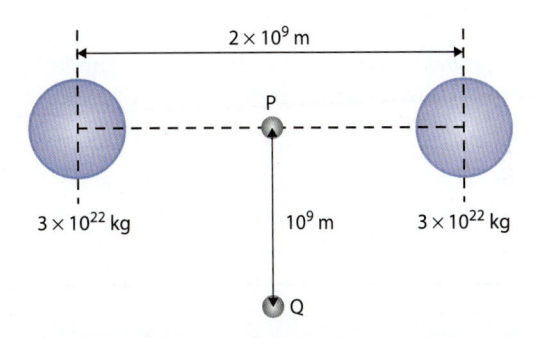

Figure 17.10: For question 8.

9. Two satellites of mass m and $2m$ orbit the earth with the same orbit radius. Which satellite experiences the larger force from earth? Which satellite experiences the larger acceleration?

10. Two satellites, X and Y, orbit the earth in circular orbits. The orbit radius of X is double that of Y. What is the ratio of the acceleration of X to that of Y?

11. A satellite orbits the earth above the equator with a period equal to 24 hours.

CONTINUED

  a   Determine the height of the satellite above the earth's surface.

  b   Suggest an advantage of such a satellite.

12 The Hubble Space Telescope is in orbit around the earth at a height of 560 km above the earth's surface.

  a   Calculate Hubble's speed.

  b   In a servicing mission, a space shuttle spotted the Hubble telescope a distance of 10 km ahead. Estimate how long it took the shuttle to catch up with Hubble, assuming that the shuttle was moving in a circular orbit just 500 m below Hubble's orbit.

13 The solar system is at a distance of about 27,000 light years from the centre of the Milky Way galaxy. A light year is the distance travelled by light in one year. The solar system orbits the galactic centre in a circular orbit with a speed that is roughly 200 km s^{-1}.

  a   The speed of light is 3.0×10^8 m s^{-1}. Convert a light year into metres.

  b   How long, in years, does it take the solar system to perform one full revolution?

  c   The mass of the galaxy that attracts our solar system is the mass of the galaxy that is within the orbit radius of the solar system. Estimate this mass.

14 Which planet of the solar system has the greatest orbital speed? (Don't just look it up!)

15 Assume that the force of gravity between two point masses is given by $F = \frac{Gm_1 m_2}{r^n}$ where n is a constant.

  a   Derive the law relating period to orbit radius for this force.

  b   Deduce the value of n if this law is to be identical to Kepler's third law.

16 a   Show that a moon orbiting a planet of mass M in a circular orbit of radius r has a period T given by $T^2 = \frac{4\pi^2}{GM} r^3$.

  b   Europa is a moon of Jupiter with an orbit radius 6.7×10^5 km and period 3.6 days. Triton is a moon of Neptune with an orbital radius 3.5×10^5 km and period 5.9 days. What is the ratio of the mass of Jupiter to that of Neptune?

17 The moon orbits the earth with an orbit radius 3.8×10^5 km and period 27 days. The radius of the earth is 6.4×10^3 km. From this information deduce the density of the earth.

18 Tethys is a moon of Saturn with a period of 1.9 days and an orbit radius 2.9×10^5 km. Titan is another moon of Saturn with a period of 16 days. What is the orbit radius of Titan?

17.2 Gravitational potential and energy

This section deals with the concepts of gravitational potential and gravitational potential energy that are needed to understand motion in a gravitational field.

Consider a mass M placed somewhere in space, and a second mass m that is a distance r from M. The two masses share **gravitational potential energy**, which is stored in their gravitational field. This energy is the work that was done in bringing the two masses to a distance r apart from an initial separation that was infinite. For all practical purposes we consider M to be fixed in space and so it is just the small body of mass m that is moved (Figure 17.11).

> **KEY POINT**
>
> The gravitational potential energy of two bodies is the work that was done in bringing the bodies to their present position from when they were infinitely far apart.

17 Gravitation

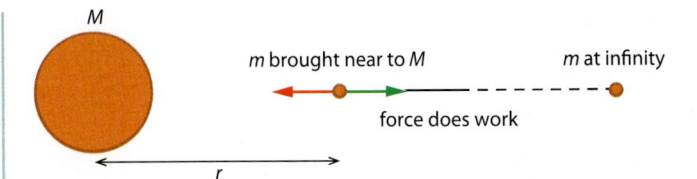

Figure 17.11: Work is done to bring the small mass from infinity to a given position near the big mass. The red arrow is the force of attraction between the two masses. We are interested in the work done by the force represented by the green arrow, i.e. the work done by the external agent. This work is negative and is stored as potential energy. The work done is independent of the actual path followed.

Notice that, strictly speaking, this is energy that belongs to the pair of masses M and m and not just to one of them. Notice also that when we say that the masses are moved from infinity we are implying that they are moved at a very small constant speed, so that no kinetic energy is involved.

The gravitational force is not constant, so we cannot straightforwardly calculate the work done. We need calculus for this calculation. The total work done in moving the mass m from infinity to a distance r from the centre of a spherical mass M is:

$$W = \int_{\infty}^{r} \frac{GMm}{r^2} dr = -\left[\frac{GMm}{r}\right]_{\infty}^{r} = -\frac{GMm}{r}$$

Note that this is the work done by an external agent in bringing the mass m from far away to a position near M at constant speed. The force this agent exerts on m is equal and opposite to the gravitational force exerted on m by M. It is important to be clear about who exerts forces on whom and who does work; otherwise things can get very confused.

So this work is now the gravitational potential energy of the two masses when their centres are separated by a distance r:

$$E_p = -\frac{GMm}{r}$$

This energy is negative. There are two ways to understand why this energy is negative:

1. Referring to Figure 17.11 we see that the force is directed to the right and motion to the left. Since $\cos 180° = -1$, the work done, and hence the potential energy, will be negative.

2. Imagine that m is very far from M. We expect no potential energy in this case. If m is free to move it will be attracted by M and so m will increase its kinetic energy. So the potential energy must decrease (that is, it will become negative).

This implies that if we have a mass m on the surface of a planet of radius R and we want to separate the two masses by moving m a large distance away we must provide an amount of energy equal to $+\frac{GMm}{R}$ to m (Figure 17.12).

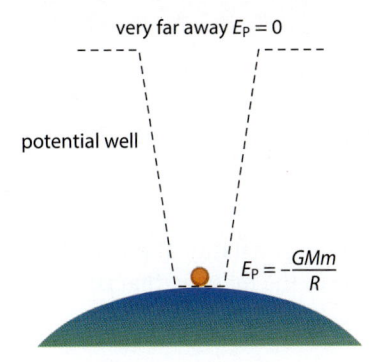

Figure 17.12: The mass m at the surface of a planet of mass M has negative potential energy. It needs energy to 'get out' of the 'well' (to move away from the planet's surface).

WORKED EXAMPLE 17.6

Calculate the difference in the potential energy of a satellite of mass 1500 kg when it is taken from the surface of the earth (mass $M = 6.0 \times 10^{24}$ kg, radius $R = 6.4 \times 10^6$ m) to a distance of 500 km above the earth's surface.

Answer

The potential energy of the system initially is:

$$E_p = -\frac{GMm}{R} = -\frac{6.67 \times 10^{-11} \times 6.0 \times 10^{24} \times 1500}{6.4 \times 10^6}$$

$$\approx -9.4 \times 10^{10} \text{ J}$$

At a distance of 520 km from the earth's surface the separation of the masses is $r = R + 520$ km. The potential energy is therefore:

$$E_p = -\frac{GMm}{r} = -\frac{6.67 \times 10^{-11} \times 6.0 \times 10^{24} \times 1500}{6.9 \times 10^6}$$

$$\approx -8.7 \times 10^{10} \text{ J}$$

The difference in these potential energies is:

$$(-8.7 \times 10^{10}) - (-9.4 \times 10^{10}) = 7.0 \times 10^9 \text{ J}$$

This difference of 7.0×10^9 J is the energy that needs to be provided to move the satellite from earth to its new position.

367

Gravitational potential

Related to the concept of gravitational potential energy is that of **gravitational potential**, V_g.

> **KEY POINT**
>
> The gravitational potential at a point P in a gravitational field is the work done per unit mass in bringing a small point mass from infinity to point P. The unit of potential is J kg^{-1}.

If the work done is W, then the gravitational potential is the ratio of the work done to the mass m, that is:

$$V_g = \frac{W}{m}$$

The gravitational potential is a *scalar* quantity.
Since $W = -\frac{GMm}{r}$, the potential a distance r from a spherical mass M is:

$$V_g = -\frac{GMm/r}{m}$$

$$V_g = -\frac{GM}{r}$$

In general, if mass M produces a gravitational potential V_g at some point and we place a mass m at that point, the gravitational potential energy of the system is $E_P = mV_g$.

If a mass m is positioned at point A in a gravitational field where the gravitational potential is V_{gA} and is then moved to another point B where the gravitational potential is V_{gB}, then the work that is done on the mass by the external agent moving the mass is the difference in gravitational potential energy:

$$W = \Delta E_P$$
$$W = mV_{gB} - mV_{gA}$$
$$W = m\Delta V_g$$

The work done does not depend on the actual path taken (Figure 17.13).

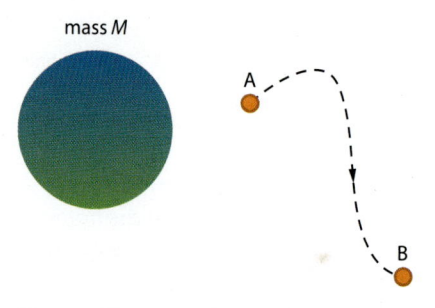

Figure 17.13: Work must be done to move a mass from one point to another in a gravitational field.

> **EXAM TIP**
>
> This formula is used when an external agent does work to move a mass m from one point in a gravitational field to another at constant small speed. The work done by the gravitational force is the opposite.

> **CHECK YOURSELF 5**
>
> The gravitational potential at a point P near a planet is -2.0×10^{10} J kg^{-1}. A body of mass 350 kg is placed at P. What is the gravitational potential energy of the body and the planet?

> **WORKED EXAMPLE 17.7**
>
> Look at Figure 17.14. The gravitational potential at A is $V_A = -5 \times 10^{12}$ J kg^{-1} and at B it is $V_B = -2 \times 10^{12}$ J kg^{-1}.
>
> What is the work done in moving a mass of 200 kg from A to B by:
>
> a an external agent (green arrow)
>
> b the gravitational force (red arrow)?

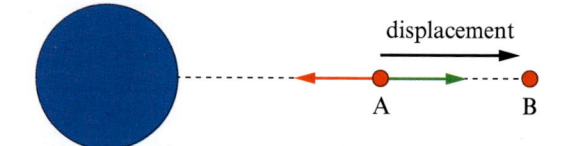

Figure 17.14

17 Gravitation

CONTINUED

Answer

The external agent has to apply a force to the right (green arrow) equal to the gravitational force (red arrow) exerted on the body by the large mass that created the gravitational potential. The forces have to be equal so that the body is moved from A to B at a small constant speed.

a The work done by the external agent is
$W = m(V_B - V_A) = 200 \times (-2 \times 10^{12} - (-5 \times 10^{12}))$
$= 6 \times 10^{14}$ J.

b The work done by the gravitational force is -6×10^{14} J.

CHECK YOURSELF 6

In worked example 17.7, the force at A is 1.7×10^9 N and the displacement from A to B is 9.0×10^5 m.

Why does the product $1.7 \times 10^9 \times 9.0 \times 10^5 = 1.5 \times 10^{15}$ J not give the right answer for the work done in moving the mass from A to B?

WORKED EXAMPLE 17.8

Figure 17.15 shows two spherical bodies. Calculate the gravitational potential at point P.

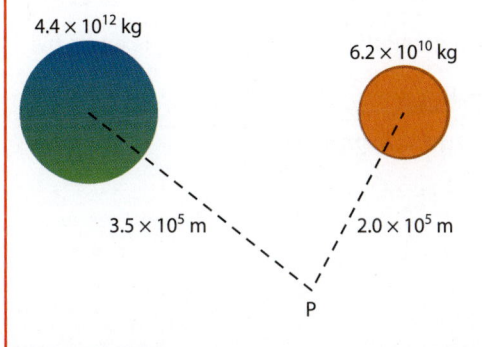

4.4 × 10¹² kg

6.2 × 10¹⁰ kg

3.5 × 10⁵ m

2.0 × 10⁵ m

P

Figure 17.15

CONTINUED

Answer

Gravitational potential is a scalar quantity, so we find the potential created by each mass separately and then add.

Potential from left mass:

$V_1 = -\dfrac{GM}{r}$

$V_1 = -\dfrac{6.67 \times 10^{-11} \times 4.4 \times 10^{12}}{3.5 \times 10^5}$

$V_1 = -8.385 \times 10^{-4}$ J kg^{-1}

Potential from right mass:

$V_2 = -\dfrac{6.67 \times 10^{-11} \times 6.2 \times 10^{10}}{2.0 \times 10^5}$

$V_2 = -2.068 \times 10^{-5}$ J kg^{-1}

The total potential is then the sum $V = V_1 + V_2 = -8.6 \times 10^{-4}$ J kg^{-1}.

WORKED EXAMPLE 17.9

The mass of the moon is about 81 times smaller than that of the earth. The distance between the earth and the moon is about $d = 3.8 \times 10^8$ m. The mass of the earth is 6.0×10^{24} kg.

a Determine the distance from the centre of the earth of the point on the line joining the earth to the moon where the combined gravitational field strength of the earth and the moon is zero.

b Calculate the combined gravitational potential at that point.

c Calculate the potential energy when a 2500 kg probe is placed at that point.

Answer

a Let the point we are looking for be point P, and the distance we are looking for be x. Let the mass of the earth be M, so the mass of the moon is $\dfrac{M}{81}$.

CONTINUED

Use the information to draw a diagram to show the situation, as in Figure 17.16.

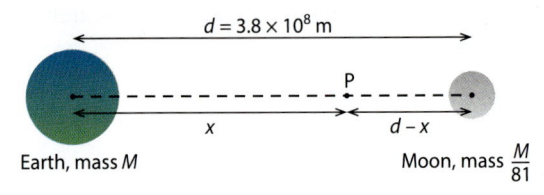

Figure 17.16

Earth, mass M; Moon, mass $\frac{M}{81}$; distance $d = 3.8 \times 10^8$ m; point P at distance x from Earth and $d-x$ from Moon.

The field due to the earth at point P is then
$$g_{earth} = \frac{GM}{x^2}.$$

The field due to the moon at point P is then
$$g_{moon} = \frac{\frac{GM}{81}}{(d-x)^2}.$$

The combined field is zero. The two fields are opposite in direction and must be equal in magnitude. Therefore:

$$g_{earth} = g_{moon}$$

$$\frac{GM}{x^2} = \frac{\frac{GM}{81}}{(d-x)^2}$$

$$\frac{1}{x^2} = \frac{1}{81(d-x)^2} \Rightarrow x^2 = 81(d-x)^2$$

$$x = 9(d-x)$$

$$\Rightarrow x = \frac{9d}{10} = \frac{9}{10} \times 3.8 \times 10^8 = 3.4 \times 10^8 \text{ m}$$

b The combined potential at this point (we add the individual potentials for the earth and the moon since potential is a scalar quantity) is:

$$V_g = -\frac{GM}{x} - \frac{\left(\frac{GM}{81}\right)}{d-x}$$

$$V_g = -\frac{6.67 \times 10^{-11} \times 6.0 \times 10^{24}}{3.4 \times 10^8} - \frac{6.67 \times 10^{-11} \times 6.0 \times 10^{24}}{0.4 \times 10^8 \times 81}$$

$$V_g = -1.3 \times 10^6 \text{ J kg}^{-1}$$

c Use the equation $E_P = mV_g$.

Substituting the mass of the probe for the mass m and using the value for V_g from part **b**:

$$E_P = 2500 \times (-1.3 \times 10^6)$$

$$E_P = -3.3 \times 10^9 \text{ J}$$

WORKED EXAMPLE 17.10

The graph in Figure 17.17 shows the variation of the gravitational potential V with distance r away from the centre of a dense compact planet of radius 2×10^6 m.

Use the graph to calculate the work required to move a probe of mass 3400 kg from the surface to a distance of 7.5×10^6 m from the centre of the planet.

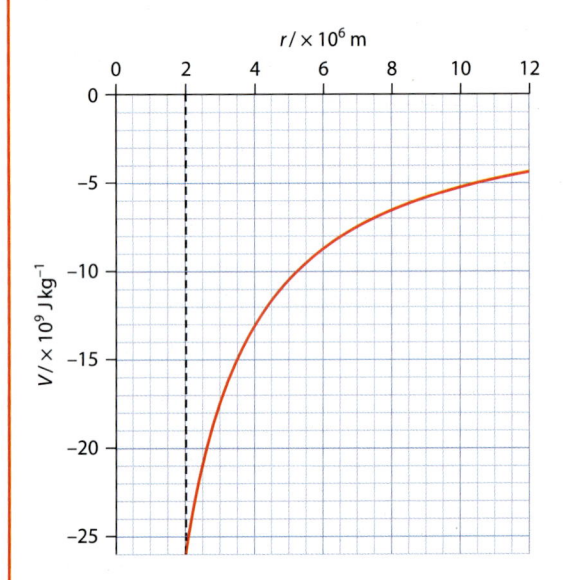

Figure 17.17

Answer

The work required can be found from $W = m\Delta V_g$ or from the completely equivalent $W = \Delta E_P$.

The change in gravitational potential ΔV_g is given by:

$$\Delta V_g = V_{final} - V_{initial}$$

$$\Delta V_g = -7.0 \times 10^9 - (-26 \times 10^9)$$

$$\Delta V_g = 19 \times 10^9 \text{ J kg}^{-1}$$

So the work done is:

$$W = m\Delta V_g$$

$$W = 3400 \times 19 \times 10^9$$

$$W = 6.5 \times 10^{13} \text{ J}$$

Field and potential

Consider two points very close to each other separated by a distance Δr and suppose that the gravitational potential difference between the two points is ΔV_g. The work done in moving a mass m from one point to the other can be calculated in two ways: $m\Delta V_g$ and $F\Delta r$. But $F = mg$ and so $mg\Delta r = m\Delta V_g$. This says that the magnitude of the gravitational field strength is:

$$g = \frac{\Delta V_g}{\Delta r}.$$

This also says that g is the gradient of a graph of V_g versus r. (If calculus is used the correct expression is $g = -\frac{dV_g}{dr}$.)

> **CHECK YOURSELF 7**
>
> The graph in Figure 17.18 shows the variation of the gravitational potential along a line joining two planets. 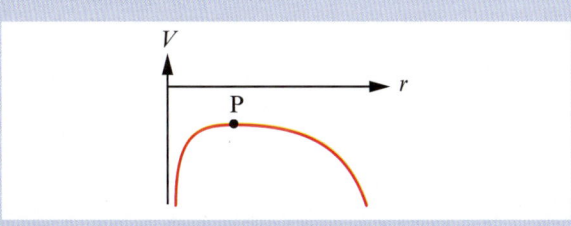
>
> **Figure 17.18:** For check yourself question 7.
>
> What is g at point P?

Equipotential surfaces

We know that a spherical uniform mass M is the source of gravitational potential which, at a distance r from the centre of the source, is given by

$$V_g = -\frac{GM}{r}$$

This means that points which are at the same distance from the centre of the mass are at the same potential. Points that have the same distance from the source lie on spheres. A two-dimensional representation of these spheres of constant potential is given in Figure 17.19. They are called **equipotential surfaces**. Notice that the field lines are normal to the equipotential surfaces.

An equipotential surface consists of those points that have the same potential.

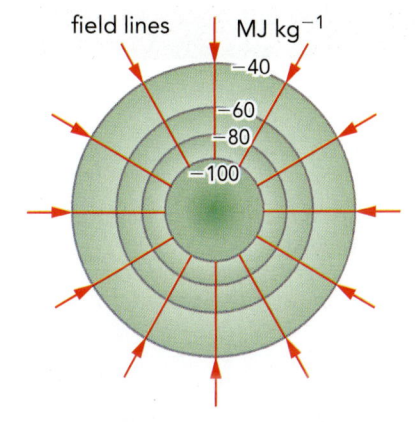

Figure 17.19: Equipotential surfaces due to one spherical mass. These surfaces are drawn so that the difference in potential between any two adjacent surfaces is the same.

Figure 17.20a shows the equipotential surfaces of two equal spherical masses, and Figure 17.20b shows the surfaces for two unequal masses.

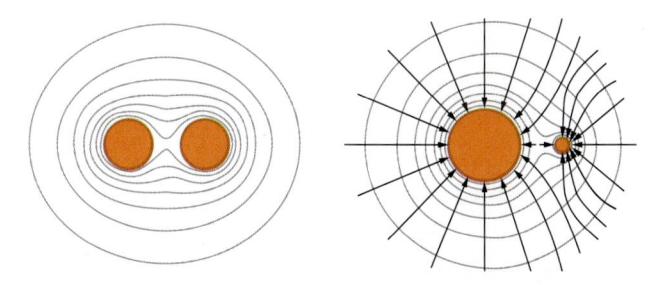

Figure 17.20: Equipotential surfaces for **a** two equal spherical masses and **b** two unequal masses. Field lines are normal to the equipotential surfaces.

The work done to move a point mass from one point to another point on the same equipotential surface is zero since $W = m\Delta V_g$ and $\Delta V_g = 0$ (Figure 17.21).

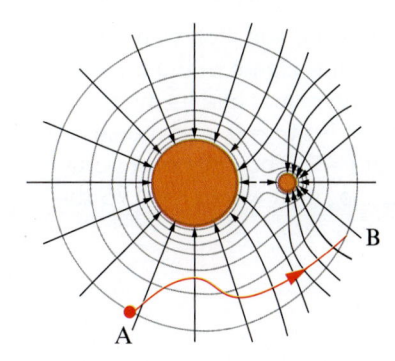

Figure 17.21: Zero work is done when moving a mass from one point to another on the same equipotential.

371

TEST YOUR UNDERSTANDING

19 Consider two particles of mass m and $16m$ separated by a distance d.

  a Deduce that at point P, a distance $\frac{d}{5}$ from the particle with mass m, the gravitational field strength is zero.

  b Determine the value of the gravitational potential at P.

20 a What is the gravitational potential at a distance from the earth's centre equal to 5 earth radii? (earth mass = 6.0×10^{24} kg, earth radius = 6.4×10^3 km.)

  b What is the gravitational potential energy of a 500 kg satellite placed at a distance from the earth's centre equal to 5 earth radii?

21 a What is the gravitational potential energy stored in the gravitational field between the earth and the moon? (earth mass = 6.0×10^{24} kg, moon mass = 7.3×10^{22} kg, separation = 3.8×10^8 m)

  b What is the earth's gravitational potential at the position of the moon?

  c Find the speed with which the moon orbits the earth.

22 A spacecraft of mass 30 000 kg leaves the earth on its way to the moon and lands on the moon. Plot the spacecraft's potential energy as a function of its distance from the earth's centre. (The earth–moon distance is 3.8×10^8 m. Take the mass of the earth to be 6.0×10^{24} kg and the mass of the moon to be 7.3×10^{22} kg.)

23 Figure 17.22 shows the variation with distance from the centre of the planet of the gravitational potential due to the planet and its moon. The planet's centre is at $r = 0$, and the centre of the moon is at $r = 1$. The units of separation are arbitrary. At the point where $r = 0.75$ the gravitational field is zero.

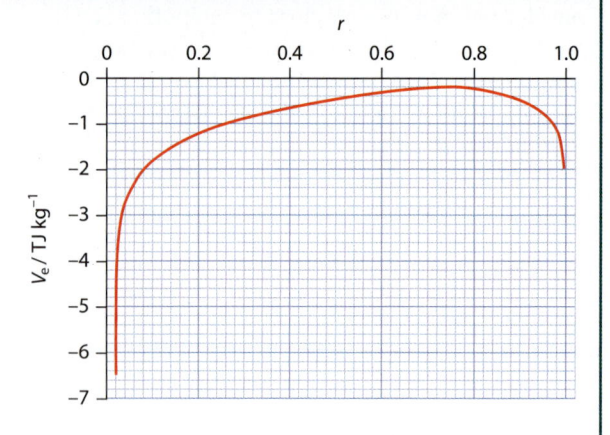

Figure 17.22: For question 23.

  a Determine the ratio of the mass of the planet to that of the moon.

  b With what speed must a probe be launched from the surface of the planet in order to arrive on the surface of the moon?

24 Figure 17.23 shows a planet orbiting the sun counterclockwise at two positions—A and B. Also shown is the gravitational force acting on the planet at each position.

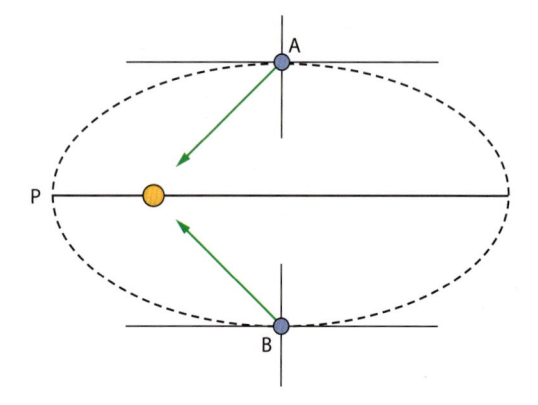

Figure 17.23: For question 24.

By decomposing the force into components normal and tangential to the path (dotted lines), explain why it is only the tangential component that does work. Hence explain why the planet will accelerate from A to P but will slow down from P to B. Reach the same conclusions by energy considerations.

CONTINUED

25 Figure 17.24 shows the variation of the gravitational force with distance between two masses.

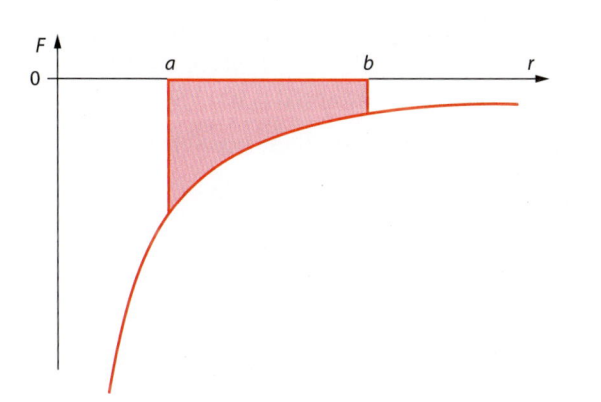

Figure 17.24: For question 25.

What does the shaded area represent?

26 Figure 17.25 shows equipotential surfaces for two spherical masses.

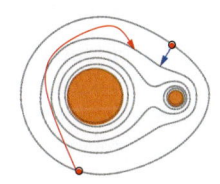

Figure 17.25: For question 26.

a Explain why the masses are unequal.

b Draw a few field lines for this arrangement.

c Why are the surfaces further out becoming spherical?

d The same mass is moved along two paths as shown. Compare the work done in each case.

17.3 Motion in a gravitational field

Orbital motion

A satellite of mass m orbits a planet of mass M with speed v. The radius of the orbit is r (Figure 17.26). The total energy E_T of this system is the sum of the kinetic energy E_K and the gravitational potential energy E_P.

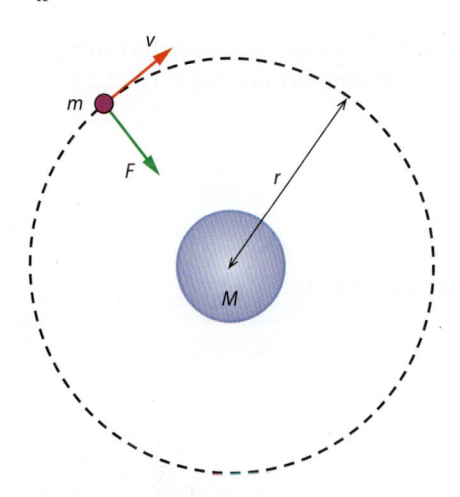

Figure 17.26: A system of a satellite orbiting a planet.

$E_K = \frac{1}{2}mv^2$ and $E_P = -\frac{GMm}{r}$

So:

$E_T = \frac{1}{2}mv^2 - \frac{GMm}{r}$

Note that we do not include any kinetic energy for the planet, as we assume it does not move.

Orbital speed is given by:

$v_{orbit} = \sqrt{\frac{GM}{r}}$

This means that the kinetic energy E_K is:

$E_K = \frac{GMm}{2r}$

The total energy of the system becomes:

$E_T = \frac{GMm}{2r} - \frac{GMm}{r} = -\frac{GMm}{2r}$

The total energy of an orbiting satellite is $E_T = -\frac{GMm}{2r}$.

> **PHYSICS FOR THE IB DIPLOMA: COURSEBOOK**

> **EXAM TIP**
>
> It is very important that you know how to derive the formula for orbital speed.

Figure 17.27 shows the kinetic energy E_K, potential energy E_P and total energy E_T of a mass of 1 kg in orbit around the earth as a function of distance from the earth's centre. This distance is measured in terms of the earth's radius R.

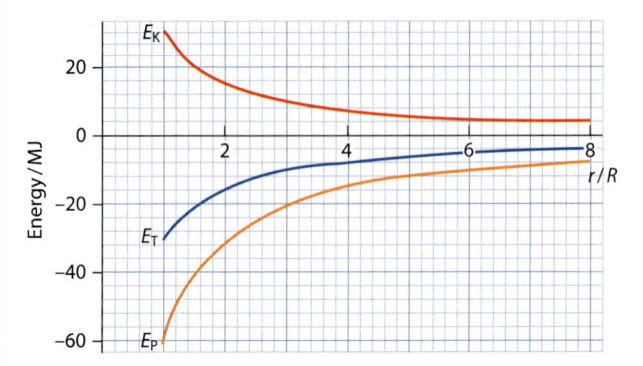

Figure 17.27: Graphs of the kinetic, potential and total energy of a mass of 1 kg in circular orbit around the earth.

The law of gravitation combined with Newton's second law of motion allows an understanding of the motion of planets around the sun, as well as the motion of satellites around the earth. Suppose you launched an object from the surface of a planet with some speed. What would be the path followed by this object? Newton's laws give several possibilities.

- If the total energy is positive, the object will follow a hyperbolic path and never return.
- If the total energy is zero, the object will follow a parabolic path to infinity, where it will just about stop. It will never return.
- If the total energy is negative, the object will go into a circular or elliptical orbit (or crash into the planet if the launching speed is too low).

Figure 17.28 illustrates these possible paths.

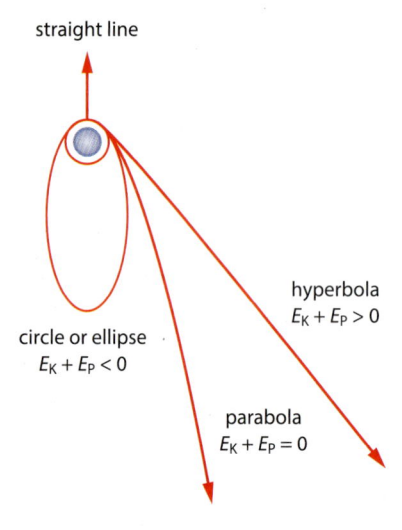

Figure 17.28: Launching a body from the surface of a planet results in various orbits, depending on the total energy E_T of the body.

> **WORKED EXAMPLE 17.11**
>
> Evaluate the speed of a satellite in orbit at a height of 500 km above the earth's surface and a satellite that just grazes the surface of the earth. (Take the radius of the earth to be 6.4×10^6 m and its mass 6.0×10^{24} kg.)
>
> **Answer**
>
> The speed is given by:
>
> $v^2 = \dfrac{GM}{r}$
>
> The radius of orbit r of the satellite at a height of 500 km above the earth's surface is:
>
> $r = (6.4 \times 10^6) + (0.5 \times 10^6) = 6.9 \times 10^6$ m

CONTINUED

Substituting for *r* and using the values from the question:

$$v = \sqrt{\frac{6.67 \times 10^{-11} \times 6.0 \times 10^{24}}{6.9 \times 10^6}}$$

$\Rightarrow v = 7.6 \times 10^3 \text{ m s}^{-1}$

For a grazing orbit, $r = 6.4 \times 10^6$ m.

Using this value and following the same method, $v = 7.9 \times 10^3 \text{ m s}^{-1}$.

WORKED EXAMPLE 17.12

A satellite in a low orbit will experience a small frictional force (due to the atmosphere) in a direction opposite to the satellite's velocity.

a Explain why the satellite will move into an orbit closer to the earth's surface.

b Deduce that the speed of the satellite will increase.

c Discuss the fate of such a satellite.

Answer

a Since there is a frictional force acting, the satellite's total energy will be reduced.

The total energy E_T of a satellite of mass *m* in a circular orbit of radius *r* around the earth of mass *M* is:

$E_T = -\frac{GMm}{2r}$

The masses do not change and *G* is a constant. The energy E_T is negative, so reducing the energy means it becomes *more* negative. This means there must be a smaller radius, i.e. the satellite comes closer to the earth by spiraling inwards.

b The speed of the satellite in a circular orbit is given by:

$v = \sqrt{\frac{GM}{r}}$

So we see that, as the satellite comes closer to earth, its speed increases.

c As the satellite gets closer to earth it experiences more friction because the atmosphere is getting denser and the satellite moves faster. So as more and more energy is converted into thermal energy, the satellite most likely burns.

WORKED EXAMPLE 17.13

A probe of mass *m* is launched from the surface of a planet of mass *M* and radius *R* with kinetic energy $E_K = \frac{4GMm}{5R}$.

a Explain why this probe will not escape the gravitational field of the planet.

b The probe eventually settles into a circular orbit around the planet with negligible work done by the engines. Calculate the radius of its orbit in terms of *R*.

CONTINUED

Answer

a The total energy at launch is the sum of the kinetic and potential energies:

$E_T = \frac{4GMm}{5R} - \frac{GMm}{R}$

$E_T = -\frac{GMm}{5R}$

This is negative and so the probe cannot escape.

b The total energy in orbit is:

$E_T = -\frac{GMm}{2r}$

By energy conservation, the total energy once the probe is in orbit must equal the total energy at launch. So:

$-\frac{GMm}{2r} = -\frac{GMm}{5R}$

$\frac{1}{2r} = \frac{1}{5R}$

$2r = 5R$

So $r = \frac{5R}{2}$

WORKED EXAMPLE 17.14

Figure 17.29 shows the variation of the gravitational potential due to a planet and its moon with distance r from the centre of the planet. The centre-to-centre distance between the planet and the moon is d. The planet's centre is at $r = 0$, and the centre of the moon is at $r = d$.

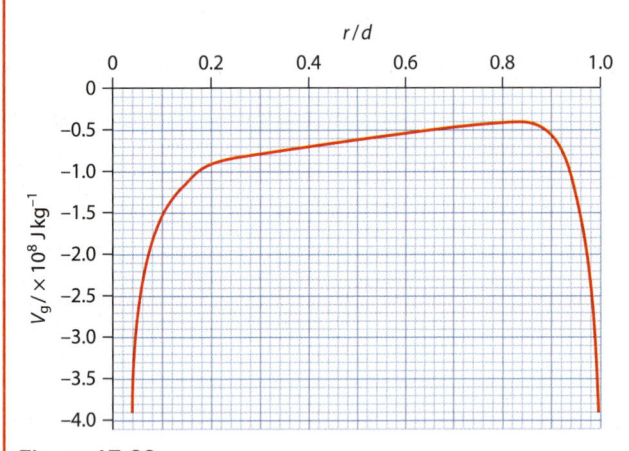

Figure 17.29

State and explain the minimum energy required so that a 850 kg probe at rest on the planet's surface will arrive on the moon.

17 Gravitation

> **CONTINUED**
>
> **Answer**
>
> The probe will arrive at the moon provided it has enough energy to get to the peak of the curve. Once there, the moon will pull it in.
>
> On the surface of the planet $V_g = -3.9 \times 10^8$ J kg^{-1}. At the peak the potential is $V_g = -0.4 \times 10^8$ J kg^{-1}. The minimum energy required is equal to the work done to move through this potential difference.
>
> $W = m\Delta V_g$
>
> $W = 850 \times (-0.4 \times 10^8 + 3.9 \times 10^8)$
>
> $W = 3.0 \times 10^{11}$ J
>
> So the minimum energy required is 3.0×10^{11} J.

Escape speed

Suppose that a body of mass m finds itself somewhere in the gravitational field of a planet or star. The object could be in orbit or just passing by or just placed there so that it is momentarily at rest. What is the minimum speed we should give to that body so that it moves far from the planet or star without returning? This is called the **escape speed** (Figure 17.30).

> **KEY POINT**
>
> Escape speed is the minimum speed a body in a gravitational field must have in order to reach infinity.

Figure 17.30: The escape speed will take the projectile from a point in the gravitational field to infinity, where it will come to rest.

When the body gets to infinity (or, at least, extremely far away) the gravitational potential energy is zero. Since escape speed is the minimum speed needed to escape, the speed at infinity will be zero. Hence the total energy will be zero. So the condition to escape from any point in a gravitational field is that the total energy at that point must be zero (and obviously you have to be moving away from the planet).

Consider an object momentarily at rest at a distance r from the centre of a planet of mass M.

The total energy is just gravitational potential energy and so equals $E_T = -\frac{GMm}{r}$.

So, we need to provide kinetic energy to make the total energy zero. In other words, the kinetic energy needed is:

$E_K = +\frac{GMm}{r}$

From $\frac{1}{2}mv_{esc}^2 = \frac{GMm}{r}$ we find $v_{esc} = \sqrt{\frac{2GM}{r}}$.

Note that the escape speed is independent of the mass of the body escaping.

If the body is initially on the surface of a planet of radius R then the formula becomes $v_{esc} = \sqrt{\frac{2GM}{R}}$.

The numerical value of this escape speed for the earth is about 11.2 km s^{-1}.

In practice, in order to escape from earth, a body must overcome not only the pull of the earth and the friction with the atmosphere but also the pull of the sun and the other planets. This means that the escape speed from the earth is larger than 11.2 km s^{-1}. This discussion does not apply to powered objects such as rockets; it applies only to objects launched from the earth like old fashioned cannon balls. In other words, it applies to ballistic motion only.

Consider now an object that in a circular *orbit* of radius r. What *additional* speed do we need to give the body in order that it escapes?

The escape speed is $v_{esc} = \sqrt{\frac{2GM}{r}}$ but the body already has an orbital speed $v_{orb} = \sqrt{\frac{GM}{r}}$ and so the *additional* speed needed is $\sqrt{\frac{2GM}{r}} - \sqrt{\frac{GM}{r}}$.

> **PHYSICS FOR THE IB DIPLOMA: COURSEBOOK**

THEORY OF KNOWLEDGE

Changing ideas

The motion of the planets is the perfect application of the theory of gravitation. The understanding of the motion of the planets has undergone very many 'paradigm shifts' since ancient times. Newton was motivated by the 'laws' discovered by Kepler. Kepler's laws were published in 1619 in a book called the *Harmony of the World*, nearly 70 years before Newton published his work. In ancient times, Ptolemy constructed an involved system in which the sun and the planets orbited the earth. The Ptolemaic worldview prevailed for centuries until Copernicus, early in the sixteenth century, asserted that the sun was at the centre of the motion of the planets in the solar system. Newton's law of gravitation has had great success in dealing with planetary motion but cannot account for some small irregularities, such as the precession of the orbit of Mercury and the bending of light near very massive bodies. In 1915, Einstein introduced the general theory of relativity, which replaced Newton's theory of gravity and resolved the difficulties of the Newtonian theory.

WORKED EXAMPLE 17.15

A probe is launched from the surface of a planet of mass M and radius R with a speed that is half the escape speed.

a Calculate, in terms of R, the largest distance from the surface of the planet the probe will get to.

b Once the probe gets to the point in part **a**, rockets are fired giving the probe a speed v. What should v be so that the probe escapes?

Answer

a Let r be the largest distance from the centre of the planet reached by the probe.

The total energy of the probe at that distance is $E_T = -\frac{GMm}{r}$, since the kinetic energy is zero.

At launch the total energy is $E_T = \frac{1}{2}mv^2 - \frac{GMm}{R}$.

CONTINUED

Now use the fact that $v = \frac{v_{esc}}{2}$ to find the total energy at launch:

$$E_T = \frac{1}{2}m\frac{v_{esc}^2}{4} - \frac{GMm}{R}$$

$$= \frac{1}{2}m\frac{\left(\frac{2GM}{R}\right)}{4} - \frac{GMm}{R}$$

$$= \frac{GMm}{4R} - \frac{GMm}{R}$$

$$= -\frac{3}{4}\frac{GMm}{R}$$

By energy conservation, the total energy at launch is equal to the total energy at the farthest distance, so:

$$-\frac{3}{4}\frac{GMm}{R} = -\frac{GMm}{r}$$

$$\frac{3}{4R} = \frac{1}{r}$$

$$\Rightarrow r = \frac{4R}{3}$$

The height from the surface is therefore $h = r - R = \frac{R}{3}$, a perhaps surprising result.

b Using our formulae, the speed must be:

$$v_{esc} = \sqrt{\frac{2GM}{r}}$$

$$= \sqrt{\frac{2GM}{\left(\frac{4R}{3}\right)}}$$

$$= \sqrt{\frac{3GM}{2R}}$$

WORKED EXAMPLE 17.16

a What must the radius of a star of mass M be such that the escape speed from the star is equal to the speed of light, c?

b Calculate this radius for the sun and the earth. (Use a mass of 2×10^{30} kg for the sun and 6×10^{24} kg for the earth.)

Answer

a Using $v_{esc} = \sqrt{\frac{2GM}{R}}$ with $v_{esc} = c$, we find $R = \frac{2GM}{c^2}$.

Since nothing can exceed the speed of light, if the radius of the star is equal to or less than $\frac{2GM}{c^2}$, nothing can escape from the star. It is a black hole.

17 Gravitation

> **CONTINUED**
>
> **b** For the sun:
>
> $R = \dfrac{2GM}{c^2}$
>
> $R = \dfrac{2 \times 6.67 \times 10^{-11} \times 2 \times 10^{30}}{(3 \times 10^8)^2}$
>
> $R \approx 3 \times 10^3$ m
>
> A similar calculation for the earth gives $R = 9$ mm. This shows that both the earth and the sun are far from being black holes!

Weightlessness

Consider an astronaut of mass m in a spacecraft in orbit around the earth a distance r from the earth's centre (Figure 17.31). Why does the astronaut 'feel weightless'? At a distance of 300 km from the earth's surface, gravity is by no means negligible. A simple answer is that the astronaut, as well as the spacecraft, are both falling freely, i.e. they have the same acceleration. Hence there are no reaction forces from the floor.

Figure 17.31: An astronaut inside a spacecraft or out in a spacewalk accelerates towards the earth with the same acceleration as the spacecraft. So whether inside or outside, there is no force of reaction on the astronaut. They feel 'weightless'.

Quantitatively, the forces on the astronaut are the reaction force N from the floor of the spacecraft and his or her weight W (i.e. the gravitational force from the earth). The net force is

$F = W - N$

The astronaut's weight is given by:

$W = \dfrac{GMm}{r^2}$

So the net force F on the astronaut is:

$F = \dfrac{GMm}{r^2} - N$

This is the force that provides the acceleration keeping the astronaut in orbit at radius r, so:

$\dfrac{GMm}{r^2} - N = \dfrac{mv^2}{r}$

$\Rightarrow N = \dfrac{GMm}{r^2} - \dfrac{mv^2}{r}$

$N = \dfrac{m}{r}\left(\dfrac{GM}{r} - v^2\right)$

But the orbital speed of the astronaut is given by:

$v_{\text{orbit}}^2 = \dfrac{GM}{r}$

Substituting this into the equation for N gives $N = 0$. Thus, the astronaut experiences no reaction forces from the floor and so 'feels' weightless.

> **NATURE OF SCIENCE**
>
> The Newtonian theory of gravity and mechanics applied to the motion of planets gives spectacular agreement with the observed motion of the planets. However, during the nineteenth century very small discrepancies between theory and observations began to arise. One of them had to do with the motion of the planet Uranus. What could be the cause of these discrepancies? One possibility was that Newtonian gravity was not correct—an unlikely possibility, given the previous successes of the theory. The French astronomer Urbain Le Verrier (1811–1877) argued that a new, unknown planet was affecting the orbit of Uranus and was responsible for the erratic behaviour of its orbit. Working backwards, Le Verrier calculated the possible orbit of the unknown planet that would give rise to the observed effects on Uranus. He communicated his results to the Berlin observatory. His letter arrived at the observatory on 23 September 1846, and on that same evening the planet Neptune was discovered!

TEST YOUR UNDERSTANDING

27 Figure 17.32 shows cross-sections of two satellite orbits around the earth. (To be in orbit means that only gravity is acting on the satellite.) Discuss whether either of these orbits is possible.

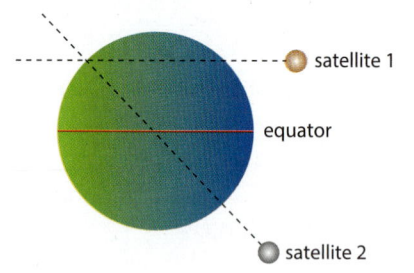

Figure 17.32: For question 27.

28 In the text it was calculated that the acceleration due to gravity at a height of 300 km above the earth's surface is far from negligible, yet astronauts orbiting in a space shuttle at such a height feel weightless. Explain why.

29 A rocket is launched from the surface of a planet. At the position shown in Figure 17.33, the rocket is a distance of $2R$ from the centre of the planet (where R is the radius of the planet) and its speed is $v = \sqrt{\frac{GM}{2R}}$. At that point the fuel runs out.

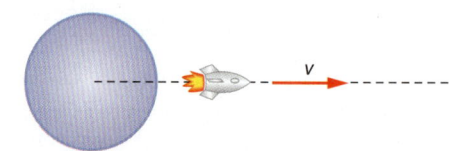

Figure 17.33: For question 29.

  a Explain why the rocket will eventually crash onto the surface of the planet.

  b Calculate, in terms of R, the maximum distance from the centre of the planet the rocket travels to.

  c Determine the speed with which the rocket crashes onto the planet surface.

  d Draw a graph to show how the speed of the rocket varies with distance r from the centre of the planet as the rocket begins to fall back towards the planet.

30 Prove that the total energy of the earth (mass m) as it orbits the sun (mass M) can be expressed as either $E = -\frac{1}{2}mv^2$ or $E = -\frac{GMm}{2r}$ where r is the radius of the earth's circular orbit.

31 A satellite orbits the earth in a circular orbit. A small frictional force acts on the satellite. State and explain the effect of this force on the following properties of the satellite:

  a the total energy

  b the orbit radius

  c the speed

  d the potential energy

  e the period.

32 Figure 17.34 shows two identical satellites in circular orbits.

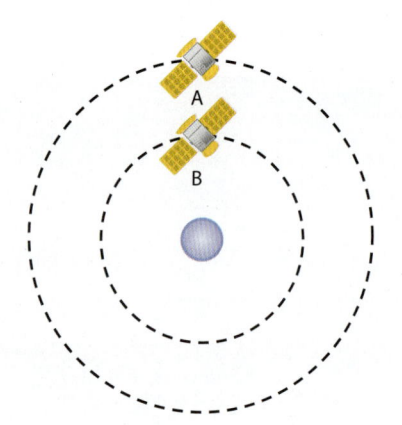

Figure 17.34: For question 32.

Which satellite has the larger:

  a kinetic energy

  b potential energy

  c total energy?

CONTINUED

33 The total energy of a satellite during launch from the earth's surface is $E = -\dfrac{GMm}{5R}$, where R is the radius of the earth.

  a Explain why this satellite will not escape the earth.

  b The satellite eventually settles into a circular orbit. Calculate the radius of the orbit in terms of R.

34 A satellite is in a circular orbit around the earth. The satellite turns on its engines and now finds itself in a new circular orbit of larger radius. State and explain whether the work done by the engines is positive, zero or negative.

35 Figure 17.35 shows a planet orbiting the sun.

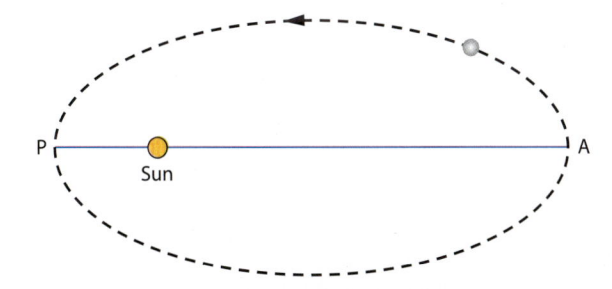

Figure 17.35: For question 35.

  a Explain why at points A and P of the orbit the potential energy of the planet assumes its minimum and maximum values, and determine which is which.

  b Hence determine at what point in the orbit the planet has the greatest speed.

  c Explain why the angular momentum of the planet is constant.

  d Hence determine the ratio of the speeds at P and A in terms of the distances of P and A to the sun.

36 Referring to the figure of the previous problem, show that the rate at which the planet sweeps area is given by $\dfrac{\Delta A}{\Delta t} = \dfrac{1}{2}r^2\omega$ where ω is the angular speed of the planet when at distance r from the sun. Hence deduce that $\dfrac{\Delta A}{\Delta t} = \dfrac{L}{2m}$ where L is the angular momentum of the planet and m is its mass, and explain Kepler's second law.

37 Show that the escape speed from the surface of a planet of radius R can be written as $v_{esc} = \sqrt{2gR}$ and $v_{esc} = \sqrt{-2V}$ where g is the gravitational field strength and V the gravitational potential at the planet's surface. Show that yet another expression for the escape speed is $v_{esc} = R\sqrt{\dfrac{8\pi G\rho}{3}}$ where ρ is the density of the planet.

38 a Deduce that a satellite orbiting a planet of mass M in a circular orbit of radius r has a period of revolution given by $T = \sqrt{\dfrac{4\pi^2 r^3}{GM}}$.

  b A grazing orbit is one in which the orbit radius is approximately equal to the radius R of the planet. Deduce that the period of revolution in a grazing orbit is given by $T = \sqrt{\dfrac{3\pi}{G\rho}}$ where ρ is the density of the planet.

  c The period of a grazing orbit around the earth is 85 minutes, and around the planet Jupiter it is 169 minutes. Deduce the ratio $\dfrac{\rho_{earth}}{\rho_{Jupiter}}$.

39 a The acceleration of free fall at the surface of a planet is g, and the radius of the planet is R. Deduce that the period of a satellite in a very low orbit is given by $T = 2\pi\sqrt{\dfrac{R}{g}}$

  b Given that $g = 4.5 \text{ m s}^{-2}$ and $R = 3.4 \times 10^6$ m, deduce that the orbital period of the low orbit is about 91 minutes.

  c A spacecraft in orbit around this planet has a period of 140 minutes. Deduce the height of the spacecraft from the surface of the planet.

CONTINUED

40 Two stars of equal mass M orbit a common centre as shown in Figure 17.36. The radius of the orbit of each star is R. Assume that each of the stars has a mass equal to 1.5 solar masses (solar mass = 2.0×10^{30} kg) and that the initial separation of the stars is 2.0×10^9 m.

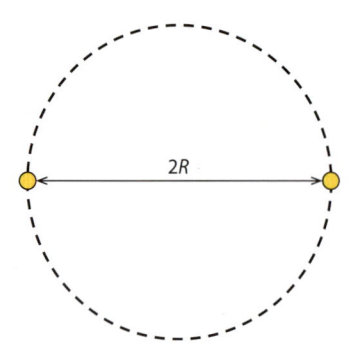

Figure 17.36: For question 40.

a State the magnitude of the force on each star in terms of M, R and G.

b Deduce that the period of revolution of each star is given by the expression:

$$T^2 = \frac{16\pi^2 R^3}{GM}$$

c Evaluate the period numerically.

d Show that the total energy of the two stars is given by:

$$E = -\frac{GM^2}{4R}$$

e The two-star system loses energy as a result of emitting gravitational radiation. Deduce that the stars will move closer to each other.

f **i** Explain why the fractional loss of energy $\left(\frac{\Delta E}{E}\right)$ per unit time may be calculated from the expression:

$$\frac{\frac{\Delta E}{E}}{\Delta t} = \frac{2}{3}\frac{\frac{\Delta T}{T}}{\Delta t}$$

where $\frac{\frac{\Delta T}{T}}{\Delta t}$ is the fractional decrease in period per unit time. (Hint: use ideas of error propagation.)

ii The orbital period decreases at a rate of $\frac{\Delta T}{\Delta t} = 72$ µs yr^{-1}. Estimate the fractional energy loss per year.

g The two stars will collapse into each other when $\Delta E \approx E$. Estimate the lifetime, in years, of this binary star system.

SELF-ASSESSMENT CHECKLIST

I am able to ...	Section	Not yet	Nearly there	Ready to move on
apply Newton's law of gravitation	17.1			
calculate the gravitational field strength from one or two spherical bodies	17.1			
apply the law of gravitation to orbiting bodies	17.1			
describe Kepler's laws	17.1			
realise that Kepler's laws are a consequence of Newton's law of gravitation and the laws of mechanics	17.1			

17 Gravitation

CONTINUED

I am able to ...	Section	Not yet	Nearly there	Ready to move on
work with gravitational potential energy and gravitational potential	17.2			
understand gravitational equipotential surfaces	17.2			
derive the expression for total energy of an orbiting body	17.3			
appreciate the significance of the sign of the total energy of a body in a gravitational field	17.3			
calculate the escape speed form any point in a gravitational field	17.3			

REFLECTION

Can you solve problems with Newton's law of gravitation? Do you understand the concept of a *gravitational field*? Can you solve problems involving gravitational field strength? Can you describe Kepler's three laws on the motion of the planets?

Do you understand the concepts of *gravitational potential* and *gravitational potential energy*? Can you solve problems involving gravitational potential and gravitational potential energy? Do you understand the concept of *escape speed*? Can you solve problems with energy conservation in gravitational fields? Can you explain the apparent weightlessness of objects in orbit?

EXAM-STYLE QUESTIONS

You can find questions in the style of IB exams in the digital coursebook.

CHECK YOURSELF ANSWERS

1. Since $F \propto \frac{1}{r^2}$, the force will become nine times smaller.

2. The acceleration is the same as the gravitational field strength. Hence $a = \frac{GM}{r^2} = \frac{GM}{(2R)^2} = \frac{1}{4}\frac{GM}{R^2} = \frac{g}{4}$.

3. The force is $mg = 0.40 \times 15 = 6.0$ N.

4. When they come near the sun they move very fast and so on the average spend most of their time away from the sun and out of sight.

5. $E_P = mV = -2.0 \times 10^{10} \times 350 = -7.0 \times 10^{12}$ J

6. The force does not stay constant as we move from A to B.

7. It is zero since the gradient at P is zero.

Chapter 18
Electric and magnetic fields

LEARNING OBJECTIVES

In this chapter you will learn how to:

- understand the concept and properties of electric charge
- charge a body by electrostatic induction
- apply Coulomb's law
- understand the concept of electric field
- work with magnetic fields
- determine the direction of the magnetic fields created by straight currents and coils
- recognize how magnetic fields exert magnetic forces on moving charges and electric currents
- > understand the concept of electric potential and electric potential energy
- > understand the connection between electric field lines and equipotential surfaces

18 Electric and magnetic fields

> **GUIDING QUESTIONS**
>
> - What is the electric force between charged particles?
> - What is the magnetic force on moving charged particles?
> - What is the connection between electricity and magnetism?

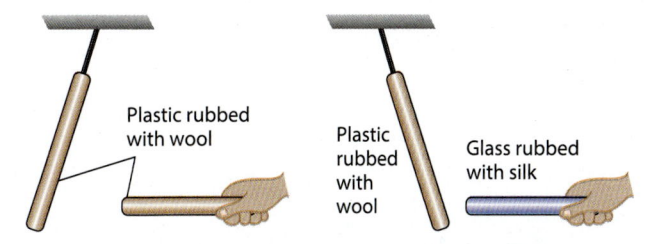

Figure 18.1: Two simple experiments to investigate properties of electric charge.

Introduction

This chapter examines the properties of electric charge and the phenomena that take place when charge is allowed to move so as to create an electric current. The concept of an electric field is crucial to understanding electric current, as it is the electric field inside a conductor that forces electric charge to move.

18.1 Electric charge, force and field

Electric charge is a property of matter. Ordinarily, matter appears electrically neutral, but we can charge a body by friction.

For example, take two plastic rods and rub each with a piece of wool. We will find that the two rods now repel each other. If we now rub two glass rods with silk, we find that the glass rods again repel each other, but the charged glass rod attracts the charged plastic rod. We can understand these observations (Figure 18.1) by assuming that:

- the process of rubbing involves the transfer of charge from one body to the other
- charge can be positive or negative
- there is a force between charged bodies that can be attractive or repulsive.

Benjamin Franklin (1706–1790) decided to call the sign of the charge on the glass rubbed with silk 'positive'. Much later, when electrons were discovered, it was found that electrons were attracted to the charged glass rod. This means that electrons must have negative charge. But if Franklin had called the charge on the glass rod negative, we would now be calling the electron's charge positive!

From experiments with charged objects, we learn that there is a force of attraction between charges of opposite sign and a force of repulsion between charges of the same sign. The magnitude of the force becomes smaller as the distance between the charged bodies increases.

Properties of electric charge

In ordinary matter, negative charge is a property of particles called electrons. Positive charge is a property of protons, which exist in the nuclei of atoms. (There are many other particles that have charge, but those do not appear in ordinary matter.)

The first important property of electric charge is that it is **conserved**. Like total energy, electric charge cannot be created or destroyed. In any process the total charge cannot change (see worked example 18.1).

In solid metals the atoms are fixed in position in a lattice, but there are many 'free' electrons that do not belong to a particular atom. When exposed to an electric field (see later) these electrons can drift in the same direction creating an electric current. In liquids, and especially in gases, positive ions can also transport charge.

Materials that have many 'free' electrons (Figure 18.2) are called **conductors**.

Materials that very few 'free' electrons, so charge cannot move freely, are called **insulators**.

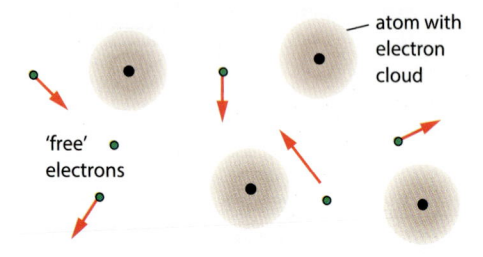

Figure 18.2: In a conductor there are many 'free' electrons that move around much like molecules of a gas.

> ### WORKED EXAMPLE 18.1
>
> Two separated, identical conducting spheres are charged with charges of 4.0 µC and −12 µC, respectively. The spheres are allowed to touch and then are separated again. Determine the charge on each sphere. Describe the transfer of charge from one sphere to the other.
>
> **Answer**
>
> The net charge on the two spheres is 4.0 − 12 = −8.0 µC. The contact of the two conducting spheres implies that charge will be transferred from one to the other. By symmetry, when the spheres are allowed to touch, they will end up with the same charge, since they are identical. The total amount of charge on the two spheres after separation must be −8.0 µC by charge conservation.
>
> When they separate, each will therefore have a charge of −4.0 µC.
>
> It is negative charge that gets transferred (electrons). The positive charges have fixed positions and do not move. So an amount of −8.0 µC gets transferred.

The second important property of electric charge is that it is a **quantised quantity**; this means that the amount of electric charge on a body is always an integral multiple of a basic unit. The basic unit is the magnitude of the charge on the proton.

This amount of charge is symbolised by e. The charge on an electron is $-e$. (If we include quarks, the particles inside protons and neutrons, then the basic unit of charge is $\frac{e}{3}$.) The SI unit of charge is the coulomb (C). $1\,e = 1.6 \times 10^{-19}$ C.

The quantisation of electric charge was determined in an experiment by Robert Millikan and is described at the end of this chapter.

Electrostatic induction

Friction is one way to charge a body. Electrostatic induction is another. Consider a positively charged rod that is placed close to, but not touching, a conducting sphere on an insulating stand.

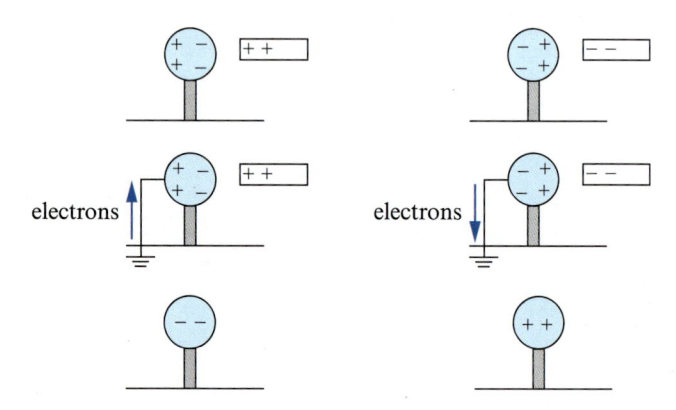

Figure 18.3: Charging a sphere by induction.

The positive charge on the rod will attract free electrons in the sphere closer to the rod. This means the left side of the sphere will be left with an excess of positive charge. The net charge on the sphere is still zero. In the second diagram the sphere is grounded. This means that we connect the sphere to the ground with a cable. Electrons from the earth will move through the cable and neutralize some of the positive charge on the left side of the sphere. The connection to the earth and the charged rod are both removed. The sphere is left with a net negative charge that will distribute itself uniformly on the surface of the sphere. The sphere is left with a net charge that is opposite to that on the charged rod.

If the rod is negatively charged, the negative charge will push electrons away leaving the right side of the sphere with an excess of positive charge. Grounding (earthing) will make electrons move to the earth leaving the sphere with a net positive charge after grounding and rod are removed. Again the charge on the sphere is opposite to that on the rod.

CHECK YOURSELF 1

A student says, referring to Figure 18.3, that when the positively charged rod is put close to the sphere, negative charge is attracted to the right side of the sphere and positive charge is repelled to the left side. Comment on this statement.

Coulomb's law for the electric force

The electric force between two electric charges, q_1 and q_2, was investigated in 1785 by Charles Augustin Coulomb (1736–1806). Coulomb discovered that this force is inversely proportional to the square of the separation of the charges and is proportional to the product of the two charges. It is attractive for charges of opposite sign and repulsive for charges of the same sign (Figure 18.4).

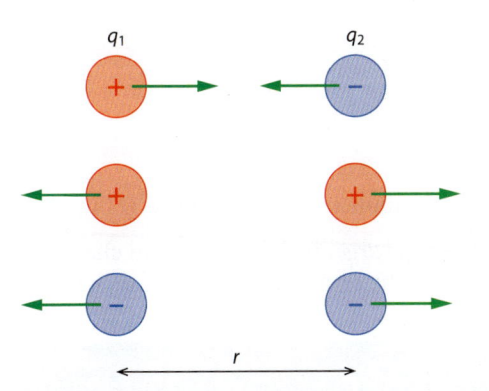

Figure 18.4: The force between two point electric charges is given by Coulomb's law and can be attractive or repulsive.

Coulomb's law states that the electric force F between two *point* charges q_1 and q_2 separated by a distance r is given by:

$$F = k\frac{q_1 q_2}{r^2}$$

The constant k is known as the Coulomb constant and equals $8.99 \times 10^9 \, \text{NC}^{-2}\text{m}^2$ in vacuum.

The constant k is also written as $k = \frac{1}{4\pi\varepsilon}$ where ε is known as permittivity. If the charges are surrounded by vacuum, the value of the permittivity is $\varepsilon_0 = 8.85 \times 10^{-12} \, \text{C}^2\text{N}^{-1}\text{m}^{-2}$. If they are surrounded by some other medium, we must use the value of the permittivity appropriate to that medium.

WORKED EXAMPLE 18.2

Two charges, $q_1 = 2.0 \, \mu\text{C}$ and $q_2 = 8.0 \, \mu\text{C}$, are placed along a straight line separated by a distance of 3.0 cm.

a Calculate the force exerted on each charge in vacuum.

b Calculate the force when the charges are surrounded by water whose permittivity is 80 times that of the vacuum.

c The charge q_1 is increased to 4.0 µC. Determine the force on each charge now (in vacuum).

Answer

a This is a straightforward application of the formula $F = k\frac{q_1 q_2}{r^2}$. We find that:

$$F = \frac{8.99 \times 10^9 \times 2.0 \times 8.0 \times 10^{-12}}{9.0 \times 10^{-4}}$$

$F = 160$ N

This is the force that q_1 exerts on q_2, and vice versa.

b The Coulomb constant is now 80 smaller so the force is 2.0 N.

c Since the charge doubles the force doubles to $F = 320$ N on *both* charges.

EXAM TIP

It is a common mistake to double the force on one charge but not the other.

WORKED EXAMPLE 18.3

A positive charge q is placed on the line joining q_1 and q_2 from worked example 2.2. Determine the distance from q_1 where this third positive charge experiences zero net force.

Answer

Let that distance be x. A positive charge q at that point would experience a force from q_1 equal to $F_1 = k\frac{q_1 q}{x^2}$ and a force in the opposite direction from q_2 equal to $F_2 = k\frac{q_2 q}{(d-x)^2}$ where $d = 3.0$ cm is the distance between q_1 and q_2.

CONTINUED

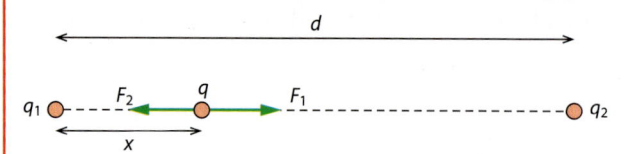

Figure 18.5: For worked example 18.3.

Charge q will experience no net force when $F_1 = F_2$, so:

$$k\frac{q_1 q}{x^2} = k\frac{q_2 q}{(d-x)^2}$$

Cancelling kq and substituting $q_1 = 2.0$ μC and $q_2 = 8.0$ μC gives:

$$\frac{2.0}{x^2} = \frac{8.0}{(d-x)^2}$$

$$(d-x)^2 = 4x^2$$

$$(d-x) = 2x$$

$$x = \frac{d}{3} = 1.0 \text{ cm}$$

EXAM TIP

We do not have to change units to C. The units on both sides of the equation are the same (μC) and cancel out.

Electric field

The space around a charge or an arrangement of charges is different from space in which no charges are present. It contains an **electric field**. We can test whether an electric field exists at a point P by bringing a small, point charge q at P. If q experiences an electric force, then there is an electric field at P. If no force is experienced, then the electric field is zero. For this reason the small charge is called a test charge: it tests for the existence of electric fields. It has to be small so that its presence does not disturb the electric field it is trying to detect. By convention test charges are assumed to be positive.

KEY POINT

We define **electric field strength**, E, as the electric force per unit charge experienced by a small, positive, point charge q:

$$\vec{E} = \frac{\vec{F}}{q}$$

Note that electric field strength is a vector quantity. The direction of the electric field is the same as the direction of the force experienced by a positive charge at the given point. The unit of electric field is NC^{-1}.

The magnitude of the force experienced by a test charge q placed a distance r from a point charge Q is (by Coulomb's law):

$$F = k\frac{Qq}{r^2}$$

and so from the definition $\vec{E} = \frac{\vec{F}}{q}$, the magnitude of the electric field strength is:

$$E = k\frac{\left(\frac{Qq}{r^2}\right)}{q}$$

$$E = k\frac{Q}{r^2}$$

The formula $E = k\frac{Q}{r^2}$ applies to a *point charge Q* but also *outside* of a *spherical charge*. If Q is a spherical charge, r is the distance from the centre of the spherical charge.

CHECK YOURSELF 2

The distance of a point from a positive charge is doubled. What happens to the electric field strength?

The left diagram in Figure 18.6a shows the electric field at various points around a positive point charge. The left diagram in Figure 18.6b shows the electric field around a negative charge. The diagrams show the direction of the electric field strength, and the fact that the arrows get smaller as we move away from the charge indicates that the magnitude of the electric field strength decreases as demanded by the formula $E = k\frac{Q}{r^2}$. Another way of representing the electric field is to imagine smooth lines going through the arrows. These are called **electric field lines**. This results in the diagrams on the right in Figure 18.6.

18 Electric and magnetic fields

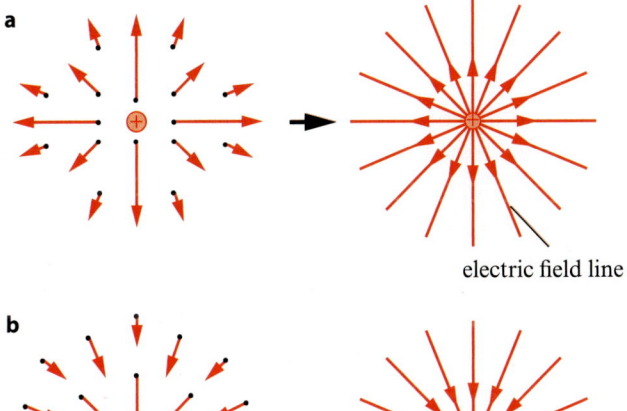

Figure 18.6: The electric force experienced by **a** positive test charge at various positions near a **a** positive and **b** a negative point charge. The diagrams on the right show the electric field lines.

The disadvantage is that we lost the information on the magnitude of the electric field strength. We make up for this by arguing that the lines are further apart as we move away. So we take the *density* of the lines to be a measure of the magnitude of the electric field strength.

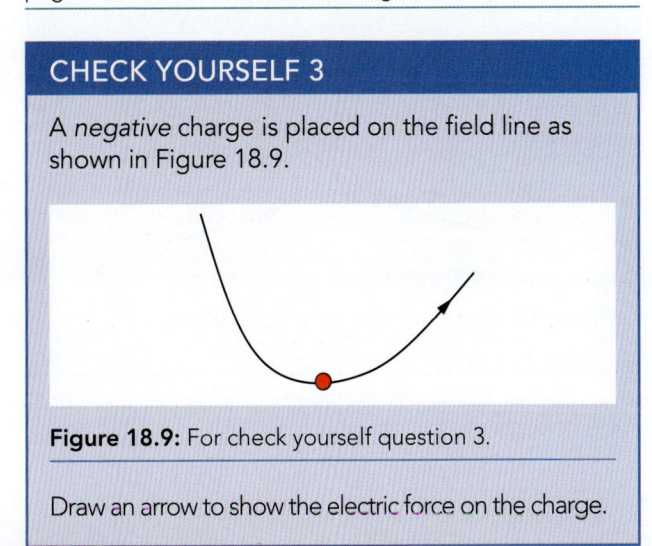

Figure 18.7a shows the field lines created by two equal, positive charges and Figure 18.7b by two equal and opposite charges.

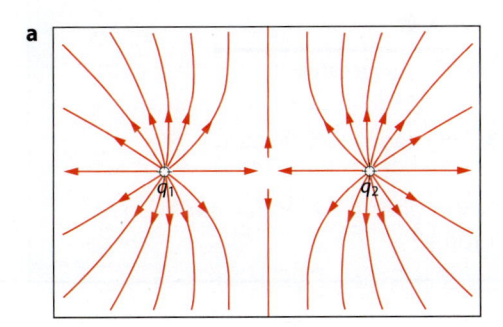

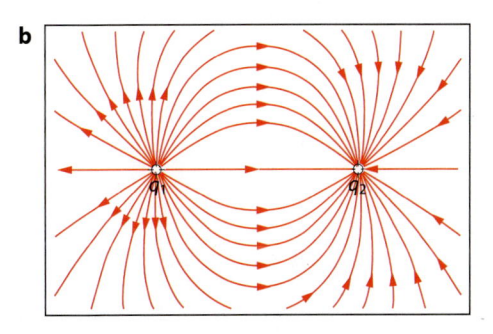

Figure 18.7: Field lines for **a** two equal positive charges and **b** two equal and opposite charges.

Unlike the case of a single charge, the field lines are no longer straight. The electric field is tangential to the field lines in the direction of the arrow, Figures 18.8a and 18.8b. Thus the electric force is also tangential to the field lines. The force on a positive charge is in the direction of the electric field, and the force on a negative charge is opposite to the electric field. The magnitude of the force is $F = qE$.

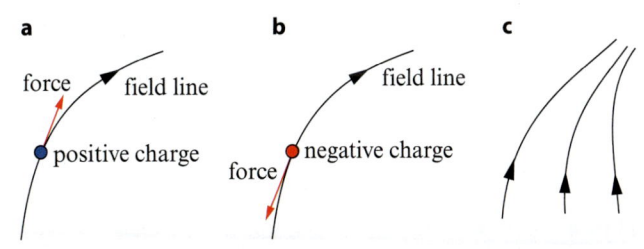

Figure 18.8: a The electric force on a positive charge is tangent to the field line in the direction of the arrow of the field line. **b** The force on a negative charge is tangent to the field line in a direction opposite to the arrow. **c** The density of field lines increases as we move towards the top of the page and so the electric field strength increases.

CHECK YOURSELF 3

A *negative* charge is placed on the field line as shown in Figure 18.9.

Figure 18.9: For check yourself question 3.

Draw an arrow to show the electric force on the charge.

389

Figure 18.10a shows the field lines created by two unequal, positive charges and Figure 18.10b the field created by two unequal and opposite charges. In Figure 18.10a $q_2 = 4q_1$ and in Figure 18.10b $q_2 = -4q_1$.

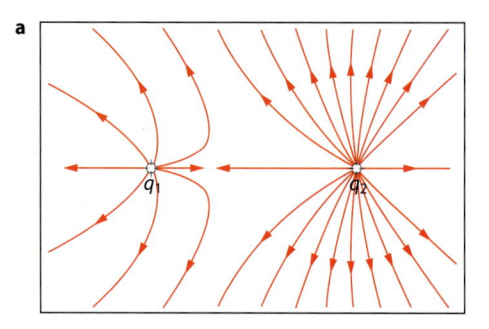

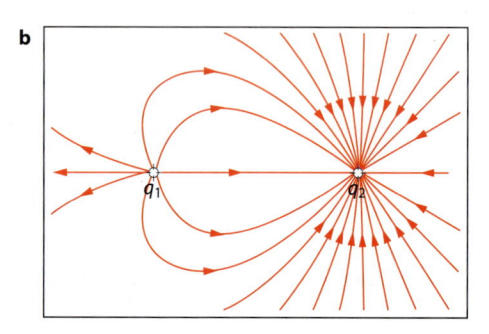

Figure 18.10: a Field lines for unequal and positive charges. **b** Field lines for unequal and opposite charges.

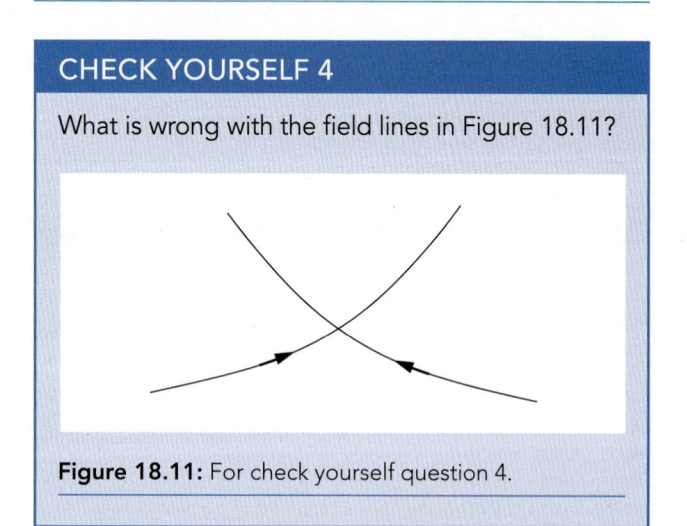

Figure 18.12 shows the electric field lines for two oppositely charged parallel plates. The lines are equally spaced in between the plates indicating that the field there is uniform (i.e. constant). The field stops being uniform at the edges of the plates. The electric field lines are directed from the positive to the negative plate.

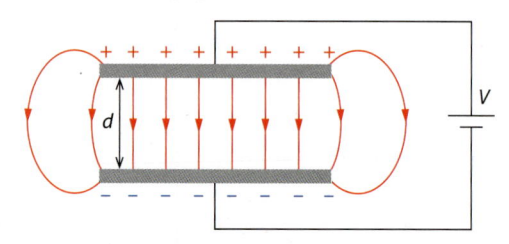

Figure 18.12: Field lines for two oppositely charged plates.

The magnitude of the uniform electric field strength in between the plates is given by

$$E = \frac{V}{d}$$

where V is the potential difference between the plates and d is the separation of the plates.

CHECK YOURSELF 4

What is wrong with the field lines in Figure 18.11?

Figure 18.11: For check yourself question 4.

CHECK YOURSELF 5

An electron is placed in position A, then B and then C in between two oppositely charged parallel plates (see Figure 18.13).

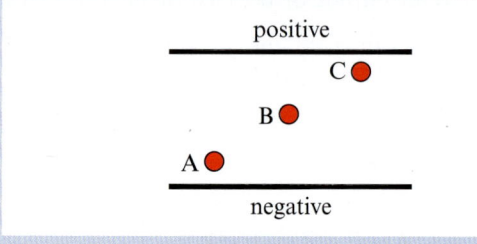

Figure 18.13: For check yourself question 5.

In which position does the electron experience the greatest force?

18 Electric and magnetic fields

WORKED EXAMPLE 18.4

A proton is placed on the positive plate in a parallel plate arrangement and is then released (see Figure 18.14).

```
─────────●─────────
         positive
         proton

─────────────────────
         negative
```

Figure 18.14: For worked example 18.4.

The potential difference between the plates is 120 V and the separation of the plates is 2.0 cm.

a Calculate the electric field strength in between the plates.

b Calculate the force on the proton.

c Determine the gain in kinetic energy of the proton when it reaches the negative plate.

d The distance between the plates is doubled but the potential difference remains the same. How do the answers to parts **a** and **b** change, if at all?

Answer

a $E = \frac{V}{d} = \frac{120}{2.0 \times 10^{-2}} = 6.0 \times 10^3 \, \text{N C}^{-1}$.

b $F = qE = 1.6 \times 10^{-19} \times 6.0 \times 10^3 = 9.6 \times 10^{-16}$ N.

c From $W = qV$ (review Chapter 11) and $W = \Delta E_K$ we find $\Delta E_K = 1.6 \times 10^{-19} \times 120 = 1.9 \times 10^{-17}$ J.

d The electric field strength will halve but the change in kinetic energy will stay the same.

WORKED EXAMPLE 18.5

A proton is placed on the positive plate in a parallel plate arrangement. An electron is placed on the negative plate. Both particles are released at the same time and will reach the opposite plate. The proton is 1840 times more massive than the electron.

```
─────────●─────────
         positive
proton

              ●
              electron
─────────────────────
         negative
```

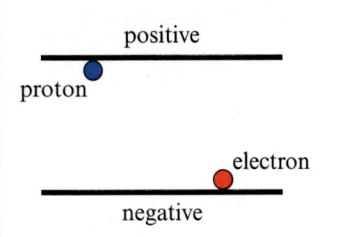

Figure 18.15: For worked example 18.5.

a What is the ratio $\frac{\text{gain in kinetic energy of proton}}{\text{gain in kinetic energy of electron}}$?

b What is the ratio $\frac{\text{time for proton to reach positive plate}}{\text{time for electron to reach negative plate}}$?

Answer

a The gain in kinetic energy is qV and so is the same. The ratio is 1:1.

b The acceleration experienced is $a = \frac{F}{m} = \frac{qE}{m}$ and so the time taken is given by (d is the plate separation):

$d = \frac{1}{2}at^2 = \frac{1}{2}\frac{qE}{m}t^2 \Rightarrow t = \sqrt{\frac{2dm}{qE}}$

Hence the required ratio is $\frac{t_p}{t_e} = \sqrt{\frac{m_p}{m_e}} = \sqrt{1840} \approx 43$.

THEORY OF KNOWLEDGE

Action at a distance and fields

These are some of the words of the Scottish theoretical physicist James Clerk Maxwell (1831–1879). Maxwell was one of the scientists who created the concept of the field.

I have preferred to seek an explanation [of electricity and magnetism] by supposing them to be produced by actions which go on in the surrounding medium as well as in the excited bodies, and endeavoring to explain the action between distant bodies without assuming the existence of forces capable of acting directly … The theory I propose may therefore be called a theory of the Electromagnetic field because it has to do with the space in the neighbourhood of the electric and magnetic bodies.

J. C. Maxwell, 1865

The Millikan oil drop experiment

Between 1910 and 1911, Robert Millikan performed an experiment that measured the charge of an electron. In this experiment, oil drops that were charged by X-rays were allowed to enter a region of uniform electric field between the parallel plates, as shown in Figure 18.16.

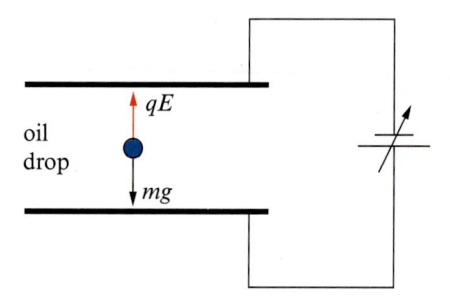

Figure 18.16: Schematic diagram of Millikan's apparatus.

Some oil drops were observed to be at rest in between the plates. This means that the weight of the oil drop is matched by the electric force:

$mg = qE$

$mg = q\dfrac{V}{d}$

and so

$q = \dfrac{mgd}{V}$

So to measure the charge, Millikan needed a method to measure the mass of the oil drop. He did that by turning off the electric field and observed the oil drop that is now falling vertically down.

The oil drop quickly achieves terminal speed because now the weight is matched by the drag force D given by Stoke's law: $D = 6\pi\eta rv$, where η is the viscosity of air:

$mg = 6\pi\eta rv$

So:

$r = \dfrac{mg}{6\pi\eta v}$

But the mass of the oil drop is given by $m = \rho V = \rho \dfrac{4\pi r^3}{3}$, where ρ is the density of oil.

So:

$r = \dfrac{\rho\left(\dfrac{4\pi r^3}{3}\right)g}{6\pi\eta v}$

Giving:

$r = \sqrt{\dfrac{9\eta v}{2\rho g}}$

Thus, by measuring the terminal speed, Millikan could find the radius of the drop and hence its mass and finally its charge. He measured the charge on more than 150 oil drops but only used the data for 58 oil drops for his published results. (This gave rise to some controversy related to correct scientific practice that you may wish to learn more about.) He found that each charge he measured was an integral multiple of a basic unit; he found that unit to be $e = 1.6 \times 10^{-19}$ C.

NATURE OF SCIENCE

Ethics in physics

The case of Robert Millikan played a central role in the discussion of ethics in physics. Millikan was accused of being a misogynist (in a letter to the president of Duke University he advised against hiring women in physics faculty positions) and he expressed anti-Semitic views in letters to his wife while he was in Europe, in contrast to the facts that he personally hired many Jewish physicists at Caltech (including Einstein) and one of his heroes, A. Michelson, was Jewish. He was also accused of mistreating his students: he demanded that a graduate student, who contributed crucially to his experiment, not be an author on the final paper announcing the discovery of the value of the elementary charge.

The big question mark for Millikan's behaviour is the blatantly false statement in his 1913 paper that "It is to be remarked, too, that this is not a selected group of drops but represents all of the drops experimented on during 60 consecutive days…".

CONTINUED

It is now accepted by all that this is a lie. Millikan only used 58 of the more than 150 oil drops he had measured. So why did Millikan include such a statement in his otherwise masterful paper? Millikan was a perfectionist. Undoubtedly, some runs with oil drops were aborted because something had gone wrong. Others, he may have rejected because he did not trust Stokes' law for very small drops which were influenced too much by Brownian motion (collisions with air molecules) and others were too big and fell too fast for accurate measurement. Modern historians of science who have gone through Millikan's notebooks note that even if he had included the data on all the drops, his result for the value of the elementary charge would not change much; only the statistical error would be larger.

TEST YOUR UNDERSTANDING

1. A charged conducting sphere with charge +12 µC is allowed to touch an identical conducting sphere of charge −6 µC. The spheres are then separated. What is the charge on each sphere after separation?

2. The electroscope is a device consisting of a metal sphere, a metallic rod connected to the sphere and two light metallic leaves attached to the rod. When charge is deposited on the sphere, rod and leaves, the leaves repel as shown. The whole arrangement (see Figure 18.17) is protected within a glass jar.

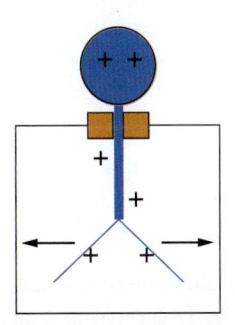

   Figure 18.17: For question 2.

   Suppose the charge on the electroscope is positive. A negatively charged rod is put close but not touching the sphere of the electroscope. What will happen to the leaves?

3. An electroscope is neutral. The following process takes place:

   a. a positively charged rod is placed close but not touching the sphere of the electroscope

   b. the sphere is earthed

   c. the earthing is removed with the charged rod still in place

   d. the rod is removed far away.

   At each stage draw a diagram to represent the state of the electroscope.

4. a. Calculate the force between charges q_1 of 2.0 µC and q_2 of 4.0 µC separated by r = 5.0 cm.

   b. Let the force calculated in **a** be F. In terms of F and without further calculations, state the force between these charges when:

      i. the separation r of the charges is doubled

      ii. q_1 and r are both doubled

      iii. q_1, q_2 and r are all doubled.

5. Three charges are placed on a straight line as shown in Figure 18.18. Calculate the net force on the middle charge.

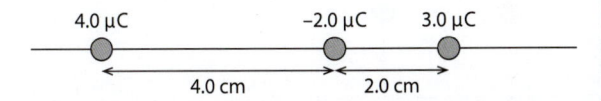

   Figure 18.18: For question 5.

6. In the previous question, determine the position of the middle charge so that it is in equilibrium.

CONTINUED

7 Calculate the force (magnitude and direction) on the charge q in Figure 18.19, where q = 3.0 μC.

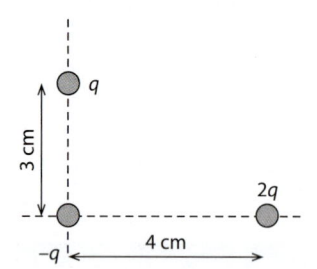

Figure 18.19: For question 7.

8 A charge of magnitude +5.0 μC experiences an electric force of magnitude 3.0×10^{-5} N when placed at a point in space. Determine the electric field at that point.

9 Figure 18.20 shows two spherical charges that are fixed in place. The spheres have the same radius.

Figure 18.20: For question 9.

Explain:

a in which region, I, II or III, could the electric field be zero?

b in which region, I, II or III, does the electric field attain its maximum magnitude?

10 Four charges, each of magnitude q, are fixed at the vertices of a square of side a, as shown in Figure 18.21.

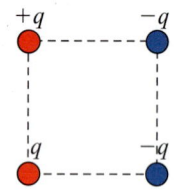

Figure 18.21: For question 10.

a What is the direction of the electric field at the centre of the square?

b What is the magnitude of the field in **a**?

11 Two plastic spheres each of mass 100.0 mg are suspended from very fine insulating strings of length 85.0 cm, as shown in Figure 18.22.

When equal positive charges are placed on the spheres, the spheres repel and are in equilibrium when 10.0 cm apart.

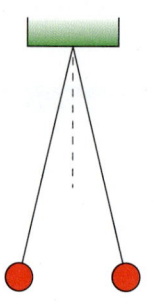

Figure 18.22: For question 11.

a Determine the charge on each sphere.

b Estimate how many electron charges this corresponds to.

c The charge on the left sphere is increased. Draw a diagram to show how the two charges hang.

12 Consider two people, each of mass 60 kg, a distance of 10 m apart.

a Assuming that all the mass in each person is made out of water, estimate how many electrons there are in each person.

b Hence, estimate the electrostatic force of repulsion between the two people due to the electrons.

c List any other simplifying assumptions you have made to make your estimate possible.

d No such force is observed in practice. Suggest why this is so.

13 The electric field is a vector, and so two electric fields at the same point in space must be added according to the laws of vector addition. Consider two equal positive charges q, each 2.00 μC, separated by a = 10.0 cm and a point P a distance of d = 30.0 cm, as shown in Figure 18.23.

CONTINUED

Figure 18.23 shows the directions of the electric fields produced at P by each charge. Determine the magnitude and direction of the net electric field at P.

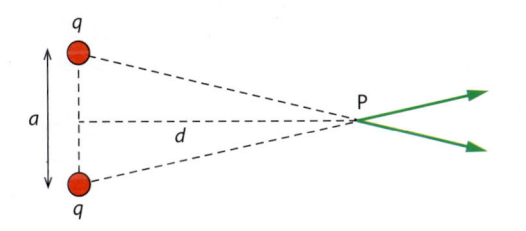

Figure 18.23: For question 13.

14 Repeat the previous question where the top charge is +2.00 µC and the bottom charge is –2.00 µC.

15 The formula for the radius of the oil drop derived in the text ignores the buoyant force on the oil drop. Show that if this force is taken into account the radius is given by $r = \sqrt{\dfrac{9\eta v}{2(\rho - \rho_{air})g}}$.

16 In a hypothetical Millikan type experiment the following charges were measured on hypothetical oil drops: 96×10^{-20} C, 144×10^{-20} C, 192×10^{-20} C, 240×10^{-20} C, 288×10^{-20} C. What is the unit of electric charge in this 'experiment'? Explain your reasoning.

18.2 Magnetic field and force

Effects of magnetic fields have been known since ancient times, and the magnetic compass has been used in navigation since the twelfth century and probably earlier. In modern times the use of magnetic fields is abundant in modern devices such as computers and mobile phones. Very powerful magnets are used to steer charged particles in circular paths in accelerators such as the Large Hadron Collider at CERN.

What produces magnetic fields?

Simple experiments reveal that bar magnets have two poles; these are called north and south. Two like poles repel and two unlike poles attract. This is very similar to positive and negative electric charges, but the poles of a magnet and electric charge are different things.

It is well known that the needle of a compass (the needle is a small bar magnet) aligns itself in an approximately north–south direction. This can be explained by assuming that the earth is itself a large magnet. The north pole of the compass needle is attracted by the earth's *magnetic south pole* (which is in the *geographic north*). Just as an electric charge creates an electric field in the space around it, a magnet creates a similar (but distinct) field, a **magnetic field**. The magnetic needle of a compass can be used to investigate the presence of magnets. Since the compass needle aligns itself with a magnetic field (Figure 18.24), it follows that we can use the direction in which a compass needle is pointing to define the direction of the magnetic field at the location of the compass. In 1819 the Danish scientist H. C. Ørsted (1777–1851) noticed a compass needle change direction when a current was turned on in a nearby wire. Although he could not explain why this happened, Ørsted had demonstrated that electric currents produce magnetic fields. (The earth's magnetic field is also thought to be created by currents in the earth's molten iron core.)

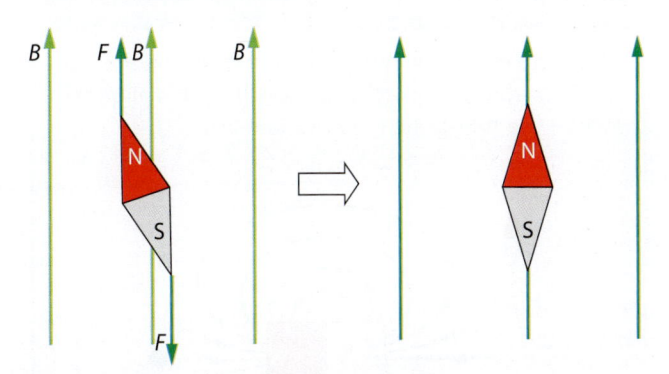

Figure 18.24: A magnetic needle in an external magnetic field experiences forces that will align it with the direction of the magnetic field. The direction of the needle (from its south to the north pole) gives the direction of the external magnetic field.

A magnetic field is produced by electric currents.
An electric field is produced by electric charges.

The vector representing a magnetic field is called **magnetic flux density** and its symbol is B. Its unit is the tesla, T, which will be defined later on. B is the analogue in magnetism of E in electricity.

In permanent magnets, such as bar magnets and horseshoe magnets, the magnetic field is created by microscopic currents due to the motion of electrons in the atoms of the material. These microscopic currents create microscopic magnetic fields; in materials called ferromagnetic these tiny fields are aligned so that a large observable macroscopic magnetic field is produced. Figure 18.25 shows the magnetic field lines for a bar magnet and a horseshoe magnet.

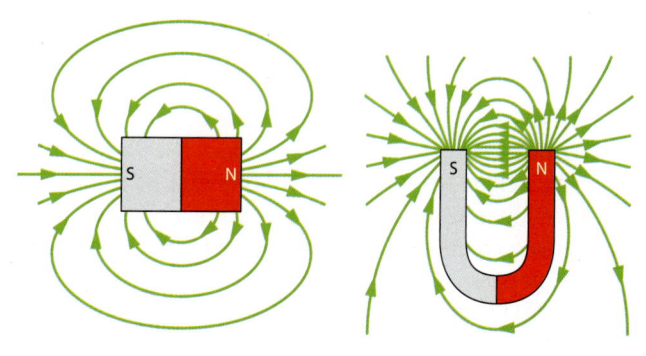

Figure 18.25: Magnetic field lines of a bar magnet and a horseshoe magnet. Notice that the arrows exit the north poles.

CHECK YOURSELF 6

Place the magnetic needle shown (red = North) at the two points marked and show how it is aligned. Ignore the magnetic field of the earth.

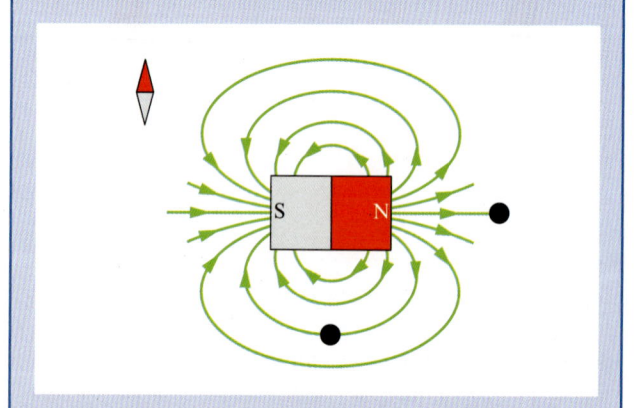

Figure 18.26: For check yourself question 6.

THEORY OF KNOWLEDGE

Magnetic poles appear similar to electric charges. We have north and south magnetic poles and positive and negative charges. The big difference is that we can isolate charges of the same sign but we cannot isolate, say, a north pole. If you cut a bar magnet in half you will only succeed in creating two smaller bar magnets, not isolated north and south poles. Yet theories of particle physics suggest that there may exist particles called magnetic monopoles which would be isolated north or south magnetic poles. Paul Dirac (1902–1984), one of the greatest but least well known physicists of the twentieth century, showed that the existence of magnetic monopoles would automatically explain why electric charge is quantised. Despite much search, no magnetic monopole has ever been found.

The field of a straight current carrying wire

How do we find the direction of the magnetic field created by a straight wire carrying electric current? Figure 18.27 shows small magnetic compasses around a long straight wire that carries current upwards. The compass needles align with the magnetic field. The direction of the needles at each point gives the direction of the magnetic field at that point.

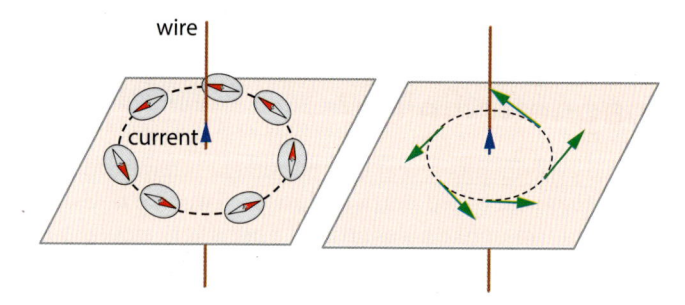

Figure 18.27: Magnetic field around a straight wire.

Drawing a smooth curve through the compass needles gives a circle. The magnetic field is *tangent* to this circle (Figure 18.18). The imaginary curves whose tangents give the magnetic field are called **magnetic field lines**.

18 Electric and magnetic fields

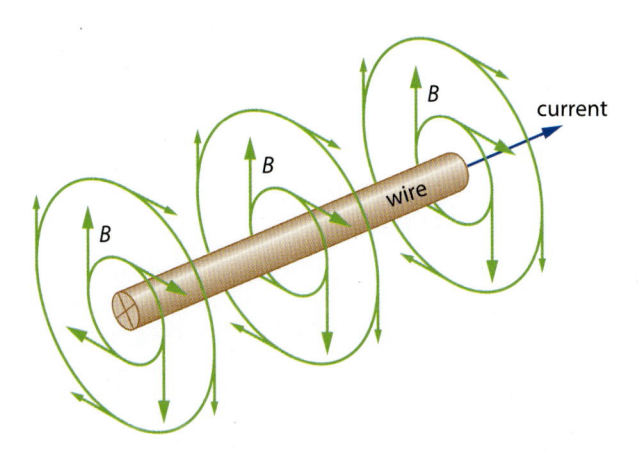

Figure 18.28: A three-dimensional view of the magnetic field pattern around a long straight wire. The magnetic field is symbolized by B. The cross in the wire indicates that the current is entering from left to right. The magnitude of the field decreases as we move away from the wire.

Drawing conventions in this chapter

A circle with a cross (⊗) indicates current or vector *into* the plane of the page.

A circle with a dot (⊙) indicates current or vector *out of* the plane of the page.

But which tangent do we take? The direction of the magnetic field around a straight wire carrying a current is given by the right-hand grip rule illustrated in Figure 18.29.

Grip the wire with the fingers of the right hand in such a way that the thumb points in the direction of the current. Then the direction in which the fingers curl is the direction of the 'flow' of the magnetic field vectors.

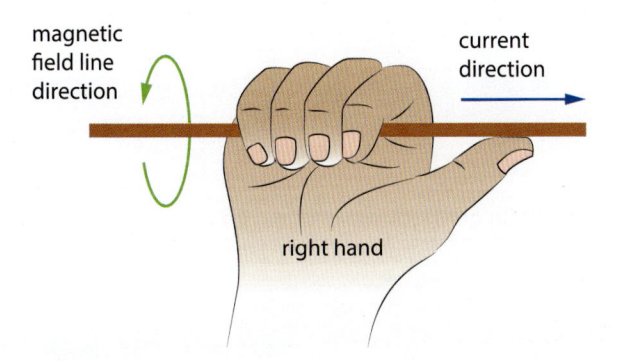

Figure 18.29: The right-hand grip rule for the magnetic field around a straight current-carrying wire. The thumb is in the direction of the current. The fingers curl in the direction of the magnetic field.

CHECK YOURSELF 7

Figure 18.30 shows a wire that goes vertically through a horizontal table. The current goes into the plane of the page.

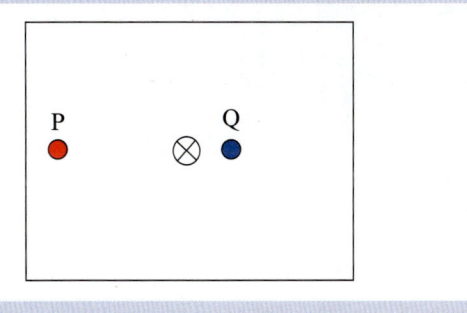

Figure 18.30: For check yourself question 7.

Copy the diagram and draw arrows to show the direction and relative magnitude of the magnetic field at points P and Q.

The solenoid

Figure 18.31 shows the magnetic field lines for a solenoid (a coil). They are no longer circular as they were for the straight wire. The magnetic field lines within the solenoid are fairly uniform, indicating that the field is roughly constant in both magnitude and direction. Notice the similarity between the field outside the solenoid and that around the bar magnet. Notice also that magnetic field lines always exit from a north (N) pole and enter at a south (S) pole.

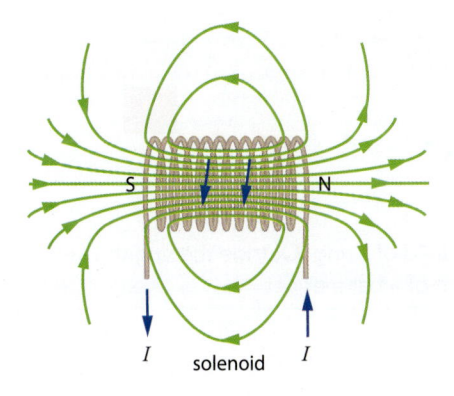

Figure 18.31: The magnetic field lines for a solenoid.

A different right-hand grip rule gives the direction of the magnetic field for a solenoid, illustrated in Figure 18.32. The fingers curl in the direction of the current. The thumb points in the direction of the magnetic field.

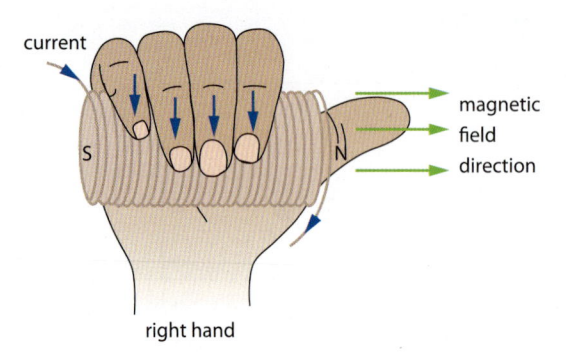

Figure 18.32: The right-hand grip rule for the magnetic field around a solenoid.

The field of a single loop of current

There is one last arrangement for which we need to know the magnetic field: a loop, i.e. a ring that carries a current. In Figure 18.33 the current flows clockwise if looked at from above. The magnetic field lines are closed loops around every point in the ring. Shown here are loops around just two points; you have to imagine similar loops around every point on the ring. For all practical purposes the field of a ring, just like that in the exterior of a coil, may be taken to be the same as that of a bar magnet.

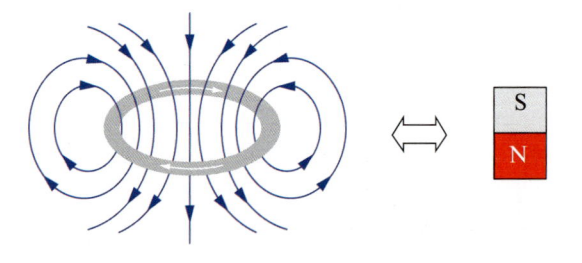

Figure 18.33: The field of a ring. Outside the ring the field is very similar to that of a bar magnet.

CHECK YOURSELF 8

a   A ring carrying current which is clockwise when looked at from above is brought near a bar magnet (Figure 18.34a). Do they attract or do they repel?

b   Two rings with counterclockwise currents when looked at from above have a common vertical axis (Figure 18.34b). Do they attract or do they repel?

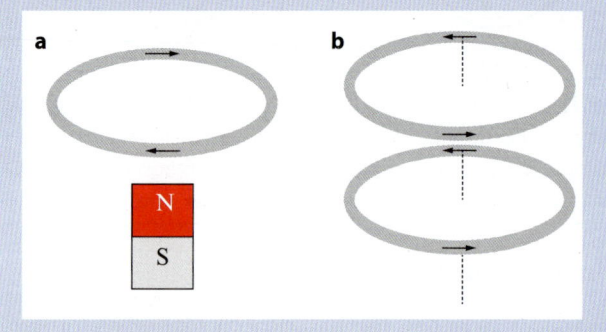

Figure 18.34: For check yourself question 8.

WORKED EXAMPLE 18.6

Figure 18.35 shows two wires carrying equal currents into the page. State the direction of the magnetic field at point P which is equidistant from the two wires.

Figure 18.35: For worked example 18.6.

18 Electric and magnetic fields

CONTINUED

Answer

Using the right-hand grip rule for each wire, the magnetic fields are as shown in the following figure. The arrows representing the field are at right angles to the line joining P to each wire. Both fields have the same magnitude, as P is equidistant from both wires and the current is the same in both wires. The resultant field points to the left.

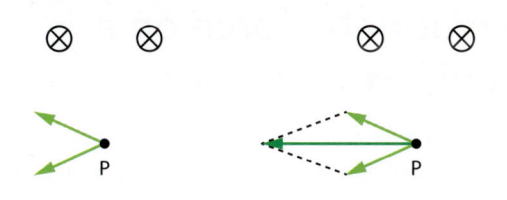

Figure 18.36: The magnetic fields from each wire are added as vectors to give the net magnetic field at P.

The magnetic force on a moving charge

Experiments show that an electric charge moving in a region of magnetic field experiences a new type of force called a **magnetic force**.

There is an exception to this rule: if the velocity of the charge is parallel to the direction of the field, the magnetic force is zero (Figure 18.37).

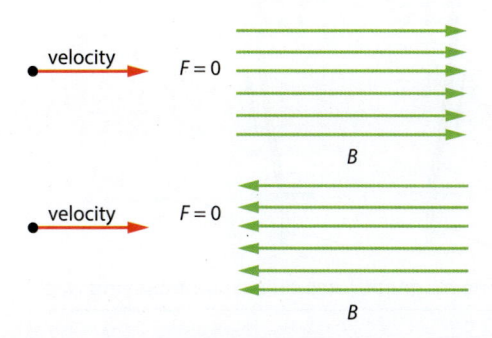

Figure 18.37: There is no magnetic force if the velocity is parallel to the magnetic field.

In any other direction there will be a force on the charge. A charge q moving with speed v in a region of magnetic field of magnetic flux density B will experience a magnetic force F given by:

$$F = qvB \sin\theta$$

where θ is the angle between the velocity direction and the B field direction.

In most of what we will do here $\theta = 90°$ so that the magnetic force will be given by the simpler formula

$$F = qvB$$

We see that there is no magnetic force if the charge is *not* moving. This is different from the electric force on a charge, which is always non-zero whether the charge moves or not. The magnetic force on particles that are electrically neutral ($q = 0$) is, of course, zero.

The magnetic force is what we use to define the magnetic flux density.

If the magnetic force is F when a charge q moves with velocity v that makes an angle θ with the direction of the field, then the magnitude of the magnetic field, B, also called the magnetic flux density, is defined to be:

$$B = \frac{F}{qv \sin\theta}$$

The unit of the magnetic flux density is the tesla (T). A magnetic flux density of 1 T produces a force of 1 N on a charge of 1 C moving at 1 m s^{-1} at right angles to the direction of the field.

What about the direction of the magnetic force? An example is shown in Figure 18.38. The force is at right angles to both the velocity vector and the magnetic field.

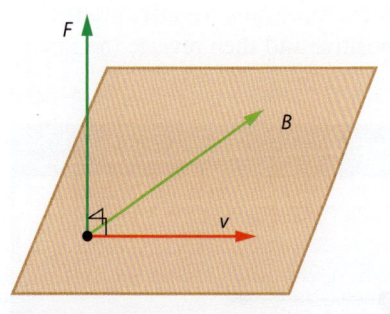

Figure 18.38: The charge shown is positive. The direction of the force is perpendicular to both the velocity vector and the magnetic field vector.

There are a number of 'rules' to help us find this direction. Three of these are shown in Figure 18.39.

399

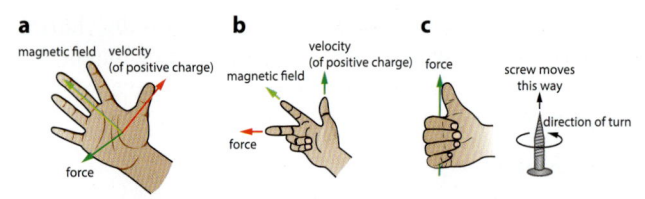

Figure 18.39: The right-hand rule gives the direction of the force on a positive charge. The force on a negative charge is in the opposite direction.

Try the different versions and choose the one that you are comfortable with.

- *Figure 18.39a.* Hold your right hand as if you are going to shake hands. Place your hand so that the four fingers point in the direction of the field and the thumb in the direction of the velocity. The direction *away* from the palm is the direction of the force.

- *Figure 18.39b.* Hold your right hand as in Figure 18.39a, but then bend the middle finger at right angles to your palm. The middle finger now represents the force, the index finger the field and the thumb the velocity.

- *Figure 18.39c.* Curl the right-hand fingers so that they rotate from the vector v to the vector B (along the smallest of the two possible angles). The direction of the thumb is the direction of the force. (In this version you can also imagine you are rotating a screw in the direction from v to B. The direction the screw moves is the force direction.)

If you are familiar with the vector product of two vectors, you may recognise that $\vec{F} = q\vec{v} \times \vec{B}$.

These rules give the direction of the magnetic force on a *positive* charge. To find the force on a negative charge, pretend the charge is positive and then reverse the force direction you find.

> **CHECK YOURSELF 9**
>
> Figure 18.40 shows the magnetic force on a moving electron.
>
> **Figure 18.40:** For check yourself question 9.
>
> What is the direction of the magnetic field?

> **WORKED EXAMPLE 18.7**
>
> Express the tesla in terms of fundamental units.
>
> **Answer**
>
> From the definition $B = \dfrac{F}{qv\sin\theta}$ it follows that:
>
> $$T = \dfrac{N}{C \times m\,s^{-1}} = \dfrac{N}{A \times m} = \dfrac{kg\,m\,s^{-2}}{A \times m} = kg\,s^{-2}\,A^{-1}$$

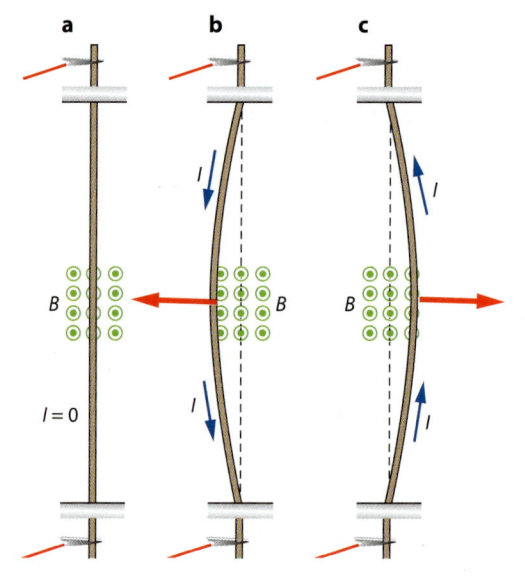

The magnetic force on a current-carrying wire

A current in a wire consists of moving charges. So a current-carrying wire placed in a magnetic field will experience a magnetic force because there is a force on the moving charges in the wire.

Part of the wire in Figure 18.41 is in a region of magnetic field directed out of the page. In Figure 18.41a the current in the wire is zero and there is no force. Figure 18.41b and Figure 18.41c show the forces on the wire when there is current.

Figure 18.41: The magnetic force on a current-carrying wire.

The formula for the magnetic force on a length L (L is that length of the wire that finds itself in the region of the field) is:

$F = BIL \sin\theta$

where θ is the angle between the current and the direction of the magnetic field.

To find the direction of the force, use the right-hand rules for the force on a charge (Figure 18.39) and replace velocity by current.

The force between two current-carrying wires

Consider two long, straight, parallel wires carrying currents I_1 and I_2 (Figure 18.42). The first wire (wire 1) creates a magnetic field in space. This field has magnitude B_1 at the position of the second wire (wire 2). This means wire 2 experiences a magnetic force. Similarly, wire 2 creates a magnetic field of magnitude B_2 at the position of wire 1, so that wire 1 also experiences a magnetic force. By Newton's third law, the force that wire 1 exerts on wire 2 must be accompanied by an equal and opposite force of wire 2 on wire 1. Therefore the forces experienced by the two wires are equal and opposite.

The currents are different in the two wires, so the magnetic fields are different, but the two forces are equal in magnitude.

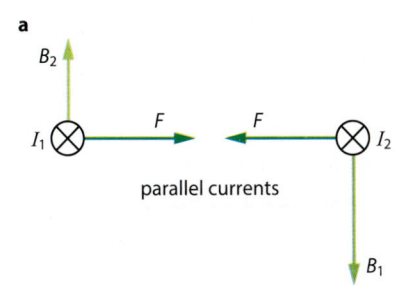

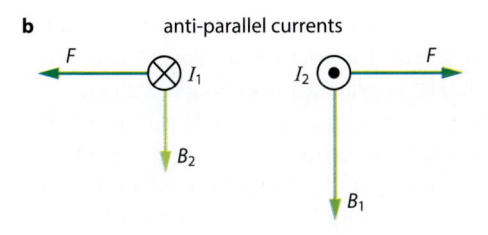

a parallel currents

b anti-parallel currents

Figure 18.42: The forces on two parallel currents are equal and opposite. **a** Force between parallel currents. **b** Force between anti-parallel currents.

We can use the right-hand rule to find the directions of these forces. Assume first that both currents are flowing into the page. Then the magnetic fields are as shown in Figure 18.42a and the forces are attractive. If wire 1 carries current into the page and wire 2 carries current out of the page, as shown in Figure 18.42b, the forces are repulsive. In both cases the forces are equal and opposite, consistent with Newton's third law. So we have found that if the currents are parallel, the forces are attractive, and if they are anti-parallel, the forces are repulsive.

It is useful to know that the magnitude of the magnetic flux density created at a distance r from a long straight wire carrying current I is given by the formula (which is not on the syllabus) $B = \frac{\mu_0 I}{2\pi r}$. Here μ_0 is a constant of physics called magnetic permeability. Its value in vacuum is defined to be $\mu_0 = 4\pi \times 10^{-7}$ T m A^{-1}. This constant is to magnetism what permittivity (ε_0) is to electricity. Looking at Figure 18.43, the magnetic flux density created by the left wire at the position of the right wire is $B_1 = \frac{\mu_0 I_1}{2\pi r}$ where r is the separation of the wires. Therefore the force experienced by a length L of the right wire is $F = B_1 I_2 L = \frac{\mu_0 I_1 I_2 L}{2\pi r}$. This gives the syllabus formula for the force per unit length:

$$\frac{F}{L} = \mu_0 \frac{I_1 I_2}{2\pi r}$$

Notice that the magnetic field produced by the right wire at the position of the left is given by $B_2 = \frac{\mu_0 I_2}{2\pi r}$.

The force on the left wire is then $F = B_2 I_1 L = \frac{\mu_0 I_2 I_1 L}{2\pi r}$ which, as expected from Newton's third law, is equal to the force on the right wire.

> **CHECK YOURSELF 10**
>
> Calculate the unit and value of the quantity $\sqrt{\frac{1}{\varepsilon_0 \mu_0}}$.

> **WORKED EXAMPLE 18.8**
>
> Figure 18.43 shows three wires, X, Y and Z, carrying equal currents I. The directions of the currents are as shown. The separation of two adjacent wires is d. 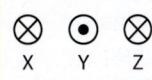
>
> **Figure 18.43:** For worked example 18.8.

CONTINUED

Find the magnitude and direction of the force per unit length on wire Z when $I = 4.0$ A and $d = 2.0$ cm.

Answer

Parallel currents attract and anti-parallel repel. So X attracts Z and Y repels it. Y is closer to Z so the force it exerts is larger. Hence the force is to the right. The force per unit length from X is $\mu_0 \frac{I^2}{2\pi(2d)}$ to the left and that from Y is $\mu_0 \frac{I^2}{2\pi d}$ to the right. The net force per unit length is then $\mu_0 \frac{I^2}{2\pi d} - \mu_0 \frac{I^2}{4\pi d} = \mu_0 \frac{I^2}{4\pi d}$ to the right. For $I = 4.0$ A and $d = 2.0$ cm the force per unit length is $4\pi \times 10^{-7} \times \frac{4.0^2}{4\pi \times 2.0 \times 10^{-2}} = 8.0 \times 10^{-5}$ N m^{-1}.

EXAM TIP

It is simpler to remember that parallel currents attract rather than having to work out the direction of the magnetic field at Z's location and then find the force.

NATURE OF SCIENCE

Introduced in the nineteenth century by Michael Faraday as 'lines of force', the concept of magnetic field lines allowed scientists to visualize the magnetic field around a magnet and the magnetic field around a moving charge.
A few years later, in one of the greatest unifications in physics, James Clerk Maxwell showed that all magnetic and electric phenomena are different sides of the same general phenomenon, electromagnetism, and that light is a combination of electric and magnetic fields. In the early twentieth century, Albert Einstein showed that viewing electric and magnetic phenomena from different frames of reference leads naturally to the theory of relativity. At about the same time, trying to understand magnetism in different materials required the introduction of quantum theory, so magnetism played a crucial role in the development of physics.

WORKED EXAMPLE 18.9

An electron approaches a bar magnet, as shown in Figure 18.44. What is the direction of the force on the electron?

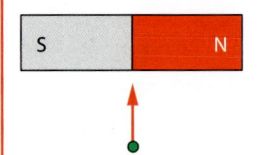

Figure 18.44: For worked example 18.9.

Answer

The magnetic flux density at the position of the electron is to the left. Placing the right hand so that the thumb points up the page (velocity direction) and the fingers to the left (field direction), the palm is pointing out of the page. But the charge is negative and so the force is into the page.

Links

We have now added two new forces to our list of forces which up to now really only included the gravitational force. All the other forces we met (normal forces, friction, tension etc.) are really macroscopic manifestations of electric or magnetic phenomena. Maxwell showed that electric and magnetic phenomena are closely linked and joined the electric and the magnetic force into one, the electromagnetic force, achieving the first unification in physics. Later on, in Chapter 23, we will meet two new forces, the weak and strong nuclear forces. These are forces that are relevant in the subatomic world. In order of increasing strength of interaction the list is gravitational, weak nuclear, electromagnetic and strong nuclear. But this is a rather meaningless list since the comparison of interaction strength depends heavily on the context in which the comparison is made. Adding to the unification of Maxwell, the theory of Glashow, Salam and Weinberg that gave us the presently accepted standard model of particles implies that the electromagnetic force and the weak nuclear force are two aspects of the same force called the electroweak force. Are there other forces that we have not discovered yet?

TEST YOUR UNDERSTANDING

17 Two wires carry equal currents into the plane of the page (Figure 18.45).

⊗ P ⊗ Q
  •   •

Figure 18.45: For question 17.

What is the direction of the magnetic field at point P halfway between the charges and at point Q?

18 Two wires carry equal currents into the plane of the page (Figure 18.46).

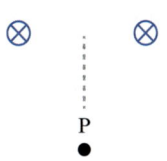

⊗   ⊗

   P
   •

Figure 18.46: For question 18.

What is the direction of the magnetic field at point P which is on the perpendicular bisector of the line joining the wires?

19 Two wires carry equal currents in opposite directions at right angles to the plane of the page (Figure 18.47).

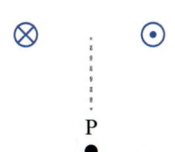

⊗   ⊙

   P
   •

Figure 18.47: For question 19.

What is the direction of the magnetic field at point P which is on the perpendicular bisector of the line joining the wires?

20 The current in a horizontal loop of wire is as shown in Figure 18.48.

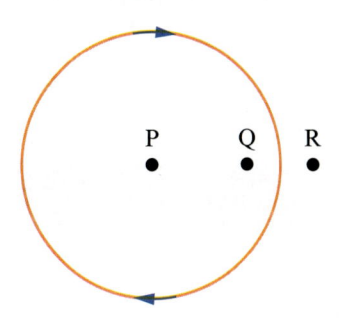

P   Q   R
•   •   •

Figure 18.48: For question 20.

What is the direction of the magnetic field at points P, Q and R?

21 Determine the direction of the missing quantity from B, v and F in each of the cases shown in Figure 18.49. The circle represents a positive charge.

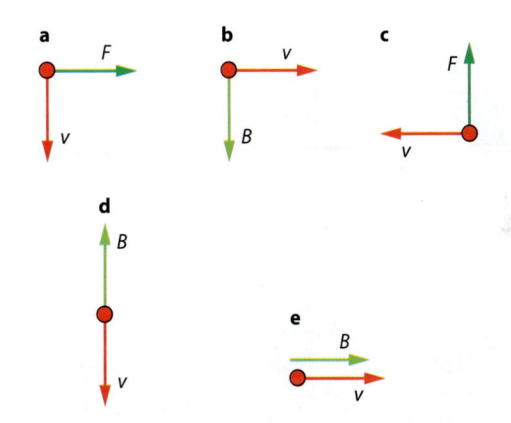

Figure 18.49: For question 21.

CONTINUED

22 The north pole of a bar magnet is brought close to a ring that carries current. For clarity only a cross section of the ring is shown (Figure 18.50).

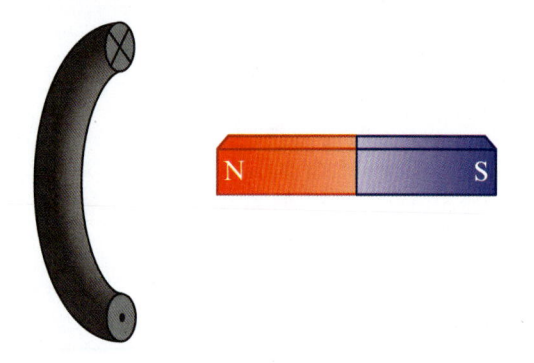

Figure 18.50: For question 22.

Describe the force between the bar magnet and the ring.

23 Currents are established in two parallel rings as shown in Figure 18.51. For clarity, only a cross section of each ring is shown.

Figure 18.51: For question 23.

Describe the force between the rings.

24 A wire carrying current into the plane of the page is put in between two bar magnets as shown in Figure 18.52.

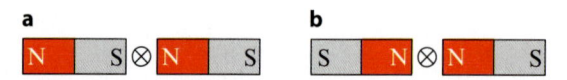

Figure 18.52: For question 24.

What is the direction of the force on the wire in each case?

25 A current carrying wire is placed in between two bar magnets as shown in Figure 18.53.

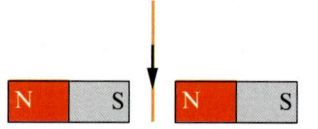

Figure 18.53: For question 25.

What is the direction of the force on the wire?

26 A bar magnet attracts a metallic ball hanging from a thread (Figure 18.54).

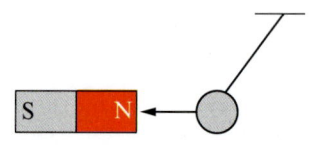

Figure 18.54: For question 26.

The magnet is reversed so that the south pole is facing the ball. What will happen now?

27 Two wires carry equal currents into the plane of the page (Figure 18.55).

X ⊗   ⊗ Y

Figure 18.55: For question 27.

a   On the diagram draw:

   i   the magnetic field created by wire X at the position of wire Y

   ii   the magnetic field created by wire Y at the position of wire X

   iii the magnetic forces on each wire.

b   The current in wire X is doubled. Make new drawings for **ai**, **aii** and **aiii**.

CONTINUED

28 Two wires carry equal currents in opposite directions at right angles to the plane of the page (Figure 18.56).

Figure 18.56: For question 28.

Wire X carries current into the page and is equidistant from the other two wires. What is the direction of the magnetic force on wire X?

29 A ring carries current as shown in Figure 18.57. For clarity only a cross section of the ring is shown. A proton moves parallel to the plane of the ring.

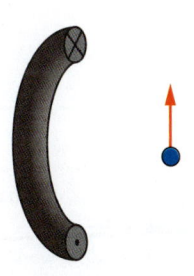

Figure 18.57: For question 29.

What is the direction of the magnetic force on the proton?

30 A square loop of wire is placed close to a straight wire (Figure 18.58).

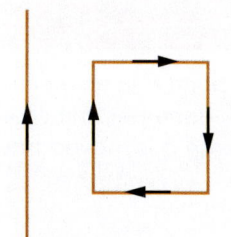

Figure 18.58: For question 30.

Both wires have currents in them as shown. Carefully describe the force between the straight wire and the loop.

31 Draw the magnetic field lines for two parallel wires carrying equal currents into the page. Repeat for anti-parallel currents.

32 Copy Figure 18.59. Draw the magnetic field lines that result when the magnetic field of a long straight wire carrying current into the page is superimposed on a uniform magnetic field pointing to the right that lies on the page.

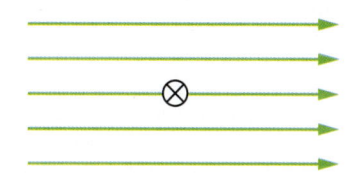

Figure 18.59: For question 32.

33 A long straight wire carries current as shown in Figure 18.60. Two electrons move with velocities that are parallel and perpendicular to the current. Determine the direction of the magnetic force experienced by each electron.

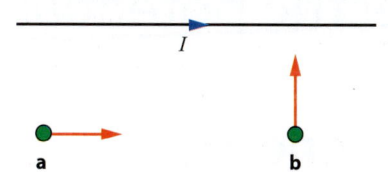

Figure 18.60: For question 33.

34 A proton moves past a bar magnet as shown in Figure 18.61. Find the direction of the force it experiences in each case.

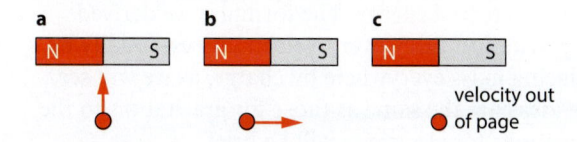

Figure 18.61: For question 34.

PHYSICS FOR THE IB DIPLOMA: COURSEBOOK

> **CONTINUED**

35 A bar magnet is placed in a uniform magnetic field as shown in Figure 18.62.

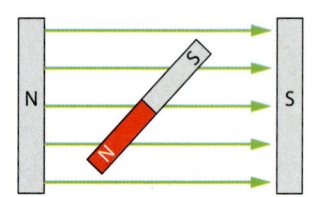

Figure 18.62: For question 35.

a Suggest whether there is a net force on the bar magnet.

b Describe how it will move.

36 A high-tension electricity wire running along a north–south line carries a current of 3000 A. The magnetic field of the earth at the position of the wire has a magnitude of 5.00×10^{-5} T and makes an angle of 30° below the horizontal.

Calculate the force experienced by a length of 30.0 m of the wire.

37 A uniform magnetic field is established in the plane of the paper as shown in Figure 18.63. Two wires carry equal *parallel* currents normally to the plane of the paper at P and Q. Point R is on the line joining P to Q and closer to Q. The magnetic field at position R is zero.

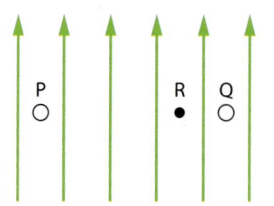

Figure 18.63: For question 37.

a Determine whether the currents are going into the paper or out of the paper.

b The magnitude of the current is increased slightly. Determine whether the point where the magnetic field is zero moves to the right or to the left of R.

18.3 Electric potential and electric potential energy

Most of what we learned about gravitational potential energy and gravitational potential applies also to electricity. Just as a mass creates a gravitational potential around it, an electric charge creates **electric potential**. And just as two masses have gravitational potential energy between them, two electric charges also share **electric potential energy**. The formulas we derived for gravitation carry over to electricity essentially by replacing mass everywhere by charge, as we will see. The ideas are the same as those for gravitation so the derivations for electricity will be brief.

Suppose that at some point in space we place a large positive charge Q. If we place another positive charge q at infinity and try to move it closer to the large charge Q, we will have to exert a force on q, since it is being repelled by Q (Figure 18.64). That is, we have to do work in order to change the position of q and bring it closer to Q.

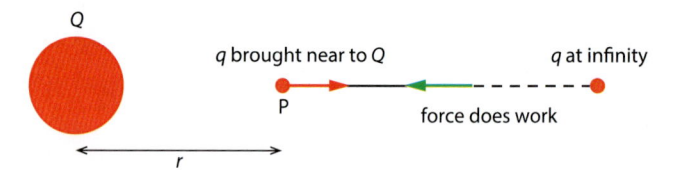

Figure 18.64: Work is done to bring the positive charge q from infinity to a given position away from positive charge Q. The red arrow is the force of repulsion between the two charges. The green arrow represents the force that moves charge q towards Q.

> **KEY POINT**
>
> The electric potential at a point P in an electric field is the amount of work done per unit charge as a small positive test charge q is moved from infinity to P
>
> $$V_e = \frac{W}{q}$$
>
> The unit of potential is the volt (V), and $1\text{ V} = 1\text{ J C}^{-1}$.

The work done in moving a charge q from infinity to point P is the electric potential energy, E_p of the system.

If the electric potential at some point P is V_e, and we place a charge q at P, the electric potential energy E_p of the system is given by:

$$E_p = qV_e$$

Using calculus to calculate the work done in moving the charge q from infinity to a separation r, as we did for gravitation, results in:

$$W = \frac{kQq}{r}$$

Therefore:

$$V_e = \frac{kQ}{r}$$

and

$$E_p = \frac{kQq}{r}$$

Electric potential and electric potential energy are scalar quantities, just like gravitational potential and gravitational potential energy. For gravitational and electric fields, the work done is independent of the path followed.

Moving a charge q from one point in an electric field to another requires work (Figure 18.65).

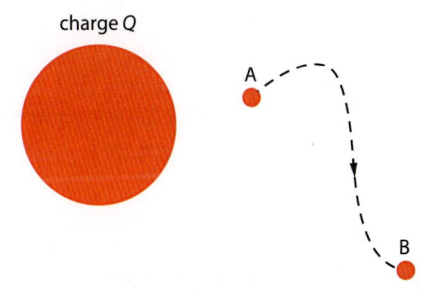

Figure 18.65: Work must be done in order to move a charge from one point to another where the potential is different.

The work done W in moving charge q from A to B is:

$$W = q\Delta V_e = q(V_{eB} - V_{eA})$$

The quantity $V_{eB} - V_{eA}$ is the potential difference between A and B.

In all these formulas, the charges must be entered with their correct sign.

> **WORKED EXAMPLE 18.10**
>
> The hydrogen atom has a single proton and a single electron, as shown in Figure 18.66. 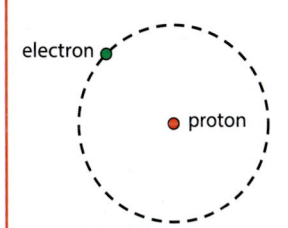
>
> **Figure 18.66:** For worked example 18.10.
>
> **a** Find the electric potential a distance of 0.50×10^{-10} m from the proton of the hydrogen atom. The proton has a charge 1.6×10^{-19} C, equal and opposite to that of the electron.
>
> **b** Use your answer to **a** to calculate the electric potential energy between the proton in a hydrogen atom and an electron orbiting the proton at a radius 0.50×10^{-10} m.
>
> **Answer**
>
> **a** $V_e = \frac{kQ}{r}$
>
> Substituting the values from the question:
>
> $$V_e = \frac{8.99 \times 10^9 \times 1.60 \times 10^{-19}}{0.50 \times 10^{-10}}$$
>
> $$V_e = 28.77 \approx 29 \text{ V}$$
>
> **b** The electric potential energy is given by:
>
> $$E_p = \frac{kQq}{r} = qV_e$$
>
> Substituting the value for V_e from part **a**:
>
> $$E_p = 28.77 \times (-1.6 \times 10^{-19})$$
>
> $$E_p = -4.6 \times 10^{-18} \text{ J}$$

Electric potential is a scalar quantity. So if we have two charges q_1 and q_2, the electric potential at a point P that is a distance r_1 from q_1 and a distance r_2 from q_2 is just the sum of the individual electric potentials:

$$V_e = \frac{kq_1}{r_1} + \frac{kq_2}{r_2}$$

That is, we first find the potential at P from q_1 alone, then from q_2 alone, and then add up the two (Figure 18.67). We find the electric potential for more than two charges in the same way—by adding the individual potentials.

PHYSICS FOR THE IB DIPLOMA: COURSEBOOK

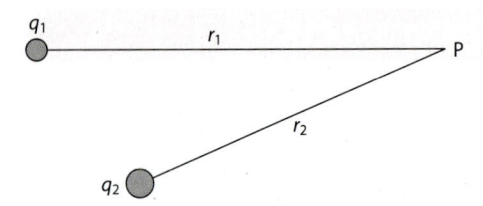

Figure 18.67: The potential at P is found by finding the potential there from the first charge, then finding the potential from the second charge, and finally adding the two.

The simple formula for electric potential works for point charges. (By point charges we mean that the objects on which the charges q_i are placed are mathematical points, or close to it.) The formula also works in another special case—when the object on which the charge q is placed is a sphere.

For a point P outside the sphere and at a distance r from the centre of the sphere, the potential at P is indeed:

$$V_e = \frac{kQ}{r}$$

On the surface of the sphere the potential is:

$$V_e = \frac{kQ}{R}$$

where R is the radius of the sphere.

But at any point inside the sphere, the electric potential is constant and has the same value as the potential at the surface (Figure 18.68).

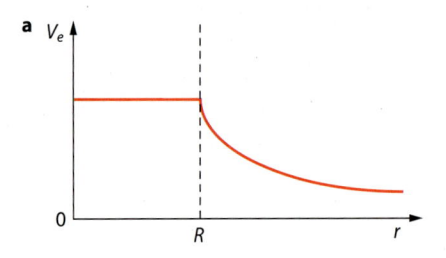

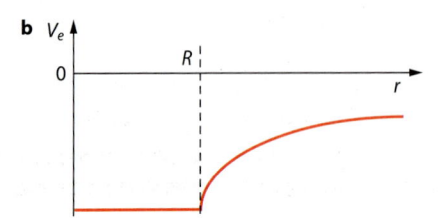

Figure 18.68: The electric potential is constant inside the sphere and falls off as $\frac{1}{r}$ outside. Shown here are **a** a positively charged sphere and **b** a negatively charged sphere.

The connection between potential and field

There is a deep connection between potential and field for both gravitation and electricity. To see this connection let us move a point charge q from a point P to a neighbouring point Q. There is a potential difference ΔV_e between the two points, and the points are a distance Δr apart, Figure 18.69.

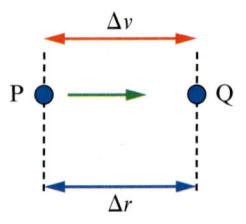

Figure 18.69: A point charge q is to be moved between points P and Q at different potential. This requires work.

We know that this requires an amount of work W given by:

$$W = q\Delta V_e$$

But we may also calculate the work from W = force × distance. The force on the point mass is the electric force $F = qE$, where E is the magnitude of the electric field strength at the position of the charge q. Assuming that the two points are very close to each other means that E will not change very much as we move from one point to the other, and so we may take E to be constant. Then the work done is also given by:

$$W = qE\Delta r$$

Equating the two expressions for work done gives:

$$E = \frac{\Delta V_e}{\Delta r}$$

(A more careful treatment using calculus gives $E = -\frac{dV_e}{dr}$.)

In a graph showing the variation with distance of the potential, the gradient (slope) of the graph is the magnitude of the field strength. This applies to both gravitational and electric fields.

> **KEY POINT**
>
> We conclude, see Figure 18.68, that the electric field inside a charged conducting sphere is zero since the potential is constant.

18 Electric and magnetic fields

WORKED EXAMPLE 18.11

Figure 18.70 shows two unequal positive charges, $+Q$ and $+q$.

distance from larger charge x

$+Q$ ---------- $+q$

Figure 18.70: For worked example 18.11.

Which one of the four graphs in Figure 18.71 shows the variation with distance x from the larger charge of the electric potential V_e along the line joining the centres of the charges?

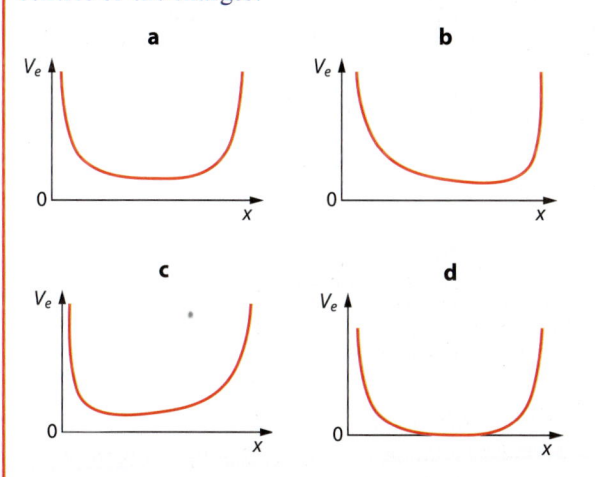

Figure 18.71: Variation of electric potential with distance.

Answer

The electric field is the gradient of the graph. It is zero closer to the smaller charge, and so the answer has to be B.

THEORY OF KNOWLEDGE

Are fields real?

Are electric (and gravitational) fields real, or are they just convenient devices for doing calculations and visualizing situations?

Feynman describes a situation of two protons moving at right angles to each other:

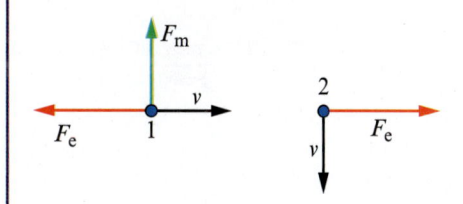

The protons repel each other with the electric force (red arrows). These forces are equal in magnitude and opposite in direction. Proton 2 creates a magnetic field at the position of proton 1 directed into the plane of the page and so there is a magnetic force on proton 1 (green arrow). However, proton 1 does not create a magnetic field at the position of proton 2 because (at this instant) proton 2 is along the direction of the velocity of proton 1. Hence there is no magnetic force on proton 2. This appears to violate Newton's third law but as we know Newton's third law is crucial in deriving the law of conservation of momentum. It can be shown that there is a rate of change of the momentum *carried by the electromagnetic field of the protons* of the right magnitude and direction so as to restore Newton's third law. Fields carry energy and momentum and are as real as protons and electrons.

The connection between field lines and equipotential surfaces

Consider a single charge Q. The electric potential it creates in the space around is given by $V_e = k\frac{Q}{r}$. This means that points in space that have the same distance from the charge have the same potential. These points lie on spheres centred at the charge. Spheres of different radii correspond to different values of the potential. We call surfaces of the same potential **equipotential surfaces**. Figure 18.72a shows equipotential surfaces for a point charge (the surfaces are spheres surrounding the charge; we only show a

409

two-dimensional version of them as circles here). Figure 18.72b adds field lines (the charge is assumed negative) along with the equipotential surfaces.
We see that the field lines are normal (perpendicular) to the equipotential surfaces.

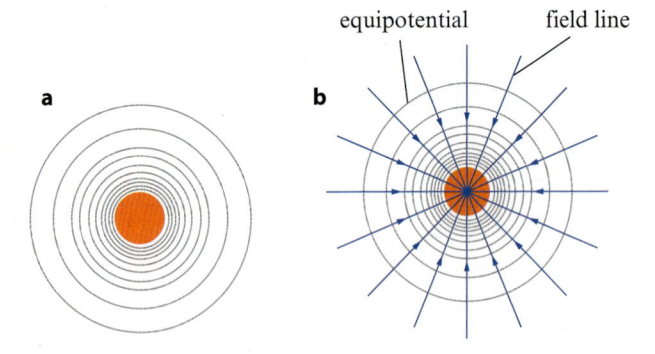

Figure 18.72: a Equipotential surfaces for a point charge. **b** The field lines are at right angles to the equipotential surfaces.

The explanation of why the field lines are at right angles to the equipotential surfaces is as follows: to move a charge from one point on an equipotential surface to another requires zero work because $W = q\Delta V$ and $\Delta V = 0$. If the field lines were not normal to the equipotential surfaces, there would be a component of the field along the equipotential and so a force on the charge. As the charge moved this force would do work, which contradicts the fact that the work should be zero.

Equipotential surfaces are spheres only for an isolated charge. With more than one charge present, the equipotential surfaces are complicated surfaces. Figure 18.73 shows the equipotential surfaces (in black) and field lines (in red) for two charges. In Figure 18.73a $q_2 = q_1$ (both positive) and in Figure 18.73b $q_2 = -q_1$. The field is zero halfway between the charges along the line joining the charges in Figure 18.73a.

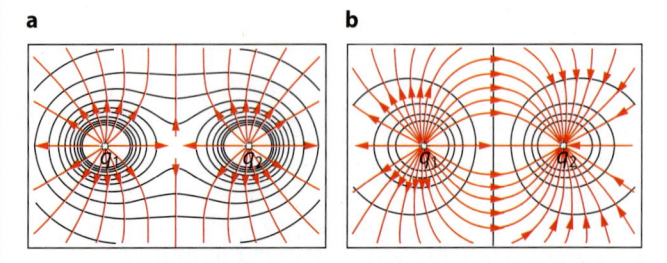

Figure 18.73: Field lines and equipotential surfaces for **a** two equal charges of the same sign and **b** two equal and opposite charges.

Figure 18.74 shows the equipotential surfaces (in black) and field lines (in red) for two unequal charges. The field is zero closer to the smaller charge along the line joining the charges in Figure 18.74a. In Figure 18.74a $q_2 = 4q_1$ and in Figure 18.74b $q_2 = -4q_1$.

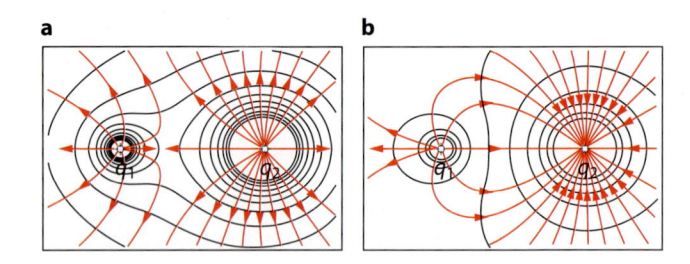

Figure 18.74: Field lines and equipotential surfaces for **a** two unequal charges of the same sign and **b** two unequal and opposite charges.

Figure 18.75 shows equipotential surfaces and field lines for the case of parallel charged plates.

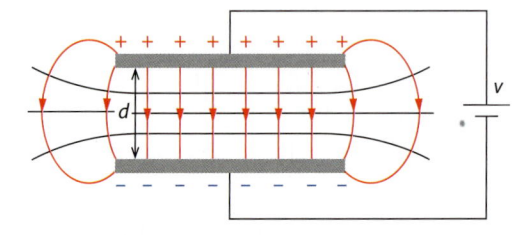

Figure 18.75: Field lines and equipotential surfaces for parallel charged plates.

WORKED EXAMPLE 18.12

A wire of length L has a potential difference V across its ends.

a Find the electric field inside the wire.

b Hence find the work done when a charge q is moved from one end of the wire to the other.

Answer

a From $E = \frac{\Delta V}{\Delta r}$ it follows that $E = \frac{V}{L}$.

b The work done can be found in two ways.

1 Use $W = q\Delta V = qV$.

2 Use $W = Fd = qEL = q\frac{V}{L}L = qV$.

The answer is $W = qV$ in both cases.

TEST YOUR UNDERSTANDING

38 a Determine the electric potential at the mid-point of the line joining two equal positive charges q in terms of q, the Coulomb constant and the charge separation d.

  b Repeat **a** for two equal but opposite charges.

39 Two charges, $q_1 = 2.0$ μC and $q_2 = -4.0$ μC, are 0.30 m apart. Find the electric potential at a point P, which is 0.40 m from q_1 and 0.60 m from q_2.

40 Four equal charges of 5.0 μC are placed at the vertices of a square of side 10 cm.

  a Calculate the value of the electric potential at the centre of the square.

  b Determine the electric field at the centre of the square.

  c How do you reconcile your answers to **a** and **b** with the fact that the electric field is the derivative of the potential?

41 A charge q of 10.0 C is placed somewhere in space.

  a What is the work required to bring a charge of 1.0 mC from a point X, 10.0 m from q, to a point Y, 2.0 m from q?

  b Does the answer depend on which path the charge follows?

42 An electron is brought from infinity to a distance of 12 cm from a charge of −15 nC. How much work was done on the electron by the agent moving the electron?

43 An electron moves from point A where the potential is 100.0 V to point B where the potential is 200.0 V. The electron started from rest. Calculate the speed of the electron as it passes point B.

44 A proton is placed on the surface of a positively charged sphere of charge 2.0 nC and radius 0.25 m. The proton is released.

  a What is the speed of the proton when it gets very far away from the sphere?

  b Draw a graph to show the variation with distance travelled, of the proton speed. (No numbers required, just the shape.)

45 Four charges are placed at the vertices of a square of side 5.00 cm, as shown in Figure 18.76.

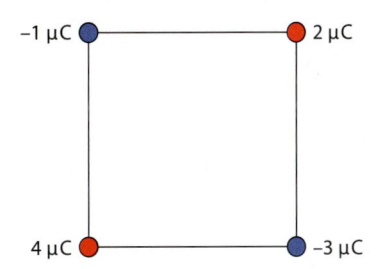

Figure 18.76: For question 45.

  a On a copy of Figure 18.76, show the forces acting on the 2.0 μC charge. Find the magnitude and direction of the net force on the 2.0 μC charge.

  b Calculate the value of the electric potential at the centre of the square.

  c Determine the work that must be done in order to move a charge of 1 nC initially at infinity to the centre of the square.

46 An electron is launched with speed 1.5×10^6 m s^{-1} from the positively charged plate, directed towards the opposite plate (Figure 18.77).

The potential difference between the plates is 8.0 V. The plates are separated by 12 cm. (The potential at the negative plate may be taken to be zero and that at the positive plate 8.0 V.)

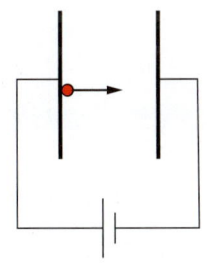

Figure 18.77: For question 46.

CONTINUED

a Show that the electron will not make it to the negative plate.

b Determine the distance at which the electron stops and turns back.

c What should the minimum electron initial speed be such that the electron makes it the negative plate?

d The electron has the minimum speed found in **c**. Draw a sketch graph to show the variation of the electron speed with distance travelled.

47 Two conducting spheres are separated by a distance that is large compared with their radii. The first sphere has a radius of 10.0 cm and has a charge of 2.00 µC on its surface. The second sphere has a radius of 15.0 cm and is neutral. The spheres are then connected by a long conducting wire.

a Find the charge on each sphere.

b Calculate the charge density on each sphere (charge density is the total charge on the sphere divided by the surface area of the sphere).

c Calculate the electric field on the surface of each sphere.

d Comment on your result in the light of your answer to part **b**. Why is it stated that the wire is long?

48 Figure 18.78 shows the equipotential lines for two equal and opposite charges. Draw the electric field lines for these two charges.

Figure 18.78: For question 48.

49 Two long parallel plates are separated by a distance of 15.0 cm. The bottom plate is kept at a potential of −250 V and the top at +250 V. A charge of −2.00 µC is placed at a point 3.00 cm from the bottom plate.

a Find the electric potential energy of the charge.

The charge is then moved vertically up to a point 3.00 cm from the top plate.

b What is the electrical potential energy of the charge now?

c How much work was done on the charge?

50 An electron is shot with a speed equal to 1.59×10^6 m s^{-1} from a point where the electric potential is zero toward an immovable negative charge q (see Figure 18.79).

Figure 18.79: For question 50.

a Determine the potential at P so that the electron stops momentarily at P and then turns back.

b Calculate the magnitude of q.

51 Two equal and opposite charges are placed at points with coordinates $x = 0$, $y = a$ and $x = 0$, $y = -a$, as shown in Figure 18.80.

Figure 18.80: For question 51.

a Find the electric field at the point with coordinates $x = d$, $y = 0$.

CONTINUED

b Repeat for two equal negative charges $-q$ on the y-axis.

c Sketch graphs to show the variation of these fields with the distance d.

52 Three protons are initially very far apart. Calculate the work that must be done in order to bring these protons to the vertices of an equilateral triangle of side 5.0×10^{-15} m.

53 A charge $-q$ whose mass is m moves in a circle of radius r around another positive stationary charge q located at the centre of the circle, as shown in Figure 18.81.

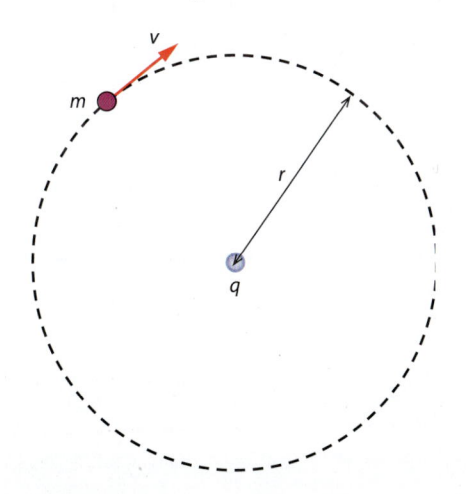

Figure 18.81: For question 53.

a Draw the force on the moving charge.

b Show that the velocity of the charge is given by:
$$v^2 = k\frac{q^2}{mr}$$

c Show that the total energy of the charge is given by:
$$E = -k\frac{q^2}{2r}$$

d Hence determine how much energy must be supplied to the charge if it is to orbit around the stationary charge at a radius equal to $2r$.

54 An electron of charge $-e$ and mass m orbits the proton in a hydrogen atom as in the previous problem.

a Show that the period of revolution of the electron is given by $T^2 = \frac{4\pi^2 m}{ke^2} r^3$ where k is the Coulomb constant and r the radius of the orbit.

b Calculate this period for an orbit radius of 0.5×10^{-10} m.

c Using the results of the previous problem calculate the energy that must be supplied to the electron so it orbits the proton in an orbit of radius 2.0×10^{-10} m.

55 An alpha particle (mass = 6.6×10^{-27} kg, charge = $+2e$) is directed towards a nucleus of electric charge $+79e$. The radius of this nucleus is 7.0×10^{-15} m. Initially the alpha particle is very far from the nucleus. What should the initial speed of the alpha particle be so that it just stops on the nuclear surface?

PHYSICS FOR THE IB DIPLOMA: COURSEBOOK

SELF-ASSESSMENT CHECKLIST

I am able to ...	Section	Not yet	Nearly there	Ready to move on
appreciate that electric charge is conserved and quantised	18.1			
state and apply Coulomb's law	18.1			
understand the concept of an electric field	18.1			
solve problems with electric fields	18.1			
draw the electric field patterns for simple arrangements of charges	18.1			
describe Millikan's experiment	18.1			
understand the concept of a magnetic field	18.2			
draw the magnetic field patterns for straight wires, coils and loops of current as well as for permanent magnets	18.2			
solve problems with magnetic forces on moving charges and currents	18.2			
understand the concept of electric potential and electric potential energy	18.3			
calculate the work done when a charged particle is moved in an electric field	18.3			
calculate the total energy of a charged particle in an electric field	18.3			
appreciate that electric field lines and equipotential surfaces are normal to each other	18.3			

REFLECTION

Do you understand what is meant by *charge conservation*? Do you understand what is meant by charging by *induction*? Can you solve problems with Coulomb's law? Do you understand the concept of *electric field*? Can you solve problems involving electric field strength? Can you describe the Millikan experiment and its consequences? Do you understand the concept of *magnetic field*? Can you draw the magnetic field patterns due to a bar magnet and current carrying straight wires, circular loops and coils? Can you find the direction of the magnetic force on moving charged particles and between current carrying straight wires, circular loops and coils? Can you solve problems involving the formula for *magnetic force per unit length*?

Do you understand the concepts of *electric potential* and *electric potential energy*? Can you solve problems involving electric potential and electric potential energy? Can you solve problems with energy conservation in electric fields?

EXAM-STYLE QUESTIONS

You can find questions in the style of IB exams in the digital coursebook.

CHECK YOURSELF ANSWERS

1 The student is wrong. Positive charges are fixed and cannot move.

2 Since $E \propto \frac{1}{r^2}$ and r is doubled E will decrease by a factor of 4.

3

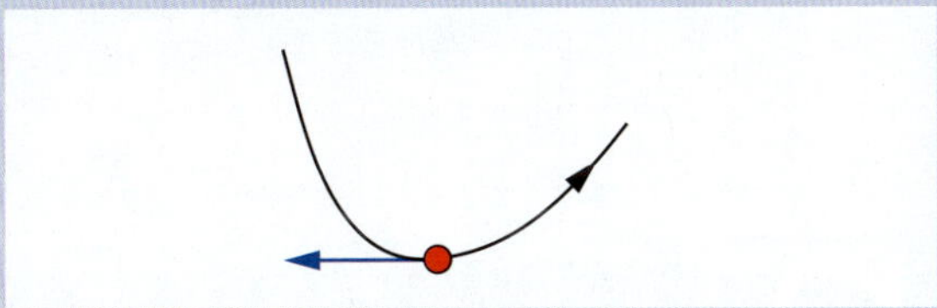

4 Field lines cannot cross since at the crossing point the direction of the field would not be defined.

5 It is the same everywhere because the electric field is uniform.

6

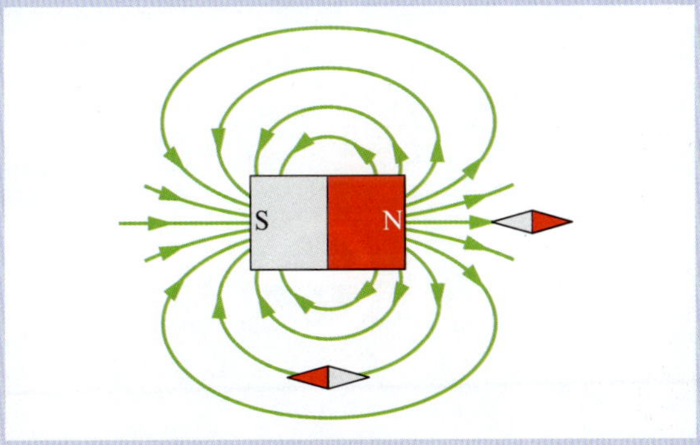

7

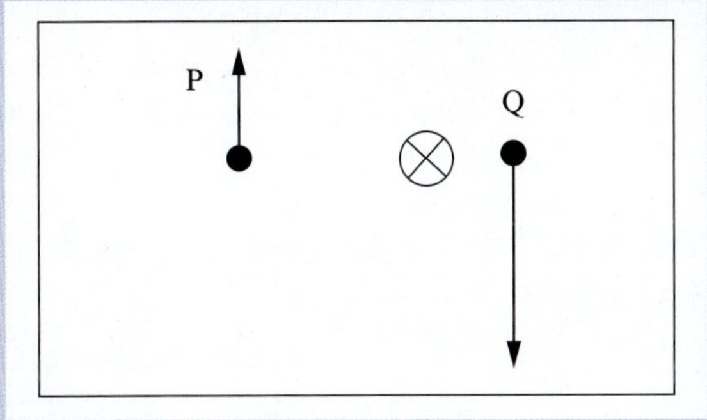

8 **a** Repulsion; **b** attraction.

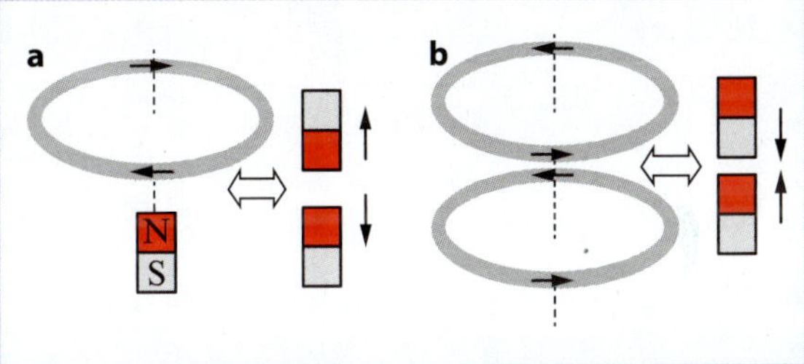

9 Out of the page

10 $3.0 \times 10^8\ \mathrm{m\,s^{-1}}$, the speed of light in a vacuum. This is worth looking into!

Chapter 19

Motion in electric and magnetic fields

LEARNING OBJECTIVES

In this chapter you will learn how to:

- describe the motion of a charged particle in a uniform electric field
- appreciate the similarity of motion in a uniform electric field with motion in uniform gravitational field
- solve problems on motion in uniform electric fields
- describe the motion of a charged particle in a uniform magnetic field
- solve problems on motion of charged particles in uniform magnetic fields
- understand motion of a charged particle in electric and magnetic fields that are perpendicular to each other.

19 Motion in electric and magnetic fields

> **GUIDING QUESTION**
>
> What is the path of a charged particle in uniform electric or magnetic fields?

19.1 Motion in an electric field

The path of an electric charge in a uniform electric field is either a straight line or a parabolic path. We have a straight line if the charge is initially at rest or if its original velocity is parallel to the electric field. In all other cases we have a parabolic path.

The diagram in Figure 19.1 shows a positively charged particle in a region of uniform electric field E. There is a potential difference V across the dotted lines X and Y.

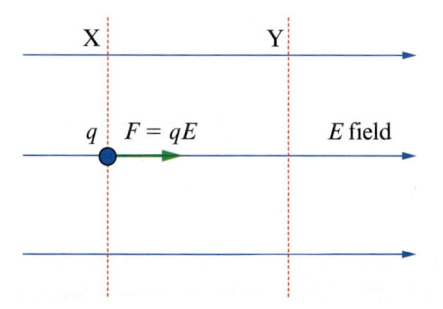

Figure 19.1: A positively charged particle accelerates along a straight field line.

The particle will experience a force qE in the direction of the field (because the charge is positive) and so will accelerate in the direction of the field. It will move along a straight line with acceleration $a = \frac{qE}{m}$. (A negative charge would move in the opposite direction.) The positive charge increases its kinetic energy as it moves to the right. The gain in kinetic energy from X to Y is equal to the work done by the electric force, and that is qV.

> **CHECK YOURSELF 1**
>
> A proton and an alpha particle (mass $4m_p$, charge $+2e$) are placed on the positive plate inside a parallel plate arrangement, as shown in Figure 19.2. The particles are released at the same time. 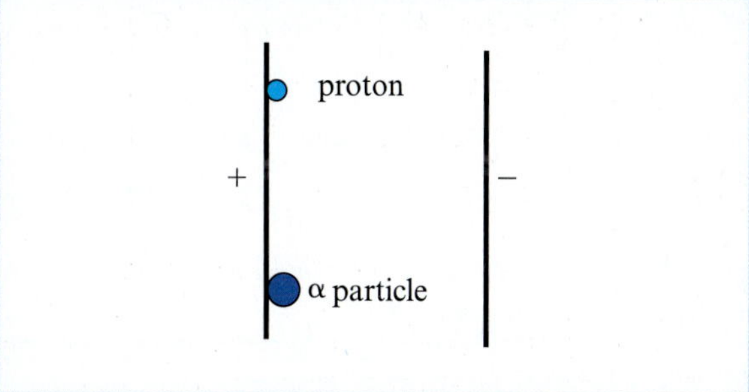
>
> **Figure 19.2:** For check yourself question 1.
>
> Which particle will reach the negative plate first?

> **WORKED EXAMPLE 19.1**
>
> A potential difference of 120 V is established between two oppositely charged parallel plates. A proton is placed on the positive plate and is then released, as shown in Figure 19.3. 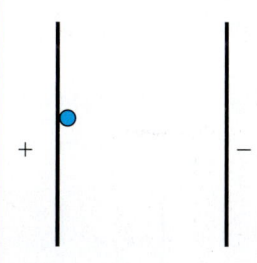
>
> **Figure 19.3:** For worked example 19.1.
>
> What is the speed of the proton as it hits the negatively charged plate?
>
> **Answer**
>
> The work done by the electric field in moving the proton from one plate to the other is $qV = 1.6 \times 10^{-19} \times 120 = 1.92 \times 10^{-17}$ J. This goes into kinetic energy for the proton and so $\frac{1}{2}mv^2 = 1.92 \times 10^{-17}$ J. This gives $v = \sqrt{\frac{2 \times 1.92 \times 10^{-17}}{1.67 \times 10^{-27}}} = 1.5 \times 10^5$ m s^{-1}.

417

A more interesting case is when the charge enters a region of uniform electric field with an initial velocity u that is at right angles to the electric field, Figure 19.4. Consider a particle with positive charge q and mass m.

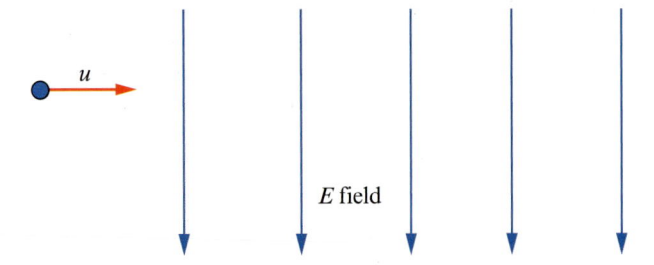

Figure 19.4: Motion in an electric field when the initial velocity is normal to the field.

When the particle enters the region of electric field it will experience a constant electric force qE directed along the field lines (i.e. downward). We are assuming that the mass is quite small so the weight of the particle is negligible compared to the electric force. Its acceleration will be $a = \frac{qE}{m}$. But we have seen this situation before! This is exactly the same as a projectile that is fired horizontally (Chapter 1). Here the role of the acceleration of gravity is played by the acceleration $a = \frac{qE}{m}$. So everything we learned in Chapter 1 applies here as well. Thus we know that, in Figure 19.5:

- the particle will follow a parabolic path
- the component of velocity normal to the field will remain constant: $v_x = u$
- the component of velocity parallel to the field will increase uniformly: $v_y = \frac{qE}{m}t$.

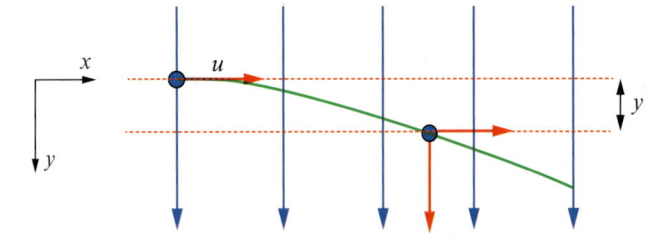

Figure 19.5: The path of the particle is parabolic.

The kinetic energy of the particle increases as time goes on because the electric force is doing work on the particle. After time t, the particle will move a horizontal distance $x = ut$ and fall a vertical distance:

$$y = \frac{1}{2}\frac{qE}{m}t^2$$

Its kinetic energy will be:

$$E_K = \tfrac{1}{2}mv^2 = \tfrac{1}{2}m(v_x^2 + v_y^2) = \tfrac{1}{2}m\left(u^2 + \left(\tfrac{qEt}{m}\right)^2\right)$$

The change in kinetic energy is, therefore:

$$\Delta E_K = \tfrac{1}{2}m\left(\tfrac{qEt}{m}\right)^2.$$

We can rewrite this as:

$$\Delta E_K = (qE) \times \left(\left(\tfrac{1}{2}\right)\left(\tfrac{qE}{m}\right)t^2\right) = Fy.$$

In other words, the change in kinetic energy is the work done by the electric force, as we know it should be from mechanics.

WORKED EXAMPLE 19.2

An electron moving at speed 6.0×10^6 m s^{-1} enters two oppositely charged parallel plates at a point near the lower plate, as shown in Figure 19.6. The length of the plates is 12 cm, and their separation is 4.8 cm. There is a potential difference of 60 V between the plates. The upper plate is positively charged.

Figure 19.6: For worked example 19.2.

a Determine:

  i the magnitude and direction of the electric field in between the plates

  ii the magnitude and direction of the acceleration of the electron when inside the region of electric field.

b Suggest whether the electron will hit the upper plate or not.

Answer

a i The electric field is directed from the upper plate to the lower plate. Its magnitude is $\frac{V}{d} = \frac{60}{4.8 \times 10^{-2}} = 1.25 \times 10^3$ N C^{-1}.

 ii The acceleration is directed from the lower to the upper plate and has magnitude $\frac{qE}{m} = \frac{1.6 \times 10^{-19} \times 1.25 \times 10^3}{9.1 \times 10^{-31}} = 2.2 \times 10^{14}$ m s^{-2}.

CONTINUED

b The time for the electron to reach the end of the plates is $\frac{0.12}{6.0 \times 10^6} = 2.0 \times 10^{-8}$ s. In this time the electron will move upwards a distance of $\frac{1}{2}at^2 = \frac{1}{2} \times 2.2 \times 10^{14} \times (2.0 \times 10^{-8})^2 = 4.4 \times 10^{-2}$ m.

This means the electron does not hit the upper plate.

CHECK YOURSELF 2

The potential difference between the plates in worked example 19.2 is increased. Will the electron get closer to the top plate or not?

Now consider a proton that is launched as in Figure 19.7 at an angle of 30° to the horizontal. The separation of the plates is 4.8 cm, and the potential difference is 60 kV.

Figure 19.7: A proton launched at an angle inside an electric field.

The initial vertical component of velocity is $u_y = 6.0 \times 10^6 \times \sin 30° = 3.0 \times 10^6$ m s^{-1}. At the highest point the proton will cover a vertical distance found from $0 = u_y^2 - 2ay$, i.e. $y = \frac{u_y^2}{2a}$ where $a = \frac{eV}{md}$ is the acceleration of the proton. The acceleration is

$a = \frac{1.6 \times 10^{-19} \times 60 \times 10^3}{1.67 \times 10^{-27} \times 4.8 \times 10^{-2}} = 1.20 \times 10^{14}$ m s^{-2}

The vertical distance is then

$y = \frac{(3.0 \times 10^6)^2}{2 \times 1.20 \times 10^{14}} = 3.75 \approx 3.8$ cm

which means the proton will not hit the upper plate. This discussion continues in worked example 19.3.

WORKED EXAMPLE 19.3

The length of the plates in Figure 19.7 is 22 cm. Figure 19.8 shows the proton at its highest point.

Calculate:

a the horizontal distance covered by the proton when it is at its highest point

b the work done on the proton by the electric field.

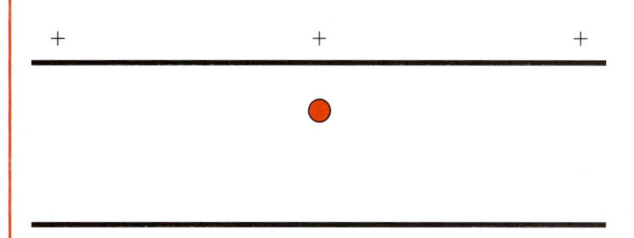

Figure 19.8: The proton at its highest point.

Answer

a The time to get to the highest point is

$t = \frac{u_y}{a} = \frac{3.0 \times 10^6}{1.2 \times 10^{14}} = 2.5 \times 10^{-8}$ s

In this time the proton moved a horizontal distance $6.0 \times 10^6 \times \cos 30° \times 2.5 \times 10^{-8} \approx 13$ cm.

b The work done on the proton by the electric field is the change in kinetic energy, which is $-\frac{1}{2}mu_y^2$

$= -\frac{1}{2} \times 1.67 \times 10^{-27} \times (3.0 \times 10^6)^2 = -7.5 \times 10^{-15}$ J.

It can also be calculated from

$W = -Fy = -may$
$= -1.67 \times 10^{-27} \times 1.2 \times 10^{14} \times 0.0375$
$= -7.5 \times 10^{-15}$ J.

TEST YOUR UNDERSTANDING

1. Why can't a charged particle follow a circular path in a uniform electric field?

2. Two parallel plates are oppositely charged. An electron is positioned on the negative plate and a proton on the positive plate (Figure 19.9).

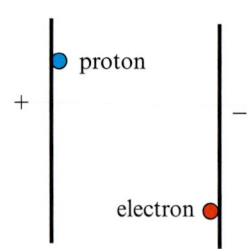

   Figure 19.9: For question 2.

   The particles are released. Compare, for when the particles reach the opposite plate:

   a the kinetic energy
   b the speed
   c the time to move across.

3. Two parallel plates are oppositely charged. A proton (charge +e, mass m) and an alpha particle (charge +2e, mass 4m) are placed on the positively charged plate (Figure 19.10).

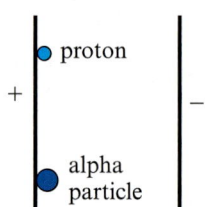

   Figure 19.10: For question 3.

   When the particles reach the opposite plate, what is the ratio of:

   a the proton speed to the alpha particle speed
   b time of travel of the proton to time of travel of the alpha particle?

4. A proton is injected with speed 1.8×10^5 m s^{-1} into the region between two oppositely charged parallel plates (Figure 19.11). The top plate is the negative plate, and there is a potential difference of 60 V between the plates. The plates are 8.0 cm apart and 24 cm long.

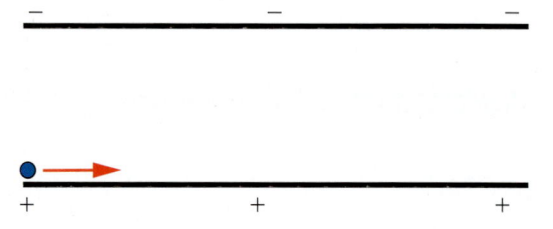

   Figure 19.11: For question 4.

   How far above the positive plate will the proton be when it leaves the plates?

5. A proton is injected into the region between two oppositely charged parallel plates (Figure 19.12). The top plate is the positive plate, and there is a potential difference of 150 V between the plates. The plates are 4.0 cm apart. The velocity of the proton makes an angle of 30° with the horizontal.

   Figure 19.12: For question 5.

   a What is the maximum speed of the proton so that it does not hit the top plate?
   b The length of the plates is 12 cm. Show that when the proton has the maximum speed found in part **a**, the proton will not hit the lower plate either.
   c How would your answer to part **a** change if the separation of the plates was made 8.0 cm without any other changes?

> **CONTINUED**
>
> **6** We know that a positively charged particle launched between charged parallel plates will follow a parabolic path just like a projectile under gravity (as shown in Figure 19.13). 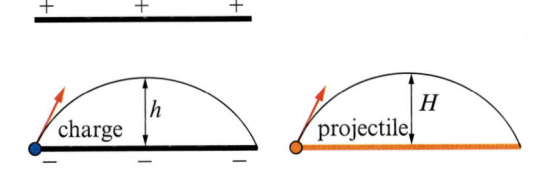
>
> Figure 19.13: For question 6.
>
> **a** The mass of the charged particle and the mass of the projectile are both doubled. How do h and H change?
>
> **b** The mass of the charged particle is the original mass, but the charge is doubled. How does h change?

19.2 Motion in a magnetic field

We just saw that the path of a charged particle in a uniform electric field is a straight line or a parabola. What is the shape of the path of a charged particle in a uniform magnetic field?

In the simple case where the velocity of the charged particle is parallel or anti-parallel to that of the uniform magnetic field, the magnetic force is zero and so the particle will move along a straight line, Figure 19.14.

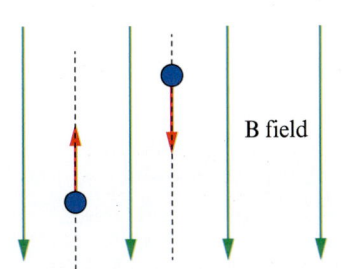

Figure 19.14: When the velocity is parallel or anti-parallel to the magnetic field the force is zero.

Figure 19.15 shows a positive charge in a uniform magnetic field that is directed into the plane of the paper. The particle has a velocity v at the instant shown. The velocity is at right angles to the magnetic field. The magnetic force is at right angles to both the velocity and the magnetic field so the particle will follow a circular path; the centripetal force is provided by the magnetic force.

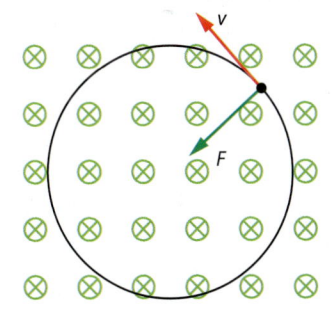

Figure 19.15: A charge in a magnetic field moves in a circle.

Consider a charge q moving with speed v at right angles to a magnetic field B. The force on the charge is $F = qvB$ at right angles to the velocity. The charge moves in a circle of radius R, and so by Newton's second law:

$qvB = m\dfrac{v^2}{R}$

Rearranging, we get:

$R = \dfrac{mv}{qB}$

Very massive or very fast charges will move in large circles; large charges and large magnetic fields will result in small circles. The time T to make one full revolution in a magnetic field is found from:

$T = \dfrac{2\pi R}{v}$

$T = \dfrac{2\pi}{v}\dfrac{mv}{qB}$

$T = \dfrac{2\pi m}{qB}$

This shows that T is independent of the speed. This is an important result in experimental particle physics and forms the basis for an accelerator called the *cyclotron*.

> PHYSICS FOR THE IB DIPLOMA: COURSEBOOK

CHECK YOURSELF 3

A particle of mass m and charge q moves on a circular path in a region of magnetic field B at right angles to the velocity. What is the average magnetic force experienced by the particle during half a revolution?

radius will also decrease. This means that the circular path will become a spiral, Figure 19.16.

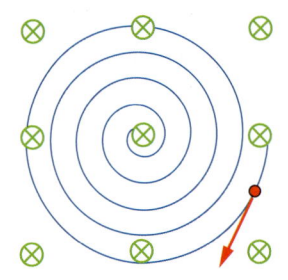

Figure 19.16: A negatively charged particle spiraling inwards in a region of magnetic field directed into the page.

Suppose, however, that the charged particle loses energy as it moves along the circular path. (This could be because the particle is colliding with other particles or it radiates electromagnetic waves.) The speed will decrease, and from the formula for the radius we see that the

WORKED EXAMPLE 19.4

Figure 19.17 shows a charged particle entering a region of magnetic field that is directed into the plane of the page.

The path of the particle is a quarter circle. The speed of the particle is 5.2×10^6 m s^{-1}.

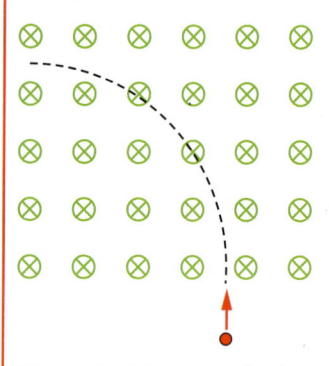

Figure 19.17: For worked example 19.4.

a Justify why the charge is positive.

b The particle is in fact a proton with mass 1.67×10^{-27} kg and charge 1.6×10^{-19} C. The magnetic flux density is 0.25 T. Calculate the radius of the proton's circular path.

c Calculate the time the proton spends in the region of magnetic field.

Answer

a The force must be directed towards the centre of the circle. The field is into the page so by the right-hand force rule the charge must be positive.

b From $qvB = \frac{mv^2}{R}$ we deduce that $R = \frac{mv}{qB}$. Thus:

$R = \frac{1.67 \times 10^{-27} \times 5.2 \times 10^6}{1.6 \times 10^{-19} \times 0.25}$

$R = 0.217 \approx 0.22$ m

> **CONTINUED**
>
> **c** The path is a quarter of a circle of radius R, so the length of the path is:
>
> $\frac{2\pi R}{4} = \frac{2\pi \times 0.217}{4} = 0.34$ m
>
> The time in the field is therefore:
>
> $\frac{0.34}{5.2 \times 10^6} = 6.6 \times 10^{-8}$ s

> **WORKED EXAMPLE 19.5**
>
> Figure 19.18 shows the path of a charged particle. The particle goes through a thin metallic foil.
>
> State and explain the direction of motion of the particle and the sign of its charge.
>
> **Figure 19.18:** For worked example 19.5.
>
> **Answer**
>
> The path consists of two circular arcs of different radius. The radius gets smaller because the particle loses energy as it passes through the foil. Therefore the direction of motion is counterclockwise. Since the field is directed into the plane of the page the charge must be positive by the right-hand force rule so that the force is directed towards the centre of the arcs.

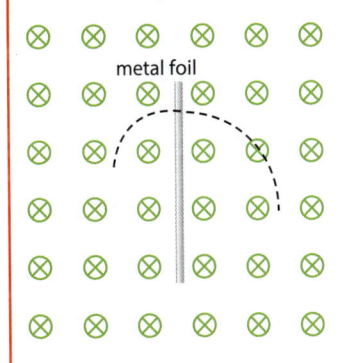

Work done and magnetic forces

Since the magnetic force is always normal to the velocity of the charge, it follows that it cannot do any work. The big magnets in particle accelerators are used only to deflect particles, not to increase the particles' kinetic energy (that job is done by electric fields). This means the kinetic energy of the particle cannot change while in the region of magnetic field.

> **EXAM TIP**
>
> $W = Fs \cos\theta$
>
> For the magnetic force, $\theta = 90°$ giving $W = 0$.

> **CHECK YOURSELF 4**
>
> Why does the proton in worked example 19.4 exit the region of magnetic field with the same speed as that at the entry point?

Motion in crossed electric and magnetic fields

Finally, we examine the motion of a charged particle in a region where an electric field and a magnetic field are both present. We will deal with the case in which the electric field is at right angles to the magnetic field. Figure 19.19 shows a positively charged particle entering, with speed v, a region of crossed E and B fields.

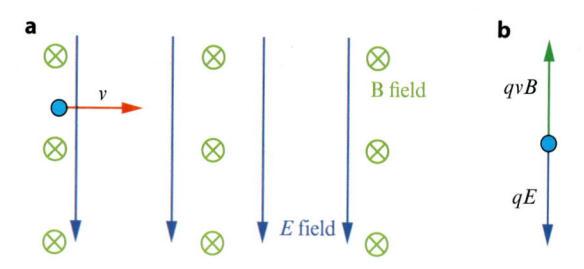

Figure 19.19: a A positively charged particle entering a region of crossed electric and magnetic fields. **b** A free-body diagram showing the forces on the particle.

The particle will be acted upon by an electric force $F_e = qE$ directed along the electric field and a magnetic force $F_m = qvB$ directed opposite to the electric force. *If* these forces are equal, the particle will continue moving on a straight line undeflected from its original path. This means that

$$qE = qvB \Rightarrow E = vB.$$

The interesting fact in this case is that the charge has cancelled out; so if the condition $E = vB$ holds, *any* charge of any value and any sign will continue undeflected through the crossed fields as long as it enters with velocity v.

If the particle enters with speed greater than v, the magnetic force is larger and the particle will move upwards; it will move downwards if the speed is less than v.

Links

The study of the motion of charged particles in electric and magnetic fields has made possible the construction of particle accelerators. For example, in synchrotrons like the Large Hadron Collider at CERN, a beam of protons is accelerated to speeds very close to the speed of light by electric fields. Powerful magnets force the protons to move along a circular track. As the speed of the protons increases the strength of the magnets must also increase in order to keep the protons on the same circular track, thus requiring the development of sophisticated superconducting electromagnets. Because the speeds involved are close to that of light, relativity (Chapter 6) must be taken into account in constructing these machines. The accelerated particles collide with another beam of accelerated particles travelling in the opposite direction and during the collision energy gets converted into matter, producing new particles. We have obtained much of our knowledge about the structure of matter (Chapters 21 through 25) through the results of accelerator experiments.

TEST YOUR UNDERSTANDING

7 How can a charged particle follow a straight line path in a uniform magnetic field?

8 An electron with speed 3.2×10^7 m s^{-1} enters a region of uniform magnetic field 0.025 T. The direction of velocity is at right angles to the field. Calculate the radius of the circular path.

9 Protons move in a circular path of radius 0.75 m with speed 3.0×10^7 m s^{-1}.

What is the magnetic field required?

10 A proton moves in a circular path of radius 12 cm in a region of magnetic field of flux density 0.35 T. The field is at right angles to the velocity. What is the speed of the proton?

11 **a** A proton of mass m_p moves in a circular path in a region of magnetic field B directed normally to its velocity. Show that the number of revolutions per second is $\dfrac{eB}{2\pi m_p}$.

   b The proton is replaced by an alpha particle (mass $4m_p$, charge $+2e$). How does the answer to **a** change, if at all?

CONTINUED

12 An electron is accelerated from rest by a potential difference 250 V. It then enters a region of uniform magnetic field where it is bent into a semicircular path (Figure 19.20). The time to complete the semicircle is 1.5 ns.

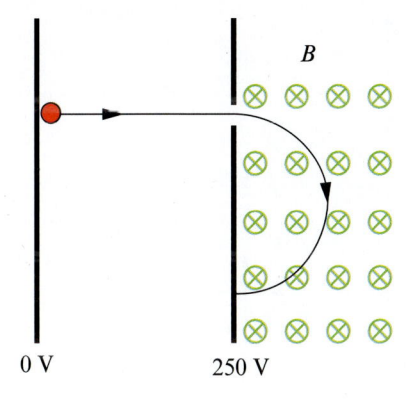

Figure 19.20: For question 12.

- **a** Calculate the speed of the electron as it enters the region of magnetic field.
- **b** Hence, calculate the radius of the semicircle.
- **c** Determine the magnetic field.

13 An electron is accelerated from rest by a potential difference V. It then enters a region of magnetic field of strength B as shown in Figure 19.21. The electron follows a semicircular path of radius R.

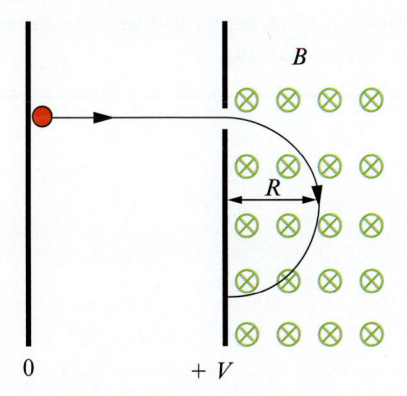

Figure 19.21: For question 13.

- **a** Show that the charge-to-mass ratio of the electron is given by $\frac{e}{m} = \frac{2V}{B^2 R^2}$.
- **b** In one experiment $V = 490$ V, $B = 1.2$ mT and $R = 6.1$ cm. Calculate the charge-to-mass ratio of the electron.
- **c** Using a value 1.6×10^{-19} C for the charge, estimate the mass of the electron from these data.

14 A singly ionised beam of ions enters a region of magnetic field with speed 1.3×10^6 m s^{-1}. The beam contains two types of different atoms of the same element. The two types of atoms differ in the number of neutrons they contain.

The magnetic flux density is 0.21 T. The ions are bent into two circular paths that differ in radius by 0.13 m (Figure 19.22).

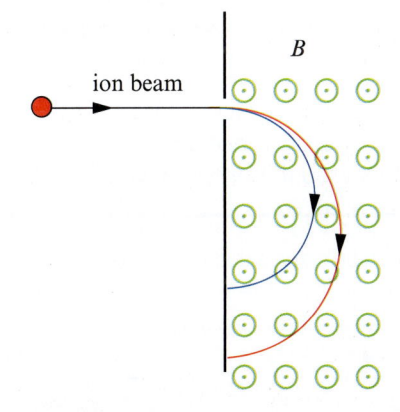

Figure 19.22: For question 14.

What is the difference in mass of the two types of atoms in the beam?

CONTINUED

15 Figure 19.23 shows two parallel plates. The electric field is directed from top to bottom and has magnitude 2.4×10^3 NC^{-1}. The shaded region is a region of magnetic field normal to the page.

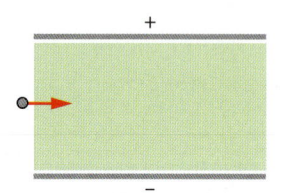

Figure 19.23: For question 15.

a Deduce the magnetic field magnitude and direction so that an electron experiences zero net force when shot through the plates with a speed of 2.0×10^5 m s^{-1}.

b Suggest whether a proton shot with the same speed through the plates experiences zero net force.

c Would an alpha particle (mass 4 times that of a proton, charge double that of a proton) be undeflected if it entered with the same speed as in **a**?

d The electron's speed is doubled. Suggest whether the electron would still be undeflected for the same magnetic field found in **a**.

16 An electron enters a region of uniform vertical magnetic field, B (Figure 19.24). The initial velocity v of the electron makes an angle θ with the horizontal.

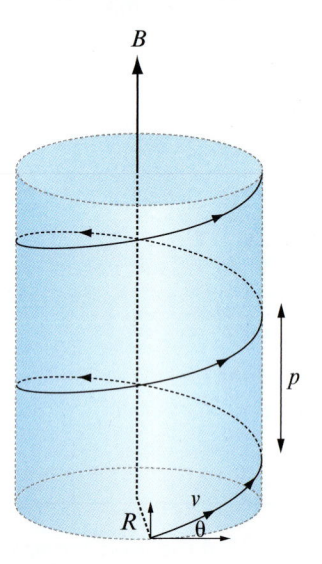

Figure 19.24: For question 16.

a By reference to the horizontal and vertical components of the velocity of the electron, explain why the path of the electron will be a spiral.

b Show that the radius of the spiral is $R = \frac{mv \cos\theta}{eB}$.

c Derive an expression for the pitch, p, of the spiral. The pitch is the vertical distance travelled in a time equal to the time taken for one full revolution.

19 Motion in electric and magnetic fields

SELF-ASSESSMENT CHECKLIST

I am able to …	Section	Not yet	Nearly there	Ready to move on
know what path a charged particle can follow in an electric field	19.1			
appreciate that motion in a uniform electric field is similar to motion in a uniform gravitational field	19.1			
solve problems of motion in a uniform electric field by exploiting the analogy with motion in a gravitational field	19.1			
know what path a charged particle can follow in a magnetic field	19.2			
explain why a magnetic force does zero work	19.2			
calculate the radius of the circular path in magnetic field	19.2			
solve problems of motion in a uniform magnetic field	19.2			
solve problems of motion in crossed electric and magnetic fields	19.2			

REFLECTION

Do you appreciate the similarity of motion of charged particles in uniform electric fields with projectile motion? Can you solve problems of motion of charged particles in electric fields? Can you explain why charged particles follow circular paths in magnetic fields? Can you solve problems of motion of charged particles in magnetic fields? Can you solve problems of motion of charged particles in crossed electric and magnetic fields?

EXAM-STYLE QUESTIONS

You can find questions in the style of IB exams in the digital coursebook.

CHECK YOURSELF ANSWERS

1. The proton because it has double the acceleration.

2. The acceleration of the electron will increase. The time to reach the end of the plates will be the same and since $s = \frac{1}{2}at^2$ the distance will increase and so the electron will get closer to the plate.

3. The average force is $\bar{F} = m\frac{\Delta v}{\Delta t}$. During half a revolution, $\Delta v = 2v$ and $\Delta t = \frac{1}{2} \times \frac{2\pi m}{qB}$ so that $\bar{F} = \frac{2vqB}{\pi}$.

4. The work done on the proton by the magnetic force is zero. But the work done is the change in kinetic energy. So the kinetic energy does not change and neither does speed.

Chapter 20
Electromagnetic induction

LEARNING OBJECTIVES

In this chapter you will learn how to:

> identify situations where flux changes and an emf is induced.

> distinguish between magnetic flux and magnetic flux linkage.

> solve problems using Faraday's law of electromagnetic induction.

> apply Lenz's law in different situations.

> understand how alternating current is produced in a generator.

20 Electromagnetic induction

> **GUIDING QUESTIONS**
> - Can a magnetic field produce a current?
> - How is electric current produced?

Introduction

This chapter deals with Faraday's law of electromagnetic induction which states that a changing magnetic flux through a loop induces an emf in the loop. The principles of electromagnetic induction are the result of ingenious experimenting by the English physicist Michael Faraday (1791–1867) and form the basis of most of the electromechanical technology we use daily today.

20.1 Electromagnetic induction

We know a current produces a magnetic field. Can a magnetic field produce a current? This is the question this chapter deals with.

Motional emf

A rod of length L is moved with velocity v in a region of a magnetic flux density B. B is directed into the plane of the page; the rod moves from left to right (Figure 20.1).

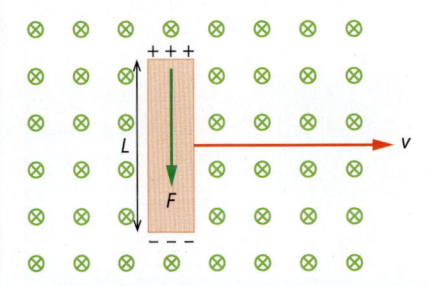

Figure 20.1: The rod is made to move normally to the magnetic field at constant speed. An emf develops between the ends of the rod.

The rod is conducting—that is, it has many 'free' electrons. As it moves, the electrons within it also move from left to right. The magnetic field will exert a force on these moving electrons. The force on the electrons is directed downward (green arrow) and therefore the electrons are pushed downward. This means that the lower end of the rod has a net negative charge and the top end has an equal net positive charge. (The net charge of the rod is zero.) The flow of electrons towards the bottom end of the rod will stop when the electrons already there are numerous enough to push any new electrons back by electrostatic repulsion. There is, in other words, an electric field established in the rod whose direction is from top to bottom.

The value of this electric field E is given by:

$$E = \frac{\varepsilon}{L}$$

where ε is the potential difference between the ends of the rod, known as the induced emf. The flow of electrons will stop when the electric force eE pushing the electrons back equals the magnetic force evB. Thus:

$$eE = evB$$

Dividing both sides by e and substituting for the electric field, this becomes:

$$\varepsilon = BvL$$

We have found the extraordinary result that a conducting rod of length L moving with speed v normally to a magnetic field B will have a potential difference BvL across its ends. This is called a **motional emf**, as it has been induced as a result of the motion of the conductor in the magnetic field.

We can check that the quantity BvL has the unit of potential difference (volt):

$[B \times v \times L]$ = Tesla × metre per second × metre = T × m s^{-1} × m

Substitute Tesla for $\frac{\text{Newton}}{\text{Ampere metre}}$:

$$\left(\frac{N}{A\,m}\right) \times (m\,s^{-1}) \times m$$

Cancel out:

$$\left(\frac{N}{A\,m}\right) \times (m\,s^{-1}) \times m \Rightarrow \left(\frac{N}{A}\right) \times s^{-1} \times m$$

Rearrange;

$$\frac{Nm}{A} s^{-1}$$

Substitute Amperes for Coulombs per second, and Newton metres for Joules, then cancel out:

$$\frac{J}{C\,s^{-1}} s^{-1} \Rightarrow \frac{J}{C}$$

1 Joule per Coulomb = 1 Volt $\Rightarrow \frac{J}{C} = V$

It is important to note that except for a very short interval of time initially, no current exists in the rod. But this example opens the way for generating an electric current out of magnetic fields.

CHECK YOURSELF 1

Three loops enter a region of magnetic field with the same speed as shown in Figure 20.2.

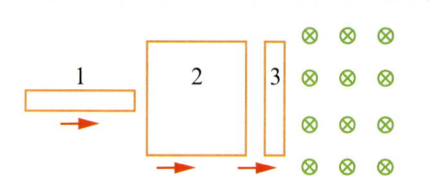

Figure 20.2: For check yourself question 1.

Just as the loops enter the region of magnetic field, which loop has the larger induced emf and which has the smallest?

Suppose we modify things by letting the rod slide on two wires that are joined by resistor of resistance R, as shown in Figure 20.3. Now the moving rod behaves like a battery. There is a potential difference between the top and the bottom equal to BvL (this is the emf of the 'battery') and a current equal to $I = \frac{BvL}{R}$ is established in the resistor and the moving rod, i.e. in the circuit on the left side of the diagram. This is because electrons in the bottom part of the circuit now have the opportunity to move *up* through the resistor; thus there is a *counterclockwise* current in the circuit.

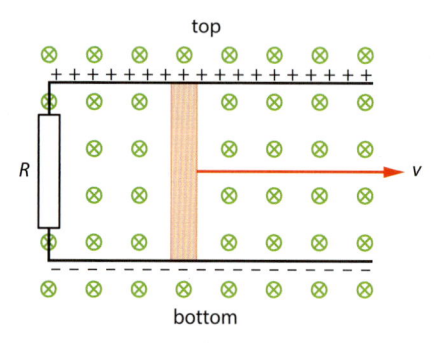

Figure 20.3: As the rod is pushed along, a current is established in the circuit.

Notice also that now that we have a current, the rod needs to be pushed if it is to continue to move at constant speed. This is because the rod carries current I and is in a magnetic field, so it experiences a magnetic force F directed to the left (use the right-hand rule for force and the fact that the current is counterclockwise) given by:

$$F = BIL = B\frac{BvL}{R}L = \frac{vB^2L^2}{R}$$

For speed to remain constant a force of equal magnitude needs to act on the rod, directed to the right. The power P generated by this force is:

$$P = Fv = \frac{v^2B^2L^2}{R}$$

The power dissipated in the circuit as thermal energy in the resistor is:

$$P = \frac{\varepsilon^2}{R} = \frac{v^2B^2L^2}{R}$$

This is in perfect agreement with conservation of energy: the work done by the agent pushing the rod is dissipated in the resistor. Here, mechanical work (pushing the rod) is transferred into thermal energy.

EXAM TIP

The work done to move an electron from top to bottom in the wire is $W = FL$. The force is eE which equals evB and so the work done is $W = evBL$. The work done per unit charge is the emf, i.e. $\varepsilon = BvL$, as expected.

CHECK YOURSELF 2

A sheet of metal moves at constant speed in a region of uniform magnetic field that is directed into the plane of the page.

On a copy of Figure 20.4, show how charge separates in the sheet of metal.

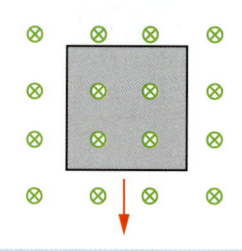

Figure 20.4: For check yourself question 2.

20 Electromagnetic induction

Magnetic flux and magnetic flux linkage

In 1831, Faraday experimented with coils of wire wrapped around an iron ring (Figure 20.5). He was hoping that somehow the current in the left circuit might induce a current in the right circuit. No such current was observed in the right circuit, but Faraday did notice that a small current was induced only during the opening and closing of the switch.

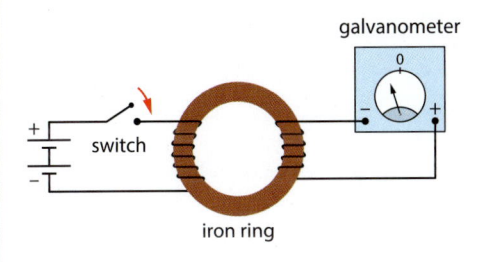

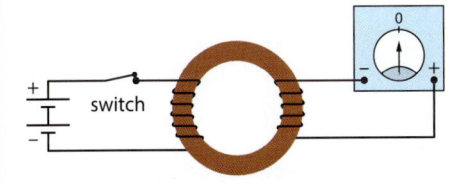

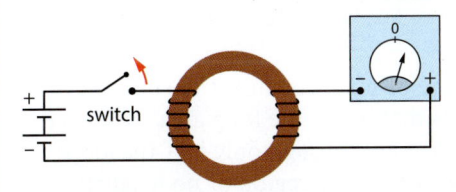

Figure 20.5: As the switch is closed a small current is registered by the galvanometer. While the switch remains closed a current exists in the circuit to the left but the current in the right circuit is zero. As the switch is opened another small current is established in the right circuit.

Similar results are obtained when a magnet is moved in or out of a coil of wire that is connected to a sensitive galvanometer (Figure 20.6). A current is induced.

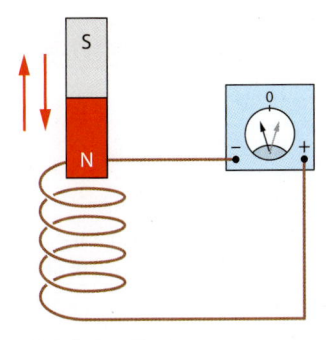

Figure 20.6: As the magnet is allowed to enter the coil a current is induced in the coil and is registered by the galvanometer. If the magnet is then pulled out of the coil the induced current is opposite.

If the magnet is simply placed near the coil but does not move relative to it, nothing happens. The current is created as a result of the *motion* of the magnet relative to the coil. If we move the coil toward the magnet, we again find a current. This indicates that it is the relative motion of the coil and magnet that is responsible for the effect. If the magnet moves towards the coil faster, the reading on the galvanometer is greater. If a magnet of greater strength is used, the current produced is greater. If we try a coil with more turns of wire, we again find a greater current. We also observe that if the area of the loop is increased, the current also increases. But if the magnet is moved at an angle to the plane of the loop other than a right angle, the current decreases. To summarise, the observations are that the current registered by the galvanometer *increases* when:

- the relative speed of the magnet and the coil increases
- the strength of the magnet increases
- the number of turns increases
- the area of the loop increases
- the magnet moves at right angles to the plane of the loop.

Faraday found that the common thread behind these observations is the concept of **magnetic flux**. Imagine a loop of wire, which for simplicity we take to be planar (i.e. the entire loop lies on one plane). If this loop is in a region of magnetic field whose magnitude and direction is constant, then we define magnetic flux as follows.

> PHYSICS FOR THE IB DIPLOMA: COURSEBOOK

> **KEY POINT**
>
> The magnetic flux Φ through the loop is:
>
> Φ = BA cos θ
>
> where B is the magnetic flux density, A is the area of the loop and θ is the angle between the magnetic field direction and the direction normal to the loop area (Figure 20.7).

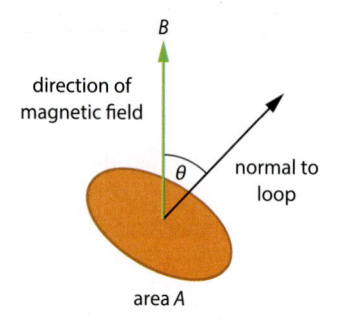

Figure 20.7: The definition of magnetic flux, Φ = BA cos θ.

> **EXAM TIP**
>
> Normal surfaces have two sides and so two normals: it does not matter which one we take.

If the loop has N turns of wire around it, the flux is given by:

Φ = NBA cos θ

The unit of magnetic flux is the weber (Wb).
1 Wb = 1 T m².

> **KEY POINT**
>
> The magnetic flux multiplied by the number of turns in a loop is called the **flux linkage**.

This means that if the magnetic field is along the plane of the loop, then θ = 90° and hence Φ = 0 (Figure 20.8a). The maximum flux through the loop occurs when θ = 0°, when the magnetic field is normal to the loop area and its value is then BA (Figure 20.8b).

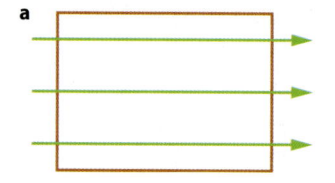

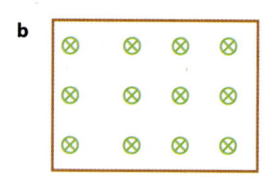

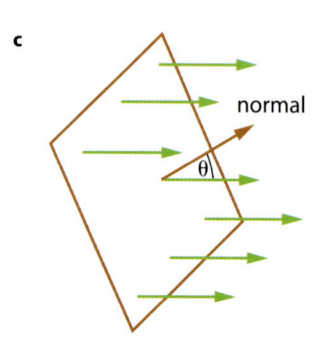

Figure 20.8: a The loop is not pierced by any magnetic field lines, so the flux through it is zero. **b** The magnetic field is normal to the loop, so the flux through it is the largest possible. **c** The flux here is BA cos θ.

The intuitive picture of magnetic flux is the number of magnetic field lines that pierce the loop area. Note that if the magnetic field went through only half the loop area, the other half being in a region of no magnetic field, then the flux would be $\Phi = \frac{BA}{2}$. In other words, what counts is the part of the loop area that is pierced by magnetic field lines.

> **WORKED EXAMPLE 20.1**
>
> A loop of area 8.0 cm² is in a constant magnetic field of B = 0.15 T. What is the magnetic flux through the loop when:
>
> a the loop is perpendicular to the field
>
> b the loop is parallel to the field
>
> c the normal to the loop and the field have an angle of 60° between them?

CONTINUED

Answer

a In this case $\theta = 0°$ and $\cos 0° = 1$. The area of the loop is 8.0×10^{-4} m². Substituting in $\Phi = BA \cos\theta$, the flux Φ is given by:

$\Phi = 0.15 \times 8.0 \times 10^{-4}$

$\Phi = 1.2 \times 10^{-4}$ Wb

b In this case $\theta = 90°$ and $\cos 90° = 0$, so $\Phi = 0$.

c In this case $\theta = 60°$, so:

$\Phi = 0.15 \times 8.0 \times 10^{-4} \times 0.5$

$\Phi = 6.0 \times 10^{-5}$ Wb

Faraday's law

What does magnetic flux have to do with how a magnetic field can create an electric current? The answer lies in a *changing* magnetic flux linkage. In Figure 20.6 we had a magnetic flux linkage through the coil, which was changing with time. As a magnet is brought closer to the loop area, the value of the magnetic field at the loop position is increasing and so is flux. If the magnet is held stationary near the loop, there is flux through the loop but it is not changing—so nothing happens. If the number of turns is increased, so is the flux linkage. Thus, we are led to consider the *rate of change of magnetic flux linkage* through the loop.

A changing flux creates an induced emf, not necessarily a current. There will only be a current if the loop is conducting; that is, if the resistance of the circuit is not infinite. For example, a loop containing an ideal voltmeter cannot let current through, but there will be an emf if the flux is changing.

KEY POINT

Faraday found that the induced emf is equal to the (negative) rate of change of magnetic flux linkage, that is:

$\varepsilon = -\frac{N\Delta\Phi}{\Delta t}$. This is known as **Faraday's law** of electromagnetic induction.

The minus sign need not concern us too much, as mostly we will be dealing with the magnitude of the induced emf. However, if we use calculus, we need the minus sign:

$\varepsilon = -\frac{N d\Phi}{dt}$

CHECK YOURSELF 3

Figure 20.9 shows how the flux in a loop changes with time.

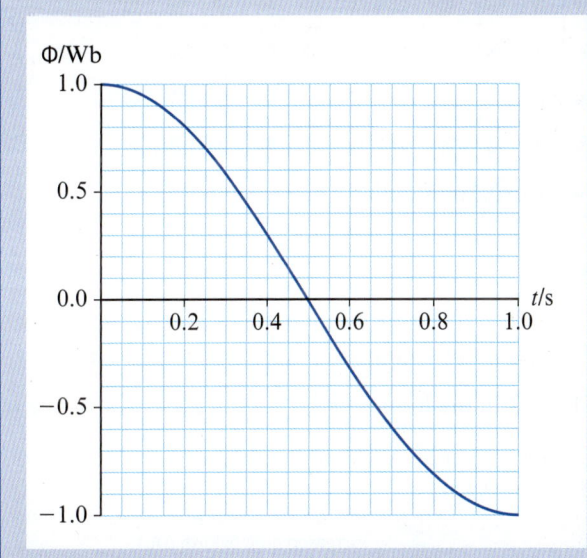

Figure 20.9: For check yourself question 3.

State a time at which the magnitude of the induced emf is a maximum.

WORKED EXAMPLE 20.2

The magnetic field through a single loop of area 0.20 m² is changing at a rate of 4.0 T s⁻¹. What is the induced emf?

Answer

The magnetic flux through the loop is changing because of the changing magnetic field.

Using $\Phi = BA$ and $\varepsilon = \frac{\Delta\Phi}{\Delta t}$:

$\varepsilon = \frac{\Delta(BA)}{\Delta t} = A\frac{\Delta B}{\Delta t}$

$= 0.20 \times 4.0$

$= 0.80$ V

WORKED EXAMPLE 20.3

A pair of conducting rails is placed in a uniform magnetic field of magnitude 0.40 T directed downward, as shown in Figure 20.10. The rails are a distance $L = 0.20$ m apart. A rod is placed on the rails and pushed to the right at constant speed $v = 0.60$ m s^{-1}. What is the induced emf in the loop formed by the rod and the rails?

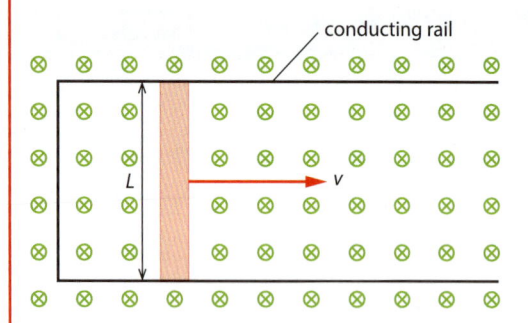

Figure 20.10: A rod on a pair of conducting rails.

Answer

We looked at this problem at the beginning of this section, but now we will solve it the 'easy' way using the concept of a changing flux and Faraday's law.

The flux in the loop is changing since the area of the loop is increasing. Therefore there will be an emf induced.

In a time interval Δt the rod will move to the right a distance $v \Delta t$ and so the area will increase by $\Delta A = Lv \Delta t$ (Figure 20.11).

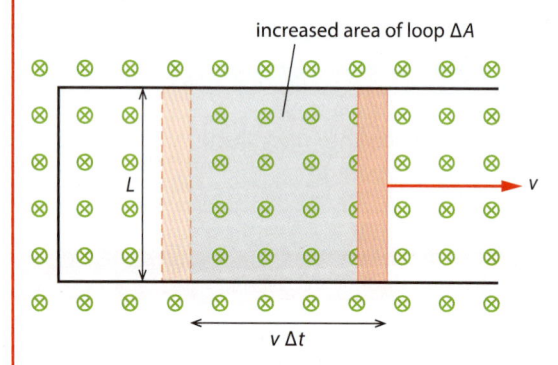

Figure 20.11: As the rod moves along the rails, the area of the loop increases.

Using $\varepsilon = \frac{\Delta \Phi}{\Delta t}$ and $\Phi = BA$, we see that $\varepsilon = B\frac{\Delta A}{\Delta t}$ and so:

$\varepsilon = B \times \frac{Lv\Delta t}{\Delta t}$

$= BLv$

$= 0.40 \times 0.20 \times 0.60$

$= 48$ mV

20 Electromagnetic induction

> **CHECK YOURSELF 4**
>
> A loop of conducting wire is in a region of uniform magnetic field directed out of the plane of the page. The loop can be rotated about any one of the three axes shown in Figure 20.12. 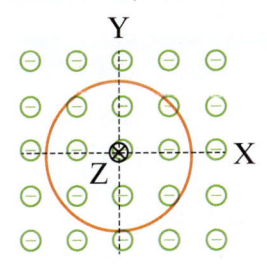
>
> **Figure 20.12:** For check yourself question 4.
>
> Rotation about which axis will give no change in magnetic flux?

Lenz's law

Having seen that a changing magnetic flux will produce an emf and therefore a current in a conducting loop of wire, we now move to the interesting problem of determining the direction of this induced current. This is given by a law discovered by the German-Russian physicist Heinrich Lenz (1804–1865).

> **KEY POINT**
>
> **Lenz's law** states that the induced emf will be such so as to oppose the change in the magnetic flux. It is equivalent to energy conservation.

What does this mean in practice? The flux in the loop is created by a magnetic field which we will call the external field. Now:

If the flux *increases*, the induced emf will create a current whose magnetic field is *opposite* to the external field.

If the flux *decreases*, the induced emf will create a current whose magnetic field is *parallel* to the external field.

This is a subtle and tricky formulation so let us try to understand it. Look at Figure 20.13. We know that the flux is increasing in the loop so an emf and a current will be induced.

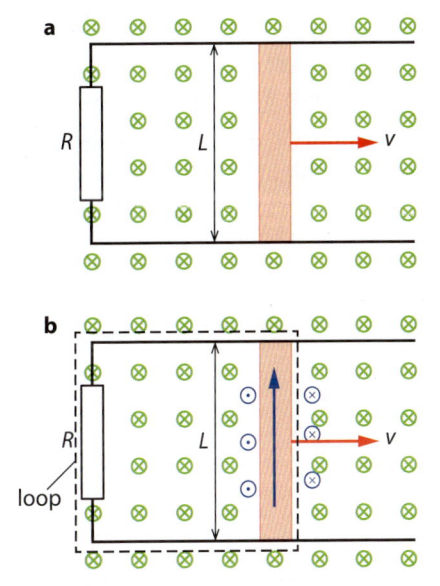

Figure 20.13: a The rod is made to move to the right. The magnetic flux through the loop is increasing and a current will be established in the rod. **b** By Lenz's law, the current must produce a magnetic field opposite to the existing magnetic field, i.e. out of the page. So the current must be counterclockwise.

Lenz's law says we have to oppose the *change* in magnetic flux. This change is an *increase* in flux. Opposing the increase means we have to *decrease* the flux. One way of decreasing the flux is to reduce the magnetic field by creating *another magnetic field* inside the loop in the *opposite* direction, i.e. out of the page. This is the field in blue in Figure 20.13b.
This is produced by the induced current. So now we ask: what should the direction of the induced current be, so that the field it produces is out of the page in the loop. By the right-hand rule, the current must be counterclockwise. (Alternatively, you can argue as follows: we want to oppose the increase in flux. A way of doing that is to prevent the rod from moving to the right. We can do that by having a force act on the rod, directed to the left. This force would be generated if a counterclockwise current flows in the loop.)

435

Notice that Lenz's law is just a statement of energy conservation: imagine that the current in the loop was *clockwise*. What would happen then? By the right-hand rule, the magnetic force on the rod would be directed towards the right—in the direction of motion of the rod. The rod will therefore accelerate and its kinetic energy will increase. But there is nowhere that this energy can come from; energy conservation would be violated.

Let us look at another example. Consider the situation in which the current in the straight wire is *decreasing*. A loop of conducting wire is next to the wire, as shown in Figure 20.14a.

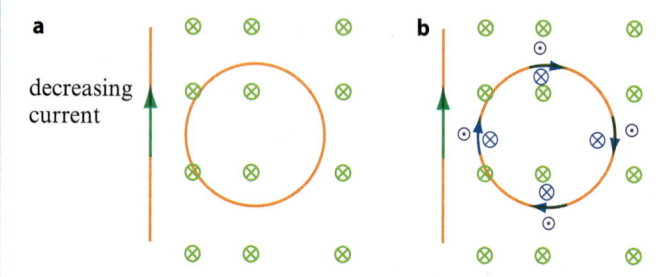

Figure 20.14: **a** A loop of wire near a straight wire in which the current is decreasing. **b** The current in the straight wire creates a magnetic field into the page at the position of the loop. The induced current in the loop produces a magnetic field in the same direction as to oppose the change in flux.

There will be an emf induced in the loop because the flux is changing; it is changing because the current is decreasing and so the magnetic field it produces decreases. What is the direction of the induced current? The change in the magnetic flux is a *decrease* in magnetic flux (the green field created by the green current in the wire is decreasing). We must oppose this decrease, i.e. we must create a magnetic field in the *same* direction as the green field, i.e. into the page inside the loop, Figure 20.14b. So the question now is: what is the direction of the current in the loop such that the field it produces is into the page inside the loop? From the right-hand rule, the current must be clockwise.

(Alternatively, you can argue as follows: we want to oppose the decrease in flux. A way of doing that is to make the loop come closer to the wire where the magnetic field is stronger. We can do that by having a force act on the loop, directed to the left. This force would be generated if a clockwise current flows in the loop.)

> **EXAM TIP**
>
> To work with Lenz's law you must be very familiar with the rules for giving the direction of a magnetic field created by a current and the rule that gives the magnetic force on a current.

> **CHECK YOURSELF 5**
>
> A conducting loop enters and then leaves a region R of uniform magnetic field directed into the page, as shown in Figure 20.15. The loop moves with constant speed. 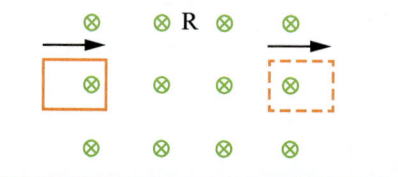
>
> **Figure 20.15:** For check yourself question 5.
>
> What is the direction of the induced current as the loop:
>
> **a** enters region R
>
> **b** leaves region R?

Let us make sure that we understand what is going on by looking at another example.

> 20 Electromagnetic induction

> **WORKED EXAMPLE 20.4**

A loop of wire has its plane horizontal, and a bar magnet is dropped from above so that it falls through the loop with the north pole first, as shown in Figure 20.16. Find the direction of the current induced in the loop.

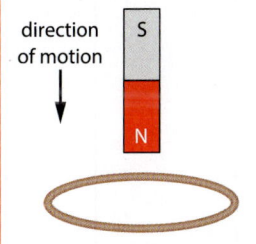

Figure 20.16: A magnet is dropped into a loop of wire.

Answer

The flux in the loop is increasing because the magnetic field at the loop is getting larger as the magnet approaches. The induced current must then oppose the increase in the flux. This can be done if the induced current produces a magnetic field in the opposite direction to that of the bar magnet, as shown by the blue arrow in Figure 20.17a. Thus, the current will flow in a counterclockwise direction when looked at from above. This also means that there is force of repulsion between the coil and the magnet so the magnet slows down.

As the magnet leaves the loop from the other side, the flux is decreasing. So the current induced must produce a magnetic field in the same direction, i.e. down. This means the current is clockwise looked at from above, as shown in Figure 20.17b. (It follows that since the current changes from counterclockwise to clockwise, at some point it must be zero.) There is now a force of attraction between the coil and the magnet so the magnet again slows down.

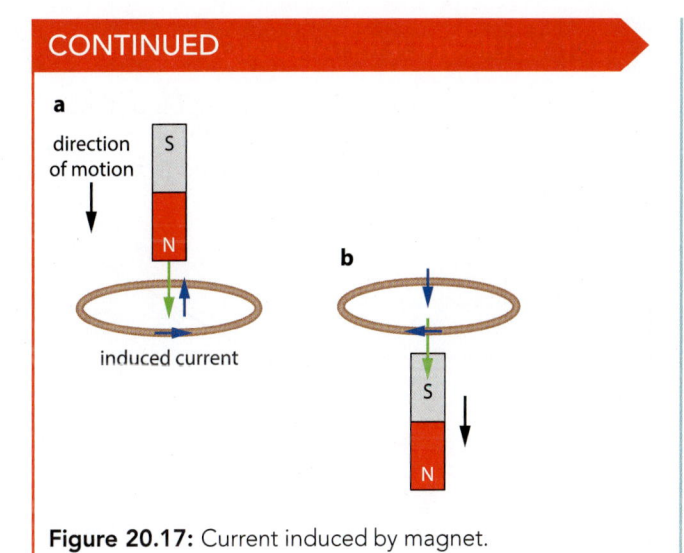

> **CONTINUED**

Figure 20.17: Current induced by magnet.

Self induction

Suppose we connect a coil to a cell and a variable resistor R. By changing the resistance of R the current in the circuit will be changing; the magnetic flux linkage in the coil will therefore also be changing and an emf ε_L will be induced in the coil. We call this phenomenon **self induction**. By Lenz's law, the induced emf will oppose the change in the current. For example, suppose that the current in a coil is increasing, Figure 20.18a.

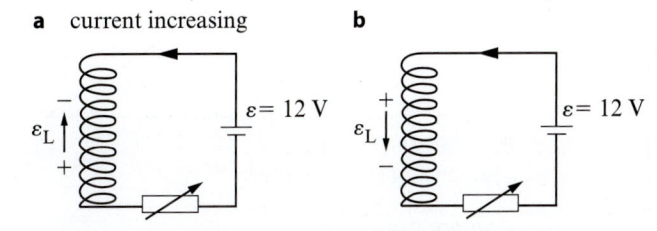

Figure 20.18: When the current is **a** increasing or **b** decreasing there is an induced emef in the coil.

The polarity of the induced emf is such as to drive current in the opposite direction to that of the current from the cell. In this way the induced emf opposes the increase in the current by decreasing the current in the circuit. If, instead, the current is decreasing, the polarity of the induced emf is shown in Figure 20.18b.

437

TEST YOUR UNDERSTANDING

1 The flux through a loop as a function of time is given by the graph in Figure 20.19. Sketch a graph of the emf induced in the loop as a function of time.

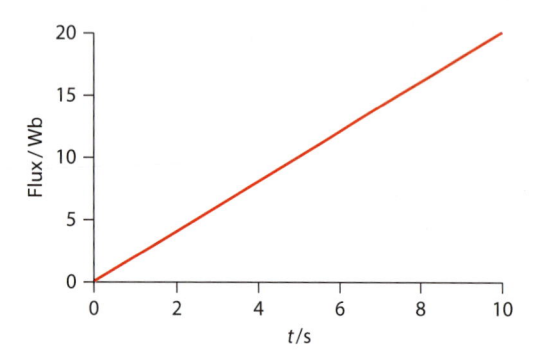

Figure 20.19: For question 1.

2 The flux through a loop as a function of time is given by the graph in Figure 20.20. Sketch a graph of the emf induced in the loop as a function of time.

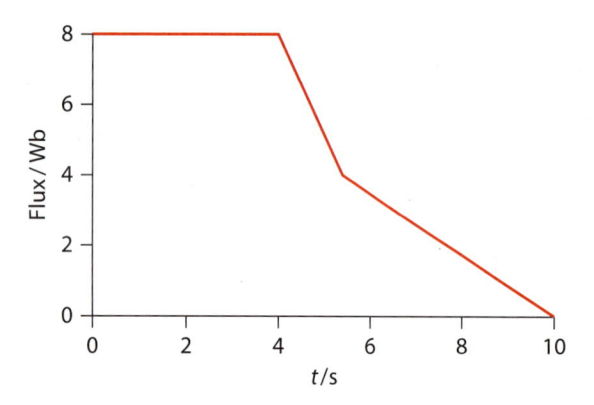

Figure 20.20: For question 2.

3 Figure 20.21 shows the emf induced in a loop as a result of a changing flux in the loop.

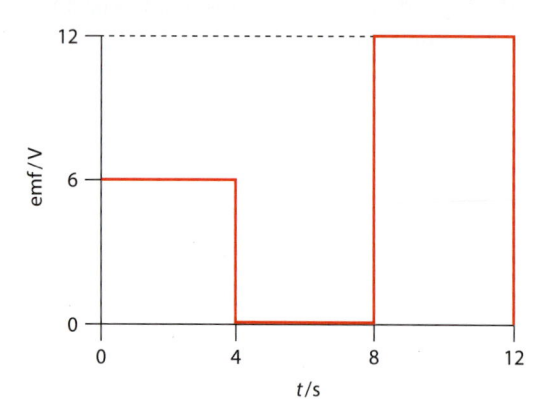

Figure 20.21: For question 3.

   a Sketch a possible flux versus time graph that would give rise to such an emf.
   b Explain why there isn't a unique answer.

4 A loop of area 0.20 m² has five turns of wire around it and finds itself in a region of uniform magnetic field 0.35 T, as shown in Figure 20.22. Initially the field is normal to the loop.

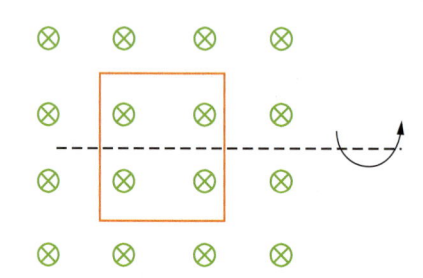

Figure 20.22: For question 4.

The loop is rotated by 180° about the axis shown in a time equal to 0.50 s.
What is the average emf induced in the loop?

CONTINUED

5   Two loops of wire enter a region of uniform magnetic field directed into the plane of the paper, as shown in Figure 20.23. The loops have the same area and speed.

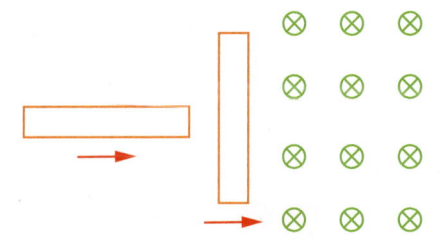

Figure 20.23: For question 5.

Is the induced emf in the loops the same? Explain your answer.

6   A current carrying wire is placed along the axis of a cylinder of length L and radius R, as shown in Figure 20.24.

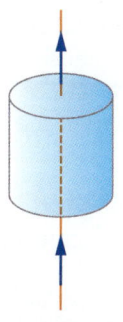

Figure 20.24: For question 6.

The magnetic flux density created by the current on the surface of the cylinder is B. What is the magnetic flux through the cylinder's surface area?

7   Figure 20.25 shows a top view of three solenoids with their axes parallel. One of the small solenoids fits within the larger one. The third solenoid is outside the big solenoid. The bigger solenoid has a current flowing in the clockwise direction (looked at from above) and the current is increasing in magnitude.

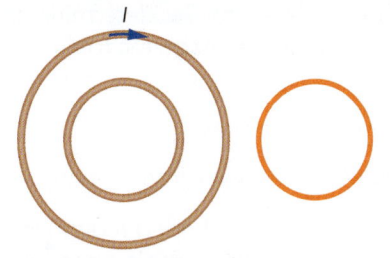

Figure 20.25: For question 7.

Find the direction of the induced current in the smaller solenoids.

8   A metallic ring is dropped from above a bar magnet as shown in Figure 20.26.

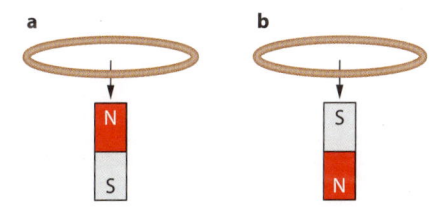

Figure 20.26: For question 8.

Determine the direction of the induced current in the ring as the ring falls over the magnet in each case, giving full explanations for your choices.

9   A magnet is dropped from above into a metallic ring as shown in Figure 20.27.

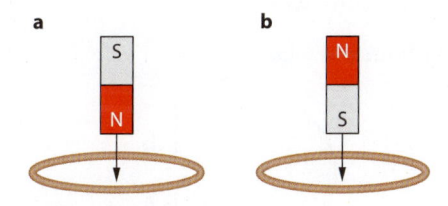

Figure 20.27: For question 9.

Determine the direction of the current induced in the ring in each case.

439

CONTINUED

10 For the diagram in question **9a**, determine and justify the direction of the magnetic force on the ring as:

   a the magnet approaches the ring.

   b the magnet moves away from the ring.

11 A metallic rod of length L (shaded region) is dragged with constant velocity v in a region of magnetic field directed into the page, as shown in Figure 20.28.

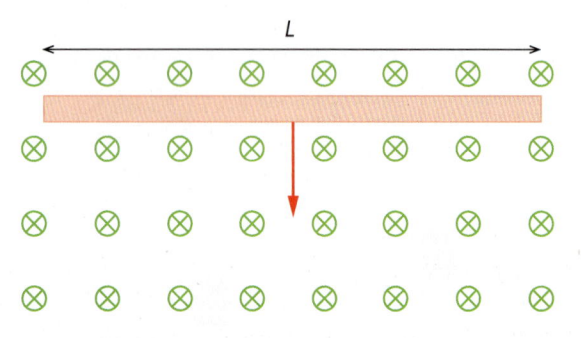

Figure 20.28: For question 11.

By considering the force on electrons inside the rod, show that the ends of the rod will become oppositely charged. Determine the end that is positively charged.

12 Find the direction of the current in the loop shown in Figure 20.29 as the loop is moved:

   a towards to the wire

   b away from the wire.

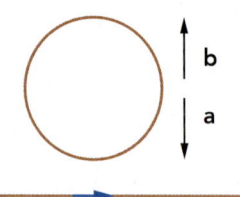

Figure 20.29: For question 12.

13 An aluminium ring hangs from a string. A magnet is moved closer to the ring, as shown in Figure 20.30.

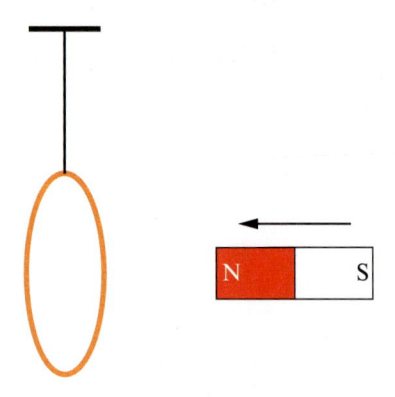

Figure 20.30: For question 13.

Determine which way the ring will move as the magnet approaches.

14 A large coil has a smaller coil inserted inside it so that their axes are parallel. The smaller coil has 200 turns and a diameter of 2.0 cm. A changing current in the large coil causes the magnetic field to be increasing at a rate of 0.45 T s^{-1}. Calculate the emf induced in the smaller coil.

15 Look at Figure 20.31. The conducting rod AB is free to move. The magnetic field is increasing.

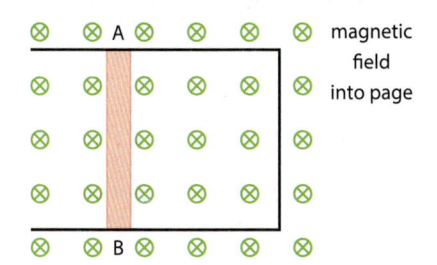

Figure 20.31: For question 15.

Determine what will happen to the rod AB.

CONTINUED

16 When lightning strikes, large magnetic fields are produced. This can be modelled by a long, straight, current-carrying wire vertical to the surface of the earth. In one strike, the magnetic field at the position of a rectangular loop of wire some distance from the strike point drops from 6.0 T to zero in a time of 8.0 μs. The loop has area 0.40 m² and has 50 turns of wire around it.

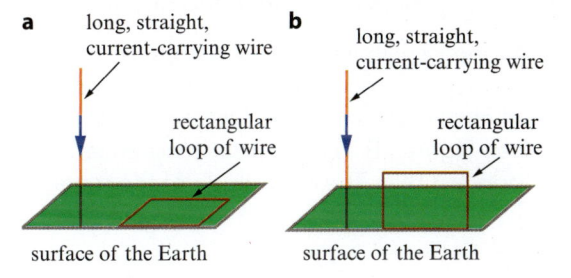

Figure 20.32: For question 16.

What is the average induced emf in the loop if the plane of the loop is:

- **a** parallel to the ground (Figure 20.32a)
- **b** normal to the ground (Figure 20.32b)?

17 A loop of wire is placed in a region of magnetic field. In half the loop the magnetic field is out of the page and in other half the field is into the page. The area of the loop is A and the magnetic field in both directions has magnitude B. (See Figure 20.33.)

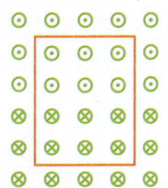

Figure 20.33: For question 17.

- **a** What is the flux in the loop?
- **b** The magnitude of the magnetic field is increasing at the same rate in both directions. Is there an induced emf in the loop?
- **c** The magnitude of the field out of the page is increasing, and the field into the page is decreasing at the same rate. Is there an induced emf in the loop?

18 A magnet is attached to a spring. The magnet oscillates in and out of a coil, as shown in Figure 20.34.

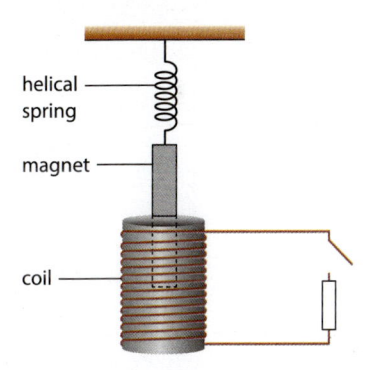

Figure 20.34: For question 18.

- **a** Draw a sketch graph to show the variation with time of the displacement of the magnet when:
   - **i** the switch is open
   - **ii** the switch is closed.
- **b** Explain your sketches in part **a**.

19 Two identical rings made out of conducting material are released from rest, from the same height above the ground and at the same time. One ring will fall through a region of a horizontal magnetic field. (See Figure 20.35.)

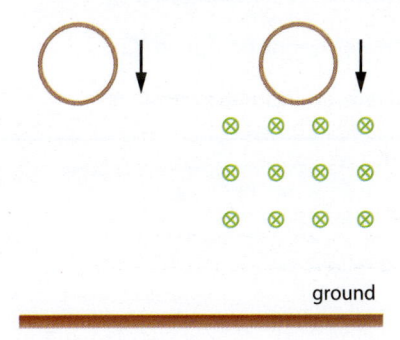

Figure 20.35: For question 19.

CONTINUED

State and explain which ring will reach the ground first.

20 A clockwise current, when looked at from above, is established in a loop of wire X. (See Figure 20.36; note: connections to a battery are not shown.) A second conducting loop Y is placed underneath X so their planes are parallel.

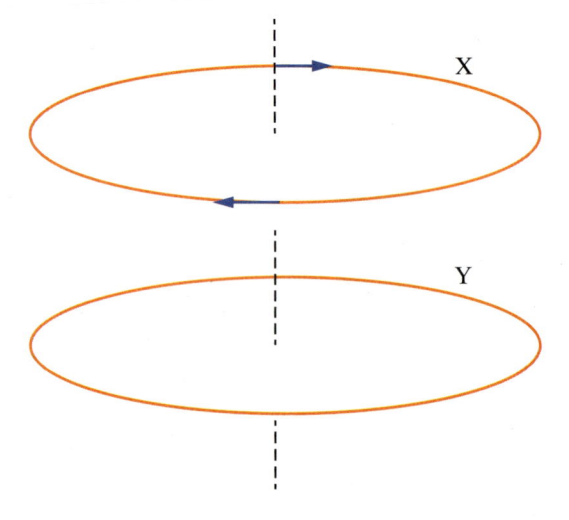

Figure 20.36: For question 20.

a The current in X is increasing.

  i What is the direction of the induced current in Y?

  ii What is the direction of the magnetic force on Y?

b The current in X is now constant.

  i Is there magnetic flux in Y?

  ii Is there an induced emf in Y?

c The current in X is now switched off. It takes 0.10 ms for the current to be reduced to zero.

  i Explain why there will be an emf induced in Y during the 0.1 ms time interval.

  ii What is the direction of the magnetic force on Y during this time?

21 A loop of wire including a battery of emf 1.5 V is moved at speed 5.0 m s^{-1} into a region of uniform magnetic field directed into the page (see Figure 20.37). The total resistance of the loop is $3.0 \text{ }\Omega$. The magnitude of the magnetic field is 0.30 T. The length of the coloured wire is 0.20 m.

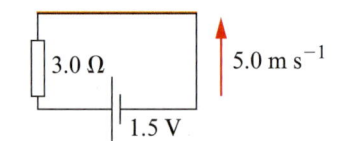

Figure 20.37: For question 21.

a What is the current in the loop *before* it enters the field?

b What is the current in the loop as it enters the region of magnetic field?

20.2 Generators and alternating current

The ac generator

One very important application of electromagnetic induction is the ac generator—the method used universally to produce electricity (Figure 20.38). A coil is made to rotate in a region of magnetic field. This can be accomplished in a variety of ways: by a diesel engine burning oil, by falling water in a hydroelectric power station, by wind power and so on. The ends of the coil are firmly attached to two slip rings that rotate along with the coil. The slip rings touch carbon brushes that transfer the current into an external circuit.

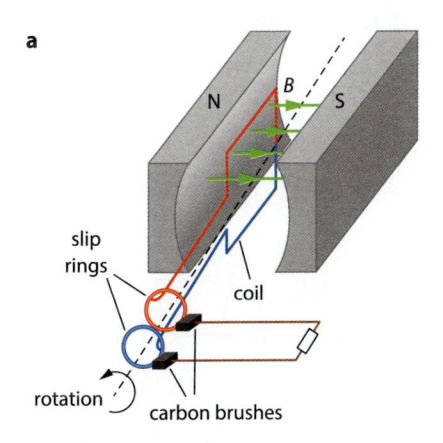

Figure 20.38: a A coil that is forced to turn in a region of magnetic field will produce an emf. **b** Generators at the Hoover hydroelectric power plant in the United States.

The flux in the coil changes as the coil rotates and so an emf is produced in it. We assume that the coil has $N = 10$ turns of wire around it, the magnetic field is $B = 0.21$ T, the coil has an area of 0.50 m^2 and the coil rotates with frequency $f = 50$ revolutions per second. The flux linkage in the coil changes as time goes on according to a cosine function as shown in Figure 20.39.

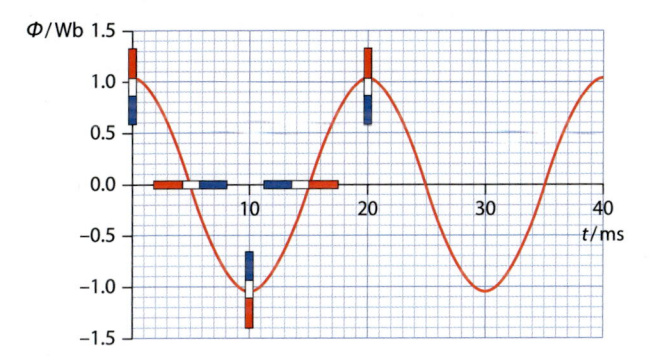

Figure 20.39: The flux linkage in the coil is changing with time.

The red, white and blue bar that is superposed on the graph indicates the position of the coil as we look at it along the axis of rotation: at $t = 0$ for example the coil is vertical with the part painted red on top. The equation of the flux (linkage) is, in general:

$$\Phi = NBA \cos\theta$$

where θ is the angle between the magnetic field and the normal to the coil and N is the number of turns in the coil.

The coil rotates with angular speed of rotation ω; it follows that $\theta = \omega t$.

But, since $\omega = 2\pi f$, we also have $\theta = 2\pi f t$. So the flux linkage becomes:

$$\Phi = NBA \cos(2\pi f t)$$

By Faraday's law, the emf induced in the coil is (minus) the rate of change of the flux linkage and is given by:

$$V = -\frac{d\Phi}{dt}$$
$$= 2\pi f NBA \sin(2\pi f t)$$

The important thing here is that $V \propto f$.

The quantity $V_0 = 2\pi f NBA$ is the peak voltage produced by the generator. The variation of the induced emf with time is given by the graph in Figure 20.40. The peak voltage in this example is 325 V.

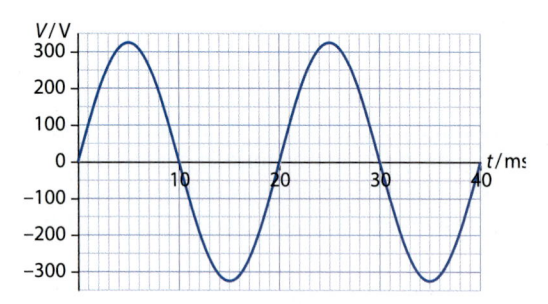

Figure 20.40: The emf induced in the loop as a function of time. The peak voltage is 325 V.

Note that the induced emf is zero whenever the flux assumes its maximum or minimum values and, conversely, it is a maximum or minimum whenever the flux is zero. The noteworthy thing here is that the voltage can be negative as well as positive. This is what is called **alternating voltage** and the current that flows in the coil is **alternating current (ac)**. This means that, unlike the ordinary direct current (dc) that flows in a circuit connected to a battery, the electrons do not drift in the same direction but oscillate back and forth with the same frequency as that of the voltage. The flux and the emf are out of phase by $\frac{\pi}{2}$ or 90°.

The current in a circuit of resistance R can be found from:

$$I = \frac{V}{R}$$

$$= \frac{V_0 \sin(2\pi f t)}{R}$$

$$= I_0 \sin(2\pi f t)$$

where $I_0 = \frac{V_0}{R}$ is the peak current. Notice that since $V \propto f$ it follows that also $I \propto f$. For the emf of Figure 20.40 and a resistance of 16 Ω, the current is shown in Figure 20.41.

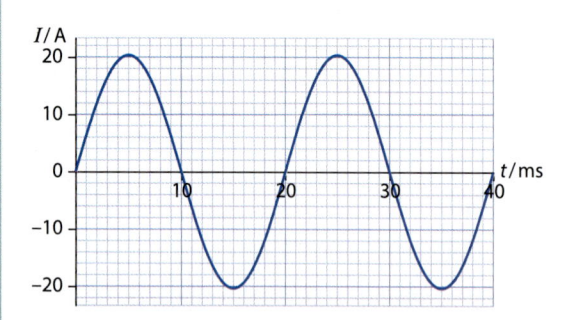

Figure 20.41: The induced current in the rotating loop. Note that the current is in phase with the emf. The peak current is found from peak voltage divided by resistance, i.e. $\frac{325}{16}$, which is about 20 A.

CHECK YOURSELF 6

The average current produced by a generator is zero. How then can it produce a heating effect in a resistor?

Power in ac circuits

The power P generated in an ac circuit is given by:

$P = VI$

Because both the current I and voltage V vary with time, the expression for power becomes:

$P = V_0 I_0 \sin^2(2\pi f t)$

This means that, just like the current and the voltage, power is not constant in time. It has a peak value P_{max} given by the product of the peak voltage and peak current:

$P_{max} = V_0 I_0$

The power as a function of time is shown in Figure 20.42. The *average* power dissipated is half the peak value.

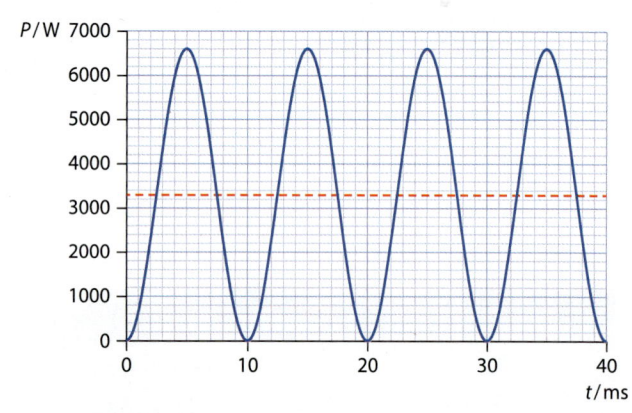

Figure 20.42: The power dissipated in a resistor as a function of time. Note that the period of one rotation of the coil is 20 ms. The power becomes zero with every half rotation of the coil. The horizontal dotted line indicates the average power, which is half the peak value.

The relationship between voltage, current and power in an ac circuit is shown in Figure 20.43.

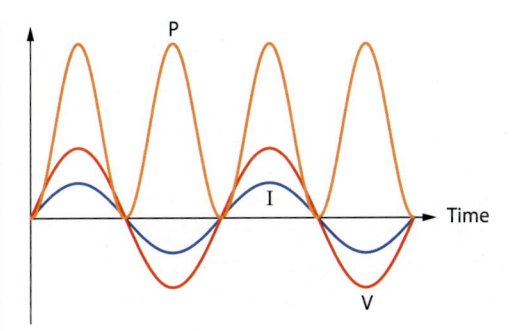

Figure 20.43: Power (orange), voltage (red) and current (blue) in an ac circuit resistor.

Since $P = VI$, and $V \propto f$ as well as $I \propto f$ it follows that $P \propto f^2$.

> ### CHECK YOURSELF 7
> The frequency of rotation of the coil of a generator is doubled. By what factor do **a** the peak voltage and **b** the peak power change?

> ### WORKED EXAMPLE 20.5
> The graph of Figure 20.44 shows the variation with time of the power delivered by an ac generator.
>
> a State the frequency of rotation of the generator.
> b On a copy of the graph, sketch the graph of the power delivered when the frequency of rotation is halved.

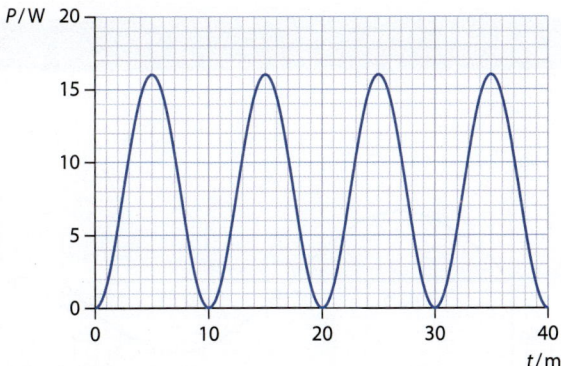

Figure 20.44: The variation with time of the power delivered by an ac generator.

> ### CONTINUED
> **Answer**
>
> a The period T is found by looking at *two* loops, i.e. it is 20 ms.
>
> So the frequency is found from $f = \dfrac{1}{T}$
>
> $f = \dfrac{1}{0.020}$
>
> $= 50$ Hz
>
> b Since $P \propto f^2$, if you halve the frequency, the power is reduced by a factor of 4. So the peak of the graph will be at 4 W.
>
> Changing the frequency also changes the period. If the frequency is halved, then the period is doubled to 40 ms.
>
> So we get the graph in red shown in Figure 20.45.

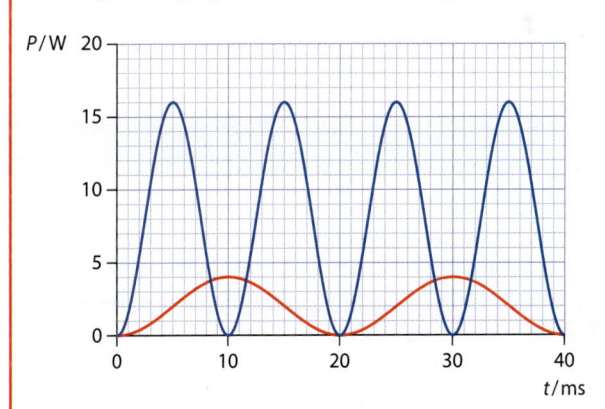

Figure 20.45: The power delivered when the frequency of rotation is halved.

> ### EXAM TIP
> It is important to understand how to get the period from a graph of power against time. The interval between two consecutive times when the power is zero is half a period.

445

PHYSICS FOR THE IB DIPLOMA: COURSEBOOK

Links

Maxwell's intuition about the symmetry between electric and magnetic fields led to electromagnetic waves and a unification of electric and magnetic phenomena. Einstein carried this connection further. Imagine a charged particle that moves parallel to a straight wire that carries current; there will be a magnetic force on this particle. But what does an observer who travels along with the charged particle see? For this observer, the particle is at rest and so there can be no magnetic force. For this observer, the wire is moving and so suffers length contraction. A detailed analysis shows that as a result the density of positive charges in the wire increases and so there is now an electric force on the particle. So not only are electric and magnetic phenomena related, but what is called 'electric' and what is called 'magnetic' also depends on the frame of reference one uses to describe the situation.

SCIENCE IN CONTEXT

The discovery of EM waves and EM induction has brought endless applications and uses. A very small selection includes all modern communications with cell phones and similar devices as well as ordinary radio and television which involve EM waves; so do antitheft devices and countless other types of radio frequency identification devices (RFIDs, for example the transponder you use to raise the bar at toll stations on a highway); levitating trains; electric cars; and most of our electromechanical technology; we owe much to what we know about the early universe by studying the cosmic microwave background radiation (CMB); the exploitation of solar energy and the greenhouse effect that sustains life on earth are both based on understanding EM waves; X rays are used in medical imaging, radar and navigation, microwave ovens and so forth.

NATURE OF SCIENCE

Much of the electromechanical technology we use today is due to the discoveries made by Michael Faraday. In 1831, using very simple equipment, Faraday observed a tiny pulse of current in one coil of wire when the current in a second coil was switched on or off, but nothing while a constant current was flowing. In further experiments he found these transient currents when he slid a magnet quickly in and out of a coil of wire. Faraday explained this electromagnetic induction using the idea of lines of force but did not provide a mathematical relationship. The mathematical description of these phenomena was given much later by the Scottish physicist James Clerk Maxwell (1831–1879).

TEST YOUR UNDERSTANDING

22 A coil is rotated in a magnetic field. The graphs show the variation of the flux with rotation angle and the variation of the induced emf with time, Figure 20.46.

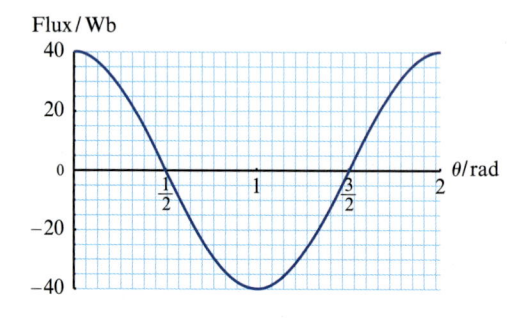

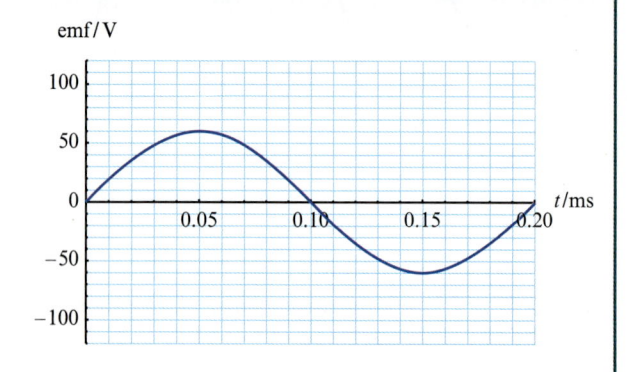

Figure 20.46: For question 22.

CONTINUED

a Draw a graph to show the variation of the induced emf with **angle**.

The same coil is now rotated at double the speed in the same magnetic field. Draw graphs to show:

b the variation of the flux with **angle**

c the variation of the induced emf with **angle**

d the variation of the induced emf with **time**.

23 A transformer consists of two coils wrapped around an iron core (Figure 20.47a). When alternating current is established in the primary coil, a varying magnetic field is created in the primary coil. The iron core ensures that all the magnetic field lines stay within the core and so also go through the secondary coil.

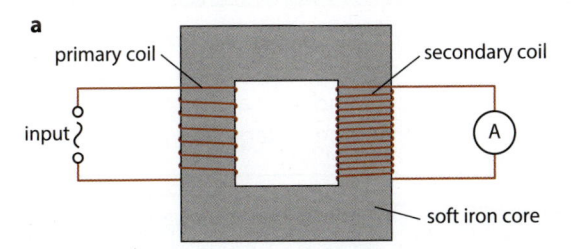

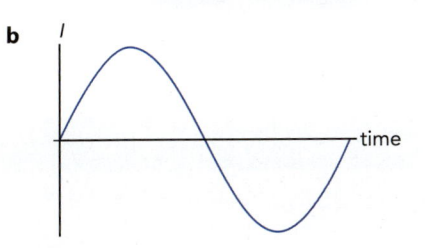

Figure 20.47: For question 23.

a Explain why a current will be established in the secondary coil.

The input current in the primary coil varies with time, as shown in Figure 20.47b.

b Draw a sketch graph (no numbers required) to show how the current in the secondary coil varies with time.

24 Figure 20.48 shows the variation with time of the power dissipated in a resistor when an alternating voltage from a generator is established at its ends.

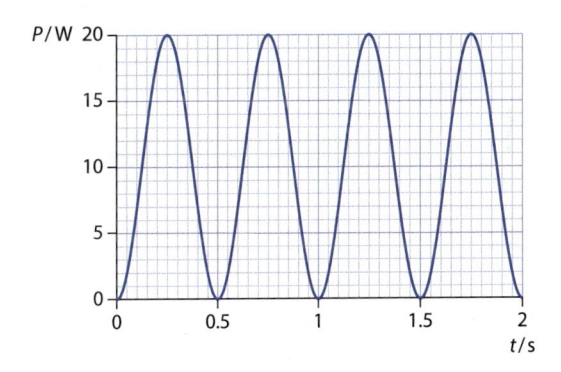

Figure 20.48: For question 24.

a Find the period of rotation of the coil.

b The coil is now rotated at double the speed. Draw a graph to show the variation with time of the power dissipated in the resistor.

SELF-ASSESSMENT CHECKLIST

I am able to …	Section	Not yet	Nearly there	Ready to move on
define and understand the concept of magnetic flux	20.1			
distinguish between magnetic flux and magnetic flux linkage	20.1			
state Faraday's law	20.1			
solve problems with Faraday's law	20.1			
understand and apply Lenz's law	20.1			
describe the production of alternating current	20.2			
solve problems with alternating current, voltage and power	20.2			
describe an electromagnetic wave	20.2			

REFLECTION

Do you understand how a *motional emf* comes about? Do you understand the concepts of *magnetic flux* and *magnetic flux linkage*? Do you understand *Faraday's law of electromagnetic induction*? Can you solve problems with Faraday's law? Do you understand *Lenz's law*? Do you understand how a generator works? Do you know how the frequency and number of turns of a generator coil affect the voltage and power produced?

EXAM-STYLE QUESTIONS

You can find questions in the style of IB exams in the digital coursebook.

CHECK YOURSELF ANSWERS

1 Loop 1 has the least, and loops 2 and 3 have the same larger emf.

2

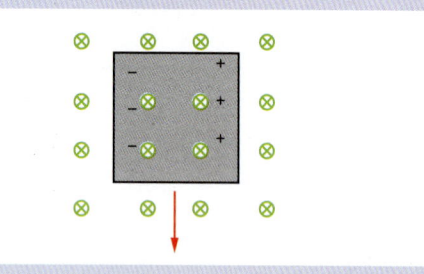

3 At 0.5 s where the rate of change of flux is greatest.

4 Axis Z.

5 a Counterclockwise
   b Clockwise

6 Mathematically, power has to do with the square of the current and the average of that is not zero. Physically, the electrons making up the AC current oscillate back and forth and in so doing collide with the lattice ions just as in the DC case, generating thermal energy.

7 a Increases by 2.
   b Increases by 4.

Unit E
Nuclear and quantum physics

INTRODUCTION

In Quantum Mechanics we can only calculate probabilities as to what the future state of a system will be. Many of the familiar concepts from classical physics break down: the energy of a system in classical mechanics, for example the kinetic energy of a ball or the total energy of an orbiting satellite are continuous quantities. This is not the case in Quantum Mechanics. The energy of the hydrogen atom is discrete. It can have a possible set of values and no other. The same applies to the energy of a nucleus. The quantum world is discrete whereas the classical world is continuous.

Einstein's explanation for the photoelectric effect required another paradigm shift: the accepted theory of light as a wave could not explain the features of the phenomenon. Einstein suggested that light consists of a large number of bundles of energy, massless particles moving at the speed of light and behaving the way particles do. Years later de Broglie would suggest that just as light that was thought to be a wave sometimes behaved as particles, particles too sometimes behave as waves. Experiments would soon verify this hypothesis and "the duality of matter" entered Physics.

At the same time our understanding of the structure of the atom increased with the discovery of the nucleus and the phenomenon of radioactivity. Most nuclei are unstable and decay by emitting energy and particles. New fundamental forces were discovered adding to the already known electromagnetic and gravitational forces. The strong nuclear force was necessary to keep nucleons bound together and the weak nuclear force was needed to explain beta decay.

Nuclear fission provided a way to harness the energy of the atom in peace and, unfortunately, war. The laws of nuclear physics applied to fusion in stars explain the creation of the elements and, at the same time, in an incredible combination of the laws of the very small with the laws of the very large predict the correct abundances of helium 4, deuterium, helium 3 and lithium 7 providing astonishing support for the Big bang model of the Universe.

> Chapter 21
Atomic physics

LEARNING OBJECTIVES

In this chapter you will learn how to:

- understand the discovery of the atomic nucleus in the Geiger–Marsden–Rutherford experiment.
- describe and explain gas emission and absorption spectra in terms of energy levels.
- solve problems with atomic transitions.
- > understand the consequences of a quantised angular momentum in the Bohr model for hydrogen.

> **GUIDING QUESTIONS**
>
> - Why is energy in atomic systems discrete?
> - What is matter made out of?

Introduction

In 1911, Ernest Rutherford (1871–1937) and his assistants Hans Geiger (1882–1945) and Ernest Marsden (1889–1970) performed a series of experiments that marked the beginning of modern particle physics, the quest to unravel the mysteries of the structure of matter. At that time it was believed that an atom was a sphere of positive charge of diameter of about 10^{-10} m with the electrons moving inside the sphere. This picture is the Thomson model of the atom. This is the picture of the atom that the Rutherford experiment challenged.

21.1 The structure of the atom

In the Rutherford experiment, positively charged particles, called alpha particles, were directed at a thin gold foil in an evacuated chamber, Figure 21.1. The number of particles deflected at a particular angle was recorded. They found that:

- the great majority of the alpha particles went straight through the foil with no or little deflection; they were detected at very small scattering angles, such as at positions A, B and C in Figure 21.1a.
- very occasionally, alpha particles were detected at very large scattering angles, such as position L.

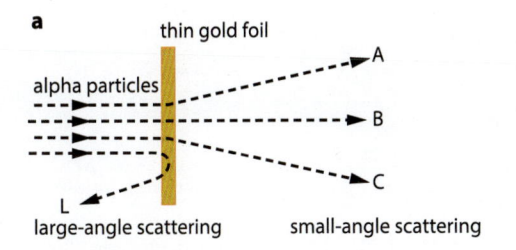

The small deflections could be understood within the Thomson model: they were due to the electric force of repulsion between the positive charge of the gold atoms and the positive charge of the alpha particles. (An alpha particle is about 7000 times more massive than the electron, so the effect of the electrons of the gold atoms on the path of the alpha particles is negligible.)

But the large-angle scattering events could not be understood within the Thomson model. Rutherford said that 'it was as if you fired a 15-inch shell at tissue paper and it came back and hit you'.

Consequences of the Rutherford experiment

The very large deflection showed that there was an enormous force of repulsion between the alpha particle and the positive charge of the atom. Since the electric force is given by $F = k\frac{q_1 q_2}{r^2}$ to get a large force implies that the separation r must be very small.

How can we get a large force in the Thomson model? Figure 21.2a shows two alpha particle paths. Suppose the alpha particle approaches along the top path. The closest distance to the centre of the positive charge is the atomic radius and this is of order 10^{-10} m. Calculations show that the resulting force is 10^{10} times too small, so this does not work. What if the alpha penetrates the atom? Then, the distance r can become as small as we like. But this does not work either. In this case, only the charge within the smaller dotted sphere would produce a force on the alpha particle, and the result is again a very small force and a small deflection. The only way out is to imagine that the positive charge on the atom is within a sphere that is much smaller than the sphere that Thomson had imagined.

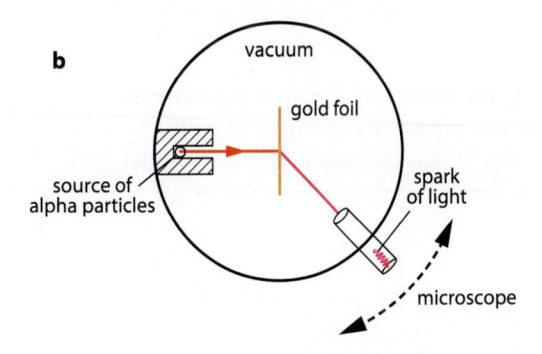

Figure 21.1: a The majority of alpha particles are slightly deflected by the gold foil. Very occasionally, large-angle scatterings take place. b The alpha particles are detected by the sparks of light they create when they hit a zinc sulfide screen in the microscope.

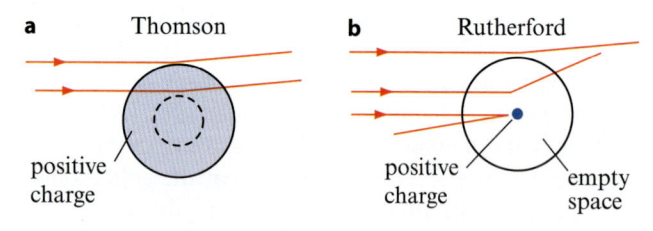

Figure 21.2: a We cannot get a large force out of the Thomson model, but **b** with a tiny nucleus we can.

Rutherford calculated theoretically the number of alpha particles expected at particular scattering angles based on Coulomb's force law. He found agreement with his experiments if the positive atomic charge was confined to a region of linear size approximately equal to 10^{-15} m. This and subsequent experiments confirmed the existence of the nucleus inside the atom—a small, massive object carrying the positive charge of the atom and most of its mass.

WORKED EXAMPLE 21.1

A sphere of charge Q has radius 10^{-15} m. Another sphere has the same charge and a radius of 10^{-10} m. Calculate the ratio of the electric fields at the surface of the two spheres.

Answer

Apply the formula for the electric field:

$$E = \frac{kQ}{r^2}$$

We find the ratio of the fields E_1 and E_2 for the two spheres as:

$$\frac{E_1}{E_2} = \frac{\frac{kQ}{(10^{-15})^2}}{\frac{kQ}{(10^{-10})^2}}$$

$$\frac{E_1}{E_2} = 10^{10}$$

This is why the deflecting forces in Rutherford's nuclear model are so large compared with what one might expect from Thomson's model.

EXAM TIP

You must be prepared to explain why the old model can account for the small deflections but not the large deflections, and why the proposed new model by Rutherford explains both the small as well as the large deflections.

CHECK YOURSELF 1

Which feature of the Rutherford experiment led to the idea of the existence of a tiny nucleus?

KEY POINT

The Rutherford experiment established the Rutherford model of the atom: the atom consists of a very small, massive, positively charged nucleus, and the electrons orbit the nucleus like planets around the sun.

Discrete energy

If you expose a container of gas at low pressure to a strong electric field, light will be emitted from the gas. You can show that the emitted light contains many different wavelengths by passing it through a prism or diffraction grating. The result is a series of bands of light at different wavelengths. Figure 21.3 shows the wavelengths that are present in the light emitted by hydrogen, helium and mercury vapour.

The set of possible wavelengths that can be emitted is called the **emission spectrum**.

21 Atomic physics

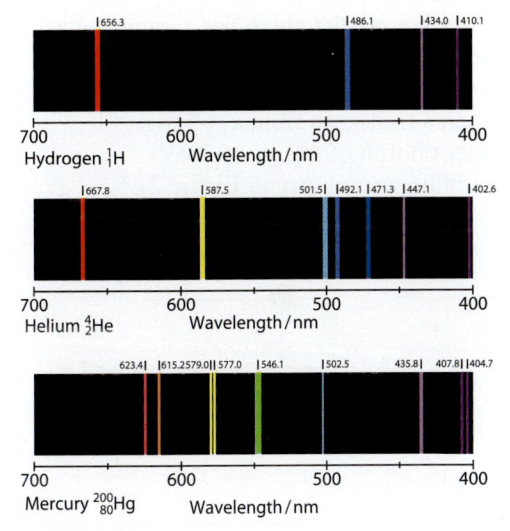

Figure 21.3: The emission spectra of hydrogen, helium and mercury vapour.

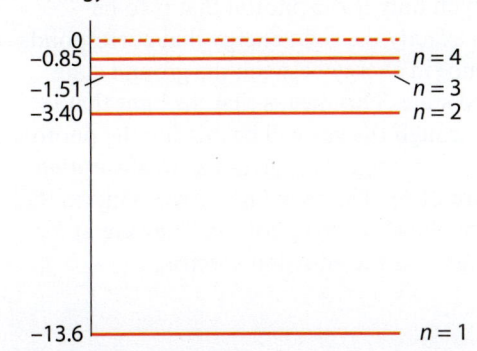

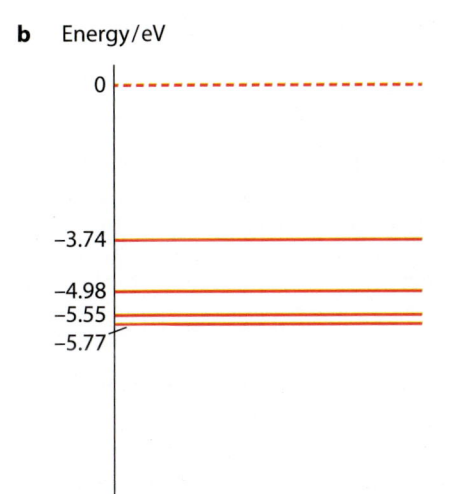

Figure 21.4: Energy level diagrams according to Bohr: **a** for hydrogen, and **b** for mercury.

How can these spectra be understood? Niels Bohr (1885–1962) provided the first radical explanation in 1913. He argued that an atom has **discrete energy**, i.e. it can have one out of a specific set of values. He represented the possible energies with an **energy level diagram**. Each horizontal level represents a possible energy of the atom. By 'energy of the atom' we mean the kinetic energy of the electrons plus the electrical potential energy of the electrons and the nucleus. The diagrams for hydrogen and mercury are shown in Figure 21.4.

Bohr applied his theory to hydrogen, the simplest atom with just one electron. He was able to show that the energy of the hydrogen atom in the nth state is given by:

$$E = -\frac{13.6}{n^2} \text{ eV} \quad n = 1, 2, 3, \ldots$$

> **EXAM TIP**
>
> This formula only applies to hydrogen.

The negative sign in the energy tells us that the electron is trapped within the atom. To have the electron leave the atom, energy must be provided. A hydrogen atom can only have an energy of −13.6 eV, −3.40 eV, −1.51 eV, −0.87 eV and so on. No other value is possible. Energy in the atomic world is discrete.

> **CHECK YOURSELF 2**
>
> How much energy must be given to a hydrogen atom in its ground state (the lowest energy state) so that the electron is knocked out of the atom? This is known as the ionisation energy.

How does this energy level structure help explain emission spectra? Bohr suggested that an atom can make a transition from a state of higher energy to a state of lower energy by emitting a **photon**, the particle of light.

The energy of the emitted photon is the difference in energy between the two levels. Think of the photon as a 'tiny flash of light'. There would be one photon for each transition. With very many transitions from very many atoms the 'tiny flashes of light' in each transition add up to the observable light we see in the emission spectrum. The photon had been introduced earlier into physics by Einstein, who suggested that its energy is given by:

$$E = hf \quad \text{or} \quad E = \frac{hc}{\lambda}$$

453

where f and λ are the frequency and wavelength of the light (the photon), c is the speed of light and h a new constant introduced by Planck a few years earlier. The Planck constant has a value 6.63×10^{-34} J s.

In a transition from a high to lower energy state, such that the *difference* in energy between the two states is ΔE, the photon emitted has a wavelength given by

$\frac{hc}{\lambda} = \Delta E$ and therefore

$\lambda = \frac{hc}{\Delta E}$

As an example, consider the transition from the level $n = 3$ (whose energy is -1.51 eV) to the level $n = 2$ (whose energy is -3.40 eV). The difference in energy between these two levels is $-1.51 - (-3.40) = 1.89$ eV, and this is the energy that will be carried by the photon emitted in this transition. Therefore:

$\frac{hc}{\lambda} = 1.89 \text{ eV} = 1.89 \times 1.6 \times 10^{-19} = 3.024 \times 10^{-19}$ J

$\lambda = \frac{6.63 \times 10^{-34} \times 3.0 \times 10^{8}}{3.024 \times 10^{-19}}$

$\lambda = 6.58 \times 10^{-7}$ m

> **EXAM TIP**
>
> Remember to convert eV into joules!

This is in excellent agreement with the red line in the spectrum of hydrogen in Figure 21.3.

In hydrogen, most transitions from higher levels to the level $n = 2$ emit photons of visible light.

When undisturbed, the electron in each hydrogen atom will occupy the lowest energy state, i.e. the one with $n = 1$ and energy -13.6 eV. This lowest energy state is called the **ground state**. If energy is supplied to the atom, the electron may move to a higher energy level, an **excited state**, by absorbing exactly the right amount of energy needed to move up. For example, to move from $n = 1$ to the state with $n = 3$ the energy needed is exactly $13.6 - 1.51 = 12.09$ eV. Suppose that precisely this amount of energy is supplied to an electron in the ground state. The electron will absorb this energy and make a transition to the level $n = 3$. At this point the atom is said to be *excited*.

From the excited state, the electron will immediately (within nanoseconds) make a transition down to one of the available lower energy states. From $n = 3$ the electron can either go directly to $n = 1$ (emitting a photon of energy 12.1 eV) or it can first make a transition to $n = 2$ (emitting a photon of energy 1.89 eV) and then a transition from $n = 2$ to $n = 1$ (emitting another photon of energy 10.2 eV). These two possibilities are shown in Figure 21.5.

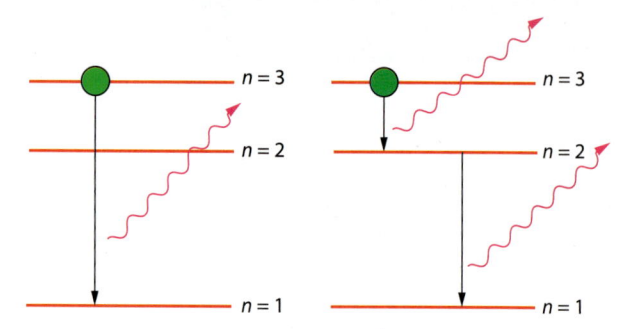

Figure 21.5: Transitions from $n = 3$ in hydrogen.

Whether the electron will choose to make the direct or the indirect transition is an issue of chance: there is a probability for the one option and another probability for the other. (The Bohr model cannot predict these probabilities, but the theories that followed years later can.)

So the emission spectra of elements can be understood if we accept that electrons in atoms exist in energy levels with discrete energy.

> **CHECK YOURSELF 3**
>
> When does an atom emit a photon?

Absorption spectra

Now imagine sending a beam of white light through a gas. The majority of the atoms in the gas are in their ground state. Electrons in the atoms may absorb photons in the beam and move to an excited state. This will happen only if the photon that is to be absorbed has exactly the right energy that corresponds to the difference in energy between the ground state and an excited state. This means that the light that is transmitted through the gas will be missing the photons that have been absorbed. This gives rise to **absorption spectra** (Figure 21.6). The dark lines correspond to the wavelengths of the absorbed photons. They are at the same wavelengths as the emission spectra.

Figure 21.6: The absorption spectrum of hydrogen (top) and the emission spectrum (bottom). The emission lines and the absorption lines are at the same wavelength.

CHECK YOURSELF 4

Figure 21.7 shows four atomic transitions.

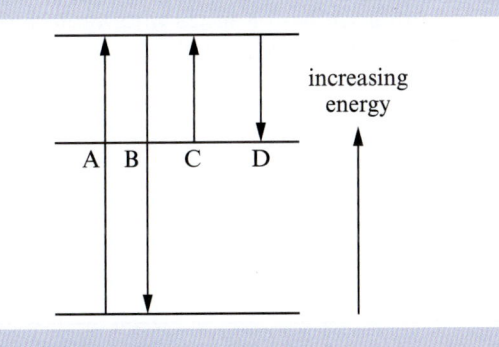

Figure 21.7: For check yourself question 4.

Which one results in the emission of a photon with the largest wavelength?

EXAM TIP

The electrons that absorb photons will move to an excited state, but once there, they will make a down transition, emitting the photons they absorbed. So why are the photons missing? This is because the photons are emitted in all directions and not necessarily along the direction the observer is looking. You must be able to explain this in an exam.

Experiments show that no two elements have the same wavelengths in their emission and absorption spectra. These wavelengths are like fingerprints—they are unique to each element and so can be used to identify the element. This has been used to identify the chemical composition of stars.

WORKED EXAMPLE 21.2

Calculate the wavelength of the photon emitted in the transition from the first excited level to the ground state of mercury.

Answer

From Figure 21.4b the energy difference is:

$-5.77 - (-10.44) = 4.67$ eV

So the wavelength is found from:

$\frac{hc}{\lambda} = 4.67 \, \text{eV} = 4.67 \times 1.6 \times 10^{-19}$ J

$\lambda = \frac{6.63 \times 10^{-34} \times 3.0 \times 10^8}{7.472 \times 10^{-19}}$

$\lambda = 2.7 \times 10^{-7}$ m

This is an ultraviolet wavelength and so does not show up in the emission spectrum in Figure 21.1.

Atoms are very particular when it comes to absorbing energy! If the energy is provided by a photon, the energy will be accepted only if the photon energy corresponds to exactly a difference of energies between levels. If the energy is provided by an incoming electron, then the atom may accept what is needed to make a transition to a higher level and the electron then bounces off with an energy reduced by the energy absorbed.

CHECK YOURSELF 5

An electron is in the ground state of hydrogen. The difference in energy between the ground state and the first excited state is 10.2 eV. What will happen to this electron if **a** a photon and **b** an electron each of energy 10.3 eV is incident on the atom?

Links

E. Hubble discovered that spectral lines emitted from distant galaxies show a redshift, i.e. the measured wavelength on earth is longer than that emitted. This led to the notion of the expanding universe and Hubble's law. Measuring the redshift allows a measurement of speed and through Hubble's law the distance to the galaxy. Also, as mentioned earlier, study of the spectral lines of stars allows the determination of the elements in the star.

NATURE OF SCIENCE

Figure 21.8: Ernest Rutherford.

Ernest Rutherford (Figure 21.8) was a very practical man with a cheerful personality. For his achievements he was compared to Newton—they are buried near each other in Westminster Abbey, London.

Rutherford has many famous quotes, such as:

'Don't let me catch anyone talking about the Universe in my department'.

'All of Physics is either impossible or trivial. It is impossible until you understand it, then it becomes trivial'.

'Equipment costs money, so we have to use our heads'.

'A theory you can't explain to a bartender is probably no damn good'.

Of the many stories about Rutherford, one involves the Russian physicist Pyotr Kapitza who wanted to become Rutherford's student. Rutherford declined, saying he had more than 10 students already and had no room for another. Kapitza asked Rutherford what error he was willing to accept in his experiments, to which Rutherford replied 10%. 'Then you can take me' said Kapitza. Rutherford did! Five of Rutherford's students, including Kapitza, went on to receive Nobel prizes in physics.

TEST YOUR UNDERSTANDING

1. What is the approximate value of the ratio of the radius of an atom to the radius of its nucleus?

2. Name the force that keeps electrons attached to the nucleus in Rutherford's model of the atom.

3. In the gold foil experiment explain why:
   a. the foil was very thin
   b. the experiment was done in an evacuated container.

4. a. Discuss what is meant by the statement that the energy of atoms is *discrete*.
   b. Outline the evidence for this discreteness.

5. Explain why the dark lines of an absorption spectrum have the same wavelengths as the bright lines of an emission spectrum for the same element.

6. What is the energy of a photon whose wavelength is 480 nm?

7. The energy of a photon is 3.8 eV. What is its wavelength?

8. Calculate the wavelength of the photon emitted in a transition from $n = 4$ to $n = 2$ in hydrogen.

9. Refer to Figure 21.3. Explain why the distance between the emission lines of hydrogen decreases as we move to the right.

10. A hydrogen atom is in its ground state.
    a. Explain the term *ground state*.
    b. Photons of energy 10.4 eV are directed at hydrogen gas in its ground state. Suggest what, if anything, will happen to the hydrogen atoms.
    c. In another experiment, a beam of electrons of energy 10.4 eV are directed at hydrogen atoms in their ground state. Suggest what, if anything, will happen to the hydrogen atoms and the electrons in the beam.

21 Atomic physics

> **CONTINUED**
>
> **11 a** What is the evidence for the existence of energy levels in atoms?
>
> **b** Electrons of kinetic energy:
>
>   **i** 10.10 eV
>
>   **ii** 12.80 eV
>
>   **iii** 13.25 eV
>
>   collide with hydrogen atoms and can excite these to higher states.
>
>   In each case, find the largest n corresponding to the state the atom can be excited to. Assume that the hydrogen atoms are in their ground state initially.
>
> **12 a** What do you understand by the term *ionisation energy*?
>
> **b** What is the ionisation energy for a hydrogen atom in the state $n = 3$?
>
> **13** What is the minimum speed an electron must have so that it can ionise an atom of hydrogen in its ground state?

21.2 Quantisation of angular momentum

Niels Bohr (1885–1962), Figure 21.9a, was a Danish physicist who studied the hydrogen atom. This is the simplest atom, consisting of a nucleus of a single proton and a single electron orbiting it, Figure 21.9b.

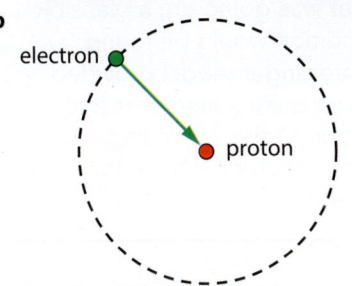

Figure 21.9: a Niels Bohr. **b** An electron orbiting a proton. The force on the electron is the electric force.

> **EXAM TIP**
>
> There is a lot of algebra in this derivation that must be learned carefully.

Bohr objected to the Rutherford model because an electron in orbit experiences centripetal acceleration. It was a prediction of the classical theory of electromagnetism that accelerated charges emit electromagnetic radiation and so the electron would lose energy and plunge into the nucleus. Bohr assumed that the electron could only exist in certain special orbits satisfying the condition:

$$mvr = n\frac{h}{2\pi} \quad n = 1, 2, 3, \ldots$$

In these orbits the electron would not radiate, in other words, the classical laws of electromagnetism would not apply to these states. This was a revolutionary step! Notice that the quantity $L = mvr$ is the angular momentum of the electron. The condition states that the angular momentum is quantised; in other words, it is an integral multiple of a basic unit (in this case, $\frac{h}{2\pi}$).

What is the consequence of this condition?

The total energy E_T of the orbiting electron is (k is the Coulomb constant):

$$E_T = \underbrace{\tfrac{1}{2}mv^2}_{\text{kinetic energy}} + \underbrace{\left(-\frac{ke^2}{r}\right)}_{\text{electric potential energy}}$$

This is because the proton has charge e and the electron charge $-e$. But the electron is acted upon by the electric force, and so:

$$\frac{ke^2}{r^2} = \frac{mv^2}{r}$$

457

From this we deduce that $mv^2 = \frac{ke^2}{r}$, and so the total energy becomes:

$$E_T = \frac{1}{2}\frac{ke^2}{r} - \frac{ke^2}{r}$$

$$E_T = -\frac{1}{2}\frac{ke^2}{r}$$

Squaring both sides of the Bohr condition equation:

$$m^2v^2r^2 = n^2\frac{h^2}{4\pi^2}$$

and so $mv^2 = \frac{n^2h^2}{4\pi^2 mr^2}$

But earlier we found that $mv^2 = \frac{ke^2}{r}$, so substituting for mv^2 we get:

$$\frac{ke^2}{r} = \frac{n^2h^2}{4\pi^2 mr^2}$$

This gives the extraordinary result that the orbital radius cannot be anything we wish:

it equals $r = \frac{h^2}{4\pi^2 ke^2 m} \times n^2$.

We define $a_0 = \frac{h^2}{4\pi^2 ke^2 m}$ to be the Bohr radius. Numerically,

$$a_0 = \frac{(6.626 \times 10^{-34})^2}{4\pi^2 \times 8.988 \times 10^9 \times (1.602 \times 10^{-19})^2 \times 9.109 \times 10^{-31}}$$

$= 5.29 \times 10^{-11}$ m so that $r = a_0 \times n^2$.

Figure 21.10 shows the radii corresponding to $n = 1, 2$ and 3.

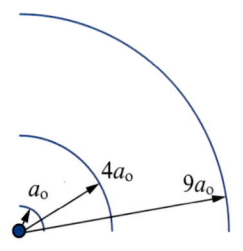

Figure 21.10: The lowest three allowed orbits of the electron in the Bohr model of hydrogen.

If we substitute this value of the orbit radius in the formula for the total energy of the electron, $E_T = -\frac{1}{2}\frac{ke^2}{r}$, we get:

$$E_T = -\frac{1}{2}\frac{ke^2}{a_0} \times \frac{1}{n^2}.$$

Putting in accurate values of the constants we finally get:

$$E = -\frac{13.6}{n^2}\text{eV}$$

In other words, the theory predicts that the electron in the hydrogen atom has discrete or **quantised energy**. As we saw in Section 21.1, this explains the emission and absorption spectra of hydrogen.

Links

Much of what you have learned in this chapter will be familiar from the work we did on gravitation in Sections 17.2 and 17.3 showing the combined use of conservation of energy and Newton's second law.

WORKED EXAMPLE 21.3

In gravitation the period of revolution T of a planet in a circular orbit of radius R around the sun obeys $T^2 \propto R^3$. Deduce the corresponding relation in the Bohr hydrogen model for an electron.

Answer

We know that $v^2 = \frac{ke^2}{mr}$ and so $\left(\frac{2\pi r}{T}\right)^2 = \frac{ke^2}{mr}$, leading to $T^2 = \frac{4\pi^2 m}{ke^2}r^3$ i.e. $T^2 \propto r^3$, just as in gravitation.

THEORY OF KNOWLEDGE

Where did the Bohr angular momentum quantisation condition come from? And why did the scientific community accept it even though no explanation was given for it? The answer is that this condition led to an explanation of a long-standing unsolved problem, namely atomic spectra. The fact that such a convincing explanation was found implied that most likely the assumptions behind the theory were correct or almost correct; that was the beginning of a new era in physics and everyone suspected that with more developments and better understanding of what was going on, a plausible argument for this condition would be found. Sure enough, the Schrödinger model provided the missing explanation quite a few years later through the introduction of the wavefunction. (But try the last end-of-chapter problem for Bohr's own explanation.)

21 Atomic physics

TEST YOUR UNDERSTANDING

14 Calculate, for an electron in the $n = 2$ state of hydrogen,

  a the orbit radius

  b the linear momentum

  c the angular momentum

  d the kinetic energy

  e the potential energy.

15 a Show that the speed of an electron in the nth state of hydrogen is given by $v = \frac{2\pi ke^2}{nh}$.

  b Hence calculate the ratio of the speed of the electron in the state $n = 2$ to that in the state $n = 1$.

16 a Show that the relation between the period of revolution T_n of an electron in the nth state of hydrogen is related to the period in the $n = 1$ state T_1 by $T_n = n^3 T_1$.

  b Find an expression for T_1 in terms of fundamental constants.

  c Evaluate T_1 in seconds and $\frac{1}{T_1}$ in Hz.

  d Use the result in **a** and the formula for the radius of the nth orbit to deduce Kepler's third law for the hydrogen electron.

17 The Balmer series consists of transitions from a state n down to the state $n = 2$.

  a Show that the wavelengths, in nanometers, of the Balmer series are given by $\lambda = 365 \times \frac{n^2}{n^2 - 4}$.

  b Evaluate this wavelength for the transition from $n = 3$.

  c Calculate the frequency of revolution of the electron in the states $n = 3$ and $n = 2$ and compare with the frequency of the photon in the transition from $n = 3$ to $n = 2$.

18 A planet (mass m) circling the sun (mass M) in a circular orbit has its angular momentum quantised as in the Bohr model.

  a Show that the allowed radii of the orbit are given by $r = n^2 \frac{h^2}{4\pi^2 GMm^2}$.

  b Apply this to the earth whose orbit radius is 1.5×10^{11} m. What value of n corresponds to this radius?

  c Is the assumption of a quantised angular momentum meaningful in this case?

19 A particle of electric charge q moving in a circle in a region of magnetic field B has its angular momentum quantised as in the Bohr model. Show that the allowed radii are given by $r = \sqrt{\frac{nh}{2\pi qB}}$.

20 The Bohr model can also be applied to the singly ionised atom of helium. By retracing the derivations in the Bohr model for hydrogen, determine for the $n = 1$ state of ionised helium:

  a the radius in terms of the Bohr radius a_0,

  b the energy in eV.

21 Show that when n is very large, in the transition from the state $n + 1$ to the state n the frequency of the emitted photon equals the frequency of revolution of the electron in the state n.

22 For the really interested: Bohr introduced his *correspondence principle* which states that as the quantum number of a system becomes very large, the quantum system behaves like the corresponding classical system. In the case of the hydrogen atom, the corresponding classical system would be an orbiting electron radiating EM waves with a frequency equal to the frequency of revolution of the electron around the proton, exactly as predicted by Maxwell's classical theory. We can use this to show why angular momentum has to be quantised!

Consider an electron that orbits a proton with angular frequency ω.

  a Show that the angular momentum can be written as $L = m\omega r^2$.

  b Applying Coulomb's law to the orbiting electron, show that $L^3 = \frac{mk^2e^4}{\omega}$.

CONTINUED

c Show that $r = \dfrac{L^2}{mke^2}$.

d Hence show that the total energy of the electron is given by $E = -\dfrac{mk^2e^4}{2L^2}$ and therefore $\dfrac{dE}{dL} = \dfrac{mk^2e^4}{L^3}$.

e Using your answer to part **b**, deduce that $\dfrac{dE}{dL} = \omega$.

f Take dE to be the energy of the photon emitted when an electron makes a transition from a state $n + 1$ to a state n where n is large. According to the correspondence principle this photon must have a frequency equal to the frequency of revolution of the electron, i.e. d$E = hf = \dfrac{h\omega}{2\pi}$.

Hence deduce that $\dfrac{h\omega}{2\pi} = \omega dL$ i.e. $dL = \dfrac{h}{2\pi}$.

This says that the angular momentum increases in steps of $\dfrac{h}{2\pi}$, i.e. it is quantised.

SELF-ASSESSMENT CHECKLIST

I am able to ...	Section	Not yet	Nearly there	Ready to move on
describe the structure of an atom	1.1			
appreciate the significance of the Rutherford scattering experiment	1.1			
appreciate the meaning of the term *discrete energy*	1.1			
calculate the wavelength of emitted photons in atomic transitions	1.1			
appreciate the consequences of a quantised electron angular momentum.	1.2			

REFLECTION

Can you describe *Rutherford's scattering* experiment? Can you discuss the implications of Rutherford's scattering experiment for the *structure of the atom*? Can you explain how *emission* and *absorption spectra* are formed? Do you understand the concepts of *energy levels* and discrete *energy*? Do you understand what is meant by an *atomic transition*? Can you calculate the wavelength of the photon emitted in an atomic transition?

Do you appreciate the consequences of the *Bohr quantisation condition* for angular momentum?

EXAM-STYLE QUESTIONS

You can find questions in the style of IB exams in the digital coursebook.

CHECK YOURSELF ANSWERS

1. The very large scattering angles.
2. 13.6 eV or more.
3. When making a transition from a high to a low energy state.
4. The one with the least energy difference so D.
5. a. The photon will not be absorbed because it is not providing the exact amount of energy needed. The photon will just bounce off the atom leaving the atom in the same state.
   b. An energy 10.2 eV will be absorbed, moving the atom to the first excited state, and the electron will bounce off the atom with energy 0.1 eV.

Chapter 22
Quantum physics

LEARNING OBJECTIVES

In this chapter you will learn how to:

- understand the nature of photons
- understand details of the photoelectric effect
- understand why the photoelectric effect cannot be explained by the wave theory of light
- understand Compton scattering
- explain the concept of matter waves
- describe an experiment that shows the wave nature of electrons.

22 Quantum physics

> **GUIDING QUESTIONS**
> - How does radiation interact with matter?
> - What is the nature of light?

Introduction

For decades, physicists of the nineteenth century knew of the photoelectric effect: the emission of electrons from a metallic surface when light fell on the surface. But an understanding of the phenomenon was lacking until Einstein explained it in 1905 with a radical theory. The basic ingredient of the theory was that light behaved as a collection of particles called photons and not as a wave. Years later, de Broglie made the equally radical suggestion that particles have wave properties.

22.1 Photons and the photoelectric effect

Photons

Light is said to be an **electromagnetic wave** consisting of oscillating electric and magnetic fields. This was Maxwell's great discovery in the nineteenth century. The wave has a wavelength λ and a frequency f and, as with all waves, the wave speed c is given by:

$c = f\lambda$

where in this case the wave speed is the speed of light.

Through Maxwell's theory, complex phenomena such as diffraction, interference, polarisation and others could be understood. The successful application of Maxwell's theory meant that light was definitely and without any doubt a wave. It therefore came as a shock that in a phenomenon known as the photoelectric effect, light did not behave as a wave should.

As we will see, Einstein suggested that light should be thought of as a collection of quanta, or bundles of energy. Each **quantum** or bundle of light has energy E given by $E = hf$, where f is the frequency of the light and h is Planck's constant. A beam of light of frequency f is now to be thought of as a very large number of these quanta moving at the speed of light. The total energy of the beam is then the product of hf (the energy of one quantum) times N, the number of quanta in the beam.

The energy of the beam is therefore an integral multiple of the basic unit hf. These quanta have energy and momentum and are localised in space; this means they behave as particles. But the theory of relativity states that if a particle moves at the speed of light it has to have zero mass. So this quantum of light, which came to be known as the **photon**, is a particle with zero mass and zero electric charge.

> **CHECK YOURSELF 1**
>
> Which has more energy, a photon of blue light or a photon of red light?

In Chapter 21 we saw that a photon will be emitted when an atom makes a transition from a high to a lower energy state. Its energy is the energy difference of the two levels. A photon can also be absorbed by an atom. An atom in a low energy state can absorb a photon of just the right energy and make a transition to a higher energy level. When we look at the light from a light bulb we see a continuous emission of light. But if we could slow down the process by a few billion times, the continuity in the emission of light would stop. We would see different spots on the filament emit tiny flashes of light (photons) at random intervals of time; the spots on the filament would be on (emitting) and off (not emitting) randomly. The discreteness of energy we talked about in Chapter 21 would surface again.

In Einstein's theory of special relativity the total energy E, the momentum p and the mass m of a particle are related according to:

$E^2 = p^2c^2 + m^2c^4$

The mass of the photon is zero, so $E = pc$. The photon therefore has momentum $p = \frac{E}{c}$. (The conventional Newtonian formula for momentum, $p = mv$, does not apply to particles with zero mass.) So the momentum of the photon is:

$p = \frac{E}{c} = \frac{hf}{c} = \frac{h}{\lambda}$

> **CHECK YOURSELF 2**
>
> The wavelength of a beam of light is decreased, but the intensity of the beam stays the same. What happens to the number of photons in the beam?

WORKED EXAMPLE 22.1

Estimate how many photons of wavelength 5.0×10^{-7} m are emitted per second by a 60 W lamp, assuming that 10% of the energy of the lamp goes into photons of this wavelength.

Answer

Let there be N photons per second emitted. Then the energy emitted is $\frac{Nhc}{\lambda}$ in one second.

This has to be 10% of 60 J, that is 6.0 J.

So:

$\frac{Nhc}{\lambda} = 6.0$

$N = \frac{6.0\lambda}{hc}$

$N = \frac{6.0 \times 5.0 \times 10^{-7}}{6.63 \times 10^{-34} \times 3.0 \times 10^{8}}$

$\Rightarrow N = 1.5 \times 10^{19}$ photons per second

WORKED EXAMPLE 22.2

All the photons from worked example 1 are incident normally on a mirror of area 0.5 m² and are reflected by it. Estimate the pressure these photons exert on the mirror.

Answer

Each photon has momentum $\frac{h}{\lambda}$. The momentum change upon reflection is $2\frac{h}{\lambda}$ (momentum is a vector!).

Since there are N such reflections per second, the force F on the mirror is:

$F = 2N\frac{h}{\lambda}$

$F = 2 \times 1.5 \times 10^{19} \times \frac{6.63 \times 10^{-34}}{5.0 \times 10^{-7}}$

$\Rightarrow F = 4.0 \times 10^{-8}$ N

The pressure is thus:

$\frac{F}{A} = 8.0 \times 10^{-8}$ N m^{-2}

(Note that if the photons were absorbed rather than reflected, the pressure would be half that obtained here.)

The photoelectric effect

The **photoelectric effect** is the phenomenon in which light (or other forms of electromagnetic radiation) incident on a metallic surface causes electrons to be emitted from the surface.

To investigate the facts about the photoelectric effect, apparatus like the one in Figure 22.1 may be used.

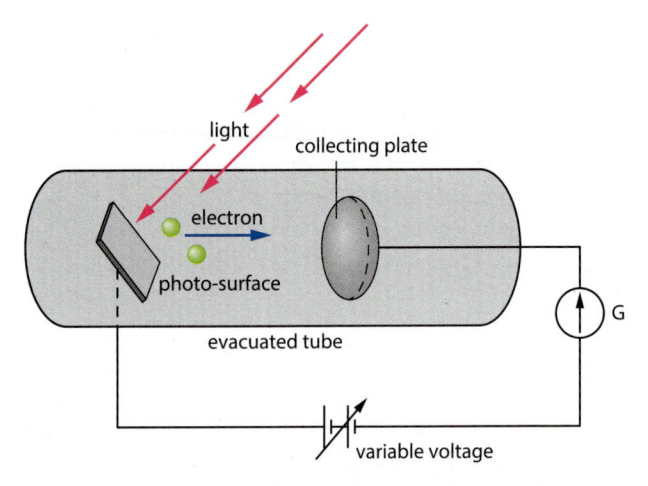

Figure 22.1: Apparatus for investigating the photoelectric effect. The collecting plate is negatively charged and so decelerates the emitted electrons. At the right voltage the electrons can be stopped, resulting in zero current in the circuit.

It consists of an evacuated tube, inside which is the **photo-surface** (the metallic surface that light is incident on). Light passes through the tube and falls on the photo-surface, which emits electrons. The emitted electrons are called **photoelectrons**. Some of the emitted electrons arrive at the collecting plate. The photo-surface and the collecting plate are part of a circuit as shown. Those electrons that make it to the collecting plate complete the circuit and so we have an electric current that is recorded by the sensitive galvanometer.

Notice that in Figure 22.1 the terminal of the variable power supply connected to the collecting plate is the negative terminal. This means that the collecting plate actually repels the emitted electrons. Only the very energetic electrons will make it to the plate. As the magnitude of the voltage is increased (i.e. made more negative) fewer and fewer electrons make it to the plate; eventually no electron will arrive there and at that point the current becomes zero. The voltage at which the current becomes zero is called the **stopping voltage**, V_s. Its significance is that the maximum kinetic energy of the emitted electrons is eV_s. We see this as follows: the maximum kinetic energy of an electron is E_{max} as it leaves the photo-surface; the electrical potential energy is $(-e)V_s$, and so the total energy at the photo-surface is $E_{max} - eV_s$. At the collecting plate the total energy is zero (zero kinetic and zero potential) and so $eV_s = E_{max}$.

We now connect the positive terminal of the power supply to the collecting plate. The electrons are now attracted to the collecting plate and the current increases. As the voltage is increased even more the current saturates, i.e. it approaches a constant value. This is because the collecting plate is so positive that it attracts every single emitted electron (even those that were not directed at the collected plate). So we have a current–voltage graph like the one in Figure 22.2.

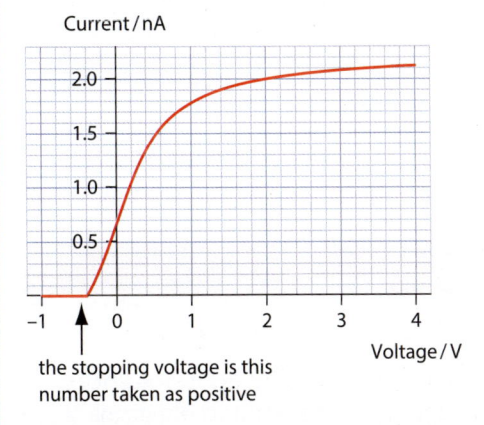

Figure 22.2: When the collecting plate is connected to the negative terminal of the power supply, there is a voltage at which the current becomes zero (Vs). This is 0.4 V in this example.

EXAM TIP

It is important to understand that the stopping voltage is related to the maximum kinetic energy of the emitted electrons.

WORKED EXAMPLE 22.3

Using the graph of Figure 22.2 determine:

a the stopping voltage

b the maximum energy of the emitted electrons

c the maximum speed of the emitted electrons.

Answer

a The current becomes zero when the voltage is -0.40 V, so the stopping voltage is 0.40 V.

b The maximum kinetic energy of the emitted electrons is 0.40 eV $= 6.4 \times 10^{-20}$ J.

c From $E_{max} = \frac{1}{2}mv^2$, we find $v = \sqrt{\frac{2E_{max}}{m}}$, giving:

$$v = \sqrt{\frac{2 \times 6.4 \times 10^{-20}}{9.1 \times 10^{-31}}} = 3.8 \times 10^5 \text{ m s}^{-1}$$

The results of this experiment reveal two immediate surprises:

The first is that changing the intensity of the light (without changing the wavelength) does not affect the stopping voltage. Light from a candle and light from an airport searchlight release electrons of the same kinetic energy, and so the stopping voltage is the same, Figure 22.3. Higher intensity means more electrons are emitted with no change in kinetic energy.

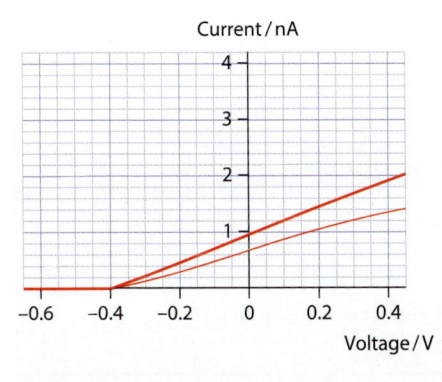

Figure 22.3: The stopping voltage for weak light (thin line) and intense light (thick line) of the same frequency. The stopping voltage is independent of the intensity of the light source.

The second is that the kinetic energy of the emitted electrons increases with increasing light frequency. This means the stopping voltage also increases with frequency. This is shown in Figure 22.4: the violet curve corresponds to violet light and the green curve to green light of lower frequency. The stopping voltages are 0.40 V for green and 0.90 V for violet.

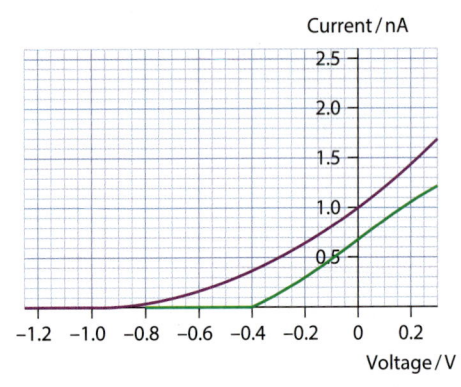

Figure 22.4: The stopping voltages for green and violet light.

> ### CHECK YOURSELF 3
>
> Which of the graphs, X or Y, in Figure 22.5 corresponds to light of higher frequency?
>
> **Figure 22.5:** For check yourself question 3.

If we plot the kinetic energy of the electrons (which equals eV_s) versus frequency, we find a straight line as shown in Figure 22.6a.

The puzzling feature of this graph is that there exists a frequency, called the critical (or threshold) frequency f_c, such that no electrons at all are emitted if the frequency of the light source is less than f_c. This is true even if very intense light is allowed to fall on the photo-surface.

When the experiment is repeated with a different photo-surface and the kinetic energy of the electrons is plotted versus frequency, a line parallel to the first is obtained, as shown in Figure 22.6b.

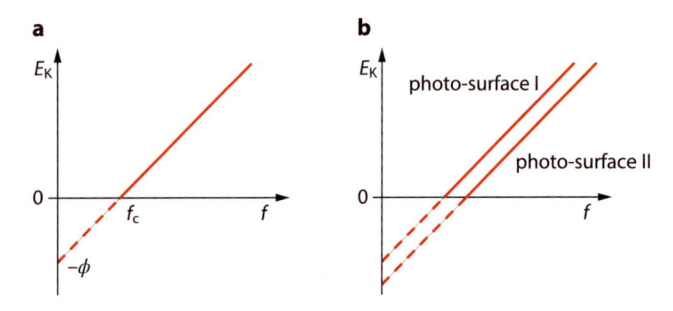

Figure 22.6: a The graph of kinetic energy versus frequency is a straight line. The horizontal intercept is the critical frequency, f_c. **b** When another photo-surface is used, a line parallel to the first is obtained.

The final puzzling observation in these experiments is that the electrons are emitted immediately after the light is incident on the photo-surface, with no apparent time delay.

> ### KEY POINT
>
> We now have four surprising observations:
>
> - The intensity of the incident light does not affect the energy of the emitted electrons.
> - The electron kinetic energy depends on the frequency of the incident light.
> - There is a certain minimum frequency of light below which no electrons are emitted.
> - Electrons are emitted with no time delay.

> ### CHECK YOURSELF 4
>
> The intensity of light incident on a metal is increased without any change to the wavelength. State the effect this change has on:
>
> a the kinetic energy of the emitted electrons
>
> b the rate at which electrons are emitted.

These four observations cannot be understood in terms of light as a wave for several reasons:

- If light is a wave, then an intense beam of light carries a lot of energy, and so it should cause the emission of more energetic electrons.
- The formula for the energy of a light wave does not include the frequency, and so frequency should play no role in the energy of the emitted electrons. For the same reason, there can be no explanation for why we have a critical frequency.
- Finally, a very low intensity beam of light carries little energy. An electron might have to wait for a considerable length of time before it accumulated enough energy to escape from the metal. This would cause a delay in its emission.

> **EXAM TIP**
>
> A simple analogy to see the difference between light as a wave and light as a particle is the following: imagine winning one million euro in a lottery. If this were to be given to you in the wave model of light you would have to wait 10 years to get all the money if the money were paid to you at a rate of 100 000 a year. In the photon model, all the money would be given to you at once.

Einstein's explanation

The explanation of all these strange observations was provided by Albert Einstein in 1905 (his 'annus mirabilis').

Einstein's mechanism for the photoelectric effect assumes that light is made up of photons, i.e. particles. A single photon of frequency f is absorbed by a single electron in the photo-surface, and so the electron's energy increases by hf. The electron will have to spend a certain amount of energy, ϕ, to free itself from the pull of the nuclei of the atoms of the photo-surface. The electron will be emitted (become free) if hf is bigger than ϕ. The difference $E_K = hf - \phi$ will be the kinetic energy E_K of the (now) free electron, Figure 22.7.

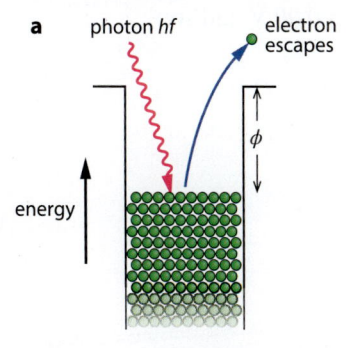

The value of ϕ (called the **work function**) is read off the graph in Figure 22.6, from the intercept of the straight line with the vertical axis. Note that the work function and the critical frequency are related by $hf_c = \phi$, since $E_K = 0$ when $f = f_c$.

In the photoelectric apparatus, the maximum kinetic energy of the electrons is measured to be $eV_s = E_{max}$. So, from $E_{max} = hf - \phi$, it follows that:

$$eV_s = hf - \phi$$
$$V_s = \frac{h}{e}f - \frac{\phi}{e}$$

That is, in a graph of *stopping voltage* against *frequency*, the graph is a straight line with slope $\frac{h}{e}$.

> **WORKED EXAMPLE 22.4**
>
> A photo-surface has a work function of 1.50 eV.
>
> **a** Determine the critical frequency.
>
> **b** Light of frequency 6.10×10^{14} Hz falls on this surface. Calculate the energy and speed of the emitted electrons.
>
> **Answer**
>
> **a** The critical frequency f_c is given in terms of the work function by $hf_c = \phi$ and thus:
>
> $$f_c = \frac{\phi}{h}$$
> $$= \frac{1.50 \times 1.6 \times 10^{-19}}{6.63 \times 10^{-34}}$$
> $$= 3.62 \times 10^{14} \text{ Hz}$$

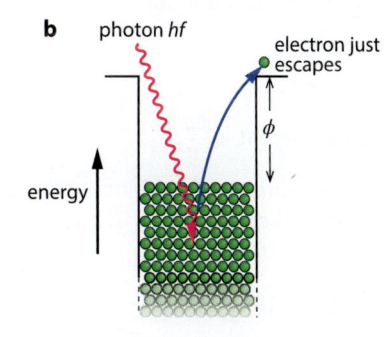

Figure 22.7: a A single photon of light may release a single electron from a metal. **b** A more tightly bound electron needs more energy to release it from the metal.

CONTINUED

b The maximum kinetic energy of the electron is $E_{max} = hf - \phi$, so:

$$E_{max} = hf - hf_c$$
$$= h(f - f_c)$$
$$= 6.63 \times 10^{-34} \times ((6.10 - 3.62) \times 10^{14})$$
$$= 1.64 \times 10^{-19} \text{ J}$$

From $E = \frac{1}{2}mv^2$ we find:

$$v = \sqrt{\frac{2E_{max}}{m}}$$
$$= \sqrt{\frac{2 \times 1.64 \times 10^{-19}}{9.1 \times 10^{-31}}}$$
$$= 6.0 \times 10^5 \text{ m s}^{-1}$$

EXAM TIP

Remember to use energy in joules for calculations.

WORKED EXAMPLE 22.5

Monochromatic light of intensity I and wavelength 4.0×10^{-7} m falling on a photo-surface whose critical frequency is 6.0×10^{14} Hz releases 2.0×10^{10} electrons per second.

a Determine the current leaving the surface.

b The intensity of the light is increased to $2I$. Predict the value of the new current.

c Light of intensity $2I$ and wavelength 6.0×10^{-7} m falls on this photo-surface. Determine the current in this case.

Answer

a The definition of electric current is $\frac{\Delta q}{\Delta t}$.

In a time of 1 second, the number of electrons emitted is 2.0×10^{10} and so the magnitude of the charge they carry is $e \times 2.0 \times 10^{10}$.

The current is thus $e \times 2.0 \times 10^{10}$, i.e. 3.2×10^{-9} A.

CONTINUED

b If the intensity doubles, the number of photons will double, and so the number of electrons emitted will double. Thus, so will the current, giving 6.4×10^{-9} A.

c The critical frequency f_c is 6.0×10^{14} Hz. The incident frequency is:

$$f = \frac{c}{\lambda}$$
$$= \frac{3 \times 10^8}{6.0 \times 10^{-7}}$$
$$= 5.0 \times 10^{14} \text{ Hz}$$

This is less than the critical frequency and so no electrons will be emitted at all.

WORKED EXAMPLE 22.6

The green light in Figure 22.4 has a wavelength of 496 nm.

a Determine the work function of the photo-surface.

b Estimate the wavelength of the violet light in that experiment.

Answer

a The stopping voltage is 0.40 V and so using $eV_s = hf - \phi$ we deduce that:

$$\phi = \frac{hc}{\lambda} - eV_s$$
$$= \frac{1.24 \times 10^{-6}}{4.96 \times 10^{-7}} - 0.40$$
$$= 2.10 \text{ eV}$$

b We again use $eV_s = hf - \phi$ to get that $\frac{hc}{\lambda} = eV_s + \phi$.

The stopping voltage is 0.90 V and so:

$$\frac{hc}{\lambda} = 0.90 + 2.1$$
$$= 3.0 \text{ eV}$$

Hence:

$$\lambda = \frac{hc}{3.0}$$
$$= \frac{1.24 \times 10^{-6}}{3.0}$$
$$= 4.1 \times 10^{-7} \text{ m}$$

> **EXAM TIP**
>
> Notice the use of $hc = 1.24 \times 10^{-6}$ eV m, which makes calculations much faster.

Compton scattering

We saw how Einstein's explanation of the photoelectric effect requires that light must be thought of as a stream of particles called photons. Even more convincing evidence for the particle nature of light is provided by **Compton scattering**. This is the scattering of light off an electron. The scattered light bounces off the electron with a longer wavelength. We can understand this in terms of photons easily: the light gives some energy to the electron which recoils with kinetic energy. The energy of the light has therefore been reduced. Thinking of light in terms of photons means that the energy of the photon is given by $E = \frac{hc}{\lambda}$ and so a reduced photon energy means an increased wavelength, which is what was observed in experiments carried out by Arthur Holly Compton in 1923.

Figure 22.8 shows a photon of wavelength λ that is incident on an electron at rest. The photon scatters off the electron in a direction making an angle θ with the original direction of the photon. The wavelength of the scattered photon is λ'. The electron gains kinetic energy and moves off in some direction.

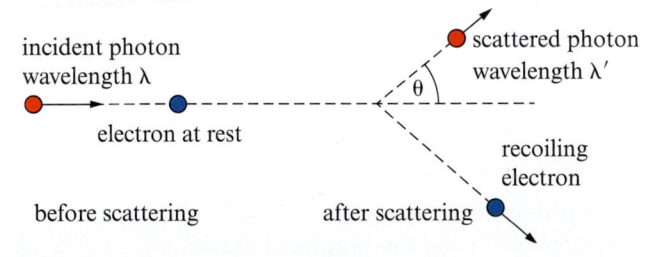

Figure 22.8: A photon incident on an electron scatters off the electron; the electron recoils.

This diagram should be compared to Figure 4.22 in Chapter 4. It is an identical diagram to the diagram we drew for a two-dimensional collision of two balls. Here the one 'ball' is replaced by a photon. The methods of Chapter 4 can be applied here as well, namely applying the laws of conservation of momentum and energy to derive the formula

$$\lambda' - \lambda = \frac{h}{m_e c}(1 - \cos\theta)$$

which relates the change in the wavelength to the scattering angle θ and the electron mass m_e. It is in this sense that Compton scattering is solid evidence that light behaves as particles. We treated the photon as if it were an ordinary particle with momentum in mechanics.

This formula is an interesting one. The presence of Planck's constant implies this is a quantum effect; this is not surprising since we are treating light as particles, photons, each of energy hf as Einstein said. But the speed of light c also enters the formula. Right away, this tells us that this is a relativistic effect which means we need the theory of relativity to derive this formula. (An end-of-chapter problem guiding to this derivation is provided for those interested.)

The largest wavelength shift occurs when $\theta = \pi$. In this case:

$$\lambda' - \lambda = \frac{h}{m_e c}(1 - \cos\pi) = \frac{h}{m_e c}(1 - (-1)) = \frac{2h}{m_e c},$$

and the energy transferred to the electron is the largest possible. The energy that is transferred to the electron is $\frac{hc}{\lambda} - \frac{hc}{\lambda'}$. There is no shift when $\theta = 0$.

The quantity $\frac{h}{m_e c}$ is known as the Compton wavelength. Its numerical value for the electron is

$$\frac{h}{m_e c} = \frac{6.63 \times 10^{-34}}{9.11 \times 10^{-31} \times 3.0 \times 10^8} \approx 2.4 \times 10^{-12} \text{ m}.$$

The smallness of this number means that observable effects are possible only with high-energy photons whose wavelength is comparable to this number (X-rays and gamma rays).

> **CHECK YOURSELF 5**
>
> Photons of energy 40 keV and 60 keV scatter off an electron with the same scattering angle. How do the wavelength shifts compare?

WORKED EXAMPLE 22.7

A photon of energy 54 keV is scattered off an electron at rest with a scattering angle of 82°.

a What is the shift in the photon wavelength?

b What energy is transferred to the electron?

Answer

a The shift is $\lambda' - \lambda = \frac{h}{mc}(1 - \cos\theta) = 2.4 \times 10^{-12} \times (1 - \cos 82°) = 2.1 \times 10^{-12}$ m.

b The incident photon wavelength is found from $\frac{hc}{\lambda} = 54 \times 10^3 \Rightarrow \lambda = \frac{hc}{54 \times 10^3} = \frac{1.24 \times 10^{-6}}{54 \times 10^3} \frac{\text{eV m}}{\text{eV}} = 2.3 \times 10^{-11}$ m. The scattered wavelength is $\lambda' = 2.3 \times 10^{-11} + 2.1 \times 10^{-12} = 2.5 \times 10^{-11}$ m. The difference in photon energies is therefore

$\frac{hc}{\lambda} - \frac{hc}{\lambda'} = 54 \times 10^3 - \frac{1.24 \times 10^{-6}}{2.5 \times 10^{-11}} = 4.4$ keV.

This is the energy transferred to the electron; it is about 8% of the original photon energy.

INTERNATIONAL MINDEDNESS

This list contains a few of the names associated with the development of quantum theory in the twentieth century: A. Einstein, N. Bohr, M. Planck, L. de Broglie, M. Born, E. Schrödinger, W. Heisenberg, W. Pauli, P. Dirac, R. Feynman. How many nationalities are represented here? In the twenty-first century, at the Large Hadron Collider at CERN alone, more than 10 000 scientists and engineers from dozens of laboratories and universities from more than 100 countries contribute to its development and operation. What does this say about how international mindedness in physics has evolved?

TEST YOUR UNDERSTANDING

1 A light source has power 60 W and emits photons of wavelength 550 nm. How many photons per second are emitted?

2 A beam of light of wavelength 620 nm is incident normally on a surface. The intensity of the beam at the surface is 25 W m^{-2}. How many photons are incident on the surface per unit time per unit area?

3 A beam of photons of intensity 660 W m^{-2} and wavelength 480 nm is incident normally on a surface. The photons are absorbed by the surface. What is the pressure exerted on the surface?

4 In an experiment, the stopping voltage was measured to be 0.32 V. What is the maximum kinetic energy of the emitted electrons?

5 In an experiment, electrons are emitted from a photo-surface with kinetic energy 1.8 eV. The photo-surface is at zero potential, and the collecting plate is at potential +2.2 V. What is the kinetic energy of the electrons as they arrive at the collecting plate?

6 In an experiment, electrons are emitted from a photo-surface with kinetic energy 2.1 eV. The photo-surface is at potential +1.2 V and the collecting plate is at zero potential. What is the kinetic energy of the electrons as they arrive at the collecting plate?

7 In photoelectric experiments with different photo-surfaces, the graphs of maximum electron kinetic energy versus light frequency are parallel straight lines. Why is that?

8 Light is incident on a photo-surface.

State and explain the change, if any, to the stopping voltage when the following two independent changes are made:

a the wavelength of the light stays the same but the intensity of the light increases

b the wavelength is decreased and the intensity of the light increases.

CONTINUED

9 A photo-surface is moving away at high speed from a source of monochromatic light that emits in all directions. State and explain what happens to:

  a the energy of the emitted electrons

  b the rate at which electrons are being emitted.

10 A photo-surface has a work function of 3.00 eV. Determine the critical frequency.

11 a What evidence is there for the existence of photons?

  b A photo-surface has a critical frequency of 2.25×10^{14} Hz. Radiation of frequency 3.87×10^{14} Hz falls on this surface. Deduce the stopping voltage.

12 Light of wavelength 5.4×10^{-7} m falls on a photo-surface and causes the emission of electrons of maximum kinetic energy 2.1 eV at a rate of 10^{15} per second. The light is emitted by a 60 W light bulb.

  a Explain how light causes the emission of electrons.

  b Calculate the electric current that leaves the photo-surface.

  c Determine the work function of the surface.

  d Estimate the maximum kinetic energy of the electrons when the power of the light becomes 120 W.

  e Estimate the current from the photo-surface when the power is 120 W.

13 a State *three* aspects of the photoelectric effect that cannot be explained by the wave theory of light. For each, outline how the photon theory provides an explanation.

  b Light of wavelength 2.08×10^{-7} m falls on a photo-surface. The stopping voltage is 1.40 V.

  i Outline what is meant by *stopping voltage*.

  ii Calculate the largest wavelength of light that will result in emission of electrons from this photo-surface.

14 a The intensity of the light incident on a photo-surface is doubled while the wavelength of light stays the same. For the emitted electrons, discuss the effect of this, if any, on:

  i the energy of the electrons emitted

  ii the number of electrons emitted.

  b To determine the work function of a given photo-surface, light of wavelength 2.3×10^{-7} m is directed at the surface and the stopping voltage, V_s, recorded. When light of wavelength 1.8×10^{-7} m is used, the stopping voltage is twice as large as the previous one. Determine the work function.

15 Light falling on a metallic surface of work function 3.0 eV gives energy to the surface at a rate of 5.0×10^{-4} W per square metre of the metal's surface. Assume that an electron on the metal surface can absorb energy from an area of about 1.0×10^{-18} m².

  a Estimate how long will it will take the electron to absorb an amount of energy equal to the work function.

  b Outline the implication of this.

  c Describe how the photon theory of light explains the fact that electrons are emitted almost instantaneously with the incoming photons.

16 a From the graph (Figure 22.9) of electron kinetic energy E_k versus frequency of incoming radiation, deduce:

  i the critical frequency of the photo-surface

  ii the work function.

b What is the kinetic energy of an electron ejected when light of frequency $f = 8.0 \times 10^{14}$ Hz falls on the surface?

c Another photo-surface has a critical frequency of 6.0×10^{14} Hz. On a copy of Figure 22.9, sketch the variation with frequency of the emitted electrons' kinetic energy.

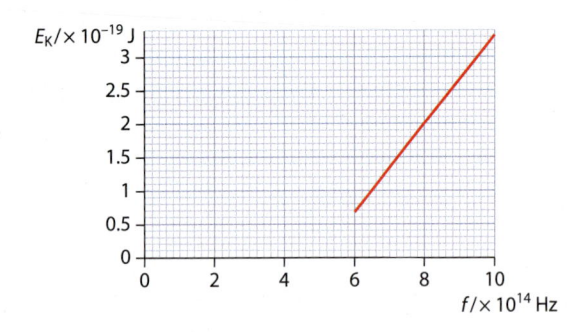

Figure 22.9: For question 16.

d Hence explain why light of wavelength $\lambda = 4.0 \times 10^{-7}$ m and of the same intensity as that of light of wavelength $\lambda = 5.0 \times 10^{-7}$ m will result in fewer electrons being emitted from the surface per second.

e State *one* assumption made in reaching this conclusion.

18 If a photon scatters off an entire atom instead of a single electron, how would you expect the wavelength shifts to compare for the same scattering angle?

19 What is the wavelength shift when a photon of wavelength 4.0×10^{-12} m scatters off an electron at rest with a scattering angle of 120°?

20 What is the wavelength shift when a photon of wavelength 4.0×10^{-12} m scatters off a *proton* at rest with a scattering angle of 120°?

17 This question will look at the intensity of radiation in a bit more detail. The intensity of light, *I*, incident normally on an area *A* is defined to be $I = \frac{P}{A}$, where *P* is the power carried by the light.

a Show that $I = \Phi h f$, where Φ is the photon flux density, i.e. the number of photons incident on the surface per second per unit area, and *f* is the frequency of the light.

b Calculate the intensity of light of wavelength $\lambda = 5.0 \times 10^{-7}$ m incident on a surface when the photon flux density is $\Phi = 3.8 \times 10^{18}$ m^{-2} s^{-1}.

c The wavelength of the light is decreased to $\lambda = 4.0 \times 10^{-7}$ m. Calculate the new photon flux density so that the intensity of light incident on the surface is the same as that found in **b**.

21 In a Compton scattering experiment the incident photon has wavelength λ and the scattered photon has wavelength λ'. Show that the fraction of the *incident* photon energy that is transferred to the electron is given by $\frac{\lambda' - \lambda}{\lambda'}$.

22 How much energy is transferred to the electron for a photon scattering angle of 0°?

23 A photon of wavelength 3.0×10^{-12} m scatters off an electron at rest with a scattering angle of 90°. How much energy is transferred to the electron?

24 a Using your graphics calculator or otherwise, find the angle at which the energy transferred to an electron during Compton scattering is a maximum.

b If the maximum energy that can be transferred to an electron is 30 keV, what is the wavelength of the incident photon?

CONTINUED

25 Derivation of the Compton formula—*not for exam purposes.*

Refer to Figure 22.8.

a Show by applying conservation of momentum that the momentum components of the electron after the photon scatters off it are $p_x = \frac{h}{\lambda} - \frac{h}{\lambda'}\cos\theta$ and $p_y = \frac{h}{\lambda'}\sin\theta$.

b Hence deduce that $p^2 = p_x^2 + p_y^2 = \left(\frac{h}{\lambda'}\right)^2 + \left(\frac{h}{\lambda}\right)^2 - \frac{2h^2\cos\theta}{\lambda\lambda'}$.

c Now apply energy conservation. You will need the result from relativity that the total energy of an electron of momentum p is given by $E = \sqrt{p^2c^2 + (mc^2)^2}$. What is the total energy of an electron at rest? Therefore deduce that energy conservation leads to

$$\frac{hc}{\lambda} + mc^2 = \frac{hc}{\lambda'} + \sqrt{p^2c^2 + (mc^2)^2}$$

d Isolate the term with the square root, square both sides and then use the result in **b**. After a few lines of algebra you should get the Compton formula.

22.2 Matter waves

In 1923, Louis de Broglie suggested that to any particle of momentum p there corresponds a wave of wavelength given by the formula (h is Planck's constant):

$$\lambda = \frac{h}{p}$$

The de Broglie hypothesis, as this is known, thus assigns wave-like properties to something that is normally thought to be a particle. This state of affairs is called the **duality of matter**. All moving particles (not just electrons) are assigned a wavelength.

What does it mean to say that the electron has wave-like properties? One thing it does *not* mean is to think that the electron oscillates up and down as it moves along. Having wave-like properties means exhibiting the two basic phenomena of waves: diffraction and interference. A wave of wavelength λ will diffract around an obstacle of size d if λ is comparable to or bigger than d. In worked example 22.8 we calculate a typical electron wavelength to be of order 10^{-10} m. This distance is typical of the separation of atoms in crystals, and it is there that electron diffraction and interference will be seen.

But what does a matter wave actually represent? What kind of wave is it? The answer to this question came long after de Broglie announced his hypothesis and played a key role in the development of quantum mechanics, through the work of E. Schrödinger and M. Born: the interpretation given was that the matter wave is a wave of probability. The square of the amplitude of the wave is proportional to the probability of finding the particle near a particular point in space at a particular time.

WORKED EXAMPLE 22.8

Find the de Broglie wavelength of an electron that has been accelerated from rest by a potential difference of 54 V.

Answer

The kinetic energy of the electron is given by $E_K = \frac{p^2}{2m}$.

The work done in accelerating the electron through a potential difference V is qV, and this work goes into kinetic energy:

$$\frac{p^2}{2m} = qV \Rightarrow p = \sqrt{2mqV}$$

So:

$$\lambda = \frac{h}{\sqrt{2mqV}}$$

$$= \frac{6.63 \times 10^{-34}}{\sqrt{2 \times 9.1 \times 10^{-31} \times 1.60 \times 10^{-19} \times 54}}$$

$$= 1.7 \times 10^{-10} \text{ m}$$

EXAM TIP

It is preferable to use $E_K = \frac{p^2}{2m}$ for kinetic energy rather than $E_K = \frac{1}{2}mv^2$.

The formula $\lambda = \frac{h}{\sqrt{2mqV}}$ is very useful in paper 1 questions, where it is often required to know that $\lambda \propto \frac{1}{\sqrt{V}}$.

Experiments showing the wave nature of the electron were carried out in 1927 by Clinton J. Davisson (1881–1958) and Lester H. Germer (1896–1971), and also by George Thomson (1892–1975), son of J. J. Thomson, the discoverer of the electron. In the Davisson–Germer experiment, electrons of kinetic energy 54 eV were directed at a surface of nickel where a single crystal had been grown and were scattered by it (Figure 22.10).

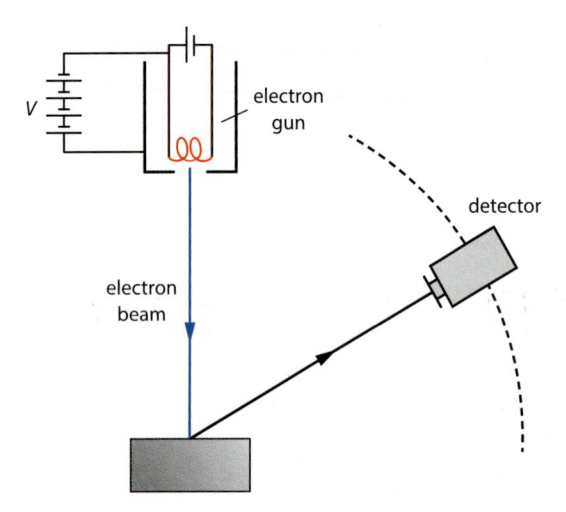

Figure 22.10: The apparatus of Davisson and Germer. Electrons emitted from the hot filament of the electron gun are accelerated through a known potential difference V and are then allowed to fall on a crystal. The positions of the scattered electrons are recorded by a detector.

Figure 22.11 shows rays of a wave incident on layers of crystal atoms. The wave scatters off atoms in two layers. The distance between the layers is d. The path difference between the two rays is indicated in thick lines and equals $d \sin\theta + d \sin\theta = 2d \sin\theta$.

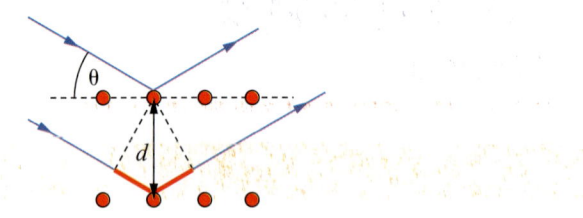

Figure 22.11: Waves scattering off atoms in two layers of the crystal. The path difference is $2d \sin\theta$.

When this path difference is an integer number of the wavelength, $2d \sin\theta = n\lambda$, constructive interference takes place i.e. a maximum in the intensity of the scattered wave. In the Davisson-Germer experiment it was known that $d = 0.107$ nm. The first maximum ($n = 1$) was observed at an angle $\theta = 50°$ which means that the number of electrons observed at this angle was a maximum. Hence $\lambda = 2 \times 0.107 \times 10^{-9} \times \sin 50° = 1.64 \times 10^{-10}$ m.

We have already calculated the de Broglie wavelength of the electron that had been accelerated by a potential difference 54 V in worked example 22.8; it was found to be 1.7×10^{-10} m. This is in excellent agreement with the experiment, thus verifying the de Broglie hypothesis.

CHECK YOURSELF 6

Electrons, protons and alpha particles pass through a narrow slit with the same speed. Which will produce the widest diffraction pattern?

WORKED EXAMPLE 22.9

Show that the Bohr condition for the quantisation of angular momentum is equivalent to $2\pi r = n\lambda$, where λ is the de Broglie wavelength of the electron and r the radius of its orbit.

Answer

The Bohr condition is that:

$mvr = \dfrac{nh}{2\pi}$

This can be rewritten as:

$2\pi r = \dfrac{nh}{mv}$

But according to de Broglie:

$\dfrac{h}{mv} = \lambda$

So we have the result.

The result of worked example 22.9 shows that the allowed orbits in the Bohr model of hydrogen are those for which an integral number of electron wavelengths fit on the circumference of the orbit. Figure 22.12 shows the electron wave for $n = 6$. The circle in blue is the actual orbit. The solid red and the dotted red lines show the extremes of the electron wave. This is reminiscent of standing waves: the electron wave is a standing wave on the circumference. We know that standing waves do not transfer energy. This is a partial way to understand why the electrons do not radiate when in the allowed orbits.

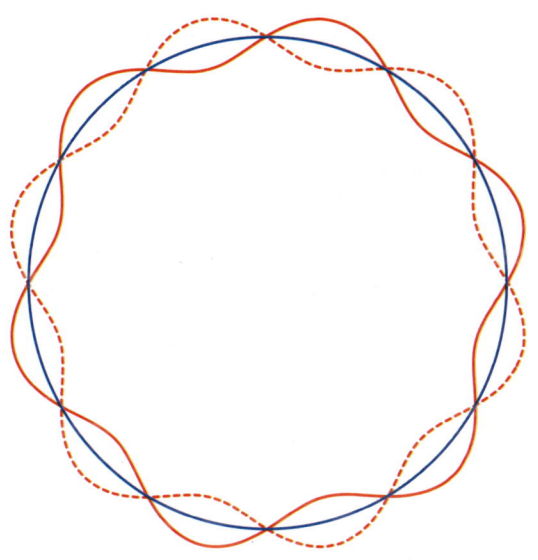

Figure 22.12: The allowed electron orbits are those for which an integral number of electron wavelengths fits on the circumference of the orbit.

> **THEORY OF KNOWLEDGE**
>
> Davisson and Germer investigated the scattering of low-energy electrons from a nickel surface. Initial results showed that, for fixed electron energy, the intensity of the electron beam decreased sharply as the scattering angle θ increased. A container of liquid air was accidentally dropped, breaking the glass jar housing the apparatus and exposing the nickel surface (which was surrounded by vacuum) to air, oxidising it. To remove the oxide, Davisson and Germer heated the surface in an atmosphere of hydrogen. The scattering of electrons was continued but now the results were very different. The intensity of the scattered electron beam varied strongly with scattering angle. After much thought, Davisson and Germer realised that they were dealing with scattering from a single crystal of nickel (that had grown on the surface as a result of heating it). Using crystals of known interatomic spacing, they eventually concluded they were seeing electron diffraction with a wavelength given by the de Broglie formula.

Links

How can electrons diffract? In Section 14.2 we learned about the principle of superposition and in Section 14.3 about diffraction and interference of waves. The key idea there was that depending on the path (or phase) difference between two waves that meet the resultant wave may have a large amplitude or zero amplitude. What is the amplitude involved with electrons? It is not the actual displacement of the electron but an abstract quantity called the electron wavefunction, about which you may want to learn more.

> **TEST YOUR UNDERSTANDING**
>
> 26 A proton and an alpha particle have the same momentum. What is the ratio $\frac{\lambda_p}{\lambda_a}$ of de Broglie wavelengths?
>
> 27 A proton and an alpha particle have the same speed. What is the ratio $\frac{\lambda_p}{\lambda_a}$ of de Broglie wavelengths?
>
> 28 A proton and an alpha particle have the same kinetic energy. What is the ratio $\frac{\lambda_p}{\lambda_a}$ of de Broglie wavelengths?
>
> 29 Consider a brick of mass 0.250 kg moving at 10 m s^{-1}.
>
>   a Estimate its de Broglie wavelength.
>
>   b Comment on whether it makes sense to treat the brick as a wave.
>
> 30 a Describe an experiment in which the de Broglie wavelength of an electron can be measured directly.
>
>   b Determine the speed of an electron whose de Broglie wavelength is equal to that of red light (680 nm).

CONTINUED

31 **a** Show that the de Broglie wavelength of an electron that has been accelerated from rest through a potential difference V is given by $\lambda = \dfrac{h}{\sqrt{2meV}}$.

   b Calculate the ratio of the de Broglie wavelength of a proton to that of an alpha particle when both have been accelerated from rest by the same potential difference.

   c Calculate the de Broglie wavelength of an electron accelerated from rest through a potential difference of 520 V.

32 Find the de Broglie wavelength of a proton (mass 1.67×10^{-27} kg) whose kinetic energy is 200.0 MeV.

33 What is the de Broglie wavelength of an electron in the $n = 2$ state of hydrogen? Give your answer in terms of the Bohr radius.

34 What is the ratio of the de Broglie wavelength of the electron in the $n = 2$ state of hydrogen to that in the $n = 3$ state?

35 A beam of electrons moving left to right is incident on an aperture of size 8×10^{-10} m, as shown in Figure 22.13. Each electron has kinetic energy 5.0 eV.

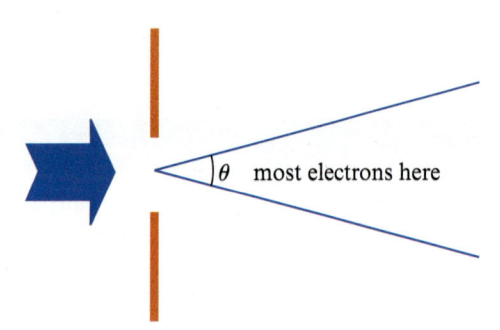

Figure 22.13: For question 35.

Most of the electrons will be observed within an angle θ.

   a Explain why the electrons do not continue to move strictly left to right.

   b Estimate the angle θ.

36 **This is a continuation of question 35.**

The electrons must have acquired a small vertical component of momentum, Δp_y, as a result of going through the aperture, as shown in Figure 22.14.

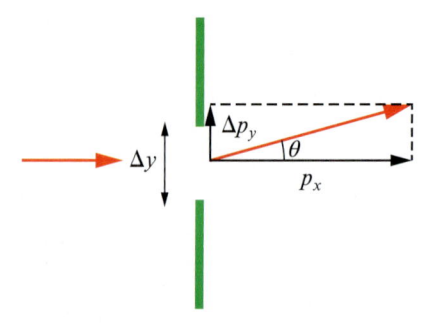

Figure 22.14: For question 36.

If the aperture size is Δy, show that $\Delta y \times \Delta p_y \approx h$.

37 Show that the quantity $\sqrt{\dfrac{hG}{2\pi c^5}}$ has units of time and the quantity $\sqrt{\dfrac{hG}{2\pi c^3}}$ units of length (h = Planck constant, G = Newton constant of gravitation, c = speed of light). These are called Planck time and Planck length. Evaluate these quantities. Do some research on their significance.

22 Quantum physics

SELF-ASSESSMENT CHECKLIST

I am able to ...	Section	Not yet	Nearly there	Ready to move on
describe the concept of a photon	22.1			
calculate the energy of a photon from its frequency or wavelength	22.1			
describe the photoelectric effect	22.1			
understand the terms *stopping voltage* and *critical frequency*	22.1			
explain the features of the photoelectric effect in terms of photons	22.1			
understand why the features of the photoelectric effect are not compatible with light as a wave	22.1			
calculate the wavelength shift in Compton scattering	22.1			
describe the de Broglie hypothesis	22.2			
calculate the de Broglie wavelength	22.2			
describe an experiment that supports the wavelike characteristics of an electron	22.2			

REFLECTION

Can you describe light in terms of *photons*? Can you explain the main features of the *photoelectric effect*? Do you understand the role of frequency and of intensity in the *photoelectric effect*? Do you understand why the *Compton effect* is significant? Can you apply the Compton formula? How would you describe the concept of *matter waves*? Can you provide the experimental evidence for matter waves?

EXAM-STYLE QUESTIONS

You can find questions in the style of IB exams in the digital coursebook.

CHECK YOURSELF ANSWERS

1. Blue, since $E = hf$ and blue has larger frequency.
2. Since the energy of each photon increases, their number has to decrease to keep the intensity the same.
3. X because the stopping voltage is greater, so kinetic energy of electrons is greater so photon energy is greater.
4. a The energy of the electrons does not change.
   b The number of emitted electrons is proportional to intensity so the number of electrons will increase.
5. The shift is independent of the incoming wavelength so they are the same.
6. Electrons, since they will have the longest wavelength.

Chapter 23
Nuclear physics

LEARNING OBJECTIVES

In this chapter you will learn how to:

- use the nuclear notation.
- understand the fundamental forces between particles.
- recognize isotopes
- use the concept of mass defect and binding energy
- solve problems with mass defect and binding energy.
- calculate the energy released in nuclear reactions.
- describe the variation with nucleon number of the average binding energy per nucleon.
- understand radioactive decay, including background radiation, and work with radioactive decay equations.
- recognize the properties of alpha, beta and gamma particles.

> understand basic nuclear properties.
> calculate the distance of closest approach

23 Nuclear physics

> **CONTINUED**
> - evaluate the evidence for the strong nuclear force
> - recognize why the existence of the neutrino was postulated.
> - use nuclear energy levels
> - work with the radioactive decay law.

> **GUIDING QUESTIONS**
> - What are the forces acting inside a nucleus?
> - Why are some nuclei stable and others unstable?

Introduction

This chapter is an introduction to the physics of atomic nuclei. We will investigate the stability of nuclei and find out that most nuclei are unstable and decay by emitting particles and energy. We will learn methods to calculate the energy released in nuclear reactions. The discreteness that we have met earlier in the atomic world will appear again at the nuclear level.

23.1 Mass defect and binding energy

Nuclear notation

We now move deep into the atom in order to describe the structure of its nucleus. Atomic nuclei are made up of smaller particles, called protons and neutrons. The word **nucleon** is used to denote a proton or a neutron.

The number of protons in a nucleus is denoted by Z and is called the **proton number**.

The total number of nucleons (protons + neutrons) is called the **nucleon number** and is denoted by A.

The number of neutrons in a nucleus is denoted by N and $N = A - Z$.

The electric charge of the nucleus is Ze, where $e = +1.6 \times 10^{-19}$ C is the charge of a proton. We use the proton and nucleon numbers to denote a nucleus in the following way: the symbol $^A_Z X$ stands for the nucleus of element X, whose proton number is Z and nucleon number is A. For example:

$^1_1 H$	hydrogen nucleus with 1 proton and no neutrons
$^4_2 He$	helium nucleus with 2 protons and 2 neutrons
$^{40}_{20} Ca$	calcium nucleus with 20 protons and 20 neutrons
$^{238}_{92} U$	uranium nucleus with 92 protons and 146 neutrons

A nucleus with a specific number of protons and neutrons is also called a **nuclide**.

> **CHECK YOURSELF 1**
> How many neutrons are there in the nucleus $^{21}_{10} Ne$?

We can apply this notation to the nucleons themselves. For example, the proton (symbol p) can be written as $^1_1 p$ and the neutron (symbol n) as $^1_0 n$. If we notice that the proton number is not only the number of protons in the nucleus but also its electric charge in units of e, then we can extend this notation to electrons as well. The charge of the electron in units of e is -1 and so we represent the electron by $^0_{-1} e$. The nucleon number of the electron is zero since the nucleon number is defined as the total number of neutrons plus protons.

The photon (the particle of light) can also be represented in this way: the photon has the Greek letter

479

gamma (γ) as its symbol. Since it has zero electric charge and is neither a proton nor a neutron, it is represented by $^0_0\gamma$.

The neutrino (we will learn more about this later) is neutral and is represented by $^0_0\nu$.

For every particle in nature, there exists an anti-particle: this is a particle with the same mass as the particle but all other properties, including electric charge, are opposite. Some neutral particles are identical with their antiparticle (the photon for example), but others are not (the neutron for example). Anti-neutrons are distinguished from neutrons by other properties that we will not discuss here. Ordinary matter is made of protons, neutrons and electrons. Table 23.1 gives a summary of these particles and their symbols.

Particle	Symbol
proton	$^1_1 p$
anti-proton	$^1_{-1} \bar{p}$
neutron	$^1_0 n$
anti-neutron	$^1_0 \bar{n}$
electron	$^0_{-1} e$
positron	$^0_{+1} e$
photon	$^0_0 \gamma$ (or just γ)
neutrino	$^0_0 \nu$ (or just ν)
anti-neutrino	$^0_0 \bar{\nu}$ (or just $\bar{\nu}$)
alpha particle	$^4_2 He$ or $^4_2 \alpha$

Table 23.1: Some particles and their symbols

Fundamental forces

There are four fundamental interactions or forces in nature. (Knowledge of the weak nuclear force and the electroweak force is not required in this course.)

These are:

1. the **electromagnetic interaction**: it acts on any particle that has electric charge. The force is given by Coulomb's law. It has infinite range.

2. the **weak nuclear interaction**: it acts on protons, neutrons, electrons and neutrinos in order to bring about beta decay. It has very short range (10^{-18} m).

3. the **strong nuclear interaction**: it acts on protons and neutrons to keep them bound to each other inside nuclei. It has short range (10^{-15} m).

4. the **gravitational interaction**: it acts on any particle with mass. The small mass of atomic particles makes this force irrelevant for atomic and nuclear physics. It has infinite range.

(It is known that the electromagnetic interaction and the weak interaction are two sides of one force—the **electroweak interaction**.)

CHECK YOURSELF 2

Nuclei contain protons which repel each other electrically. Why then don't nuclei break apart?

Isotopes

Nuclei of the same element have the same number of protons but may have different number of neutrons; these are called **isotopes** of each other.

KEY POINT

Isotopes have the same proton number Z but different neutron number N and nucleon number A.

For example, $^1_1 H$, $^2_1 H$ and $^3_1 H$ are three isotopes of hydrogen, and $^{235}_{92}U$, $^{236}_{92}U$ and $^{238}_{92}U$ are just three (of many) isotopes of uranium. Since isotopes have the same number of protons, their atoms have the same number of electrons as well. This means that isotopes have identical chemical properties but different physical properties. The existence of isotopes is evidence for the existence of neutrons inside atomic nuclei.

CHECK YOURSELF 3

How many electrons are there in each of the neutral atoms of $^{48}_{22}Ti$ and $^{50}_{22}Ti$?

The atomic mass unit

In atomic and nuclear physics, it is convenient to use a smaller unit of mass than the kilogram.

> **KEY POINT**
>
> The **atomic mass unit** is defined to be $\frac{1}{12}$ of the mass of an atom of carbon-12, $^{12}_{6}C$.

The symbol for the atomic mass unit is u. In terms of the kg, $1\ u = 1.6605402 \times 10^{-27}$ kg.

As we will see in the next worked example, this means that the mass of a proton and the mass of a neutron are both *approximately* equal to 1 u. In turn this means that a nucleus with nucleon number A has a mass that is approximately A u.

> **WORKED EXAMPLE 23.1**
>
> Determine to six decimal places, in units of u, the masses of the proton, neutron and electron. Use $m_p = 1.6726231 \times 10^{-27}$ kg, $m_n = 1.6749286 \times 10^{-27}$ kg, and $m_e = 9.1093897 \times 10^{-31}$ kg.
>
> **Answer**
>
> Using the relationship between u and kg, we find:
>
> $m_p = \frac{1.6726231 \times 10^{-27}}{1.6605402 \times 10^{-27}} = 1.007276$ u
>
> Similarly:
>
> $m_n = 1.008665$ u
>
> $m_e = 0.0005486$ u
>
> (This shows that, approximately, $m_p \approx m_n \approx 1$ u).

The mass defect and binding energy

Protons and neutrons are very tightly bound to each other in a nucleus through the action of the strong nuclear force. To separate them, energy must be supplied to the nucleus. Conversely, energy is released when a nucleus is assembled from its constituent nucleons.

In Einstein's theory of relativity, a mass m is equivalent to an energy E according to the equation:

$E = mc^2$

where c is the speed of light.

It is very convenient to find out how much energy corresponds to a mass of 1 u. Then, given a mass in u, we can easily find the energy that mass corresponds to. The energy corresponding to 1 u is:

$1\ u \times c^2 = 1.6605402 \times 10^{-27} \times (2.9979 \times 10^8)^2$ J

$= 1.4923946316 \times 10^{-10}$ J

Changing this to eV, using $1\ eV = 1.602177 \times 10^{-19}$ J, gives an energy equivalent to a mass of 1 u of:

$\frac{1.4923946316 \times 10^{-10}\ J}{1.602177 \times 10^{-19}\ J\,eV^{-1}} = 931.5 \times 10^6\ eV = 931.5$ MeV

So:

$1\ u \times c^2 = 931.5$ MeV   or $1\ u = 931.5$ MeV c^{-2}

Let us find the energy equivalent of the mass of a proton, a neutron and an electron whose masses in u are $m_p = 1.007276$ u, $m_n = 1.008665$ u and $m_e = 0.0005486$ u.

For the proton, the energy is $m_p c^2$: $1.007276\ u \times c^2 = 1.007276 \times 931.5$ MeV $c^{-2} \times c^2 = 938.3$ MeV

> **KEY POINT**
>
> We multiply the mass in u by 931.5 to get the energy in MeV.

For the neutron, the energy equivalent is 1.008665×931.5 MeV $c^{-2} \times c^2 = 939.6$ MeV.

And for the electron: $0.0005486 \times 931.5 = 0.511$ MeV.

Notice that the mass-energy equivalence allows us to express mass in a new unit: for the proton for example we know that $m_p c^2 = 938$ MeV. We can then say that $m_p = 938$ MeV c^{-2}. Similarly, for the neutron, $m_n = 940$ MeV c^{-2}. The energy equivalent to the mass of a nucleus of helium-4 is 3727 MeV and so the mass of the nucleus may also be expressed as 3727 MeV c^{-2}. To convert a mass in MeV c^{-2} to u we divide by 931.5. So if $m = 1800$ MeV c^{-2}, the mass in u is $\frac{1800}{931.5} \approx 1.93$ u.

Since we must supply energy to a nucleus to separate the nucleons and since energy is equivalent to mass, it follows that the total mass of the separated nucleons is greater than the mass of the nucleus.

Take the nucleus of helium, ^4_2He, as an example. The mass of a neutral atom of helium is 4.0026 u. This includes the mass of two electrons. So the nuclear mass is:

$M_{nucleus} = (4.0026 - 2 \times 0.0005486)$ u $= 4.0015$ u

The helium nucleus is made up of two protons and two neutrons. Adding their masses we find:

$2m_p + 2m_n = 2 \times 1.007276 + 2 \times 1.008665 = 4.031882$ u.

This is larger than the mass of the nucleus by 0.030382 u. This leads to the concept of **mass defect**.

> **KEY POINT**
>
> The mass defect μ is the total mass of the nucleons minus the mass of the nucleus.

This can be written as:

$\mu = Zm_p + Nm_n - M_{nucleus}$

where $N = A - Z$ is the number of neutrons in the nucleus. Because $M_{nucleus} = M_{atom} - Zm_e$ where m_e is the mass of an electron, we can rewrite the mass defect as

$\mu = Zm_p + Nm_n - (M_{atom} - Zm_e) = Z(m_p + m_e) + Nm_n - M_{atom}$.

But $m_p + m_e = 1.007825$ u is the mass of the hydrogen atom, M_H, and so a more useful formula is

$\mu = ZM_H + Nm_n - M_{atom}$

(This is more useful because tables usually give atomic masses rather than nuclear masses.)

> **WORKED EXAMPLE 23.2**
>
> Find the mass defect of the nucleus of gold, $^{197}_{79}$Au, whose nuclear mass is 196.923229 u and that of iron, $^{54}_{26}$Fe, whose atomic mass is 53.939611 u.
>
> **Answer**
>
> For gold, we have been given the nuclear mass directly; the nucleus has 79 protons and 118 neutrons, so:
>
> $\mu = (79 \times 1.007276$ u$) + (118 \times 1.008665$ u$) - 196.923229$ u $= 1.674$ u.
>
> For iron we use the second formula in terms of atomic mass to get
>
> $\mu = (26 \times 1.007825$ u$) + (28 \times 1.008665$ u$) - 53.939611$ u $= 0.5065$ u.

The energy equivalent to the mass defect is called **binding energy**.

> **KEY POINT**
>
> The binding energy, E_b, of a nucleus is the minimum energy required to completely separate the nucleons of that nucleus: $E_b = \mu c^2$.

The energy required to remove *one* nucleon from the nucleus is roughly the binding energy divided by the total number of nucleons. Thus, the binding energy per nucleon is a measure of how tightly bound the nucleus is—the higher the binding energy per nucleon, the more tightly bound the nucleus.

The binding energy of gold-197 is $1.674 \times 931.5 = 1559$ MeV and so the binding energy per nucleon is $b = \frac{1559}{197} = 7.914$ MeV. The binding energy for iron-54 is $0.5065 \times 931.5 = 471.8$ MeV with a binding energy per nucleon of $b = \frac{471.8}{54} = 8.737$ MeV.

> **WORKED EXAMPLE 23.3**
>
> Determine the binding energy per nucleon of the nucleus of carbon-12.
>
> **Answer**
>
> The atomic mass is 12.000000 u, and we will use $\mu = ZM_H + Nm_n - M_{atom}$.
>
> The nucleus has 6 protons and 6 neutrons, so the mass defect is:
>
> $\mu = (6 \times 1.007825$ u$) + (6 \times 1.008665$ u$) - 12.000000$ u $= 0.098940$ u
>
> Hence the binding energy is:
>
> 0.098940×931.5 MeV $= 92.163$ MeV.
>
> The binding energy per nucleon is then:
>
> $b = \frac{92.163}{12} = 7.68$ MeV.

23 Nuclear physics

The binding energy curve

Figure 23.1 shows the variation with nucleon number A of the binding energy (E_b) per nucleon, $b = \frac{E_b}{A}$.

The main features of the graph are:

- The binding energy per nucleon for hydrogen, $^{1}_{1}\text{H}$, is zero because there is only one particle in the nucleus and there is nothing to separate.
- The curve rises sharply for low values of A.
- The curve has a maximum for $A = 62$ corresponding to nickel, which makes this nucleus particularly stable.
- There are peaks at the position of the nuclei $^{4}_{2}\text{He}$, $^{12}_{6}\text{C}$ and $^{16}_{8}\text{O}$, which makes these nuclei unusually stable compared to their immediate neighbours.
- The curve drops gently from the peak at $A = 62$ and onwards.
- Most nuclei have a binding energy per nucleon between 7 and 9 MeV.

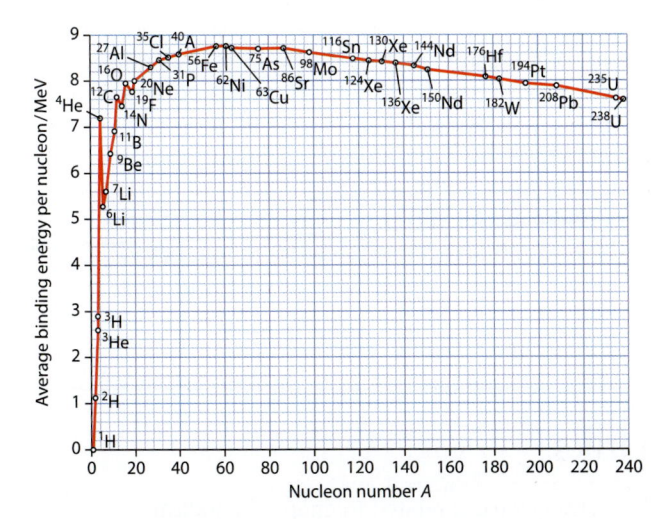

Figure 23.1: The binding energy per nucleon is almost constant for nuclei with $A > 20$.

Energy released in nuclear reactions

The reactions $^{226}_{88}\text{Ra} \rightarrow\ ^{222}_{86}\text{Rn} +\ ^{4}_{2}\alpha$, $^{14}_{7}\text{N} +\ ^{4}_{2}\alpha \rightarrow\ ^{17}_{8}\text{O} +\ ^{1}_{1}\text{p}$ and $^{2}_{1}\text{H} +\ ^{6}_{3}\text{Li} \rightarrow\ ^{4}_{2}\text{He} +\ ^{4}_{2}\text{He}$ are all examples of nuclear reactions in which a nucleus may split into other nuclei or nuclei collide and form new nuclei and nucleons. Notice that the total proton number on the left of the reaction is equal to the total proton number on the right. This is a consequence of electric charge conservation. The nucleon numbers on the left and right also match. This is consequence of nucleon number conservation (formally known as baryon number conservation).

To decide whether energy is released in any nuclear reaction, we have to calculate the mass difference Δm:

Δm = total mass of reactants − total mass of products

If Δm is positive, then energy will be released and the decay will occur. If Δm is negative, the reactants will not react and the reaction can take place only if energy is supplied.

We can see how this works by looking at the reaction:

$^{226}_{88}\text{Ra} \rightarrow\ ^{222}_{86}\text{Rn} +\ ^{4}_{2}\text{He}$

(This is a type of reaction called alpha decay, which we will meet later on.)

The masses involved are:

Ra-226: 226.0254 u	Rn-222: 222.0176 u	He-4: 4.0026 u

These are atomic masses; we should be using nuclear masses. To get the nuclear mass from the atomic mass we must subtract the mass of the electrons from the atomic mass. We need to subtract 88 electron masses from the left of the reaction and $86 + 2 = 88$ from the right, i.e. the same number. Since we will calculate the mass *difference*, using atomic or nuclear masses will give the same answer. When the number of electron masses that must be subtracted from each side is not the same, we need to use nuclear masses.

So the mass difference is:

$\Delta m = 226.0254\text{ u} - (222.0176 + 4.0026)\text{ u}$

$\Delta m = 226.0254\text{ u} - 226.0202\text{ u}$

$\Delta m = 0.0052\text{ u}$

This is positive, so energy will be released. The quantity of energy Q released is the energy equivalent of the mass difference and is given by:

$Q = 0.0052 \times 931.5\text{ MeV} = 4.84\text{ MeV}$

This energy is released in the form of kinetic energy, which is shared by the helium and radon nuclei. Helium, being much lighter than radon, has greater speed and greater kinetic energy as the next worked example shows.

WORKED EXAMPLE 23.4

Calculate the ratio of the kinetic energies of the helium nucleus to that of the radon nucleus in the decay of radium ($^{226}_{88}$Ra) to radon ($^{222}_{86}$Rn). Assume that the radium nucleus decays at rest. Determine how much energy the helium nucleus carries.

Answer

The radium nucleus is at rest, so the initial momentum is zero. By conservation of momentum, the momenta of the products are opposite in direction and equal in magnitude. Thus $p_{He} = p_{Rn}$.

Kinetic energy is related to momentum by $E_K = \frac{p^2}{2m}$, so:

$$\frac{E_{He}}{E_{Rn}} = \frac{\left(\frac{p_{He}^2}{2M_{He}}\right)}{\left(\frac{p_{Rn}^2}{2M_{Rn}}\right)}$$

$$= \frac{M_{Rn}}{M_{He}}$$

$$\approx \frac{222}{4}$$

$$\approx 56$$

This means that the energy carried by helium is $\frac{56}{57} \times 4.84 \approx 4.76$ MeV; in other words, practically all the energy released.

EXAM TIP

Momentum conservation applies to nuclear physics as well!

Consider the reaction in which an alpha particle collides with a nucleus of nitrogen producing a nucleus of oxygen and a proton:

$^{14}_{7}$N + $^{4}_{2}\alpha$ → $^{17}_{8}$O + $^{1}_{1}$p

Nuclear masses: m_N = 13.9992 u; m_α = 4.0015 u; m_O = 16.9947 u; m_p = 1.0073 u

This is a famous reaction called the transmutation of nitrogen; the nucleus produced (oxygen) is heavier than the original nucleus (nitrogen). It was studied by Rutherford in 1909.

In this reaction the mass difference is negative:

Δm = 18.0007 − 18.0020 = −0.0013 u

This reaction will only take place if the alpha particle has enough kinetic energy to make up for the deficit. The minimum kinetic energy needed is 0.0013 × 931.5 = 1.21 MeV. (But this is not quite correct. With this kinetic energy the total kinetic energy of the oxygen and the proton would be zero, and hence the total momentum of the products would also be zero. But this would violate conservation of momentum since the incoming alpha particle has kinetic energy and so must have non-zero momentum. A more careful calculation shows that the minimum kinetic energy required is about 1.53 MeV.)

THEORY OF KNOWLEDGE

The belief in unification

In the early nineteenth century there were three known forces: gravitational, electric and magnetic. Through the work of James Clerk Maxwell (1831–1879) physicists realised that electric and magnetic forces were two sides of the same force, the electromagnetic force. Thus began the notion (for some a belief, for others a prejudice) that all interactions, as more were being discovered, were part of the same 'unified' force. In the twentieth century two new forces were discovered: the weak nuclear force and the strong nuclear force. In the late 1960s the electromagnetic and the weak nuclear force were unified in the standard model of particles. All efforts to unify this electroweak force with the strong nuclear force in a grand unified force have failed. All attempts to unify any of these forces with gravity have also failed. Yet the dream of unification remains.

Links

Everything we did related to energy in nuclear reactions is based on the equivalence of mass and energy discovered by Einstein in his theory of relativity. A theory that rested on the postulate that the speed of light is a universal constant independent of the speed of the source of light has led to radical changes in Newtonian mechanics including the famous $E = mc^2$ equation that we have used heavily in the preceding chapters.

TEST YOUR UNDERSTANDING

1. State the electric charge of the nucleus $^3_2$He.

2. State the number of protons and the number of neutrons in the nucleus $^{209}_{82}$Pb.

3. What is the energy equivalent
   a. in J to a mass of 65 kg and
   b. in MeV to a mass of 65 u?

4. a. State what is meant by the term *isotope*.
   b. State *three* ways in which the nuclei of the isotopes $^{16}_8$O and $^{18}_8$O differ from each other.

5. What is the existence of isotopes evidence for?

6. Why are the chemical properties of isotopes of the same element identical?

7. Explain why a nucleus stays bound despite the fact that the protons in it repel each other.

8. State the name of the dominant force between two protons separated by a distance of:
   a. 1.0×10^{-15} m
   b. 1.0×10^{-10} m.

9. Why do we ignore the gravitational force in nuclear interactions?

10. Find the mass defect and binding energy of the nucleus $^7_3$Li. The nuclear mass is 7.0144 u.

11. Find the mass defect and binding energy of the nucleus $^{12}_7$N. The atomic mass is 12.0186 u.

12. The binding energy per nucleon of the nucleus $^{56}_{26}$Fe is 8.7903 MeV. What is the binding energy of this nucleus?

13. The binding energy per nucleon of $^{91}_{40}$Zr is 8.6933 MeV. What is the mass defect of this nuclide in MeV c^{-2} and in u?

14. The binding energy of the nucleus $^3_2$He is 7.7180 MeV. What is the nuclear mass of $^3_2$He in MeV c^{-2} and in u?

15. The binding energy per nucleon of $^{131}_{54}$Xe is 8.4237 MeV. What is the nuclear mass of $^{131}_{54}$Xe in MeV c^{-2} and in u?

16. Find the binding energy and binding energy per nucleon of the nucleus $^{62}_{28}$Ni. The atomic mass is 61.9283 u.

17. The isotopes $^{12}_6$C and $^{13}_6$C are both stable. Which nucleus is more tightly bound? The atomic mass of carbon-13 is 13.0033 u.

18. Identify particle X by finding the missing numbers:
    a. $^{27}_{13}$Al + n → $^{24}_{11}$Na + $^?_?$X
    b. $^1_1$H + $^7_3$Li → $^7_4$Be + $^?_?$X
    c. $^{22}_{11}$Na + n → $^{22}_{10}$Ne + $^?_?$X

19. How much energy is required to remove one proton from the nucleus of $^{238}_{92}$U? A rough answer to this question is obtained by giving the binding energy per nucleon (7.57 MeV). A better answer is obtained when we write a reaction that removes a proton from the nucleus. In this case $^{238}_{92}$U → $^1_1$p + $^{237}_{91}$Pa. Calculate the energy required for this reaction to take place, known as the proton separation energy. Compare the two energy values. (The nuclear mass of uranium is 238.0003 u; that of protactinium is 237.0012 u.)

20. The reaction $^{254}_{98}$Cf → $^{118}_{46}$Pd + $^{132}_{52}$Te + 4$^1_0$n is an example of spontaneous fission. What is the energy released? (Atomic masses: californium = 254.0873 u, palladium = 117.9190 u, tellurium = 131.9086 u.)

21. What is the energy released in the reaction $^1_0$n + $^{14}_7$N → $^{14}_6$C + $^1_1$p? (Nuclear masses: nitrogen = 13.9992 u, carbon = 14.0000 u.)

22. Calculate the energy released in the reaction $^2_1$H + $^6_3$Li → $^4_2$He + $^4_2$He. (Atomic masses: deuterium = 2.0141 u, lithium = 6.0151 u, helium = 4.0026 u.)

23.2 Radioactivity

At the end of the nineteenth century and in the early part of the twentieth century, it was discovered that most nuclides are unstable. This means that the nuclei emit particles and energy. This discovery was mainly due to the work of Henri Becquerel (1852–1908), Marie Sklodowska-Curie (1867–1934) and Pierre Curie (1859–1906).

Radioactive decay

An unstable nucleus is one that **randomly** and **spontaneously** emits particles that carry energy away from the nucleus.

The emission of particles and energy from a nucleus is called **radioactivity**. It was soon realised that three distinct emissions take place. The emissions are called **alpha particles**, **beta particles** and **gamma rays**. They have different ionising power (i.e. ability to knock electrons off atoms) and penetrating power (distance travelled through matter before they are stopped).

Alpha particles and alpha decay

An example of **alpha decay** is uranium decaying into thorium:

$$^{238}_{92}U \rightarrow {}^{234}_{90}Th + {}^{4}_{2}\alpha$$

An alpha particle is emitted from the **parent nucleus** (uranium) creating the **daughter nucleus** (thorium).

The alpha particles were shown to be identical to nuclei of helium in an experiment by E. Rutherford and T. Royds in 1909. They collected the gas that the alpha particles produced when they came in contact with electrons and then investigated its spectrum. The spectrum was found to be identical to that of helium gas. Alpha particles have a mass that is about four times the mass of the hydrogen atom and an electric charge equal to $+2e$.

Notice the balancing of the total proton and nucleon numbers on both sides of the reaction equation as we discussed in Section 23.1.

The energy released in this decay can be calculated with what we learned in Section 23.1. The atomic masses are U = 238.0508 u, Th = 234.0436 u, He = 4.0026 u. The mass difference is then

238.0508 − 234.0436 − 4.0026 = 0.0046 u

The energy released is 0.0046 × 931.5 = 4.3 MeV.

Two other examples of alpha decay are:

$$^{224}_{88}Ra \rightarrow {}^{220}_{86}Rn + {}^{4}_{2}\alpha$$

$$^{212}_{84}Po \rightarrow {}^{208}_{82}Pb + {}^{4}_{2}\alpha$$

Why does a nucleus emit alpha particles (helium nuclei) rather than other nuclei (or even single protons or neutrons)? A partial reason is the fact that helium-4 has a very large binding energy and so the decay is energetically possible. For most nuclei, emitting a proton would *require* energy rather than releasing it, and so it does not happen (but there are exceptions to this statement).

Beta particles and beta decay

In **beta minus decay**, a neutron in the decaying nucleus turns into a proton, emitting an electron and an anti-neutrino. An example is the nucleus of thorium decaying into a nucleus of protactinium:

$$^{234}_{90}Th \rightarrow {}^{234}_{91}Pa + {}^{0}_{-1}e + {}^{0}_{0}\bar{\nu}$$

The 'beta minus particle' is just the electron. It was called beta minus before experiments showed it was identical to the electron. Note again how the proton and nucleon numbers balance in the reaction equation.

Also note that unlike alpha decay, where two particles are produced, here we have three. The third is called the 'anti-neutrino', $\bar{\nu}$. The bar over the symbol indicates that this is an anti-particle. (It was predicted theoretically and subsequently verified in experiments that all particles in nature have a corresponding anti-particle of the same mass but opposite electric charge.)

Notice that in beta minus decay, one neutron in the parent nucleus gets converted into a proton. This explains why the proton number of the daughter nucleus increases by one, whereas the nucleon number stays the same.

Two other examples of beta minus decay are:

$^{214}_{82}Pb \rightarrow {}^{214}_{83}Bi + {}^{0}_{-1}e + {}^{0}_{0}\bar{\nu}$

$^{40}_{19}K \rightarrow {}^{40}_{20}Ca + {}^{0}_{-1}e + {}^{0}_{0}\bar{\nu}$

Another type of beta decay is **beta plus decay**. Instead of emitting an electron the nucleus emits its anti-particle, the positron, which is positively charged. The third particle is the neutrino. Two examples of beta plus decay are:

$^{22}_{11}Na \rightarrow {}^{22}_{10}Ne + {}^{0}_{+1}e + {}^{0}_{0}\nu$

$^{13}_{7}N \rightarrow {}^{13}_{6}C + {}^{0}_{+1}e + {}^{0}_{0}\nu$

It is tempting to think that the electron in beta minus decay (and the positron in beta plus decay) was emitted from within the nucleus, where the electron found itself. It can be shown that an electron *cannot* exist within a nucleus. The electron and the antineutrino were *created* through the action of the weak nuclear force in a process that is beyond the level of this book.

Gamma rays and gamma decay

In **gamma decay** a nucleus emits a gamma ray, in other words a photon of high-frequency electromagnetic radiation:

$^{238}_{92}U \rightarrow {}^{238}_{92}U + {}^{0}_{0}\gamma$

Unlike alpha and beta decay, in gamma decay the nucleus does not change identity. It just moves from a higher to a lower nuclear energy level. The wavelength of the photon emitted is given by:

$\lambda = \dfrac{hc}{E}$

just as with atomic transitions. Here E is the energy of the emitted photon. In contrast to the photons in atomic transitions, which can correspond to visible light, these photons have very small wavelength (smaller than 10^{-12} m), and they are called gamma rays.

Other examples of gamma decay are:

$^{60}_{28}Ni \rightarrow {}^{60}_{28}Ni + {}^{0}_{0}\gamma$

$^{24}_{12}Mg \rightarrow {}^{24}_{12}Mg + {}^{0}_{0}\gamma$

The identification of gamma rays with photons was made possible through diffraction experiments in which gamma rays from decaying nuclei were directed at crystals. The wavelengths were measured from the resulting diffraction patterns.

> **CHECK YOURSELF 4**
>
> A nucleus of $^{137}_{55}Cs$ decays into a nucleus of $^{137}_{56}Ba$. What kind of decay is this?

Properties of alpha, beta and gamma radiations

Table 23.2 summarises the properties of alpha, beta and gamma radiations. Notice that alpha particles are the most ionising and gamma rays the most penetrating.

Characteristic	Alpha particle	Beta particle	Gamma ray
Nature	Helium nucleus	(Fast) electron	Photon
Charge	$+2e$	$-e$	0
Mass	6.64×10^{-27} kg	9.1×10^{-31} kg	0
Penetrating power	A few cm of air	A few mm of metal	Many cm of lead
Ions per mm of air for 2 MeV particles	10 000	100	1
Detection	Affects photographic film	Affects photographic film	Affects photographic film
	Is affected by electric and magnetic fields	Is affected by electric and magnetic fields	Is not affected by electric and magnetic fields

Table 23.2: Properties of alpha, beta and gamma radiations.

Decay series

The changes in the proton and nucleon numbers of a nucleus when it undergoes radioactive decay can be represented in a diagram of nucleon number against proton number. A radioactive nucleus such as thorium ($Z = 90$) decays first by alpha decay into the nucleus of radium ($Z = 88$). Radium, which is also radioactive, decays into actinium ($Z = 89$) by beta decay. Further decays take place until the resulting nucleus is stable. The set of decays that takes place until a given nucleus ends up as a stable nucleus is called the **decay series** of the nucleus. Figure 23.2 shows the decay series for thorium. Successive decays starting with thorium end with the stable nucleus of lead ($Z = 82$, $A = 208$).

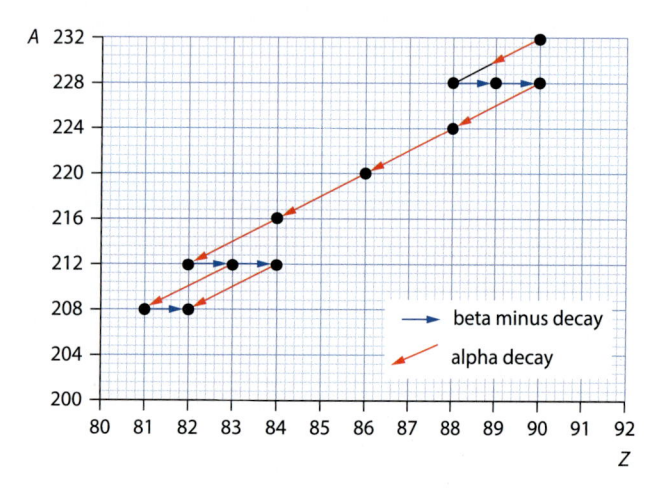

Figure 23.2: The decay series of thorium ($Z = 90$, $A = 232$). One alpha decay reduces the nucleon number by 4 and the proton number by 2. One beta minus decay increases the proton number by one and leaves the nucleon number unchanged. The end result is the nucleus of lead ($Z = 82$, $A = 208$).

> ### CHECK YOURSELF 5
> Part of the decay series of polonium-215 includes polonium-211. By what series of decays does this happen?

> ### WORKED EXAMPLE 23.5
> A nucleus $^A_Z X$ decays by alpha decay followed by two successive beta minus decays.
>
> Find the proton and nucleon numbers of the resulting nucleus.
>
> **Answer**
>
> The decay equation for alpha decay is:
>
> $^A_Z X \rightarrow {}^{A-4}_{Z-2} Y + {}^4_2 \alpha$
>
> Then we have two beta decays:
>
> $^{A-4}_{Z-2} Y \rightarrow {}^{A-4}_{Z-1} Y' + {}^0_{-1} e + \bar{\nu}$ and $^{A-4}_{Z-1} Y' \rightarrow {}^{A-4}_{Z} X + {}^0_{-1} e + \bar{\nu}$
>
> The nucleon number doesn't change in beta minus decay, but the proton number increases by one for each decay (since in beta minus decay a neutron turns into a proton).
>
> So the proton number of the resulting nucleus is Z and the nucleon number is $A - 4$.

The law of radioactive decay

Radioactive decay is random and spontaneous. By *random* we mean that we cannot predict which unstable nucleus in a sample will decay or when there will be a decay. It is *spontaneous* because we cannot affect the rate of decay of a given sample in any way. Although we cannot predict or influence when a particular nucleus will decay, we know that the number of nuclei that will decay per second is proportional to the number of nuclei in the sample that have not yet decayed.

The law of radioactive decay states that the rate of decay is proportional to the number of nuclei that have not yet decayed:

$\frac{\Delta N}{\Delta t} \propto N$

A consequence of this law is that the number of radioactive nuclei decreases exponentially.

Consider the beta minus decay of thallium (the parent nucleus) into lead (the daughter nucleus):

$^{208}_{81} \text{Tl} \rightarrow {}^{208}_{82} \text{Pb} + {}^0_{-1} e + {}^0_0 \bar{\nu}$

The isotope of lead is stable and does not decay. Figure 23.3a shows how the number of thallium nuclei decreases with time. Initially (at $t = 0$) there are 1.6×10^{22} nuclei of thallium. This corresponds to a mass of about 6 g of thallium. After 3 min the number of thallium nuclei left is *half* of the initial number (0.8×10^{22}). After *another* 3 min, the number is one-quarter of the initial number (0.4×10^{22}). After yet another 3 min the number of thallium nuclei is one-eighth of the initial number (0.2×10^{22}).

The time of 3.0 min is called the **half-life** of thallium. It is the time after which the number of the radioactive nuclei is reduced by a factor of 2. The blue curve in Figure 23.3b shows how the number of lead nuclei increases with time.

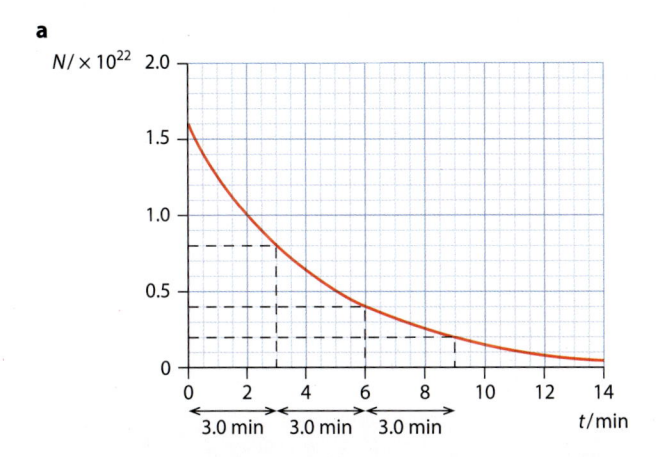

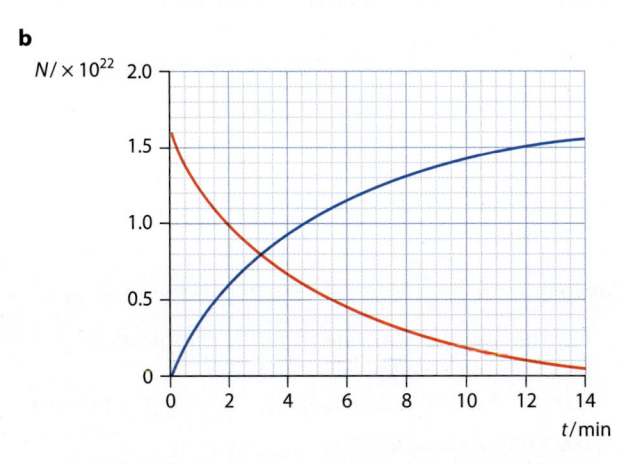

Figure 23.3: **a** The number of thallium nuclei decreases exponentially. **b** As thallium decays (red curve) lead is produced and so the number of lead nuclei increases (blue curve).

CHECK YOURSELF 6

The half-life of an element is one month. Does this mean that, after two months, *all* the radioactive material will have decayed away?

A concept that is useful in experimental work is that of decay rate or **activity** A: this is the number of decays per second. We cannot easily measure how many unstable nuclei are present in a sample, but we can detect the decays. The unit of activity is the becquerel (Bq): 1 Bq is equal to one decay per second.

Activity obeys the same exponential decay law as the number of nuclei. In a time equal to the half-life the activity is reduced by a factor of 2. This is shown in Figure 23.4.

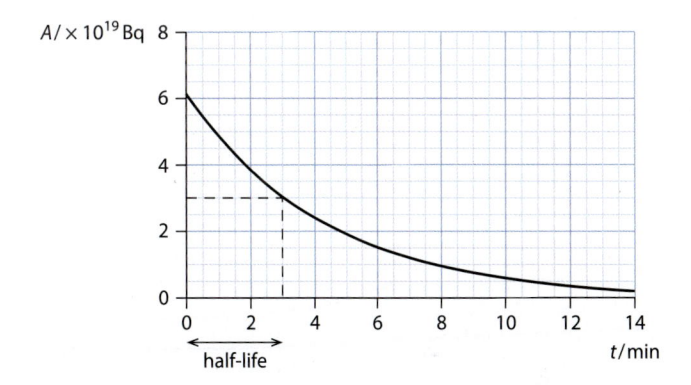

Figure 23.4: The activity of thallium decreases exponentially with time. You can also use this graph to determine half-life.

It is best to define the half-life in terms of activity:

KEY POINT

Half-life is the interval of time after which the activity of a radioactive sample is reduced by a factor of 2.

CHECK YOURSELF 7

There are 100×10^{25} nuclei of a radioactive isotope. After how many half-lives will 75×10^{25} nuclei decay?

Provided the half-life is not too long, a graph of activity against time can be used to determine the half-life. In Figure 23.4 the activity approaches zero as the time increases. In practice, however, this is not the case. The detector that measures activity from the radioactive sample under study also measures the activity from natural sources. As a result, the activity does not approach zero; it approaches the activity due to all other sources of **background radiation**. These background sources include cosmic rays from the sun, radioactive material in rocks and the ground, radiation from nuclear weapons testing grounds, and so on.

The effect of background radiation can be seen in the activity curve of Figure 23.5a. This shows a background rate of 40 Bq. By subtracting this value from all data points we get the graph in Figure 23.5b. Using the corrected graph we get a half-life of 6.0 min. Using Figure 23.5a without correcting for the background gives a half-life of 6.9 min, which is inaccurate by 15%.

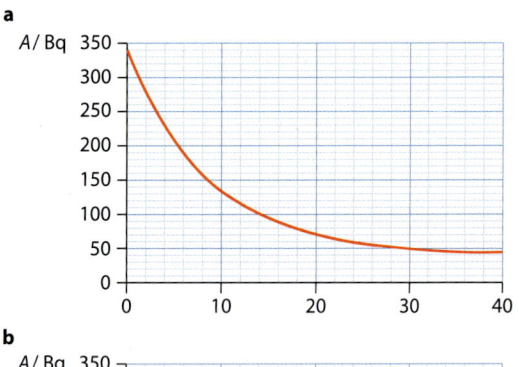

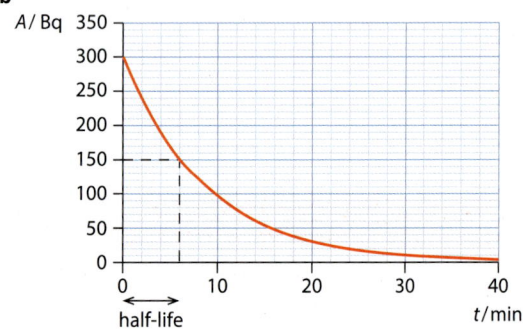

Figure 23.5: **a** An activity curve that includes a background rate of 40 Bq. This curve cannot be used to measure half-life as it is. The background needs to be subtracted as shown in **b**.

Activity measures the total number of decays per second of a radioactive sample. In practice, an instrument, such as a Geiger–Muller tube, will be used to measure this activity. Obviously, the instrument will only record those α, β or γ particles that enter the tube and not all the particles emitted by the sample. The reading of the instrument is called count rate and, like activity, is measured in Bq or in counts per minute. Count rate is also exponentially decreasing with time and may also be used to measure half-lives.

WORKED EXAMPLE 23.6

An isotope has a half-life of 20 min. Initially there are 1024 g of this isotope. Determine the time after which 128 g are left.

Answer

Find the fraction remaining: $\frac{128}{1024} = \frac{1}{8}$.

This corresponds to three half-lives, as $\frac{1}{2} \times \frac{1}{2} \times \frac{1}{2} = \frac{1}{8}$.

Since the half-life is 20 min, three half-lives is:

$3 \times 20 = 60$ min

After 60 min, 128 g are left.

WORKED EXAMPLE 23.7

The count rate for a sample is initially 80 counts per minute. After one half-life the count rate becomes 48 counts per minute.

a What is the background count rate?

b What is the count rate after an additional two half-lives go by?

Answer

a Let the initial count rate from the sample alone be C_0 and the background rate be b. Then $80 = C_0 + b$. After one half-life, the count rate from the sample alone becomes $\frac{C_0}{2}$ and so $48 = \frac{C_0}{2} + b$. Solving, we find $b = 16$ counts per minute (and $C_0 = 64$ counts per minute).

b After three half-lives from the initial time the count rate from the sample alone will be $64 \to 32 \to 16 \to 8$ counts per minute. With the background, the count rate will then be $8 + 16 = 24$ counts per minute.

> **WORKED EXAMPLE 23.8**
>
> The activity of a sample is 15 decays per minute. The half-life is 30 min. Predict the time when the activity was 60 decays per minute.
>
> **Answer**
>
> One half-life before the sample was given to us the activity was 30 decays per minute, and one half-life before that it was 60 decays per minute.
>
> So the activity was 60 decays per minute two half-lives earlier, which is 60 minutes earlier.

Half-life and probability

The meaning of a half-life can also be understood in terms of probability. Any given nucleus has a 50% chance of decaying within a time interval equal to the half-life. If a half-life goes by and the nucleus has not decayed, the chance that it will decay in the next half-life is still 50%. This is shown as a tree diagram in Figure 23.6.

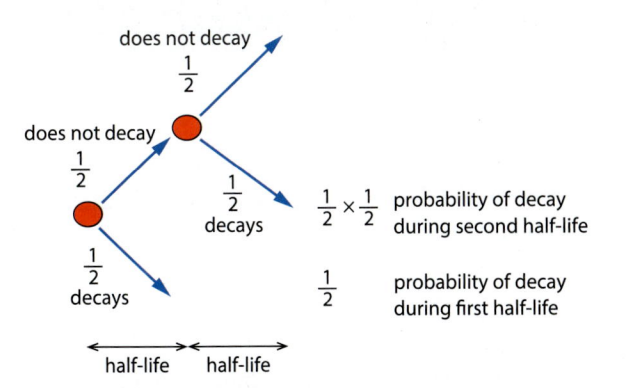

Figure 23.6: Tree diagram for nuclear decay.

The probability that a nucleus will have decayed by the second half-life is the sum of the probability that it decays in the first half-life and the probability that it decays during the second half-life:

$$\frac{1}{2} + \left(\frac{1}{2} \times \frac{1}{2}\right) = \frac{3}{4} = 0.75 \text{ or } 75\%$$

> **CHECK YOURSELF 8**
>
> The half-life of a radioactive element is 5 minutes. A nucleus of this element has not decayed after the passage of 5 minutes. What is the probability that this nucleus will decay in the next 5 minutes?

> **NATURE OF SCIENCE**
>
> **Accidental discovery**
>
> The discovery of radioactivity is an example of an accidental discovery. Henri Becquerel, working in Paris in 1896, believed that minerals made phosphorescent (emitting light) by visible light might give off X-rays. His idea was to wrap a photographic plate in black paper and place on it a phosphorescent uranium mineral that had been exposed to bright sunlight. But the sun did not shine, and he stopped the experiment, placing the wrapped plate and the mineral in a drawer. A few days later he developed the photographic plate, expecting to see only a very weak image. To his surprise, there was a very strong image. Becquerel concluded that this image was formed by a new kind of radiation that had nothing to do with light. The radiation came from the uranium mineral.

> **SCIENCE IN CONTEXT**
>
> Radioactivity has many practical applications. A common household device is a smoke detector. The device contains a very small quantity of a radioactive element. The radiation produced when this element decays ionises the surrounding air molecules, and a small current is established in a circuit. When smoke enters the device, the radiation is absorbed by the larger smoke particles and the current is reduced, triggering an alarm.
>
> Radioactive dating is another important application. Using isotopes with very long half-lives, it has been established that earth and moon rocks are equally old, about 4.5 billion years, providing stringent tests of theories about the formation of the solar system. Use of carbon-14, with a half-life of 5730 years, has made possible the determination of the age of ancient objects. Living things (trees or animals) contain a fixed amount of carbon-14 as long as they are alive.

> **CONTINUED**

After death, the amount of carbon-14 is reduced according to the exponential decay law. Measuring the content of carbon-14 in the object therefore allows a determination of its age. So if a bone, say, contains half the amount of carbon-14 it would have in a living bone, its age must be 5730 years.

Radioactivity can also be used to find a leak in a water pipe buried into the ground: a small amount of a radioactive isotope that emits gamma rays is inserted in the pipe. Water collects at the point of the leak, and therefore that area becomes a strong gamma ray emitter. The gamma rays are penetrating enough to go through the soil, so they can be detected at the surface, thus locating the leakage point. An alpha particle emitter isotope would not be appropriate since the alpha particles would be absorbed by the soil. (Some beta emitting isotopes can also be used.) The half-life of the isotope used must be a few days: this is long enough for detectable emissions to reach the surface but short enough to limit exposure and contamination to people and animals that drink the water.

Nuclear physics has found significant applications in medicine for example in the use of radioisotopes for the treatment of cancer as well as in imaging using radioisotope tracing. The injection of radioactive materials in the human body carries risks, and so the choice of isotope and the dosage must be carefully calculated to maximize the intended effect and minimize damage to the rest of the body. Other imaging techniques involving important nuclear physics phenomena include positron emission tomography (PET scans), magnetic resonance imaging (MRI) and many other applications.

TEST YOUR UNDERSTANDING

(You can look at the periodic table for names of elements.)

23 Describe what is meant by *radioactivity*.

24 Radioactive decay is described as *random* and *spontaneous*. Explain these terms in the context of radioactivity.

25 Write down the equation for the beta minus decay of $^{3}_{1}H$.

26 Write down the equation for the beta plus decay of $^{23}_{12}Mg$.

27 Bismuth ($^{210}_{83}Bi$) decays by beta minus decay, followed by gamma emission. State the equation for the reaction and the proton and nucleon numbers of the nucleus produced.

28 Plutonium ($^{239}_{94}Pu$) decays by alpha decay. State the equation for this reaction and name the nucleus plutonium decays into.

29 By what sequence of decays would a nucleus $^{A}_{Z}X$ end with an isotope of X?

30 Small, stable nuclei tend to have equal numbers of protons and neutrons. A small ($Z < 20$) unstable nucleus has fewer neutrons than protons. What is the likely decay of this nucleus?

31 Small, stable nuclei tend to have equal numbers of protons and neutrons. A small ($Z < 20$) unstable nucleus has more neutrons than protons. What is the likely decay of this nucleus?

32 Alpha decay occurs mainly for large, heavy nuclei, but one exception to this is the decay of beryllium ($^{8}_{4}Be$). Write down the equation for the decay and calculate the energy released. The atomic mass of beryllium is 8.0053 u.

33 What sequence of decays of a nucleus $^{A}_{Z}X$ will end with a nucleus with proton number $Z - 3$ and nucleon number $A - 4$?

34 What sequence of decays of a nucleus $^{A}_{Z}X$ will end with a nucleus with proton number $Z - 3$ and nucleon number $A - 8$?

35 What sequence of decays of a nucleus $^{A}_{Z}X$ will end with a nucleus with proton number $Z - 4$ and nucleon number $A - 4$?

CONTINUED

36 Outline what is meant by the activity of a radioactive sample.

37 What is the activity in Bq of a sample that has 3600 decays per minute?

38 A radioactive source has a half-life of 3.0 min. At the start of an experiment 32.0 mg of the radioactive material is present. Determine how much will be left after 18.0 min.

39 An unstable isotope X decays into a stable isotope Y. What is the ratio of the number of nuclei Y to the number of nuclei X after 3 half-lives? No nuclei of Y were present initially.

40 An unstable isotope X decays into a stable isotope Y. After 12 minutes the ratio of the number of nuclei Y to the number of nuclei X is 3. No nuclei of Y were present initially. What is the half-life of X?

41 The half-life of an isotope is 5 minutes. It is observed that a nucleus in a sample of the isotope has not decayed after 5 minutes. A student claims that it is now more likely that this nucleus will decay in the next 5 minutes. Comment on this statement.

42 The count rate for a radioactive sample is 10 000 counts per minute. After 36 days the count rate is reduced to 625 counts per minute. What is the half-life?

43 At a particular location, the background count rate is 20 counts per minute. An experiment at this location shows a count rate of 310 counts per minute for a radioactive sample. The half-life is four days. What will be the count rate 4 days from the start of the experiment?

44 At a particular location, the background count rate is 25 counts per minute. An experiment at this location shows a count rate of 565 counts per minute for a radioactive sample. The count rate becomes 160 counts per minute after 12 days. What is the half-life?

45 In a study of the intensity of gamma rays from a radioactive source it is suspected that the counter rate C at a distance d from the source behaves as $C \propto \left(\frac{1}{d + d_0}\right)^2$ where d_0 is an unknown constant. A set of data for C and d is given. Outline how the data must be plotted in order to get a straight line.

46 The isotope $^{40}_{19}K$ of potassium is unstable, with a half-life of 1.25×10^9 years. It decays into the stable isotope $^{40}_{18}Ar$. moon rocks were found to contain a ratio of potassium to argon atoms of 1 : 7. Find the age of the moon rocks. (You may assume that no argon was present in the rocks when they were formed.)

47 Figure 23.7 shows the variation with time of the activity of a radioactive sample.

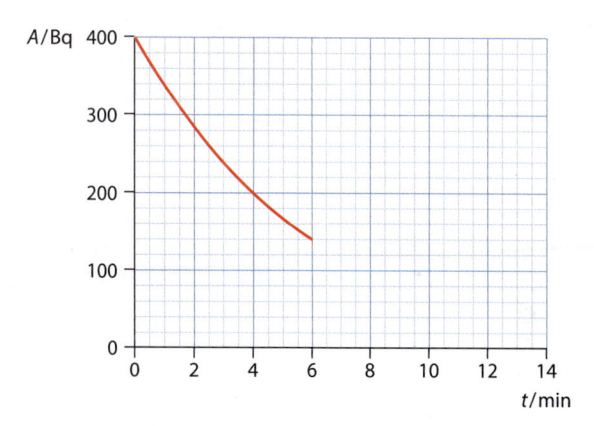

Figure 23.7: For question 47.

a State what is meant by *activity*.

b Use the graph to estimate the half-life of the sample.

c On a copy of the graph, extend the curve to show the variation of the activity for a time up to 12 minutes.

d The sample contains a radioactive element X that decays in to a stable element Y. At $t = 0$, no atoms of element Y are present in the sample. Determine the time after which the ratio of Y atoms to X atoms is 7.

23.3 Nuclear properties and the radioactive decay law

Nuclear radii

When an alpha particle of kinetic energy E_K is directed at a nucleus of proton number Z, the distance of closest approach, d, is found by equating the kinetic energy far from the nucleus to the electric potential energy at the point of closest approach (Figure 23.8). That is:

$$E_K = k\frac{(2e)(Ze)}{d} \Rightarrow d = \frac{2kZe^2}{E_K}$$

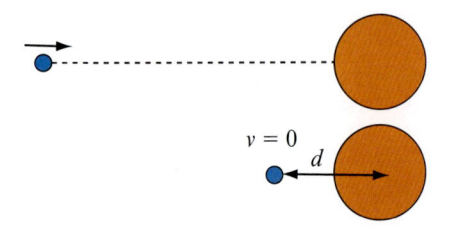

Figure 23.8: The alpha particle momentarily stops at the distance of closest approach d.

So for an alpha particle of kinetic energy 4.5 MeV that is directed at a nucleus of nickel of proton number 28 we will find a distance of:

$$d = \frac{2kZe^2}{E_K} = \frac{2 \times 8.99 \times 10^9 \times 28 \times (1.6 \times 10^{-19})^2}{4.5 \times 10^6 \times 1.6 \times 10^{-19}}$$

$$= 1.8 \times 10^{-14} \text{ m}$$

As the energy of the incoming alpha particles increases, the distance of closest approach decreases and will eventually approach the nuclear surface. When the alpha particle is near the nuclear surface deviations from Rutherford scattering will be observed (see next section) because the nuclear force will start acting on the alpha particle. The number of scattered alpha particles will not be what is expected based on Rutherford scattering. Thus, the distance of closest approach measured in this case will essentially be the nuclear radius. In this way it was discovered that the radius of a nucleus is given by the empirical formula

$$R = R_0 A^{\frac{1}{3}}$$

where $R_0 = 1.2 \times 10^{-15}$ m and A is the nucleon number of the nucleus, i.e. the total number of protons and neutrons in the nucleus. A nucleus has a typical radius of order of magnitude 10^{-15} m whereas the atom has a radius of order 10^{-10} m.

> **WORKED EXAMPLE 23.9**
>
> Explain why the empirical formula for the nuclear formula implies that all nuclei have the same density. Estimate this density.
>
> **Answer**
>
> The density of a nucleus is given in terms of mass and volume by $\rho = \frac{M}{V}$. A nucleus with nucleon number A has a mass of approximately Au. The volume is given by $V = \frac{4\pi}{3}R^3 = \frac{4\pi}{3}(R_0 A^{\frac{1}{3}})^3 = \frac{4\pi}{3}R_0^3 A$. Both mass and volume are proportional to the nucleon number so in the ratio the dependence on A disappears. Specifically,
>
> $$\rho = \frac{Au}{\frac{4\pi}{3}R_0^3 A} = \frac{3u}{4\pi R_0^3} = \frac{3 \times 1.66 \times 10^{-27}}{4\pi(1.2 \times 10^{-15})^3}$$
>
> $$\approx 2 \times 10^{17} \text{ kg m}^{-3}.$$
>
> (The only macroscopic body with a density of this order of magnitude is a neutron star.)

Deviations from Rutherford scattering—evidence for the strong nuclear force

Rutherford derived a theoretical formula for the scattering of alpha particles from nuclei. The Rutherford formula states that as the scattering angle θ increases, the number of alpha particles scattered at that angle decreases very sharply. This is shown in Figure 23.9a. In fact, Rutherford's formula states that the number N of alpha particles scattering at an angle θ is proportional to $\frac{1}{\sin^4\left(\frac{\theta}{2}\right)}$. If this is the case, the product $N \sin^4\left(\frac{\theta}{2}\right)$ should be constant.

Table 23.3 contains some of the original data in the Geiger–Marsden experiment with a gold foil. The last column in the table shows that the product $N \sin^4\left(\frac{\theta}{2}\right)$ is indeed fairly constant, which is strong evidence in support of the Rutherford formula.

The derivation of the Rutherford formula is based on a number of assumptions. The most important is that the only force in play during the scattering process is the electric force. As the energy of the alpha particles increases, the alpha particles can get closer to the nucleus. When the distance of closest approach gets to be about 10^{-15} m or less, deviations from the Rutherford formula are observed (Figure 23.9b). This is due to the fact that the alpha particles are so close to the nucleus that the strong nuclear force begins to act on the alpha particles. Therefore, the presence of these deviations from perfect Rutherford scattering is additional evidence for the existence of the strong nuclear force.

Scattering angle θ / °	N	$N \sin^4\left(\frac{\theta}{2}\right)$
15	132 000	38.4
30	7 800	35.0
45	1 435	30.8
60	477	29.8
75	211	29.1
105	69	27.5
120	52	29.0
150	33	28.8

Table 23.3: Data from the Geiger–Marsden experiment, reproduced in the book by E. Rutherford, J. Chadwick and C. D. Ellis, *Radiations from Radioactive Substances*, Cambridge University Press, 1930.

> **WORKED EXAMPLE 23.10**
>
> Suggest how the results of the scattering of alpha particles would change if the gold ($^{197}_{79}$Au) foil was replaced by an aluminium ($^{30}_{13}$Al) foil of the same thickness.
>
> **Answer**
>
> Aluminium has a smaller nuclear charge and so the alpha particles would approach closer to the nucleus. This means that the alpha particles would start feeling the effects of the nuclear force and deviations from perfect Rutherford scattering would be observed at lower alpha particle energies compared to those in the case of gold.

Approximate constancy of the binding energy per nucleon

We have already noted that a feature of the binding energy curve, Figure 23.1, is that the binding energy per nucleon is approximately constant for nuclei with $A > 20$. How do we explain this observation? The short range of the force implies that a given nucleon can interact with its immediate neighbours only and not with all of the nucleons in the nucleus. So, for large nuclei (roughly $A > 20$) any one nucleon is surrounded by the same number of immediate neighbours, Figure 23.10,

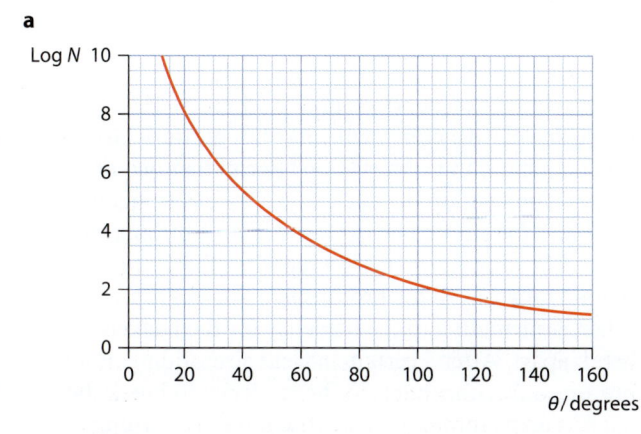

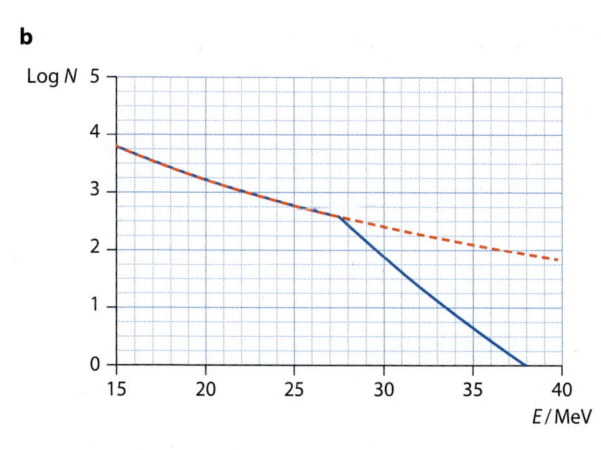

Figure 23.9: a The logarithm of the number of alpha particles scattered at some angle θ as a function of θ. **b** The logarithm of the number of alpha particles scattered at an angle of 60° as a function of the alpha particle energy. The dotted curve is based on Rutherford scattering. The blue curve is the observed curve. We see deviations when the energy exceeds about 28 MeV. The energy at which deviations start may be used to estimate the nuclear radius.

and so the energy needed to remove that nucleon from the nucleus is the same. Thus, the short-range nature of the nuclear force explains why the binding energy per nucleon is roughly constant above a certain value of A. Conversely, this feature of the curve is evidence for the short-range nature of the nuclear force.

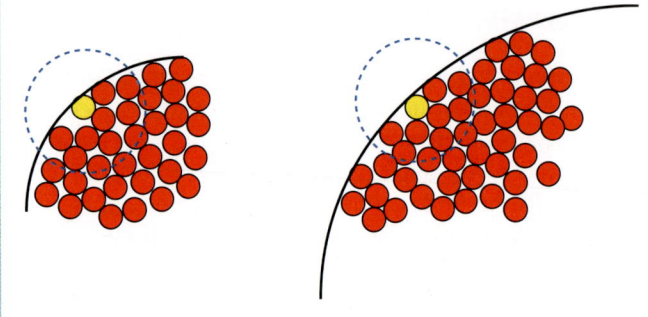

Figure 23.10: For nuclei that are large enough, any one nucleon has the same number of closest neighbours that fall within the range of the strong nuclear force (dotted circle). The nucleon painted yellow has about 12 closest neighbours in both nuclei (in this unrealistic two-dimensional representation).

CHECK YOURSELF 9

State and explain the evidence for

a   the existence of the strong nuclear force

b   the short range of the nuclear force.

Nuclear stability—the role of neutrons

Figure 23.11 shows that very few nuclides are stable; there are about 250 of them and are shown as points in black. Most nuclides (about 2500) are unstable.

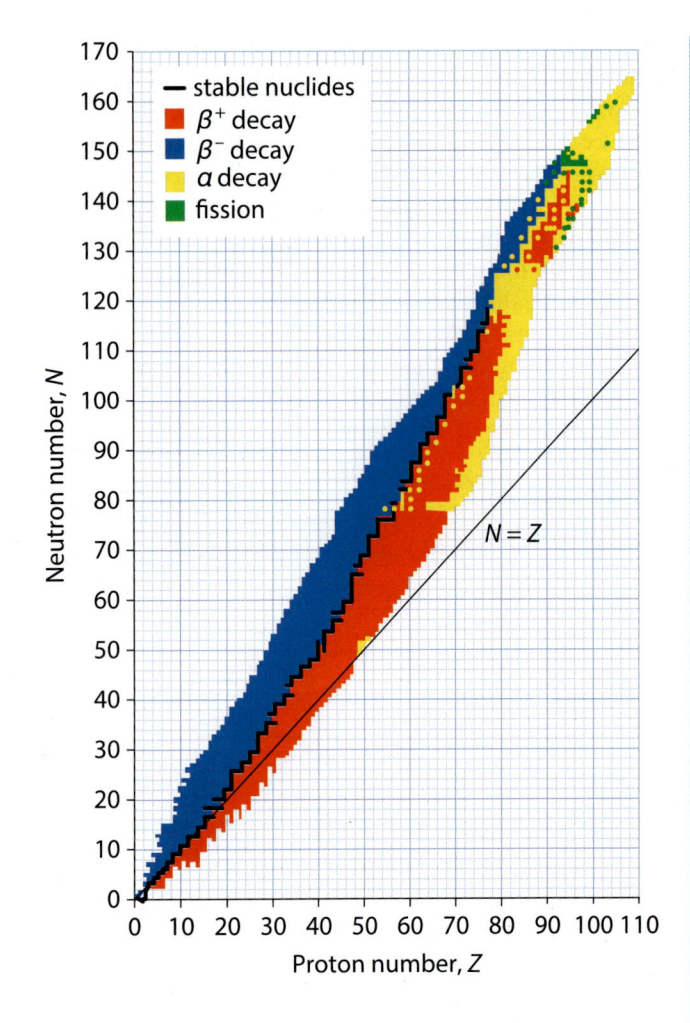

Figure 23.11: A plot of neutron number versus proton number for nuclides. The stable nuclides are shown in black. Most nuclides are unstable.

Notice that stable nuclei with small values of Z have equal numbers of neutrons and protons. As Z increases, stable nuclei have more neutrons than protons. How do we understand this observation? Recall that two of the forces acting within the nucleus are the electromagnetic force and the strong nuclear force. The electromagnetic force acts on protons and is a repulsive force. It has infinite range so all the protons in a nucleus repel each other, contributing to the tendency for the nucleus to break apart. After a certain nuclear size, adding more protons only contributes to the tendency to break the nucleus apart through the electric force. The strong nuclear force does not help because for large enough nuclei the number of nearest neighbours of a given proton is the same and because of the short range of

23 Nuclear physics

the force only these act on a given proton. So, to keep a larger nucleus stable, more neutrons are needed, both because the extra neutrons make the distance between protons larger and because the neutrons contribute to binding.

Nuclear energy levels

The nucleus, like the atom, exists in discrete energy levels. The main evidence for the existence of nuclear energy levels comes from the fact that the energies of the alpha particles and gamma ray photons that are emitted by nuclei in alpha and gamma decays are discrete. This is to be contrasted with beta decays, in which the electron has a continuous range of energies, a fact that we will explain shortly.

Figure 23.12 shows the lowest nuclear energy levels of the magnesium nucleus $^{24}_{12}$Mg. Also shown is a gamma decay from the level with energy 5.24 MeV to the first excited state. The emitted photon has energy 5.24 − 1.37 = 3.87 MeV.

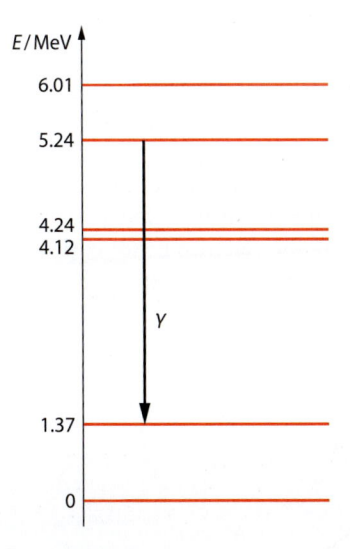

Figure 23.12: Nuclear energy levels of magnesium, $^{24}_{12}$Mg. Notice the difference in scale between these levels and atomic energy levels.

Figure 23.13 shows an energy level of plutonium ($^{242}_{94}$Pu) and a few of the energy levels of uranium ($^{238}_{92}$U). Also shown are two transitions from plutonium to uranium energy levels. These are alpha decays:

$$^{242}_{94}\text{Pu} \rightarrow {}^{238}_{92}\text{U} + {}^{4}_{2}\alpha$$

The energies of the emitted alpha particles are 4.983 − 0.148 = 4.835 MeV and 4.983 − 0.307 = 4.676 MeV.

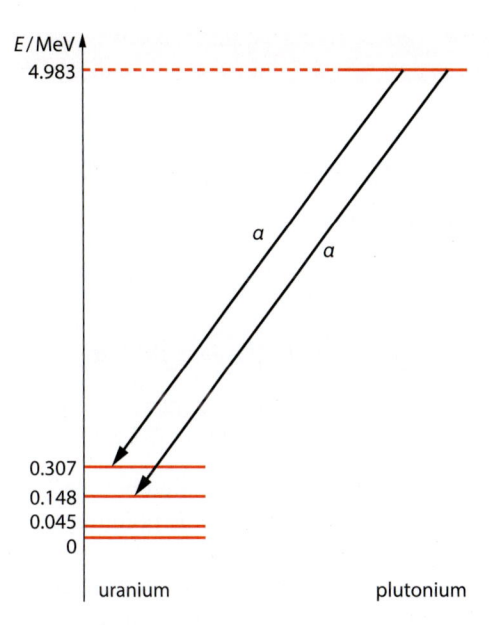

Figure 23.13: Energy levels for plutonium and uranium. Transitions from plutonium to uranium energy levels explain the discrete nature of the emitted alpha particle in the alpha decay of plutonium. Photons may emitted as uranium makes transitions from excited states to lower energy states.

WORKED EXAMPLE 23.11

The nucleus of bismuth ($^{211}_{83}$Bi) decays into lead ($^{207}_{82}$Pb) in a two-stage process. In the first stage, bismuth decays into polonium ($^{211}_{84}$Po). Polonium then decays into lead. The nuclear energy levels that are involved in these decays are shown in Figure 23.14.

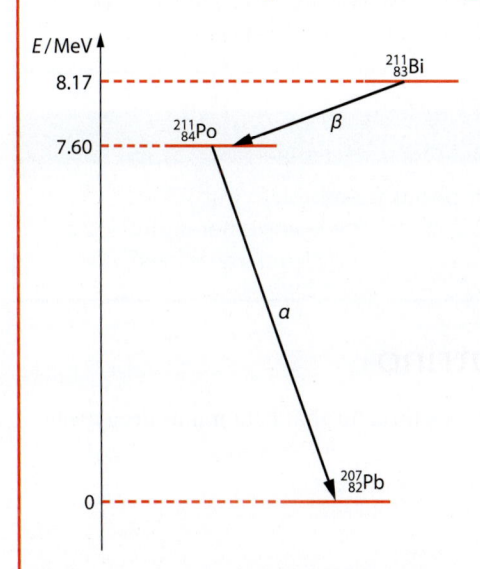

Figure 23.14: For worked example 23.11.

497

> **CONTINUED**
>
> a Write down the reaction equations for each decay.
>
> b Calculate the energy released in the beta decay.
>
> c Explain why the electron does not always have this energy.
>
> **Answer**
>
> a $^{211}_{83}\text{Bi} \rightarrow {}^{211}_{84}\text{Po} + {}^{0}_{-1}\text{e} + {}^{0}_{0}\bar{\nu}$ and $^{211}_{84}\text{Po} \rightarrow {}^{207}_{82}\text{Pb} + {}^{4}_{2}\alpha$
>
> b The energy released is the difference in the energy levels involved in the transition, i.e. 0.57 MeV.
>
> c The energy of 0.57 MeV must be shared between the electron, the anti-neutrino and the polonium nucleus. So the electron does not always have the maximum energy of 0.57 MeV. Depending on the angles (between the electron, the anti-neutrino and the polonium nucleus), the electron energy can be anything from zero up to the maximum value found in **b**.

> **INTERNATIONAL MINDEDNESS**
>
> Research into neutrino physics is a great example of very large international research teams that work together and collaborate widely, including the Kamiokande and the super-Kamiokande Japanese–American collaboration, the GALLEX and SAGE groups in Italy and Russia and the Solar Neutrino Observatory (SNO) in Canada with Canadian, American and British participation.

> **CHECK YOURSELF 10**
>
> How are the photons emitted in transitions between nuclear energy levels different from the photons in atomic energy level transitions?

The neutrino

In the 1930s it was thought that beta minus decay was described by:

$${}^{1}_{0}\text{n} \rightarrow {}^{1}_{1}\text{p} + {}^{0}_{-1}\text{e}$$

The mass difference for this decay is:

1.008665 u – (1.007276 + 0.0005486) u = 0.00084 u

and corresponds to an energy of:

$Q = 0.00084 \times 931.5$ MeV $= 0.783$ MeV

If only the electron and the proton are produced, then the electron, being the lighter of the two, will carry most of this energy away as kinetic energy. To see this, assume that the neutron is at rest when it decays. Then the total momentum before the decay is zero. After the decay the electron and the proton will have equal and opposite momenta, each of magnitude p. Equating the total kinetic energy after the decay to the energy released, Q:

$$\frac{p^2}{2m_e} + \frac{p^2}{2m_p} = Q$$

$$p^2 = \frac{2Qm_e m_p}{m_e + m_p}$$

And so:

$$E_e = \frac{p^2}{2m_e} = \frac{Qm_p}{(m_e + m_p)}$$

$$E_e = \frac{0.783 \times 1.007}{5.49 \times 10^{-4} + 1.007}$$

$$E_e = 0.78257 \approx 0.783 \text{ MeV}$$

Thus, we should observe electrons with kinetic energies of about 0.783 MeV. In experiments, however, the electron has a *range* of energies, from zero up to 0.783 MeV (Figure 23.15). If the electron is not carrying 0.783 MeV of energy, where is the missing energy?

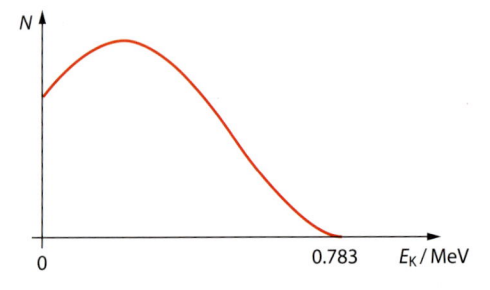

Figure 23.15: The number of electrons that carry a given energy as a function of energy.

Wolfgang Pauli (1900–1958) hypothesised the existence of a third particle in the products of a beta decay in 1933. Since the energy of the electron in beta decay has a range of possible values, it means that a third very light particle must also be produced so that it carries the remainder of the available energy.

Enrico Fermi coined the word *neutrino* for the 'little neutral one' (Fermi is shown with Heisenberg and Pauli in Figure 23.16).

Figure 23.16: E. Fermi (left), W. Pauli (right) and W. Heisenberg in happy times, before they were separated by World War 2.

As the neutrino is electrically neutral, it has no electromagnetic interactions. Its mass is negligibly small and so gravitational interactions are irrelevant. It also does not have strong nuclear interactions. This leaves the weak interaction as the only interaction with which the neutrino can interact. This means that the neutrino can go through matter with very few interactions. In fact, about 10 billion neutrinos pass through your thumbnail every second, yet you do not feel a thing. For every 100 billion neutrinos that go through the earth only one interacts with an atom in the earth! Most of the neutrinos that arrive at earth are produced in the sun in the fusion reaction $p + p \rightarrow {}^2_1H + e^+ + \nu_e$. Read the fascinating story of the solar neutrino problem in the Nature of Science section at the end of this topic.

Links

Pauli had an additional argument suggesting the existence of a third particle in beta decay in addition to energy conservation that we talked about above. A nucleus with zero angular momentum can decay by beta minus decay into a nucleus with zero angular momentum. But the electron produced in the decay has a property called spin, which is a kind of angular momentum. So to conserve angular momentum another particle had to be produced with an angular momentum equal and opposite to that of the electron.

The radioactive decay law

The law of radioactive decay states that the rate of decay is proportional to the number of nuclei present that have not yet decayed:

$$\frac{dN}{dt} = -\lambda N$$

The constant of proportionality is denoted by λ and is called the **decay constant**.

To see the meaning of the decay constant we argue as follows: in a short time interval dt the number of nuclei that will decay is $dN = \lambda N \, dt$ (we ignore the minus sign). The probability that any one nucleus will decay is therefore:

probability $= \frac{dN}{N}$

probability $= \frac{N \lambda dt}{N}$

probability $= \lambda \, dt$ (this is valid provided λdt is smaller than one)

and finally, the probability of decay per unit time is:

$\frac{\text{probability}}{dt} = \lambda$

KEY POINT

The decay constant λ is the probability of decay per unit time.

CHECK YOURSELF 11

The decay constant of a radioactive isotope is $\lambda = 6 \text{ hr}^{-1}$. What is the probability of decay in 1 hour?

The decay law is a differential equation, which when integrated gives:

$N = N_0 \, e^{-\lambda t}$

This is the number of nuclei present at time t given that the initial number (at $t = 0$) is N_0.

As expected, the number of nuclei of the decaying element decreases exponentially as time goes on (Figure 23.17).

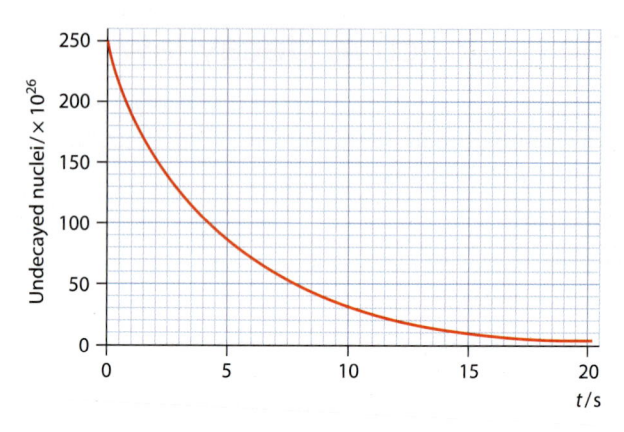

Figure 23.17: Radioactive decay follows an exponential decay law.

The (negative) rate of decay (i.e. the number of decays per second) is called activity, A:

$$A = -\frac{dN}{dt}$$

It follows from the exponential decay law that activity also satisfies an exponential law:

$$A = \lambda N_0 e^{-\lambda t}$$

Thus, the initial activity of a sample is given by the product of the decay constant and the number of atoms initially present, $A_0 = \lambda N_0$. Notice also that $A = \lambda N$.

After one half-life, $T_{\frac{1}{2}}$, half of the nuclei present have decayed and the activity has been reduced to half its initial value. So using either the formula for N or A (here we use the N formula):

$$\frac{N_0}{2} = N_0 e^{-\lambda t}$$

Taking logarithms we find:

$$\lambda T_{\frac{1}{2}} = \ln 2$$

$$\lambda T_{\frac{1}{2}} = 0.693$$

This is the relationship between the decay constant and the half-life.

> **WORKED EXAMPLE 23.12**
>
> Carbon-14 has a half-life of 5730 yr, and in living organisms it has a decay rate of 0.25 Bq g^{-1}. A quantity of 20 g of carbon-14 was extracted from an ancient bone, and its activity was found to be 1.81 Bq. What is the age of the bone?
>
> **Answer**
>
> Using the relationship between decay constant and half-life:
>
> $$\lambda = \frac{\ln 2}{T_{\frac{1}{2}}}$$
>
> $$\lambda = \frac{\ln 2}{5730} \text{ yr}^{-1}$$
>
> $$\lambda = 1.21 \times 10^{-4} \text{ yr}^{-1}$$
>
> When the bone was part of the living body the 20 g would have had an activity of $20 \times 0.25 = 5.0$ Bq. If the activity now is 1.81 Bq, then:
>
> $$A = A_0 e^{-\lambda t}$$
>
> $$1.81 = 5.0 e^{-1.21 \times 10^{-4} t}$$
>
> $$e^{-1.21 \times 10^{-4} t} = 0.362$$
>
> Taking logarithms of both sides: $-1.21 \times 10^{-4} t = -1.016$
>
> $$t = \frac{1.016}{1.21 \times 10^{-4}}$$
>
> $$t \approx 8400 \text{ yr}$$

> **EXAM TIP**
>
> It is important to know that the initial activity A_0 is λN_0.
>
> A graph of A against N gives a straight line whose slope is the decay constant.

23 Nuclear physics

> **WORKED EXAMPLE 23.13**
>
> **a** A container is filled with a quantity of a pure radioactive element X whose half-life is 5.0 minutes. Element X decays into a stable element Y. At time zero no quantity of element Y is present. Determine the time at which the ratio of atoms of Y to atoms of X is 5.
>
> **b** Polonium-208 decays by alpha decay into a stable isotope of lead. The half-life is 2.90 years. Initially there were 8.00 mg of Po in a sample and none of lead. What is the mass of lead produced after 1.30 years?
>
> **Answer**
>
> **a** After time t the number of atoms of element X is given by $N = N_0 e^{-\lambda t}$. The number of atoms of element Y is given by $N = N_0 - N_0 e^{-\lambda t}$. The decay constant is $\lambda = \frac{\ln 2}{5.0} = 0.1386$ min^{-1} and so we have that:
>
> $$\frac{N_0 - N_0 e^{-0.1386t}}{N_0 e^{-0.1386t}} = 5$$
>
> $$1 - e^{-0.1386t} = 5 e^{-0.1386t}$$
>
> $$e^{-0.1386t} = \frac{1}{6}$$
>
> $$0.1386 \times t = 1.7918$$
>
> $$t = 12.9 \text{ min}$$
>
> **b** The number of lead nuclei produced in 1.30 years is $N_0 - N_0 e^{-\frac{\ln 2}{2.90} \times 1.30} = 0.267 N_0$, where N_0 is the initial number of Po nuclei. $N_0 = \frac{8.00}{208} \times N_A$ so the mass M of lead is $M = \underbrace{0.267 \times \frac{8.00}{208} \times N_A}_{\text{number of lead nuclei}} \times \underbrace{\frac{204}{N_A}}_{\text{lead atom mass}} = 0.267 \times 8.00 \times \frac{204}{208} = 2.09$ mg.

NATURE OF SCIENCE

The solar neutrino problem

In 1968, Ray Davis announced results of an experiment that tried to determine the number of neutrinos arriving at earth from the sun. The idea was that the very rare interaction of neutrinos with ordinary chlorine would produce radioactive chlorine atoms that could then be detected, and hence the number of neutrinos determined. The results showed that the number of neutrinos was about one-third of what the theoretical calculation predicted. This created the 'solar neutrino problem'. There were three ways out: either the Davis experiment was wrong or the theory was wrong, or there was new physics involved.

Happily, it turned out that it was the last possibility that actually was in play. The number of neutrinos predicted by theory was based on the assumption that the neutrino was massless. If the neutrino had mass, then the theory would have to be modified because in that case 'neutrino oscillations' would take place. This is a rare quantum phenomenon, in which the three types of neutrinos could turn into each other. The Davis and subsequent experiments all measured electron neutrinos. Much later, when advances in instrumentation and computing power allowed experiments to detect all three types of neutrinos, the number was in agreement with the theory.

But the neutrinos produced in the sun were only electron neutrinos!

By this time, experiments in Japan and elsewhere provided convincing evidence that neutrinos had a tiny mass. So, because of neutrino oscillations, by the time the electron neutrinos reached earth some of them had turned into muon neutrinos and some into tau neutrinos. On the average, about one-third would be electron neutrinos, in agreement with Davis' results! Ray Davis shared the 2002 Nobel Prize in Physics.

TEST YOUR UNDERSTANDING

48 Large, stable nuclei have more neutrons than protons. Explain this observation by reference to the properties of the strong nuclear force.

49 An alpha particle of energy 4.10 MeV is fired at a nucleus of iron 56 (proton number 26). Calculate the distance of closest approach assuming the iron nucleus does not move.

50 An alpha particle directed towards a nucleus of platinum ($^{195}_{78}$Pt) stops at a distance d from the centre of the nucleus. If the nucleus is replaced by the isotope $^{198}_{78}$Pt, how does d change, if at all?

51
  a Estimate the nuclear radii of an alpha particle and a nucleus of platinum ($^{195}_{78}$Pt).

  b Determine the initial energy of an alpha particle directed towards the platinum nucleus such that the alpha particle stops just as the nuclear surfaces touch.

52 An alpha particle is fired head-on at a stationary gold nucleus from far away. Calculate the initial speed of the particle so that the distance of closest approach is 8.5×10^{-15} m. (Take the mass of the alpha particle to be 6.64×10^{-27} kg.)

53 A particle of mass m and charge e is directed from very far away toward a massive ($M \gg m$) nucleus of charge $+Ze$ with a velocity v, as shown in Figure 23.18. The distance of closest approach is d. Sketch (on the same axes) a graph to show the variation with separation of:

  a the particle's kinetic energy

  b the particle's electric potential energy.

  c The incoming particle is a proton and $Z = 28$; $v = 3.0 \times 10^7$ m s^{-1} and $d = 2.0 \times 10^{-14}$ m. Using energy and angular momentum conservation find b, the distance by which the proton misses the nucleus.

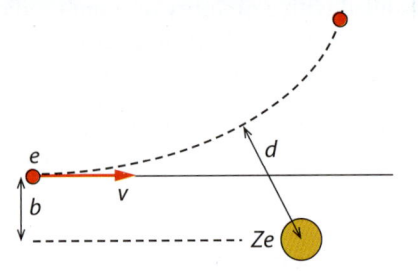

Figure 23.18: For question 53.

54 Show that the nuclear density is the same for all nuclei.

55
  a Deviations from Rutherford scattering are expected when the alpha particles reach large energies. Suggest an explanation for this observation.

  b Some alpha particles are directed at a thin foil of gold ($Z = 79$) and some others at a thin foil of aluminium ($Z = 13$). Initially, all alpha particles have the same energy. This energy is gradually increased. Predict in which case deviations from Rutherford scattering will first be observed.

56 Plutonium ($^{242}_{94}$Pu) decays into uranium ($^{238}_{92}$U) by alpha decay. The energy of the alpha particles takes four distinct values: 4.90 MeV, 4.86 MeV, 4.76 MeV and 4.60 MeV. In all cases a gamma ray photon is also emitted except when the alpha energy is 4.90 MeV. Use this information to suggest a possible nuclear energy level diagram for uranium.

57 The first excited state of the nucleus of uranium-235 is 0.051 MeV above the ground state.

  a What is the wavelength of the photon emitted when the nucleus makes a transition to the ground state?

  b What part of the spectrum does this photon belong to?

CONTINUED

58 Figure 23.19 shows a few nuclear energy levels for $^{40}_{18}$Ar, $^{40}_{19}$K and $^{40}_{20}$Ca.

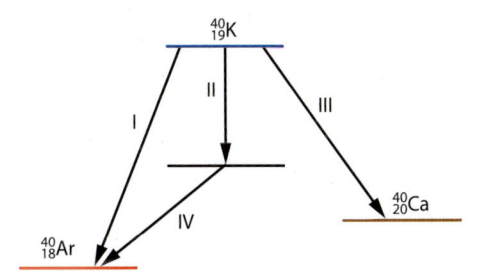

Figure 23.19: For question 58.

Identify the *four* indicated transitions.

59 a State the evidence in support of nuclear energy levels.

Radium's first excited nuclear level is 0.0678 MeV above the ground state.

b Write down the reaction that takes place when radium decays from the first excited state to the ground state.

c Calculate the wavelength of the photon emitted in **b**.

60 a Find the decay constant for krypton-92, whose half-life is 3.00 s.

b Suppose that you start with $\frac{1}{100}$ mol of krypton. Estimate how many undecayed atoms of krypton there are after

 i 1 s

 ii 2 s

 iii 3 s.

61 a State the probability that a radioactive nucleus will decay during a time interval equal to a half-life.

b Calculate the probability that it will have decayed after the passage of three half-lives.

c A nucleus has not decayed after the passage of four half-lives. State the probability it will decay during the next half-life.

62 a Estimate the initial activity of 1.00 g of polonium-210. The half-life of polonium-210 is 138 days.

b Polonium-210 decays into lead-206 by alpha decay. Estimate the mass of lead produced after 31 days.

63 The half-life of an unstable element is 12 days. Find the activity of a given sample of this element after 20 days, given that the initial activity was 3.5 MBq.

64 The half-life of a radioactive isotope is 6.0 days. The activity of the sample now is 0.50 MBq. What was the activity one day before?

65 The age of very old rocks can be found from uranium dating. Uranium is suitable because of its very long half-life: 4.5×10^9 yr. The final stable product in the decay series of uranium-238 is lead-206. Find the age of rocks that are measured to have a ratio of lead to uranium atoms of 0.80. You must assume that no lead was present in the rocks when the rocks were formed.

66 A piece of an ancient bone has a mass of 150 g. The ratio of carbon-14 to carbon-12 atoms in a living bone is constant at 1.3×10^{-12}. The activity of the bone is measured to be 11 Bq. The half-life of carbon 14 is 5730 years. How old is the bone?

67 Two unstable isotopes are present in equal numbers (initially). Isotope A has a half-life of 4 min and isotope B has a half-life of 3 min. Calculate the ratio of the activity of A to that of B after:

a 0 min

b 4 min

c 12 min.

68 The decay constant of an isotope is 1.2 hr^{-1}.

a Using the radioactive decay law, calculate the fraction of nuclei that will decay in 1 hr.

b By expressing the decay constant in min^{-1} calculate the probability of decay within 1 hr.

c How do the answers to **a** and **b** compare?

CONTINUED

69 The half-life of an isotope with a very long half-life cannot be measured by observing its activity as a function of time, since the variation in activity over any reasonable time interval would be too small to be observed. Let m be the mass in grams of a given isotope of long half-life.

   a Show that the number of nuclei present in this quantity is $N_0 = \frac{m}{\mu} N_A$ where μ is the molar mass of the isotope in g mol^{-1} and N_A is the Avogadro constant.

   b From $A = N_0 \lambda e^{-\lambda t}$ show that the initial activity is $A_0 = \frac{m N_A}{\mu} \lambda$ and hence that the half-life can be determined by measuring the initial activity (in Bq) and the mass of the sample (in grams).

70 In a pure sample of a radioactive material the number of nuclei that have not yet decayed is 2.0×10^{20}. The half-life is 5.0 min. What is the activity?

SELF-ASSESSMENT CHECKLIST

I am able to ...	Section	Not yet	Nearly there	Ready to move on
calculate the mass defect and binding energy of a nucleus	23.1			
describe the main features of the binding energy curve	23.1			
calculate the energy released in a nuclear reaction	23.1			
appreciate the three different types of radioactive decay	23.2			
describe the properties of alpha, beta and gamma ray particles	23.2			
understand the meaning of the terms *activity* and *half-life*	23.2			
apply the radioactive decay law for an integral number of half-lives	23.2			
describe nuclear fission	23.3			
calculate the energy released in nuclear fission	23.3			
describe the role of the main features of a nuclear reactor	23.3			
calculate distances of closest approach	23.4			
calculate nuclear radii and densities	23.4			
understand deviations from Rutherford scattering	23.4			
apply the radioactive decay law	23.4			
appreciate the necessity of the neutrino	23.4			
describe the role of neutrons in nuclear stability	23.4			
explain why the binding energy per nucleon is almost constant for larger nuclei	23.4			
give evidence for the existence of nuclear energy levels	23.4			

23 Nuclear physics

> **REFLECTION**
>
> Do you understand *nuclear notation*? Do you understand why a *strong nuclear force* must be acting between nucleons? Can you explain why the mass of nucleons is greater than the mass of the nucleus? Do you appreciate the significance of *binding energy per nucleon*? Can you describe the main features of the graph of binding energy per nucleon versus nucleon number? Can you calculate the energy released in a nuclear reaction? Do you understand the term *radioactivity*? Can you state the properties of *alpha*, *beta* and *gamma* particles? Do you understand what is meant by *half-life* and *activity*? Can you solve problems with half-life and activity?
>
> Can you describe how *nuclear radii* are determined? Can you explain why deviations from Rutherford scattering are observed? Can you explain why the binding energy per nucleon is approximately constant for large nuclei? Can you explain why large stable nuclei have more neutrons than protons? Can you provide the evidence for *nuclear energy levels*? Can you explain why the *neutrino* was hypothesized to exist? Can you solve problems with half-life and activity?

EXAM-STYLE QUESTIONS

You can find questions in the style of IB exams in the digital coursebook.

CHECK YOURSELF ANSWERS

1. 21 − 10 = 11.

2. Because the strong nuclear force keeps them bound.

3. 22 in both cases.

4. Beta minus decay.

5. One alpha decay and two beta minus decays.

6. No. After another half-life, half of what was there before will decay.

7. 25×10^{25} nuclei of the radioactive isotope are left so 2 half-lives went by.

8. It is still 0.5, the decays are random.

9. a Deviations from Rutherford scattering. The deviations imply that a new force is acting on the alpha particles as they get too close to the nuclear surface.

   b The approximate constancy of the binding energy per nucleon for larger nuclei. For large nuclei, any one nucleon is surrounded by the *same* number of nucleons, thus the *same* energy would be required to remove that nucleon from the nucleus.

10. Nuclear energy levels differ in energy by MeV and atomic energy levels by eV. So the photons in nuclear transitions have wavelengths that are of order 10^6 smaller than those in atomic transitions.

11. It is not 6! Express the decay constant as λ = 6 hour^{-1} = 0.1 min^{-1}. The probability of decay within 1 min is 0.1. The probability of *no* decay within 1 min is then 0.9. The probability of *no* decay in 60 min is then 0.9^{60} and so the probability of decay in 1 hour is $1 - 0.9^{60}$ = 0.998. Similarly, λ = 6 hour^{-1} = 0.1 min^{-1} = 1.667×10^{-3} s^{-1}. What is the probability of a decay in 1 min? We expect the answer to be 0.1. Indeed: probability of no decay within 1 s = $1 - 1.667 \times 10^{-3}$ = 0.9983. Probability of no decay in 60 s = 0.9983^{60}. So probability of decay in 60 s is $1 - 0.9983^{60}$, which is about 0.1 as expected.

Chapter 24
Nuclear fission

LEARNING OBJECTIVES

In this chapter you will learn how to:

- calculate the energy released in a fission reaction
- recognize the functions of the main components of a nuclear reactor
- approach some issues related to safety of nuclear power
- understand issues that have to do with the storage of nuclear waste products.

24 Nuclear fission

> **GUIDING QUESTION**
>
> How can we extract energy from the atom?

Introduction

Nuclear fission is the splitting of a heavy nucleus into smaller ones with the release of energy and neutrons. This makes possible the extraction of energy in nuclear reactors.

24.1 Nuclear fission

We will now discuss nuclear fission, a special kind of nuclear reaction in which the ideas we learned in Section 23.1 will come to be applied. *Nuclear fission* is the process in which a heavy nucleus splits up into two lighter nuclei. This can happen when the nucleus is bombarded by a neutron, and in this case we speak of **induced fission**. When a neutron is absorbed by a nucleus of uranium-235, the nucleus momentarily turns into uranium-236. It then splits into lighter nuclei plus neutrons. One possibility is:

$${}^{1}_{0}n + {}^{235}_{92}U \rightarrow {}^{236}_{92}U \rightarrow {}^{144}_{56}Ba + {}^{89}_{36}Kr + 3{}^{1}_{0}n$$

In **spontaneous fission** a nucleus may split into two smaller nuclei without neutron absorption. An example is the reaction: ${}^{254}_{98}Cf \rightarrow {}^{118}_{46}Pd + {}^{132}_{52}Te + 4{}^{1}_{0}n$.

The production of neutrons is a key feature of fission reactions, and use is made of this in a nuclear reactor (see next section).

The energy released can be calculated through mass differences as follows:

$$\Delta m = \underbrace{(235.0439299 + 1.008665)}_{\text{total mass of reactants}} u -$$

$$\underbrace{(143.92292 + 88.91781 + 3 \times 1.008665)}_{\text{total mass of products}} u$$

$$= 0.18587 \text{ u}$$

Thus for this reaction, the energy released is:

$$Q = \Delta mc^2 = 0.18587 \times 931.5 \approx 173 \text{ MeV}.$$

This energy appears as kinetic energy of the products, mostly for the produced neutrons. The energy can be released in a controlled way, as in a fission reactor (see next section), or explosively in a very short time, as in a nuclear bomb (Figure 24.1a).

Figure 24.1: a Vast amounts of energy are released in the detonation of a nuclear weapon. **b** The results are catastrophic, as this photograph of Hiroshima shows.

> **WORKED EXAMPLE 24.1**
>
> One fission reaction of uranium-235 releases 173 MeV for each reaction. Estimate the energy released by 1 kg of uranium-235.
>
> **Answer**
>
> A quantity of 1 kg of uranium-235 is $\frac{1000}{235}$ mol of uranium.
>
> The number of nuclei is therefore:
>
> number of nuclei = $\frac{1000}{235} \times 6 \times 10^{23}$
>
> Each nucleus produces about 173 MeV of energy, so:
>
> total energy = $\frac{1000}{235} \times 6 \times 10^{23} \times 173$ MeV
>
> This is 4.4×10^{26} MeV or about 7×10^{13} J.

Fission and the binding energy curve

The release of energy in fission is expected on the basis of the binding energy per nucleon graph, Figure 23.1 and Figure 24.2, as we will now explain. For the fission reaction $^1_0n + ^{235}_{92}U \rightarrow ^{144}_{56}Ba + ^{89}_{36}Kr + 3^1_0n$ we calculated the energy released by finding the total mass of the reactants on the left and subtracting the total mass of the products on the right. But this energy can also be calculated in a different way.

We know that

$$Q = ((m_n + M_U) - (M_{Ba} + M_{Kr} + 3m_n))c^2$$
$$= (M_U - M_{Ba} - M_{Kr})c^2 - 2m_n c^2$$

Recalling the definition of binding energy,

$$B_{bU} = (92m_p + 143m_n - M_U)c^2 \Rightarrow$$
$$M_U c^2 = (92m_p + 143m_n)c^2 - B_{bU}$$

$$B_{bBa} = (56m_p + 88m_n - M_{Ba})c^2 \Rightarrow$$
$$M_{Ba} c^2 = (56m_p + 88m_n)c^2 - B_{bBa}$$

$$B_{bKr} = (36m_p + 53m_n - M_{Kr})c^2 \Rightarrow$$
$$M_{Kr} c^2 = (36m_p + 53m_n)c^2 - B_{bKr}$$

We now substitute these values for the masses in the expression for Q to get

$$Q = (92m_p + 143m_n)c^2 - B_{bU} - (56m_p + 88m_n)c^2$$
$$+ B_{bBa} - (36m_p + 53m_n)c^2 + B_{bKr} - 2m_n c^2$$
$$= B_{bBa} + B_{bKr} - B_{bU}$$

We have the result that the energy released can also be calculated by subtracting from the total binding energy *on the right* of the reaction the total binding energy *on the left* of the reaction. The binding energy curve involves binding energy per nucleon, so let us express the energy released in terms of binding energy per nucleon, b:

We find that

$$Q = 144b_{Ba} + 89b_{Kr} - 235b_U$$

This is where the binding energy curve comes in: krypton and barium are to the left of uranium in the graph and so have *higher binding energy per nucleon*, $b_{Kr} > b_{Ba} > b_U$. These inequalities of binding energy per nucleon are enough to show that $Q > 0$, i.e. energy will be released. The actual numbers are $b_{Kr} = 8.616959$ MeV, $b_{Ba} = 8.265467$ MeV and $b_U = 7.590907$ MeV so that

$$Q = 144 \times 8.265467 + 89 \times 8.616959 - 235 \times 7.590907$$
$$= 173 \text{ MeV}.$$

The dashed vertical line at nickel-62 in Figure 24.2 is at the peak of the binding energy curve—this is the most energetically stable nucleus. Fission means heavy nuclei split into lighter nuclei with *higher binding energy per nucleon*. Fusion (see next chapter) means light nuclei join to form heavier nuclei with *higher binding energy per nucleon*. By the argument of the previous paragraph, in both cases energy is released.

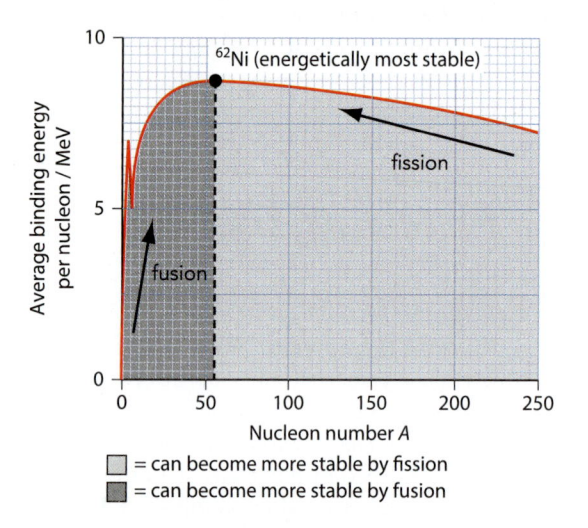

Figure 24.2: When a heavy nucleus splits up, energy is released because the produced nuclei have a higher binding energy per nucleon than the original nucleus. When two light nuclei fuse, energy is produced because the products again have a higher binding energy per nucleon.

WORKED EXAMPLE 24.2

Consider the fission reaction: $^{238}_{92}U \rightarrow ^{145}_{57}La + ^{90}_{35}Br + x^1_0n$.

Is this an example of induced or spontaneous fission? What is x? What is the energy released? Data available:

Binding energy per nucleon for $^{238}_{92}U = 7.57$ MeV, for $^{145}_{57}La = 8.26$ MeV and for $^{90}_{35}Br = 8.48$ MeV.

Answer

No neutrons are used to bombard uranium, so it is a spontaneous fission reaction. Balancing mass numbers gives $x = 3$. The energy released is $Q = 145 \times 8.26 + 90 \times 8.48 - 238 \times 7.57 = 159$ MeV.

24 Nuclear fission

Nuclear fission reactors

A nuclear reactor is a machine in which nuclear fission reactions take place, producing energy.

Schematic diagrams of the cores of two types of nuclear reactor are shown in Figure 24.3.

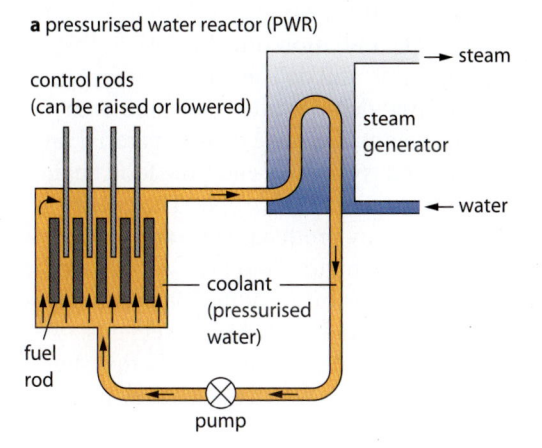

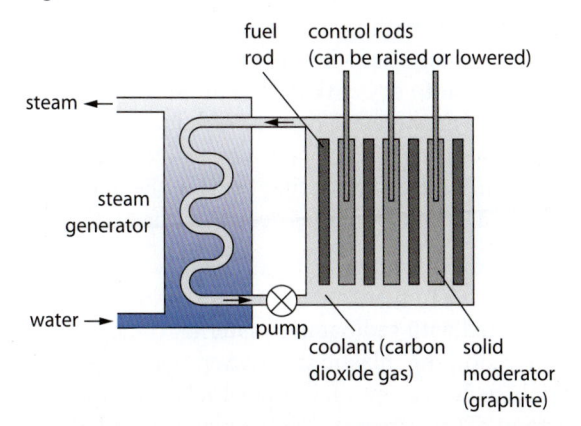

a pressurised water reactor (PWR)

b gas-cooled reactor

Figure 24.3: Schematic diagrams of two types of fission reactor.

The fuel of a nuclear reactor is typically uranium-235. Neutrons initiate the reaction. One possible fission reaction is:

$$^{1}_{0}n + ^{235}_{92}U \rightarrow ^{140}_{54}Xe + ^{94}_{38}Sr + 2^{1}_{0}n$$

The energy released is about 185 MeV.

The neutrons produced can be used to collide with other nuclei of uranium-235 in the reactor, producing more fission, more energy and more neutrons. The reaction is thus self-sustaining; it is called a **chain reaction**. For the chain reaction to get going, a certain minimum mass of uranium-235 must be present, otherwise the neutrons escape without causing further reactions. This minimum mass is called the **critical mass** (for pure uranium-235, this is about 15 kg and rises to 130 kg for fuels containing 10% uranium-235). Uranium-235 will only capture neutrons if the neutrons are not too fast. The neutrons produced in the fission reactions are much too fast and so must be slowed down before they can initiate further reactions.

The slowing down of neutrons is achieved through collisions of the neutrons with atoms of the **moderator**, the material surrounding the **fuel rods** (the tubes containing uranium). The moderator material can be graphite or water, for example. As the neutrons collide with moderator atoms, they transfer energy to the moderator, increasing its temperature. A **heat exchanger** is therefore needed to extract the heat from the moderator. This can be done using cold water that circulates in pipes throughout the moderator. The water is turned into steam at high temperature and pressure. The steam is then used to turn the turbines of a generator, finally producing electricity.

The rate of the reactions is determined by the number of neutrons available to be captured by uranium-235. Too few neutrons would result in the reactions stopping, while too many neutrons would lead to an uncontrollably large release of energy. Thus **control rods** are introduced into the moderator. These absorb neutrons when too many neutrons are present, thus decreasing the rate of reactions. If the rate of reactions needs to be increased, the control rods are removed. The core of the reactor where the fission reactions take place has to be shielded (by thick concrete walls) to prevent radiation leaking to the surroundings.

CHECK YOURSELF 1

a   What would happen to a nuclear reactor if a moderator was not present?

b   What would happen to a nuclear reactor if the mass of the fuel were less than the critical mass?

> **PHYSICS FOR THE IB DIPLOMA: COURSEBOOK**

> **WORKED EXAMPLE 24.3**
>
> a Assuming the energy released in one fission reaction involving U-235 is 185 MeV, show that one kilogram of uranium-235 will release an energy equal to about 8×10^{13} J.
>
> b Natural uranium (mainly uranium-238) contains about 0.7% of uranium-235 (by mass). Calculate the energy released by 1 kg of natural uranium.
>
> **Answer**
>
> a The energy released by one nucleus of U-235 is $185 \times 10^6 \times 1.6 \times 10^{-19} = 2.96 \times 10^{-11}$ J. One kilogram of U-235 contains $\frac{1000}{235} \times 6.02 \times 10^{23} = 2.56 \times 10^{24}$ nuclei of uranium and so the energy released by 1 kg of U-235 is $2.96 \times 10^{-11} \times 2.56 \times 10^{24} = 7.58 \times 10^{13}$ J.
>
> b One kilogram of natural uranium contains 0.7% of uranium-235 and so the energy E of *natural* uranium that can be extracted from 1 kg is:
>
> $E = \frac{0.7}{100} \times 7.58 \times 10^{12} = 5.3 \times 10^{11}$ J kg^{-1}
>
> $E = 530$ GJ kg^{-1}
>
> This value is substantially higher than that of fossil fuels.

Risks with nuclear power

The fast neutrons produced in a fission reaction may be used to bombard uranium-238 and produce plutonium-239. The reactions leading to plutonium production are:

$^{1}_{0}n + ^{238}_{92}U \rightarrow ^{239}_{92}U$

$^{239}_{92}U \rightarrow ^{239}_{93}Np + ^{0}_{-1}e + \bar{\nu}$

$^{239}_{93}Np \rightarrow ^{239}_{94}Pu + ^{0}_{-1}e + \bar{\nu}$

The importance of these reactions is that non-fissionable material (uranium-238) is being converted to fissionable material (plutonium-239) as the reactor operates. The plutonium-239 produced can then be used as the nuclear fuel in other reactors. It can also be used in the production of nuclear weapons, which therefore raises serious concerns.

The spent fuel in a nuclear reactor and the products of the reactions are all highly radioactive with long half-lives. There are now about 400 000 tons of radioactive waste worldwide, and about one third of this has been reprocessed. Radioactive waste is broadly classified as higher level and low level waste.

Higher level waste is mainly the left-over uranium fuel in a reactor's fuel rods and the lighter elements produced in the fission of the uranium fuel, such as strontium-90 and cesium-137 and others that we looked at in fission reactions earlier. These elements are highly radioactive. The radiation produced when they decay is very penetrating and delivers fatal doses even during short exposures, decades after they have been removed from the reactor. Leakage of this material into groundwater, lakes and rivers may enter the food chain, contaminating a large number of people. The energy produced when they decay produces heat, and so their storage must ensure cooling to avoid fires. As we saw, the absorption of neutrons by uranium-238 eventually produces plutonium-239 and other heavy elements. These produce less heat and penetrating radiation, but they have very long half-lives which means they pose a danger even after thousands of years. Higher level waste products are kept in steel containers surrounded by thick reinforced concrete which are filled with water. The water serves both as a coolant as well as a radiation shield. After many years in these containers, the waste can be moved into dry casks; these are steel vessels surrounded by concrete. These storage facilities are temporary until satisfactory permanent storage is found. Many countries are considering burying the material in containers in special facilities deep into the earth.

Low level waste includes material that has become radioactive due to neutron absorption or has been contaminated with radioactive material. It includes protective clothing, plastic shoe covers, cleaning materials such as mops and filters, tools and other equipment. These are not very radioactive, and after storage for some time, so that their radioactivity drops to below background, they can be disposed of as ordinary trash. Also included in low level waste are products generated in the mining of uranium and in the process of extracting the uranium from the ore.

In addition, there is always the possibility of an accident due to uncontrolled heating of the moderator, which might start a fire or explosion. This would be a conventional explosion—the reactor cannot explode in the way a nuclear weapon does. In the event of an explosion, radioactive material would leak from the sealed core of a reactor, dispersing radioactive material into the environment. Both explosions shown in Figure 24.4 resulted in widespread contamination.

24 Nuclear fission

Advantages of power by nuclear fission
- High power output
- Large reserves of nuclear fuels
- Nuclear power stations do not produce greenhouse gases

Disadvantages of power by nuclear fission
- Radioactive waste products difficult to dispose of
- Major public health hazard should 'something go wrong'
- Problems associated with uranium mining
- Possibility of producing materials for nuclear weapons

> **WORKED EXAMPLE 24.4**
>
> A nuclear power plant produces 800 MW of electrical power with an overall efficiency of 35%. The energy released in the fission of one nucleus of uranium-235 is 170 MeV. Estimate the mass of uranium used per year.
>
> **Answer**
>
> Let P be the power produced from nuclear fission. Since the efficiency is 35%, then:
>
> $0.35 = \frac{800}{P}$
>
> $\Rightarrow P = 2286$ MW
>
> The energy produced in one year is:
>
> $2286 \times 10^6 \times 365 \times 24 \times 3600 = 7.21 \times 10^{16}$ J
>
> The energy produced in the fission of one nucleus is:
>
> $170 \times 10^6 \times 1.6 \times 10^{-19} = 2.72 \times 10^{-11}$ J
>
> and so the number of fission reactions in a year is:
>
> $\frac{7.21 \times 10^{16}}{2.72 \times 10^{-11}} = 2.65 \times 10^{27}$
>
> The mass of uranium-235 used up in a year is therefore $2.65 \times 10^{27} \times 235 \times 1.66 \times 10^{-27}$, which is about 1000 kg.

Figure 24.4: The effects of two of the world's worst nuclear accidents. **a** The devastation after the explosion at the Fukushima nuclear plant in Japan on March 11, 2011. **b** Reactor number 4 in the Chernobyl nuclear power plant after the explosion on April 26, 1986.

PHYSICS FOR THE IB DIPLOMA: COURSEBOOK

Ethics and morals

This section has shown how Einstein's famous formula $E = mc^2$ applies to nuclear reactions. This formula describes the conversion of mass into energy—something that violates the law of conservation of mass as described by chemists. At the same time this formula made possible nuclear weapons that exploit the fission and fusion processes. Is this dangerous knowledge? J. R. Oppenheimer, who led the American effort to make the atomic bomb during World War II, said, quoting from the Hindu holy book *The Bhagavad Gita*: 'I am become Death, the Destroyer of Worlds'. If some knowledge is dangerous, can it ever be prevented from becoming widely available? If yes, by whom?

Figure 24.5: J. R. Oppenheimer (1904–1967).

TEST YOUR UNDERSTANDING

1 Consider the nuclear fission reaction of uranium: $^{235}_{92}U + ^{1}_{0}n \rightarrow ^{98}_{40}Zr + ^{135}_{52}Te + 3^{1}_{0}n$.

   a Calculate the energy released in two ways: using the masses, U = 235.0439 u, Zr = 97.9128 u, Te = 134.9165 u; and using the binding energies per nucleon, U = 7.5909 MeV, Zr = 8.5814 MeV, Te = 8.3465 MeV.

   b Use the binding energy curve in Figure 23.1 to explain carefully why energy is released in fission reactions.

2 Assume uranium-236 splits into two nuclei of palladium-117 (Pd).

   The atomic mass of uranium is 236.0456 u; that of palladium is 116.9178 u.

   a Write down the reaction.

   b What other particles must be produced?

   c What is the energy released?

3 Consider the decay $^{238}_{92}U \rightarrow ^{234}_{90}Th + ^{4}_{2}\alpha$.

   Calculate the energy released.

   (Binding energy per nucleon: U = 7.57 MeV; Th = 7.60 MeV; He = 7.07 MeV.)

4 Consider the reaction $^{235}_{92}U + ^{1}_{0}n \rightarrow ^{145}_{57}La + ^{y}_{x}X + 3^{1}_{0}n$.

   What is x and y? Calculate the energy released.

   (Binding energy per nucleon: $^{235}_{92}U$ = 7.59 MeV, $^{145}_{57}La$ = 8.26 MeV, X = 8.56 MeV.)

5 State and explain two advantages of energy production by nuclear fission over energy production by fossil fuels.

6 State and explain two reasons for concern in the energy production by nuclear fission.

7 a In what form is the energy from a nuclear fission reactor produced?

   b How does the nuclear reactor produce electricity?

8 A U-235 fission reaction involves the release of 170 MeV of energy which is used to light a 60 W light bulb for 12 hours. What mass of U-235 would be needed?

9 What is meant by nuclear waste?

10 Distinguish between higher level and low level nuclear waste.

11 Outline some of the problems with nuclear waste storage.

24 Nuclear fission

SELF-ASSESSMENT CHECKLIST

I am able to ...	Section	Not yet	Nearly there	Ready to move on
describe nuclear fission	24.1			
calculate the energy released in nuclear fission	24.1			
explain why energy is released in fission using the binding energy curve	24.1			
describe the role of the main features of a nuclear reactor	24.1			
understand the risks of nuclear power	24.1			
understand the problem of nuclear waste storage	24.1			

REFLECTION

Can you describe *nuclear fission*? Can you calculate the energy released in a nuclear fission reaction? Can you list the main parts of a nuclear reactor and describe their function? Can you discuss efforts to store nuclear waste?

EXAM-STYLE QUESTIONS

You can find questions in the style of IB exams in the digital coursebook.

CHECK YOURSELF ANSWERS

1 a No useful energy would be produced.
  b The neutrons would escape without causing further reactions.

Chapter 25
Nuclear fusion and stars

LEARNING OBJECTIVES

In this chapter you will learn how to:

- recognize the conditions for nuclear fusion to occur
- calculate the energy released in fusion reactions
- explain why energy is released in fusion
- understand why the conditions for fusion exist in stellar cores
- recognize the role of stellar mass in the evolution of the star
- understand the proton–proton chain
- use stellar radii and the Hertzsprung–Russell (HR) diagram
- describe the evolution of a star off the main sequence
- understand the Chandrasekhar and Oppenheimer–Volkoff limits, white dwarfs, neutron stars and black holes

25 Nuclear fusion and stars

> **GUIDING QUESTIONS**
> - What determines the evolution of a star?
> - What is the origin of the elements?

Introduction

Here we will extend the work of the previous chapter to nuclear fusion reactions. We will see that nuclear fusion is the source of energy in stars and that stellar evolution and nuclear fusion reactions go hand in hand. We will discover that stars are the birthplace of the elements: either in stellar cores or in the explosive stages that end the life of a star.

25.1 Nuclear fusion

Nuclear fusion is the joining of two light nuclei into a heavier one with the associated production of energy. An example of a fusion reaction is:

$${}^{2}_{1}H + {}^{3}_{1}H \rightarrow {}^{4}_{2}He + {}^{1}_{0}n$$

In this reaction a deuterium nucleus joins with a tritium nucleus to form a nucleus of helium and a neutron. We can work out the energy released from the mass difference for the reaction:

Mass of deuterium:	2.014102 u
Mass of tritium:	3.016049 u
Mass of helium:	4.002602 u
Mass of neutron:	1.008665 u

$\Delta m = 2.014102 + 3.016049 - (4.002602 + 1.008665)$
$\quad\;\; = 0.0189\ u$

Therefore:

$Q = \Delta mc^2 = 0.0189 \times 931.5 = 17.6$ MeV,

which is a lot of energy!

Conditions for fusion to take place

There are three main conditions for fusion to take place.

Temperature: For fusion to occur, the reacting nuclei must join. They have to come very close to each other, within the range of the strong nuclear force, so that they attract each other (through the strong nuclear force) and join. But nuclei are positively charged so they repel each other (through the electric force). One way to get the nuclei to come close to each other is by raising the temperature at which the nuclei are kept. At high temperatures the nuclei would be moving fast enough to overcome the Coulomb repulsion and crash into each other.

Density: The second condition is that the number density of the nuclei (number of nuclei per unit volume) must be high so that there are lots of them around for fusion to occur.

Confinement time: The third condition is that the nuclei must be maintained at high temperature and density for a time long enough for many fusion reactions to take place.

The problem is that the temperatures required are in the millions of degrees. At these temperatures matter is in the plasma state, i.e. the electrons have left the atoms, and the problem is that it is not easy to confine this very hot plasma at high density for sufficiently long times.

Whereas we face serious problems in our attempts to extract energy from nuclei through fusion, stars perfectly satisfy all criteria for nuclear fusion. Nuclear fusion provides the energy that is radiated by stars into space, the pressure to keep a star from collapsing under its own weight and the nuclear fusion reactions and related processes that are responsible for **nucleosynthesis**, the creation of the chemical elements. Therefore, the natural place to study fusion is the stars so we begin in Section 25.2 by discussing basic stellar properties.

> **CHECK YOURSELF 1**
>
> Why are high temperatures required for fusion to occur?

> **PHYSICS FOR THE IB DIPLOMA: COURSEBOOK**

WORKED EXAMPLE 25.1

Consider the fusion reaction:

$^{2}_{1}H + ^{2}_{1}H \rightarrow ^{3}_{2}He + ^{1}_{0}n$

Mass of deuterium: 2.014102 u

Mass of helium: 3.016029 u

Mass of neutron: 1.008665 u

Calculate the energy released.

Answer

$\Delta m = 2 \times 2.014102 - (3.016029 + 1.008665)$ u

$\Delta m = 0.00351$ u

Therefore:

$Q = \Delta m c^2 = 0.00351 \times 931.5 = 3.27$ MeV

WORKED EXAMPLE 25.2

The two deuterium nuclei in worked example 25.1 will fuse when their distance apart is of order 10^{-15} m. The electrostatic potential energy at this separation is of order 10^{-13} J. To overcome the electrostatic repulsion, a kinetic energy of this order of magnitude is required. The deuterium nuclei are kept at a temperature T. Estimate T.

Answer

Using $E = \frac{3}{2}kT$, we find

$\frac{3}{2}kT \times 2 = 10^{-13} \Rightarrow T = \frac{10^{-13}}{3 \times 1.38 \times 10^{-23}} \approx 2 \times 10^9$ K

In stars, deuterium fusion reactions take place at temperatures of order 5×10^8 K, which shows that at this lower temperature, some deuterium nuclei have energies that are way above the average.

TEST YOUR UNDERSTANDING

1. State and explain the conditions necessary for nuclear fusion to occur.

2. Calculate the energy released in the fusion reaction:

   $^{1}_{1}H + ^{2}_{1}H \rightarrow ^{3}_{2}He + \gamma$

   (Atomic masses: $^{1}_{1}H$ = 1.007825 u; $^{2}_{1}H$ = 2.014102 u; $^{3}_{2}He$ = 3.016029 u.)

3. Deuterium–tritium fusion, $^{2}_{1}H + ^{3}_{1}H \rightarrow ^{4}_{2}He + ^{1}_{0}n$, happens at a lower temperature than deuterium–deuterium fusion, $^{2}_{1}H + ^{2}_{1}H \rightarrow ^{3}_{2}He + ^{1}_{0}n$. Can you suggest a reason for this observation?

4. State and explain one difficulty that still prevents the commercial production of energy through nuclear fusion.

5. Suggest two advantages of energy production that nuclear fusion would have over energy production by nuclear fission.

25.2 Stellar properties and the Hertzsprung–Russell diagram

The Hertzsprung–Russell diagram

For this section you may need to review the material on luminosity and apparent brightness in Section 7.3. In the early part of the twentieth century, the Danish astronomer Ejnar Hertzsprung and the American Henry Norris Russell independently pioneered plots of stellar luminosities. They plotted luminosity on the vertical axis and surface temperature on the horizontal axis (increasing to the left). Such plots are now called **Hertzsprung–Russell (HR) diagrams**. In the HR diagram of Figure 25.1 luminosity is given in terms of the sun's luminosity (i.e. 1 on the vertical axis corresponds to the solar luminosity $L_\odot = 3.9 \times 10^{26}$ W; astronomers use the symbol ⊙ to denote quantities pertaining to the sun). The surface temperature is given in thousands of kelvin.

The luminosity in this diagram varies from 10^{-4} to 10^4, a full 8 orders of magnitude, whereas the temperature varies from 3000 K to 30 000 K. For this reason, the scale on both axes is not linear so that all data can fit.

25 Nuclear fusion and stars

> **EXAM TIP**
>
> It is important that you understand the HR diagram very well.

The slanted dotted lines represent stars with the same radius. So our sun and Procyon A have about the same radius. The symbol $R_\odot$ stands for the radius of our sun.

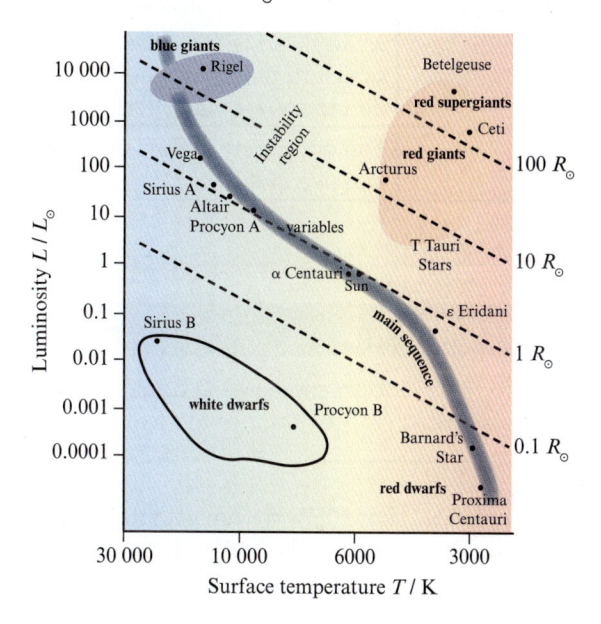

Figure 25.1: The Hertzsprung–Russell diagram. The (surface) temperature increases to the left. Note that the scales are not linear. The dotted lines represent stars with the same radius. $R_\odot$ is the radius of the sun.

> **CHECK YOURSELF 2**
>
> Sirius A and Sirius B occupy very different places on the HR diagram. Can we conclude that these stars are physically far from each other in space?

As more and more stars were placed on the HR diagram, three clear features emerged:

Most stars fall on a strip extending diagonally across the diagram from top left to bottom right. This is called the **main sequence**.

Some large stars, reddish in colour, occupy the top right—these are the **red giants** (large and cool). Above these are the super red giants (also known as red supergiants) and are even larger and brighter than red giants.

The bottom left is a region of small stars known as **white dwarfs** (small and hot).

As we move along the *main sequence* toward hotter stars, the mass of the stars increases. Thus, the right end of the main sequence is occupied by red dwarfs and the left by blue giants.

An almost vertical strip above the main sequence is known as the **instability region**. We will discuss this region a bit later in the section on stellar evolution. It contains stars that have a variable luminosity.

Note that, once we know the temperature of a star (for example, through its spectrum), the HR diagram can tell us the luminosity of the star with an acceptable degree of accuracy, provided we know what type of star it is.

Main sequence stars

Our sun is a typical member of the main sequence. It has a mass of 2×10^{30} kg, a radius of 7×10^8 m, an average density of 1.4×10^3 kg m^{-3} and radiates at a rate of 3.9×10^{26} W. Main sequence stars produce energy in their core from nuclear fusion of hydrogen into helium. The outflow of energy from the core creates an outward radiation pressure that exactly counterbalances the tendency of the star to collapse under its own weight. The common characteristic of all main sequence stars is the fusion of hydrogen into helium.

> **KEY POINT**
>
> Stable stars are in equilibrium due to a balance of the inward gravitational pressure and the outward radiation pressure.

Red giants and super red giants

Red giants are very large, cool stars with a reddish colour. The luminosity of red giants is considerably greater than the luminosity of main sequence stars of the same temperature. Treating them as black bodies radiating according to the Stefan–Boltzmann law means that a luminosity of 10^6 times larger corresponds to an area of 10^6 times larger, which means a radius of 10^3 times larger, Figure 25.2. The mass of a red giant can be as much as 1000 times the mass of our sun, but their huge size also implies small densities. A red giant will have a central hot core surrounded by an enormous envelope of extremely tenuous gas.

517

PHYSICS FOR THE IB DIPLOMA: COURSEBOOK

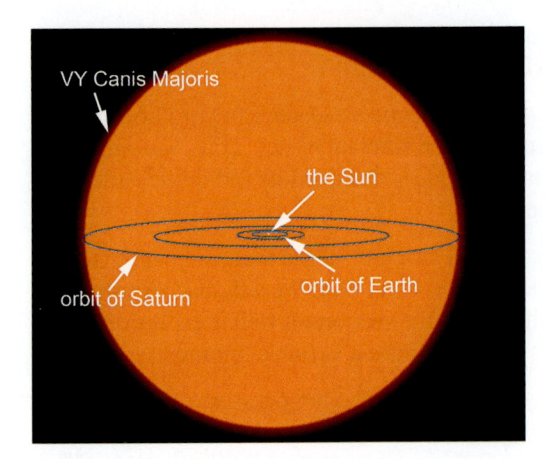

Figure 25.2: Artist's impression of the comparison between our sun and the red supergiant VY Canis Majoris.

White dwarfs

These are common stars, but their faintness makes them hard to detect. A well-known white dwarf is Sirius B, the second star in a binary star system (double star system), the other member of which, Sirius A, is the brightest star in the evening sky, Figure 25.3.

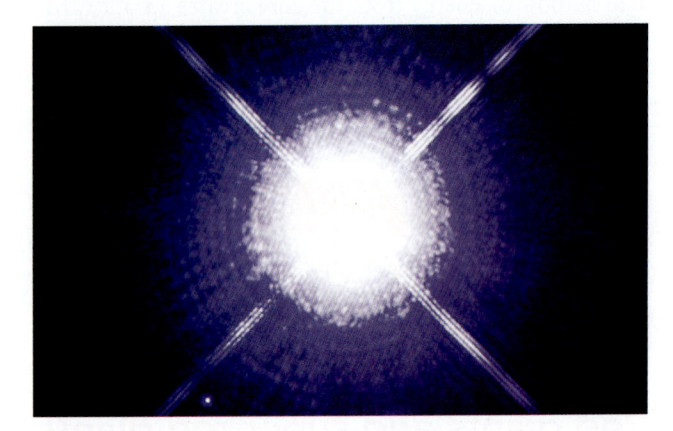

Figure 25.3: Sirius A is the bright star in the middle of the photograph. The white dwarf companion Sirius B is the tiny speck of light lower left. The rings and spikes are artifacts of the telescope's imaging systems. The photograph has been overexposed so that the faint Sirius B could be seen.

Sirius A and B have about the same surface temperature (about 10 000 K), but the luminosity of Sirius B is about 10 000 times smaller. This means that Sirius B has a radius that is 100 times smaller than that of Sirius A. Here is a star of mass roughly that of the sun with a size similar to that of the earth. This means that its density is more than about 10^6 times the density of the earth!

Type of star	Main characteristic
Main sequence star	Fuses hydrogen into helium
Red giant	Bright, large, cool, reddish, tenuous
Super red giant	Even larger and brighter than red giants
White dwarf	Dim, small, hot, whitish, dense
Neutron star	Dimmer and smaller than a white dwarf with a density similar to that of nuclei. Too dim to show on an HR diagram
Black hole	The end point of the very massive stars.

Table 25.1

CHECK YOURSELF 3

One star appears reddish and another appears bluish. Explain which is the hotter of the two.

Worked example 25.3 shows how we can get information on stellar radii. The key idea is the Stefan–Boltzmann law that states that $L = \sigma A T^4$. Since the area is given by $A = 4\pi R^2$ we find

$$R = \sqrt{\frac{L}{4\pi \sigma T^4}}$$

WORKED EXAMPLE 25.3

The HR diagram (Figure 25.4) shows three stars, A, B and C.

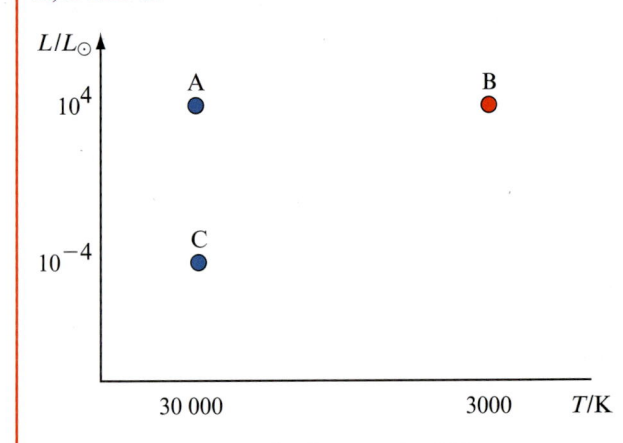

Figure 25.4: For worked example 25.3.

25 Nuclear fusion and stars

> **CONTINUED**
>
> **a** Calculate the ratio of radii $\frac{R_A}{R_C}$ and $\frac{R_B}{R_A}$.
>
> **b** Estimate the wavelength at which star C emits most of its light.
>
> **Answer**
>
> **a** $\dfrac{L_A}{L_C} = 10^8 = \dfrac{\sigma(4\pi R_A^2)T_A^4}{\sigma(4\pi R_C^2)T_C^4} = \dfrac{R_A^2}{R_C^2}$
>
> Hence:
>
> $\dfrac{R_A}{R_C} = 10^4$
>
> Similarly:
>
> $\dfrac{L_B}{L_A} = 1 = \dfrac{\sigma(4\pi R_B^2)T_B^4}{\sigma(4\pi R_A^2)T_A^4} = \left(\dfrac{R_B^2}{R_A^2}\right)\left(\dfrac{3000}{30\,000}\right)^4$
>
> Hence:
>
> $\dfrac{R_B}{R_A} = \left(\dfrac{30\,000}{3000}\right)^2 = 100$.
>
> **b** From Wien's law: $\lambda \times 30000 = 2.9 \times 10^{-3}$ K m and so $\lambda = 9.7 \times 10^{-8}$ m.

To measure the radius of a star through its temperature and lumininosity assumes we know the temperature and luminosity! Temperature can be measured using Wien's law. But what about luminosity? We can find it, if we know its apparent brightness (which is easily measured) and the distance. So what about distance? There are various methods for doing that. In this course we will learn about a method that works for nearby stars. It is called the **parallax** method. It is based on the fact that when you look at an object from two different positions, the object *appears to shift relative to the very distant background*. You can easily see this: hold up a finger in front of you and look at it with the left eye closed. Now look at it with the right eye closed. The finger looks shifted relative to distant objects.

Figure 25.5 shows two observations of the star from two positions six months apart.

The parallax angle is the angle at which the star subtends a distance equal to the earth orbit radius R.

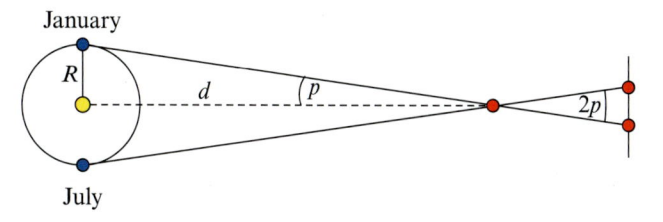

Figure 25.5: The earth (blue circles) in orbit around the sun. The star is observed from two positions six months apart.

Figures 25.6a and 25.6b show the two images of the star taken six months apart. In Figure 25.6c the two images are put together.

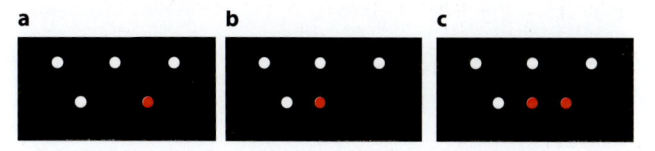

Figure 25.6: The white stars represent the distant background. **a** The star observed from one position. **b** The star observed from another position six months later. **c** The two images are put together to determine the parallax angle. The shift shown here is greatly exaggerated.

Parallax angles are very small. It is convenient to express them in arc seconds (arcsec): one degree contains 60 arc minutes and one arc minute contains 60 arc seconds. So 1° = 3600 arcsec. Now suppose we define a new unit of distance, the parsec, pc. One parsec is the distance at which the parallax is 1 arcsec. So if we are told that a star has parallax p in arcsec, the distance in pc is

$$d \text{ (in pc)} = \dfrac{1}{p \text{(in arcsec)}}$$

How many metres are there in a pc? From Figure 25.5, we see that

$$\tan p = \dfrac{R}{d}$$

The distance d is 1 pc when p = 1 arcsec; $R = 1.496 \times 10^{11}$ m and so

$$1 \text{ pc} = \dfrac{1.496 \times 10^{11}}{\tan\left(\frac{1}{3600}\right)^\circ} = 3.086 \times 10^{16} \approx 3.09 \times 10^{16} \text{ m}$$

This is a convenient unit for distance in astronomy. Another is the light year, ly, which is the distance travelled by light in one year: 1 ly = $3.0 \times 10^8 \times 365 \times 24 \times 60 \times 60 = 9.461 \times 10^{15}$ m. It follows that:

$$1 \text{ pc} = \dfrac{3.086 \times 10^{16}}{9.461 \times 10^{15}} = 3.26 \text{ ly}$$

So, a star with a parallax angle of 0.125 arcsec is at a distance of 8.0 pc or 26 ly or 2.5×10^{17} m.

The method is restricted to nearby stars. Stars far away have parallax angles that are too small to measure accurately. The limit for earth-bound telescopes is about 100 pc. However, satellite-based systems such as the Hubble space telescope, the JWST (James Webb Space Telescope) and ESA's Gaia can measure parallaxes to distances up to 3000 pc.

The proton–proton chain

The main series of nuclear fusion reactions taking place in the cores of low mass main sequence stars is the **proton–proton chain**:

$${}^1_1H + {}^1_1H \rightarrow {}^2_1H + {}^0_1e^+ + {}^0_0\nu$$

$${}^1_1H + {}^2_1H \rightarrow {}^3_2He + {}^0_0\gamma$$

$${}^3_2He + {}^3_2He \rightarrow {}^4_2He + 2{}^1_1H$$

Notice that the deuterium and helium-3 produced in the first and second stages are used up again. In this cycle, the net effect is to turn four hydrogen nuclei into one nucleus of helium. We can see this by rewriting the reaction equations above after having multiplied the first two by 2. Nuclei in the same colour 'cancel out', i.e. what is produced is used up again:

$$2 \times {}^1_1H + 2 \times {}^1_1H \rightarrow 2 \times {}^2_1H + 2 \times {}^0_1e^+ + 2 \times {}^0_0\nu$$

$$2 \times {}^1_1H + 2 \times {}^2_1H \rightarrow 2 \times {}^3_2He + 2 \times {}^0_0\gamma$$

$$\underline{{}^3_2He + {}^3_2He \rightarrow {}^4_2He + 2 \times {}^1_1H}$$

$$4 \times {}^1_1H \rightarrow {}^4_2He + 2 \times {}^0_1e^+ + 2 \times {}^0_0\nu + 2 \times {}^0_0\gamma$$

WORKED EXAMPLE 25.4

Our sun emits energy at a rate (luminosity) of about 3.9×10^{26} W.

The mass of the sun = 2.0×10^{30} kg.

When the sun was created, 75% of its mass was hydrogen.

Estimate the mass of hydrogen that undergoes fusion in a year.

Assuming that the energy loss is maintained at this rate, find the time required for the sun to convert 12% of its original hydrogen into helium.

(Assume that energy is produced in the proton–proton chain with an energy released per reaction of about 3.98×10^{-12} J.)

CONTINUED

Answer

Since the luminosity of the sun is 3.9×10^{26} W, it follows that the number of fusion reactions required per second is

$$\frac{3.9 \times 10^{26}}{3.98 \times 10^{-12}} = 9.8 \times 10^{37}$$

For every such reaction, four hydrogen nuclei turn into helium, and thus the mass of the fused hydrogen is:

$$9.8 \times 10^{37} \times 4 \times 1.67 \times 10^{-27} \text{ kg s}^{-1} = 6.5 \times 10^{11} \text{ kg s}^{-1}$$

or 2×10^{19} kg per year.

At the time of its creation, the sun consisted of 75% hydrogen, corresponding to a mass of

$$0.75 \times 2.0 \times 10^{30} \text{ kg} = 1.5 \times 10^{30} \text{ kg}$$

The limit of 12% results in a hydrogen mass to be fused of 1.8×10^{29} kg. The time for this mass to fuse is thus

$$\frac{1.8 \times 10^{29}}{6.5 \times 10^{11}} \text{ s} = 2.8 \times 10^{17} \text{ s}$$

$$= 9 \times 10^9 \text{ yr}$$

Since the sun has existed for about 5 billion years, it still has about 4 billion years left in its lifetime as a main sequence star.

In stars more massive than our sun the CNO cycle dominates. Its net effect is to convert four hydrogen nuclei into one of helium just like the proton-proton chain. See extension material at the end of the chapter.

Stellar evolution

When about 12% of the hydrogen in the star is used up in nuclear fusion, a series of instabilities develop in the star. These have the result that the delicate balance between the radiation and gravitational pressures is upset. The star will then begin to move away from the main sequence. What happens next is determined mainly by the mass of the star. Other types of nuclear fusion reactions will take place and the star changes in size and surface temperature (and hence colour).

25 Nuclear fusion and stars

> **KEY POINT**
>
> The mass of the star is the main factor that determines its evolution off the main sequence.

Figure 25.7 shows a schematic summary of the life history of a star.

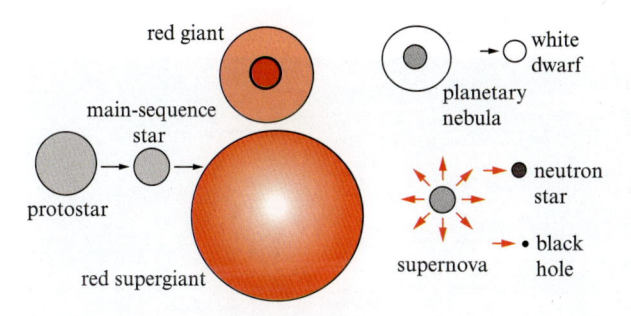

Figure 25.7: The birth and death of a star. The star begins as a protostar, evolves to the main sequence and then becomes a red giant or supergiant. After a planetary nebula or supernova explosion, the core of the star develops into one of the three final stages of stellar evolution, a white dwarf, a neutron star or a black hole.

The star is called a protostar when it is first formed. It then settles on the main sequence according to its temperature and luminosity.

A low mass star (this means of mass less than about 12 solar masses) will follow the top path leading to red giant, an explosion called a **planetary nebula** and the final remnant of a white dwarf. A heavier star will follow the lower path leading to a red supergiant and a more violent explosion called a **supernova** leaving behind a neutron star or a black hole.

The paths shown schematically in Figure 25.8 can also be shown on HR diagrams.

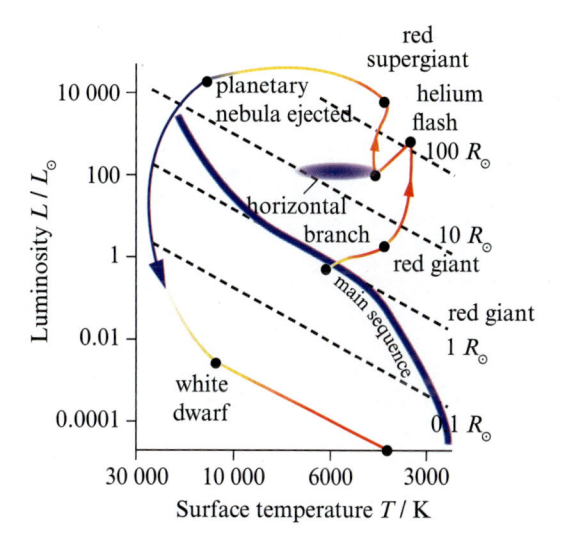

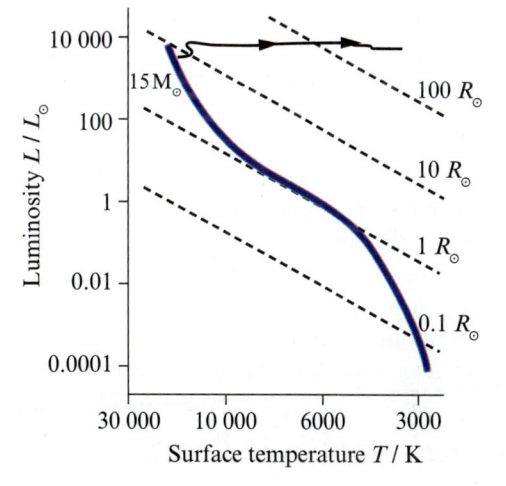

Figure 25.8: a Evolutionary path of a low mass star. This is the path of a star of one solar mass that ends up as a white dwarf, which continues to cool down, moving the star ever more to the right on the HR diagram. **b** This is the path of a star of 15 solar masses. It becomes a red supergiant that explodes in a supernova. After the supernova, the star becomes a neutron star, whose luminosity is too small to be plotted on the HR diagram.

As seen in Figure 25.8a, a star will leave the main sequence following an almost horizontal path on the HR diagram. A star more massive than the sun may go back and forth on the HR diagram several times as shown in Figure 25.9; the star is now in the instability region of the HR diagram.

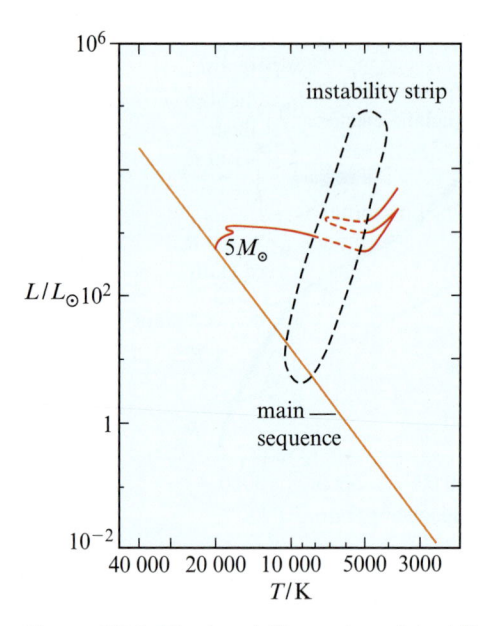

Figure 25.9: The instability region of the HR diagram.

The delicate balance between radiation and gravitational pressures has been disturbed; the star tries to find a new equilibrium state but instead the star pulsates, i.e. it grows and then shrinks in size. So the star cools and heats up during these pulsations and that affects the rate and type of nuclear fusion reactions taking place. This makes its luminosity variable, and this is a general characteristic of all stars in the instability region.

The Chandrasekhar limit

Low mass stars after ejecting mass into space in the planetary nebula explosion leave behind a core, Figure 25.10. The conditions in the core mean that the electrons behave as a gas, and the pressure they generate is what keeps the core from collapsing further under its weight. This pressure (electron degeneracy pressure) is a quantum effect and beyond the level of this course.

The core has now become a white dwarf star. Now exposed, and with no further energy source, the star is doomed to cool down and will then become what is called a *black dwarf*.

This pressure is able to stop the further collapse of the core only if the mass of the core is less than a certain limit.

> ### KEY POINT
> This is known as the **Chandrasekhar limit** and is the largest mass a white dwarf star can have. It equals $1.4M_\odot$.

The limit is named after the astrophysicist S. Chandrasekhar, Figure 25.12, who discovered it in the 1930s.

Figure 25.10: The Helix: a planetary nebula. The star that produced this nebula can be seen at the exact centre.

> ### CHECK YOURSELF 4
> What is the minimum mass that must be ejected by a 3 solar mass star so that it ends up as a white dwarf?

The Oppenheimer–Volkoff limit

If the Chandasekhar limit is exceeded, electrons will be forced into protons, turning them into neutrons. The star is now made almost entirely of neutrons, and it is still contracting rapidly. The neutrons get too close to each other, and a pressure develops to prevent them from getting any closer. But the neutrons have overshot. They have become too close together, and the entire core will now rebound to a larger size. The rebounding of the core is catastrophic for the star. It creates an enormous shockwave travelling outward that tears apart the outer layers of the star. The explosion that takes place is much more violent than a planetary nebula and is called a supernova, Figure 25.11. The core that is left behind is called a neutron star.

The core is kept stable by quantum effects similar to those in the white dwarf case provided the mass of the core is not more than the **Oppenheimer–Volkoff limit**. The Oppenheimer–Volkoff limit is the largest mass a neutron star can have and equals about $3M_\odot$.

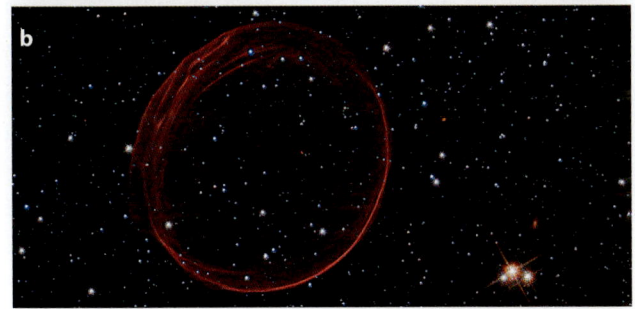

Figure 25.11: a The Crab nebula, the remnant of a supernova observed by the Chinese in 1054 and perhaps also by Native Americans. It was visible for weeks even during daytime. **b** This majestically serene bubble of gas is the remnant of a supernova that happened 400 years ago.

If the original mass of the star is very high ($M > 40M_\odot$), nothing can stop further collapse and the core will become a black hole. Black holes are predicted by Einstein's theory of general relativity.

> **CHECK YOURSELF 5**
>
> A main sequence star increases its luminosity when it becomes a red supergiant even though its temperature decreases. How is this explained?

25.3 Stellar evolution extension

The creation of the elements

The hydrogen in the universe and most of the helium (and some lithium) were produced at the very earliest times in the life of the universe. The rest of the elements were produced in a process known as **nucleosynthesis** in stars, in the process of stellar evolution.

We have seen that for low mass stars, the dominant nuclear fusion reaction is the proton-proton chain which results in the fusion of four hydrogen nuclei into one nucleus of helium. For stars more massive than about 1.5 solar masses there is a second way to fuse hydrogen into helium. This is the CNO (carbon, nitrogen, oxygen) cycle and is described by the series of fusion reactions:

$${}^{1}_{1}H + {}^{12}_{6}C \rightarrow {}^{13}_{7}N + \gamma$$

$${}^{13}_{7}N \rightarrow {}^{13}_{6}C + {}^{0}_{1}e^{+} + \nu$$

$${}^{1}_{1}H + {}^{13}_{6}C \rightarrow {}^{14}_{7}N + \gamma$$

$${}^{1}_{1}H + {}^{14}_{7}N \rightarrow {}^{15}_{8}O + \gamma$$

$${}^{15}_{8}O \rightarrow {}^{15}_{7}N + {}^{0}_{1}e^{+} + \nu$$

$${}^{1}_{1}H + {}^{15}_{7}N \rightarrow {}^{12}_{6}C + {}^{4}_{2}He$$

Notice that the net effect is just to turn four hydrogen nuclei into one of helium just like the proton-proton chain. The heavier elements produced in intermediate stages are all used up. Carbon has 6 units of positive charge so the Coulomb barrier that needs to be overcome for carbon to fuse is much higher. This requires higher temperatures which can be found in the more massive stars.

The proton-proton chain and the CNO cycle are both main sequence star processes. What happens beyond the main sequence? Almost everything that happens to a star from now on depends on the mass of the star.

For low mass stars, the helium produced in the p-p chain is collecting in the core of the star surrounded by a thin shell of hydrogen and a bigger hydrogen envelope, Figure 25.12.

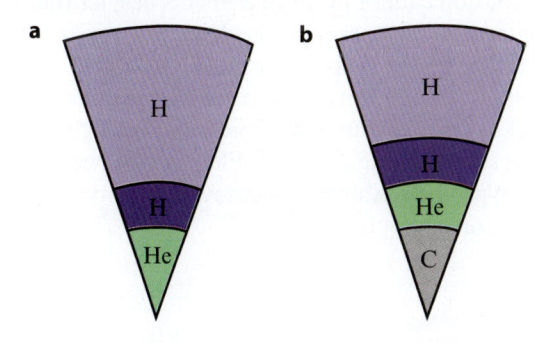

Figure 25.12: a The structure of a low mass star after it leaves the main sequence. **b** After helium begins to fuse, carbon collects in the core.

523

In more massive stars, carbon will replace helium in the core once carbon starts getting produced in the *triple alpha process*:

$${}^4_2\text{He} + {}^4_2\text{He} \rightarrow {}^8_4\text{Be} + \gamma$$

$${}^4_2\text{He} + {}^8_4\text{Be} \rightarrow {}^{12}_6\text{C} + \gamma$$

Only hydrogen in the thin shell is undergoing nuclear fusion. The temperature and pressure of helium build up and eventually helium begins to fuse through the triple alpha process. This called the 'helium flash'. This only lasts a few minutes but during this time enormous amounts of energy are produced. Carbon collects in the core, with helium now fusing in a thin shell around carbon. The hydrogen in the thin shell is still fusing so the star now has nuclear fusion in two shells, the H and He shells. This release of energy blows away the outer layers of the star in an explosion called a planetary nebula; mass is thrown into space leaving behind a helium or carbon core.

For high mass stars (those with more than 8 solar masses) helium fuses with carbon to produce oxygen:

$${}^4_2\text{He} + {}^{12}_6\text{C} \rightarrow {}^{16}_8\text{O} + \gamma$$

For even more massive stars neon, sodium and magnesium are produced:

$${}^{12}_6\text{C} + {}^{12}_6\text{C} \rightarrow {}^{20}_{10}\text{Ne} + {}^4_2\text{He}$$

$${}^{12}_6\text{C} + {}^{12}_6\text{C} \rightarrow {}^{23}_{11}\text{Na} + {}^1_1\text{H}$$

$${}^{12}_6\text{C} + {}^{12}_6\text{C} \rightarrow {}^{23}_{12}\text{Mg} + {}^1_0\text{n}$$

Silicon is then produced through fusion of oxygen:

$${}^{16}_8\text{O} + {}^{16}_8\text{O} \rightarrow {}^{28}_{14}\text{Si} + {}^4_2\text{He}$$

The process continues until iron is formed. This creates the onion like layered structure of the star with progressively heavier elements as we move in towards the centre. Fusion cannot produce elements heavier than iron, since the binding energy per nucleon peaks near iron and further fusion is not energetically possible. Thus, a massive star ends its cycle of nuclear reactions with iron at its core surrounded by progressively lighter elements, as shown in Figure 25.13. Elements heavier than iron are produced during supernova explosions through neutron absorption.

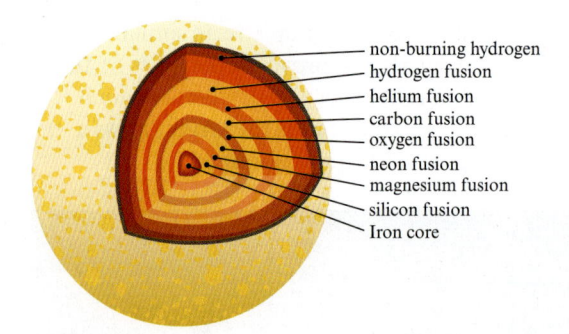

Figure 25.13: The central core of fully evolved massive star consists of iron with layers of successively lighter elements surrounding it.

In summary:

- A star with an initial mass $M < 0.25 M_\odot$ ends up as a white dwarf with a helium core.

- A star with an initial mass $0.25 M_\odot < M < 8 M_\odot$ ends up as a white dwarf with a carbon core.

- A star with an initial mass $8 M_\odot < M < 12 M_\odot$ ends up as a white dwarf with an oxygen/neon/magnesium core.

- A star with an initial mass $12 M_\odot < M < 40 M_\odot$ ends up as a neutron star.

- A star with an initial mass $M > 40 M_\odot$ ends up as a black hole.

Links

The study of stars requires knowledge from very many different areas of physics including gravitation, hydrodynamics, atomic physics, plasma physics, electrodynanics, magnetohydrodynamics, condensed matter physics, relativity and of course nuclear physics. Treating the material in a star as an ideal gas gives approximately correct results for some main sequence stars but fails completely for white dwarf and neutron stars where the ideal gas approximation has to be replaced by other more exotic states of matter.

25 Nuclear fusion and stars

NATURE OF SCIENCE

The supreme problem solver and the death of a star

Figure 25.14: Hans Bethe (1906–2005) and Subrahmanyan Chandrasekhar (1910–1995).

Much about the nature of nuclear fusion in stars was discovered by Hans Bethe. Freeman Dyson, one of Bethe's greatest students, called him the 'supreme problem solver of the twentieth century'. Bethe was active as a physicist well into his nineties! After providing the details of the proton–proton chain, he wrote a paper on what was to become known as the carbon–nitrogen–oxygen cycle (the CNO cycle), a series of reactions taking place in heavier stars as they evolve. Bethe found out that the New York Academy of Sciences was offering a $500 prize for the best paper on energy production in stars. Originally planning publication in another journal, Bethe entered the competition, won it and with the prize money managed to do a great favour for his mother: relocate her furniture from Germany to the United States. The family, fearing persecution, had left Germany in 1939. For his work on the production of energy in stars, Bethe received the 1967 Nobel Prize in Physics. Bethe is also famous for a paper he did *not* write: in a paper written by G. Gamow and R. Alpher, Gamow added the name of Bethe so the paper is now known as the alpha, beta, gamma paper. He was in charge of the theoretical division of the Manhattan project that developed the atomic bomb during World War II. He later became a critic of the nuclear arms race and warned of the dangers of nuclear weapons.

Subrahmanyan Chandrasekhar was an Indian, and later American, astrophysicist. His work on collapsed stars was started on the long boat ride from India to England where he was going to study at the University of Cambridge.

His work was presented in 1935 at a meeting of the Royal Astronomical Society in England. His ideas were publicly ridiculed by Sir Arthur Eddington, his colleague and mentor at Cambridge. Undeterred, Chandraseshkar continued his work, and seven years later he moved to the University of Chicago where he remained for the rest of his academic career, becoming one of the greatest and most influential astrophysicists of the twentieth century. A long overdue Nobel Prize in Physics was awarded to Chandrasekhar in 1983. A moving article on Chandrasekhar's work, in *Nature* **438**, 1086 (2005), by Freeman Dyson, is aptly entitled 'The death of a star'.

TEST YOUR UNDERSTANDING

6   a   State what is meant by an HR diagram.

    b   Describe the main features of the HR diagram.

7   a   Estimate the ratio of radii of two stars, A and B, of the same luminosity and temperatures $T_A = 3.2 \times 10^4$ K and $T_B = 2.9 \times 10^3$ K.

    b   Estimate the ratio of radii of two stars, C and D, of the same temperature and luminosities $L_C = 5.0 \times 10^{28}$ W and $L_D = 2.4 \times 10^{22}$ W.

    c   Place the stars A, B, C and D on a copy of the HR diagram (Figure 25.15).

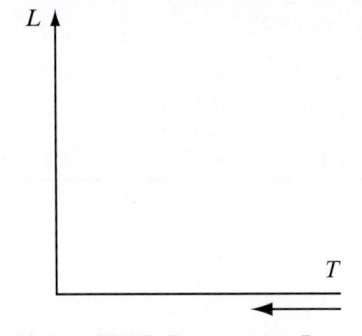

Figure 25.15: For question 7.

CONTINUED

8. A main sequence star has temperature 3000 K. Use the HR diagram in the text to estimate its radius in terms of the solar radius.

9. The parallax of a star is 0.0125 arc seconds. What is its distance in metres?

10. The parallax of a star is 0.022 arc seconds. The apparent brightness of the star is 5.0×10^{-10} W m^{-2} and its surface temperature is 4500 K. What is the radius of this star?

11. Lunar occultation is a method for finding the radius of a star. The idea is to measure how long it takes for the moon to cover the star as the moon passes in front of the star.

    a The moon makes a full revolution around the earth in 27 days. Show that the angular speed of the moon is 2.7×10^{-6} rad s^{-1}.

    b A star is covered by the moon in 17 ms. What is the angular diameter of the star?

    c The parallax of the star is 0.167 arcsec. What is the radius of the star?

12. Describe the formation of a red giant star.

13. a Describe what is meant by a planetary nebula.

    b Suggest why most photographs show planetary nebulae as rings—doesn't the gas surround the core from all directions?

    c To eject mass from a star in a planetary nebula, the core of the star must exert a force on the outer layers of the star. What force is then exerted on the core and what does this imply?

14. Verify that at each stage of the proton–proton chain the indicated energies are released.

    $\underbrace{{}^{1}_{1}H + {}^{1}_{1}H \rightarrow {}^{2}_{1}H + {}^{0}_{1}e^+ + {}^{0}_{0}\nu}_{0.42 \text{ MeV}}, \underbrace{{}^{1}_{1}H + {}^{2}_{1}H \rightarrow {}^{3}_{2}He + {}^{0}_{0}\gamma}_{5.49 \text{ MeV}}$

    $\underbrace{{}^{3}_{2}He + {}^{3}_{2}He \rightarrow {}^{4}_{2}He + 2{}^{1}_{1}H}_{12.86 \text{ MeV}}$

    Hence determine the *total* energy produced when four protons fuse to make one helium nucleus. (You will need the off-syllabus information that when one positron collides with one electron an amount of energy equal to 1.02 MeV is produced. The positron in stage 1 will certainly do that with a surrounding electron.)

    Atomic masses: ${}^{1}_{1}H$ = 1.007825 u, ${}^{2}_{1}H$ = 2.014103 u, ${}^{3}_{2}He$ = 3.016029 u, ${}^{4}_{2}He$ = 4.002603 u.

15. Describe the evolution of a main sequence star of mass:

    a 2 solar masses

    b 20 solar masses.

16. a Describe the formation of a white dwarf star.

    b State two properties of a white dwarf.

17. Describe two differences between a main sequence star and a white dwarf.

18. A white dwarf of mass half that of the sun and radius equal to one earth radius is formed. Estimate the density of this white dwarf. ($M_\odot = 2.0 \times 10^{30}$ kg, $R_E = 6.4 \times 10^{6}$ m.)

19. Explain what is meant by the terms

    a instability region

    b supernova.

20. State and explain two changes in the appearance of a main sequence star as it moves into the red giant phase.

21. Describe two differences between a main sequence star and a neutron star.

22. a Describe the formation of a neutron star.

    b State two properties of a neutron star.

23. a The triple alpha process is the series of reactions

    ${}^{4}_{2}He + {}^{4}_{2}He \rightarrow {}^{8}_{4}Be + \gamma$

    ${}^{4}_{2}He + {}^{8}_{4}Be \rightarrow {}^{12}_{6}C + \gamma$

CONTINUED

Show that the net effect of the triple alpha process is to fuse three helium nuclei into one of carbon-12.

b Show that the energy released in the triple alpha process is 7.27 MeV. (Helium mass = 4.0026 u.)

c Assume that all the mass of a star is made entirely of helium. The mass is 3.0×10^{32} kg and the luminosity is 1.6×10^{34} W. How long would it take this star to convert all the helium to carbon?

24 The CNO cycle is a series of nuclear fusion reactions taking place in massive stars. It consists of the reactions

$${}^{1}_{1}H + {}^{12}_{6}C \rightarrow {}^{13}_{7}N + \gamma$$

$${}^{13}_{7}N \rightarrow {}^{13}_{6}C + {}^{0}_{1}e^{+} + \nu$$

$${}^{1}_{1}H + {}^{13}_{6}C \rightarrow {}^{14}_{7}N + \gamma$$

$${}^{1}_{1}H + {}^{14}_{7}N \rightarrow {}^{15}_{8}O + \gamma$$

$${}^{15}_{8}O \rightarrow {}^{15}_{7}N + {}^{0}_{1}e^{+} + \nu$$

$${}^{1}_{1}H + {}^{15}_{7}N \rightarrow {}^{12}_{6}C + {}^{4}_{2}He$$

a Explain why the CNO cycle happens only in massive stars.

b Explain why the net effect of the CNO cycle is to turn four hydrogen nuclei into one of helium.

SELF-ASSESSMENT CHECKLIST

I am able to …	Section	Not yet	Nearly there	Ready to move on
describe nuclear fusion	25.1			
calculate the energy released in a nuclear fusion reaction	25.1			
describe the conditions necessary for nuclear fusion	25.1			
explain why nuclear fusion takes place in stellar cores	25.1			
appreciate the role of mass in stellar evolution	25.2			
show the evolution of a star on an HR diagram	25.2			
find the distance to a star using the method of parallax	25.2			
calculate the radius of a star from its temperature and luminosity	25.2			
appreciate the role of the Chandrasekhar and Oppenheimer–Volkoff limits	25.2			

REFLECTION

Can you describe the conditions necessary for *nuclear fusion* to occur? Do you appreciate the role of fusion in energy production in stars? Do you understand the main features and regions of a *Hertzsprung-Russel diagram*? Do you understand the role of mass in *stellar evolution*? Do you appreciate the role nuclear fusion for nucleosynthesis? Can you describe the stages in the evolution of a *main sequence star*? Can you solve problems with luminosity and *apparent brightness*? Do you understand what is meant by *stellar parallax*?

PHYSICS FOR THE IB DIPLOMA: COURSEBOOK

EXAM-STYLE QUESTIONS

You can find questions in the style of IB exams in the digital coursebook.

CHECK YOURSELF ANSWERS

1. The nuclei have to overcome the Coulomb repulsion of their positive electric charges. High temperatures imply high nuclei speeds so they can crash into each other.

2. No, being close to each other on the HR diagram says nothing about the actual distances between stars.

3. By Wien's law, the bluish star is hotter since blue has a shorter wavelength than red.

4. 1.6 solar masses in order to satisfy the Chandrasekhar limit.

5. The surface area increases massively.

Glossary

absolute zero the temperature at which all random motion of molecules stops

absorption spectrum the set of wavelengths that can be absorbed

acceleration the rate of change of velocity; it is a vector

acceleration of free fall the acceleration, g, due to the pull of the earth on a body; $g = 9.8 \text{ m s}^{-2}$ near the surface of the earth

activity the rate of decay (number of decays per second)

adiabatic a thermodynamic process in which no heat enters or leaves the system

albedo the ratio of reflected to incident power or intensity; it has no unit

alpha decay a decay of a nucleus producing an alpha particle

alternating current (ac) current which varies between positive and negative values

alternating voltage voltage which varies between positive and negative values

ammeter an instrument that measures the electric current through it

amplitude the maximum displacement from equilibrium of a wave or oscillation

angular acceleration the rate of change of angular velocity; measured in rad s^{-2}

angular displacement the change in angular position; measured in rad

angular impulse the change in angular momentum

angular momentum the product of moment of inertia and angular velocity, $L = I\omega$

angular position the angle defining the position of a particle relative to some arbitrary reference line; measured in rad

angular speed, ω the rate of change of the angle swept by an object as it moves along a circular path: $\omega = \frac{2\pi}{T} = 2\pi f$

angular velocity the rate of change of the angular position; measured in rad s^{-1}

antinode a point on a standing wave where the displacement is a maximum (at some instant)

apparent brightness the power received from a star per unit area (of the detector)

atmosphere a non-SI unit of pressure

atomic mass unit $\frac{1}{12}$ of the mass of the neutral atom of carbon-12.

average speed total distance travelled divided by the time taken

average velocity total displacement divided by total time

Avogadro constant the number of particles in one mole: $6.02214076 \times 10^{23}$

background radiation radiation from natural sources such as cosmic rays and radioactive material in rocks

beta minus decay a decay of a nucleus producing an electron and an anti-neutrino

beta plus decay a decay of a nucleus producing a positron and a neutrino

binding energy the minimum energy required to separate the nucleons of a nucleus; $E_b = \mu c^2$

black body a theoretical body that absorbs all the radiation incident on it and radiates the maximum possible intensity for a given temperature

blue-shift the shift in wavelength towards smaller wavelengths for an approaching source

Boltzmann constant the ratio of the gas constant to Avogadro's number

buoyant force the force acting on an object in a fluid due to a difference in pressure at the top and bottom of the body; force is opposite to weight

Carnot cycle a thermodynamic cycle consisting of two isothermal and two adiabatic curves

centripetal acceleration the rate of change of velocity of a body in circular motion; given as $a = \frac{\Delta v}{\Delta t} = \frac{v^2}{r} = r\omega^2 = v\omega$ and is directed towards the centre of the circle

centripetal force the force directed toward the centre of a circular path; given as $F = \frac{mv^2}{r} = m\omega^2 r = mv\omega$

chain reaction a reaction in which the products are used to keep the reaction going

Chandrasekhar limit the maximum possible mass of a white dwarf, about 1.4 solar masses

closed system a system that can transfer energy, but not matter (mass), into or from its surroundings

coefficient of dynamic friction the ratio of the force of friction to the normal contact force on a on a body that is sliding along a surface

coefficient of static friction the ratio of the maximum force of friction between two bodies to the normal contact force when an object is at rest

coherent sources sources with the same frequency and a constant phase difference between them

compression a point where the density of the medium is highest

Compton scattering the scattering of light off an electron

condensation when a vapour changes into a liquid (thermal energy is transferred away from the vapour)

conduction method of thermal energy transfer based on collisions of electrons with atoms

conductors materials with many free electrons per unit volume, through which thermal energy and electric current can pass easily

conservation of angular momentum when the net torque on a system is zero, the angular momentum is conserved; that is, it stays constant

conservation of momentum when the net force on a system is zero, the total momentum of the system remains constant

conserved a quantity that stays the same before and after an interaction

constructive interference superposition of waves leading to maximum amplitude

control rods rods that can easily absorb neutrons that are raised and lowered into the core of the reactor in order to control the rate of the reactions

convection method of thermal energy transfer due to the rising of lower density hot fluids

convection currents motion of a fluid as result of differences in fluid density

Coulomb's law the force between two point charges is inversely proportional to the square of the separation and proportional to the product of the charges

critical mass the smallest mass of the nuclear fuel that can sustain a chain reaction

damping the loss of energy of an oscillating system due to the presence of resistance forces

daughter nucleus the nucleus produced by radioactive decay

decay constant probability of decay per unit time

decay series the series of decays until a nucleus reaches a stable nuclide

destructive interference superposition of waves leading to zero (or minimum) amplitude

diffraction the spreading of a wave through an aperture or past an obstacle

diffraction grating a very large number of closely separated slits of negligibly small width

direct current (dc) rate of flow of charge through the cross sectional area of a conductor

discrete energy energy taking a set of specific values rather than a continuous set of values

displacement change in position; the difference between the position of the oscillating body and the position at equilibrium

distance length of path followed

Doppler effect the change in observed frequency when there is relative motion between the source and the observer

drag force the force acting against the motion of an object that is moving through a fluid (gas or liquid)

driven oscillations oscillations when an external periodic force acts on the system

driving frequency the frequency of the external force acting on the system

duality of matter matter has both particle and wave-like characteristics

dynamic friction a force opposing motion when a body moves

efficiency, η the ratio of useful work or power to input work or power:
$$\eta = \frac{\text{useful energy out}}{\text{actual energy in}} \text{ or } \frac{\text{useful power out}}{\text{actual power in}}$$

Einstein's postulates 1. All the laws of physics are the same in all inertial frames; 2. the speed of light in vacuum is the same for all inertial observers

elastic collision a collision in which the total kinetic energy before the collision equals the total kinetic energy after the collision; that is, E_K is conserved

elastic potential energy (E_H) the energy stored in a spring that has been stretched or compressed:
$$E_H = \tfrac{1}{2}kx^2$$
where k is the spring constant and x is the amount by which the spring has been stretched or compressed

electric charge a conserved property of matter

electric field a region of space where an electric charge experiences an electric force

Glossary

electric field lines   curves, tangents to which give the direction of the electric field strength

electric field strength   the electric force per unit charge on a small positive point charge

electric potential   the work done by an external agent per unit charge in bringing a small point positive charge from infinity to a point in an electric field

electric potential energy   the work that needs to be done by an external agent in order to bring a set of charges from where they were separated by an infinite distance to their current position

electric power   the energy per unit time dissipated in a conductor

electrical resistance   the ratio of voltage across conductor to current through it

electromagnetic interaction   force given by Coulomb's law; acts on any particle that has electric charge; has infinite range

electromagnetic (EM) wave   a transverse wave moving at the speed of light in vacuum and consisting of oscillations of an electric and a magnetic field at right angles to each other

electromotive force (emf)   the work done per unit charge in moving charge across a battery's terminals

electroweak interaction   represents the unification of the electromagnetic and weak nuclear interactions

emission spectrum   the set of wavelengths of light emitted by an atom

emissivity   the ratio of the intensity radiated by a body to the intensity radiated by a black body of the same temperature

energy balance equation   an equation expressing the equality of incoming and outgoing intensities of radiation

energy level diagram   a representation of the discrete energies of an atom

enhanced greenhouse effect   the augmentation of the greenhouse effect due to human activities

entropy   a measure of a system's disorder

equations of kinematics $v = u + at$, $\Delta s = ut + \frac{1}{2}at^2$, $\Delta s = \left(\frac{u+v}{2}\right)t$, $v^2 = u^2 + 2a\Delta s$
where u = initial velocity, v = final velocity, s = final position, a = acceleration, t = time and Δs = displacement

equilibrium   the state when the net force on a system is zero

equilibrium position   the position where an oscillator has no net force acting on it

equipotential surfaces   surfaces where all points are at the same potential

escape speed   the minimum speed, v_{esc}, of an object in a gravitational field so that the object reaches infinity

excited state   any state above the ground state

evaporation   vaporisation taking place at the surface of a liquid at any temperature

event   something that happens at a particular point in space and time

Faraday's law   (of electromagnetic induction) the induced emf is the rate of change of magnetic flux linkage

first harmonic   the longest wavelength (and the lowest frequency) at which a standing wave forms

fluid resistance force   a speed dependent force opposing the motion of a body through a fluid

flux linkage   magnetic flux multiplied by the number of turns in a loop

force   the action of one body on a second body; unbalanced forces cause changes in velocity or shape

free-body force diagram   a diagram showing a body in isolation with all forces acting on it drawn as arrows

freezing   when a liquid changes into a solid (thermal energy is transferred away from the liquid)

frequency, f   the number of complete revolutions or full waves made in one second; $f = \frac{1}{T}$

friction laws   empirical 'laws' about frictional forces

Galilean transformation equations
$x' = x - vt$
$t' = t$
$u' = u - v$

gamma decay   a decay of a nucleus producing a short wavelength photon

gas constant   the constant, R that appears in the ideal gas law

gravitational field   a region of space where a mass experiences a gravitational force

gravitational field strength   gravitational force per unit mass exerted on a small point mass

gravitational interaction   force that acts on any particle with mass; has infinite range

gravitational potential   the work done per unit mass by an external agent in bringing a small point mass from infinity to a point

gravitational potential energy (E_p)   the work done by a force in moving a body to a position above its initial position; for an earth–mass system,

$E_P = mgh$

where m is the mass of the body, g is the gravitational field strength near the surface of the earth and h is the height above the earth's surface; also the work done to bring two bodies to their present position from when they were infinitely far apart

greenhouse effect the phenomenon in which re-radiated energy from the greenhouse gases returns to earth, warming the earth

greenhouse gases gases in the atmosphere that are capable of absorbing infrared radiation

ground state the state of lowest energy

half-life time after which the activity is reduced by a factor of 2

harmonics standing wave with a frequency that is an integral multiple of the first harmonic frequency

heat engine a device that transfers thermal energy to mechanical or electrical energy, which can then be used to do mechanical work

heat exchanger The part of the reactor where the thermal energy generated in the moderator is extracted

Hooke's law the tension in a spring is proportional to the extension or compression

ideal ammeter an ammeter with zero resistance

ideal gas a theoretical gas in which the particles do not exert forces on each other except during contact

ideal gas law (also known as the equation of state) equation relating pressure, volume and temperature of an ideal gas: $PV = RnT$

ideal voltmeter a voltmeter with infinite resistance (takes no current when connected to a resistor)

impulse the product of force and the time interval for which the force acts; it equals the change in momentum: $\vec{J} = \Delta \vec{p}$

impulse = area under a graph of *force* against *time*

induced fission the splitting of a large nucleus into two smaller nuclei after it has absorbed a neutron

inelastic collision a collision in which the total kinetic energy after a collision is less than the total kinetic energy before the collision; that is, some E_K is lost during the collision

inertia the tendency of a massive body to remain in its current state of motion

inertial reference frame a reference frame which is not accelerating

instability region a region on the HR diagram with stars of variable luminosity

instantaneous speed the magnitude of the instantaneous velocity

instantaneous velocity the rate of change of position; it is a vector

insulators materials with few free electrons per unit volume, through which thermal energy and electric current cannot readily pass

intensity the power of radiation *received* or *emitted* per unit area; its unit is W m^{-2}

interactions a process in which two or more systems exchange energy or momentum

interference when two or more waves meet to form a resultant wave of greater, lower or the same amplitude

internal energy the sum of the random kinetic energy of particles and the intermolecular potential energy in a system

internal resistance a resistance in series to the cell due to the chemicals in the cell

isobaric a thermodynamic process in which pressure stays constant

isolated a system whose total energy stays constant

isolated system a system where no energy or matter (mass) can be transferred into or from its surroundings

isothermal a thermodynamic process in which temperature stays constant

isothermal curve a curve on a pressure–volume diagram where all points have the same temperature

isotopes nuclei of the same element containing different numbers of neutrons

isovolumetric a thermodynamic process in which volume stays constant

Kepler's first law planets move on ellipses with the sun at one of the foci of the ellipse

Kepler's second law the line joining a planet and the sun sweeps equal areas in equal times

Kepler's third law the period of revolution of a planet around the sun is proportional to the $\frac{3}{2}$ power of the semi-major axis of the ellipse

kinetic energy the energy possessed by a body that is moving:
$E_K = \frac{1}{2}mv^2$

where m is the mass of the body and v is its velocity

kinetic energy of rotational motion $E_K = \frac{1}{2}I\omega^2$

law of conservation of energy energy cannot be created or destroyed—it can only be transferred from one form to another

law of conservation of total mechanical energy in the absence of resistive forces and other external forces the total mechanical energy of a system stays the same

law of reflection the angle of incidence i is equal to the angle of reflection r

length contraction the length of an object that moves past an observer is shorter than the length of the object in a frame where it is at rest; $L' = \frac{L}{\gamma}$

Lenz's law the induced emf will be such so as to oppose the change in the magnetic flux; it is equivalent to energy conservation

light dependent resistor (LDR) resistor where resistance decreases as light intensity increases

linear momentum $\vec{p}$, is the product of the mass of a body and its velocity:
$\vec{p} = m\vec{v}$

longitudinal a wave where the displacement is parallel to the direction of energy transfer

luminosity the power radiated by a star

magnetic field a region of space where a bar magnet would experience a magnetic force

magnetic field lines imaginary lines the tangents to which give the direction of the magnetic field

magnetic field lines imaginary lines the tangents to which give the direction of the magnetic field

magnetic flux the product of the magnetic field flux density times the area of a loop times the cosine of the angle between the magnetic field direction and the normal to the loop

magnetic flux density the force per unit charge on a charge moving with unit velocity at right angles to the field

main sequence the stable phase in the life of a star; the stars produce energy in their core, from nuclear fusion of hydrogen into helium

mass defect the difference between the mass of the nucleons and the mass of a nucleus

mechanical wave a disturbance that transfers energy and momentum through oscillations of the particles of a medium

melting when a solid changes to a liquid (thermal energy is transferred to the solid)

moderator the fast neutrons produced in fission must be slowed down and this is achieved by collisions of the neutrons with the moderator atoms

molar mass the mass in grams of one mole of a substance

mole a quantity of a substance containing as many particles as atoms in 12 g of carbon-12

moment of inertia a measure of the distribution of mass of an extended body about an axis of rotation: $I = \sum m_i r_i^2$

monochromatic light light of a single wavelength

motional emf an emf produced due to the motion of a conductor in a magnetic field

natural frequency the frequency of free oscillations of a body

Newton's first law of motion when the net force on a body is zero, the body will move with constant velocity (which may be zero); in other words, it will move on a straight line with constant speed (which may be zero)

Newton's law of gravitation there is a force of attraction between any two point masses that is proportional to the product of the masses and inversely proportional to the square of their separation; the force is directed along the line joining the two masses

Newton's second law of motion the net force on a body of constant mass is proportional to that body's acceleration and is in the same direction as the acceleration

Newton's third law of motion if body X exerts a force on body Y, then body Y will exert an equal and opposite force on body X

node a point on a standing wave where the displacement is always zero

normal contact force the force that arises when two bodies are in contact directed normally to the surface creating the force

nuclear fusion the joining of light nuclei to form heavier nuclei, releasing energy

nucleon a proton or a neutron

nucleon number the total number of protons and neutrons in a nucleus

nucleosynthesis the formation of the elements

nuclide a nucleus with a specific atomic and nucleon number

Ohm's law at constant temperature the current through a metallic conductor is proportional to the voltage across the conductor

Oppenheimer–Volkoff limit the maximum possible mass of a neutron star, about 3 solar masses

parallax the fact that when you look at an object from two different positions, the object appears to shift relative to the very distant background

parallel connection resistors connected so that they have the same potential difference across them

parent nucleus the decaying nucleus

path difference the difference in distance of a point from each of the two sources

peak wavelength the wavelength corresponding to the peak of the black body spectrum curve

period, T the time it takes for an orbiting object to make one complete revolution; the time for one full oscillation or one full wave

phase the state of a substance depending on the separation of its molecules; we consider the solid, liquid and vapour phases in this course

phase angle the angle that appears in the formula for displacement, determined by the initial position and velocity

phase difference $\Delta\phi = \frac{\Delta t}{T} \times 2\pi$, where T is the period and Δt the time difference between two neighbouring peaks

photoelectric effect the emission of electrons from a metallic surface when light is incident on the surface

photoelectrons the electrons emitted in the photoelectric effect

photon the particle of light (a quantum of energy), a massless particle moving at the speed of light

photo-surface technical term for the metallic surface that releases electrons when light is incident on it

planetary nebula the explosion of a red giant hurling mass and energy into space

point mass an idealised body with no physical size

position the coordinate on the number line

position vector the vector from the origin of a coordinate system to the position of a particle

potential difference the work done per unit charge in moving a point charge from one point to another

power the rate at which work is being done (or energy being transferred or dissipated):

$P = \frac{W}{t}$

where W is the work done and t the time taken

pressure the normal force on an area per unit area

principle of superposition when two or more waves of the same type arrive at a given point in space at the same time, the displacement of the medium at that point is the algebraic sum of the individual displacements

proper length the length of an object measured by an observer in a frame of reference in which the object is stationary with respect to the observer

proper time interval the time interval between two events that occur in a reference frame in which both events occur at the same position

proton number the number of protons in a nucleus

proton–proton chain the production of helium through the fusion of hydrogen

quantised energy discrete energy given by a formula involving an integer

quantised quantity a quantity whose magnitude is an integral multiple of a basic unit

quantum a small quantity of something, for example, energy

radial the direction towards or away from the centre of a spherical body

radiation method of thermal energy transfer though the emission of electromagnetic waves from a hot surface

radioactivity the phenomenon where particles and energy are emitted by an unstable nucleus

random it cannot be predicted when or which nucleus will decay

rarefaction a point where the density of the medium is lowest

ray a line perpendicular to a wavefront that gives the direction of energy transfer of the wave

real gas a gas obeying the gas laws approximately for limited ranges of pressures, volumes and temperatures

red giants very large, cool stars with a reddish colour; the core is hot enough for the helium to fuse to form carbon

red-shift the shift in wavelength towards larger wavelengths for a source getting further away

reference frame a set of co-ordinate axes and a set of clocks at every point in space

resistivity the resistance of a conductor of unit length and unit cross-sectional area

resonance the condition when the driving frequency is equal or slightly less than the natural frequency of a system, resulting in maximum amplitude

rest frame a reference frame in which a particular object is at rest

resultant or net force the one force whose effect is the same as that of a number of forces combined

Glossary

rotational equilibrium the net torque on the body is zero

series connection wire connecting resistors does not have any junctions so both resistors take the same current

simultaneity events that take place at the same time are said to be simultaneous

solar constant, S the intensity of solar radiation received at the upper atmosphere of the earth

spacetime diagram a graph in which the y-axis represents time (although it is more usually given as ct), and the x-axis represents position, x; single events are then shown by a dot on the diagram

spacetime interval $(\Delta s)^2 = (c\Delta t)^2 - (\Delta x)^2$, has the same value in all inertial reference frames

specific heat capacity the energy required to change the temperature of a unit mass by one degree

specific latent heat of fusion the energy needed to change a unit mass from the solid to the liquid phase at constant temperature

specific latent heat of vaporisation the energy needed to change a unit mass from the liquid to the vapour phase at constant temperature

spontaneous the decay cannot be prevented from happening or forced to happen

spontaneous fission the splitting of a large nucleus into two smaller nuclei without neutron absorption

standing wave a wave formed by the superposition of two identical travelling waves in opposite directions

state of a gas a gas with a specific value of pressure, volume, temperature and number of moles

states of matter matter can exist in one of three states: solid, liquid or gaseous form

static friction a force opposing the tendency to motion when a body is at rest

Stefan–Boltzmann law the radiated intensity is proportional to the fourth power of the kelvin temperature

strong nuclear interaction force that acts on protons and neutrons to keep them bound to each other inside nuclei; has short range (10^{-15} m)

stopping voltage the voltage in the photoelectric effect that makes the current zero

supernova the explosion of a red super giant hurling mass and energy into space

temperature a measure of the average random kinetic energy of particles

tension the force arising when a body is being stretched or compressed

terminal speed the constant speed attained when the resistance force becomes equal to the force pushing the body

thermistor temperature dependent resistor where resistance decreases as temperature increases

time dilation an observer with respect to whom a clock moves measures a longer time interval between the ticks of the clock than an observer at rest relative to that clock $\Delta t = \gamma \Delta t'$

torque the product of the magnitude of the force and the perpendicular distance between the line of action of the force and the axis of rotation:
$\tau = Fd$ or $\tau = Fr \sin \theta$

total internal reflection when the angle of incidence is greater than the critical angle, the incident ray only reflects with no refracted ray

total mechanical energy the sum of the kinetic energy, gravitational potential energy and elastic potential energy of a body

transfer of thermal energy the transfer of energy from one body to another as a result of a temperature difference

translational equilibrium the net force of the body is zero

transverse a wave where the displacement of the particles of the medium is at right angles to the direction of energy transfer

travelling wave A wave that transfers energy from one place to another through oscillations of a medium

uniform motion motion with constant velocity

vaporisation (or **boiling**) when a liquid changes into vapour (thermal energy is transferred to the liquid)

velocity is the displacement divided by the time to achieve that displacement: $v = \frac{\Delta s}{\Delta t}$, the rate of change of position.

voltage the potential difference across a conductor

voltmeter an instrument that measures the potential difference across its ends

wavefront a surface through crests and normal to the direction of energy transfer of the wave

wavelength the length of one full wave

weak nuclear interaction force that acts on protons, neutrons, electrons and neutrinos in order to bring about beta decay; has very short range (10^{-18} m)

weight the gravitational force between the mass of a planet and a body:
$W = mg$

where m is the mass of the body and g is the gravitational field strength of the planet

white dwarfs small, hot stars no longer undergoing fusion; they get dimmer as they cool down

Wien's law the peak wavelength is inversely proportional to the kelvin temperature

work done is the product of the force in the direction of the displacement multiplied by the distance travelled: $W = Fs \cos\theta$

where θ is the angle between the direction of the force, F, and the direction of the displacement, s

work–energy relation the net work done on a system is equal to the change in kinetic energy of the system

work function ϕ, the amount of energy required to free an electron from a photo-surfrace

worldline a line on a spacetime diagram relating a sequence of events, the angle of which is related to the speed at which something is moving; $\tan\theta = \frac{x}{ct} = \frac{v}{c}$

Index

absolute (kelvin) temperature, 158, 179
absolute zero, 158
absorption of photons, 183
absorption spectra, 454–5, 458
acceleration, 7–16
   angular acceleration, 103–4
   centripetal, 54–5
   Newton's second law, 42–9
   and projectile motion, 21–5
   in SHM, 266, 268, 273
      maximum, 273–5
acceleration-displacement graphs, 268
acceleration of free fall, 13–16
   air resistance in, 25–6
   and gravitational field strength, 30, 360, 361
   and Newton's law, 42–3
   and weight, 30
   see also projectile motion
acceleration-time graphs, 8–10, 17, 19
   SHM, 268
ac circuits, 444–5
ac generators, 443–4
activity, 489–90, 500
ac voltage, 444–5
adiabatic process, 207–9, 226
air molecules, 293, 335
air resistance, 25–6, 32
   and power, 78
   see also frictional forces
albedo, 178, 181, 182
alpha decay, 486, 488
   discrete energies in, 497
alpha particles, 417, 480, 486
   energies of, 484, 494, 495
   scattering with, 451–2, 494–5
alternating current (ac), 443–5
alternating voltage *see* ac voltage
ammeters, 254–5
ampere, 233, 234, 429
amplitude, 265, 267
   from energy graphs, 280–2
   of oscillations, 340
   in SHM, 267, 270, 273, 274
   standing waves, 330–3
   of waves, 291–3, 312, 313, 315

angle of diffraction, 319
angle of incidence, 303, 305
angle of reflection, 303
angle of refraction, 303–5
angular acceleration, 103–4, 112
angular displacement, 103
angular frequency in SHM, 266, 273
angular momentum, 119–20, 123
angular momentum, quantisation of, 457–8
angular position, 103
angular separation, 318
angular speed, 52–3
angular velocity, 103–4, 111–12
anti-neutrinos, 480, 486, 487, 498
antinodes, 331
   waves in pipes, 334, 335
   waves on strings, 332, 333
anti-particles, 480, 486–7
apparent brightness, 173, 516, 519
asperities, 33
atmosphere (unit), 191
atomic mass, 189, 483
atomic mass unit, 481
atomic (proton) number, 479, 480, 483
   on decay series, 488
atoms, 157
   electron collisions with, 235
   energy level diagrams of, 453, 497
   hydrogen, 453–4, 457–8
   models of, 451–5
   in a mole, 189
   transitions, 453–5, 463, 487, 497–8
average power, 78, 79, 444
average speed, 4, 5, 200, 331, 333
average velocity, 7
Avogadro constant, 189, 222
axis scale, 145–6

background radiation, 490
ballistic motion, 377
bar magnets, field round, 396
baryon numbers *see* mass (nucleon) number
batteries, 257–8
   in circuits, 239
   see also cells

beta decay, 480, 486–8
beta minus decay, 486–7, 498, 499
   in decay series, 488
beta particles, 486–7
beta plus decay, 487
binding energy, 481–2, 486, 495–6, 508
binding energy curve, 483, 508
black-body radiation, 169, 173, 178, 179, 181
black dwarf, 522
black holes, 299, 518, 521, 523
blue-shift, 348
Bohr model, 123, 364, 453, 454, 457–8
boiling, 162
   see also vaporisation
Boltzmann equation, 196, 199–201, 222
Boyle's law, 193
buoyant forces, 32

calorimetry, 161–2, 165–6
carbon, 523–4
carbon dioxide, 182, 183
Carnot cycle, 226–7
cells, in circuits, 239, 241, 242
Celsius scale, 158
centrifugal force, 57
centripetal acceleration, 54–5
centripetal forces, 55–9, 62–4
   charges in fields, 421–2
   gravitational force as, 363
chain reactions, 509
Chandrasekhar limit, 522
change of phase, 162–5
charge, 232–3, 385
   conservation of, 232, 385
   in electric fields, 388–90
      equipotential surfaces, 371, 409–10
      force on, 388–9, 406, 408, 417–18
      motion of, 417–19
   in magnetic fields, 399–401, 421–4
   moving *see* moving charge
   of nuclei, 452, 479
   point, 387–9, 408–10
   properties, 385–6
charge carriers, 232, 233
   see also electrons
Charles' law, 193–4
chemical energy, 94, 239
circuits, 241–6
   ac circuits, 444–5
   meters in, 254–5
   potential dividers in, 258
   resistors in, 234, 235, 242–6

circular motion, 52–9, 63–4
   and angular speed, 52–3
   charges in fields, 421–2
   see also orbits
climate change, 184
closed system, 207, 210
CNO cycle, 523
coefficient of dynamic friction, 33–4
coefficient of static friction, 33–4
coherent light, 315
collisions, 90–1, 97
   of electrons with lattice atoms, 235
comets, 364
compasses, 395, 396
components of forces, 40–1
compression
   of gases, 207–11, 218–19
   in springs, 31
   in waves, 292
      sound waves, 293
Compton scattering, 469
condensation, 162
   specific latent heat of, 162
conduction, 168
conductors, 233, 234
   free electrons in, 233, 386
conservation of energy, 70–1, 81
   and induced current/emf, 435–6
conservation of momentum, 90–2, 100, 119, 409
   in nuclear physics, 484
conservation of total energy of systems, 71, 211
constant velocity, 3–4
constructive interference, 312, 313
   diffraction gratings, 324
   of electrons, 474
   two sources, 313–15
contact forces, 31–2
control rods, 509
convection, 169
convection currents, 169
cooling, 166
coulomb (unit), 232, 386
Coulomb's law, 387, 452, 480
crest of waves, 288, 291, 302, 331
critical angle, 305
critical (threshold) frequency, 466, 467
critical mass, 509
current, 233–5, 238–9
   in ac circuits, 444–5
   and battery emf, 257–8
   in circuits, 241–6
      parallel resistors, 244–6

Index

series resistors, 242–3, 245–6
induced *see* induced current
measuring with ammeters, 254–5
peak, 443, 444
in potential dividers, 258
current-carrying wires, 233
    force between two, 401
    magnetic field around, 396–7
    magnetic force on, 400–1
current-voltage graphs, 234–5
    photoelectric effect, 464–5
cycle, thermodynamic, 219, 224, 226

damping, 340
Davisson–Germer experiment, 474, 475
de Broglie hypothesis, 473–5
decay
    of particles, 480, 483
    radioactive, 486–92, 496–500
decay constant, 499–500
decay rate, 489, 500
decay series, 488
destructive interference, 312, 313
    and path difference, 312–13
    and single-slit diffraction, 319
    on standing waves, 331
deterministic systems, 359
deuterium, 515
diffraction, 311–14
    of electrons, 473–5
    multiple-slit, 322–3
    single-slit, 318–22
diffraction gratings, 323–5
direct current (dc), 233
discrete energy, 452–4, 458, 463, 479, 497
    and nuclear transitions, 497–8
displacement, 3–7
    angular displacement, 103
    in free fall, 13–16
    and longitudinal waves, 292–4
    and projectile motion, 20–6, 418
    in SHM, 265–8, 270, 279–80, 281
        equation for, 273
    of standing waves, 330, 331
    and transverse waves, 290–2
    uniformly accelerated motion, 7–16
    and work done, 62, 65–6
    see also distance travelled; position
displacement-distance graphs
    wave motion, 290, 291
        longitudinal waves, 293
displacement-energy graphs, 279

displacement-time graphs
    SHM, 267–8, 279
    standing waves, 330
    waves, 290, 291, 313
distance travelled, 4
    and work done, 62–4
Doppler effect, 347–55
double-slit interference, 313–15
double-source interference, 312–13
drag forces, 32
    see also air resistance
drift speed, 236
driven oscillations, 340–2
driving frequency, 340, 341
duality of matter, 473
dynamic friction, 33–4

earth
    albedo of, 181, 182
    energy from the sun, 169, 178, 180–1
    escape speed, 382
    greenhouse effect, 182–3
    magnetism of, 40, 39, 51
    motion of, 53
    temperature of, 158, 181–3
        and energy balance, 181
efficiency, 79–80, 225
elastic collisions, 93
elastic potential energy, 80–1
    in simple harmonic motion, 279
    of stretched springs, 67
    and total mechanical energy, 71
electrical devices, rating of, 239
electrical energy, 79, 238–9
electric cells, 239, 241, 242
electric charge *see* charge
electric current *see* current
electric fields, 388–90, 406–8
    in EM waves, 298
    equipotential surfaces, 371, 409–10
    motion of charges in, 417–19, 424
    between parallel plates, 390
    and potential difference, 232–4
    in the Rutherford model, 452
electric field strength, 388–90
    on potential-distance graphs, 408–9
electric force, 40, 387
    and electric fields, 388–90, 417–18
    particle acceleration, 232
electricity
    generation, 443–4
        fossil fuels, 183

hydroelectric power, 443
nuclear power, 509
wind power, 443
electric potential, 406–10
  connection with fields, 408–10
  equipotential surfaces, 371, 409–10
  between parallel plates, 390, 410
electric potential energy, 406–7
electric power, 238–9
  dissipation in circuits, 239, 253, 430, 444
  see also power
electromagnetic force, 402, 484, 496
electromagnetic induction, 429–37
  in ac generators, 443–4
  Faraday's law, 433
  Lenz's law, 435–7
  magnetic flux, 431–2
electromagnetic interaction, as fundamental force, 480
electromagnetic radiation
  in the photoelectric effect, 464
  wavelength emitted, 170
  see also gamma rays; infrared; light
electromagnetic spectrum, 298
electromagnetic waves, 298–9
  all bodies emit, 169
  light as, 463
  polarisation, 310
electromotive force *see* emf
electron microscopes, 325
electrons
  in atoms
    and binding energy, 482, 483
    Bohr model, 123, 364, 457–8
    transitions and spectra, 454–5, 458
  in beta minus decay, 486, 487, 498
  and charge, 232, 233, 385, 392
  collision with lattice atoms, 235
  diffraction, 473–5
  discovery of, 385
  Feynman diagrams, 149, 409
  free, 232, 385–6
  interference of, 473–5
  kinetic energy
    in conduction, 168
    in the photoelectric effect, 464–6, 469
    in radiation, 169
  in photoelectric effect, 464–7
  symbol for, 480
  wave-like properties, 473–5

electrostatic induction, 386
electroweak interaction, 480
elements, spectra of, 452–4
emf (electromotive force), 239
  of batteries, 257–8
  induced, 429–33, 435–7, 443–4
  motional, 429–30
emission spectra, 170, 452–4
emissivity, 174, 178
EM waves *see* electromagnetic waves
energy, 64–5
  of alpha particles, 484, 494, 497
  of beta particles/electrons, 497, 498
  binding energy, 481–3, 486, 495–6, 508
  change of state, 162
  conservation of, 70–1, 81, 211, 342
    and induced current/emf, 435–6
  converting to mass/matter, 481–4
  discrete energy, 452–4, 458, 463, 479, 497
  and greenhouse effect, 182–3
  internal, 159–60, 201, 206, 207
  mechanical energy, 70–8
  nuclear fission produces, 507–8, 510
    in reactors, 509–10
  nuclear fusion produces, 515–17
  of photons, 183, 463, 469
    gamma emission, 487, 497
  potential *see* potential energy
  quanta of, 463
  radioactive decay releases, 483, 486
  resistors generate, 238
  in SHM, 279–81
  sun gives, 169, 178, 181
  thermal *see* thermal energy
  transfers *see* energy transfer
  waves carry, 302
energy balance equation, 181
energy-displacement graphs, SHM, 279
energy, kinetic *see* kinetic energy
energy level diagrams, 453, 497
energy levels
  molecular, 183
  nuclear, 487, 497–8
  transitions, 452–4, 487, 497–8
    nuclear, 497–8
energy transfer, 80–2
  heat engines, 224–5
  rate and power, 78
  on Sankey diagrams, 81

Index

and temperature difference, 82, 159, 162, 166
thermal energy/heat, 75, 79, 159, 162, 164–5, 168–74
    by waves, 287
        longitudinal waves, 292, 293
        standing waves, 331
        transverse waves, 290, 298
engines, 224–6
entropy, 218–19, 220, 222
equation of state, 189, 192, 196
equations of kinematics, 10
equilibrium, 35–8, 40–2, 108–9, 265
equilibrium temperature, 181
equipotential surfaces, 371, 409–10
    between parallel plates, 390, 410
error propagation, 382
escape velocity, 377
ethics, 392–3, 512
evaporation, 162
excited state, 454, 455
explosions
    nuclear explosions, 507
    in nuclear reactors, 510–11
    planetary nebulae and supernovas, 521, 522, 524

Faraday's law, 433
Feynman diagrams, 149, 409
field lines, 388–90, 396–8, 402, 409–10
fields, 357–448
    connection with potential, 371, 408–10
    electric see electric fields
    gravitational see gravitational fields
    magnetic see magnetic fields
field strength, 408
    electric, 388, 408
    gravitational, 30, 360–3, 365
        on potential-distance graphs, 370, 372
    magnetic, 431
first law of thermodynamics, 211
fission see nuclear fission
fluid resistance, 25–6
    see also frictional forces
fluids, 32
    convection in, 169
flux linkage, 431–2, 437
    in ac generators, 443
    Faraday's law, 433
force-distance graphs, 63
force-extension graphs, 67, 70
force pairs, 40

forces, 30–60
    centripetal, 55–9, 421–2
    electric see electric force
    and equilibrium, 35–8, 40–2
    fluid resistance, 25–6
    free-body diagrams, 34–5, 45–7
    fundamental, 480
    in ideal and real gases, 192, 201, 202
    inter-particle, 157, 159, 160, 164
    line of action, 106
    magnetic see magnetic forces
    and momentum, 85–101
    in Newton's first law of motion, 39
    in Newton's second law of motion, 42–9, 113–14
    in Newton's third law of motion, 39–40
    in orbital motion, 363
    and pressure, 191–2
    resistance forces, 340–2
    restoring, 266
    in SHM, 266
    in thermodynamic processes, 209, 225
    torque, 106–8
    work done by, 62–5
        in heat engines, 225
        on a particle, 64
force-time graphs, 87–90
fossil fuels, 183
free-body diagrams, 34–5, 45–7
free electrons, 232, 385–6
free fall see acceleration of free fall
freezing, 162
frequency
    in circular motion, 53
    critical, 466, 467
    and Doppler effect, 347–53
    driving frequency, 340, 341
    natural, 340–2
    in the photoelectric effect, 464–7
    of rotation of ac generators, 443
        power from, 444–5
    in SHM, 266, 273, 274
        angular, 266, 273
    and standing waves, 331–3
    of waves, 288, 290, 292
frictional forces
    centripetal, 55–6
    and efficiency, 79–80
    in orbital motion, 363
    in rotational motion, 114

work done by, 64, 68, 69, 76–9
    see also air resistance
friction laws, 33
fringes and slit width, 323
fringe separation, 315, 323
fringe spacing, 314
fuel rods, 509
fuels
    fossil fuels, 183
    in nuclear power reactors, 509–11
fundamental forces, 480
fundamental interactions, 480
    see also interactions
fundamental units, 400
fusion, nuclear see nuclear fusion
fusion, specific latent heat of, 162

Galilean transformation, 127, 128
gamma decay, 487, 497
gamma rays, 486
    energies of, 487, 497
gas constant, 194, 196
gases
    adiabatic process, 207–9
    Boltzmann equation, 196, 199–201, 222
    change of phase, 162, 163
    convection in, 169
    equation of state, 189, 192, 196
    gas laws, 193–6, 207–8
        graphs of, 193–5
    ideal, 192, 196, 206, 207, 210
        internal energy of, 201, 206
    modelling, 192–6
    particles in, bonds between, 159
    pressure-temperature law, 195–6
    pressure-volume law, 193
    real gases, 192, 194
    speed of molecules in, 192, 199–200
    volume-temperature law, 193–4, 207
    work done on or by, 209–10, 218–19
Gay-Lussac's law, 195–6
Geiger–Marsden experiment, 494, 495
gravitation, 359–62
    and planetary motion, 363–4
gravitational fields, 360–2
    connection with potential, 368, 371
gravitational field strength, 360–3
    between earth and moon, 365
    graphs of, 362
    potential-distance graphs give, 370, 372
    and weight, 30

gravitational force
    and gravitational field strength, 360–1
    inverse square law for, 360
    and Newton's third law, 40
    in orbital motion, 363, 373–4
    between point masses, 359–62
    and work done, 65–6, 367
gravitational interaction, 480
gravitational potential, 368, 371
    connection with fields, 368, 371
    equipotential surfaces, 371
gravitational potential energy, 66, 366–8
    and escape speed, 377
    in orbital motion, 373–4
    and total mechanical energy, 71, 73, 75
gravitational potential well, 367
gravitational waves, 299
gravity, work done by, 65–6
greenhouse effect, 182–3
greenhouse gases, 182–3, 183, 342
ground state, 453, 454

Hafele-Keating experiment, 136
half-life, 489–91, 500
harmonics, 332–8
    waves in pipes, 334–6
    waves on strings, 332–3
heat, 159
    and change of phase, 162–5
    see also thermal energy; thermodynamic laws;
        thermodynamic process
heat engines, 224–6
heat exchangers, 509
heat transfer, 75, 82, 159, 168–74
    and temperature difference, 82, 159, 162, 164–5, 166
height reached of projectiles, 24, 26, 27
helium, 479, 481–3, 486, 487, 515, 517–18, 523–4
Hertzsprung–Russell (HR) diagrams, 516–17, 521, 522
Hooke's law, 31, 66
horseshoe magnets, field around, 396
Hubble's law, 455
hydroelectric power, 443
hydrogen
    electrons in
        Bohr model, 457–8, 474
        transitions, 454
    in nuclear fusion, 517, 518, 520, 523–4
    spectra, 453, 455, 458
    transitions of, 454

ideal ammeters, 254
ideal gases, 192, 196

equation of state, 189, 192, 196
    internal energy of, 201, 206
ideal voltmeters, 254
impulse, 87–9
impulse (angular), 119
inclined planes, 33, 44–5
induced current, 429–31
    ac generators produce, 444–5
    Lenz's law, 435–7
induced emf, 429–33, 435–7
    ac generators produce, 443–4
induction, electrostatic, 386
inelastic collisions, 93
inertia, 39, 109–11
inertial reference frames, 123
infrared radiation (IR), 182–3
instability region, 517, 521, 522
instantaneous speed, 8, 12
instantaneous velocity, 7–8
insulators, 233, 386
intensity
    and Doppler effect, 348
    in the photoelectric effect, 464–5
    of radiation, 169, 170, 178–9
    in two-slit interference, 313–15, 321
    of waves, 320–4
        in interference, 313
intensity patterns
    diffraction gratings, 324
    multiple-slit diffraction, 322, 323
    single-slit diffraction, 320
    in two-slit interference, 315, 321
interactions, fundamental, 480
interference, 312
    double-slit, 313–15
    and double-slit diffraction, 321
    double-source, 312–13
    of electrons, 473–5
    and multiple-slit diffraction, 322–3
    thin film, 325–6
internal energy, 159–60, 206, 207
    of ideal gases, 201, 206
internal resistance, 239, 257
inter-particle forces, 157, 159, 160, 164
inter-particle potential energy, 164
inverse square law, 360
ionising power, 486, 487
isobaric process, 207
isolated systems, 71, 207
isothermal process, 193, 207, 218, 224, 226
isotopes, 480, 492
isovolumetric process, 207

joule (unit), 62, 160, 468

kelvin, 158, 194, 196, 201
Kepler's laws of planetary motion, 363–4, 378
kinetic energy, 64
    of accelerated particles, 232, 423
    of electrons
        in hydrogen atoms, 453
        in the photoelectric effect, 464–6
    and escape speed, 377
    of molecules
        and phase changes, 162
        and temperature, 158, 164, 189, 201, 209
    and momentum, 91, 93–5
    in orbital motion, 373–4
    of particles, 158–60, 162, 418
        in conduction, 168
        in decay, 494, 498
        in fission, 507
    of projectiles, 22
    of rotational motion, 110, 112
    in SHM, 279–81
    and total mechanical energy, 71, 75, 80
    and work done, 64–5, 75
kinetic friction, 33

lamp filament, I-V graph, 235
latent heat, 162–3, 165
length contraction, 135–6, 139, 146–7
Lenz's law, 435–7
light
    diffraction, 312, 318–21, 323–5
    and Doppler effect, 348–9
    interference, 313–15
    in the photoelectric effect, 464–7
    and photons, 463, 469
    polarisation, 310, 316
    reflection of, 303, 305
    refraction, 303–5
    stars and escape speed, 378
    total internal reflection, 305
    wave nature of, 303–5, 310, 321, 463
light bulbs, 234, 238–9, 463
light dependent resistors (LDRs), 235
light year (unit), 519
linear momentum, 85
linear motion, 113, 116, 119–20
linear speed in circular motion, 53–4
line of action, 106
liquids, 157
    change of phase, 162–4
    convection in, 169

positive ion charge carriers in, 385
longitudinal waves, 292–4
loops, magnetic field around, 398
Lorentz transformations, 130, 132, 133, 136, 137, 140, 148
loudness and Doppler effect, 348
luminosity, 173, 516–19, 521–3

magnetic field lines, 396–8, 402
magnetic fields, 395–402
   in EM waves, 298
   induced emf in, 429–32
   and Lenz's law, 435–7
   and magnetic flux, 399, 431–2
   motion of charges in, 421–4
   see also electromagnetic induction
magnetic field strength, 431
magnetic flux, 431–2, 435–6
magnetic flux density, 396, 401, 429, 432
magnetic flux linkage *see* flux linkage
magnetic forces
   on a current-carrying wire, 400–1
   on moving charges, 399–400
   two current-carrying wires, 401
   work done, 406–8, 423
magnetic permeability, 401
main sequence stars, 517, 518, 520–4
mass
   converting to energy, 481–4
   and gravitation, 359–62, 366–8, 371
     equipotential surfaces, 371
   and moment of inertia, 109–10
   and momentum, 85, 87
   point masses, 359–62
   in second law of motion, 42–9, 85, 113–14
   solar, 517, 518, 520–4
mass defect, 481–2
mass (nucleon) number, 479, 483, 486
   and binding energy, 483
   on decay series, 488
mass-spring system, 266
matter
   duality of, 473
   interaction with radiation, 463–75
   particle model of, 157
   structure of, 451–5
matter waves, 299, 473–5
Maxwell's electromagnetic theory of light, 129
measurements
   current and voltage, 254–5
   heat capacity and latent heat, 161, 165–6
   temperature, 158

mechanical energy, 70–8, 224
mechanical waves, 287, 299
melting, 162–4
melting temperature, 163–5
metals
   free electrons in, 232, 233, 385
   resistivity, 235
methane as a greenhouse gas, 182, 183
method of mixtures, 165–6
Michelson-Morley experiment, 140
microscopic–macroscopic connection, 261
Millikan oil drop experiment, 392–3
modelling climate change, 184
modelling gases, 192–202
moderator, 509
modulated intensity, 321
molar mass, 189
molecular energy levels, 183
molecules, 157
   of air and waves, 293, 335
   in ideal and real gases, 192
   kinetic energy
     and adiabatic process, 209
     and conduction, 168
   in a mole, 189
   motion of, 192, 199–200
moles, 189–90
   in the equation of state, 192, 196
moment of inertia, 109–11
momentum, 85–101
   angular, 119–20, 123
   angular, quantisation of, 457–8
   conservation of, 90–2, 100, 119, 409
     in nuclear physics, 484
   and impulse, 87–9
   and kinetic energy, 91, 93–5
   of photons, 409, 463
   quanta of, 463
   rocket equation, 92
   transfer by waves, 287
monochromatic light, 320
morals and ethics, 512
motion, 3–28
   acceleration of free fall, 13–16
     and air resistance, 25–6
     and gravitational field strength, 361, 363
     linear motion, 113, 116, 119–20
     and Newton's law, 42–3
   circular, 52–9, 63–4, 421–2
   in crossed electric and magnetic fields, 424
   in electric fields, 417–19, 424
   fluid resistance, 25–6

Index

graphs of, 16–20
    acceleration-time, 8–10, 17, 19, 268
    position-time *see* position-time graphs
    velocity-time *see* velocity-time graphs
in magnetic fields, 421–4
Newton's laws of, 39–52, 113–14
non-uniform, 7–13
orbital *see* orbits
projectile motion, 20–6, 418
rotational *see* rotational motion
uniformly accelerated, 7–16
and weight, 25
see also rotational motion
motional emf, 429–30
moving charge
    magnetic force on, 399–400
    work done, 232, 406–7
        and emf, 239
        in wires, 410
multiple-slit diffraction, 322–3
muon decay, 139
muons, 501

natural frequency, 340–2
negative feedback, 184
net force, 35–6, 57
neutrinos, 480, 487, 498–9
    solar, 501
    symbol for, 480
neutron number, 479, 480
neutrons
    anti-particle of, 480
    in beta minus decay, 486, 498
    in fission, 507, 509
    in nuclei, 479–80, 496–7
        and binding energy, 481–2
neutron stars, 518, 521–3
Newton's constant of universal gravitation, 359
Newton's first law of motion, 39
Newton's law of gravitation, 359–60, 364, 378
Newton's second law of motion, 42–9, 85–6, 113–14
Newton's third law of motion, 39–40
nitrous oxide as a greenhouse gas, 182, 183
nodes, 331
    waves in pipes, 334, 335
    waves on strings, 332, 333
non-ohmic conductors, 235
non-renewable energy, 183
normal contact forces, 31–2
normal reaction forces, 278
    and weightlessness, 379
nuclear energy levels, 497–8

in gamma emission, 487
nuclear explosions, 507, 510–11
nuclear fission, 507–8
    nuclear reactors, 507, 509–10
nuclear fusion, 515, 517, 520, 523–5
nuclear power, 510
nuclear reactions, 483–4
nuclei, 479–80
    binding energy of, 481–3, 495–6
    density of, and fusion, 515
    discovery of, 452
    energy levels, 497–8
    in fission, 507–8
    in radioactive decay, 486–91, 499–500
        decay series, 488
        energy released, 483
        numbers of, 499–500
    radius of, 494, 495
    stability of, 496–7
    and strong interaction, 480
nucleon number *see* mass (nucleon) number
nucleons, 479, 481–3, 495–6
    see also neutrons; nuclei; protons
nucleosynthesis, 515, 523
nuclides, 479, 486, 496
    see also nuclei

Ohm's law, 234–5, 259
Oppenheimer–Volkoff limit, 522–3
optical fibres, total internal reflection in, 305
orbital radius, Bohr model of, 458
orbital speed, 363, 373–4
orbits, 52, 299, 363, 373
    of electrons, Bohr model, 123, 364, 457–8, 474
    of planets, 55, 359, 360, 363–4, 374
    and weightlessness, 379
oscillations, 265–71
    and damping, 340
    and resonance, 340–2
    simple harmonic motion, 266–71
    see also waves

parallax angle, 519–20
parallel plates, 390, 410
parallel, resistors in, 244–6
particle accelerators, 136, 421, 463
particle model of matter, 157
particle nature of light, 463–4, 469
particles, 157
    atoms *see* atoms
    decay of, 480, 483
    electrons *see* electrons

545

kinetic energy of, 158–60, 162, 418, 423
   in conduction, 168
molecules *see* molecules
motion in phase changes, 160
neutrinos *see* neutrinos
neutrons *see* neutrons
protons *see* protons
quarks, 157, 386
standard model, 402, 484
wave nature, 320, 473–4
work done by forces on, 40
path difference, 312
  diffraction gratings, 324
  interference from two sources, 313–15
  single-slit diffraction, 319
peak current, 444
peak power, 445
peak voltage, 443–5
peak wavelength, 170
pendulums, 53, 55, 183, 341
  simple, 265, 266, 276
penetrating power, 486, 487
period, 265
  in circular motion, 52
  of orbits, 363, 364
    electrons, 410
  in SHM, 265–7, 268, 270, 273
    energy graphs, 279–80
    mass-spring system, 266
    simple pendulum, 266
  of waves, 287, 288, 290–2
periodic motion, 265
permittivity, 387
phase angle, 273
phase changes, and reflection, 309
phase difference
  and interference, 315
  in SHM, 270
  and waves, 294
phases of matter, change of, 162–5
photoelectric effect, 464–7
photons, 342, 463–4
  absorption of, 183
  discovery of, 453
  emission, 453–5, 487
  in Feynman diagrams, 409
  in the photoelectric effect, 467
  symbol for, 479–80
photo-surface, 464
photovoltaic cells, 239
pions, 129, 142
pipes, standing waves in, 334–6

Planck's constant, 123, 454, 463, 469, 473
planetary nebulae, 521, 522, 524
planets, 360, 363–4, 374, 378, 379
  escape speed, 377
plastic collisions, 93
plutonium, 497, 510
point charges, 387–9, 408–10
point masses, 359–62
point particle, 35, 113, 114, 119
point sources and wavefronts, 302
polarisation, 310, 316, 463
poles, 395, 396
position, 3–28
  in uniformly accelerated motion, 7, 9–13
  see also displacement; distance travelled
position-time graphs, 5–7, 10, 17–18
  projectiles, 23, 26
  uniform acceleration, 7–9
  uniform motion, 5
positive feedback, 184
positive ions as charge carriers, 385
positrons, 480, 487, 492
potential
  connection with field, 408–10
  electric, 406–10
  equipotential surfaces, 371, 409–10
  gravitational, 66, 366–8, 371, 373–4
potential difference, 232, 238
  across a battery, 257
  in circuits, 241–2, 244, 246
  measuring, voltmeters, 254–5
  and potential dividers, 258
  and resistance, 234–5, 238
  terminal, 257
  see also voltage
potential-distance graphs
  electric fields, 408–9
  gravitational fields, 370, 372
potential dividers, 258
potential energy, 66
  elastic, 67, 80–1
  electric, 406–7
  gravitational *see* gravitational potential energy
  inter-particle, 159–60, 164
  in SHM, 279–81
power, 78–9, 116
  in ac circuits, 444–5
  and albedo, 178
  average power, 78, 79, 444
  in batteries, 246, 257
  electric, 238–9, 253, 430, 444
  and energy carried by waves, 302

hydroelectric power, 443
and intensity, 178–9
radiated/emitted, and temperature, 178–9
wind power, 443
power stations
ac generation in, 443
hydroelectric, 443
nuclear power, 509–11
predictions, 364
pressure, 191–2
in gases, 192, 200–1, 207–10
in gas laws, 193–6
and sound waves, 293
pressure-temperature law, 195–6
pressure-volume diagrams, 207, 209, 210, 224, 226
pressure-volume law, 193
prisms, 304, 452
probability, in radioactive decay, 491, 499
probability waves, 299
projectile motion, 20–6, 418
proper length, 136
proper time interval, 135
proton–proton chain, 520, 523
protons, 386, 409, 417, 419, 424
in beta minus decay, 486, 488
in nuclei, 479, 482, 484, 494, 496–7
pulses, 287, 308–9

quanta
of angular momentum, 457–8
of energy, 463
of momentum, 463
quantised charge, 386
quantum mechanics, 449, 473
quarks, 157, 386

radial fields, 361
radiation
black-body, 169, 173, 178, 179, 181
electromagnetic *see* electromagnetic radiation
as heat transfer, 169
interaction with matter, 463–75
thermal, 169
see also radioactive decay
radioactive decay, 486–92
energy released in, 483, 486
law of, 488–90, 499–500
radioactivity, 486, 491–2
radius of nuclei, 494, 495
radius of stars, 517–19
rarefaction in waves, 292
sound waves, 293

rays, 302–3
reaction forces, 278, 379
real gases, 192, 194
red giants, 517–18
red-shift, 348
reference frames, 126–7
reflection
of light, 303, 305
of pulses, 309
total internal, 305
refraction, 303–5
refrigerators, 225, 227
relativity
addition of velocities, 128, 136–7
Galilean relativity, 127–8, 137
length contraction, 135–6, 139, 146–7
Lorentz transformations, 130, 132, 133, 136, 137, 140
muon decay, 139
reference frames, 126–7
simultaneity, 137–8, 148
spacetime diagrams, 143–9
special relativity, 129–32, 136, 463
time dilation, 134–5, 136, 139, 147–8
resistance, 234–5
in ac circuits, 444
in parallel, 244–6
and power generated, 238
in series, 242
resistivity, 235
resistors, 234
in ac circuits, 444–5
in parallel, 244–6
and potential dividers, 258
power and energy generated in, 238–9
in series, 242–3, 245–6
resonance, 183, 341–3
rest frame, 136
restoring force, 266
resultant force, 35
rings, magnetic field around, 398
risk and nuclear power, 510–11
rms, 189, 201
rocket equation, 92
rolling without slipping, 111–12
root mean square (rms), 189, 201
rotational equilibrium, 108–9
rotational motion, 103–24
angular acceleration, 103–4
angular displacement, 103
angular velocity, 103–4
equilibrium, 108–9
moment of inertia, 109–11

Newton's second law, 113–14
rolling without slipping, 111–12
torque, 106–8
Rutherford experiment, 451–2, 494–5

Sankey diagrams, 81
satellites, 361, 363, 373
scattering experiments, 451–2, 469, 474, 475, 494–5
Schrödinger theory, 458
second law of thermodynamics, 218–19
self induction, 437
series, resistors in, 242–3, 245–6
SHM *see* simple harmonic motion
simple harmonic motion, 266–85
- defining equation, 273
- energy in, 279–81
- graphs of, 268
  - acceleration-displacement, 268
  - acceleration-time, 268
  - displacement-energy, 279, 280
  - displacement-time, 79, 267–8
  - energy-displacement, 279, 280
  - velocity-time, 267, 268
- and waves, 290
simple harmonic oscillations, 265–73
simple pendulums, 265, 266, 276
simultaneity, 137–8, 148
single-slit diffraction, 318–22
slits, width of, 314, 315, 318–21
see also interference
small angle approximation, 314
Snell's law, 304
solar constant, 175, 179
solar mass, 517, 518, 520–4
solar neutrinos, 501
solenoids, magnetic fields round, 397–8
solids
- change of phase, 162–4
- particles in, bonds between, 159
sound, 293
- and Doppler effect, 347–53
- speed of, 348, 351
spacetime diagrams, 143–9
spacetime interval, 133
special relativity, 129–32, 136, 463
specific heat capacity, 161–2
- measuring, 165–6
specific latent heat, 162–3
spectra
- absorption, 454–6
- black-body, 170
- electromagnetic spectrum, 298

emission, 170, 452–4
- of hydrogen, 453, 458
speed
- angular speed, 52–3
- average speed, 4, 6
- in circular motion, 52–6
- drift speed, 236
- escape speed, 377
- instantaneous speed, 8, 12
- of light, 128–30, 135–7, 140, 143–5, 152, 298, 304, 463
- maximum in SHM, 275, 279
- of molecules, 199–201
- orbital speed, 363, 373–4
- and power, 78
- of rockets, varying with mass, 92
- of sound, 348, 351
- terminal speed, 25–6
- of waves, 287, 288, 291
spheres, charge around, 386, 408–10
spring constant, 31
springs, stretching, 31, 66–7
standard model of particles, 402, 484
standing waves, 330–4, 475
stars, 173, 299
- black dwarfs, 522
- Chandrasekhar limit, 522
- evolution, 520–4
- luminosity, 516–19, 521–3
- main sequence, 517, 518, 520–4
- mass, 517, 518, 520–4
- Oppenheimer–Volkoff limit, 522–3
- radius of, 517–19
- red giants and super red giants, 517–18
- temperature, 516–19
- white dwarfs, 517–20, 522, 523
state of a gas, 192
static friction, 33–4
Stefan-Boltzmann law, 169, 173, 178, 517, 518
Stoke's law, 32, 392, 393
stopping voltage, 464–5, 467
straight line motion, 3–5
stretching springs, 31, 66–7
strings, standing waves on, 331–4
strong interaction, 499
- as a fundamental force, 480
strong nuclear force, 494–6
structure of matter, 451–5
sun, 169, 178–9, 239, 363–4
supernovas, 521, 524
superposition, 308–9, 312
- standing waves from, 330, 331
super red giants, 517–18

Index

surface temperature, 182
surroundings, 75, 166, 178, 206–7
symbols
    for circuits, 241
    for nuclides and particles, 479–80
system, 70–1, 75, 80–1
    closed system, 207
    isolated system, 207
    and momentum, 85, 90–1
systems, deterministic, 359

taus, 501
temperature, 158–9
    and adiabatic process, 207–9
    of earth, 158, 181–3
    and energy transfer, 159, 160, 164–5, 166
    of gases in gas laws, 193–201
    and nuclear fusion, 515
    and power of emitted radiation, 178–9
    and resistance of conductors, 234, 235
    and specific heat capacity, 161–2
    and speed of molecules, 199–201
    of stars, 516–19
tension, 30–1
    and centripetal forces, 56
terminal speed, 25–6
tesla, 396, 399
thermal energy, 159–66
    Carnot cycle, 226–7
    and entropy, 218–19, 220, 222
    generated in resistors, 238
    heat engines, 224–5
    work done by frictional forces, 75, 79
thermal energy transfer, 75, 79, 80, 165–6, 168–74, 182, 224–5
thermal equilibrium, 159, 165
thermal radiation, 169
    see also radiation
thermistors, 235
thermodynamic laws
    first law, 211
    second law, 218–19
thermodynamic process, 207
thin film interference, 325–6
Thomson model, 451–2
time
    and oscillations, 265, 266, 290
    proper time interval, 135
time dilation, 134–5, 136, 139, 147–8
torque, 106–8
total energy, 75, 80–1, 112, 373–4
    and escape speed, 377

mechanical energy, 71–7
    in orbital motion, 373–4
    in SHM, 279, 281
total internal reflection, 305
total mechanical energy, 71–7
transfer of energy see energy transfer
transformations of energy, 279
transformers, 447
transitions, 453–5, 487
    nuclear energy levels, 497–8
translational equilibrium, 108
transmutation, 484
transverse waves, 290–2, 298
travelling waves, 287–99, 330–4
trough of waves, 288
tubes, standing waves in, 334–6

unification, 484
uniform fields, gravitational, 361
uniformly accelerated motion, 7–16
uniform motion, 4–5
units
    ampere, 233
    atomic mass unit, 481
    of charge, 232, 386
    tesla, 396, 399
Universe, 158, 219, 227, 348
upthrust, 32
uranium nuclear fuel, 509–10

vacuum, 298, 304, 387
vaporisation, 162–3
vapours, change of phase of, 162–3
    see also gases
velocity
    in acceleration of free fall problems, 13–14
    angular velocity, 103–4
    average velocity, 7, 12, 16, 292
    in circular motion, 54–5
    constant velocity, 3–4
    and impulse, 89
    instantaneous velocity, 7–8
    and momentum, 85–6
    in Newton's first law of motion, 39
    in non-uniform motion, 7–13
    in projectile motion, 20–5
    in SHM, 267–8
        equations for, 273, 279, 281
    in uniformly accelerated motion, 7–16
    in uniform motion, 4–5
velocity-addition formula, 128, 136–7
velocity-time graphs, 10, 17–19

projectiles, 22, 25, 26
SHM, 267, 268
uniform acceleration, 7–9
uniform motion, 5
voltage, 238
   in ac circuits, and power, 444–5
   peak, 443–5
   stopping voltage, 464–5, 467
   see also potential difference
voltmeters, 254–5
volume of gases, 192–6, 207
volume-temperature law, 193–4

water vapour as a greenhouse gas, 182, 183
wavefronts, 302–3
   in diffraction, 311–12, 318–19
   Doppler effect, 347, 351
wavefunction, 458
wavelength, 288, 291
   in diffraction, 311–12, 452
   diffraction gratings, 324
   and Doppler effect, 347–52
   of electrons, 473–6
   in emission spectra, 170, 178, 452–4
   in interference, 312–13
      two sources, 313–15
   multi-slit, 323
   of particles, 463–4
   of photons, 454, 455, 469, 487
   of standing waves, 330–2, 335, 336
   in Wien's displacement law, 170
wave nature of electrons, 473–5
wave nature of light, 303–5, 310, 463
wave-particle duality, 473
waves, 287–8
   behaviour of, 263–356
   diffraction of, 311–15, 322–3
   Doppler effect, 347–55
   electromagnetic, 298–9
   energy carried by, 302
   graphs of
      displacement-distance, 290, 291, 293
      displacement-time, 267, 290, 291, 313
   gravitational, 299
   interference, 312–13
   longitudinal, 292–4
   matter, 299, 473–5
   probability, 299
   standing, 330–4, 475
   superposition, 308–9, 312, 330, 331
   transverse, 290–2, 298
   travelling, 287–99, 330–4

   see also oscillations
wave speed of EM waves, 463
weak interaction, 499
   as a fundamental force, 480
weight, 30, 32
   and gravitation, 359, 360
   work done by, 65–6
weightlessness, 379
white dwarfs, 517–20, 522, 523
white light, 304, 320, 325
Wien's displacement law, 170
wind power, 443
wires
   current-carrying, 233, 400–1
   magnetic fields around, 396–7, 400–1
   resistance of, 234
work done
   in a battery, 239
   by forces, 62–5
      frictional forces, 64, 68, 69, 76–9
      gravity/weight, 65–6
      magnetic forces, 406–8, 423
      rotational motion, 116
      in thermodynamic processes, 224–6
   and gravitational potential, 66, 368, 371
   and gravitational potential energy, 366–7
   and heat engines, 224–5
   and heating, 160
   moving charge, 232, 406–7
      and emf, 239
      in wires, 410
   on or by gases, 209–10, 218–19
   and potential difference, 232
   and power, 78–9, 116
   in stretching springs, 66–7
work function, 467
work-kinetic energy relation, 64–5, 75
worldline, 143–5

Young's double-slit experiment, 313–15

> Acknowledgements

The authors and publishers acknowledge the following sources of copyright material and are grateful for the permissions granted. While every effort has been made, it has not always been possible to identify the sources of all the material used, or to trace all copyright holders. If any omissions are brought to our notice, we will be happy to include the appropriate acknowledgements on reprinting.

Thanks to the following for permission to reproduce images:

Cover Davespilbrow/GI; *Inside* Chapter 1 Jon Feingersh/GI; Stocktrek Images/GI; Design Pics/GI; Chapter 2 pippee/GI; fStop Images - Caspar Benson/GI; wragg/GI; Max Mumby/Indigo/GI; RossHelen/GI; Kevin Jones/EyeEm/GI; Chapter 3 Andriy Onufriyenko/GI; Chapter 4 imaginima/GI; drbueller/GI; Stocktrek/GI; Chapter 5 Adrienne Bresnahan/GI; Chapter 6 Design Cells/GI; DEA PICTURE LIBRARY/GI; Choumoff/GI; Chapter 7 Cultura RF/Joseph Giacomin/GI; EUROPEAN SPACE AGENCY,THE PLANCK COLLABORATION/SCIENCE PHOTO LIBRARY; Leighton Lum/500px/GI; Chapter 8 CHRISTOPH BURGSTEDT/SCIENCE PHOTO LIBRARY/GI; Chapter 9 Agustín Faggiano - Fotografía/GI; Chapter 10 ROBERT BROOK/SCIENCE PHOTO LIBRARY/GI; Chapter 11 Fotokot197/GI; RICHARD MEGNA/FUNDAMENTAL/SCIENCE PHOTO LIBRARY; Chapter 12 Ali Kahfi/GI; Chapter 13 Andy_R/GI; Chapter 14 Abstract Aerial Art/GI; ANDREW LAMBERT PHOTOGRAPHY/SCIENCE PHOTO LIBRARY (x2); GIPHOTOSTOCK/SCIENCE PHOTO LIBRARY (x2); Nancybelle Gonzaga Villarroya/GI; Chapter 15 Claverie Olivier/EyeEm/GI; Keystone/Hulton Archive/GI; Chapter 16 Elerium/GI; chapter 17 dottedhippo/GI; Heritage Images/GI; Chapter 18 sakkmesterke/GI; Chapter 19 sarayut Thaneerat/GI Chapter 20 Javier Zayas Photography/GI; Ronda Churchill/Bloomberg/GI; Chapter 21 Guido Mieth/GI; Print Collector/GI; Bettmann/GI; Chapter 22 Yuichiro Chino/GI; Chapter 23 ratpack223/GI; AMERICAN PHILOSOPHICAL SOCIETY/SCIENCE PHOTO LIBRARY; Chapter 24 pixelparticle/GI; CORBIS/Corbis via GI; Hulton Archive/GI; figure 24.4 sources unconfirmed; SCIENCE SOURCE/SCIENCE PHOTO LIBRARY; Chapter 25 MARK GARLICK/SCIENCE PHOTO LIBRARY; Stocktrek Images, Inc./Alamy Stock Photo; H. E. BOND/E. NELAN/M. BARSTOW/M. BURLEIGH/J. B. HOLBERG/NASA/ESA/STSCI/SCIENCE PHOTO LIBRARY; CORBIS/Corbis via GI; Handout/GI; NASA/ESA/STSCI/SCIENCE PHOTO LIBRARY; CORBIS/Corbis via GI; Bettmann/GI

Key: GI = Getty Images